COMPUTERS
AND
INFORMATION
SYSTEMS
IN
BUSINESS

Nai-yuan Wu
June 30, 1993

COMPUTERS AND INFORMATION SYSTEMS IN BUSINESS

Robert A. Szymanski

MERRILL PUBLISHING COMPANY
A Bell & Howell Information Company
Columbus I Toronto I London I Melbourne

Published by Merrill Publishing Company
A Bell & Howell Information Company
Columbus, Ohio 43216

This book was set in Meridien.

Administrative Editor: Vernon R. Anthony
Developmental Editor: Peggy H. Jacobs
Production Editor: Sharon Rudd
Art Coordinator: Lorraine Woost
Cover Designer: Brian Deep
Text Designer: Cynthia Brunk
Photo Editor: Terry L. Tietz

Library of Congress Catalog Card Number: 89–62923
International Standard Book Number:
0–675–20905–6
Printed in the United States of America
1 2 3 4 5 6 7 8 9—94 93 92 91 90

Front cover photo: Steve Chenn/Westlight
Back cover photo: Pierce Kopp/Westlight
Background cover photo: Larry Hamill

Title page photo (pp. ii–iii): courtesy of International
Business Machines Corp.

Part opener photos: pp. xix, xxvi, xxviii–1, 404–405,
Larry Hamill; pp. xx, xxii, xxiv, 78–79, 212–213,
322–323, courtesy of International Business Machines
Corp. Part opener background photo (pp. xxviii–1,
78–79, 212–213, 322–323, 404–405): Larry Hamill.

Chapter opener photos: pp. 3, 35, 81, 127, 259, 293,
325, courtesy of International Business Machines
Corp.; pp. 169, 407, 437, courtesy of Compaq
Computer Corp.; p. 359, courtesy of Honeywell, Inc.
Chapter opener marginal photo (pp. 2–3, 34–35,
80–81, 126–127, 168–169, 214–215, 258–259,
292–293, 324–325, 358–359, 406–407, 436–437):
Larry Hamill.

Application Module marginal photo (pp. 73, 75–77,
206–210, 317–321, 398–402, 457–461): Larry
Hamill.

To Laura for her love and support throughout this project and always

THE MERRILL SERIES IN COMPUTER AND INFORMATION SYSTEMS

BARKER	*Developing Business Expert Systems with LEVEL5*, 20951−X
BROQUARD/WESTLEY	*Fundamentals of Assembler Language Programming for the IBM PC and XT*, 21058−5
CAFOLLA/KAUFFMAN	*Turbo Prolog: Step by Step*, 20816−5
CHANDLER/LIANG	*Developing Expert Systems for Business Applications*, 21102−6
CHIRLIAN	*Programming in C++*, 21007−0 *Turbo Prolog: An Introduction*, 20846−7 *UNIX for the IBM PC: An Introduction*, 20785−1
DENOIA	*Data Communication: Fundamentals and Applications*, 20368−6
ERICKSON/ISAAK	*Easy Ventura: A Guide to Learning Ventura Desktop Publishing for the IBM PC*, 21304−5
GEE	*A Programmer's Guide to RPG II and RPG III*, 20908−0
HOBART/OCTERNAUD/ SYTSMA	*Hands-On Computing Using WordPerfect 5.0, Lotus 1−2−3 and dBase IV*, 21110−7
HOUSTON	*Looking into C*, 20845−9
INGALSBE	*Using Computers and Applications Software Featuring VP-Planner, dBase III/III Plus, and WordPerfect*, 21097−6
	Using Computers and Applications Software Featuring Lotus 1−2−3, dBase III/III Plus, and WordPerfect, 21179−4
	Business Applications Software for the IBM PC Alternate Edition with VP-Planner, dBase III/III Plus, and WordPerfect, 21000−3
	Business Applications Software for the IBM PC Alternate Edition with Lotus 1−2−3, dBase III/III Plus, and WordPerfect, 21042−9
	Business Applications Software for the IBM PC with Lotus 1−2−3, dBase III/III Plus, and WordPerfect, Third Edition, 21175−1
KHAN	*Beginning Structured COBOL*, 21174−3
LETRAUNIK	*MVS/XA JCL: A Practical Approach*, 20916−1
LIPNER/KALMAN	*Computer Law: Cases and Materials*, 21104−2
MELLARD	*Introduction to Business Programming Using Pascal*, 20547−6
MORGAN	*Introduction to Structured Programming Using Turbo Pascal Version 5.0 on the IBM PC*, 20770−3
MORIBER	*Structured BASIC Programming, Second Edition*, 20715−0
REYNOLDS/RIECKS	*Introduction to Business Telecommunications, Second Edition*, 20815−7
ROSEN	*Office Automation and Information Systems*, 20557−3

Preface

Based on the premise that information is essential to survival in the business world and that computers and information systems are essential to the best use of information, this book explains how computers and information systems work, where they work, and how they affect a business's physical, political, and ethical environment. The text reflects my commitment to students and their need to prepare for the demands of the Information Age. Whether a student wishes simply to understand the use of computers and information systems and their role in today's business world, to use computers and information systems to manage information in his or her work place, or to design information systems, this text offers comprehensive up-to-date information.

Computers in Preparation of This Text

The existence of this textbook confirms the relevance and importance of Information Age technologies to business. From the contract negotiation stage, when the publishing company ran computer budgeting and production analyses, to the drafting, revising, and typesetting of the manuscript, the computer was a team member in creating the finished product and presenting it in a way that is pleasing to the reader.

The manuscript was prepared using microcomputer and word processing software, then sent on floppy diskette to the editor. After the necessary copy-editing changes, the manuscript was transmitted electronically through the telephone lines to a compositor's larger computers and typesetting equipment located in another state. There, exact margins were set and text lines justified; then the text was retransmitted electronically to the publisher for further corrections. Final composition of the pages was executed on computer; then pages were printed out for editorial review. Final film was sent to the printer, and computer-controlled presses produced the finished book.

While computers played an important role in the preparation of this text, so did a talented group of publishing professionals. Computers and people working together—that partnership is responsible for making this book, as well as numerous other business ventures, possible.

Note to the Student

Computers will play an important part in your future, whether in your personal life or at your work place. Some experts think that, eventually, the person who does not know how to use a computer will be just as handicapped at his or her job as the person today who cannot read.

To be computer literate, you should know how and where computers and information systems can be used, the kinds of tasks they perform, how they affect our society and economy, and how to use them to benefit your own career and life. If you are taking this course to familiarize yourself with the world of computers and information systems, *Computers and Information Systems in Business* serves as an interesting and informative guide on your journey to computer literacy. If you intend to become a computer professional, this book will give you the broad-based background you will need to pursue more advanced course work in the area.

Key Features of the Text

To present thorough coverage of concepts, hardware and software, computer systems, information systems, and other related topics that educators have indicated they feel important, these features have been incorporated:

- **Understandable coverage of the major functional areas of a business,** through the use of subchapters called Application Modules, which can be used to give the beginning student an understanding of business functions and the role of computers and information systems in them.
- **Readability** at the appropriate reading level and a conversational writing style that holds the student's interest
- **Effective motivation,** provided to the student through an opening section in each chapter called Impact on Management Problem Solving and Decision Making, which answers the question "Why is the material in this chapter important to study?"
- **Sound and effective pedagogy** designed to facilitate student interest in and understanding of the subject matter
- **Encouragement to think and apply concepts** through the use of minicases at the end of Chapters 2 through 12. The Case Analysis section in Chapter 1 instructs the student about how to solve and get the most out of the minicases.
- **Current examples** of computer applications that relate concepts to actual situations
- **Comprehensive coverage** that, beyond the usual core coverage, includes discussions of such contemporary issues as:

    - Artificial intelligence
    - Expert systems
    - Computer-assisted software engineering (CASE)
    - Information resource management (IRM)
    - Increasing use of networks and communication technology
    - Work monitoring

- o Robotics
- o Legal issues and computer-related legislation
- o Trends in new chip technologies, optoelectronics, parallel processing, and communication
- o Popular types of application packages

- **Written for everyone**—not only introductory level students who may be interested in continuing their study of computers and information systems as a career, but also students who plan to enter noncomputer fields

Pedagogy

These pedagogical devices were chosen with both the student and the instructor in mind:

- **Chapter objectives** alert students and instructors to the major points or concepts to be gleaned from the chapter.
- **Chapter outlines** preview chapter topics and organization so students can see the relationships among the topics covered.
- **Profiles** acquaint students with the various issues that concern modern MIS management and expose them to the wide variety of personalities and backgrounds of MIS managers.
- **Highlight boxes** focus on interesting illustrations of current computer uses and issues.
- **Summaries** review major concepts in the chapter.
- **Key terms** spotlight words that are important to understanding the material. They are listed alphabetically at the end of each chapter.
- **Review questions** check the student's understanding of the main topics in the chapter. They appear at the end of each chapter as a self-test.
- **Minicases** let the student apply the chapter's concepts to a business situation. In lieu of minicases Chapter 1 contains a discussion of how to solve and get the most out of the minicases presented in subsequent chapters.
- **Application Modules** provide coverage of the major functional areas of a business and the role computers and information systems play in each. These subchapters (one per part) offer flexibility in structuring course content. If students do not have a sufficient understanding of the basic functional areas of a business, the Application Modules can be assigned. Covering this material can significantly increase a student's understanding and appreciation of the material presented in Chapter 2.
- A **glossary,** at the end of the book, contains definitions of all key terms and serves as a handy reference.
- An **index** supplies a detailed guide to text and Application Module topics.

Finally, full-color functional illustrations and more than 60 photographs clarify concepts, depict applications, and show equipment.

Coverage

Comprehensive coverage of topics in the text includes chapters on hardware, software, data communications, information systems, and business concerns and trends. Basic concepts and how these concepts are integrated into business situations and activities are also discussed. Each chapter opens with a section entitled Impact on Management Problem Solving and Decision Making that explains the relevance of the chapter to the student's larger understanding of business.

Because microcomputers are the easiest-to-use computers and because most people (many of whom never become involved with larger systems) will encounter them in their daily work lives, I have included significant coverage of microcomputers throughout the text.

In addition to the core text, two opportunities for hands-on computer lab experience are provided:

- The appendix offers hands-on instruction in the BASIC programming language.
- An affordable worktext provides tutorials for VP-Planner Plus (or Lotus 1-2-3), dBase III, and WordPerfect 5.0. Limited student versions of VP-Planner Plus and dBase III Plus are available from the publisher on a site-license basis.

Organization

The text is divided into five logical parts. Part One (Chapters 1 and 2) provides an overview of computers and information systems, Part Two (Chapters 3 through 5) describes business computer systems, and Part Three (Chapters 6 through 8) explains business information systems concepts. Part Four (Chapters 9 and 10) describes business information systems development, while Part Five (Chapters 11 and 12) discusses the implications of business information systems for business and social concerns and trends. The text also contains an appendix covering structured programming concepts and providing instruction in the BASIC programming language.

Chapter 1, "Computer and Information System Concepts," introduces the student to the concepts of data, information, computers, and information systems. It describes examples of where computers are used, briefly explains how they work and what they can and cannot do, and describes their role in an information system.

Chapter 2, "Information Systems in Business," describes the types of information needed by managers and offers a brief overview of the major types of business information systems. It also surveys the application of information systems in functional areas of business as well as in selected industries. The chapter closes with a brief discussion of the history of computers that provides the student with a summary of events and significant people and their contributions.

Chapter 3, "Components of Business Computer Systems," opens with a discussion of data representation and then examines the internal design and operation of the central processing unit. Input and output concepts and devices for both large and small systems are described, as are secondary storage devices and media.

Chapter 4, "Software for Business Computer Systems," discusses system and application software. Operating systems for both large and small computers are described. The basic instructions that are found in any programming language and the major categories of programming languages are also presented. The chapter introduces the five major microcomputer application packages and distinguishes among the various types of integrated packages.

Chapter 5, "Data Communication," explains how data are transferred from one computer to another and describes applications of data communications. Network topologies, local-area networks, wide-area networks, and distributed data processing are also described.

Chapter 6, "File and Database Organization and Access," describes the data hierarchy and discusses the different types of files and file storage and access methods. Batch and real-time updating processes are presented, and ways of validating file input are described. Database processing is also addressed with discussions of the kinds of databases, database structures, database management systems, database design concepts, concerns with managing databases, and distributed databases.

Chapter 7, "Principles of Business Information Systems," describes the functions and role of transaction processing systems, management information systems, decision support systems, and knowledge-based (expert) systems.

Chapter 8, "Office Information Systems," describes the various parts of an office information system and its role in a business.

Chapter 9, "System Analysis," describes the system analysis phase of the development of an information system.

Chapter 10, "System Design and Implementation," describes the system design and implementation phases of the development of an information system.

Chapter 11, "Impact of Information Systems and the Information Resource," discusses the impact business information systems have had on corporate strategy and social concerns such as privacy of data, computer crime, electronic work monitoring, health and safety, and computer ethics. In addition, the implications of information as a resource and the management of that resource are examined.

Chapter 12, "Trends in Business Information Systems," describes some technological trends—artificial intelligence, Josephson junction, parallel processing, new chip technologies, communication technologies, optoelectronics, and software innovations. Competition at the international level is discussed, and society's response to the proliferation of business information systems is also presented. The chapter closes with a discussion of trends in information system use.

The Appendix, "Structured Programming Concepts/The BASIC Programming Language," describes why it is important to learn about programming, presents structured programming concepts, and introduces the student to the BASIC programming language.

The Instructional Package

- **Worktext for VP-Planner Plus (or Lotus), dBase III Plus, and WordPerfect 5.0** is a hands-on guide to help students learn basic functions of a spreadsheet, database, and word processor.
- **Instructor's Resource Manual** contains chapter-by-chapter lecture outlines, answers to all questions in the text and worktext, and suggestions for using alternative instructional material.
- **Computerized Test Bank** includes 1,000 true/false, short answer, multiple choice, and fill-in questions. This versatile test bank program allows the instructor to generate tests, edit existing questions, and add new questions.
- **Printed Test Bank** is a hard copy version of all questions in the computerized test bank.
- **Transparency Package** consists of 75 full-color overhead transparencies that illustrate concepts presented in the text.
- **Videotapes**—Adopters of *Computers and Information Systems in Business* can purchase instructional tapes directly from the following companies at a discounted rate.

    o International Business Machines Corporation (IBM)—Using Your IBM PC, Merrill version
    A ninety-minute tape divided into seven lessons on how to use the IBM PC

    Lesson 1—Assembling Your System
    Lesson 2—Using Your Keyboard
    Lesson 3—About Disks
    Lesson 4—The Disk Directory
    Lesson 5—Programming Languages
    Lesson 6—Installing DOS
    Lesson 7—Programming in BASIC

    o American Micro Media—A series of ten videotapes, each running approximately thirty minutes. New terms are explained as they are introduced, and a review of concepts appears approximately every ten minutes.

    Electronic Words—explains key concepts related to word processors
    Keeping Track—explains key concepts related to data management packages

Computer Calc—explains key concepts of electronic spreadsheets
Computer Talk—explains key communications concepts
Computer Images—explains key graphics concepts
Computer Crime—focuses on crime awareness, prevention, and ethics
Computer Career—describes how computers affect the work place
Computer Peripherals—explains differences among computer systems
Computer Music—shows how computer sounds are generated
Computer Business—explores microcomputers and office automation

ACKNOWLEDGMENTS

So many people were involved in the development, production, and creative aspects of this project that the list of names could go on and on. All of the professionals I worked with at Merrill Publishing provided support, enthusiasm, and helpful suggestions. Special acknowledgment, however, goes to my administrative editor and friend, Vernon Anthony, who once again steadfastly led me through every phase of the publication process. The developmental editorial support of Peggy Jacobs is unrivaled. Everyone in Merrill's production, art, and design departments is to be commended for their creativity, patience, and hard work. In particular I thank Sharon Rudd, production editor, Lorry Woost, art coordinator, Cindy Brunk, text designer, and Brian Deep, cover designer. A special thanks goes to my wife, Laura, for her helpful suggestions and tireless efforts at typing and proofing this project. I am grateful to Don Szymanski, Donna Pulschen, and Norma Morris for their support in this project. Additionally, I am grateful to the organizations and businesses that provided photographs and technical materials for use in this book.

Special appreciation goes to these contributing authors: Kirk Arnett, Mississippi State University; Anthony Fabbri, University of Louisville; Thomas Harris, Ball State University; M. B. Khan, California State University; and Merle Martin, California State University.

Finally, I thank these reviewers for their thoughtful comments about the manuscript: Kenneth Forsythe, University of Wisconsin; Randy Weinberg, Saint Cloud University; Charles Small, Abilene University; David Yen, Miami University; Greg Smith, Colorado State University; G. W. Willis, Baylor University; John Schillak, University of Wisconsin; Dwight Hazlett, Texas A&I University; Robert Panian, University of Northern Michigan; Gerald Evans, University of Montana; Karen Forcht, James Madison University; Chang-tseh Hsieh, University of Southern Mississippi; Carey T. Hughes, University of North Texas; and David Paradise, Texas A&M University.

Brief Contents

Contents

Chapter 2
Information Systems in Business   35

Application Module: The Functions of Business   73

PART TWO
BUSINESS COMPUTER SYSTEMS   79

Chapter 5
Data Communication   169

PART THREE
BUSINESS INFORMATION SYSTEMS

Chapter 6
File and Database Organization and Access
215

Chapter 7
Principles of Business Information Systems
259

Chapter 8
Office Information Systems   293

Application Module: Human Resource Information Systems   317

PART FOUR
DEVELOPMENT OF BUSINESS INFORMATION SYSTEMS   323

Chapter 9
System Analysis 325

Chapter 10
System Design and Implementation 359

PART FIVE
IMPLICATIONS OF COMPUTERS IN BUSINESS INFORMATION SYSTEMS 405

Chapter 11
Impact of Information Systems and the Information Resource 407

Chapter 12
**Trends in Business Information Systems
437**

**Application Module: Marketing Information
Systems   457**

PART ONE

An Overview of Computers and Information Systems

Computer and Information System Concepts

Chapter 1

Management Profile: George Grippo
YOUNG GUN MATURES AT TV MIS DEPARTMENT

George Grippo is the first to admit he seems an unlikely MIS captain. The 26-year-old manager of information systems says he has found his niche in the small MIS shop at Secaucus, NJ's WWOR-TV. His technical background consists of personal computing experience in two jobs as a teenager.

Grippo got his foot in the door in 1985 at RKO General, which owned WWOR at the time. Grippo, who wanted to be a disk jockey, never got on the air. When the company discovered his PC background, he was shanghaied into the accounts payable department. Grippo transferred from the New York headquarters to WWOR the following year. His first task was implementing a modest PC system from scratch. From there he quickly moved up to being accounts receivable supervisor and then data-processing manager.

"I got a lot of promotions by default," Grippo says, "but always on condition that I would get the job done. I've said to those hiring me, 'Give me six months. If I can't get the job done, then you can let me go, and there are no hard feelings.'" Grippo says that throughout his career he has approached difficult projects with the straight-shooting philosophy of "Show it to me once, I'll know it, and I'll get it done again and again."

In early 1987, RKO General sold WWOR to MCA Broadcasting. Suddenly WWOR was deprived of its link to RKO General's mainframe and MIS department. Grippo knew MCA Broadcasting intended to fill the void with a new in-house MIS department, and he saw the chance to make his mark. He approached the WWOR business manager and said, "You can't lose with me—I'm cheap and I promise to get the job done." Grippo was tapped as the new MIS chief.

Learning as he went, Grippo built a department and an information system virtually from nothing. In the span of six months, he installed a mainframe computer, packaged accounting software, and numerous microcomputers. The user base at WWOR has grown from fewer than a dozen employees to about 50 and continues to expand. And Grippo's staff has expanded by 200 percent—from one person to three, including Grippo.

Despite the blossoming fortunes of his company and his personal achievements, Grippo's youth has been a handicap. "People don't believe me," he says. "I walk into a meeting and say something I know to be fact, and they'll say, 'Come on, maybe you're overreacting; you're only 26.'" Nonetheless, Grippo's credibility has mounted, though not fast enough to suit his aggressive nature. "If I had gray hair and a limp, maybe they'd say, 'Sure, look at him. He's got gray hair; he must know what he's doing,'" he jokes.

Adapted from "George Grippo: Young Gun Matures at TV MIS Department" by Richard Pastore. Copyright 1988 by CW Publishing Inc., Framingham, MA 01701. Reprinted from *Computerworld,* Dec. 5, 1988.

Computers have reached far into today's life-styles. Typical Americans experience the activity of at least twenty computers each day: computer-controlled automobile parts, computer-generated mail, computer-produced and -sorted mail, computer-maintained charge accounts, computer-assisted supermarket checkouts, computer-monitored traffic, computer-aided banking, computer-controlled office temperatures, computer-produced TV commercials, computer-controlled games, computer-activated traffic lights, and still other computer-supported functions.

From A to Z, automobiles to zoos, computers have a pervasive influence on our daily lives. The entertainment industry uses computers for movie making, MTV music production, and guiding rides and animated cartoon characters in amusement parks. Computers also abound in the sports industry, where major league baseball and football franchises use computers to recruit playing talent. The Chicago White Sox and other baseball teams use computers to chart the speed, distance, and location of a batter's hits and to determine the speed and range of the fielders. Bobby Rahal won the 1986 Indianapolis 500 with an on-board computer linked to his pit crew's computer—a common occurrence today. Doug Flutie's dad used a home computer to analyze contracts and make the 1984 Heisman Trophy winner the highest paid professional football rookie when Doug began his professional career. Hi-tech criminals use computers to match stolen vehicles with needed parts and to achieve other less desirable purposes. You probably used a computer to enroll in this course. Today's life-styles would be less fulfilling and less productive without computers, and many businesses could not continue to operate without them.

No matter what your career path, you will likely be responsible for identifying and solving problems and for making decisions every day of your career. Some decisions will be inconsequential; others may have monumental impact on you and your organization. To ensure that the decisions you make are in the best interests of your organization, you need to understand how to recognize and acquire the appropriate information. You need to be aware of and understand how to use the powerful tools of computers and information systems to their best advantage. This book teaches you how to function in a business world that makes extensive use of computers. It emphasizes the use of the computer for problem solving and decision making in the business arena.

IMPACT ON MANAGEMENT PROBLEM SOLVING AND DECISION MAKING

Information is the key to a successful business. Organizations are now realizing that, next to people, information is the most valuable resource they have. Managers must make decisions everyday about how a business is run and what direction its operation will take in the future. Information plays a major role in improving the efficiency and effectiveness of the human decision-making process.

To solve problems and make decisions that will achieve the organizations' goals, people need some means of collecting and managing the necessary information. Information systems, specifically the use of computers in information systems, have been a primary force in enabling people to collect, process, and manage the information they need for problem solving (Figure 1–1).

The computer has had a tremendous impact on business information systems, similar to the effect of the automobile and the airplane in revolutionizing travel. The computer's initial impact was in accounting, where computers served as an efficient tool for processing payrolls and other numerical data. The first computerized payroll was processed in 1954 by General Electric Company using a UNIVAC 1 computer. Today, the computer's reach has extended to almost all areas within organizations. The computer has moved from a simple number cruncher to a fundamental building block in the development and implementation of business information systems to help identify and solve problems and assist in decision making.

Computers and communications enable business people who are separated by building space or by large geographical areas to talk to each other electronically. Telecommunications and global networks have provided the means for corporations to expand their operations and have greatly increased the complexities involved in establishing and managing business information systems. The personal computer has also played a significant role in business information systems by enabling all workers to create, process, store, and distribute information. Computers have the potential to make operations more efficient, productive, and competitive.

Computers have not only impacted existing businesses but have also created a whole new industry. The computer industry includes businesses that create and supply technology as well as enterprises that educate and consult in its use.

FIGURE 1–1
At Ford Motor Company computers enable engineers to easily collect, process, and manage test data on automobiles. The acquired information can help the engineers detect and solve problems and improve designs. (Courtesy of Ford Motor Company)

Computer and Information System Concepts

Computer use in business information systems has also benefited the consumer. For example, computerized order-entry systems allow quicker response to customer orders, and computerized product design and analysis produce better quality products.

We have developed an economy based on the manipulation of information rather than the production of goods. In this Information Age, information, or knowledge, has become a primary resource. **Knowledge workers**—the people who create, process, and distribute information—currently make up over 60 percent of the work force.

Because of the changing makeup of today's businesses, it is important that employees and managers alike have an understanding of the importance of information in problem solving and decision making, the computer's role in information systems, and the effect of information systems on an organization's strategies and goals. Computers and information systems have become the foundation of most businesses and the primary tools for a manager to use in problem identification and solution and in decision making. The way in which an organization uses computers will have a profound effect on its growth, profitability, and productivity.

This text provides the basic foundation needed to understand computers and information systems and their role in problem solving and decision making, as well as a focus on the importance of information as an organizational resource and the management concerns in developing, using, and maintaining information systems. Let's begin by defining *data* and *information*.

DATA AND INFORMATION

35.4, 30.2, 28.7, 27.9, 27.6, 26.9—these numbers are data. Standing alone, they have no meaning; but when coupled with other data—such as Jordon, Malone, Ellis, Drexler, English, and Barkely—they might begin to look significant. Add NBA and PPG AVG, and these data become information to basketball fans. The numbers represent the average points per game of the scoring leaders in the National Basketball Association.

Data are facts—numbers, labels, and so on that have little meaning by themselves. **Information** is data that have been processed into an organized, usable form and are relevant and meaningful to the recipient for the task at hand. Strange as it may seem, one person's data may be another's information. For example, your first test grade of, say, 83 is information to you but is probably regarded only as data by your teacher.

Data are readily available to an organization. Every transaction that occurs supplies data. A **transaction** is a business activity or event. The receipt of an order or the sale of a product constitutes a transaction. There typically is much more data available than needs to be collected for the decision making, problem solving, and control activities of most managers. With computers and improved data communications, the problem for most managers is not the lack of data or the subsequent information that its processing can generate, but the fact that they receive more information than they can possibly absorb. This condition is referred to as "information overload"; too much of the decision maker's time is spent trying to determine what is relevant and what is not. The greatest difficulty is not in gathering data but in deciding what data need to be gathered to provide the necessary information and making sure the information gets distributed to the right people at the right time.

Information can be of two general types: qualitative or quantitative. **Quantitative information** tells how much or how many. For example, there are 12 roses in the vase. Quantitative information is used heavily throughout businesses. How many units were sold, or how many dollars are being spent on employee salaries. Quantitative information appears in one of two forms: numerical or graphical. Information represented by numbers is called **numerical information**. A business's balance sheet or income statement contains numerical information. Information represented pictorially is called **graphical information**. Common graphical representations of quantitative business information include pie charts and bar and line graphs. **Qualitative information** describes something using nonquantitative characteristics. For example, the roses in the vase are red. Qualitative characteristics can be used to describe job categories or positions, such as a programmer, system analyst, or manager.

<table>
<tr><td>

ATTRIBUTES OF INFORMATION

</td><td>

Information can be expressed in terms of its attributes, or characteristics. These give the user a framework on which to judge the meaningfulness and usefulness of information. We will look at seven basic attributes of information: accuracy, relevance, completeness, timeliness, cost-effectiveness, auditability, and reliability.

Accuracy refers to whether information is accurate (true) or inaccurate (false). Information is accurate if it represents a fact or situation as it really is. Inaccurate information can result from errors in the collecting, processing, or reporting activities involved in producing and transmitting information. Your first thought might be that inaccurate information is not really information. However, if users are unaware that information is inaccurate and they use that information in decision making, then it is information to them. This is one of the problems with the generation and distribution of information within organizations. In most cases the user of the information is not the same person(s) who collected, processed, and distributed it. Users of information assume that what they have received is accurate. It is therefore the responsibility of the information provider to ensure its accuracy.

Relevance refers to whether information is needed and useful in a particular situation. If it is needed, then the information is relevant. However, relevance is not a static attribute. What is relevant for a chief executive officer (CEO) may not be relevant for a purchasing clerk, and vice versa. In addition, what is relevant today in making a decision may not be relevant tomorrow in making the same decision.

Completeness refers to how thorough or inclusive a set of information is. A complete set of information tells everything you need to know about a situation. Because of the complexity of most business decision-making situations, it is virtually impossible to attain a complete set of information. The aim is to acquire the most complete set of information possible.

</td></tr>
</table>

Computer and Information System Concepts

Timeliness refers to two conditions: is the information available when it is needed, and is the information outdated when it is received or when it is to be used? If the information is not available when needed or if it is outdated by the time it is used, then the information has little or no value to the manager in decision making, problem solving, or control activities. Outdated information may also be counterproductive, that is, worse than no information at all.

Cost-effectiveness refers to the relationship between the benefit to be derived by using information and the cost of producing that information. If the cost of the information is more than the benefit, the information is not cost-effective and is usually not produced.

Auditability, also known as verifiability, refers to the ability to check the accuracy and completeness of information. Without auditability it is not possible to determine the accuracy of information, thus bringing into question its usefulness. The term *audit trail* is used to indicate that summarized information can be traced back to its original source(s) to verify its accuracy.

Reliability summarizes how closely information fits the other six attributes. Information is not always perfect. It may not be totally accurate, or it may not be 100 percent verifiable. Reliability takes into consideration the expected averages of the other six attributes. If they are near what was expected, then the information is considered reliable. If the information deviates significantly from what was expected, then it is considered unreliable.

SOURCES OF INFORMATION

It is important for managers to become aware of all the potential sources of information available to them. Decision-making efforts can be hampered if managers do not know where to get the information they need or fail to realize that certain information exists. Information can be acquired from two basic sources—internal and external.

Internal sources of information come from within an organization. Three common internal sources are internally generated documents, observations, and internal surveys. Internal documents—such as a balance sheet, income statement, employee files, scheduled and unscheduled reports, and other files and reports—can supply a great deal of information about how a business operates and what its financial condition is.

Observation is a method of obtaining information about a situation or event by observing it and thus gaining firsthand knowledge. It is important for an observer to be complete and accurate in recording information so that it will not be misinterpreted later on. It is also important to realize that the process of observation itself may alter the situation or event being observed. Often, observations are conducted secretly by trained observers or by movie or closed-circuit television cameras and tape recordings to avoid affecting the natural state of an event.

Internal surveys are a popular means of obtaining information about an organization from individuals within that organization. Surveys can take the form of questionnaires, telephone interviews, or personal interviews. It is very important that the survey questions be planned and chosen carefully so that they will be interpreted in the same way by all participants and the results will be meaningful.

External sources of information are produced outside an organization. Common external sources include external surveys, annual reports from other organizations, statistics from government agencies, trade publications, and research reports. External surveys are similar to internal surveys except that the individuals surveyed are outside the organization that is conducting the survey.

Government agencies provide another external source by compiling large amounts of information about a wide variety of topics, including such items as the gross national product (GNP) and population estimates, which can be very important to some businesses. Most of the information collected by government agencies is available upon request.

Publications of a commercial, trade, government, or professional business nature are available through subscriptions, libraries, or special purchase. These can provide valuable information on such topics as industry trends, new technologies, and government regulations.

Information can also be purchased from outside sources such as research houses, like A. C. Nielson Company, and public opinion polls, like those conducted by Gallup Poll. An organization can buy information from existing research and polls or can commission specific research and polls to gather needed information.

Concerns with Information Sources

Managers need to ensure that the decision-making information they receive is of the highest quality. There are several concerns about information sources for the user of information. The information supplied by a source should not contain bias but should be valid, reliable, consistent, and timely (i.e., having minimal time delay between its request and its receipt).

Bias refers to the impartiality of the information source. Unbiased information is impartial and does not attempt to distort reality.

Valid information is meaningful and relevant to the purpose for which it is used. For example, a manager might notice that a product's sales went down after its price was increased. The manager might look at this information and conclude that the increase in price caused the sales to go down. In fact, the product price might not have been the reason for the decrease in sales. Other factors, such as a decrease in quality or availability of the product, might account for the diminishing sales. An information user should examine all possible factors before determining the validity of any specific information.

Reliable information gives a true picture of a given event or situation. For example, a survey may report that 90 percent of those surveyed were using a particular brand of product and may have concluded that that brand was the most popular. However, it is important to know other things, such as what percent of the total market was surveyed. If the total market consists of 100,000 product users and the survey reflects the views of only 10, then the reliability of the results is questionable. If the survey randomly sampled 10,000 users, then the results would reflect a significant portion of the market and would be more reliable.

Information obtained from a source should be based on factors that are consistent so that the same factors can be compared each time and the information will be meaningful. For example, a manager might want to compare first quarter sales to second quarter sales. If total sales in the first quarter are based on four products, then the second quarter total sales should also be based on the same four products if the comparison is to be meaningful. If the total number of products in the second quarter report increases or decreases or the products are not the same, the comparison will not be meaningful.

The time delay in receiving information from a source is also very important in assessing the information's value. After a user has identified the need for information, the time required to collect and process data or to gain access to information is the primary reason that information becomes dated and loses its value. Many of the concerns in the design of information systems center around decreasing the delay between a user's request for information and receipt of it.

VALUE OF INFORMATION

How does one determine the value of information? This question faces managers daily. Value must be determined by the user of the information on a case-by-case basis. Valuable information for one user in one situation may have no value for another user in another situation.

The value of information should be looked at in terms of its incremental value. The important factor in determining value is not how much information an item contains but how much additional knowledge it adds to what was previously known and stored.

The costs and benefits of information must also be examined in determining its value. Figure 1–2 illustrates the relationships between costs, benefits, and value of information. The costs are relatively easy to identify because they are quantifiable. They include such things as the costs of personnel, equipment, and supplies for collecting, processing, and transmitting the information. The benefits of information are harder to pin down. They can range from the quantifiable (e.g., faster order processing) to the intangible (e.g., better decision making). The likelihood of actually obtaining the expected benefit also needs to be weighed.

Benefits may include improvement in strategic performance, management control, and cost displacement or avoidance. Improved strategic performance is difficult to quantify and achieve because of the intangible

FIGURE 1–2
Relationships among benefits, costs, and value of information.

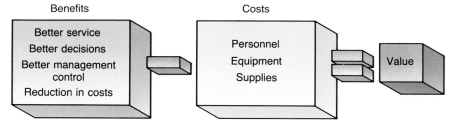

nature of such components as customer service and utilization of management talent. The benefits of improved management control can only be estimated before a system is implemented but can be quantified after implementation. For example, in a direct-order-taking system such things as an increase in business volume and a reduction in lost orders can only be estimated before controls are implemented but can be directly measured and quantified thereafter. The benefits of improved cost displacement are the easiest to quantify and attain. This type of benefit includes the elimination of staff and materials used to create a product or service. The benefits of cost avoidance—for example, not hiring a replacement when a worker retires—are more difficult to determine.

Businesses are beginning to realize that one of the most important benefits of information is the strategic role that it can have. What the competition is and will be doing, where the market is headed, what can be expected of the economy—all these pieces of information along with a host of others can be used to plan a successful corporate strategy for the future.

WHAT COMPUTERS ARE

A **computer** is simply a tool for people to use; it is a device that can help solve problems by accepting data, performing certain operations on the data, and then presenting the results of those operations. A computer is generally thought of as belonging to one of two classifications—analog or digital.

Analog computers recognize data as a continuous measurement rather than separating them into unconnected values. The output of these computers is usually in the form of readings on dials or graphs. Voltage, pressure, speed, and temperature are properties that can be measured in this way.

Digital computers are high-speed, programmable, electronic devices that perform mathematical calculations, compare values, and store the results. Numbers, letters, and special symbols are all reduced to on or off states of electrical components represented by high and low voltage when used by a digital computer.

Our focus throughout this text is on digital computers because they are the most widely used in business and are the classification of computers you are most apt to encounter. Throughout the remainder of this text the term *computer* refers to a digital computer.

COMPUTER SYSTEMS

Let's examine the components that make up a computer system: hardware, software, users, and procedures. The **hardware,** or equipment, includes

- the computer, where processing occurs
- memory, with both primary and secondary storage (discussed in Chapter 3)
- input devices, such as a keyboard and a mouse (discussed in Chapter 3)

Computer and Information System Concepts

- output devices, such as printers and monitors (discussed in Chapter 3)
- data communications devices, such as modems (discussed in Chapter 5)

The **software,** or instructions, tells the computer what to do. A person, or **user,** is required to activate the system. Finally, **procedures,** or lists of instructions, direct the user in utilizing the hardware and the software. Figure 1−3 illustrates the components of a computer system.

The size and configuration of a computer system depends on the processing requirements, necessary functions, and budget constraints of an organization. Computer systems have been traditionally grouped into these four major categories, starting with the most powerful: supercomputers, mainframes, minicomputers, and microcomputers. However, the categorical distinctions among these groups are becoming blurred as technology progresses. Today, many of the new, smaller machines have the characteristics and capabilities of the larger machines of only a few years ago. Two new categories, superminis and supermicros, have emerged as a result of the advances. Superminis bridge the gap between standard mainframes

FIGURE 1−3

Components of a computer system.

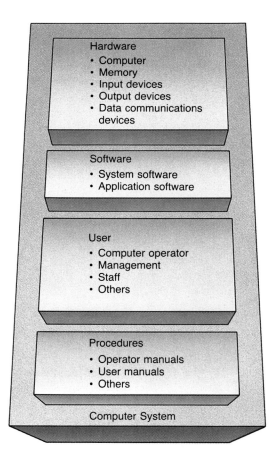

An Overview of Computers and Information Systems

and minicomputers. Supermicros bridge the gap between minicomputers and microcomputers.

In addition to relative computing power, other factors are used to categorize computers (Figure 1–4).

1. *The type of architecture used.* Architecture refers to the design of the computer circuits. It includes the number and type of the central processing unit(s) (CPUs). (The CPU performs the actual computing tasks. It can be thought of as the brains of the computer and is discussed in Chapter 3.) Architecture also includes the number and size of the processing registers. (Registers, also presented in Chapter 3, are special-purpose memory used by the CPU when performing computing tasks.)

2. *The processing speed.* Processing speed is the number of instructions that a computer can process per second. It is usually measured in millions of instructions per second (MIPS). An instruction specifies the computer operation to be performed and the data to be used. Generally, the higher the classification, the more MIPS the computer will have and the faster it will process data. Currently, microcomputers can execute up to several MIPS, whereas supercomputers have reached the 1 billion mark.

3. *The amount of primary storage that the CPU can access and use.* Primary storage is also called internal memory. (Primary storage provides the CPU with temporary storage and fast access to the instructions and data needed for processing; it is discussed further in Chapter 3.)

FIGURE 1–4

Because technological advances have increased computing power and decreased prices, categorical distinctions among computer systems are becoming increasingly blurred.

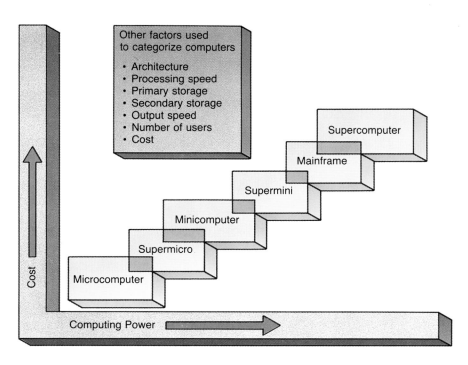

Other factors used to categorize computers

- Architecture
- Processing speed
- Primary storage
- Secondary storage
- Output speed
- Number of users
- Cost

Supercomputer

Mainframe

Supermini

Minicomputer

Supermicro

Microcomputer

Cost

Computing Power

4. *The capacity of the secondary storage devices.* Generally, the higher the computer classification, the larger the capacity of the secondary storage devices will be. (Secondary storage devices provide relatively permanent storage of instructions and data and are discussed in Chapter 3.)

5. *The speed of the system's output devices.* Typically this factor describes how fast output can be printed. Generally, the larger the system, the faster the output devices will be. Output from microcomputer systems is usually measured in characters per second (cps). For larger systems, output is usually measured in lines per minute. (Output devices are also discussed in Chapter 3.)

6. *The number of users that can simultaneously access the computer system.* Typically, microcomputers can be accessed by only a single user at one time. Supermicrocomputers generally allow several users to access at one time. Minicomputers and superminis generally support from 10 to 100 users. Mainframes and supercomputers can typically support hundreds of users.

7. *The cost of the computer.* Price is usually a reflection of the power of a computer system. Therefore, the higher the classification, the larger the price tag will tend to be. The price of a computer also depends on the options that are purchased; thus, a complete computer system that is classified in a lower category may actually cost more than one in a higher category. Microcomputer systems generally range from hundreds to several thousands of dollars. Minicomputers typically cost tens of thousands to several hundreds of thousands of dollars. Mainframes usually cost several hundred thousand dollars; supercomputers, well over one million dollars.

Supercomputers are the most powerful and most expensive computers. They are used by government agencies, scientists, and large corporations (Figure 1–5).

Mainframe computers are not as powerful as supercomputers (Figure 1–6). They are used as the "traditional" computer in companies where large databases are required and where many users at separate workstations share the same computer.

Minicomputers are somewhat less powerful than mainframes (Figure 1–7). They are usually used in small and medium-sized businesses as the primary computer; in larger businesses they may serve the computing needs of a particular department. Minicomputers can serve numerous users simultaneously but typically fewer than a mainframe can accommodate. High-end minicomputers are classified as **superminis**.

Microcomputers are the least powerful of all the classifications. Because they are small enough to fit on a standard desktop, they are often called **desktop computers** (Figure 1–8). Unlike the larger computers a single microcomputer is generally used by only one person at a time; it is also referred to as a **personal computer**. Figure 1–9 shows a typical desktop microcomputer system. Microcomputers are also available in portable, lap-top, and hand-held models. A **portable computer** is small and lightweight enough to carry around (Figure 1–10). Businesses often have por-

FIGURE 1–5
Used primarily by government and large corporations, supercomputers are the most high-powered computers made. (Courtesy of Los Alamos National Laboratory)

FIGURE 1–6
Mainframes are most often used for business processing in medium- to large-sized corporations.

FIGURE 1–7
Minicomputers are smaller and less powerful than mainframes. They are used in many small and medium-sized organizations. (Photo courtesy of Hewlett-Packard Company)

table computers available so that employees who need to work overtime on a computer-related project can take a portable computer home. A **laptop computer,** sometimes called a briefcase computer, can be used in your lap and is very portable (Figure 1–11). The manageable size enables business people to work while traveling on a commuter train and journalists to

FIGURE 1–8
Desktop microcomputers are used in offices for a wide variety of tasks.

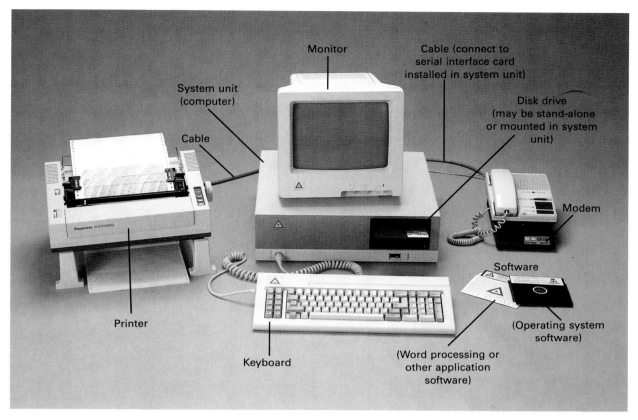

FIGURE 1–9
A typical microcomputer system.

FIGURE 1–10
Portable computers allow individuals to transport computing power between home and office.

Computer and Information System Concepts

FIGURE 1–11
Lap-top computers are convenient for salespeople who have to make client contacts either in person or by telephone. This salesman is able to give his client current prices, which are stored in the computer, and to key in the client's order as it is placed.

FIGURE 1–12
Many businesses, including grocery stores, are automating inventory using hand-held computers. These devices store data read from the bar codes on each product. The data can later be entered directly into the main computer system. (Courtesy of Albertson's)

file stories from the field. **Hand-held computers** are small enough to carry in your hand and usually have only one line for display (Figure 1–12). The hand-held size is particularly appropriate for people who work on location, such as engineers or repair and maintenance personnel.

High-end microcomputers are classified as **supermicros** and have the capability of supporting several users simultaneously. Microcomputers can also be attached to larger computer systems to allow access to and sharing of resources.

HOW COMPUTERS ARE USED AND WHAT THEY CAN DO

There are four basic ways in which computers are used: information processing, control, design and development, and communications. Information processing is a primary role of computers in information systems. **Information processing** involves the computer in transforming data into information. This function includes the processing of mathematical calculations for such items as payrolls, filing tasks, and even word processing—all traditional business applications. The information generated can then be used by management to help in problem identification and solution and to assist in decision making.

Converting data into information has traditionally been called **data processing,** but many sources now refer to it as information processing.

For simplicity's sake we will refer to all the processes involved in the conversion of data into information as information processing.

Computers are also used to control many mechanical devices and processes. Often, computers direct factory operations, assembly lines, machinery, and robots for large manufacturers.

By using computers for design and development, engineers can design a product and test it by computer before manufacturing it. For example, a new type of airplane wing can be designed by engineers using a computer and then tested by computer simulation to see how it will function under certain conditions.

Computers are also used to facilitate communications. For example, with data communications hardware and software, information can be sent to and retrieved by a computer at another location. Users at distant locations can also talk directly to each other through their computers, a process known as teleconferencing. Some people do their office work from their homes using a computer and communications. In addition, the computer can be used to communicate ideas and procedures through the use of graphic demonstrations.

Functions

Although computers have many applications, they can execute only three basic tasks:

1. performing arithmetic functions on numeric data (adding, subtracting, multiplying, and dividing)
2. testing relationships among data items (by comparing values)
3. storing and retrieving data

These tasks are really no more than people can accomplish, but the computer can accomplish the tasks faster, more accurately, and more reliably. A computer can solve complex mathematical problems in fractions of a second; it can work with the greatest accuracy imaginable; and it can store great volumes of data.

How Computers Operate

Data flow through the computer system according to the following steps: input, processing, and output. Before processing can occur, the data must get into the system by means of an input device. **Input** involves collecting, verifying, and encoding data into a machine-readable form for the computer. The computer then performs the necessary calculations or manipulations on the data. In **processing** the computer creates useful information from the data by performing such operations as classifying, sorting, calculating, summarizing, and storing the results. Finally, the organized information is displayed by output devices. **Output** includes retrieving the stored information, converting it into a human-readable form, and displaying the information to the user. Figure 1−13 illustrates the basic flow of data through a computer system.

Computer and Information System Concepts

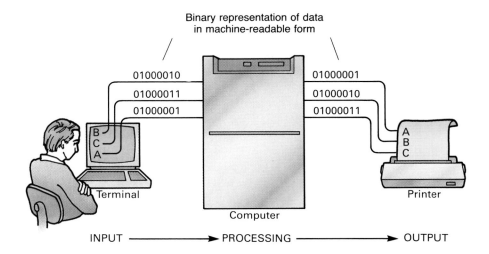

Binary representation of data
in machine-readable form

01000010	01000001
01000011	01000010
01000001	01000011

Terminal

Computer

Printer

INPUT   →   PROCESSING   →   OUTPUT

FIGURE 1–13

The basic flow of data through a computer system involves three steps: input, processing, and output. Data are entered by an input device and are converted to machine-readable form. In this example the computer's instructions specify that the data should be alphabetized. After the computer completes that procedure, the output, in human-readable form, is displayed on an output device.

Information processing requires careful planning and appropriate instructions. Accurate data must be input, or the information delivered as output is useless. This phenomenon is called "garbage-in, garbage-out," meaning that the output is only as accurate as the input and the program(s) that process the data. If you enter a meaningless series of numbers and letters, the computer will not automatically process the data into a list of names and addresses. Correct data have to be entered.

WHAT COMPUTERS CANNOT DO

Computers are very good at what they do, but there are some tasks that they cannot do. They can't do anything unless they are first programmed with specific instructions. In general, computers can't decide how they are to be programmed or provide their own input; they can't interpret the information they generate; they can't implement any decisions that they suggest; and they can't think. However, advances in artificial intelligence (AI) (the field devoted to giving computers human intelligence) are gradually changing this last inability.

It is still up to human beings to make appropriate decisions; the computer is only a tool. The better we learn to use and manage the tool, the better it will serve us.

WHAT A SYSTEM IS

A **system** is a set of components that interact with each other to form a whole and work together toward a common goal. The four major components of a system are inputs, processes, outputs, and feedback control. Figure 1–14 illustrates a simple system.

An input is anything that enters the system, such as energy, materials, or data. For example, raw material such as iron ore may be input into a production system, and data in the form of figures indicating market share may be input into a marketing system. A system may have one or many inputs.

An output is anything leaving the system. Outputs are the goal of the system, the purpose for which the system exists. Products, services, or information may be the output of a system, and the outputs of one system can become the inputs of another system. For example, the output of one system (an organization that produces tires) may be automobile tires. These tires may then be used as an input in another system (an automobile production company) that assembles automobile parts.

A process transforms an input into an output. Processes can be broken down into two general categories: white box processes and black box processes. In a **white box process** we know exactly how the process transforms an input into an output. A manual typewriter is an example of a white box process. If the *y* key is pressed, we know that the arm containing the *y* symbol will strike against the ribbon to make an imprint of the *y* on the paper. We can easily control the output of the system by managing the input into the system. In a **black box process** the transformation process is not known in detail because it is too complex. For example, a business organization constitutes a black box process. Because the organization is composed of numerous subsystems that interact in intricate and dynamic ways with each other and with systems external to the organization, it is impossible to define in detail the exact process that converts the inputs into the outputs of the system.

A process often involves a great number of inputs that may be combined in different ways or in different orders to result in different outputs. Because of the large number of components and the complexity of relationships in many business processes, managers are often unable to understand what factors contributed to the attainment of a system's goal. For example, if the goal of a system is to make a profit and it does, it is often difficult, if not impossible, for a manager to say exactly what factors led to

FIGURE 1–14

A simple system.

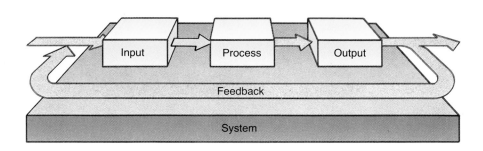

Computer and Information System Concepts

the achievement of the goal. Was it achieved because of the quality of a product, its price, the advertising, some other factor, or a combination of factors?

Feedback reintroduces a portion of a system's output as an input into the same system. It is actually a special kind of input. Feedback is used as a control mechanism within a system to indicate the difference between a system's goal and actual performance. The thermostat used in home heating and cooling systems provides feedback that controls the temperature.

THE ORGANIZATION AS A SYSTEM

We have stated that a system is made up of input, process, output, and feedback control components that all work together to achieve a common goal. Systems can be nested in a hierarchy, with the outputs of one system being the inputs of another. Let's look at an organization and see how it fits into the system model.

An organization accepts many types of inputs, including information, raw materials, and new employees. Input components such as people, material/equipment, capital, and land have a high degree of controllability by the organization. These are considered resources and are within the organizational system's boundaries. Other input components such as government, competitors, the general public, and ecology are largely outside the organization's control but nonetheless affect its goals. These factors are in the environment of the organization.

As a system, all of the components of the organization, under the direction of management, work together as a whole to process and transform these inputs to achieve the organization's goals. Goals are the output of the organization and may include profit, cost reduction, market share, customer service, and so on.

One of the main focuses of an organization as a system is to regulate itself to ensure that its goals are met. The key ingredient of regulation is information, which is required by management for decision making, problem solving, and control. Information is the binding force that brings together all the components of an organization. The manager is the control element in the organizational system, using information to help achieve the desired goals. Through feedback control managers monitor how well output matches the goals of the organization. For example, a manager might develop specific quality control processes to monitor the quality of a product and compare it to the desired goal. If the product deviates from the goal, adjustments are made to the input and/or to the process producing the product.

An organization also falls within a hierarchy of systems. If we expand the boundaries of the organizational system outward, we can define a larger system that covers an entire industry. By expanding that still further, we can cover an entire economic system. So the organization itself is a subsystem of larger systems. On the other hand, if we shrink the organizational system's boundaries, we can see that the organization itself is also composed of many subsystems—for example, the accounting subsystem, production subsystem, and so on. Each subsystem is also composed of its own subsystems. For example, within the sales subsystem the sales force for one particular product area can be defined as a system. The boundaries of a system within an organization are not hard and fast but are dependent on the observer's focus. Subsystems within the organizational system are nested, with the outputs of one becoming the inputs of others and all the subsystems working together to achieve the common goals of the organization.

DEFINITION OF AN INFORMATION SYSTEM

An **information system** is a set of people, data, and procedures that work together to achieve the common goal of information management. Information management includes the tasks of gathering and processing data into reliable and accurate information in a usable form and distributing it in a timely fashion for use in decision making, problem solving, and control activities. People, data, and procedures are the minimum components required in an information system; most of today's information systems also include computer hardware and software. These systems are the focus of this book.

The most valuable resource an organization has is its people. From the production line through top management it is people that make products, deliver services, solve problems, and make decisions. Good people are the backbone of an organization. This chapter examines three groups of people involved in an information system—system personnel, users, and management.

System personnel are the professionals responsible for designing and implementing an information system. System personnel include system analysts and programmers. A **system analyst** is the specialist who works with users to determine their information needs and then designs a system to fulfill those needs. A **programmer** codes in a programming language the instructions that solve a problem so that they can be used by a computer. A system analyst can be compared to an architect who designs a building and a programmer, to a construction worker who builds the building. In larger organizations these positions are separate and distinct jobs; in other companies they may be combined into one position known as a programmer/analyst.

The user is the person(s) who will use or benefit from the information system. Users can range from the lowest paid clerk to the highest paid executive. Information system specialists as well as those without specific information system skills are part of this group. For example, users might include the operators who run the computers, system analysts, programmers, managers, and other staff who require information from a system. **End-user** specifically refers to non–information system personnel who use an information system; the term includes managers and staff who are not professional information system personnel. End-users can be a difficult group to satisfy since their computer knowledge and experience can range from none to considerable sophistication. The importance of end-user involvement in the planning and development of information systems cannot be overemphasized. End-users are the ultimate consumers of the information system and must accept and use it if it is to be successful. The best way to ensure this acceptance is through close communication among

Computer and Information System Concepts

FIGURE 1–15
Major management functions.

system personnel, management, and end-users throughout the development and life of an information system. In the last few years there has been a rapid trend toward end-user computing, whereby end-users design and program their own applications. End-user computing is discussed further in Chapter 11.

Managers are the key decision makers and problem solvers within an organization. In order for them to perform most efficiently and effectively, an information system must supply them with the quality information they need, when they need it. A **manager** is a person responsible for using available resources—people, materials/equipment, land, information, money—to achieve an organizational goal. A manager works toward a goal through five major functions: planning, staffing, organizing, directing, and controlling resources (Figure 1–15). **Planning** is the future-oriented process of developing courses of action to meet the short- and long-term goals of the organization.

Staffing involves assembling and training personnel who will achieve the organization's goals. **Organizing** provides resources and a structure in which personnel are responsible and accountable for working toward the organizational goal. **Directing** supplies leadership in supervising personnel, working through communication and motivation. **Controlling** involves development of procedures to measure actual performance against goals and to make any necessary adjustments to ensure that the organization is moving toward its goal. The organization's performance is evaluated, and plans are provided for any needed modifications.

In addition to people, data play an important role in an information system, providing the basis for information. The data gathered must be complete and accurate. If not, the information generated from the data will not be valid or accurate, and errors in decision making may result.

A large portion of an organization's resources are put into gathering and storing data about business transactions, competitors, the market place, and a host of other topics. Collecting data for a particular decision can be a large, costly task. An organization must determine what data are essential to generate the needed information, where the data can be obtained, and whether the data gathered are correct. All of this must be done in a cost-effective manner.

The final component in an information system is procedures, the instructions that tell people how to operate and use the system. For example, procedures tell how to format data for input into the information system, what program(s) should be used to process specific data, and how the output is to be used. Procedures also explain the steps to be taken if an error occurs. Common sources of procedures include operation manuals, which provide instructions on how to operate the computer system, and user's manuals, which tell users how to utilize the information system to get the information they need.

COMPUTER-BASED INFORMATION SYSTEMS

Even though an information system does not require a computer, most people think of computer-based information systems when they read or hear the term *information system*. A **computer-based information system** is a set of people, data, procedures, hardware, and software that work together to achieve the common goal of information management. We've already discussed people, data, and procedures. Hardware is the physical devices and connections of a computer system, such as computers, disk drives, printers, modems, cables, and so on. Chapter 3 examines computer hardware in more detail. Software is the set of instructions that tells the hardware how to operate; Chapter 4 discusses software. Throughout the rest of this text, unless otherwise indicated, the term *information system* will imply a computer-based information system.

WHY COMPUTERS ARE INCLUDED IN AN INFORMATION SYSTEM

Computers are used as part of an information system to increase the efficiency and effectiveness of an information system. Computers enable us to store and process more data in less time than ever before. Because of the computer's speed in processing data and the telecommunications capability to distribute information, managers can take advantage of information that would otherwise have been impossible to gather, process, analyze, and distribute in a timely fashion. Thus, decisions can be based on better information.

However, the use of computers does not automatically create a better information system. Computers simply give us a tool to reach this goal. The computers used in information systems have the advantage of performing arithmetic functions, testing relationships, and storing and retrieving data in a manner that is faster, more accurate, and more reliable than that of humans. However, people still need to determine what data need to be collected, how they are to be processed, and how the generated information is to be used.

Computers can also act as equalizers. They can enable smaller companies to compete effectively. In many cases large companies can no longer overpower smaller companies simply by using their size to make the cost of entering the market very high.

Computers are also used as part of an information system to achieve a twofold strategic advantage. (Highlight 1–1 examines the topic of strategic information systems.) One type of strategic advantage differentiates an organization's products and services from others in the field. For example, J.C. Penney used computers to create a credit card network. This service created a new business that other companies pay to use and helped differentiate J.C. Penney from its competitors. Second, organizations are applying automation to become the low-cost producer in an industry. For example, Northeast Utilities is using the latest computer technologies, such as an integrated services digital network (ISDN), to help keep costs down. ISDN is covered in Chapter 5.

FUNCTIONS OF AN INFORMATION SYSTEM

An information system has three basic functions: to (1) accept data (input), (2) convert data to information (process), and (3) produce and communicate information in a timely fashion to users for utilization in decision making (output). Many banks and other financial institutions use information systems to help determine whether a customer applying for a loan

Strategic Information Systems

The word *strategic* is used extensively these days. It has become a favorite buzzword and has been applied to almost every type of information system in a business. Information systems are often promoted as "strategic" when funds or approval of management is sought. But just what constitutes a truly strategic system? A strategic system is an information system that makes an important difference to a company's strategic mission. The strategic mission may be to take away market share from the competition or to increase the company's return on investment. Systems that accomplish this type of action and better the company's overall position in the market are strategic systems. They are in contrast to those information systems that merely allow the company to function (e.g., accounting systems) but don't help improve the company's position in the market.

A classic example of a strategic system was put into place by the American Hospital Supply Corporation (AHS). When the system was first developed, AHS was a company that distributed products from 8,500 manufacturers to more than 100,000 health care providers. The information system was a direct-order entry system, which set up direct computer links between AHS and its customers and suppliers. The system allowed hospitals to enter orders easily and at a lower cost, without having to wait for or deal with a salesperson. The system allowed AHS to cut inventories, improve customer service, and get better terms from suppliers because of their increased volume. Other distributors that did not have this type of system were often locked out of the market because they couldn't compete in price or customer service. The direct-order entry system increased the AHS market share dramatically and can truly be classified as a strategic information system.

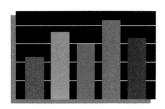

is a good risk (Table 1–1). Data about the customer, lending policies, and interest rates are input into the information system, which then processes the data, using previously defined procedures for determining credit worthiness, and generates information for the loan officer (the end-user) in the form of a recommendation to grant or deny the loan. This information is then output in a form usable by the loan officer. It is important to note, however, that no matter what the output indicates, the user of an information system must make the actual decision.

Because of the ever-increasing importance of information to an organization, the efficiency and effectiveness of an information system's functions in managing information are becoming more and more critical to the organization's and thus the manager's success. Highlight 1–2 illustrates what can happen when information systems fail.

Several reasons are often cited for the growing concerns relative to an information system's ability to manage information. Both the size of many organizations and the number of competitors have been growing. As a

Strategic Information System Failures

When an information system fails, the results can be devastating to an organization. BankAmerica experienced this when its Masternet institutional trust accounting system failed to perform. The on-line system was designed to replace a 20-year-old system and provide on-line updating and querying. However, the new system failed to deliver because of poor and inadequate design and implementation. Masternet failed to maintain current data and fell months behind in generating statements. The system cost BankAmerica $80 million and valued customers and had to be entirely scrapped. Strategic information system failures in the 1980s have helped BankAmerica go from 1st to 29th place in assets of banks worldwide.

An·ill-defined and overly ambitious driver registration system for the New Jersey Division of Motor Vehicles cost that state $6.5 million dollars. Price Waterhouse was contracted to design and implement the system, but poor judgment in the implementation phase led to the wrong programming language being used to implement the system. As a result, more than a million New Jersey drivers were unable to register their cars at all or registered them incorrectly because of computer errors.

In 1983 Blue Cross/Blue Shield of Wisconsin attempted to replace its entire financial and claims systems. Its current systems at that time included seven different claims processing systems and three different membership systems. The systems had grown into an unwieldy mass of confusion and were filled with old and outdated information. The conversion to new systems cost Blue Cross/Blue Shield $600 million. Electronic Data Systems Corporation (EDS) was contracted to design and implement the new system, but serious problems resulted in many claims not being paid at all and others being overpaid. The overpayments cost the company tens of thousands of dollars, but the system failures also cost the company 22,000 subscribers. Clearly, system failures can have serious effects on an organization.

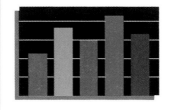

TABLE 1–1
Functions of an information system in determining customer credit.

Input	Process	Output
Data	*Data to Information*	*Information*
Customer specifics Lending policy Interest rate	Algorithms to convert data into desired information (e.g., customer credit worthiness, recommendation of whether to grant loan or not)	Transformed into a form usable by loan officer (e.g., screen display, paper copy)

result, the volume of data generated and the information needed to make decisions have increased dramatically.

The computer's ability to process large amounts of data with great speed and the advances in communication technologies permitting faster data transmission have left many managers overwhelmed with information. In addition, managers must deal with much more sophisticated technology today. Getting the needed information to choose from numerous computers, communication technologies, robots, and so on has become an ever-growing task. On top of all this, managers have less time to make decisions as technology continues to increase the pace of business transactions. For example, computers and communication technology now allow a product order to be received, processed, and shipped all in the same day.

Not only is it necessary for an information system to perform its three basic functions, but factors such as those just listed require it to perform those functions with ever-increasing efficiency and effectiveness if an organization is to remain competitive in today's fast-paced Information Age.

SUMMARY

A computer is a machine that can solve problems by accepting data, performing certain operations, and presenting the results of those operations. Analog computers recognize data as continuous measurement of a physical property. Digital computers are high-speed, programmable, electronic devices that perform mathematical calculations, compare values, and store results. A computer system includes hardware, software, users, and procedures. Computers are categorized as supercomputers, mainframe computers, superminis, minicomputers, supermicros, and microcomputers.

Computers are used in four basic ways: information processing, control, design and development, and communications. Computers can perform only three basic tasks—arithmetic functions, comparisons, and storage and retrieval—but they can do these tasks faster, more accurately, and more reliably than people. Information processing involves converting data into information. Data flow through the computer system in the following steps: input, processing, and output. Input involves collecting, verifying, and encoding data so that the machine can read them. Processing occurs as the computer classifies, sorts, calculates, summarizes, and stores the results. Output takes place when the data are retrieved and converted so that a person can read the results.

A system is a set of components that interact with each other to work together toward a common goal. The four major components of a system are input, process, output, and feedback. Input includes anything that enters the system. Output is anything that leaves the system. A process transforms an input into an output. Feedback is a control mechanism that reintroduces a portion of a system's output as an input into the same system.

Data are merely facts. Information is data that have been processed into an organized and usable form; information must be relevant and meaningful to the user for the task at hand. Information can be of two general types: Quantitative information tells how much or how many and can be presented in two forms, as numerical or graphical information. Qualitative information describes something in nonquantitative terms. A transaction is a business activity or event. The attributes of information include accuracy, relevance, completeness, timeliness, cost-effectiveness, auditability, and reliability.

The two basic sources of information are internal, those gathered within an organization, and external, those gathered outside the organization. Information received from any source should not contain bias and should be valid, reliable, consistent, and timely. The value of information is determined by how much additional knowledge the information adds to what was already known. The costs and benefits of obtaining information are also important in determining its value.

An information system is a set of people, data, and procedures that work together to achieve the common goal of information management. Information management includes the tasks of gathering and processing data into reliable and accurate information in a usable form and distributing it in a timely fashion for use in decision making, problem solving, and control activities.

System personnel are professionals responsible for designing and implementing an information system; included are system analysts and programmers. End-users are specifically non–information system personnel, such as managers and staff, who use an information system. Managers are the key decision makers and problem solvers within an organization. Managers are responsible for using available resources to achieve organizational goals. The five major functions of a manager are planning, staffing, organizing, directing, and controlling.

Data provide the basis for the information generated by an information system; procedures are the instructions that tell people how to operate and use an information system. A computer-based information system is a set of people, data, procedures, hardware, and software that work together to achieve the common goal of information management.

Every information system has three basic functions: to accept data (input), convert data to information (process), and produce and communicate information in a timely fashion to users for decision making (output).

CASE ANALYSIS

Each of the remaining chapters is followed by two minicases. Some instructors will assign them; others will not. Regardless of your instructor's requirements, you will benefit from working through these cases. Case analysis will help you understand business information systems, and that understanding will be valuable to you in this course, those that follow, and your professional career.

A case is simply a written description of a specific situation. Almost all cases in business classes contain a problem structured to provide a decision-making opportunity. The basic reason for using cases is to allow you to apply the various techniques and knowledge you have learned (in this and other courses) to real-world situations. With cases the process of analysis may be more important than generating specific, accurate answers; thinking is the most important element. Many courses require memorizing lists and facts, but case analysis is different. There are no canned answers or procedures that will always work. It may be one of the few times in your education when you really need to think.

A five-step process for case analysis is recommended.

1. Identify and define the problem.
2. Develop and evaluate alternative solutions.
3. Select the most desirable solution.
4. Develop plans to implement the solution.
5. Consider backup solutions.

These five steps do not guarantee a proper analysis, but they do offer a logical sequence that, when diligently and vigorously pursued, can be of great help in analyzing classroom cases and real-world situations.

Identify and Define the Problem

The first step of the process involves identifying the problem. A *problem* can be defined as the difference between the desired situation and the existing condition. To identify a problem area, you must (1) recognize that a problem exists, (2) define the specific problem, and (3) develop a problem statement.

Recognizing a problem area requires a careful reading to become familiar with the overall case and to gain a sense of perspective. It may be helpful to underline all problems and symptoms in the case and then organize them according to areas. One critical aspect of defining a specific problem is distinguishing between problems and symptoms. Symptoms are the outward signs or results of a problem. Treating symptoms may offer temporary relief but seldom solves the basic problem. Developing a clear and specific statement of the problem provides the basis for the next step—developing and evaluating alternative solutions to the problem.

Develop and Evaluate Alternative Solutions

Once the major problem or issue has been identified, you are ready to begin generating and evaluating alternative solutions. Virtually all problems have numerous potential answers, and it is quite helpful to evaluate several alternatives before choosing one.

An important component of evaluating alternatives is consideration of both positive and negative aspects of each alternative. Essentially, you should ask, "If I were to select this alternative, what would happen and what are the consequences?" At this point you should also consider how each solution would be implemented.

Select the Most Desirable Solution

Selecting the most desirable solution should be relatively easy if the preceding step has been performed adequately. It is important to discuss the reasons for your choice, which may range from positive (it is the best of several good solutions) to negative (it is the least onerous of several poor solutions).

Develop Plans to Implement the Solution

The best solution in the world is no good if it cannot be implemented. In some situations you will find that several solutions would be acceptable but only one can be implemented effectively and efficiently.

Consider Backup Solutions

Regardless of the quality of your solution, it may not work. Failure can occur for many reasons, including changes in the situation, inaccurate forecasts or assumptions, and so on. You should address the possibility that your solution may not work and develop a backup solution. This alternate solution should be implemented if it becomes evident that the selected solution is not working.

Key Terms

accuracy	information
analog computer	information processing
auditability	information system
black box process	input
completeness	internal source of information
computer	knowledge workers
computer-based information system	lap-top computer
controlling	mainframe computers
cost-effectiveness	manager
data	microcomputer
data processing	minicomputer
desktop computer	numerical information
digital computer	organizing
directing	output
end-user	personal computer
external source of information	planning
feedback	portable computer
graphical information	procedures
hand-held computer	processing
hardware	programmer

qualitative information

quantitative information

relevance

reliability

software

staffing

supercomputer

supermicro

supermini

system

systems analyst

system personnel

timeliness

transaction

user

white box process

Review Questions

1. In what different ways were you influenced by a computer yesterday?

2. What is the difference between *data* and *information*?

3. Do you prefer quantitative or qualitative information? What determines the type of information you prefer?

4. Do managers prefer information from an internal source or an external source? Why?

5. List and describe the five concerns about information sources discussed in the chapter.

6. How can the value of information be determined?

7. Define *digital computer*. How does it differ from an analog computer?

8. List the components of a computer system.

9. List and briefly define the major categories of computer systems.

10. Describe three types of microcomputers.

11. In what three basic ways are computers used?

12. What are the four basic tasks that a computer is capable of performing?

13. What advantages are there in using a computer as opposed to doing a task manually?

14. Describe the three steps involved in the flow of data through a computer system. Compare this flow to that of a human system.

15. Identify a system functioning at your school. List any subsystems that make up that system.

16. What is the difference between a black box and a white box process?

17. Define the terms *information system* and *computer-based information system,* and briefly describe the components of each.

18. What advantages are there in using a computer as part of an information system?

19. What are the three basic functions of an information system?

Information Systems in Business

OBJECTIVES

- Know the impact that information systems have had on businesses
- Describe the different levels of management and the types of information each needs
- List and briefly describe the six types of information systems
- List and briefly describe some functional areas of business
- Discuss several ways in which information systems are used in the functional areas of business
- Discuss several ways in which information systems have impacted entire industries

OUTLINE

IMPACT ON MANAGEMENT PROBLEM SOLVING AND DECISION MAKING

TYPES OF INFORMATION THAT MANAGERS NEED

TYPES OF INFORMATION SYSTEMS
Transaction Processing Systems I Management Information Systems I Decision Support Systems I Knowledge-Based (Expert) Systems I Office Information Systems I Computer-Integrated Manufacturing Information Systems

APPLICATION OF INFORMATION SYSTEMS IN FUNCTIONAL AREAS OF BUSINESS
Accounting Information System I Financial Information System I Marketing Information System I Production/Operations Information System I Human Resources Information System

APPLICATION OF INFORMATION SYSTEMS IN SELECTED INDUSTRIES
The Manufacturing Industry I The Banking Industry I The Investment Industry I The Retail Sales Industry I The Health Care Industry

HISTORY OF COMPUTERS

TECHNICAL EVOLUTION OF COMPUTERS
First Generation (1951–1959) I Second Generation (1959–1965) I Third Generation (1965–1971) I Fourth Generation (1971–Present) I Fifth Generation (Future)

Chapter 2

Management Profile: Patrick Rooney
ROONEY TURNS DP AT BASEBALL HALL OF FAME

Among the hundreds of exhibits in the National Baseball Hall of Fame and Museum, Patrick Rooney is particularly proud of two. One is the large aerial photograph of the Bronx, Yankee Stadium, and the old Polo Grounds; Rooney can point out the apartment building he lived in as a boy. In the summers he sold peanuts in both those historic ballparks. The other special exhibit is a user-interactive CRT screen with which visitors can spend hours. Some compare baseball statistics, and others watch videos of their diamond heroes.

Rooney began his career at the General Motors assembly plant in Tarrytown, New York, in the early 1960s. He later joined the data-processing operation of Central Hudson Gas & Electric in Poughkeepsie and rose to the top of that operation during his 17-year stay. He went on to create and teach the data-processing curriculum at a community college in Cortland, New York. He worked summers as a hall of fame attendant and was inducted as the first full-time computer professional in 1985.

Rooney heads a one-man operation facing the same challenges that many large management information system shops face: reluctant end-users. "When I first started in the business, no one knew the extent to which you could make a computer work for you," Rooney says. "Here my problem is that I know, but my people really haven't always had exposure to it. In any operation that's probably the single biggest problem. People still don't have a real good understanding of what a computer can do."

What do computers do at the Hall of Fame? Plenty now, including the traditional data-processing functions of payroll and accounting, and they will do much more in the future. Rooney has ambitious automation goals for the hall and the adjoining National Baseball Library. One of Rooney's ongoing projects is the creation of a database for the more than 24,000 baseball artifacts that have been donated. Related information, currently stored in manual ledger books, requires constant updating as the hall receives thousands of new items each year.

Rooney takes special pride in the two IBM interactive screen exhibits, and with good reason—they helped get him hired. As a hall of fame attendant, Rooney had offered his advice on where the hall could computerize. When IBM later offered to set up the interactive exhibit but needed help from an in-house professional, Rooney was in the right place at the right time.

"The mission of a museum is part educational, and the interactive exhibit adds to that," he says. "That's where the computers can really improve the means of accessing this part of American history, which is, in essence, folklore."

Hall directors say the IBM exhibits are the most popular attractions. "The computers have been a marvelous addition," says the hall's associate director.

Adapted from "Patrick Rooney: Rooney Turns DP at Baseball Hall of Fame" by Cliton Wilder. Copyright 1988 by CW Publishing Inc., Framingham, MA 01701. Reprinted from *Computerworld*, Oct. 24, 1988.

Computer use in business information systems has grown tremendously over the past two decades. Decreasing hardware costs and increasing capabilities, more and better software applications, and a better understanding of computer potential have all contributed. In addition, the acceptance of information as a strategic corporate resource and competitive pressure have forced many businesses to expand their use of computers in their information systems.

In this chapter we examine how information systems have impacted businesses and look at the types of information that managers need from information systems. We briefly examine several different types of information systems. In addition, we examine where information systems are being used in several of the more common functional areas of business, as well as how they are being used in selected industries. The chapter concludes with a discussion of the history of computers.

IMPACT ON MANAGEMENT PROBLEM SOLVING AND DECISION MAKING

Over the last several decades the management of information and, thus, information systems has become increasingly more important to the successful attainment of an organization's goals. Information is the lifeblood of an organization. Most activities performed by managers in an organization—such as problem identification and solution, control, and decision making—are based on information. Managers need to receive accurate and timely information to accomplish these activities effectively. Information systems permit information to be acquired, processed, and distributed efficiently. They can enable businesses to gain a competitive edge because accurate, timely, and more complete information allows better decisions to be made.

Many organizations are now seeing information systems as crucial. Some businesses, such as the Travelers Corporation, an insurance giant, have made information system strategy a top priority. Travelers issued a mandate that each of the company's businesses should take advantage of technology. The corporation sees its information system's management and staff as the driving force behind corporate strategy.

Travelers is moving into a new era of information systems. They have long had information systems in use in administrative and operational areas where they could provide an immediately apparent benefit. But information systems are now viewed as more than just a service. They are seen as an integral part of the organization's business. One example is Travelers' client access and risk management analysis (CARMA) program. The CARMA program makes available to large corporate customers detailed information about their employee claims so that the companies can analyze the patterns of losses and take preventive measures. Travelers also foresees information systems that will automate the writing of policies from the initial application through the underwriting and the issuance of a final policy. These uses of information systems will provide added services that will help distinguish Travelers from its competitors. Highlight 2–1 takes a look at another strategic use of information systems.

The casino and hotel business is extremely competitive. It is a business where customer service is of utmost importance. Often the difference between one establishment and the next is the customer's perception of the service received. Trump Plaza Casino and Hotel relies on three strategic systems to keep operations running smoothly and competitively. These systems include the finance system, the casino system, and the hotel system.

The finance system can do a background credit check within minutes on those seeking a gambling credit line. The system also keeps track of who is winning money, who is not, who had the biggest win in a given day and the biggest loss, and what the average bet of each gambler is. That information is entered into the system by the pit clerks in the gambling pits; they get their information from the pit bosses. If a person wants his credit increased, the credit manager looks at his current standing in the computer and can approve or deny the request immediately.

The casino system contains information about gamblers that is used to rate them as players. Those ratings are then used to determine which players will receive complimentary dinners in the hotel's restaurants, tickets to shows, or free rooms.

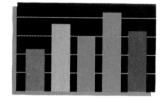

The hotel system keeps track of which hotel rooms are rented and which are vacant and clean. When a room is clean, the maid picks up the room phone and dials in a code, which alerts the system that the room is available for occupancy. The hotel system also tracks reservations and cancellations.

Information systems can also be used to help contain costs. For example, Amoco, a major company in gasoline and oil refining and distribution, has been forced to downsize its business units to cut costs. A reduction in the number of middle managers has increased the need for computer support to fill in the gaps. Amoco uses information systems as tools to create more efficient operations. Information systems may also be able to lower the costs of producing existing goods and services and developing and producing new goods and services. In addition, information systems can result in greater productivity for managers and the organization as a whole. Computer-based information systems can take advantage of computer processing speeds and allow more work to be done in a given amount of time with greater accuracy and fewer errors. Managers are able to access and manipulate information right at their desks through a personal computer linked to the information system.

Many of today's products could not be produced without the effective use of information systems on the factory floor. Aerospace, automotive, and industrial manufacturers use information systems to automate production and streamline engineering, speed development time, reduce cost, and keep up with the competition. These industries need a strong commitment to and investment in information systems to compete successfully in cost, quality, and delivery.

Most organizations are constantly changing as a result of both internal and external influences. An information system provides the means for managers to gather and manage the appropriate information needed to keep pace with that change. For example, a merger between two organizations may result in new goals and objectives. The managers must quickly acquire the information needed to meet the requirements of the new business and the philosophy of new top management. Changes in the marketplace, availability of resources, economic factors, and a host of other considerations are constantly forcing managers to reevaluate. Information systems help them do this quickly and easily.

One of the challenges in increasing the use of information systems is overcoming the reluctance of non−information system personnel to accept the importance of and use the information systems. This concern can be dealt with through ongoing dialogue between the information system group and other users in the company. Input from all end-users is important to information system success; input can result in better systems that take into account human factors, such as the design of computer screens, software interfaces, and work environments. Involvement can win the support of end-users by making them feel that the system is theirs and they have some control over it.

Communicating with an increasing number of other departments, managers, and staff; dealing with new technologies; and maintaining an edge over a growing number of competitors are all factors that increase the complexity of a manager's job. An information system can help control this increasing complexity by ensuring that appropriate information is communicated in an accurate and timely manner.

Successful information systems require

- commitment to invest funds in systems that will exceed those of the competition
- application of systems to business needs that will contribute to profit growth
- acquisition of qualified systems personnel without overspending
- provision for adequate training of systems professionals in new methods and technologies
- user access to technology throughout the company
- consideration of human factors in system designs
- commitment to developing competitive systems to capture greater market share

When designed, developed, and used correctly, information systems are a powerful tool that can increase the efficiency and effectiveness with which an organization acquires, processes, communicates, and uses information. Effective information systems can enable organizations to make better decisions and reach their goals.

TYPES OF INFORMATION THAT MANAGERS NEED

Management is divided into three basic levels: top-level (strategic) managers; middle-level (tactical) managers; and low-level (operational) managers (Figure 2–1). Although all three levels of management work toward organizational goals and are involved to varying degrees in all five management functions, each level requires different types of information. As we look at the types of decisions made and some of the informational needs of each level of management, note that the amount of detail required by a manager increases from top to bottom. The higher the management level, the broader and less detailed the information needs to be.

Consider an organization in which Pete is the top-level strategic manager, Tom is the middle-level tactical manager, and Mel is the low-level operational manager. Pete is interested in information on the capacity and use of the company's physical facility as well as a measure of the facility's revenue generation. Tom needs more detailed information regarding the efficient and effective utilization of resources, and he wants similar information on the resources available to his competitors. Mel wants even more detailed information about the resources. He is not so concerned with cost or effectiveness but is extremely concerned with short-run productivity—how the resources perform on a minute-by-minute basis.

Owner Pete O'Malley, manager Tom Lasorda, and scout Mel Didier all work for the same organization—the Los Angeles Dodgers—at differ-

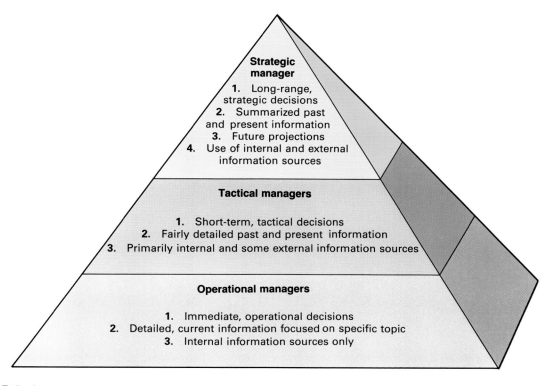

Strategic manager
1. Long-range, strategic decisions
2. Summarized past and present information
3. Future projections
4. Use of internal and external information sources

Tactical managers
1. Short-term, tactical decisions
2. Fairly detailed past and present information
3. Primarily internal and some external information sources

Operational managers
1. Immediate, operational decisions
2. Detailed, current information focused on specific topic
3. Internal information sources only

FIGURE 2–1
Levels of management, types of decision making, and information needs.

ent levels in the managerial pyramid. Mel needs much more detailed information than Tom or Pete, and Pete needs more summarized information for his decision making than do Tom or Mel. Pete has great interest in the average World Series attendance in Dodger Stadium (56,000) and the proceeds ($2,500,000). Tom is concerned with the physical and emotional health of his resources (the players). Mel wants to know whether the Oakland A's pitcher Dennis Eckersley will throw an inside slider to hobbled Dodger hitter Kirk Gibson. As it turned out, Eckersley did; but Kirk knew it was coming because of Mel's information and nailed it for the game-winning home run in the first game of the 1988 World Series.

So it is with all organizations, from baseball teams to automobile giants. Higher levels of management have different information needs to make different decisions. **Top-level (strategic) managers** make decisions involving the long-range, or strategic, goals of the organization. Of the five major management functions, top-level managers spend most of their time planning and organizing. They need summarized information covering past and present operations as well as future projections. Information drawn from internal sources gives them broad views of their companies' internal situations. Information drawn from external sources permits them to evaluate industry trends, world economic trends, government regulations, and other outside activities that influence the business health of corporations. A strategic manager such as Lee Iacocca, CEO of Chrysler, might be required to decide whether a new plant should be opened or a new sports car produced.

Middle-level (tactical) managers divide their time among all five functions of management. They are concerned with short-term, tactical decisions directed toward accomplishing the overall organizational goals established by top-level managers. Middle-level managers work on such tasks as budgets, schedules, and performance evaluations and need information that is fairly detailed to permit them to compare present and past results and make adjustments where necessary. Middle-level managers require mainly internal information but also use some external information. A tactical manager for Chrysler might decide how long to advertise a new car on television in a particular state. Many organizations are cutting costs by using computerization to reduce the number of tactical managers.

Low-level (operational) managers are directly involved with the day-to-day operations of a business. They are responsible for seeing that the tactical decisions of middle-level managers are implemented by personnel at the operations level. The information of operational managers must be detailed, current, and focused on a specific topic. It comes from sources such as inventory lists, historical records, and procedures manuals. Chrysler's operational manager might decide to use a newer and less expensive method for cleaning paint nozzle jets.

TYPES OF INFORMATION SYSTEMS

An organization can make use of different types of information systems to supply the information essential to successful operation. This section discusses six types of information systems: transaction processing systems, management information systems, decision support systems, knowledge-based (expert) systems, office information systems, and computer-integrated manufacturing information systems (Figure 2–2).

Transaction Processing Systems

A transaction, as mentioned in Chapter 1, is a business event or activity, such as selling a product or shipping an order, that involves or affects a business or organization. A **transaction processing system (TPS)** is a system that processes data about transactions or other events that affect the operation of a business. A TPS is the oldest and most common type of information system used in business. Examples of TPSs include order-entry and payroll systems. An order-entry system uses data from the sale order as input (who purchased how many of what item) and produces a customer's bill as output. Transaction processing systems are examined further in Chapter 7.

Management Information Systems

The purpose of a **management information system (MIS)** is to provide information to managers for use in problem detection and solution. An MIS is designed to support decisions regarding situations that recur and are highly structured, that is, whose information requirements are known in advance by the manager. MISs produce reports on a recurring basis to help management in predictable decision making. An MIS can use data from a transaction processing system as well as data that has been collected and processed in response to a particular decision that must be made. For example, the order-entry transactions could be collected for all customers and then summarized to show the total sales volume each month compared to that of the same month for the previous year. MISs are presented in more detail in Chapter 7.

FIGURE 2–2
Types of information systems.

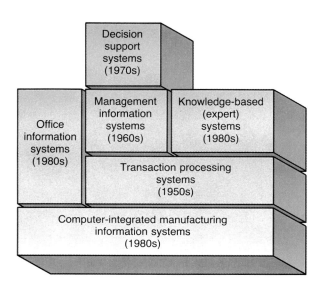

Decision Support Systems

A **decision support system (DSS)** is designed to help managers with relatively unstructured decisions. These decisions might be necessary only once or twice and cannot be predicted in advance. For example, decisions such as whether to merge with another organization or build a large industrial park can benefit from a DSS, which is designed to respond to a manager's ad hoc need for information. As changes occur or new situations arise, a manager can request needed information. For example, a manager might use sales data from the company database and compare it with a competitor's sales data found in a published financial report. The two companies' sales data could be examined side-by-side via a microcomputer DSS. A DSS analysis of a given situation or recommendation is based on mostly quantitative data that exist in factual databases. Such databases typically cover a broad range of subjects.

DSSs are used primarily by middle management and are often oriented toward models and data analysis. Managers often use microcomputers with both internal and external data to support these unstructured decisions. A DSS that caters specifically to the special information needs of managerial planning, monitoring, and analysis is called an **executive information system (EIS)**. Chapter 7 takes a closer look at DSSs.

Knowledge-Based (Expert) Systems

A **knowledge-based (expert) system** not only uses facts like a DSS, but also combines rules and assumptions to make inferences that lead to decision-making recommendations for highly structured, although often complex, problems. An expert system uses a process that is designed to mimic the decision process of a human expert; hence the name *expert system*. Much of the data used by an expert system is qualitative although some quantitative data can exist as well. Expert systems are used to troubleshoot problems in equipment, determine credit worthiness, provide medical diagnosis, guide less experienced people in jobs that require special expertise, and accomplish a host of other tasks. Chapter 7 further examines expert systems.

Office Information Systems

An **office information system (OIS)** includes a number of subsystems integrated to perform the functions of an office more efficiently and productively. These subsystems include word processing systems; data processing, storage, and retrieval systems; image-processing systems; communication systems; and office support systems. An OIS may also interact with other information systems within an organization.

Word processing systems offer computer-assisted creation, editing, and printing of text and documents. Data processing, storage, and retrieval systems are all concerned with data. Processing systems include microcomputers that are either used in a stand-alone capacity or are connected to other computers within the office or to other information systems throughout the organization. Storage and retrieval systems include disk, microforms (microfilm and microfiche), and optical devices. Image-processing systems include reprographic (copying and duplication) systems, scanners, and desktop publishing systems. Data communication systems include electronic mail, facsimile, voice messaging, electronic teleconferencing, and telecommuting. Office support systems include electronic calendars, appointment books, tickler files, and task management systems. OISs, also referred to as office automation systems, will be discussed further in Chapter 8.

Computer-Integrated Manufacturing Information Systems

Most companies have come to realize that they must either partially or fully computerize their factories in order to be competitive. The use of computers to control machines in the manufacturing process is called **computer-aided manufacturing (CAM)**. To be fully automated and integrated, a company must link all the different parts of the manufacturing process with all other aspects of the company. An information system that automates and integrates the entire manufacturing enterprise results in **computer-integrated manufacturing (CIM)**. With CIM, companies not only link product design to the manufacturing process, but also link those processes to the company computers that handle word processing, project management, general accounting, inventory control, order processing, factory-floor scheduling, and all other operations within the factory itself (Figure 2–3).

FIGURE 2–3
Information can flow from the factory floor to the boardroom with computer-integrated manufacturing systems (CIM) similar to the one used by this manufacturing company. (Courtesy of Honeywell)

**APPLICATION OF
INFORMATION SYSTEMS
IN FUNCTIONAL AREAS
OF BUSINESS**

This section takes a brief look at some of the ways in which information systems are used in several of the more common functional areas of business. Remember that these are typical descriptions and are by no means the only way that information systems and subsystems are organized and named. Figure 2–4 shows an organizational chart of the functional areas we will examine—accounting, finance, marketing, production/operations, and human resources. Each of these areas may be supported by its own information system, although there can also be some sharing of information among them.

Accounting Information System

An **accounting information system** uses primarily transaction processing systems to record transactions that affect the financial status of the organization. Such systems are referred to as operational accounting systems and maintain a historical record of the transactions. These systems are also used to produce reports, such as a balance sheet and income statement, that give a financial picture of the organization.

Accounting was one of the first functional areas to incorporate computer-based information systems; the nature of accounting readily lends itself to computerization for several reasons. Accounting transactions generate large amounts of data that need to be regularly processed and stored, accurately and quickly. The processing required is relatively simple and easy to implement on the computer, and management can establish appropriate controls and error-checking procedures to ensure the security and accuracy of the data. In addition, accounting systems are designed to

FIGURE 2–4
Several functional areas of business.

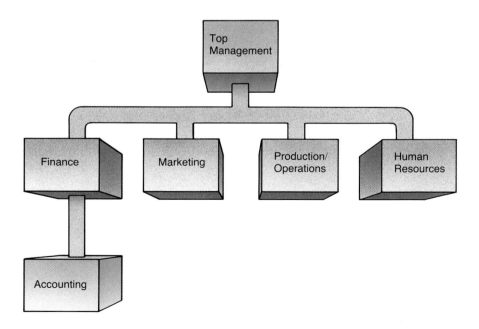

maintain an audit trail, which enables data stored in the system to be traced back to the original transactions. As Chapter 1 explained, computers can easily handle tasks with these requirements.

Accounting systems also use some MIS and DSS applications. These management accounting systems usually involve projections and estimates of the future to help in developing budgets and plans. Accounting information systems are made up of a number of subsystems. Several of the more common include the accounts receivable, accounts payable, payroll, and general ledger systems.

Financial Information System

A **financial information system** is designed to provide information concerning the acquisition of funds to finance business operations. It also provides information on the allocation and control of the organization's financial resources. Whereas an accounting information system focuses on recording data generated by the daily operation of a business, financial information systems focus on planning and control. In so doing, they rely heavily on DSSs, which in turn draw much of their data from the transaction processing systems of the accounting information system.

Financial information systems are also an excellent candidate for computerization. Many financial calculations are complex, requiring large numbers of variables with numerous possible interactions. The calculations often need to be repeated numerous times with minor data changes to answer what-if questions. A computer speeds up the recalculation process greatly. Financial information systems are less concerned with absolute accuracy than accounting information systems are because many of the financial variables are future-oriented and difficult to predict precisely.

Financial information systems are also made up of numerous subsystems. Several common ones include requirements analysis, planning, cash management, credit management, and capital expenditure systems.

Marketing Information System

A **marketing information system** involves gathering details about day-to-day sales transactions, managing and controlling marketing operations, and planning sales and marketing strategies for the future. A marketing information system must deal with existing products and markets and must plan for future products and markets. To accomplish its goals, a marketing information system relies equally on transaction processing systems, management information systems, and decision support systems.

A marketing information system can be broken into two subsystems: a sales system and a marketing system. The sales system records data about day-to-day sales transactions—for example, customer names, item numbers and quantities ordered, and billing and shipping addresses. This information is recorded using a transaction processing system. The sales system must be capable of accurately processing a high volume of data and thus is an ideal candidate for computerization.

The marketing system focuses on planning and control and relies on MISs and DSSs. The MISs use data generated by the sales system to provide information on how well products and sales staff are performing. Management may use this information to adjust activities to meet organizational goals. DSSs are used to help plan for the future by assisting in such tasks as forecasting sales, planning pricing, and designing promotional strategies. Since the marketing system must process complex calculations of many variables with numerous possible interactions, it is also an ideal candidate for computerization.

Marketing information systems are also composed of numerous subsystems. Some of the more common subsystems include order-entry, customer profile, product management, sales management, sales forecasting, advertising, and market research systems.

Production/Operations Information System

The **production/operations information system** gathers and processes data about all of the activities involved in producing goods and services. That information is then used to plan, monitor, and control the production/operations process. Such a system enables an organization to produce goods and services more efficiently. Production scheduling can be better planned and the workload balanced with the available production capacity. Production/operations information systems also enable continuous monitoring, feedback, and control of production/operations, resulting in stricter quality control and leading to better products and greater productivity. Production/operations information systems can also reduce the carrying costs of inventories by enabling better control of raw materials and finished goods and fewer occurrences of depleted inventories.

The production/operations information system is also composed of a number of subsystems. Several of the more common include the master production schedule, materials requirement planning, capacity planning, engineering, production control, plant maintenance, process and numerical control, and physical distribution systems.

Human Resources Information System

The **human resources information system** in most organizations is involved with the recruitment, placement, evaluation, compensation, and development of employees. The goal of the system is to enable management to use the organization's human resources efficiently and effectively. The information should permit the personnel needs of a business to be appropriately met and effective personnel policies and programs created.

The human resources system is also made up of a number of subsystems. Some of the more common include payroll and labor analysis; personnel records; personnel skills inventory; recruitment, training, and development analysis; compensation analysis; and human resource requirements forecasting systems.

APPLICATION OF INFORMATION SYSTEMS IN SELECTED INDUSTRIES

Applications for computers and information systems continue to proliferate in numerous industries as more and more businesspeople recognize the advantages of having computers do a wide variety of tasks for them. We will look at some of the ways that computers and information systems are used in the manufacturing, banking, investment, retail, and health care industries.

The Manufacturing Industry

A manufacturing firm is one that transforms raw materials into finished goods. It relies on engineering activities, such as the planning and design of new products, and depends heavily on information from MISs and DSSs. A manufacturer is also concerned with the procurement of raw materials, which may be another firm's finished goods. This area of manufacturing relies on TPSs to monitor inventories and generate purchase orders when needed. It also relies on MISs and DSSs in the planning and control of inventories and orders. Scheduling the efficient use of facilities to maximize productivity is another function of a manufacturing firm, one for which MISs and DSSs are also important in planning and control. Finally, a manufacturing firm is involved in the fabrication of finished goods, which requires making or acquiring components and assembling them into finished products. TPSs are used extensively to gather data about the fabrication process. MISs are used to supply management with information to help control the fabrication process. And expert systems are used by some firms to help diagnose problems with machinery.

As was mentioned earlier, most companies have come to realize that they must computerize their factories in order to be competitive (Figure 2–5). However, only a few companies have fully implemented computer-integrated manufacturing (CIM). Highlight 2–2 (p. 51) takes a look at a factory used as a CIM test ground.

To integrate all computer-controlled operations and make sure that each piece of equipment can communicate with all others, equipment manufacturers must agree on communication links. The industry standard in communication links was developed by General Motors and is called **manufacturing automation protocol (MAP)**. Although developed by an automaker, MAP standards can be implemented in other manufacturing environments.

As the computer has become more powerful over the years, it has become capable of handling more sophisticated tasks than the simple processing of numerical data. As modern manufacturing plants are built, or older ones are remodeled, they have incorporated an impressive array of computer-controlled machinery into their overall information system. Computers have been used for very practical reasons: to increase productivity and to reduce costs.

Computer-Aided Design. If you had walked into a design work area just a few years ago, you would have seen numerous drafting tables with

FIGURE 2-5

Technicians and assemblers at the Convair Division of General Dynamics Corporation in San Diego are using a "paperless" factory system that replaces up to 90 percent of manufacturing paperwork in the final assembly area of the Tomahawk cruise missile. Accessing the system through bar codes, assemblers receive instructions at their workstation computers. The system maintains configuration control and is being adapted to other factory areas to maintain high quality and reduce the cost of manufacturing. Convair produces the Tomahawk cruise missile for the U.S. Navy and the U.S. Air Force. (Courtesy of General Dynamics Corporation)

designers or engineers hovering over them. Planning and drawing a proposed new product was a pencil-and-paper operation. If you walk into that same room today, you will probably see a different scene. The room contains design and drafting workstations, plotters, graphics tablets, and digitizers. The computerized tools used to design and draw the various items may be either individual microcomputers or terminals connected to the company's large computer system.

Computer-aided design (CAD) is the integration of the computer and graphics to aid in design and drafting. Manufacturers such as Brooks Shoe, a manufacturer of footwear, use CAD systems to design their running shoes (Figure 2–6). The advantages of this new application of computers are twofold.

1. It makes the designing and drafting easier, more accurate, and better planned.
2. It increases productivity because design and drafting time are significantly shortened.

Designers find this drawing method much easier than the pencil-and-paper method because mistakes can be corrected easily and designs can be redone many times until they are just right. Designers can move, copy, mirror, or erase sections or entire images—all without eraser marks, of course. And drawings can be scaled to any size and plotted on all sizes of paper.

The computer also lets the operator draw the product or object to appear in three dimensions (3-D). By drawing in 3-D, the operator can rotate the item on any axis on the display screen to view it from different

(a)

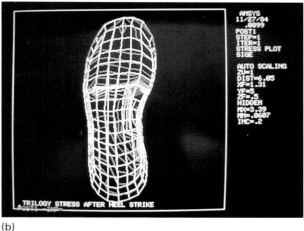

(b)

(c)

FIGURE 2-6

(a) A computer-generated model of the human foot is used to help design athletic shoes. (b) A computer generates a three-dimensional, finite-element model of an athletic shoe midsole that can be tested for stress points. (c) A two-dimensional cross-section of athletic shoe midsole. (All photos courtesy of Brooks Shoe and Michigan State University)

angles. The designer can "zoom in" to see small details or "pull back" to see the whole object, gaining a clear view of any design flaws and a glimpse of how the item will look when it is finished.

The use of a CAD system reduces production time because the initial drawing can be done more easily and quickly and it avoids repetition. Each design can be filed and used later to create different products. Often-used items or images can be stored in libraries and simply retrieved whenever needed and then inserted into a current drawing.

Automobile designers at Ford Motor Company use CAD to draw the many prototypes of a new car before creating solid models (Figure 2-7). Engineers at Ikeda Bussan Company in Tokyo use a CAD system to design automotive seats, most of which are used in Nissan's passenger cars. One facet of their system allows them to design and perform tests that measure body pressure on the seats and analyze road-induced vibrations. CAD systems are even being used by clothing manufacturers to design the patterns and fabrics for their apparel lines.

Computer Numerical Control (CNC). Manufacturing techniques have been through a tremendous transformation in recent years. A common task in the manufacturing process is the milling of parts. In the past, all

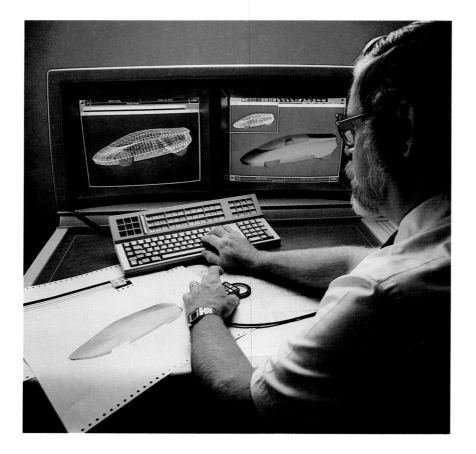

FIGURE 2–7
An engineer at Ford Motor Company uses a CAD system to assist in designing new automobiles. (Courtesy of Ford Motor Company)

operations of this sort were controlled by individual machine operators, and the quality of the end product was often directly related to the skill of the operator. Today, many of these milling operations have been turned over to **computer numerical control (CNC),** a system in which an operator programs a computer that controls the milling apparatus. The actual machine is not attended by a human being. A computer-controlled drill bit, for example, can perform the same task precisely, over and over again. This ability is particularly beneficial in forming repetitive parts.

CNC devices make it possible to cut more difficult parts and to operate with greater precision. The computer-controlled machines are even becoming easier to use. When programming is required, the commands usually appear as simple English words rather than complex computer codes.

In addition, the computer with a CNC machine can be programmed to change drill bits during a cutting operation. Operators no longer have to stop the manufacturing process to change drill bits and are therefore free to perform other duties. Often a CNC machine is connected to a CAD workstation. By watching the monitor, the CNC operator can view the part as it is being made by the machine.

GM's Vanguard axle plant in Saginaw, Michigan, incorporates the latest in computer-integrated manufacturing technology. In addition to producing axles for GM's J-cars, the plant is used to test automated processes before GM's car and truck factories put them on-line.

From a single bank of consoles in the control room all processes can be monitored and, if necessary, changed by simply pressing touch screens or using "soft keys" on console keyboards. When things go wrong, alarms are shown on-screen in the order of their priority; the highest priority is shown in red. The control room also contains a Texas Instruments knowledge-based workstation, which is used to revise the plant schedule once per shift. The plant incorporates 52 robots and 60 employees.

Technology has changed the way Vanguard employees work. Instead of spending the entire workday on the shop floor, they spend much of it in office cubicles processing data and making decisions. Because human engineering is an important consideration at the plant, employees are given some degree of choice in how they will meet production goals. In addition, they are given some discretion in scheduling their time off. All employees were given training to help change the work attitudes developed during years on a standard assembly-line operation.

Using this plant as a testing ground, GM hopes to discover automated technologies that improve the efficiency and productivity of plant operations and reduce costs. Successful technologies can then be incorporated into other GM plants.

Robotics. Many people think of robots as walking, talking androids or highly intelligent machines capable of carrying out all kinds of unusual deeds. Those are the robots of science fiction and modern-day movies rather than reality. **Robot** has been defined by the Robotics Institute of America as "a reprogrammable, multifunctional manipulator designed to move material, parts, tools, or specialized devices through variable programmed motions for the performance of a variety of tasks." More simply put, a robot is a machine that can be programmed to do a variety of useful tasks.

Although some experimental robots are made into humanlike forms, most industrial robots resemble nothing of the sort and would be impractical in that form. Far from being intelligent, robots are capable of completing only preprogrammed instructions. But they can be programmed to do some rather complicated tasks, and they can turn out products in a factory with unsurpassed precision.

Robots are used in manufacturing mainly to reduce costs and increase productivity. They are also excellent at repetitive tasks, which humans find boring; robots never tire. They are also ideal to replace humans on many jobs that are hazardous.

The first industrial robots were simply computer-controlled mechanical arms, performing a single, simple task. Today, industrial robots are still used primarily for assembly-line tasks, but some can do multiple tasks and move along on wheels or a track or belt system. Many robots have an elementary sense of touch and vision that gives them more precision.

Robots are generally delegated to three types of jobs: operating tools, lifting and handling materials or parts, and assembling parts. The operation of tools is the most common application of robots. Spot or arc welding and spray painting of automobile parts are typical tasks (Figure 2–8). The robots at Fey Manufacturing in California weld bumpers for small trucks. The drilling of hundreds or thousands of rivet holes in aircraft components is another natural task to assign to robots, and General Dynamics does just that.

The lifting and handling of materials are also fairly uncomplicated tasks for robots. Most robots are of the "pick and place" variety and simply pick up an object, such as a piece of metal, and place it somewhere else, as in a stamping machine.

Assembly is still difficult for robots, although inroads have been made in some areas. Some companies use robots to insert electrical components of standard shapes into printed circuit boards destined for many types of electrical equipment. IBM not only sells robots that can handle this type of

FIGURE 2–8
Robots are used for welding automobile parts at this Honda Plant. (Courtesy of Honda America, Marysville, Ohio)

An Overview of Computers and Information Systems

assembly task, but also uses them to assemble products in their computer and terminal plants.

As computer capabilities grow, so do the applications for robots. Robots can now be adapted with sensors that help the robot "see" and "feel" its way around the workplace. An elementary sense of sight is accomplished with digital-imaging cameras or by bouncing infrared or microwave signals off the object. These signals are received by a robot's computer and matched with previously stored images for the purpose of identification and inspection.

Robots can be programmed to pick up heavy objects or objects as delicate and lightweight as an egg without damaging either. The sense of touch, tactile sensing, is in its elementary stages of development, but robots can now distinguish many different shapes, handle each appropriately, and perform various operations. These tasks are possible because the robot's "hands," called end effectors, are available in many varieties and are often interchangeable.

Japan is the world's leader in the manufacture and use of industrial robots; about 65 percent of all robots are in Japan. The United States is the next largest user. Projections indicate that there will be more than 200,000 robots in the early 1990s. The cost of an industrial robot is between $25,000 and $125,000. Major suppliers of robots include Hitachi, Kawasaki, and Mitsubishi in Japan; Cincinnati Milacron, GMF Robotics, and DeVilbiss in the United States; Volkswagen in West Germany; and Renault in France.

Programmable Controllers. Two important aspects of running an industrial plant are monitoring and controlling the activities of the machinery. These jobs are being taken over by the **programmable controller,** which is a computer-regulated unit consisting of a microprocessor, an input and output module, and a power supply (Figure 2–9). A programmable controller is used to control the on/off functions of switches and relays and to control processes (process control).

The microprocessor of a programmable controller is programmed with a keyboard that can be attached to it when needed. When the programming is complete, the keyboard can be removed, and the programmable controller is still functional. The advantage of the programmable controller is that its microprocessor can be programmed to reflect any desired cause-and-effect relationship (e.g., throwing Switch 1 starts Motor 2). The programmable controller can also be reprogrammed if any changes are necessary.

Process control is the monitoring and controlling of various processes in a system's operation (Figure 2–10). For example, a programmable controller can play an important part in regulating the furnace temperature for melting glass. Basically, a "set point," such as a specific temperature, is programmed into the programmable controller for the glass-melting furnace. The furnace continually sends temperature data signals back to the programmable controller, which compares these signals to its preprogrammed set point. If the signals do not match, the programmable controller sends a signal to a control element that adjusts the furnace

FIGURE 2–9
The Babcock & Wilcox Company's Loose Parts Monitoring System III, a programmable controller, uses sophisticated computer-analysis techniques to evaluate the metal-to-metal impact of loose parts caught in the high velocity flows of nuclear steam systems. The controller provides real-time estimates of the location and damage potential of loose parts. (Courtesy of the Babcock & Wilcox Company)

temperature accordingly. One programmable controller can control many process-control systems, a more complex task than controlling on/off operations.

Because of fierce worldwide competition more factories are incorporating the latest computer technologies into their information systems. Factories need to keep their costs down, and with the aid of computers the productivity of each person can be increased. In addition, the precision of computer-controlled machinery reduces product defects, which also affect operating costs.

The Banking Industry

Banking is the most computer-intensive industry in the United States because of the repetition of the transactions, the accuracy required, and the speed needed to handle the great volume of daily transactions. Transaction processing systems are heavily used throughout the banking industry. In addition, computers and information systems have helped banks plan and control their accounting and reporting operations and have also enabled them to provide new and improved services.

The most widely used computer application in banking is demand-deposit, or checking account, banking. This transaction processing system generates monthly customer statements and supplies information to management on checking account activities.

FIGURE 2–10
Process control can be integrated with plant data. The system used by this factory offers touch-screen access to thousands of terminals along the plantwide reporting network. (Courtesy of Honeywell)

Computers and information systems also made possible real-time banking, in which customer accounts are immediately updated after a transaction. Each teller station has a terminal and operates on-line when accessing accounts to cash checks or make deposits (Figure 2–11). Most banks and branch offices also have installed automated teller machines (ATMs), which dispense set amounts of cash (Figure 2–12).

Lending activities have also been able to take advantage of computer-based information systems. Consumer, commercial, and mortgage loans are all analyzed by computers. Sometimes an expert system is used to evaluate the credit worthiness of a customer. The information system generates customer statements and numerous management reports, such as loan analysis, interest, and tax reports. Many banks also include credit card services and trust management, which are handled by computers.

In addition, the banking industry uses computers and information systems to enable **electronic funds transfer (EFT)**. EFT is a computerized method of transferring funds from one account to another. Many of an organization's funds are moved in this way.

Besides providing new or better services to customers, computers have created new business opportunities for banks. Many banks now take advantage of their computer facilities and expertise and offer computer services to other banks, financial institutions, businesses, and other organizations.

FIGURE 2–11
A bank teller's computer terminal and printer are linked to the bank's mainframe computer to process customer transactions.

FIGURE 2–12
Automated teller machines are linked to a bank's mainframes and offer individuals easy and convenient access to their bank accounts. (Courtesy of Diebold)

The Investment Industry

The investment industry has traditionally used computer-based information systems to record transactions, process billing information, and prepare monthly statements. Computers are now used in the stock market to keep track of the stocks being traded on the floor of the New York Stock Exchange (Figure 2–13). The average volume of shares traded daily is 140 million, far beyond the capacity of the older ticker-tape machines. In 1975 the designated order turnaround (DOT) system was implemented to handle orders. Although some transactions are still completed by specialists,

FIGURE 2–13
The New York Stock Exchange is a busy place where trade decisions are based on the most current data available. Computers are also important in individual offices, where stockbrokers keep clients informed of late-breaking developments. (Preston Lyon/Index Stock. Inset: Merrill/Cobalt Productions)

the turn-around time for a market order processed by a computer is approximately 75 seconds. This system greatly facilitates the exchange of information between involved parties.

People who invest in the stock market need current information about the financial condition of their investments. Computers permit the quick and easy retrieval of financial information through data banks, reports, and time-sharing services. The Dow Jones News Retrieval is one of many electronic information services that give traders the instant financial data they need for making decisions on stock trading. Other services include Standard and Poor's Compustat, Wharton's Econometric, and Data Resources, Inc. (DRI).

Security analysis has also benefited from the use of computers. Improved forecasts of the market prices of securities can be obtained by computer analysis of the numerous variables that affect the financial position of a firm. Many brokers manage their clients' portfolios with computers, which help them analyze their decisions to buy, sell, or hold securities. Interestingly, the computer has been blamed for aiding the stock market disaster of October 1987. Critics claim that the computer's automatic trading capability fueled the fire of the market's panic.

The Retail Sales Industry

The area of retail sales includes many repetitive transactions that lend themselves to computer technology. Although each sale is different, the basic recording process remains the same. Consequently, retail stores use TPSs to record transactions. In addition to basic applications such as accounting and customer billing, computers are used for forecasting sales, analyzing sales, and merchandising. Retail purchases made with credit cards also involve computers. The computer stops many consumers who try to charge over their approved credit limits.

A growing computer application is the **point-of-sale system (POS)**. A POS system typically consists of cash-register-like terminals that are on-line to a computer in the store or to a unit that stores and transmits data over communication lines to a computer at a regional center. A POS terminal with a laser scanner reads sales data from items containing a product code (Figure 2–14). A POS system allows management to analyze sales and advertising impact quickly and more accurately.

Many businesses, including grocery stores, are automating inventory using hand-held computerized input devices, which store information read from the bar codes on the products. These data can later be entered directly into the main computer system.

Computers can also spur sales by simulating products and services. In L. S. Ayres department stores in the Midwest, customers could try on 10 different clothing ensembles each minute. Three Ayres stores tried a leased system called Magic Mirror, programmed with the Liz Claiborne spring

FIGURE 2–14
Supermarkets use optical scanning systems to read sales data from a product code and speed the checkout process. (Courtesy of National Semiconductor Corporation)

An Overview of Computers and Information Systems

collection. While standing in front of the mirror, the customer could see her own face, but the computer projected a comparable body image with as many different outfits as the customer wanted to try. The simulation concept proved to be quite a sales promotion; Claiborne's sales increased more than 700 percent in 1 week.

The Health Care Industry

The health care industry uses computer-based information systems for traditional data-processing operations such as patient billing, accounting, inventory control, calculation of health care statistics, and maintenance of patient histories. In addition, the industry uses such systems for more challenging tasks, such as scheduling lab times and operating-room times, automating nurses' stations, monitoring intensive care patients, and providing preliminary diagnoses. Expert systems are often used to assist physicians in making diagnoses because systems can remember more facts than human doctors can.

Many physicians and medical researchers enter their fields of specialty not only with a knowledge of physical science, but also with skills in using computers. In addition to helping with the usual record-keeping and administrative types of tasks in pharmacies, doctors' offices, and hospitals, this combination of knowledge and technology enables doctors and other health-care technicians to (1) test for and diagnose diseases and illnesses faster and more accurately; (2) design prostheses and reconstruction models; (3) build and use devices to monitor vital signs and other bodily functions; (4) design and test pharmaceuticals; and (5) offer choices in life-style and job selection to people who are physically challenged.

Some computerized methods that aid physicians in diagnosing diseases and illnesses include digital subtraction angiography, sonography, computed tomography, and computerized lab testing. Digital subtraction angiography (DSA) creates a clear view of a flow or blockage of blood. Pictures are first made by a digital X-ray scanner. Then an injection of a contrasting agent (iodine) is introduced into the body, and a second image is made. The computer subtracts the first image from the second and leaves an image that shows what has changed.

In sonography, beams of high-frequency sound waves penetrate a patient's body, and the computer translates the rebounding echoes into an image that the doctor can read. Sonograms view internal organs—such as the heart, liver, and gallbladder—and help monitor the growth and condition of a developing fetus.

Computed tomography (CT) scanners can view different sections (or slices) of the body from many angles by moving X-ray tubes around the body. The scanner converts the X-ray pictures into a digital code to create high-resolution images. It is possible to create three-dimensional pictures by combining the cross sections, thus giving surgeons a total picture when planning reconstructive surgery.

Computerization of laboratory tests, such as the typing of blood and the testing of sugar levels, leads to faster and more accurate reporting of test results and, therefore, more timely and accurate diagnoses. During biopsy procedures surgeons need reports quickly to determine whether further surgery is called for. If such processes are computerized, the results can be automatically sent to the operating room, printed and forwarded to the patient's physician, placed in the main file, and updated in the billing files.

Computer technology is also important for programmers and engineers who work closely with physicians to design prostheses and create models for reconstructive surgery. Some orthopedic surgery requires the creation and implantation of artificial limbs and other replacement parts, such as hip joints. By using diagnostic scanning procedures, technicians can digitize an accurate picture of damaged bone and visually compare it with a prosthesis design for fit and function. Then the actual prosthesis is built, usually with the help of computer-aided manufacturing machinery to ensure that precise measurements are met.

Computer-controlled devices are another important area of medical technology for patients who need constant monitoring, such as those in intensive care units, post-operative recovery rooms, and premature-baby nurseries. Premature infants, especially babies whose birth weight is under 3 pounds, are at high risk for death from strokes caused by high blood pressure. These babies' vital signs, blood gases, and head movements can be computer-monitored, with measurements taken up to 32 times per minute. It would be physically impossible for nurses to obtain the same volume of data and it could be hazardous for the infant to undergo the amount of physical contact that such data gathering would require. Researchers are hopeful that the causes and possible prevention of sudden infant death syndrome (SIDS) can be learned from these computer-monitoring tactics.

Other computer-controlled medical devices have also been developed. One device frees diabetics from hypodermic needles by automatically dispensing the proper doses of insulin from a reservoir implanted in the patient's body.

Pharmaceuticals are another area impacted by computerization. Development of a new drug is time-consuming and costly, involving years of research and experimentation and costing millions of dollars. Thousands of compounds have to be made and tested before a new drug can be released for production and human use. Computer-graphics techniques save drug researchers time by simulating, in 3-D, the shapes of molecules. Because the shape of a molecule usually determines its behavior, biochemists can accurately predict how various molecules should be combined. In addition, some computers are programmed to simulate various attributes of test animals so that toxicity can be checked or the safety of certain procedures can be verified by computer simulation without endangering human or animal life.

For individuals with movement deficits, devices that stimulate muscles to move (with patterned electrical stimulation) continue to be improved. The computer stores a signal of brain-wave muscle patterns, reads the signal, and then gives an electrical stimulation to the appropriate muscle group to cause movement. Tendon injuries are being treated in this way, and improvement has been shown in patients paralyzed by strokes, accidents, or cerebral palsy. Dr. Jerrold Petrofsky at Wright State University in Dayton, Ohio, is one of the most widely recognized researchers using this type of computer technology. His patients, with damaged spinal nerves causing paralyzed limbs, are able to walk and ride bicycles by using attached electrodes and adapted equipment.

Other requirements of physically challenged individuals are being addressed in computer design. The Kurzweil Reading Machine scans printed words and then speaks them aloud through a speech synthesizer. The Versabraille is a lap-top computer that some blind people use to write letters or take notes. There are also braille keyboards, keyboards adapted for those with limited muscle control, and keyboards that can be activated merely by eye movement. Computers and information systems have had, and continue to have, a tremendous and far-reaching effect on nearly all aspects of the business community.

HISTORY OF COMPUTERS

The preceding material has illustrated how computers fit into modern businesses. To round out your perspective, this section examines how computers have evolved. The history of computers is full of remarkable advances and exciting and sometimes strange people. So remarkable is the progress that in 1981, students used a Radio Shack TRS-80 microcomputer to outperform (by 20,000 to 1) a 51-foot-long 1944 computer. Today's microcomputer would demolish the 1981 record. Imagine how a supercomputer would perform!

One view of the history of computers goes back thousands of years to the Chinese abacus as the earliest computing device. Our view will narrow that scope to advances beginning in the 1950s, the era of the first generation of commercial computers, and will concentrate on the people who are largely responsible for the advances.

In 1951 John Mauchly and J.P. Eckert formed their own company to create a commercially usable general-purpose computer, the UNIVAC I. Remington Rand bought the company when Mauchly and Eckert fell on hard times. The UNIVAC I was the first general-purpose computer designed specifically for business data-processing applications. The UNIVAC I claim to fame was its 1952 presidential election prediction, with only 5 percent of the votes counted, that Dwight Eisenhower would defeat Adlai Stevenson. Previously, computers had been used solely for scientific or military applications. The U.S. Census Bureau immediately installed UNIVAC I and used it for more than 12 years. In 1954 the General Electric Company in Louisville, Kentucky, used UNIVAC I to process the first computerized payroll. It wasn't long before other companies—including Burroughs (now called UNISYS), Honeywell, and IBM—realized the commercial value of computers to the business community and began offering their own machines.

From 1950 to 1952 the U.S. Navy and the Digital Computer Lab at MIT developed the Whirlwind computer, another early vacuum-tube, stored-program computer. One of the students involved in the Whirlwind's development was Ken Olsen, later the founder of Digital Equipment Corporation. The Whirlwind simulated high-performance trainer aircraft, contained self-diagnostics, and performed 50,000 operations per second; but it was only about 85 percent accurate.

Other innovators appeared on the scene in the late 1950s. Both Jack Kilby at Texas Instruments and Robert Noyce at Fairchild Semiconductor discovered that resistors, capacitors, and transistors could be made from the same semiconductor material at the same time. Any number of transistors could be etched on silicon and thus the integrated circuit was born and refined. It was also during this time that the integrated circuit was christened as a "chip." These 1959 discoveries were finally mass-produced in 1962 and were included in the computers of the mid-1960s.

Gene Amdahl's revolutionary IBM System/360 series of mainframe computers was also introduced in the 1960s. They were the first general-purpose, digital computers using integrated-circuit technology. The IBM System/360 offered a family of computers. Small but growing companies could start with a relatively inexpensive, small computer system; then as the company grew, larger and more powerful computers from the same family could be added. Because the software was compatible, programs could be shared by all the computers in the family. Later, in his own company Amdahl built a competitive computer that was less expensive, smaller in size, and faster.

When coupled with the commercial success of computers, miniaturization, which had come about through various technological innovations, led Ken Olsen and his Digital Equipment Corporation (DEC) to produce the first minicomputer, the PDP−1, in 1963. Its successor, the PDP−8, was the first commercial minicomputer. It was considerably less expensive than a mainframe, and small companies could afford it to computerize their operations.

However, miniaturization was not the only focus for progress; computers were also becoming more powerful. In fact, the ILLIAC IV was a supercomputer first used at the Ames Research Center in 1972 to solve aerodynamic problems that were too large and complicated for other systems.

Meanwhile, advances were being made in the field of programming languages. High-level, English-like programming languages began to be developed in the mid-1950s. FORTRAN (FORmula TRANslator) was developed by John Backus and a group of IBM engineers as the first problem-oriented, algebraic programming language. Its orientation was in line with mathematicians and scientists. Retired Rear Admiral Grace Murray Hopper was instrumental in developing COBOL (COmmon Business-Oriented Language) as the first programming language designed for business data processing. Hopper also helped develop the UNIVAC I's compiler, a program that could translate other programs into machine language, the 1s and 0s that the computer understands. During the mid-1960s Dr. John Kemeny, a mathematics professor and president of Dartmouth, and his colleague, Dr. Thomas Kurtz, developed the computer language BASIC (Beginner's All-Purpose Symbolic Instruction Code). They later developed a version called True BASIC, which uses structured programming tools to make programs easier to read, debug, and update. Today there are numerous other high-level languages in use, including Pascal, C, and Logo.

By 1970 Intel had created a memory chip that could store a kilobit of information. A kilobit translates roughly into 25 five-letter words. Another innovation at Intel came from Ted Hoff, who further improved the integrated circuit by compressing 12 chips into 4. The arithmetic and logic functions of several chips could be contained on one chip—called a microprocessor. This microprocessor, called the Intel 4004 ("forty-oh-four"), made the development of the small computer, or microcomputer, a possibility. However, this chip could handle only four bits of data at a time. Eventually, eight-bit microprocessor chips were developed and were used in the early microcomputers.

The earliest microcomputer, the Altair 8800, was developed in 1975 by Ed Roberts. Roberts, called the father of the microcomputer, founded a company called Micro Instrumentation Telemetry Systems (MITS). He developed the Altair to be sold in kit form to consumers (mainly hobbyists) for $395. This computer used an early Intel microprocessor and had less than 1K of memory.

At the same time supercomputers were being developed, too. In 1976 Seymour Cray's Cray−1 supercomputer was delivered to Los Alamos Scientific Laboratory in New Mexico, and a Control Data Corporation CYBER−205 was used by the Meteorological Service in the United Kingdom for weather predictions.

The market for software was also growing. In 1974 Bill Gates and Paul Allen developed Microsoft BASIC, a high-level language for microcomputers. The language was used by the MITS Altair in 1975. IBM then adopted Microsoft BASIC for its personal computers in 1981, a move that turned Microsoft into a thriving company. Most popular microcomputers—including the Apple II, Commodore 64, and Commodore PET—use Microsoft BASIC. Other successful Microsoft products include PC-DOS and MS-DOS, the operating system software that runs millions of personal computers.

The application software industry got its initial boost because Dan Bricklin, a Harvard Business School student, was not fond of the tedious mathematical calculations involved in preparing financial planning sheets, part of his assigned work. The worksheets were repetitive and required numerous hand calculations and recalculations to obtain meaningful results. Bricklin did not just wish for a better way; he teamed up with friend Bob Frankston and developed and marketed an electronic spreadsheet called VisiCalc. It was the first of its kind and stayed a best-selling package until 1983. At that time lawsuits prevented timely upgrades from including the 16-bit technology. Eventually, Bricklin sold VisiCalc and its rights to Lotus, a name recognizable for its spreadsheet package Lotus 1−2−3.

Competition for the Altair appeared in 1977 in the form of Tandy's TRS−80 Model 1, which was available for purchase from Radio Shack stores, and the Personal Electronic Transactor (or PET) from Commodore Business Machines. Many microcomputer companies have come and gone, but one of the great rags-to-riches stories is Apple Computer. It was founded by Steven Jobs and Stephen Wozniak, with the partners' first headquarters located in the Jobs garage. Wozniak, the technical expert, made a microcomputer small and affordable enough for both the individual and the small businessperson. Because Jobs knew very little about circuitry or coding, he provided the marketing impetus for the small company.

Even though business was booming, the total accumulated sales of microcomputers was still less than one million units until IBM came along. For years IBM had been in the business of manufacturing and marketing office equipment and large computer systems. In 1981 they presented their IBM Personal Computer (IBM PC), using a 16-bit microprocessor. This introduction helped legitimize the microcomputer's use in business. That year other computer giants, Xerox and Digital Equipment Corporation, also brought out their versions of microcomputers. Now Sony, Hewlett-Packard, NEC, North Star, Zenith, and others have microcomputers on the market.

Adam Osborne introduced a truly portable microcomputer in 1981, the Osborne 1. It weighed only 24 pounds, had a memory capacity of 64 kilobytes, and cost approximately $1,795. It could be manufactured in just over 1 hour's time, using only 40 screws to put together the easy-to-find parts.

By 1984 the IBM PC had become the industry standard with hundreds of companies designing software for it. IBM did not stay at the top of the heap for long, however. Almost every microcomputer manufacturer soon presented its version of the popular IBM PC design. These are called IBM PC compatibles, or clones—machines that run the IBM PC software and work with other IBM PC equipment. Some IBM PC compatibles are made by Tandy, Epson, Dell, Advanced Logic Research, Everex, and Compaq.

Another benchmark in the microcomputer revolution was the introduction of the Apple Macintosh in the early 1980s. The Macintosh was visually oriented, and its mouse made it remarkably easy to use. It was praised for its ability to produce graphics and print text of near-typeset quality using Apple's LaserWriter.

In 1986 the Compaq DeskPro 386 computer, the first to use the powerful 32-bit Intel 80386 microprocessor, was introduced. The year 1987 saw the introduction of new microcomputers by both IBM and Apple. IBM introduced its new line, the PS/2 series, which was based on a new architecture called microchannel architecture. Apple made its move into the business world with the introduction of the powerful Macintosh II computer. Microsoft Corporation also introduced a new operating system for microcomputers, called OS/2, that allows application programs to take advantage of the newer computers' multitasking abilities. In 1988 IBM introduced a major new series of mainframes for business users called the AS/400 series.

Time magazine annually honors someone who has made a difference in the world during the year. In 1982 *Time* chose the computer as its "Man of the Year." Table 2–1 lists many of the major contributors to the development of computers.

TECHNICAL EVOLUTION OF COMPUTERS

Over time, computers have changed; they have improved in speed, power, and efficiency. These changes are recognized as a progression of generations, each characterized by specific developments.

First Generation (1951–1959)

These early first-generation computers were powered by thousands of vacuum tubes. The UNIVAC I and others like it were large because of the massive number of tubes that were required. The tubes themselves were large (the size of today's light bulbs), they required lots of energy, and they generated lots of heat.

Second Generation (1959–1965)

The device that characterized second-generation computers was the transistor. Made of a semiconducting material, transistors controlled the flow of electricity through the circuits. The use of transistors was a breakthrough in technology that allowed computers to become physically smaller but more powerful, more reliable, and even faster than before. The transistor was developed at Bell Labs in 1947 by William Shockley, J. Bardeen, and W. H. Brattain. It was displayed for the public in 1948 and won a Nobel Prize in 1956; however, it was not used in conjunction with computers until 1959.

Transistors were less expensive and smaller, required less electricity, and emitted less heat than vacuum tubes. In addition, fewer transistors were required to operate a computer, they were not as fragile as vacuum tubes, and they lasted longer. Because the components were substantially smaller, the size of the computer itself was able to shrink considerably.

Third Generation (1965–1971)

The use of integrated circuits (ICs) signified the beginning of third-generation computers. Again, they were smaller, more efficient, and more reliable than their predecessors. Unlike transistors and circuit boards that were assembled manually, ICs could be manufactured, ultimately resulting in lower costs. Memory technology was improved and by 1969 as many as 1,000 transistors could be built on a chip of silicon.

A new computer program also came into being at this time, one that controlled the computer and its resources and used them more effectively. This new program was the operating system. It meant that human operators were no longer required and processing could be done at computer speeds rather than human speeds.

Another phenomenon of this third generation was the introduction of families of computers. Previously, businesses had bought computers and programs and then found that almost before the system was fully adapted, it was outdated, or unable to grow with the user's needs. IBM recognized this problem and created an entire product line, the IBM/360 series, which allowed necessary upgrading or expansion. Programs written for one com-

TABLE 2–1

Major contributors to computer development.

Date	Person	Contribution
1642	Pascal	Developed first mechanical digital calculator, the Pascaline.
1804	Jacquard	Used punched-cards with weaving loom.
1822	Babbage	"Father of the computer," invented difference engine with mechanical memory to store results.
1840s	Augusta Ada	"The first programmer," suggested binary rather than decimal system for data storage.
1850s	Boole	Developed Boolean logic, which later was used in design of computer circuitry.
1880s	Hollerith	Built first electromechanical, punched-card, data-processing machine, used to compile information for 1890 U.S. census.
1939	Atanasoff and Berry	Built the ABC, world's first general-purpose, electronic, digital computer to solve large equations.
1943	Turing	Used vacuum-tube technology to build British Colossus, which counteracted the German code scrambling device, Enigma.
1944	Aiken	Built the Mark I, the first automatic, sequence-controlled calculator, used by military to compute ballistics data.
1940s	von Neumann	Presented a paper outlining the stored-program concept.
1947	Mauchly and Eckert	Built ENIAC, second general-purpose electronic, digital computer, used to compute artillery firing tables.
1949	Wikes	Built EDSAC, first stored-program computer.
1949	Mauchly, Eckert, and von Neumann	Built EDVAC, second stored-program computer.

puter were compatible with any of the other machines in the line. Businesses could upgrade or expand their data-processing operations as necessary.

In addition, Digital Equipment Corporation introduced the first minicomputer in November 1968. Its PDP–1 was substantially cheaper than a mainframe, thus making these smaller computers available to yet another business market.

TABLE 2–1
(Continued)

Date	Person	Contribution
1949	Wang	Developed magnetic-core memory.
1949	Forrester	Organized magnetic-core memory to be more efficient.
1950	Turing	Built the ACE, which some consider to be the first programmable, digital computer.
1951	Mauchly and Eckert	Built UNIVAC I, first computer designed and sold commercially, specifically for business data-processing applications.
1950s	Hopper	Developed UNIVAC I compiler.
1957	Backus	With other IBM engineers helped develop FORTRAN.
1959	Kilby and Noyce	Developed and perfected the integrated circuit to be used in later computers.
1960s	Amdahl	Designed IBM System/360 series of mainframe computers, the first general-purpose, digital computers to use integrated circuits.
1961	Hopper	Helped develop the COBOL programming language.
1963	Olsen	With DEC produced the PDP–1, the first minicomputer.
1965	Kemeny and Kurtz	Developed BASIC programming language, with True BASIC following later.
1970	Hoff	Developed the famous Intel 4004 miroprocessor chip.
1975	Roberts	"Father of the microcomputer," designed the first microcomputer, the Altair 8800, in kit form.
1976	Cray	Developed the Cray–1 supercomputer.
1977	Jobs and Wozniak	Designed and built the first Apple microcomputer.

Fourth Generation (1971– Present)

The significant distinction of fourth-generation computers is the large-scale integration (LSI) of chips with several thousand transistors. Then, in the mid-1970s the development of very-large-scale integration (VLSI) produced a chip containing a microprocessor. The development of VLSI made the development of the microcomputer possible; this was followed by the

TABLE 2–2
Generations of computers and their characteristics.

First Generation (1951–1959)
- Vacuum tubes
- Magnetic tape for external storage—some magnetic drums
- Punched cards for input
- Punched cards and paper for output
- Machine and assembly languages
- Human operators to set switches
- UNIVAC I, typical example

Second Generation (1959–1965)
- Transistors
- Magnetic-core storage
- Magnetic tape most common external storage; magnetic disk introduced
- Punched cards and magnetic tape for input
- Punched cards and paper for output
- High-level languages—FORTRAN, COBOL, BASIC, PL/I, and others
- Human operator to handle punched cards
- Honeywell 200, typical example

Third Generation (1965–1971)
- Integrated circuits
- Improved disk storage
- Monitors and keyboards for input and output
- More high-level languages, including RPG and Pascal
- Complete operating systems; less involvement for human operators
- Family of computers, allowing compatibility
- Minicomputers used commercially
- IBM System/360, typical example

Fourth Generation (1971–Present)
- LSI and VLSI
- Magnetic disk most common external storage
- Introduction of microcomputer
- Fourth-generation languages; application software for microcomputers
- Microcomputers used—IBM PC, typical example
- Burroughs B7700 and HP 3000 (minicomputer), typical examples

Fifth Generation (Future)
- Development of true artificial intelligence

Intel 80386 microprocessor. Again, the Intel 80386 was faster and more powerful than its predecessors.

The proliferation of application programs for microcomputers allowed home and business users to adapt their computers for word processing, spreadsheet manipulating, file handling, graphics creation, and much more.

Fifth Generation (Future)

Although many people disagree on fifth-generation computer technology, some say that the creation and use of a computer with artificial intelligence represents that next step. The unofficial original goal was a thinking machine by 1990. Although expert systems are already being used for specialized applications, true artificial intelligence, or computers that can think, are still concepts of the mind. Table 2–2 lists the generations of computers and their respective characteristics. Note that programming languages, secondary storage, principal methods of input, and methods of operation also change with the generations. The future remains to be seen, of course. You may have some ideas or innovations of your own.

SUMMARY

The decision making, problem identification and solution, and control activities of managers are based on information. Information systems are the tool that allows the process of acquiring, processing, and distributing information to be effectively managed. Managers must gather and manage information to keep pace with change and control the increasing complexity of their jobs. A business can gain a competitive edge by using information systems to supply more accurate, timely, and complete information for better decision making. Because information systems utilize computers, they can take advantage of the computers' capabilities, such as fast processing speeds and increased productivity in an organization.

There are three basic levels of management: top-level (strategic) managers; middle-level (tactical) managers; and low-level (operational) managers. Each level has different information needs and makes different types of decisions.

The six types of information systems discussed in this chapter are transaction processing, management information, decision support, knowledge-based (expert), office information, and computer integrated manufacturing information systems.

Several common applications of information systems in functional areas of business include accounting information, financial information, marketing information, production/operations information, and human resources information systems.

The manufacturing industry has seen the incorporation of information systems into almost all aspects of its business. Innovations include computer-aided design, computer numerical control, robotics, and programmable controllers. The banking and investment industries have traditionally used computers and information systems to record their transactions. They have also used them to increase the quality and types of services they can offer their customers. The health care industry uses information systems not only to collect and process routine transactions but also to increase the quality and types of services and treatments offered to patients.

MINICASE 2-1

The Milford Novelty Company (MNC) has been in business for several years, but its information systems department is still in a maturing process. MNC currently has transaction processing systems in place to gather and record all of its transactional data. There is also a basic management information system in place that supplies middle-level managers with reports to help them with the structured decisions they need to make. Currently, all the data entered into the management information system comes from the transaction processing system and other internal sources.

The market in the novelty business changes often, and MNC's share of the existing market fluctuates. Even though the present information systems has suited the needs of the tactical and operational managers, top management has not been receiving much benefit. The strategic managers need instant access to summarized information on the internal financial condition of the organization. They also want a system that will keep them current on external information that is crucial to the business health of their organization. These managers complain that either the current system doesn't contain the external information they need about competitors, economic factors, market trends, and the like or it can't produce reports fast enough for their ad hoc inquiries.

Top management has asked you, as head of the Information Systems Department at MNC, to expand the current information systems to meet their needs.

1. What changes would you suggest for the information systems structure at MNC to ensure that it will also meet the needs of top management?

2. Describe several benefits that can be obtained by developing information systems to meet top-management information needs.

MINICASE 2-2

Several months ago Mark and Nancy Preston opened Preston Videos. Their inheritance money was enough to lease a small shop for 1 year, hire two employees, and purchase a reasonable inventory of videos to get started.

Their initial setup included a cash register and paper documents designed by Mark to record the rental data. Each document included the customer's name, address, license number, name of the movie, rental amount, and date. Mark and Nancy had good intentions of looking over all transaction documents, but there were so many that it was difficult and very time-consuming to summarize any useful information by hand.

They did notice, however, that some videos were always being requested, and often they would lose sales because they didn't have enough copies of the popular videos. Other movies were never rented and were wasting valuable shelf space both on the display floor and in the back, where the actual videos were stored.

The Prestons also experienced problems in their video inventory. Their system of keeping the videos in alphabetical order worked for the most part, but often a video was misfiled by an employee. Then they had no way of knowing whether it was misfiled, still out on rental, or stolen.

The Prestons also wanted a more efficient means of keeping track of who rented which video. It was easy to lose or misplace the paper documents that contained this information. In addition, Mark and Nancy wanted to be able to identify good customers so they could send them promotional and discount information.

1. What type(s) of information systems would be helpful to Preston Video? Explain.
2. Besides having information about transactional data recorded and supplied, in what other ways could Preston Video benefit from computer-based information systems?

Key Terms

accounting information system

computer-aided design (CAD)

computer-aided manufacturing (CAM)

computer-integrated manufacturing (CIM)

computer numerical control (CNC)

decision support system (DSS)

electronic funds transfer (EFT)

executive information system (EIS)

financial information system

human resources information system

knowledge-based (expert) system

low-level (operational) managers

management information system (MIS)

manufacturing automation protocol (MAP)

marketing information system

middle-level (tactical) managers

office information system (OIS)

point-of-sale system (POS)

process control

production/operations information system

programmable controller

robot

top-level (strategic) managers

transaction processing system (TPS)

Review Questions

1. How can information systems give an organization a competitive edge?
2. List and describe the information needs of the three basic levels of management.
3. Why are there more transaction processing systems than other types of information systems?
4. Describe a management information system (MIS).
5. Define the function of a decision support system (DSS).

6. Do MISs and DSSs serve the same levels of management?

7. What is an executive information system (EIS)?

8. Can knowledge-based (expert) systems replace humans?

9. Describe an office information system.

10. What information could be exchanged between an office information system and other information systems operating within the same company?

11. What level of management would use an office information system?

12. Describe the information needs of two functional areas of business.

13. How does an accounting information system differ from a financial information system?

14. How have robots influenced the manufacturing industry?

15. What is process control? Give an example.

16. Describe several ways in which information systems are used in the banking and investment industries.

17. Describe several ways in which information systems are used in the retail sales industry.

18. Describe several ways in which information systems are used in the health care industry.

19. List and describe the ways in which information systems might be used in two industries not covered in this chapter.

20. Describe the characteristics of each generation of computers.

APPLICATION MODULE
The Functions of Business

Our business world is often described as a free-market system, in which the economy is based on a voluntary exchange of goods or services between buyers and sellers. The underlying idea is that enough competition exists among sellers to ensure that prices are in line with what buyers are willing and able to pay. If a seller's prices are too high, buyers will make purchases from competing firms; and if prices are too low, the seller will not remain in business long.

Businesses exist in our free-market system in three basic forms: sole proprietorships, partnerships, and corporations. Each of these forms has its own positive and negative features. The form that is best depends on the circumstances of the particular firm; no single form can fit all businesses. General Motors' corporate style would not work well for Sara and Sam's video store, a partnership, or for Sal's sandwich shop, a sole proprietorship.

Regardless of the business form, however, an essential set of duties or functions is performed by most enterprises. Among these functional areas are finance, personnel, manufacturing, marketing, and research and development. For hundreds of years managers have recognized that creating organizations along functional lines leads to both efficient and effective organizations. Several universally proven management concepts also apply to the design of all organizations: division of labor; span of management; departmentalization; and authority, responsibility, and delegation.

Although there are successful firms with different organizational arrangements, many larger businesses divide their resources, including managerial skills, along the five functional lines just identified. We will follow this outline as we examine the various areas of business and the way in which computer information systems support these functions. That support takes two general forms: (1) support for the basic duties that occur daily within the functional areas and (2) support for managerial decision making that is required to maintain a business's competitive edge.

Figure A presents an organizational chart of a generic business and shows the five major functional areas, along with some of the subfunctions that apply to each. Notice that all of the major areas are on the same level of the chart and are thus equal in importance to the organization as a whole.

FINANCE

Regardless of size, all businesses have someone who manages the finances. In larger firms a number of people may be devoted to this function. Financial management includes three essential components:

1. developing a company-wide financial plan
2. acquiring funds in a timely manner to support that plan
3. deciding when and how to use those funds

Financial plans for the future depend on budgets that are used to estimate income and expenses for a specified period of time. Consider the differences in income for a swimsuit manufacturer during May and December or the change in expenses when a company decides to relocate some or all of its facilities. Timing complicates plans but is a crucial element.

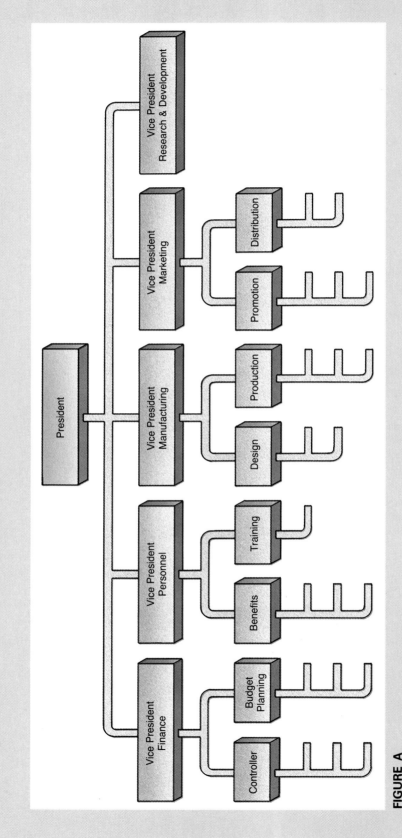

FIGURE A
A conventional organizational chart.

Sometimes a firm has enough cash on hand or sufficient investments that can be quickly converted to cash to finance future plans, but most often outside financing is needed. That financing can be obtained for the short term (1 year or less) with a note or loan. Long-term financial needs are met with bonds (debt financing) or stock issue (equity financing).

Business funds are spent for a variety of purposes: new plants, new product manufacture and promotion, employee benefits, and so on. When funds remain after actual and anticipated expenditures, financial managers must decide how to use the excess. Typically, options include dividends to stockholders and/or outside investments, such as high-yield savings, stock purchase, or government bond purchase. Here, again, the timing of any subsequent need for funds is a vital consideration.

These are the major tasks of financial managers. In the application module at the end of Part Two, we examine just how helpful computer information systems can be in the financial area of business.

PERSONNEL

Personnel decisions require attention to detail in recruiting, obtaining, developing, monitoring, and maintaining the human skills that are to be used in the firm. A prime consideration of personnel management is accommodating the wide variety of human needs that exist among employees.

Personnel managers must ensure that their recruiting efforts are cost-effective, yield the most qualified persons, and do not unfairly discriminate against certain classes, sexes, or ages of potential applicants. These efforts require that the firm sell, or market, itself to prospective employees.

Once hired, employees must be trained in the work culture of the firm (i.e., the way people think and behave at work) and in specific duties relating to their particular positions within the firm. Training and development activities are expensive, but they are crucial. Proper training results in more productive employees. You will learn that training activities can be provided on a cost-effective basis with the use of computer technologies.

It is a fact of life that not everyone performs equally. Some employees will perform a given job better than others; some will perform adequately, but not exceptionally; and still others will perform below the minimum acceptable level. The personnel function is responsible for monitoring the productive activities of employees. Although specific performance measures may be established in individual work areas, personnel management must develop a system that ties performance information to benefits and compensation for all employees of the firm. The personnel function must also ensure that the benefits and compensation are administered in a fair and comprehensible manner.

Other cultures, particularly the Japanese, have long recognized the importance of an employee's longevity with a firm. Long tenure helps employees make better decisions that are in concert with a firm's needs; long-term employees know more about what is best for the firm. Thus, a crucial personnel task is maintaining human skills within the firm. Adequate compensation and benefits help keep skilled individuals from moving their skills to other firms.

Closely linked to keeping the right employees on the job is the personnel function of maintaining the skill levels of employees. As technology moves into a firm, employee skills must often be updated to keep pace.

Computer information systems play a major role in the personnel function. Some people believe that many current personnel tasks could not be done at all without the aid of computer information systems. In the application module at the end of Part Three, we take a closer look at the role of computer information systems in support of the personnel function.

MANUFACTURING

Before products or services can be sold, they must be produced. Decisions involved in this production process are called operations decisions, or, in our more narrow context, manufacturing decisions. These decisions focus on transforming raw materials—such as fabric, foam rubber, wood, or metal—into a salable product, such as living room furniture. The goals of the manufacturing process are high-quality products, low operating costs, and high productivity from both labor and machinery.

High-quality products are a must in today's competitive business arena. Consumers are a demanding lot and, in many cases, are protected by law from purchasing inferior goods and services. Most consumers will return for a full refund any merchandise that does not meet their expectations, which are based on the merchandise promotion. Inferior products are costly to a firm in at least two ways: (1) they cannot be sold at the expected price and therefore fail to generate the expected income; and (2) they alienate customers, who are not likely to purchase more of those products or to recommend them to friends or relatives, thereby affecting the popularity of the products in the marketplace.

The competitive nature of the free-market system demands that manufacturing (operating) costs remain low to help a firm remain profitable. Obviously, there is tension between low operating costs and high-quality products. Decisions in this area must balance these two goals, keeping the satisfaction of both the consumer and the firm in mind. Technology (both computer-driven and other) assists manufacturing managers in their efforts.

High productivity helps keep operating expenses at lower levels. Studies on increasing human productivity have been undertaken for hundreds of years and center on providing better tools with which to accomplish tasks and considering the human needs that lead to improved motivation and output. The computer has been successfully used (although not without objection) to achieve both of these objectives.

The application module that concludes Part Four examines the role of computer information systems in the manufacturing process. Such information systems can be used not only to influence the process directly, but also to provide information that manufacturing managers need to monitor the process.

MARKETING

Marketing is the process of developing, pricing, promoting, and distributing products and services in a way that meets both the seller's and the buyer's needs. Whereas older marketing concerns were centered on the firm, modern marketing recognizes the satisfaction of the consumer as the primary concern. A seller's basic marketing activities are frequently summarized as the four Ps: product, price, place (distribution), and promotion.

Product strategies include an initial decision regarding what to make. Thereafter, quality, quantity, type and size, packaging, labeling, and branding must all be considered. Pricing strategies revolve around establishing a price that is competitive in the marketplace but also allows the firm to generate reasonable income from product sales. A price too low or too high does not work for long.

Place decisions relate to how the product or service will ultimately be sold to the consumer. For example, will the product be sold by mail order, TV toll-free telephone orders, specific stores, or some combination of the three? What is the best strategy to get the product to the necessary location in a timely and cost-effective way?

Promotion decisions focus on the means, cost, and effectiveness of getting product information to ultimate consumers. Personal selling, sales promotion, and advertising all come into play. Marketing specialists add an important condition to the maxim "Build a better mousetrap, and the world will beat a path to your door": only if the world knows about the mousetrap.

Computer information systems support the marketing function in two ways: (1) with operational tasks and (2) with analytical tasks. Marketing information systems are examined in detail in the application module at the end of Part Five.

RESEARCH AND DEVELOPMENT

Research and development activities (R&D) center on identifying and evaluating threats and opportunities that exist in the marketplace and in the firm's environment. R&D activities are closely tied to the planning function of managers and may differ greatly from firm to firm. For example, those firms engaged in fulfilling the needs of consumers for leisure activities are interested in the specific age categories of the work force, legislation affecting the amount of leisure time that individuals have, and trends in leisure activities. Such concerns are also impor-

tant for the tourism industry, but less so for the food industry.

Once an opportunity is identified, a firm must determine how to exploit that opportunity to its advantage. This process might involve guesswork, perhaps about the performance of a new market. Often R&D activities take place on an ad-hoc basis and require considerable human as well as computer support. The computer is commonly used to model hypothetical activities, in an attempt to predict what might happen in the marketplace given some assumed circumstances.

Computer information systems support R&D activities by manipulating large quantities of data derived from diverse sources. Computer systems can also make impressive pictures and reports to help investigate the possible results of pursuing certain trends and opportunities. Because of space limitations, the R&D function is not examined in detail in a separate application module. Nonetheless, the R&D area makes extensive use of computer information systems and data from the other functional areas as well as from external sources.

PART TWO

Business Computer Systems

Components of Business Computer Systems

Chapter 3

Management Profile: Katherine Hudson
KODAK'S HUDSON STRIVES TO CREATE MIS HARMONY

Everyone remembers when, in 1985, the U.S. District Court in Boston upheld the patent infringement charges of Polaroid Corporation against Eastman Kodak Company, forcing Kodak to stop manufacturing and selling instant cameras.

Katherine Hudson remembers it well. As then-general manager of the division, she handled the thankless task of shutting down the instant products group, redeploying 1,200 employees within Kodak, and offering trade-ins for the 16 million Kodak instant cameras already in customers' hands. "We had just ninety days to exit the business, and we did it on time," she recalls. It was a management challenge that prepared her for a January 1988 promotion to corporate vice president (a Kodak position never before held by a female) and director of corporate systems.

The latter position is as new for Kodak as it is for Hudson. Prior to her appointment no such title existed. MIS executives were scattered throughout decentralized subsidiaries, each running systems that were incompatible with those of other divisions. Hudson's mission is not an easy one. She is charged with developing a broad plan to move systems and networks ahead uniformly within each division of the $13.3 billion conglomerate.

Hudson's systems experience is broad. Her initial job was that of a systems programmer. She managed groups in Kodak's business imaging systems area and became more familiar with computer systems, Kodak's storage products, and the role of information technology in the market. "I can see clearly that you have to marry the information systems strategy to the business strategy," Hudson says.

One staff member in the MIS department commented, "It's going to be a tough job; all the business units are used to going their own way."

Hudson must define the boundaries of her job as she goes along. "Right now, I am paddling around listening to people's views—the employees', vendors', and consultants'. If our actions are not servicing customers, then we know we have done something wrong." Hudson is anxious to deliver more helpful information services to the subsidiaries. "But first, we have to understand where we are," she says. "The second priority is to determine where the company wants to go. Third, we have to move ahead."

Although Kodak is the only company at which she has ever worked, that linkage was unintentional. Years ago Hudson dreamed of becoming a university professor of economics. Hence, after receiving her bachelor's degree in business administration, she rushed off to Cornell University to secure a master's degree in economics. What didn't cooperate was the campus political climate; the Vietnam War was giving rise to student riots. Hudson decided to put a collegiate career on hold until the situation improved and went to Kodak as a systems analyst. Expecting to stay a year, Hudson says she was so impressed with the company that she has remained for eighteen years.

Hudson's view of management is simple: set a strategic direction, get the right people for the right jobs, and give the people the right tools. "Then my time can be spent communicating with people and working on the fun stuff," she says.

Adapted from "Katherine Hudson: Kodak's Hudson Strives to Create MIS Harmony" by Kathy Chin Leong. Copyright 1988 by CW Publishing Inc., Framingham, MA 01701. Reprinted from *Computerworld,* March 28, 1988.

The basic operations of the computer have not changed much over the years. What has changed, however, is the technology used to accomplish those operations. In the 1950s it took a roomful of vacuum tubes and equipment to perform the tasks that are now completed by a single chip no bigger than a child's thumbnail. As technology has advanced, the size of the chip has become smaller; as the chip continues to evolve, its size will be reduced even further. Computers just keep getting smaller and doing more work in less time.

This chapter presents some basic concepts of data representation and provides an overview of the central processing unit. In addition, input/output concepts and devices and secondary storage devices are discussed. You won't be able to build a computer after you've read this chapter, but you will know how its basic components interact.

IMPACT ON MANAGEMENT PROBLEM SOLVING AND DECISION MAKING

It is important to realize that decisions about what hardware to purchase have both an immediate and a long-term impact on an organization's productivity. Management must consider not only what hardware will get the job done today, but also whether that hardware will meet the organization's expanding needs tomorrow. Will the hardware purchased today run the applications required in the future?

When making decisions about hardware, a manager needs to consider such items as price, performance, and after-the-sale support and service. Price and performance are important considerations; the hardware must be priced within budget and have a minimum performance level to accomplish required tasks. However, the hardware with the lowest price and highest performance often is not selected by businesses. In many cases the after-the-sale support and service sway the purchase decision. Computer hardware has become vital to the operations of most organizations; the computer is the foundation of business information systems used in management problem solving and decision making. No business can wait long to have problems solved or disabled equipment repaired or replaced. This priority is evident in the microcomputer market. IBM's reputation for superior after-the-sale support and service kept their products in many corporations despite inferior performance and higher price tags than those of similar equipment of other vendors. Managers may not need specific knowledge of any particular hardware, but general knowledge of what is available now and what is expected in the future can help guide hardware choices.

DATA REPRESENTATION

Like a common light switch, a computer only identifies signals in the form of electric pulses that represent either a high voltage state, "on," or a low voltage state, "off." The on and off conditions are commonly labeled with the numbers 1 and 0, respectively. A number system using only 1s and 0s is called a **binary system**. The 1s and 0s can be arranged in various combinations to represent all the numbers, letters, and symbols that can be entered into the computer. While you perceive numbers and letters assembled to form English words and phrases, the computer is seeing things quite differently. For example, the lowercase letter *d* appears as a series of high and low voltage states to the computer (01100100).

Because the language of the computer, machine language, is based on a binary system, data and programs entered into the computer must be translated into binary code before they can be used by the computer. Language translator programs (see Chapter 4) take care of this conversion.

Bits and Bytes

The smallest piece of data that can be recognized and used by a computer is the **bit**, a *binary digit*. A bit is a single binary value, either a 1 or a 0. A grouping of eight bits is a **byte**. The term *nibble,* which is half of a byte (four bits), is used occasionally. The byte is the basic unit for measuring the size of memory, although with today's memory sizes it is more common to hear the term *kilobyte* (K or KB) or *megabyte* (MB).

There is some confusion over the prefixes *kilo-* and *mega-*. In strict scientific notation *kilo-* means 1,000 and *mega-* means 1,000,000. However, in the language of computers, *kilo-* actually means 1,024 and *mega-* is 1,048,576. The disparity occurs because the computer is a binary machine based on the powers of 2. If 2 is raised to the 10th power (2^{10}), the value is 1,024. Since this is very near 1,000, the prefix *kilo-* was adopted for computer use. The same reasoning accompanies the prefixes *mega-, giga-* (1 billion), and *tera-* (1 trillion).

Computer Words

A computer **word** is the number of adjacent bits that can be stored and manipulated as a unit. Just as English words are of varying lengths, so are computer words. Some of the newer microcomputers have the ability to manipulate a 32-bit word, whereas older models have word lengths of 8 and 16 bits. Word lengths range up to 128 bits for supercomputers.

The longer the length of the computer word that the registers can hold (registers are special-purpose memory and are discussed shortly), the faster the computer can process the data. A word's length can be misleading, however. Even though a register may be able to handle 32 bits, the data bus (electronic pathway for data transfer) may be able to handle only 16 bits at a time. A microprocessor such as the Intel E-9 series, which has a 32-bit word size but only a 16-bit data bus, requires twice the time to load a 32-bit word as would a true 32-bit microprocessor.

Encoding Systems

Computers must be capable of interpreting more than just numbers. Letters of the alphabet as well as symbols—such as @, #, *, +—are also used. Any character that can be entered from the keyboard must be converted into 1s and 0s before it can be used by the computer. The combination of letters, numbers, and symbols is collectively called alphanumeric characters.

TABLE 3–1

The ASCII encoding scheme.

Character	8-Bit ASCII (Place Values)	Character	8-Bit ASCII (Place Values)
0	1011 0000	K	1100 1011
1	1011 0001	L	1100 1100
2	1011 0010	M	1100 1101
3	1011 0011	N	1100 1110
4	1011 0100	O	1100 1111
5	1011 0101	P	1101 0000
6	1011 0110	Q	1101 0001
7	1011 0111	R	1101 0010
8	1011 1000	S	1101 0011
9	1011 1001	T	1101 0100
A	1100 0001	U	1101 0101
B	1100 0010	V	1101 0110
C	1100 0011	W	1101 0111
D	1100 0100	X	1101 1000
E	1100 0101	Y	1101 1001
F	1100 0110	Z	1101 1010
G	1100 0111	+	1010 1011
H	1100 1000	$	1010 0100
I	1100 1001	.	1010 1110
J	1100 1010	<	1011 1100

TABLE 3–2

The EBCDIC encoding scheme.

Character	8-Bit EBCDIC (Place Values)	Character	8-Bit EBCDIC (Place Values)
0	1111 0000	K	1101 0010
1	1111 0001	L	1101 0011
2	1111 0010	M	1101 0100
3	1111 0011	N	1101 0101
4	1111 0100	O	1101 0110
5	1111 0101	P	1101 0111
6	1111 0110	Q	1101 1000
7	1111 0111	R	1101 1001
8	1111 1000	S	1110 0010
9	1111 1001	T	1110 0011
A	1100 0001	U	1110 0100
B	1100 0010	V	1110 0101
C	1100 0011	W	1110 0110
D	1100 0100	X	1110 0111
E	1100 0101	Y	1110 1000
F	1100 0110	Z	1110 1001
G	1100 0111	+	0100 1110
H	1100 1000	$	0101 1011
I	1100 1001	.	0100 1011
J	1101 0001	<	0100 1100

Encoding systems, which permit alphanumeric characters to be coded in bits of 1 and 0, were developed to make the necessary conversion. The two most widely used encoding systems are EBCDIC (Extended Binary Coded Decimal Interchange Code), which was popularized by IBM in the 1960s, and ASCII (American Standard Code for Information Interchange), which is the system used by most microcomputers today. ASCII and EBCDIC codes allow computers to distinguish numbers, letters, and symbols. Tables 3–1 and 3–2 show representations of these two encoding systems. When a computer sees the ASCII bit pattern 11001011, it interprets the pattern as a capital letter *K*. A system using EBCDIC represents a capital *K* as 11010010. There is more than one encoding standard only because of competitive marketing strategies among computer vendors.

CENTRAL PROCESSING UNIT

The **central processing unit (CPU)** is comprised of the arithmetic and logic unit (ALU), the control unit, and the primary storage unit. Some sources define the CPU as including only the ALU and the control unit. However, because the ALU, the control unit, and primary storage are closely related and function as a whole, the CPU is defined here as containing all three elements (Figure 3–1).

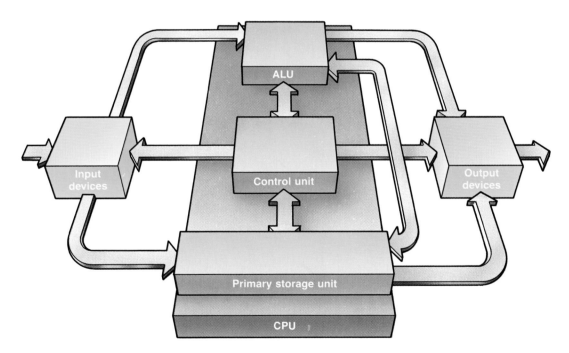

FIGURE 3–1
The relationship between a CPU and input and output devices is shown here. Arrows indicate the basic movement of data or instructions among these elements.

Advances in semiconductor technology have reduced the size of the CPU. Depending on conditions, a semiconductor can serve as a conductor (allowing the transmission of electricity) or an insulator (inhibiting the transmission of electricity). This ability is ideal because data are represented by combinations of high voltage states (conductor) and low voltage states (insulator).

A single, complete electronic semiconductor circuit contained on a small piece of silicon is called an **integrated circuit (IC). Large-scale integration (LSI)** and **very-large-scale integration (VLSI)** technology have dramatically increased the number of complete circuits residing on a small piece of silicon (from several thousand with LSI to more than 100,000 with VLSI). An IC, also called a microchip or just a **chip,** is used for the design of both logic and memory circuitry. For example, an IC can be designed to function as part of the ALU or as primary storage.

Initially, the parts of the CPU were separate units. However, developments have now allowed the parts of a CPU to be combined on a single chip called a **microprocessor** (Figure 3–2). To be called a microprocessor, a chip must contain at least the ALU and control unit, but it may also contain primary storage.

FIGURE 3–2
The Motorola MC68020 microprocessor in a protective ceramic package. (Photo courtesy of Motorola, Inc.)

In a microcomputer the components of the CPU are mounted on the main circuit board, often called the motherboard (Figure 3–3).

Arithmetic and Logic Unit

The **arithmetic and logic unit (ALU)** is the part of the CPU where all mathematical and logical functions are performed. The basic mathematical functions include addition and subtraction; multiplication and division are achieved by continuous addition or subtraction operations. Software can be used to combine these basic math functions to perform logarithmic, trigonometric, and other mathematical functions. A logic function is one in which numbers or conditions are compared to each other. Logic functions include concepts like greater than, less than, equal to, not equal to, greater than or equal to, and less than or equal to.

The Control Unit

The **control unit** interprets any instruction it receives from memory and directs the sequence of events necessary to execute the instruction. The control unit also establishes the timing of these events, acting like the traffic cop of the system.

To control all that is going on in the CPU, the control unit uses a **system clock,** which synchronizes all tasks by sending out electrical pulses. The number of pulses, or cycles, per second is a main element in determining the speed of the processor. The clock speed is measured in megahertz (MHz). Hertz is the unit of frequency that measures the number of cycles per second in a periodic signal; a megahertz is equal to 1 million

FIGURE 3–3
The motherboard, or main circuit board, of a computer.

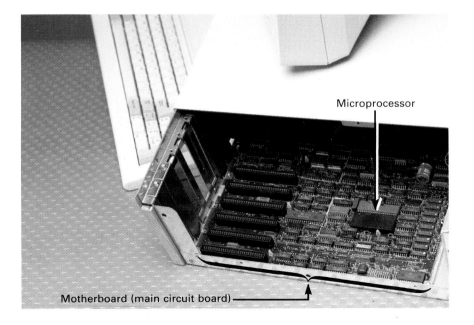

Microprocessor

Motherboard (main circuit board)

hertz. All things being equal, an 8-MHz processor does things twice as fast as a 4-MHz processor.

Other factors, such as the instruction set, also affect processing speed. An **instruction set** is the group of commands available to the CPU. It determines the basic computer operations (arithmetic, logic, and storage and retrieval) that can be performed and the commands that the control unit can use to direct and coordinate the computer's operations.

Each instruction takes a specific number of system clock cycles to complete. The same instruction may take 10 clock cycles to complete on one processor but only 5 clock cycles on another. So even though both such processors are running at 8 MHz, the first takes twice as long to complete the same instruction.

Computer speed is also measured by the number of instructions completed per second, or **millions of instructions per second (MIPS)**. This designation is usually used in comparing large computer systems, such as minicomputers, mainframes, and supercomputers. Typical speeds for minicomputers are in the 5 to 10 MIPS range. Mainframe computers generally perform in the 20 to 50 MIPS range but can go to more than 100 MIPS. Supercomputers execute instructions in excess of approximately 200 MIPS. Some microprocessors, such as the Intel 80386, can execute 3 to 4 MIPS. Most microprocessors, however, run at less than 1 MIPS and are usually classified only by their system clock speeds. A typical microcomputer can execute an instruction, such as adding two numbers, in a few milliseconds (Table 3–3). Mainframes and supercomputers can execute in the microsecond and nanosecond ranges.

The difference between a millisecond and a microsecond may seem to be insignificant; however, it equals roughly the difference between one minute and one day, or one hour and one month. Just think of how much more you can accomplish in a month than you can in an hour. Such speed differences become noticeable and important in long programs that process volumes of data. A few millionths of a second can make a big difference in the performance of a software package. For example, a computer with a slow processing speed may take minutes or even hours longer to run a complicated accounting program than a computer with a fast processing speed.

TABLE 3–3
Computer speeds compared to one second of time.

Equivalents		
1 millisecond	=	.001 second
1 microsecond	=	.000001 second
1 nanosecond	=	.000000001 second
1 second	=	1 thousand milliseconds
1 second	=	1 million microseconds
1 second	=	1 billion nanoseconds

Primary Storage Unit

The **primary storage** unit refers to the internal storage of the computer, where programs and their data are stored. Primary storage, or primary memory, provides temporary storage during program execution. Part of primary storage may also contain permanently stored instructions that tell the computer what to do when it is turned on. Because primary storage is located inside the computer and is linked directly to the other components of the CPU, access time to data is very fast.

The process of entering data into storage (primary or secondary) is called writing. When data are placed in (or written into) storage, they replace what was originally there, a procedure equivalent to deleting a word with a pencil eraser and writing a new word in its place. The process of retrieving data from storage (primary or secondary) is called reading. The reading process does not change the data in any way.

Semiconductor Memory. Most primary storage today depends on semiconductor technology. **Semiconductor memory** is made by etching electronic circuits onto a silicon chip. The two most common forms of semiconductor memory are random-access memory and read-only memory. **Random-access memory (RAM)** is that part of primary storage where data and program instructions are held temporarily while being manipulated or executed. This type of memory allows the user to enter data into memory (write) and then retrieve it (read). RAM depends on a supply of electricity to maintain data storage. When the power to the computer is shut off, everything stored in RAM is lost. In other words, RAM is volatile.

As the name implies, the contents of **read-only memory (ROM)** can be *read* only; data cannot be *written* into it. ROM may contain information on how to start the computer and even instructions for the entire operating system. The actual contents of ROM are usually set by the computer manufacturer; they are unchangeable and permanent. Because the contents cannot be altered and are not lost when the electric current is turned off, ROM is nonvolatile.

Several types of read-only memory can be programmed according to the user's specifications. **Programmable read-only memory (PROM)** allows a chip to be programmed by the user once; then it cannot be altered further. A type of ROM in which the contents *can* be changed is called **erasable programmable read-only memory (EPROM)**. An EPROM chip has the features of PROM, but it also has a transparent quartz window covering the internal circuitry. If the chip is removed from the circuit and the window is exposed to ultraviolet light, the contents are erased, and the chip can be reprogrammed for another application. Another type of ROM chip is the **electrically erasable programmable read-only memory (EE-PROM)**. This memory chip can be erased and reprogrammed electrically, eliminating the need to remove it from the circuit.

To understand the use of RAM and ROM, let's look at how they might be used in a typical microcomputer. The primary storage unit is represented by the entire cube in Figure 3–4. That cube is composed of

FIGURE 3–4
An illustration of RAM and ROM
use in a microcomputer.

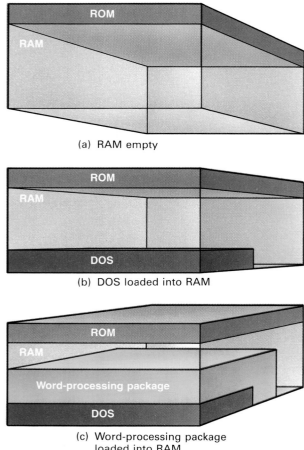

(a) RAM empty

(b) DOS loaded into RAM

(c) Word-processing package
loaded into RAM

two parts, RAM and ROM. ROM appears as the thin portion along the top of the cube. When the computer is first turned on, ROM follows predetermined instructions, such as checking the system for errors, and nothing is contained in RAM (Figure 3–4a).

Before a computer can be used, it must have operating instructions. The software that provides these instructions is called the operating system (OS). The typical microcomputer operating system resides wholly or partially on a disk and is referred to as a disk operating system (DOS). DOS must be transferred, or loaded, into RAM. Figure 3–4b shows the part of RAM that is occupied by DOS. (For more on operating systems, see Chapter 4.)

Now, let's say we want to write a letter using a word processor. The computer needs programming instructions that direct it to function as a word processor. These programming instructions as a group are called a package, or an application package. This word-processing package must also be loaded into RAM, and then it is ready to use. Application programs usually take a lot of memory space (Figure 3−4c), but RAM is volatile. If we turn the computer off now, primary storage will again contain only ROM and will look like Figure 3−4a.

The amount of primary storage is very important in determining the capabilities of a computer. More primary storage means that more instructions and data can be loaded into the computer. Many programs require a specific amount of memory and cannot be used if the computer doesn't have that amount. Most computers have provisions for adding individual RAM chips to the main circuit board or adding RAM cards. A RAM card is a group of integrated circuits already assembled on a printed circuit board. It can be plugged into the main circuit board (motherboard) of a computer to increase the amount of RAM.

Bubble Memory. One attempt to overcome the volatility of RAM was the development of bubble memory. **Bubble memory** is built on a thin piece of the mineral garnet, where certain sections are polarized (subjected to a magnetic field) to produce bubblelike areas. Data are represented by the presence or absence of these bubbles. Bubble memory is nonvolatile, but it is not used as widely as semiconductor memory because it is slower and more expensive. One advantage of bubble memory is that it is a durable storage medium not susceptible to extreme environmental conditions, such as dust, heat, and vibrations. Consequently, bubble memory is often used in factory computers where conditions make the operation of the computer risky.

Special-Purpose Memories. The two types of special-purpose memories in a computer are registers and buffers. These memories are vital to moving data in and out of primary storage and processing the data. A CPU uses them to improve the computer's overall performance. Figure 3−5 shows a generalized view of the interconnections of the components of the CPU and these special memories.

A **register** holds an instruction or data that are to be worked on immediately. It is part of the CPU and can hold only one piece of data at a time. Because registers are part of the CPU, the transfer of data in and out of primary storage is a high-speed operation. In fact, the size and number of these registers help determine the overall speed of the computer. The names and functions of the registers used most often are these:

- accumulator—stores the result of the last processing step of the ALU
- instruction register—holds an instruction in the control unit before it is decoded
- address register—holds the location of the next piece of data
- storage register—holds data on the way to or from primary storage
- program counter—holds the location of the next instruction to be executed

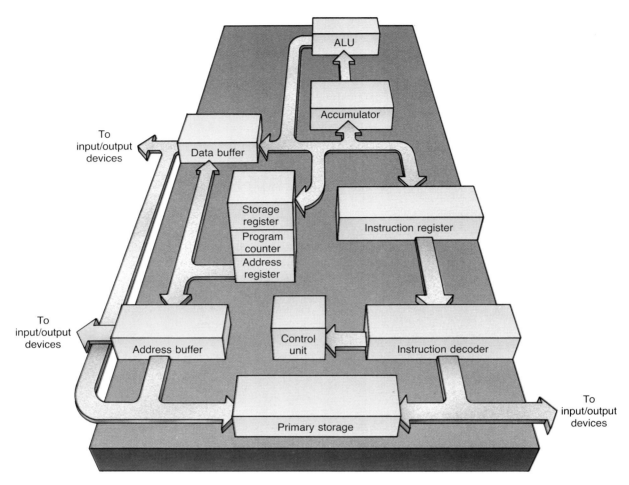

FIGURE 3–5

Arrows show a generalized view of the movement of data or instructions between registers and buffers within the CPU.

A **buffer,** another temporary holding space for data, may be part of the CPU or may be built into devices used to input or output data. Unlike a register, a buffer can hold more than one piece of data at a time. It acts as an intermediary between the CPU and any input or output device. Input and output devices operate at much slower rates than the CPU, so it is necessary to have a temporary holding place for larger amounts of data. For example, a printer cannot print data as fast as the CPU can send them. Without a place to store the data temporarily, the CPU would be idly waiting for the printer to catch up, and the CPU's operating speed would be reduced to the rate of the particular output device. A buffer allows the data to be stored temporarily, thereby freeing the CPU to do other tasks.

COMMUNICATION PATHWAYS

To function as a complete unit, the ALU, control unit, and primary storage unit must have a way to communicate. These links between and within the various units are called buses. A **bus** is no more than an electrical path on which data can flow from point to point in a circuit. A bus is classified by name according to its function. For example, the control bus is the pathway for all timing and control functions sent by the control unit to other units of the system. The address bus is the pathway used to locate the next instruction or the next piece of data in storage. The data bus is the pathway along which the actual data transfer takes place. The three bus paths are shown in Figure 3–6.

THE CPU AT WORK

Thanks in part to the control unit, the elements of the computer interact with amazing precision. Depending on the instruction executed, certain computer components may or may not be used. In one instance, an instruction may require computations within the ALU, whereas another may simply look into and display the contents of some memory location. Regardless of the actual instruction, however, the computer goes through two basic cycles to execute it: the **instruction cycle** and the **execution cycle**.

FIGURE 3–6
A generalized view of the communication pathways within a computer.

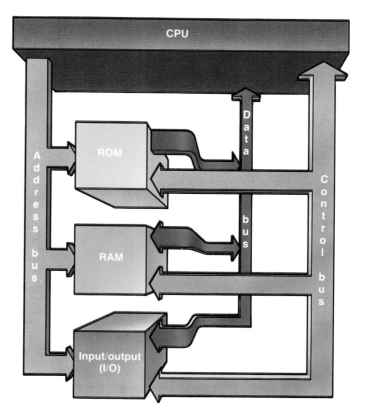

FIGURE 3–7
Instruction and execution cycles.

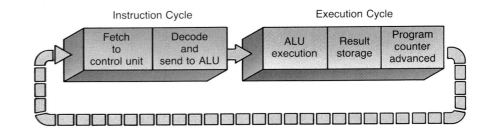

The instruction cycle is made up of two distinct steps: fetch and decode. In general, the fetch step locates an instruction in memory and sends it to the control unit. During the decode step the instruction is decoded and sent to the ALU, along with any necessary data. During the execution cycle the instruction is executed by the ALU, and the result is stored in the accumulator until needed. Then the program counter is incremented by an internally determined value to identify the location of the next instruction, and the instruction-execution sequence is repeated, continuing until the program ends. What may seem like a long process to fetch, decode, and execute a single instruction is actually done in less than the blink of an eye—and it takes only about 200 milliseconds (.2 second) to blink an eye! Figure 3–7 illustrates the sequence of events that occurs when an instruction is executed.

INPUT CONCEPTS AND DEVICES

Many of the traditional ways to input and output data were geared more to machines than to the humans who used them. However, the trend in input and output (I/O) devices is now moving toward a more natural means of communication. The most natural way for humans to communicate with computers is to use the same techniques that people use to communicate with each other. For example, entering data into a computer might be accomplished by speaking, writing, or physically pointing to specific objects on the screen. Speech, written text, and visual images such as color graphs are output forms that humans find easiest to interpret and use. Voice recognition and speech synthesis have only begun to reach their potential.

Input is the process of entering and translating incoming data into machine-readable form so that they can be processed by a computer. The data to be entered are also often referred to as input. Hardware is all the physical components of a computer system. Any hardware item that is attached to the main unit of a computer, which houses the CPU, is referred to as a **peripheral device**. An **input device** is a peripheral device through which data are entered and transformed into machine-readable form.

Keyboards

Today's most common and familiar input device is the standard keyboard. The traditional QWERTY typewriter keyboard (so called because the first six letters in the top row are *Q, W, E, R, T,* and *Y*) comprises the basic portion of today's computer **keyboard** (Figure 3–8). A typical computer keyboard contains all the letters, numbers, and symbols of a regular typewriter, plus a variety of other keys. Those other keys may include (1) a numeric keypad that looks and functions much like a calculator; (2) function keys whose operation can be determined by the user or preprogrammed by the software being used; and (3) special keys such as those used to control the movement of a cursor on the computer screen.

A **cursor** is a special character or symbol that indicates the user's position on the screen or focuses attention to a specific area on the screen. Cursor-movement keys typically include four directional arrow keys, which move the cursor one space at a time in an up, down, left, or right direction. Other keys—typically named *Home, End, PgUp* (page up), and *PgDn* (page down)—move the cursor quickly over longer distances. The cursor-movement keys are often part of the numeric keypad. In those cases, a key, such as the NumLck (number lock), acts as a toggle switch, shifting the function of these keys between cursor movement and numeric operations. Other special keys common to many keyboards are ESC (escape), CTRL (control), INS (insert), DEL (delete), and PRT SC (print screen). Many of these keys have been added to increase the user's efficiency.

The QWERTY keyboard design originated in the era of mechanical typewriters. The keys were arranged to keep the striking arms of frequently used characters far apart so that they would not get tangled up. A second keyboard design, the Dvorak keyboard designed in the 1920s, has also been introduced with electronic keyboards, with which there are no movable arms. The Dvorak keyboard rearranged the keys so that those most frequently used were placed in a single row and arranged to make more efficient use of the hands. This design is said to speed typing and thus improve productivity. However, since the vast majority of people using keyboards learned on and still use the QWERTY keyboard, it is doubtful that the Dvorak keyboard will replace it in the near future. In addition, many data entry operations involve numbers predominately, for which the type of keyboard arrangement doesn't make any difference.

In the selection of a keyboard style, it is important to consider the human factors involved, such as the touch or action of the keys and the sound they make as they are pressed. Some keyboards don't give a good response to touch, making it difficult to tell when a key has been pressed. Some keyboards are silent; others respond with a definite clicking sound when a key is struck. Users should be involved in the selection of a keyboard so that they will be satisfied and productive.

Mouse

The **mouse** has been around for more than 20 years. It was developed as an alternative to a keyboard in the 1960s. As the user rolls the mouse across a flat surface, it controls the cursor movement on the screen. When the user presses one of the buttons on the mouse (there are usually one to three buttons), the mouse either marks a place on the screen or makes selections from on-screen data (Figure 3–9).

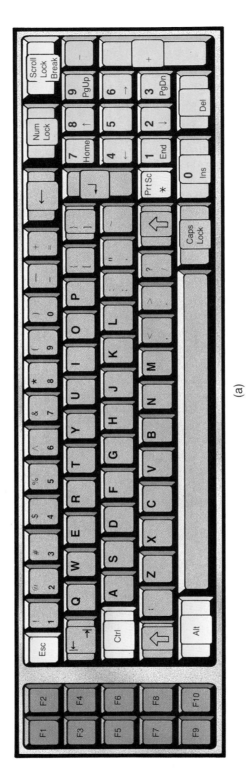

FIGURE 3–8

(a) Standard IBM PC keyboard.

(a)

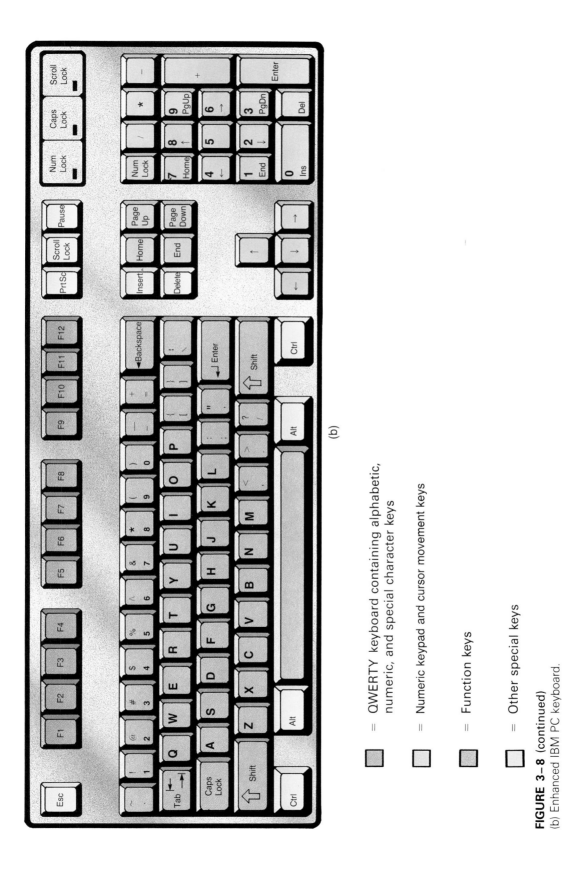

= QWERTY keyboard containing alphabetic, numeric, and special character keys

= Numeric keypad and cursor movement keys

= Function keys

= Other special keys

FIGURE 3–8 (continued)
(b) Enhanced IBM PC keyboard.

FIGURE 3–9
An electromechanical mouse.

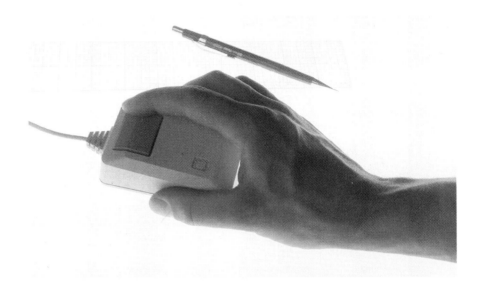

The mouse operates either electromechanically or optically. An electromechanical mouse has a partially enclosed ball on its underside. As the mouse is rolled along a flat surface, its movement is translated into a position on the screen. An optical mouse travels over a special tablet of grid lines. The computer senses the location of the mouse on the grid and turns that input into a relative position on the screen.

A mouse can be used for many applications, ranging from word processing to designing products with graphics. A mouse provides an alternative for people who are uncomfortable with a keyboard; it can also be used in combination with a keyboard to enhance input operations.

Touch Screens

A **touch screen** registers input when a finger or other object comes into contact with the screen. Two touch-screen techniques involve infrared beams and ultrasonic acoustic waves. With the first method, infrared beams crisscross the surface of the screen, and the location is recorded wherever a light beam is broken. The other technique involves ultrasonic acoustic waves that pass over the surface of the screen. Wherever the wave signals are interrupted by some contact with the screen, the location is recorded. Because the acoustic waves bend with the curved surface of the screen, they are closer to the screen and thus are more precise in locating the point of contact. Figure 3–10 shows one example of a touch screen.

Light Pens and Digitizers

A **light pen** can make selections, place objects, or indicate dimensions by simply touching the screen (Figure 3–11). A light pen does not emit light; rather, it reacts to light through a photosensitive detector in its base. A

FIGURE 3–10
A Hewlett-Packard touch screen. (Photo courtesy of Hewlett-Packard Company)

FIGURE 3–11
An X-ray technician uses a light pen to enter data into the computer. (Courtesy of Travenol Laboratories)

digitizer, or graphics tablet, is similar to a light pen; however, instead of drawing on the screen, a separate tablet is used on which a special stylus is moved (Figure 3–12). By selecting commands on the digitizer, objects can be drawn or erased, and coordinates can be marked on the screen. Light pens and digitizers are often used for mechanical and architectural drawing.

Voice Recognition

Voice recognition is one of the newest, most complex input techniques used with computers. With this approach the user inputs data by speaking into a microphone (Figure 3–13). The simplest form of voice recognition is a one-word command spoken by one person. Each command is isolated, with pauses between the words.

With a voice-recognition device some quality-control inspections can be performed more productively if inspectors can verbally list possible defects into the microphone of the computer instead of stopping to write them down. Any procedure that requires using two hands and recording data simultaneously can benefit from voice input. Voice recognition also opens up the world of computers to people who are physically challenged and are unable to use traditional types of input devices.

Today's voice-recognition systems can recognize a few hundred words; however, regional accents and words that sound alike but have different meanings, such as *hear* and *here,* are difficult to decipher and thus cause the system problems. Although research continues in this area, computer voice recognition of continuous speech or normal conversation is not currently available for widespread use.

Source Data Input

Data entered directly into a computer system without a transcription process is referred to as source data. Methods of source data input include magnetic-ink character recognition, magnetic strips, and optical recognition.

Magnetic-Ink Character Recognition. Magnetic-ink character recognition (MICR) is computer interpretation of a line of characters written in a special magnetic ink. These characters can be read by humans as well and often appear on the bottom of a check. Those numbers and odd-shaped characters, which are magnetic-ink characters, are bank-processing symbols representing the check number, customer account number, and bank identification number (Figure 3–14). When the bank receives the check, the amount of the check is also printed in magnetic ink. The check is then sent through an MICR reader to interpret the information, update the appropriate account, and in some cases sort the check afterwards.

Magnetic ink is used on documents such as bank checks and credit card slips because an MICR device can easily distinguish the appropriate magnetic characters no matter how much a user may have written over them.

FIGURE 3–12
A digitizer is used to transfer images to a computer screen. Here, an engineer digitizes a coffee maker and displays it on a computer screen. (Courtesy of the Gillette Company)

FIGURE 3–13
With a voice-recognition data-entry system, the operator's hands are free to write while commands are spoken to the computer. (Courtesy of Texas Instruments)

FIGURE 3-14

Banks use magnetic-ink characters on checks to ensure fast and efficient processing.

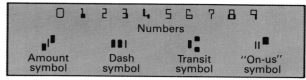

(a) Magnetic-ink character set

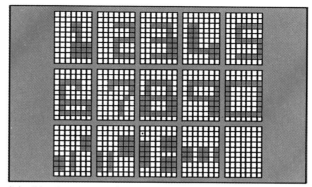

(b) Matrix patterns for magnetic-ink characters

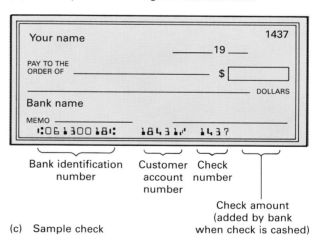

(c) Sample check

Magnetic Strips. Magnetic strips are thin bands of magnetically encoded data that are found on the backs of many credit cards and automated-teller cards. The data stored on the cards vary, but they usually include account numbers or special access codes. Magnetic-strip cards can also be used to limit access to high security areas. To enter a security area, a person would insert a card into a computerized "read" device; if the card contained the right code, the door would automatically open. Because such data cannot be seen or interpreted simply by looking at the card, the stored data can be highly sensitive or personal.

Optical Recognition. Optical recognition occurs when a device called a **scanner** scans a printed surface and translates what it sees into a machine-

Components of Business Computer Systems

readable format that can be understood by a computer. Scanning devices that use optical technology are one of the fastest growing input options today. The three types of optical recognition described here are optical-mark, optical-bar, and optical-character recognition.

Optical-mark recognition (OMR) employs mark sensing, one of the simplest forms of optical recognition, in order to scan and translate, based on their location, a series of pen or pencil marks into computer-readable form. For example, answers to multiple-choice questions can be marked in pencil on a specially designed form. A computerized optical-mark reader then scores the answers by identifying the positions of the marks, not their shapes.

A slightly more sophisticated type of optical recognition is **optical-bar recognition (OBR)**. An optical-bar reader recognizes and interprets a pattern of lines that form a bar code. **Bar codes,** also called product codes, appear on products as a series of thick and thin black bars and spaces, which are arranged to represent data, such as the name of the manufacturer and the type of product (Figure 3–15a). Interpretation of the code is based on the width of the lines. The bar code does not contain the price of the item; prices are stored in a computer, where the amount can be easily reprogrammed to reflect sales or increases. In a transaction the bar code is read by a scanner, the price and the product are matched by the computer, and the price is displayed at a checkout counter by a point-of-sale terminal. A point-of-sale (POS) terminal is a device that reads data at a transaction source and immediately turns them into usable information. These termi-

FIGURE 3–15
(a) A universal product code (UPC) is typically found on consumer products. (b) This employee is using a bar-code scanner to enter inventory data into a computer. (Courtesy of Intermec Corporation)

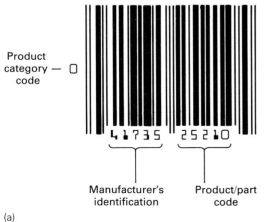

Product category — 0
code

41735   25210

Manufacturer's identification   Product/part code

(a)

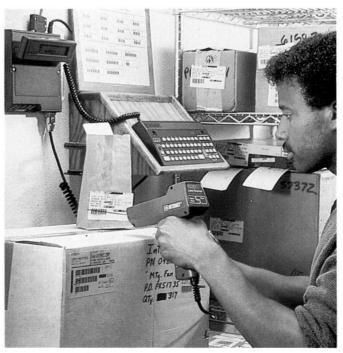

(b)

nals record the data found on the bar code or MICR price tag of each product, calculate the cost, and provide the consumer with a detailed receipt of the transaction. Some terminals also directly update inventory files (Figure 3–15b).

There are various bar-coding schemes in use; however, the most common is the universal product code (UPC). Department and grocery stores have long used OBR; now other types of stores, factories, and manufacturing operations are also using bar codes to provide more efficient, cost-effective control of inventory. Northeast Utilities is incorporating the use of bar codes to track environmental data, such as low-level radioactive wastes. The waste containers are marked with bar codes and tracked from cradle to grave by small, 32-Kbyte hand-held computers.

The most sophisticated type of optical recognition is **optical-character recognition (OCR)**. An optical-character reader works in much the same way as the human eye. It does not rely on a magnetic quality, as MICR does; rather, it recognizes specially shaped alphabetic and numeric characters. Capital and lowercase letters, as well as a variety of different optical-character typesets, can be read.

A set of optical characters can be used to print merchandise tags that can be read with an OCR wand (Figure 3–16). For a sales transaction the information on the tag, such as the item price and the inventory number, can be automatically read by a point-of-sale terminal. Pertinent data can thus be saved and transferred to a company's main computer system to be used in such activities as managing inventories and analyzing sales. State-of-the-art scanners can translate both graphic and textual material. Technical drawings can also be scanned and entered into a computer-aided design system for easy editing. Because of the variety of applications, optical-character-recognition technology is steadily increasing its role as an input method. Highlight 3–1 looks at how several organizations make use of optical-character recognition and scanners.

FIGURE 3–16
A salesclerk using an OCR wand.

Components of Business Computer Systems

Optical-Character Recognition Finds New Uses in Business

About 150 billion first class letters are mailed each year. Each piece of mail is sorted three times before it reaches its destination. The first sort is by general zip code, which gets the letter to the right post office. The second sort gets the letter to the correct carrier. The mail carrier does the final sorting, delivering the mail to the correct mailbox.

The U.S. Postal Service has incorporated optical-character readers into its mail sorters in 64 of its busiest post offices. An OCR scans each envelope, reads an address, converts it to a digitized form, and sends it to a computer. There the information is correlated with a database that contains the nine-digit zip code for that area. The mail sorter then prints the bar-code equivalent of the nine-digit zip code on the letter to be used in further sorting. The sorter can handle approximately 600 letters per minute.

This system has been credited with saving the Post Office more than $750 million in labor costs since 1982. The department expects to expand the program to nearly 200 locations by 1992. It's estimated that the optical readers can eliminate the need for human handlers to determine an address in up to 60 percent of the first class mail by 1991. Currently, the readers are scanning only 33 percent of the first class mail because of a shortage of mail sorters with optical-character-recognition ability.

Scanning the mail allows it to move from start to destination with minimum human intervention. The Post Office figures that it would have needed an additional 23,000 persons (earning $750 million) to handle the increase in mail from 1982 to 1987 if it had not been for the scanners. The department's $380 million budget for hardware and

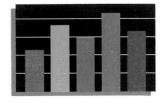

OUTPUT CONCEPTS

Output is the process of translating data in machine-readable form into a form that can be understood by humans or read by other machines. Information that results from that process is also often referred to as output. An **output device** is a peripheral device that accepts data from a computer and transforms them into a usable form, thus allowing the computer to communicate information to humans or other machines.

Output is divided into two general categories: (1) output that can be readily understood and used by humans and (2) output to secondary storage devices that hold the data to be used as input for further processing by a computer or for use by another machine.

Output that can be understood by humans can be categorized as hard copy and soft copy. **Hard copy** is output, such as paper, that can be read immediately or stored and read later. It is a relatively stable and permanent form of output. **Soft copy** is a temporary form, usually a screen-displayed software realized a 200 percent return on the investment. The Post Office hopes that the scanners will continue to cut its labor costs, which are about 83 percent of its budget.

A scanner can't always read a letter because an address is sometimes scrawled all over an envelope and the scanner is programmed to seek numbers and letters from a defined area. In about 10 percent of the letters the address information is outside these bounds. In such cases the envelopes have to be sorted by humans.

In an effort to further reduce costs, the Post Office is trying to convince big businesses to imprint their envelopes with a nine-digit bar code below the zip code. However, because of the cost of the equipment businesses have been only somewhat cooperative.

Optical-character recognition is also being used to eliminate keying errors and help track and control inventory. American President Companies is a freight company that is incorporating a newly developed, automated equipment identification (AEI) system that relies on scanners. The system incorporates microchip transponders, or electronic tags, which the company attaches to its aluminum or steel shipping containers, chassis, trucks, and rail cars. Information about the container, chassis, or truck is programmed into the tag, which can then be read by scanning devices to track the freight's movement as it moves through APC's ports and terminals. The company also uses a truck equipped with a scanner to take inventory of stacked shipping containers in rows typically 20 to 45 feet long; the truck simply drives around the containers and scans the information on the electronic tags. That information is fed into APC's worldwide equipment-management database to help track freight and manage inventories. The scanning devices eliminate the possibility of keying errors, which might introduce invalid data into the database.

output, but it may also be in the form of voice output. If the data needed to create the soft copy have been saved on a secondary storage medium, the soft copy can be reproduced at any time.

HARD-COPY DEVICES

Textual material and graphics can be produced with a wide selection of printers and plotters. A **printer** produces output, usually in the form of text, on paper; some printers also produce graphics. A **plotter** produces graphic images on paper. Printers and plotters range in price from about one hundred dollars to tens of thousands of dollars. The speed of the devices and the quality of the hard copy are the main features that determine the various prices. Descriptions of different printers and plotters could fill this text. This section will look at only the major categories, after a brief discussion of print quality, an important feature of any hard-copy device.

Print Quality

The print quality of hard-copy output can vary considerably. You may have heard the terms *typeset quality, near-typeset quality, letter-quality, near-letter quality, standard quality,* and *draft quality.* But what do these terms mean?

At the top of the list is **typeset-quality print**. This print is produced by computer-driven typeset machines. Examples of typeset-quality print can be seen in magazines and high-quality books. Near-typeset-quality print is similar to that produced by a typeset machine but is of lower quality.

Letter-quality print is the equivalent of good typewriter print. This print is made of fully formed (solid-line) characters as opposed to characters made of dots or lines (Figure 3–17). Letter-quality print is traditionally used in business letters and formal correspondence.

Printers that don't produce fully formed characters can still print high-quality documents with a near-letter-quality print. Some printers accomplish this by having the print head make multiple passes over the same letters, thus filling in the spaces between the dots or lines.

Standard-quality print is produced when characters composed of dots or lines are formed by a single pass of the print head. Generally, standard quality is suitable for most informal applications.

At the low end of the quality scale is **draft-quality print,** sometimes called compressed print. This print is sometimes used for rough drafts, informal correspondence, or computer program listings. The characters are formed with a minimum number of dots or lines and are smaller than the standard-quality characters. Figure 3–18 compares print qualities.

Impact Printers

The quality of type that a printer produces is determined by its printing mechanism. An **impact printer** produces characters by using a hammer or pins to strike an ink ribbon, which in turn presses against a sheet of paper, leaving an impression of the character on the paper. This is how an ordinary typewriter works.

FIGURE 3–17
A comparison of fully formed characters and characters composed of dots or lines.

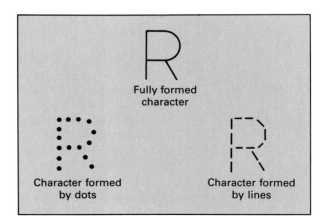

Fully formed character

Character formed by dots

Character formed by lines

FIGURE 3–18
A comparison of different qualities of print.

This is an example of near-typeset-quality print.

This is an example of letter-quality print.

This is an example of near-letter-quality print.

This is an example of standard-quality print.

This is an example of draft-quality (compressed) print.

Impact printers are often very loud. When locating impact printers in an office environment, a manager needs to be conscious of the effect of their noise on the staff's productivity. Printers can be located in separate rooms away from work areas; if they must be located near office personnel, sound hoods can be purchased to muffle the sound. Some of today's newer impact printers have been designed to operate relatively quietly.

Two popular impact printers most often used with microcomputers are the dot-matrix printer and the daisy-wheel printer. They are both character-at-a-time printers, printing one character at a time.

Dot-Matrix Printers. The **dot-matrix printer** uses print heads containing from 9 to 24 pins. These pins produce patterns of dots on paper to form individual characters. The 24-pin dot-matrix printer produces more dots than a 9-pin dot-matrix printer; the larger number of dots results in much crisper, clearer characters. Some dot-matrix printers can produce better quality characters by using a near-letter-quality mode. However, this mode drastically reduces printing speed because it makes multiple passes over the same line. Dot-matrix printers are relatively inexpensive.

Many printers have built-in buffers to store succeeding lines of text. In other systems output may be temporarily stored (buffered) on a separate secondary storage device. The process of sending output to a secondary storage device for temporary storage before printing is called **spooling**. (Input may also be spooled before processing.) Buffer storage allows bidirectional printing, that is, printing in both directions as the print head moves back and forth across the paper. This capability significantly increases print speed.

Daisy-Wheel Printers. In order to get the quality of type found on typewriters, a daisy-wheel impact printer can be used. The **daisy-wheel printer** is so called because the print mechanism looks like a daisy; at the end of each "petal" is a fully formed character that produces solid-line print. A hammer strikes a petal against the ribbon, and the character prints on the paper.

The daisy wheel can be replaced to change styles and sizes of typeface (fonts). For example, daisy wheels can shift from pica to elite or from characters to symbols, or they can print text in a foreign language. When one feature of a printer, such as the print quality, is enhanced, it is usually at the expense of another. These letter-quality printers are much slower.

Line Printers. For certain operations in businesses where enormous amounts of material are printed, character-at-a-time printers are just too slow; these users need line-at-a-time printers. **Line printers,** or line-at-a-time printers, use special mechanisms that can print a whole line at once; such printers can typically print from 1,200 to 6,000 lines per minute. Drum, chain, and band printers are all line-at-a-time printers.

A **drum printer** has complete character sets engraved around the circumference of the drum at each of the print positions. The number of print positions across the drum equals the number available on the page, typically ranging from 80 to 132. Individual print positions rotate until the desired letter is in the proper place; then a bank of hammers strikes the paper against the ribbon and the drum, producing an entire line of print.

A **chain printer** uses a chain of print characters wrapped around two pulleys. Like the drum printer, there is one hammer for each print position. Circuitry inside the printer detects when the correct character appears at the desired print location on the page. The hammer then strikes the page, pressing the paper against a ribbon and the character located at the desired print position. An impression of the character is left on the page. The chain keeps rotating until all of the required print positions on the line have been filled. Then the page moves up to print the next line.

A **band printer** operates in a similar way except that it uses a band instead of a chain and has fewer hammers. The hammers on a band printer are mounted on a carriage that moves across the paper to the appropriate print positions. Characters are rotated into place and struck by the hammers. Font styles can easily be changed by replacing a band or chain.

Nonimpact Printers

Nonimpact printers do not use a striking device to produce characters on paper and are therefore much quieter. A disadvantage is that a document must be reprinted for each needed copy because multipart, or carbon, forms cannot be successfully used with nonimpact printers. Major technologies in this area include the ink-jet, thermal-transfer, and laser printers.

Ink-Jet Printers. Ink-jet printers form characters on paper by spraying ink from tiny nozzles through an electrical field that arranges the charged ink particles into characters at the rate of approximately 250 characters per second. The ink, which can be of various colors, is absorbed into the paper and dries instantly. Ink-jet printers are reliable but expensive.

Thermal-Transfer Printers. An inexpensive alternative to the ink-jet printer is the **thermal-transfer printer,** which uses heat to transfer ink to paper. These printers bond the ink to the paper by heating pins that press against a special ink ribbon. A thermal-transfer printer produces near-letter-quality characters and can give color printouts by using a color ribbon.

Laser Printers. When speed and quality that is comparable to typeset material are required, a laser printer is the solution. **Laser printers** produce characters and other images on paper by directing a laser beam at a mirror, which bounces the beam onto a drum. The laser leaves a negative charge on the drum, to which positively charged black toner powder will stick. As the paper rolls by the drum, the toner is transferred to the paper. A hot roller then bonds the toner to the paper.

Laser printers use buffers that store an entire page at a time. When a whole page is loaded, it will be printed. Many laser printers designed to be used with microcomputers can print eight pages per minute. Laser printers designed for commercial use are much faster and print approximately 21,000 lines per minute, or 437 pages with each containing 48 lines. Laser printer prices range from several thousand dollars to tens of thousands of dollars. Developments in the last few years have provided relatively low-cost laser printers for use in small businesses.

Plotters

The growth of computer-aided design and drafting has created a demand for devices that can produce high-quality graphics in multiple colors. A plotter reproduces drawings using pens that are attached to movable arms and are directed across the surface of a stationary piece of paper (Figure 3–19). Many plotters, however, combine a movable pen arm with paper that can also roll back and forth to make the drawing. This two-way movement allows any configuration to be drawn.

Plotter applications are not limited to computer-aided design. High-quality bar graphs and pie charts created with a plotter can add interest and meaning to business presentations.

Computer Output Microform

Computer output microform (COM) is hard copy in the form of photographic images recorded on a microform, such as microfilm or microfiche cards. In some cases the computer can output directly to a COM machine. In other cases data are first recorded on magnetic tape, and that tape is used as input to a COM machine. The advantage of COM is that it provides a low-cost storage option for large amounts of data requiring infrequent access. It is ideal for businesses such as hospitals that must keep old data for such things as patients' medical, financial, and insurance claim records. Microfilm and microfiche readers are used to read the data.

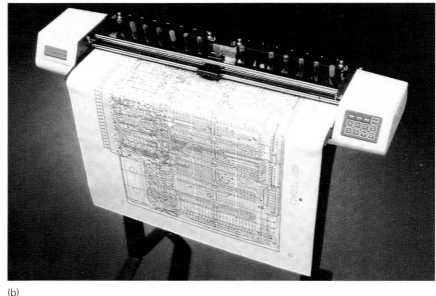

(a)   (b)

FIGURE 3–19
(a) Desktop plotters are used in offices to generate graphics that enhance
business presentations. (b) Large plotters allow images such as this circuit
diagram to be drawn to a size that enables users to view the image in detail.
(Courtesy of Houston Instrument)

SOFT-COPY DEVICES

Usually, a user prefers to see what the output looks like before making a permanent copy of it. Viewing the work allows corrections or rearrangement of material to suit specific needs. Although most soft-copy output is seen on a display device, voice synthesis devices let us hear it as well.

Monitors and Terminals

The most popular and certainly the most viewed form of output is found on the monitor. A **monitor** is a television-like device used to display data or information. Just like other output devices, it comes in many styles and price ranges. A monitor allows a user to view the results of processing but can also be combined with a keyboard so that input data can be viewed and checked as they are entered. This combination of keyboard and monitor is often called a **terminal,** or a **video display terminal (VDT).** Terminals are categorized as dumb terminals, smart terminals, and intelligent terminals.

Dumb terminals do not contain a microprocessor and cannot do any of their own processing. These basic devices are attached to a computer system and are used for data entry and output display. If these terminals are disconnected from the computer system, they cannot function on their own. **Smart terminals** allow limited editing and data storage without interacting with the computer system. However, these terminals cannot be used to program or run sophisticated applications. **Intelligent terminals** incorporate a microprocessor that enables them to process data independently.

Monitor quality is often compared in terms of **resolution,** a measure of the number of picture elements, or pixels, that a screen contains. A **pixel** is the smallest increment of a display screen that can be controlled individually—the more pixels, the clearer and sharper the image. A 640 × 460 pixel screen contains 640 horizontal pixels and 460 vertical pixels.

Several human factors should be considered by a manager selecting monitors. Employees who work at monitors for long periods of time can suffer eye strain and fatigue resulting from the glare and flicker of some monitors. Monitors should be positioned in a manner that makes them easy to read, and antiglare screens should be used wherever needed to reduce glare. The resolution should be sufficient so that text can be comfortably read, and personnel should be given frequent breaks away from the monitor. Health concerns regarding the emission of radiation by monitors are still unresolved. Because of the potential danger, managers should stay current on research findings and should take reasonable precautions, as in the case of pregnant employees.

Cathode-Ray Tube. There are two kinds of viewing screens used for monitors: cathode-ray tube and flat-panel display. To produce a data image on a **cathode-ray tube (CRT),** an electron beam moves across a phosphor-coated screen. Intensifying the strength of the beam causes the phosphor coating to glow in certain places, forming the characters. The most common type of CRT has a display screen of 24 lines with 80 characters in each. Other sizes are available, including those that can display a full 8½-by-11-inch page.

The least expensive of the CRTs is the single color, or monochrome, monitor. Monochrome monitors are used where output is mainly text and numbers; with appropriate circuitry, however, some monochrome monitors can display graphics. Monochrome monitors usually display green, amber, or white characters on a black screen.

A color monitor is often preferable for output containing graphics. Three colors of phosphor dots form a pixel on color monitors. These colors are blended to make other colors by varying the intensity of the electron beam focused on the phosphor dots.

Two types of color monitors are commonly used: composite and red-green-blue. A composite color monitor uses only one electron gun to control the intensity of all three phosphor dots in each pixel. In a red-green-blue (RGB) monitor, three electron guns, one for each dot in a pixel, are used to control the intensity of the phosphor dots. A much sharper picture is produced with the RGB monitor because the three electron guns allow finer control of the intensity of the phosphor dots. Artists may wonder why red, green, and blue are used as the primary colors instead of red, yellow, and blue. Simply stated, the difference between electronic waves and color pigments requires that green be used instead of yellow to get the appropriate color mixes.

Flat-Panel Display. As computers become smaller and more powerful, a CRT can become cumbersome for use with portable computers. However, a **flat-panel display** does not have a picture tube and can be made small enough to fit on little battery-powered portables. Some desktop microcomputers also use flat-panel displays.

The most common type of flat-panel display is the liquid-crystal display (LCD), which produces images by aligning molecular crystals. When a voltage is applied, the crystals line up in a way that blocks light from passing through them; that absence of light is seen as characters on the screen.

Besides size, another advantage of LCD displays is that flat panels do not flicker. The flicker of a CRT, caused by the electron beam moving across the screen, can cause eye strain and fatigue during prolonged sessions at the computer.

The flat-panel display is still in its infancy; better resolution and contrast, as well as other new features, are being developed. One advance is the gas-plasma screen, which offers flicker-free viewing and a much higher contrast than LCDs have. Gas-plasma displays contain an ionized gas (plasma) between two glass plates. One glass plate contains a set of horizontal wires; the other has a set of vertical wires. The intersecting point of each horizontal and vertical wire identifies a pixel, which is turned on when current is sent through the appropriate vertical and horizontal wires. The plasma at the pixel emits light as the current is applied, and characters are formed by lighting the appropriate pixels.

Voice Synthesis

Another emerging technology involves **voice synthesis** and the computers that produce it. Voice synthesis is the process of electronically reproducing the human voice in recognizable patterns. Producing such patterns is not an easy task; the English language and its rules of syntax are enough to confuse many humans. Imagine the difficulty in programming a computer to decipher this expression: "I can record a record." There are still many obstacles to overcome.

SECONDARY STORAGE

John von Neumann realized the importance of having instructions and data readily available in internally stored programs for the computer to process. His realization led to the development of primary storage and the stored-program concept. However, in some applications a computer's primary storage capabilities are so expensive that they are of limited practical value in handling the instructions and data needed for processing.

Another limitation of primary storage is its volatility. In many cases a particular set of data is used more than once. However, when the power is turned off, data in primary storage are erased and require reentry for each new use, a time-consuming and costly way to process data. In addition, it is often desirable to save the results of processing for use as input in further processing or for printing purposes later.

Thus, because primary storage may not be large enough to hold all the required instructions and data and because RAM is volatile and doesn't provide long-term memory, supplemental storage is necessary. The solution to these limitations is the use of secondary storage.

Secondary storage is the nonvolatile memory that is stored outside the computer. It is less expensive, per storage character, than primary storage is and is usually used for storage of large amounts of data or for permanent or long-term storage of data or programs. Secondary storage is also used for storing backups, or copies, of data and programs so that they are not permanently lost if primary storage power is interrupted. Three secondary storage media that are used with all sizes of computers are magnetic tapes, magnetic disks, and optical media. Although these media are cheaper and can hold much more data than primary storage can, access to the data is slower.

Magnetic Tape

Typically, **magnetic tape** is a ½- or ¼-inch ribbon of mylar (a plasticlike material), coated with a thin layer of iron oxide. An I/O device, the tape drive, reads and writes the data as the tape passes by a read/write head, the electromagnetic component in the drive. When the tiny, haphazardly arranged particles of iron oxide are aligned by magnetization, data are stored as magnetized spots. Magnetic tape is usually divided into nine separate strips, or tracks. Eight of these tracks are usually used for the codes that represent data characters; the ninth track is reserved for an error-checking bit (Figure 3–20). To store data, the write head aligns the iron-oxide particles. If they are aligned (polarized) in one direction, the particle represents a 1; in the opposite direction, the iron-oxide particle represents a 0. To read the tape, the drive sends the tape past the read head, and the patterns of 1s and 0s are interpreted as pieces of data.

Magnetic tape stores records or groups of related data sequentially, that is, one after another. To access a data record, you must read every record preceding it. Not every inch of tape is used for data, however. Between two records is a space called an **interrecord gap (IRG)**. The IRGs

FIGURE 3–20

Data representation of EBCDIC code on magnetic tape: 1 represents a magnetized spot or bit; 0 represents a nonmagnetized spot.

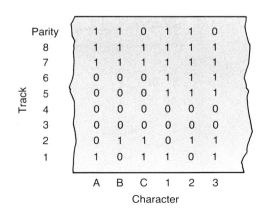

Track	A	B	C	1	2	3
Parity	1	1	0	1	1	0
8	1	1	1	1	1	1
7	1	1	1	1	1	1
6	0	0	0	1	1	1
5	0	0	0	1	1	1
4	0	0	0	0	0	0
3	0	0	0	0	0	0
2	0	1	1	0	1	1
1	1	0	1	1	0	1

Character

FIGURE 3-21

An unblocked tape with interrecord gaps (IRGs) between every two records.

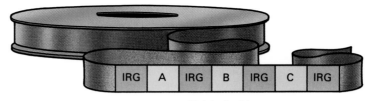

Unblocked tape

identify where the tape stops and starts and allow the tape to attain the proper speed before data are read from or written on it.

When an IRG is located between every two records, the tape is referred to as unblocked, and much of it is unavailable for data storage because of the space needed for the IRGs (Figure 3-21). In addition, data access is slow because the tape drive has to stop and start after each record. In practice, more than one record is usually stored between two IRGs. In such cases the tape is said to be blocked, and each space is referred to as an **interblock gap (IBG)** (Figure 3-22). The number of records stored between IBGs is referred to as the **blocking factor**. Blocking increases the storage capacity of a tape because it decreases the spaces needed. Since an entire block of records is written or read all at once, blocking also increases the speed of writing data on or reading data from magnetic tape.

Tapes can store large quantities of data inexpensively and thus are often used as backup storage media. Magnetic tapes are erasable, reusable, and durable. They can be easily registered in a catalog and stored in a tape library. They can also be easily stored off-site to guard against catastrophic events (e.g., earthquakes) that might seriously damage an information center. However, magnetic tape is not well suited to data files that are revised or updated often. Such files should be stored on a medium that allows faster and more direct access to data. Some appropriate media are discussed later in this chapter.

Although used mainly with large computers, magnetic tapes can be utilized with all sizes of computers. They are made in reel-to-reel, cassette, and cartridge forms. Each form stores data magnetically, but each holds different amounts of data and accesses them at different rates. The amount of data that can be held depends on the length of the tape, the number of interrecord gaps, and the density of the tape. **Density** describes how tightly data can be packed and stored on a storage medium; we use it as a measure of the number of characters or bytes of data that can be recorded on one

FIGURE 3-22

A blocked tape with a blocking factor of 5, that is, with five records between interblock gaps (IBGs).

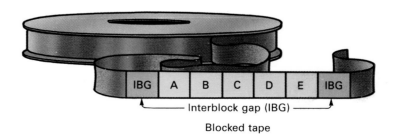

Blocked tape

inch of tape. The data transfer rate—the number of characters or bytes per second that can be transferred from the tape drive to the medium, or vice versa—also varies among the different tape forms.

Reel-to-Reel Tape.   A reel-to-reel tape consists of magnetic tape placed on a reel about 10½ inches in diameter (Figure 3–23). A typical tape is about 2,400 feet long, ½ inch wide, and able to hold about 40 megabytes of data. Data transfer rates vary from approximately 5,000 bytes per second to more than 1 million bytes per second. The more common tape drives have rates of 60,000 bytes per second. These tapes usually store data at a density of 1,600 bytes per inch, but that figure can range from 800 to 6,250 bytes per inch. Reel-to-reel tapes are relatively inexpensive, durable, and capable of holding a large quantity of data. They are used mainly with large computer systems to store backups of important data and data that do not change often.

Cassette Tape.   A cassette tape resembles the cassette tape used for audio recording. The tape, about ¼ inch wide, is enclosed in a plastic case and is used mainly with small computers. Such tapes are inexpensive; but they

(a)

(b)

FIGURE 3–23
(a) A magnetic reel-to-reel tape. (Courtesy of BASF Corporation Information Systems) (b) Magnetic reel-to-reel tapes mounted on tape drives. (Courtesy of Boise Cascade Corporation)

FIGURE 3–24
This cartridge tape is approximately one-half the size of a videocassette and holds about 20,000 pages of information. (Courtesy of BASF Corporation Information Systems)

cannot hold much data, and access to the stored data is fairly slow. Cassette-tape storage, once very popular with personal computer users, has been largely replaced by the more popular and versatile disk storage systems, which will be discussed shortly.

Cartridge Tape. Cartridge tape (Figure 3–24) is another form of magnetic tape. Its packaging is similar to that of a cassette tape, but a cartridge tape has a much greater data storage density (i.e., it has more storage in less area). Cartridge tapes and reel-to-reel systems are popular as secondary storage media for large computer systems.

Magnetic Disk

A **magnetic disk** is a mylar or metallic platter on which electronic data can be stored. Although disks resemble phonograph records, they do not have a record's characteristic spiraling groove. Nonetheless, data are accessed in much the same way that an individual song is selected on a long-playing record.

A magnetic disk's main advantages over magnetic tape include these capabilities:

1. accessing any data immediately without having to start at the beginning
2. holding more data in a smaller space
3. attaining faster data transfer speeds

Floppy Diskette. Magnetic disks are manufactured in both floppy-diskette and hard-disk styles. A **floppy diskette**, also called simply a diskette or a disk, is a small, flexible mylar disk coated with iron oxide (similar to the coating on magnetic tape) and used to store data. Floppy diskettes have been around since the early 1970s. Originally, they were 8 inches in diameter; today they are available in three sizes—the 3½-inch microfloppy, as well as the 5¼-inch and 8-inch sizes (Figure 3–25).

The 8-inch and 5¼-inch diskettes are covered by stiff, protective jackets with various holes and cutouts that serve special functions (Figure 3–26). The hub ring is where the disk drive holds the disk to rotate it. The elongated read/write window allows the read/write head of the drive to write data on or read data from the floppy disk. The small hole next to the hub ring is the index hole, through which the computer determines the relative position of the disk for locating data. The cutout on the side of the floppy disk is the write-protect notch. Covering this opening with a piece of tape prevents data on the disk from being erased or written over.

The 3½-inch diskettes have hard plastic coverings and protective metal pieces that cover the read/write window when the disk is not in use. This additional protection makes them less prone to damage from handling, dust, or other contaminants. The 3½-inch disk is growing in popularity. Many microcomputers, such as the IBM PS/2 series and the Apple Macintosh series, now use the 3½-inch disk as their standard.

FIGURE 3–25
Floppy diskettes are available in three different sizes.

A diskette must be prepared for use before data or programs can be stored on it. Each diskette, regardless of size, is divided into concentric circles called **tracks,** where data are stored. Each diskette is also divided into pie-shaped wedges called **sectors,** which further specify data storage locations (Figure 3–27). The number of tracks and sectors is usually determined by a computer's operating system during a formatting operation. The operating system labels each sector of each track with an address so that the computer can go directly to a specific area.

FIGURE 3–26
A floppy diskette jacket.

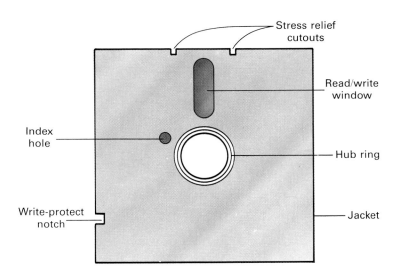

Components of Business Computer Systems

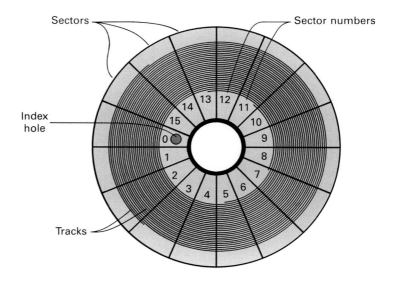

FIGURE 3–27
A diskette is divided into tracks and sectors.

Sectors — Sector numbers

Index hole

Tracks

Increased use of 3½-inch disks has created the problem of transferring data between 3½-and 5¼-inch disks. Managers can solve this problem in several ways. One approach is to use software and cables to directly connect computers through their parallel or serial ports, enabling them to transfer or share data. It is also possible to send a file to an electronic bulletin board (the electronic equivalent to a conventional bulletin board) from one computer and then retrieve it by another computer. In addition, managers might buy desktop computers that have both types of diskettes or an external floppy drive of the appropriate size.

Hard Disk. **A hard disk** is just that—hard and inflexible. It is made from materials such as aluminum instead of mylar. The I/O device used to transfer data to and from a hard disk is called a hard-disk drive. The read/write head of a hard-disk drive floats above the surface of the disk at a height of about 0.00005 of an inch. In comparison, the diameter of a human hair is 100 times larger. Because of the high rotation speed of the hard disk (approximately 3,600 revolutions per minute [rpm]), any particles of dirt, dust, or even smoke that encounter the read/write head result in a **head crash**. When this occurs, a foreign particle is pushed into the disk, and the head actually bounces and comes into physical contact with the disk. Severe damage can result to either the head or the disk, destroying the stored data.

A hard disk has several advantages over a floppy disk. The rigid construction of a hard disk allows it to be rotated very fast (3,600 rpm) compared to the rotation speed of a floppy diskette (360 rpm). Thus, data can be transferred much faster to or from a hard disk because it takes less time to find the storage location. Also, because of its hard construction, a hard disk allows data to be stored more densely, giving a hard disk more storage capacity than a floppy diskette of the same size.

FIGURE 3-28

The top of the case has been removed from this fixed disk to show the hard disk and a read/write head. (Courtesy of Seagate Technology)

Hard-disk drives are available for all sizes of computers, from microcomputers to business-oriented large-system computers. A hard disk may be permanently installed in a drive or may appear as a removable cartridge or disk pack.

A **fixed disk** is enclosed permanently inside a sealed case for protection from the elements (Figure 3-28). Fixed-disk systems contain one or more hard disks and can be used in all types of computers. The 5¼-inch fixed-disk systems used with microcomputers have typical storage capacities of between 10 and 70 megabytes. In large computers the fixed-disk system provides storage capacities in the gigabyte range (billions of bytes).

A storage system using **removable cartridges** (Figure 3-29) has the same speed and capacity as a hard-disk system. Such cartridges usually contain only one or two disks. Many hard-disk drives used with small computers are designed to use removable cartridges. The advantage of the

FIGURE 3-29

Removable-cartridge storage systems allow users more flexibility than fixed-disk systems. The cartridges can be removed and stored in a secure location. The Bernoulli Box is a removable-cartridge storage device.

removable cartridge is that it can be removed at any time and a new or different cartridge can be inserted. Thus, a user could have a separate cartridge for each application.

A **disk pack** (Figure 3–30) is another removable device in which several hard disks (a common number is 11) are packed into a single plastic case. Disk-pack drives are designed for large systems that require larger storage capacities. Because a disk pack is susceptible to damage by scratching, the top of the first disk and the bottom of the last disk are generally not used. However, 20 sides remain, in a disk pack containing 11 disks, permitting storage of hundreds of megabytes. Disk packs can also be interchanged, giving a computer a virtually unlimited amount of secondary storage.

Optical Media

Optical technology involves the use of lasers—highly concentrated beams of light. This technology has created new types of secondary storage media for computers, including optical laser disks, optical cards, and optical tape. Predictions suggest that by the end of this century most storage will be optical. Highlight 3–2 examines digital paper, a new optical storage medium.

FIGURE 3–31
A CD-ROM optical laser disk.

Optical Laser Disk. Sometimes technological developments created for one application result in an improvement in other areas. **Optical laser disks** (Figure 3–31) are hard metal disks ranging in size from 4.72 inches to 14 inches. They were originally developed as compact disks for video and audio applications. The same method of using laser beams to encode binary data (by burning microscopic "pits" on audio and video disks to represent 1s and 0s) is used to encode the data stored on optical laser disks.

Digital paper could be just the solution that businesses need to solve the cost and storage-space problems associated with mass storage of data. Digital paper is a flexible plastic film made of polyester-based fabric coated with a dye that is sensitive to infrared light. It stores data optically in the same way that optical disks do, but at much higher densities.

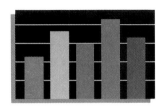

Digital paper can be slit into lengths like tapes, stamped into disks, or wound into cassettes. It can be produced inexpensively and—according to its manufacturer, ICI Electronics of London—can store data at a cost of only ½ cent per megabyte. Because of its low cost ICI believes that digital paper can become an alternative to paper and microfilm by the early 1990s. A 2,400-foot reel of ½-inch digital-paper tape could store 600 gigabytes (600,000 millions) of data, equivalent to the storage capacity of 1,000 compact disks.

Digital paper has a 15-year shelf life. Because it requires much less physical storage space than current media and because it is available at low cost, digital paper could become a business user's primary medium of storage in the future.

Most optical disks are read-only storage devices. A common version of the optical disk is the CD-ROM (compact disk, read-only memory); the user can only read data from and cannot write data on the disk. A **write-once-read-many (WORM) optical disk** is a blank optical disk that allows the user to write data on the disk once, after which the disk can only be read from. Although not suited to applications where data change, WORM optical disks are very convenient for storing data that remain constant. Some of the more expensive optical disks can be written on and erased; they are called **erasable optical-storage disks.**

Optical Card. The **optical card,** or laser card, is the size of a credit card and has an optical-laser-encoded strip that can store approximately 2 megabytes of data. These cards have many potential uses, most notably for credit records or medical histories.

Optical Tape. Continuing developments and refinements in optical technology include optical tape. **Optical tape** is similar in appearance to magnetic tape, but data are stored by optical-laser techniques. Optical tapes, which are in cassette form, can store more than 8 gigabytes each; and the tape drives can hold 128 cassettes, providing total data storage of about 1 terabyte (1,000 gigabytes). Like other optical methods of data storage, optical tape is read-only. As optical technology develops, higher densities and expanded uses will result.

SUMMARY

Within a computer, data are represented as binary system numbers. The smallest piece of data that a computer understands is a bit. A grouping of eight bits is a byte. A kilobyte is 1,024 bytes.

A central processing unit (CPU) is comprised of an arithmetic and logic unit (ALU), a control unit, and a primary storage unit. Modern technology has put the ALU, the control unit, and, in some cases, the primary storage unit onto one integrated circuit (also known as a microchip or a chip) called a microprocessor.

There are several forms of primary storage, including semiconductor memory and bubble memory. Semiconductor memory is the most common and is of two basic types: RAM and ROM. RAM is volatile and is used primarily for temporary storage. ROM is nonvolatile (i.e., it does not rely on a source of power) and is used for permanent storage.

Two special-purpose memories are registers and buffers. A register is a temporary holding place for instructions or data to be worked on immediately. A buffer holds data on their way in and out of the CPU.

Data are transferred out of memory and into the ALU for processing by way of the control, address, and data buses. The process of executing an instruction involves both an instruction cycle and an execution cycle.

Before the CPU can process data and make the results available, there must be a way of communicating data to and from the computer. The process of entering and translating data into machine-readable form is called input. The data to be entered are also often referred to as input. Input devices include any hardware used to enter and translate data. There are many kinds of input devices, including keyboards, a mouse, light pens, and voice recognition, as well as optical-mark, optical-bar, and optical-character recognition.

The process of translating machine-readable data into a form that can be understood by humans or read by other machines is called output. An output device is any hardware that performs the translation and produces a hard or soft copy of the processing results. Output that humans can read can be separated into hard copy and soft copy. Hard-copy output devices include printers, plotters, and computer output microform devices. Soft-copy output devices include monitors and voice-synthesis systems. Two popular types of monitors are cathode-ray tube (CRT) and flat-panel displays.

Primary storage is often inadequate because of its limited size and its volatility. To supplement primary storage, secondary storage—memory that is external to the computer and nonvolatile—is used. Three types of secondary storage media are magnetic tape, magnetic disk, and optical media. Magnetic tape is a ribbon of mylar, coated with a thin layer of iron oxide. Magnetic disks are mylar or metallic platters coated with iron oxide. Optical technology involves the use of lasers to store data on various media.

MINICASE 3–1

The Lucas County Historical Society maintains information on historical facts related to the county. Because of the former director's lack of understanding about computers the society has never computerized. It has maintained all its information in paper files, making topic research a slow and tedious process. Often, requests for specific information have taken up to a month to satisfy. In addition, the society is running out of physical space to store any more documents. The new director recognizes the benefits of computerization and has been able to raise about $20,000 to purchase a new system.

The director wants a computer system that can be easily operated by his staff. He is also concerned that there be features to help physically challenged individuals operate it. In addition, the system should be able to print informal documents quickly and inexpensively, as well as providing near-typeset-quality print and high resolution graphics to enable the society to produce its monthly newsletter in-house. The director also wants the capability of storing large amounts of data easily, to allow quick access. Since the historical data stored by the society remains constant, it rarely has to be updated.

1. What category of computer system would best fit the society's needs? Why?

2. What types of input and output components would satisfy the director's concerns?

3. What types of storage components would accommodate the society's records?

MINICASE 3–2

Shared-Use Network (SUN) is a firm that provides long-distance customers with access to several major phone networks at discounted prices. Its operations involve numerous states throughout the nation. Each office is currently processing its own accounting and billing data, but SUN has decided to centralize the data-processing activities for each geographic region into a single regional data center. Each data center will process all of the general accounting and billing data within its region. The volume of accounting and billing data is high and is very important to the successful operation of the company. Any loss of data could be devastating. Numerous accounting reports and a large number of customer bills need to be generated each month.

1. What type of computer system would best suit the needs of each regional data center? Why?

2. What type of output components do you think are needed?

Key Terms

arithmetic and logic unit (ALU)	bubble memory
band printer	buffer
bar code	bus
binary system	byte
bit	cathode-ray tube (CRT)
blocking factor	central processing unit (CPU)

chain printer

chip

computer output microform (COM)

control unit

cursor

daisy-wheel printer

density

digitizer

disk pack

dot-matrix printer

draft-quality print

drum printer

dumb terminal

electrically erasable programmable read-only memory (EEPROM)

encoding system

erasable optical-storage disks

erasable programmable read-only memory (EPROM)

execution cycle

fixed disk

flat-panel display

floppy diskette

hard copy

hard disk

head crash

impact printer

ink-jet printer

input device

instruction cycle

instruction set

integrated circuit (IC)

intelligent terminal

interblock gap (IBG)

interrecord gap (IRG)

keyboard

large-scale integration (LSI)

laser printer

letter-quality print

light pen

line printer

magnetic disk

magnetic-ink character recognition (MICR)

magnetic strips

magnetic tape

microprocessor

millions of instructions per second (MIPS)

monitor

mouse

nonimpact printer

optical-bar recognition (OBR)

optical card

optical-character recognition (OCR)

optical laser disk

optical-mark recognition (OMR)

optical tape

output device

peripheral device

pixel

plotter

primary storage

printer

programmable read-only memory (PROM)

random-access memory (RAM)

read-only memory (ROM)

register

removable cartridge

resolution

scanner

secondary storage

sectors

semiconductor memory

smart terminal

soft copy

spooling

standard-quality print

system clock

terminal

thermal-transfer printer

touch screen

tracks

typeset-quality print

very-large-scale integration (VLSI)

video display terminal (VDT)

voice recognition

voice synthesis

word

write-once-read-many (WORM) optical disk

Review Questions

1. What number system is used to represent the electrical conditions of "on" and "off" in computers?
2. What is the smallest unit of data that a computer can recognize?
3. What is a byte? How many bytes are in a kilobyte?
4. Describe a computer word.
5. What is an encoding system?
6. Describe the three major units that comprise the CPU.
7. What is a microprocessor?
8. What does the term *volatile* mean as it pertains to computer memory?
9. Explain the differences among RAM, ROM, PROM, EPROM, and EEPROM chips.
10. What purposes do registers and buffers serve?
11. Describe the purpose of the control bus, data bus, and address bus.
12. Briefly describe the two cycles involved in the execution of an instruction.
13. What does it mean to input data into a computer?
14. Which input device would be best for a computerized record shop? Why?
15. Discuss the difference between hard copy and soft copy output.
16. Which type of output would be best for an accounting firm? Why?
17. Name and describe three types of impact printers and three types of nonimpact printers.
18. Would year-end tax forms (W2) be printed on a nonimpact printer? Why?
19. How do resolution and pixels relate to monitors?
20. Do CRTs pose a health problem to clerical workers?
21. What advantages do flat-panel displays have over CRT displays?
22. Describe secondary storage and explain why it is needed.
23. Is magnetic-tape storage faster than hard-disk storage?
24. Which type of storage is the least expensive on a per-character basis?
25. What might cause a head crash?

Software for Business Computer Systems

OBJECTIVES

- Define *software* and differentiate between system and application software
- Describe an operating system and list several different types
- Define *application package* and describe how it might be used
- Describe the differences between specialized and generalized application packages
- Identify three sources of application software
- List and describe the five major microcomputer application packages discussed in this chapter
- Discuss integrated application packages
- Define the purpose of a programming language
- Identify the basic instructions included in all programming languages
- Discuss the four categories of programming languages
- List and discuss several major high-level programming languages
- Discuss some considerations in the selection of a programming language

OUTLINE

IMPACT ON MANAGEMENT PROBLEM SOLVING AND DECISION MAKING

SYSTEM AND APPLICATION SOFTWARE

OPERATING SYSTEMS

Control and Service Programs I Types of Operating Systems I Popular Microcomputer Operating Systems

APPLICATION PACKAGES

Sources of Application Software

MICROCOMPUTER APPLICATION PACKAGES FOR BUSINESS

Word Processors I Data Managers I Electronic Spreadsheets I Graphics Packages I Communication Packages

TYPES OF INTEGRATED PACKAGES

Integrated Family of Programs I All-in-One Integrated Packages I Integrated Operating Environment I Background Integration

PROGRAMMING LANGUAGES

Basic Instructions of a Programming Language I Categories of Programming Languages I Procedural vs. Nonprocedural Languages I Major High-Level Languages I Choosing a Programming Language

Chapter 4

Management Profile: Robert C. Walsh
MIS IN WITH SCHWINN

Ninety-three-year-old Schwinn Bicycle Company is booming today, in part because of the efficiencies brought about by Robert C. Walsh, MIS director. Walsh took Schwinn's computer operation from a state of decay to state of the art. "You can't look at a company's technology structure as separate from the company's business functions: what it makes, what it sells, how it's organized," Walsh says. "To believe in tech for tech's sake, as existing outside the business, is to court catastrophe."

He first worked in MIS at Little Company of Mary Hospital in Chicago and recalls meeting with constant frustration. "People would come to MIS with legitimate needs and get told, 'I'll have it for you in a year.' That is answering in an MIS time frame, not a business time frame," Walsh says. When he left the hospital for Moraine Valley Community College in Palos Hills, Illinois, where he headed systems operations for 8 years, his philosophy was in place: "Ask what does the business need?"

Walsh brought that philosophy to Schwinn in 1980, when he arrived with a mandate to turn a 20-year-old system into a lean, mean, competing machine "preferably yesterday," he recalls. Five years and more than $600,000 later, Schwinn has gone through a series of system upgrades. Sophisticated software, Walsh says, "allows the systems folks to have a great amount of empathy with the end-users. For example, because you can add data elements so easily, you don't find yourself saying, 'What's your 2-year plan?' to an employee who's thinking, 'If I don't get this inventory in order in 4 months, I'm not gonna be here in 2 years.' "

"Bob's great strength is being able to work within a company structure to get things taken care of for both the MIS department and the corporate guys," says Steve Arnold, systems programmer at Schwinn. "He's great at wheelin' and dealin'—he really gets into the game."

In 1986 Mike Fritz, new arrival at Schwinn as director of engineering, set out to automate the bicycle design department. As a new guy in town trying to sell an IBM-loyal administration on costly CAD workstations, Fritz turned somewhat reluctantly to the MIS director. "My initial feeling was that Bob would be a problem. He was an IBM loyalist, and design was his territory," Fritz says. "But I couldn't have been more wrong." Walsh "went to bat and did a great job for us," Fritz says. Not only did he deploy his negotiating skills on Fritz's behalf, both in dealing with the computer manufacturer and in selling Schwinn's "true blue" front office on the CAD workstation concept, but he also suggested that Fritz double the number of systems he was requesting.

"The key to the company's real benefit is getting one of these babies on every designer's desk," Fritz remembers Walsh saying. "All I could think was, this guy's got to be Santa Claus." Today Fritz oversees a $500,000 CAD operation; Schwinn Bicycle ranks as the leading U.S. bicycle maker; and Walsh has a $3 million MIS budget to play Santa Claus with—a far cry from the $700,000 budgeted for MIS in 1979.

Adapted from "Robert C. Walsh: MIS in with Schwinn" by Nell Margolis. Copyright 1988 by CW Publishing Inc., Framingham, MA 01701. Reprinted from *Computerworld,* May 2, 1988.

Computer hardware cannot perform alone. In order to accomplish any task, that hardware must be supplied with a series of instructions, or software, telling it what to do. This chapter introduces two types of software, system software and application software. The most important type of system software, the operating system, is presented first. We then look at application packages and examine several popular ones used for business. Then we examine integrated packages. Finally, we discuss programming languages used to write both system and application software.

IMPACT ON MANAGEMENT PROBLEM SOLVING AND DECISION MAKING

Like hardware decisions, the software decisions that a manager makes will also have immediate and long-term impact on an organization's productivity. The software selected must meet today's needs as well as the needs of the future. For example, if your business is growing fast, you should not choose software that barely meets your current needs. Instead, you should select software that will be able to handle your needs for some time to come in order to get the most from your investment.

Managers need to stay abreast of new software to take advantage of new technologies. They also need to decide whether the productivity gains resulting from new software are enough to warrant the upgrading or whether they should protect their investment in past training and existing technologies. If an organization chooses to develop its own software, a manager will be faced with the decision of which programming language to use. The material in this chapter will help familiarize you with several types of software and programming languages commonly used in many organizations.

SYSTEM AND APPLICATION SOFTWARE

The series of instructions telling the hardware what to do is called a **program,** or software. The two general types of software are system and application. Programs that control and direct the operation of the computer hardware are **system software**. For example, system software controls the saving of data as well as data retrieval from secondary storage devices. Operating systems and language translator programs are examples of system software.

Programs that help the user, the system software, and the hardware work together to solve end-user problems are **application software**. For example, application software enables a user to perform such tasks as writing a letter or creating a graph. Application packages create a communication bridge whereby the user can tell the system software how to direct the hardware to perform the desired functions. Figure 4–1 shows the relationships among system software, application software, hardware, and the user.

OPERATING SYSTEMS

When computers were first invented, every detail of how the hardware operated had to be programmed into the computer manually by setting switches or hand-wiring circuits. This was a long, tedious process that had

FIGURE 4–1

Relationships among system software, application software, hardware, and the user.

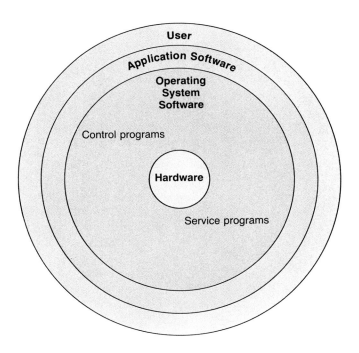

to be repeated for each program executed. The programmer required specific and detailed knowledge about how a particular computer system operated, and the CPU sat idle most of the time, while these details were being programmed. Because hardware costs for the early computers were so high, users wanted to increase the efficiency of the CPU. To accomplish this goal, a program called an operating system was created.

An **operating system** is a set of programs that controls and supervises a computer system's hardware and provides services to application software, programmers, and users of a computer system. The purpose of an operating system is to manage the hardware for the most efficient use of computer resources and to provide an interface between the hardware and a user or an application program. An operating system dramatically increases the efficiency of a CPU, because it takes the burden of detailed programming off the programmer.

There is not, however, one universal operating system. Some operating systems are developed by computer manufacturers specifically to take advantage of an individual machine. Others are developed by computer manufacturers or third-party (nonhardware) vendors and are intended to be used across a wide range of computers. For example, the IBM 360 operating system was developed for selected IBM mainframe models, whereas Microsoft's MS-DOS is the operating system of choice for microcomputers produced by a host of vendors.

The portion of the operating system in use resides in primary storage, so the details of an operation are received and executed by the computer at computer speeds, thus eliminating the long delays that existed when humans had to intervene. An operating system can also execute another program immediately without human involvement.

Control and Service Programs

The programs that make up an operating system are generally divided into two categories: control programs and service programs. **Control programs** manage the computer hardware and resources. The major functions of these programs are

- resource management
- data management
- job (task) management

With resource management, computer resources such as CPU time, primary storage, secondary storage, and input and output devices are allocated for use by other system software and application software. Data management control programs govern the input and output of data and their location, storage, and retrieval.

Jobs that are being submitted for execution are prepared, scheduled, controlled, and monitored by job management control programs to ensure the most efficient processing. A **job** is a collection of one or more related job steps and their data. A job step is the execution of one program. A **job control language (JCL)** is used to tell the operating system what a job requires in terms of computer resources and operating system services. JCL is the user's language for communication with the operating system, and each operating system has its own JCL. Some JCLs, such as those for mainframe operating systems, can be very complex and difficult to learn. Others, such as those found with many microcomputer operating systems, use simple one-line commands—for example, RUN to execute a program or ERASE to delete a file from a disk. Many operating systems keep a record of all the jobs processed. A job record, or log, can then be printed and reviewed by management to determine the status of a job: has it been processed, and were there any errors?

The main program in most operating systems is the supervisor program. The **supervisor program** is a control program that is known in some operating systems as the monitor, executive, or kernel; it is responsible for controlling all other operating system programs as well as other system and application programs. The supervisor program controls the activities of all the hardware components of the computer system.

Many of the processing and input/output operations of an operating system are controlled with the use of interrupts. An **interrupt** is a signal that tells the operating system that some action needs to be taken or an earlier action is now completed. For example, an interrupt may signal that data need to be input, that input of data is complete, that data need to be output, or that output of data is complete. Interrupts based on events are referred to as event interrupts. In some systems interrupts are generated at specific time intervals, and processing is automatically switched to another program or operation. These signals are referred to as time-slice interrupts.

Service programs are programs in the operating system that provide a service to the user or the programmer of the computer system. Examples include language-translator programs and utility programs. **Language-translator programs** convert programmer-authored programs into machine-language instructions that can be executed by the computer. Such programs are discussed with programming languages later in this chapter. **Utility programs** perform routine but essential functions, such as loading, saving, or copying a program; keeping track of the files stored on a disk; and preparing a disk for use.

Operating system programs are stored on a **system resident device**—one that is always available. Depending on the particular computer, the system resident device may be a hard disk, floppy diskette, or tape. When the computer is turned on, essential portions of the supervisor program are loaded into primary storage from the system resident device and remain there throughout the computer's operation. Other portions of the supervisor program and the rest of the operating system programs are loaded into primary storage as needed and are removed when they have completed their tasks.

Types of Operating Systems

There are several basic types of operating systems, including single-program, concurrent, time-sharing, multiprocessing, virtual-storage, real-time, and virtual-machine operating systems. A particular operating system may exhibit characteristics from one or more of the various types.

Single-Program Operating System. A **single-program operating system** allows one program to execute at a time, and that program must finish executing completely before the next can begin. This type of operating system is often found with personal computers. For example, Microsoft's MS-DOS is a single-program operating system for the IBM PC, its compatibles, and the IBM PS/2. The goal of this type of operating system is maximum ease of use and minimum professional support.

Concurrent Operating System. A **concurrent operating system** allows **multiprogramming,** in which a single CPU can execute what appears to be more than one program at the same time but is, in fact, only one program. The CPU switches its attention between two or more programs in primary memory as it receives requests for processing from one program and then another. This processing happens so fast that the programs appear to be executed simultaneously. Multiprogramming can increase the overall performance of a CPU because it can devote its time to processing instructions from one program while another goes through input/output operations. The Unix operating system is an example of a concurrent operating system.

Time-Sharing Operating System. A **time-sharing operating system** allows multiple users to access a single computer system. The attention of the CPU is shifted among users on a timed basis, which is controlled by the operating system. As long as the computer system does not have more users than the operating system can handle, it appears as if each user has uninterrupted access to the CPU. However, if the number of users exceeds the operating system's capability, noticeable delays in processing result.

TSO is an example of a time-sharing operating system used on many mainframes.

Time-sharing operating systems allocate specific periods of time, or time-slices, for the execution of instructions of a particular program. These time-slices are usually only a fraction of a second long and are controlled by the operating system through the use of time-slice interrupts generated by a hardware clock. The time-sharing concept enables each user's program to receive processor time at regular intervals, thus preventing any one program from monopolizing the CPU. When an event interrupt occurs (e.g., an input/output request), the operating system may switch to another program before a full time-slice is used. This capability allows the CPU to be used more efficiently. Keeping track of which job is next in line for processing is one of the responsibilities of the operating system.

In many time-sharing environments the number of jobs waiting to be processed exceeds what can fit into the computer's primary storage. The technique of program swapping was developed to get around this limitation. **Program swapping** involves moving jobs between primary storage and secondary storage. The active program's instructions are then executed during its allotted time-slice. Depending on the procedures defined for a particular system, that program may reside in primary memory for several time-slices or may be immediately moved back to secondary storage. A number of factors can influence the scheduling routine, such as the priority of the job, the primary memory size of the job, the number of other jobs in memory, and so on. When a job or program is swapped, it is the responsibility of the operating system to keep track of where the execution of the program ceased and where the program is temporarily stored on the secondary storage device.

Multiprocessing Operating System. A **multiprocessing operating system** allows the simultaneous execution of programs by a computer that has two or more CPUs. Each CPU can be dedicated to one program, or each CPU can be dedicated to specific functions and then used by all programs. Many computer systems such as mainframes and supercomputers have more than one CPU.

Virtual-Storage Operating System. A **virtual-storage operating system** (also called virtual-memory operating system) allows the use of a secondary storage device as an extension of primary storage. A problem experienced by some computer users is insufficient primary storage to contain an entire program. A virtual-storage operating system can resolve this problem by rapidly accessing the part of the program residing in secondary storage. Portions of a program can be swapped between a secondary storage device and primary storage as needed, giving the illusion of having the maximum amount of primary storage in the CPU available to each user. With a virtual-storage operating system, the user need not worry about how much primary storage is available since the program is segmented into pages. A page is a storage area of predetermined size that contains a certain number of instructions. Pages are kept on secondary storage devices and are swapped in and out of primary storage as needed.

Real-Time Operating System. A **real-time operating system** allows a computer to control or monitor the task performance of other machines and people by responding to input data in a specified amount of time. To control processes, immediate response is usually necessary; to simply monitor processes, periodic response is generally adequate. Real-time operating systems generally have fewer functions than other more general-purpose operating systems; real-time systems offer only those services required to respond to a set of monitored events in minimum time and within certain set periods. Often, real-time operating systems are specifically written for an intended application, for example, monitoring the position of a rocket. With real-time operating systems CPU efficiency is often sacrificed in favor of quicker response time.

Virtual-Machine (VM) Operating System. A **virtual-machine (VM) operating system** is a very powerful program that can run several different operating systems at one time. It allows several users of a computer system to operate as if each had the only terminal attached to the computer. Thus, users feel as if each is on a dedicated system and has sole use of the CPU and input and output devices.

After a VM operating system is loaded, the user chooses the operating system that is compatible with the intended application. Other operating systems, such as the virtual-storage operating system, appear as just another application program to the VM operating system. Thus, the VM system gives users flexibility and allows them to choose an operating system that best suits the needs of a particular application.

Popular Microcomputer Operating Systems

All or part of a microcomputer operating system usually resides on a disk and is referred to as a **disk operating system (DOS)**. Several of the most common disk operating systems include MS-DOS (Microsoft disk operating system), the Apple Macintosh operating system, OS/2, and various versions of the UNIX operating system.

MS-DOS is the current defacto standard for IBM PCs and compatibles. The Apple Macintosh operating system is a graphical operating system used on the Macintosh series of computers. OS/2 is a multitasking operating system that makes working with several applications at once natural and efficient. It requires at least an 80286 microprocessor and needs at least one MB of memory—preferably several megabytes.

The Unix operating system was developed at AT&T's Bell Labs in the late 1960s. It has been used on minicomputers by colleges and universities across the country since early 1970. In the past few years, however, there has been an increased interest by IBM, Apple, Microsoft, AT&T, and others in Unix as a microcomputer operating system. Several versions of UNIX—including AT&T's System V, Microsoft's Xenix, and IBM's AIX—currently exist. Joint industry efforts are being planned to combine the many UNIX variants into one operating system.

Personal computer operating systems are becoming more sophisticated. They now include such features as multitasking, multithreading, and interprocessing.

- **Multitasking** allows several different applications to run simultaneously.
- **Multithreading** supports several simultaneous functions with the same application.
- **Interprocessing** (also called dynamic linking) allows any change made in one application to be automatically reflected in any related, linked applications.

Most operating systems allow users to develop and run programs on 32-bit microprocessors, such as the Intel 80386, but the systems are not designed to take full advantage of the power of these chips. Only UNIX currently taps the inherent memory management advantages of an 80386 microprocessor. The OS/2 version will also take advantage of the 80386 microprocessor soon. Newer, more powerful microcomputer operating systems, such as Concurrent DOS/386 and PC-MOS/386, are designed to take full advantage of the capabilities offered by the 32-bit microprocessors.

Managers are faced with a wide variety of options when choosing among operating systems. The correct choice can best be made by considering the tasks to be performed, the number of people needing to perform the tasks simultaneously, and the kinds of applications that will be run.

APPLICATION PACKAGES

The key to making the computer useful is to combine it with software for a particular application. An **application** is the job or task a user wants to accomplish through the computer. An **application package** is prepared software that, in conjunction with the system software, instructs the computer in how to perform the user's task. Application packages help the user work faster, more efficiently, and thus more productively than manual performance would allow. Table 4–1 shows some examples of application packages.

Application packages come in varying levels of sophistication and complexity. The demand for better human-oriented interfaces has made software developers more sensitive to the needs of the novice and the nontechnical user. The term **user-friendly** has come to refer to a software interface that is easy to learn and use. But whether software really is easy to learn and use is dependent on the skills, sophistication, and needs of the user. What may be easy to use for the novice may be so simple that it's not useful to the more experienced user, who needs more features and sophistication. The market has seen the development of some powerful and complex packages that are also user-friendly, and some software packages provide two or more interfaces suited to the skill levels of different users. Regardless of the user's technical level, there should be an application package to match those needs and abilities.

TABLE 4-1
Some business application packages.

Application	Selected Vendor Product Names
Word processing	Word, WordPerfect, WordStar, DisplayWrite, MultiMate, PC-Write
Data managers	Paradox, dBase, R:Base, FoxBASE
Spreadsheets	Lotus 1-2-3; Excel, VP-Planner Plus, SuperCalc
Inventory control	BPI Inventory Control, CCC Materials Inventory, CYMA Inventory, EZ MRP, INMASS
Accounting	BPI Enterprise Series, ABS Accounting Modules, Harmony, Solomon III
Financial Analysis	IFPS, TurboTax, Managing Your Money, Money Counts, Profit Planner

Application packages can be grouped into two broad categories: specialized and generalized. A specialized application package performs a specific task and cannot be changed or programmed to perform a different task. For example, a payroll package is designed to be used exclusively for payroll functions. It cannot be programmed to do other tasks, such as cost analysis.

A generalized application package is one that can be applied to a wide variety of tasks. A spreadsheet, for example, can create one worksheet to calculate a payroll and another to perform cost analysis. In Table 4-1 the first three applications are generalized; the last three are specialized.

Sources of Application Software

Software is created and acquired in three main ways:

- prewritten by an outside source for public sale
- custom developed in-house
- custom developed by an outside source

Prewritten software packages have been written by another person or group and made available to computer users. Generally, prewritten software is available for purchase through a vendor, a distributor such as a computer store, or the author. The use of prewritten software packages has several advantages:

1. Prewritten software packages can be quickly installed, ready for immediate use.
2. They are usually less expensive than packages produced in-house.
3. They are available for almost any required task.
4. They have already been tested.
5. Some prewritten application packages can be quickly customized or modified to meet a user's specialized requirements.

The primary disadvantage of prewritten software packages is that they may not precisely fit the special needs of the user.

Instead of purchasing prewritten software, programmers or skilled users sometimes write their own software. In-house custom-developed software packages are designed and coded by skilled personnel within the firm. The main advantage of in-house software is that it can be tailored to the user's exact specifications. An additional advantage is that the creator may, in turn, be able to market and sell the software to others. A major disadvantage of this approach is the cost. Skilled programmers are expensive, and determining precise specifications can be time-consuming.

If the needed personnel, expertise, time, or money is not available for in-house custom development, another option is to contract with a person or group that specializes in developing software. Many such firms employ skilled programmers to develop customized software for the specialized needs of their clients.

Users must balance the need for customized software against the costs involved. The wise decision may be to select a prewritten package that comes close but doesn't precisely meet the user's needs rather than spending the time and/or money in-house or out of house for development of customized software.

MICROCOMPUTER APPLICATION PACKAGES FOR BUSINESS

There are many types of application packages for microcomputers on the market today, and new ones are being developed as microcomputers become faster and more powerful. Applications that have been traditionally large-system applications, such as CAD systems and expert systems, are now available for microcomputers. In addition, the applications themselves have grown in number, size, speed, power, and capability. For example, when the first electronic spreadsheet for microcomputers was conceived, most microcomputers had 48K or less of RAM to work with. This capacity severely limited the software that could run on them. Today, however, microcomputers have at least 640K of RAM and can add up to several more megabytes of RAM. Obviously, today's spreadsheets can be a lot more powerful than the first one.

Application packages, such as accounting and financial packages (including payroll, accounts receivable, accounts payable, general ledger, budgeting, and financial planning), are used in almost every kind of business. Vertical-market packages—software designed to handle the unique needs of specific markets (businesses), such as medical offices, law firms, car dealerships, and hotel management—are also being sold. Highlight 4–1 looks at how the presidential campaign of 1988 made use of microcomputer application packages.

Five application packages, often labeled the "big 5" productivity tools, have emerged as the most popular and widely used with business microcomputers: word processors, data managers, electronic spreadsheets, graphics, and electronic communications.

Word Processors

Several distinctions should be made among similar terms with different meanings: *word processor, word processing,* and *word-processing system*. A **word processor** is the software, or program, that creates, edits, manipulates, and prints text. WordPerfect, Wordstar, Multimate, MS-Word, and DisplayWrite are five of the most popular word processors. Word processors have had a tremendous impact on businesses and can be found in almost all offices. **Word processing** is the activity of entering, viewing, storing, retrieving, editing, rearranging, and printing text material, using a computer and appropriate software. A **word-processing system** is the combination of hardware and software used for word processing; it usually consists of a general-purpose computer and software.

Some businesses use a dedicated word-processing system, which employs a computer made mainly for the purpose of word processing. A few years ago such a system was the dominant one. Today, dedicated word-processing systems are still used by many companies, despite the advent of inexpensive and powerful word processors for microcomputers.

Individual word processors have many features and functions to help manipulate text, but the basic functions common to all of them are text editing and formatting. **Text editing** activities include entering the words that make up the text, making deletions or insertions, and moving words, phrases, or blocks of text from one place to another. When text is entered, it is displayed on the screen and stored in the computer as a document (also called a file); revisions can be made until it is exactly the way the writer wants it.

Formatting refers to establishing the way the document should look on the screen and in print. Margins can be justified (made to appear even) on the left or the right; line spacing can be adjusted; headings can be centered and underlined, boldfaced, or italicized; and headers can be placed at the tops of pages and footers at the bottoms. Automatic page numbering is also a feature of formatting capability. Formatting specifications and parameters are communicated from the computer to the printer before printing.

Word processors handle files (documents) in different ways. A page-oriented word processor brings forward only one page at a time from the disk into primary storage. Pages are swapped between disk and primary storage as the user makes corrections on the pages. A document-oriented word processor brings the entire document from the disk into primary storage. Remember that text stored in primary storage is volatile, and changes are not saved until a save command is given. If substantial changes are being made, it is advisable to save the document to disk every 15 minutes so that all changes are not lost if power is interrupted.

Some word processors employ a virtual-memory scheme that transfers portions of the document from primary storage to disk and vice versa as primary storage is filled. This process happens automatically and gives the illusion of an unlimited amount of primary storage.

Computers and Application Software on the Campaign Trail

Numerous tasks involved in electing a president rely heavily on computers and application software. These tasks include tracking financial contributions with spreadsheets and using database management systems to identify voters, target them with specific pitches, and tally the vote.

The Bush campaign headquarters, which had more than 400 campaign workers, used almost 100 stand-alone personal computers for tasks such as word processing and spreadsheet tabulation. IBM portables and word processors were used on the road to draft speeches and write reports. The staff worked on the keep-it-simple principle; no mainframes, networks, or other sophisticated technologies were used. They believed that these would add unneeded complexity to an already-hectic situation. In addition, because there is a large turnover of personnel throughout a campaign, the constant training of new personnel to use the system would be difficult, time-consuming, and expensive. The staff couldn't see much sense in pouring money and technological know-how into something that would die so quickly; according to the Federal Election Commission, each candidate's headquarters must be dismantled within 30 days after an election.

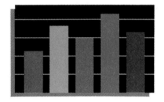

The Dukakis campaign used a supermicrocomputer with 12 terminals, six networked Apple Macintosh computers, and a variety of application and development tools including word processors, databases, spreadsheets, and graphics software. Staff used the computers mostly for routine tasks, thus freeing volunteers to make phone calls or get out and talk to voters.

Data Managers

The need for data and information to be organized and accessible in different formats has exceeded what can be done manually in a reasonable amount of time. **Data managers** were developed in answer to this demand; they store, organize, manipulate, retrieve, display, and print data.

A data manager can be one of two general types of programs used to manage data: a file-management system or a database-management system. A **file-management system** creates, stores, manipulates, and prints data stored in separate files, but it can access and manipulate only one file at a time (Figure 4–2a). Using a file-management system has its limitations. It makes locating and manipulating data from different files difficult and time-consuming, and data such as employee name and number are unnecessarily duplicated in each file.

Another limitation of file-management systems is poor data reliability. When data are updated, each file must be individually accessed for

An example of how Dukakis workers used technology can be seen in their public relations use of a digitizer to quickly exploit photo opportunities. They recorded and digitized photographs on diskettes, using graphics software, and then loaded the images into a Macintosh, where they were combined with text in a word processor and were quickly printed out. If Dukakis was photographed shaking hands with a mayor at noon, the press could have a release and accompanying photo one hour later.

Databases were used by the media to store quotes by and about the leading candidates. Whenever a candidate talked on an issue, anything he had said in the past on that issue could be acquired within minutes.

Computers were also used heavily by independent firms to target voters for their clients. Information on voters—such as party affiliation, date of birth, gender, race, and voting regularity—was compiled using a database and a mainframe computer. In addition, the firms could add ethnic identifiers and telephone numbers and could sort the voters into households. They could ask the computer for all the Democrats in a particular state, all the Reagan Democrats in that state, or even all the black, Jewish, Spanish-speaking Democrats. The input process was significantly aided by the use of hand-held computer scanners, which could read bar codes from coded telephone lists into a PC or into a phone that sent the information to mainframes. This technology allowed the candidates to incorporate a degree of personalization into mailings and phone calls that was not possible before computers.

changes to be made. Imagine how difficult it is for a business that maintains many files in separate locations to ensure that data updates occur in all files containing the changed data.

The database concept was developed to solve the problems associated with a file-management system. A **database** is a collection of related files stored together in a logical fashion. A **database management system (DBMS)** creates, stores, manipulates, and prints data in a database. With this system data from more than one file can be accessed at the same time (Figure 4–2b). Paradox, dBASE, and RBASE are popular database management systems.

DBMSs have certain advantages over file-management systems. First, they usually require data to be entered only once. As soon as an item is entered, it can be used by any file in combination with any other data in the database. This feature eliminates excessive data duplication. In addition, because data are generally stored only once, updates have to be entered only once.

FIGURE 4-2
(a) A file-management system
can access only one file at a
time. (b) A database
management system can
access more than one file at a
time.

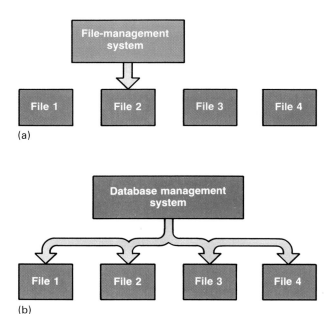

(a)

(b)

Because a file-management system is not as powerful or sophisticated as a DBMS, the types of applications for which it is suited are also less sophisticated. Examples of appropriate applications for a file-management system include maintaining a mailing list; a file of names, addresses, and phone numbers; or an inventory list or list of any other items.

Because a DBMS allows its user to create and access multiple files, it lends itself to more complex applications. One of its most popular applications is with an accounting system, which involves the integration of several different files, including general ledger, accounts receivable, accounts payable, and payroll. Other applications that require the integration of several files include financial management, travel-agency management, medical-office management, and real-estate management.

Electronic Spreadsheets

A **spreadsheet** is little more than a means of keeping track of and manipulating numbers, separating them into rows and columns. Paper spreadsheets are forms with horizontal and vertical lines that separate each row and column of numbers. You may have seen paper spreadsheets similar to the one in Figure 4-3. A spreadsheet can take other forms, too; each user can adapt a spreadsheet to individual applications and formats.

With the development of the computer, the paper spreadsheet was converted to a computerized format called an electronic spreadsheet, which could display, manipulate, and print rows and columns of numbers; make calculations; and actually evaluate formulas. The first electronic spreadsheets operated only on large computer systems, and most businesses and individuals continued to use paper spreadsheets. The develop-

FIGURE 4–3
Part of a paper spreadsheet.

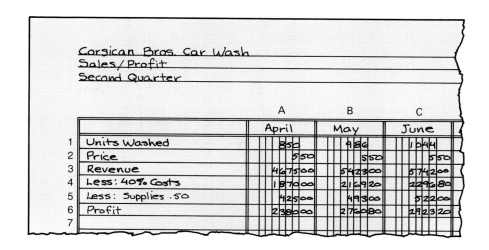

Corsican Bros. Car Wash
Sales/Profit
Second Quarter

		A	B	C
		April	May	June
1	Units Washed	850	986	1044
2	Price	5.50	5.50	5.50
3	Revenue	4675.00	5423.00	5742.00
4	Less: 40% Costs	1870.00	2169.20	2296.80
5	Less: Supplies .50	425.00	493.00	522.00
6	Profit	2380.00	2760.80	2923.20
7				

ment of VisiCalc in 1979, the first electronic spreadsheet for microcomputers, permitted easy and affordable access to this powerful tool. But even VisiCalc was rather crude by today's standards because of its limitations. With the continuing development of more sophisticated hardware and software, programs have improved to such an extent that most of today's computer spreadsheets allow as many as 256 columns and 2,048 rows—more than one-half million cells. (A cell is the intersection of a column and a row.)

Instead of writing and calculating entries by hand, a person can now sit at a computer keyboard and use an electronic-spreadsheet program to make necessary entries. The computer then makes all the calculations. In addition, the spreadsheet program can accept a correction in one item and can recalculate any affected numbers throughout the document. Furthermore, if the user wonders just how an increase or decrease in one particular entry might affect the end result, the program allows the user to pose various what-if questions. For example, if a manager wanted to see the effect of a price change on the projected earnings for a product, a spreadsheet would allow her to simply update the price and have the computer recalculate the affected numbers in just a few seconds.

The shortcuts and speed of the electronic spreadsheet certainly explain its popularity. Hundreds of spreadsheet programs are available for almost any brand of computer. Figure 4–4 illustrates an electronic version of the paper spreadsheet shown in Figure 4–3. Spreadsheet processing is one of the most popular computer applications; it brings to accounting functions the shortcuts, speed, and accuracy that word processors bring to writing. Lotus 1–2–3, Microsoft Excel, VP-Planner Plus, Multiplan, and SuperCalc are examples of popular spreadsheets.

Graphics Packages

A **graphics package** allows people to use a computer to create, edit, display, and print graphic images, which can range from simple bar charts to

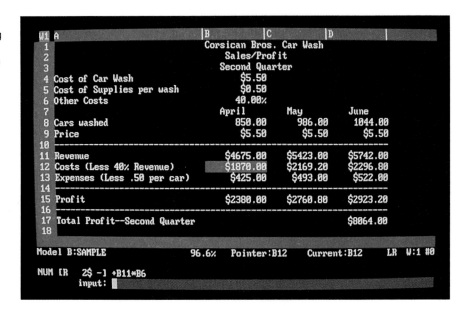

very complex designs and pictures. Graphics packages create images with one of two types of graphics:

1. **Text graphics**—in which any character the keyboard generates is used to create shapes and lines.
2. **High-resolution graphics**—in which the individual dots, called pixels, that make up a display screen are turned on and off to form various shapes. Resolution refers to the sharpness or clarity of an image. Display screens have varying numbers of pixels; the more pixels a display screen has, the higher the resolution, or quality, of the image.

Graphics packages for microcomputers can be divided into three basic types: painting and drawing, design, and business and analytical programs. A **painting and drawing program** lets the user become an artist without paint, canvas, or brushes; however, the creativity must still come from the user. This type of package can be used by small businesses to create forms, logos, and letterheads. With input devices such as a mouse, light pen, or graphics tablet, these programs let users choose from many different pointer (or "brush") sizes and shapes to paint an image, draw and fill shapes, or change color and texture. MacPaint is an example of a paint-and-draw program (Figure 4–5). Because of the availability of very high resolution screens and sophisticated graphics programs, computer images are now rivaling those of canvas or film in clarity and crispness.

A **design program** helps designers complete the tasks associated with hand-drafted designs more easily and efficiently. Such a program eliminates the need to manually erase or redraw a design. It can also create three-dimensional drawings that can be rotated and viewed from any an-

FIGURE 4–5

This graphic was created on a Macintosh microcomputer using MacPaint, a paint-and-draw program. (Courtesy of Apple Computer, Inc.)

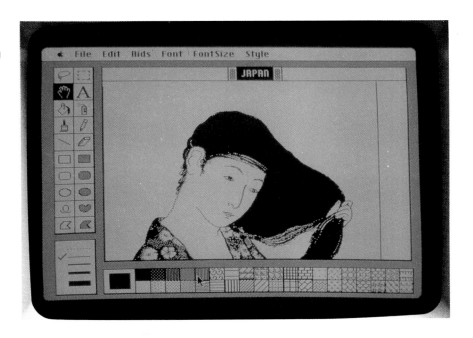

gle. Some packages also provide simulation capabilities. For example, a skyscraper design might be mathematically tested to see whether it could withstand the forces of an earthquake or to determine where its shadow would fall at 3:00 P.M. on a sunny day. Design programs are used primarily by engineers and architects.

A **business and analytical program** transforms numerical data into pictorial representations—charts and graphs—that show the relationships among data. Typical graphs that can be produced include bar, line, pie, scatter, stacked-bar, three-dimensional, and surface graphs. These are sometimes referred to as presentation-graphics programs, although strictly speaking they do not all provide high-quality graphics. **Presentation graphics** are suitable for a formal presentation. Highlight 4–2 looks at important aspects of business graphs.

A business and analytical program may be a stand-alone package or part of a spreadsheet or integrated package. A spreadsheet program incorporating business and analytical graphics was used to produce the graph in Figure 4–6. Many of the graphics programs incorporated in spreadsheets are adequate for informal uses, but they are not appropriate in a formal presentation. Many of the stand-alone programs, such as Grafix Partner and PC Storyboard, can enhance charts and graphs generated by other programs.

Some graphics packages combine elements of all three types of programs—paint and draw, design, and business and analytical—in one program. As hardware capabilities and software sophistication increase, more graphics programs will accommodate the functions of all three program types.

FIGURE 4–6
A business and analytical graph
created with a spreadsheet
package.

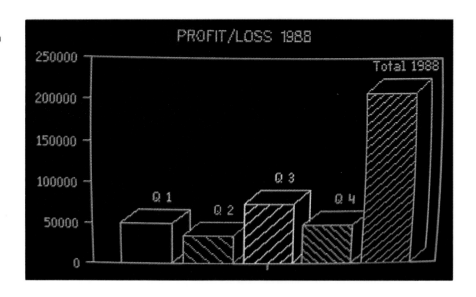

Communication Packages

A **communication package** is designed to control communication between two computers. The purpose of communication software is to

- establish and maintain communication with another computer
- tell the computer how to send data (i.e., determine the communication parameters)
- direct outgoing data from the keyboard or disks through the communication port, and direct incoming data from the communication port to the screen or disk

There are many communication packages with a wide variety of options. However, they must all be able to perform two general functions: (1) set essential communication parameters and (2) emulate a dumb terminal. The four essential **communication parameters** are these:

- speed of transmission
- number of data bits used to create each character
- number of bits to signify the end of a character
- type of error checking during transmission

These parameters are discussed in detail in Chapter 5.

The second general function is that a communication package must cause the user's microcomputer to emulate a dumb terminal—that is, to operate in what most programs call the terminal mode. A dumb terminal is a stand-alone keyboard and display screen unit that can send data to or receive data from only a computer to which it is connected; a dumb terminal cannot function as a stand-alone computer. Most minicomputers and mainframes used in business or information services communicate with only this kind of terminal.

Creating Business Graphs

Many of you readers are headed into managerial positions. A study by the Wharton Business School's Applied Research Center found that people who created and used visuals in their business and analytical presentations were perceived to be more professional and more interesting than those who did not. Pictorial representations of data make it easy to compare data or to spot trends that might otherwise be difficult to determine from just numerical data. Business and analytical graphics programs provide the tools to create a graph.

Numerous design options are available and vary from program to program. To be the most effective in a formal presentation, a graph should be dynamic and should impress upon an audience the point that needs to be made. Attention to proper design is important; a poorly designed chart or graph can be very misleading.

In general, a good presentation graph should be simple, accurate, and easy to interpret and should make an impact on the intended audience. First of all, the graph should be simple. Too much information can make it difficult to grasp the meaning of the graph. In addition, a graph should not show finite details or figures but should focus on general ideas, such as trends, comparisons, and movement. Keeping a graph simple increases its clarity and effectiveness.

The use of appropriate scales makes a graph easier to interpret. A poorly designed scale on either the horizontal or the vertical axis may distort the relationship of the data. And when two graphs are to be compared, the increments between grid marks should be the same on the horizontal and vertical axes of both graphs. Changing the distance between grid lines for a portion of a graph may cause identical data to appear different or different data to appear identical (Figure A).

Several factors contribute to making a favorable impact on an audience. Proper balance and spacing of elements should be maintained. Elements in a graph should fill the available space and should balance with other dimensions. Bars and columns should be wider than the space between them (Figure B).

Important elements of a graph should be emphasized. For example, a segment of a pie chart might be exploded, or one bar might be colored or shaded differently to make it stand out (Figure C).

In addition, design elements such as color, shape, and texture should be chosen carefully; they can alter the visual effect of a graph. When shades of color and textured patterns are used, they should move from darker in the foreground to lighter in the background because lighter colors tend to jump forward. Blues and greens are generally considered good background colors for graphs. In business situations it is usually wise to avoid red (it suggests failure to most business people) unless failure is what is being conveyed. Also, if red and green appear

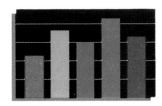

next to each other, a person with red-green color blindness will see only brown. This affliction affects approximately 4 percent of males in the United States.

Textures or patterns that can cause distortion should be avoided in graphs. For example, solid bars stand out more than outlined bars, and vertical lines in a horizontal plane make the surface appear higher. Furthermore, multiple plot lines, the lines that connect the data points in a graph, should be of different thicknesses, or weights. Plot lines should be the heaviest, grid lines the lightest. Color shades or textures can also be used to differentiate among plot lines. Grid lines should not overlay solid areas on charts. Finally, numbers and titles should be large enough to be read easily, and titles should to be horizontal whenever possible, again for easier reading.

Design elements may influence where a viewer's attention is focused and which part of a graph is perceived as the most important. Not all software programs give the user control over every aspect of creating a graph; some allow more flexibility than others.

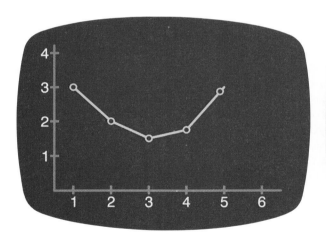

Equal distance between grid marks on horizontal and vertical axes gives the graph a smoother, more realistic appearance.

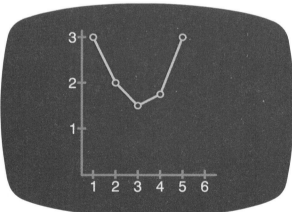

Contracted and uneven grid marks make the curve appear to have a severe dip.

FIGURE A
A correct and a distorted scale.

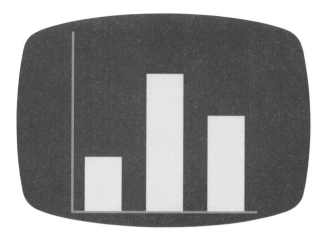

Balanced graph

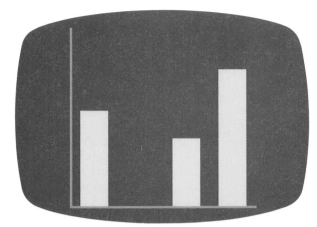

Unbalanced graph

FIGURE B
A balanced and an unbalanced bar graph.

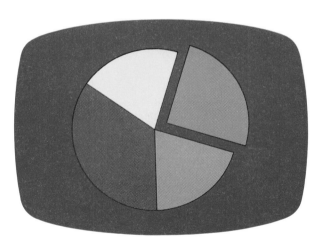

Exploded pie chart

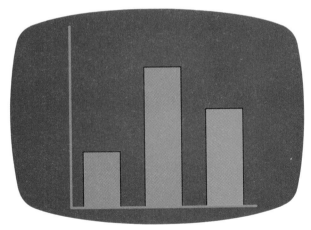

Colored bar for emphasis

FIGURE C
An exploded pie chart and a colored bar graph.

TYPES OF INTEGRATED PACKAGES

The data files of many programs designed for microcomputers are incompatible with each other. Such programs are not integrated, that is, data cannot be electronically moved from one program to the other. In such cases transferring data from one program to another can be either impossible or complex and tedious. Typically, the user's only recourse is to retype all data into the receiving program.

For example, if you were asked to analyze and then make a presentation of the sales performance of all 36 sales regions in a company, you could purchase a spreadsheet for all the necessary calculations and a separate graphics package to produce the graphs. Although it takes you 5 hours to enter the data and formulas into the spreadsheet, the results are impressive. Now you need a series of graphs for the presentation. You spend the next hour poring over the manuals to find a way to transfer the data from the spreadsheet to the graphics program. No luck! Your only option is to spend another several hours reentering the spreadsheet figures into the graphics program.

Integrated software allows several programs to share the same data. For example, the graphics package in the previous example could have used data directly from the spreadsheet file if the two programs had been integrated. Integration also implies the use of familiar functions and a common set of commands and keystrokes among programs. However, in reality this commonality occurs in varying degrees. The result of integration is that the user can work faster, more efficiently, and thus more productively than is possible with nonintegrated programs. The demand for integrated software has led to the development of four distinct approaches to integration.

Integrated Family of Programs

An **integrated family of programs** is a group of independent application programs that can share data and use common commands and keystrokes. For example, if one program in the set uses the function key F10 to save (store), then all the other programs will also use F10 to save. Using the same commands and keystrokes for the same operations makes it faster and easier to learn each program. A disadvantage of this approach is that sharing and merging data between applications can be slower than in other approaches.

All-in-One Integrated Packages

An **all-in-one integrated package** combines several types of applications into a single program. Most of these packages combine some or all of these programs: word processor, spreadsheet, data manager, graphics, and communication. The user can conveniently switch among applications and use a common set of commands. A limitation of all-in-one packages is that they require large amounts of primary storage capacity. Many require well over 256K because the single program contains all applications and is, therefore, quite large.

Some programs, such as Open Access II and the Smart Software System, are designed to function either as an integrated family or in combination as an all-in-one integrated package. Popular all-in-one integrated packages include Enable, Framework, and Symphony.

Integrated Operating Environment

An **integrated operating environment** uses a program called a window manager, or integrator, that permits independent applications—such as WordStar (a word processor), Lotus 1−2−3 (a spreadsheet), and dBase (a database manager)—to work concurrently in an integrated way. With this combination a user can retain the power and capabilities of separate packages and yet share and merge data among them.

These programs work by using **windows,** separate areas or boxes on the screen, to enclose independent applications. Several applications or documents can then be displayed on the screen concurrently, and data can be transferred among them. DesQ and Windows are popular integrated-operating-environment packages.

Background Integration

Utilities are programs that assist users in various administrative tasks. **Background integration** places utilities in memory so that they are available instantly at the touch of a key while other software is still running. These types of programs are often referred to as transient stay resident (TSR) programs. Typical utilities in background integration are a calculator, calendar, appointment book, notepad, and telephone directory and dialer. Utilities can be useful additions to any software. SideKick Plus is a popular example.

PROGRAMMING LANGUAGES

To take advantage of the capabilities of computer hardware, people need some means of communicating exactly what they want done. The computer must be instructed through each detail of an operation. For example, if a user wants to print a document, the computer must be given detailed instructions on how to access the file, initialize the printer, send the data to the printer, and so on. A **programming language** is a set of written symbols that instruct the computer hardware to perform specified operations. Use of these symbols is governed by a set of rules called **syntax,** the equivalent to grammar in English and other languages.

Basic Instructions of a Programming Language

Several hundred programming languages are used for computers today. Although the specifics of each language may vary, certain basic instructions are included in all programming languages.

- Input/output instructions—to transfer instructions and data between the central processing unit and input and output devices.

- Arithmetic instructions—to perform mathematical operations, such as addition, subtraction, multiplication, and division.
- Logic instructions—to determine comparisons—such as equal to, not equal to, less than, greater than, greater than or equal to, and less than or equal to—and test conditions. A condition involves testing the values or logical relationships of one or more data items. For example, in the statement "If $x > 10$, then $y = 1$, else $y = 2$," the condition being tested is $x > 10$. If x is greater than 10, then the value of y is set to 1. If x is not greater than 10, the value of y is set to 2.
- Control instructions—to alter the order in which the program instructions are to be executed.
- Data movement instructions—to copy and move data within primary storage.
- Specification instructions—to specify various parameters, such as constants, portions of memory to be used, file access method, and so on.

Even though every programming language is capable of these basic functions, the methods used to accomplish them vary widely.

Categories of Programming Languages

Of the hundreds of different programming languages available, all fit into one of four general categories: machine, assembly, high-level, and fourth-generation languages. Figure 4–7 illustrates the various general categories.

Machine Language. Machine language is made up of 1s and 0s and is the only programming language that the computer can understand. There is not, however, one universal machine language. The arrangement of 1s

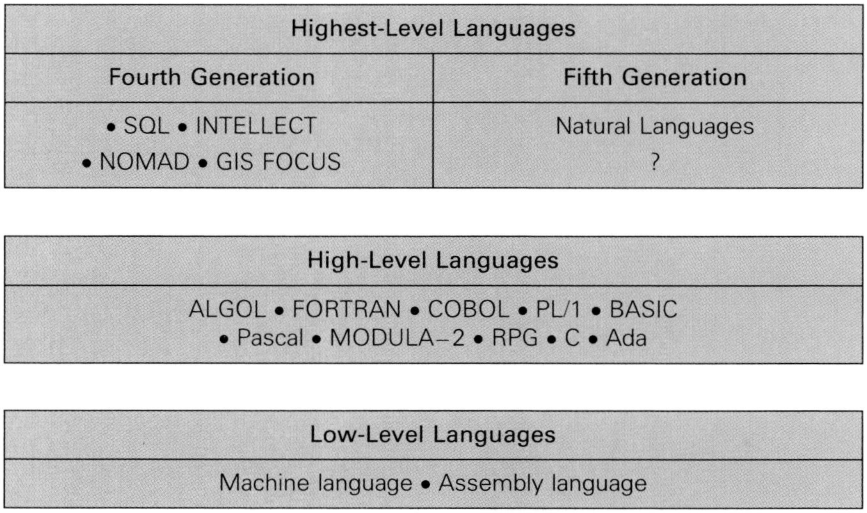

FIGURE 4–7
General categories of programming languages.

Highest-Level Languages	
Fourth Generation	Fifth Generation
• SQL • INTELLECT • NOMAD • GIS FOCUS	Natural Languages ?

High-Level Languages
ALGOL • FORTRAN • COBOL • PL/1 • BASIC • Pascal • MODULA–2 • RPG • C • Ada

Low-Level Languages
Machine language • Assembly language

and 0s to represent similar instructions, data, and memory locations differs among computers because of different hardware designs.

Machine-language programs have the advantage of fast execution speeds and efficient use of primary memory. However, writing machine language is a very tedious, difficult, and time-consuming method of programming. As a **low-level language** it requires that the programmer have detailed knowledge of how the computer works since every detail of an operation must be specified. As you might imagine, it is easy to make an error but very difficult to remove it from (debug) a machine-language program.

If machine language were the only means of programming a computer, there probably wouldn't be many programmers, and there certainly wouldn't be the vast number of application programs available for use. To make programming simpler, other easier-to-use programming languages have been developed. These languages, however, must ultimately be translated into machine language before the computer can understand and use them.

Assembly Language. The next higher level of programming language is assembly language. It is also classified as a low-level language because detailed knowledge of hardware specifics is still required. An **assembly language** uses mnemonics in place of 1s and 0s to represent the instructions (Figure 4−8). A **mnemonic** is an alphabetical abbreviation used as a memory aid. For example, instead of using a combination of 1s and 0s to represent an addition operation, the mnemonic *AD* might be used.

Assembly languages use symbolic addressing capabilities that simplify the programming process because the programmer does not need to know or remember the exact storage locations of instructions or data. Symbolic addressing is the expression of an address in terms of symbols chosen by the programmer rather than an absolute numerical location. Instead of assigning and remembering a number that identifies the address of a piece of data, a programmer can assign data to a symbolic name, such as TOTAL. The assembly language then automatically assigns an address when it encounters that symbolic name and remembers all addresses assigned.

Before it can be used by a computer, an assembly language must be translated into a machine language. This conversion is done by a language-translator program called an **assembler**. Assembly languages provide an easier and more efficient way to program than machine languages do, while still maintaining control over the internal functions of a computer at the most basic level. In addition, assembly languages produce programs that are efficient, use less storage, and execute much faster than programs using high-level languages. However, assembly languages are still machine-oriented and require a thorough knowledge of computer hardware. Compared to high-level languages, they are tedious and prone to errors.

High-Level Language. A **high-level language** is one with instructions that closely resemble human language and mathematical notation. High-

```
                Assembler code (mnemonics)                                    Machine-language instructions

sseg                    segment stack                      0100
                        db 256  dup (?)                     110010  100000  1111000  100000  110100  100000
                                                            111101  100000  100000
sseg                    ends                               11110
dseg                    segment                            10111000
data                    db "2 x 4 = "                      1010000
                                                           11101000
dseg           ends                                        11111100
cseg                    segment                            10111000
assume         cs:cseg,ds:dseg,ss:sseg,es:nothing          10001110  11011000
start          proc far                                    10111000
                        push ds                            10001110  11000000
                        mov ax,0                            10111010
                        push ax                             10111011
                        call main                           10001101  110110
start          endp                                         10111111
                                                            10110000  00000010
main                    proc near                           10110011  00000100
                        cld                                 11110110  11100011
                        mov ax, dseg                        00001100  110000
                        mov ds, ax                          10100000
                        mov ax, 0b000h                      10111001
                        mov es, ax                          10100100
                        mov dx, 0                           1000111
                        mov bx, 0                           10110000  10000111
                        lea si, data                        10001000  00000101
                        mov di, 32848                       11100010  1111000
                        mov al, 02h
                        mov bl, 04h
                        mul bl
                        or al, 30h
                        mov al, data+9
    msgsb:     mov cx,9
    1b1:                movsb
                        inc di
                        mov al, 135
                        mov [di], al
                        loop 1b1
    main       endp
    cseg       ends
               endstart
```

FIGURE 4-8

A comparison of machine-language instructions and assembler codes
(mnemonics) for a program that computes and prints out the result of 2 × 4.

level languages do not require that the programmer have detailed knowledge about the internal operations of a computer. Because of the close resemblance to human language, high-level languages are much easier to learn and use than either machine or assembly languages. Typically, less time and effort are required for high-level programming because errors are easier to avoid and correct.

Many high-level languages are also designed to be machine-independent; they can be transported from computer to computer and executed with few changes. As a result, high-level languages are used more often than machine or assembly languages. The American National Standards Institute (ANSI) has developed standards to help make high-level languages more machine-independent.

Sometimes, portions of a program may require more speed or efficiency than can be achieved with the high-level programming language being used. Most high-level languages allow assembly language programs to be used (called) to supply the needed boost in capabilities.

Business Computer Systems

A high-level language must also be translated into a machine language before it can be used by a computer. One of two different language-translator programs is used to translate high-level languages: a compiler or an interpreter. A **compiler** translates a whole program, called the source code, into machine language at once before the program is executed. Once converted, the program is stored in machine-readable form, called the object code. The object code can be immediately executed anytime thereafter. The source code remains intact after the conversion and can be updated and changed as required and then recompiled into the object code.

An **interpreter** translates a program into machine language one line at a time, executing each line of the program after it is translated. With most interpreters the machine-readable form is not stored in primary storage or on a secondary storage medium. Therefore, the program must be interpreted each time it is executed.

Fourth-Generation Language. The different categories of languages are sometimes labeled by generations—from lowest to highest. Machine languages are considered the first generation; assembly languages, the second generation; and high-level languages, the third generation. A **fourth-generation language** is one of a variety of programming languages that allow end-users to expend much less effort creating programs than is required by high-level languages. The objectives of a fourth-generation language include

- increasing the speed of developing programs
- minimizing end-user effort to obtain information from a computer
- decreasing the skill level required of end-users so that they can concentrate on the application rather than the intricacies of coding and thus solve their own problems without the aid of a professional programmer
- minimizing maintenance by reducing errors and making programs easy to change

The sophistication of fourth-generation languages varies widely. These languages are usually used in conjunction with a database and its data dictionary and are often found as part of an MIS or DSS. Fourth-generation languages include database query languages, report generators, and application generators. A **database query language** permits user formulation of queries that may relate to records from one or more files. The appropriate records can then be printed or displayed in a suitable format. Examples include IBM's SQL and Artificial Intelligence's INTELLECT.

A **report generator** allows data from a database to be extracted and formatted into reports. It also allows substantial arithmetic and logic operations to be performed on the data before they are displayed or printed. NOMAD by NCSS and GIS by IBM are two examples of report generators.

An **application generator** allows data entry and permits the user to specify how the database will be updated, what calculations or logic operations will be performed, and what output will be created. This language allows a user to build an entire application. Examples include FOCUS by Information Builders and MANTIS by Cincom Systems.

Fifth-Generation Languages. Many individuals consider natural languages to be **fifth-generation languages**. **Natural languages** are similar to query languages but eliminate the need for the user or programmer to learn a specific vocabulary, grammar, or syntax. A natural language closely resembles human speech.

Procedural vs. Nonprocedural Languages

Programming languages are classified into two different types: procedural and nonprocedural languages. **Procedural languages** specify how something is accomplished. Common procedural languages include BASIC, Pascal, C, Ada, COBOL, and FORTRAN. **Nonprocedural languages** specify what is accomplished without going into the details of how. Database query languages and report generators are examples of nonprocedural languages.

The difference between procedural and nonprocedural languages can be illustrated with the analogy of giving directions to a taxi driver. Using a procedural language, the directions might go as follows: "Drive 600 yards forward. Turn right. Drive 350 yards forward. Turn left. Drive 500 yards forward. Stop." Using a nonprocedural language, you would simply tell the driver what you want: "Take me to the Fairview Hotel."

Major High-Level Languages

FORTRAN. FORTRAN (FORmula TRANslator) was introduced in 1957 and is the oldest high-level programming language. It was designed primarily for use by scientists, engineers, and mathematicians in solving mathematical problems. However, most early business applications were written in FORTRAN and later converted to COBOL. And it is not uncommon, even today, to find business application programs written in FORTRAN. FORTRAN is well-suited to complex numerical calculations; but because it lacks strength for some input/output and nonnumeric operations, it is not widely used for manipulation of large data files. Figure 4–9 gives a brief example of a FORTRAN program.

COBOL. COBOL (COmmon Business-Oriented Language) is a widely used programming language for business data processing. It was developed in the late 1950s by a Conference on Data Systems Languages (CODASYL) committee that consisted of manufacturers, users, and government agencies. It was specifically designed to manipulate the large data files typically encountered in business.

COBOL uses descriptive English-like statements that offer a self-documenting quality. This feature makes it easy to understand and follow the logic of a program. A COBOL program is generally much longer than other high-level language programs that accomplish the same task because COBOL is designed to make future program changes more efficient. The language is deliberately redundant so that program maintenance becomes easier. This approach is important because an organization typically spends

FIGURE 4–9

A FORTRAN program that computes the sum and average of 10 numbers.

```
C    COMPUTE THE SUM AND AVERAGE OF 10 NUMBERS
C
        REAL NUM, SUM, AVG
        INTEGER TOTNUM, COUNTR
C
        SUM = 0.0
C   INITIALIZE LOOP CONTROL VARIABLE
        COUNTR = 0
        TOTNUM = 10
C
C   LOOP TO READ DATA AND ACCUMULATE SUM
    20 IF (COUNTR .GE. TOTNUM) GO TO 30
        READ, NUM
        SUM = SUM + NUM
C       UPDATE LOOP CONTROL VARIABLE
        COUNTR = COUNTR + 1
        GO TO 20
C   END OF LOOP - COMPUTE AVERAGE
    30 AVG = SUM / TOTNUM
C   PRINT RESULTS
        PRINT, SUM
        PRINT, AVG
        STOP
        END
```

85 percent of its business programming dollars on maintenance programming.

Although other programming languages perform the same operations more efficiently, COBOL is likely to be the predominant language in business for some time to come because the expense in time and money to convert existing programs and retrain programmers would be prohibitive. With COBOL programs already in place and operating satisfactorily, the attitude of many people in business is, "If it isn't broken, don't fix it." Figure 4–10 is a brief example of a COBOL program.

PL/1. PL/1, Programming Language One, was created in the early 1960s. It was designed to be all things to all people. In particular it was designed to replace FORTRAN, ALGOL, and COBOL. The users of each of these languages found themselves needing more than any one of the languages could provide. They wanted a true general-purpose language that allowed powerful computations and sophisticated data structures. Although the designers of PL/1 produced a very detailed and good programming language, it failed to gain a large following. One reason may be that the initial version of PL/1 was finished too late. The COBOL revolution had already begun, as most businesses wrote their applications in or converted them to COBOL. In addition, the size of the PL/1 language posed a drawback for users who needed only a fraction of its capabilities. After failing to capture the business and scientific markets, PL/1 was promoted as a systems programming language. However, it is not competitive with modern languages like C, which were specifically designed for systems programming. PL/1 is largely used in the oil industry today. Figure 4–11 shows an example of a simple PL/1 program.

FIGURE 4-10
A COBOL program that
computes the sum and average
of 10 numbers.

```
IDENTIFICATION DIVISION.
PROGRAM-ID.      AVERAGES.
AUTHOR.          DEB KNUDSEN.
DATE-COMPILED.
ENVIRONMENT DIVISION.
CONFIGURATION SECTION.
    SOURCE-COMPUTER. HP-3000.
    OBJECT-COMPUTER. HP-3000.
INPUT-OUTPUT SECTION.
FILE-CONTROL.
    SELECT NUMBER-FILE ASSIGN TO "NUMFILE".
    SELECT REPORT-FILE ASSIGN TO "PRINT,UR,A,LP(CCTL)".
DATA DIVISION.
FILE SECTION.
FD  NUMBER-FILE
    LABEL RECORDS ARE STANDARD
    DATA RECORD IS NUMBER-REC.
01  NUMBER-REC                      PIC S9(7)V99.
FD  REPORT-FILE
    LABEL RECORDS ARE STANDARD
    DATA RECORD IS REPORT-REC.
01  REPORT-REC                      PIC X(100).

WORKING-STORAGE SECTION.
01  END-OF-NUMBER-FILE-FLAG         PIC X(3) VALUE SPACES.
    88  END-OF-NUMBER-FILE                   VALUE "YES".
01  SUM-OF-NUMBERS                  PIC S9(7)V99.
01  AVERAGE-OF-NUMBERS              PIC S9(7)V99.
01  NUMBER-OF-NUMBERS               PIC 9(5).

01  WS-REPORT-REC.
    05  FILLER                      PIC X(2)    VALUE SPACES.
    05  FILLER                      PIC X(17)   VALUE
                                    "Sum of Numbers = ".
    05  WS-SUM-OF-NUMBERS           PIC Z,ZZZ,ZZZ.99-.
    05  FILLER                      PIC X(3)    VALUE SPACES.
    05  FILLER                      PIC X(15)   VALUE
                                    "# of Numbers = ".
    05  WS-NUMBER-OF-NUMBERS        PIC ZZZZ9.
    05  FILLER                      PIC X(3)    VALUE SPACES.
    05  FILLER                      PIC X(21)   VALUE
                                    "Average of Numbers = ".
    05  WS-AVERAGE-OF-NUMBERS       PIC Z,ZZZ,ZZZ.99-.
    05  FILLER                      PIC X(8)    VALUE SPACES.
```

BASIC. BASIC (Beginner's All-Purpose Symbolic Instruction Code) was developed at Dartmouth College in the mid-1960s to provide students with an easy-to-learn, interactive language on a time-sharing computer system. In an interactive language each statement is translated into machine language and executed as soon as it is entered into the computer. If there is an error in the statement, BASIC also provides error messages immediately.

BASIC was developed as a shortened and simplified version of FORTRAN. It allowed novice programmers to learn and begin programming in a few hours. Because it is easy to learn and use, BASIC became the most popular language for microcomputers and is available for most microcomputers in use today.

Many extensions to BASIC have been developed to take advantage of specific hardware, resulting in many different, nonstandardized versions of

FIGURE 4–10
(Continued)

```
PROCEDURE DIVISION.

100-MAIN-PROGRAM.
    OPEN INPUT  NUMBER-FILE
         OUTPUT REPORT-FILE.
    MOVE SPACES TO REPORT-REC.
    MOVE ZEROS TO SUM-OF-NUMBERS.
    MOVE ZEROS TO AVERAGE-OF-NUMBERS.
    MOVE ZEROS TO NUMBER-OF-NUMBERS.

    READ NUMBER-FILE
      AT END MOVE "YES" TO END-OF-NUMBER-FILE-FLAG.

    IF END-OF-NUMBER-FILE
      NEXT SENTENCE
    ELSE
      PERFORM 200-PROCESS-NUMBER-FILE
        UNTIL END-OF-NUMBER-FILE.

    PERFORM 300-COMPUTE-AVERAGE.

    PERFORM 400-PRINT-RESULTS.

    CLOSE NUMBER-FILE
          REPORT-FILE.

    STOP RUN.

200-PROCESS-NUMBER-FILE.
    ADD 1 TO NUMBER-OF-NUMBERS.
    ADD NUMBER-REC TO SUM-OF-NUMBERS.

    READ NUMBER-FILE
      AT END MOVE "YES" TO END-OF-NUMBER-FILE-FLAG.

300-COMPUTE-AVERAGE.
    DIVIDE SUM-OF-NUMBERS BY NUMBER-OF-NUMBERS
      GIVING AVERAGE-OF-NUMBERS.

400-PRINT-RESULTS.
    MOVE SUM-OF-NUMBERS TO WS-SUM-OF-NUMBERS.
    MOVE NUMBER-OF-NUMBERS TO WS-NUMBER-OF-NUMBERS.
    MOVE AVERAGE-OF-NUMBERS TO WS-AVERAGE-OF-NUMBERS.

WRITE REPORT-REC FROM WS-REPORT-REC.
```

the language. The American National Standards Institute (ANSI) set standards for the most essential portion of the BASIC language, called Minimal BASIC, in 1978. However, because Minimal BASIC and its various extensions are not well-suited to structured programming methods, structured versions of BASIC, such as True BASIC, have also emerged. Figure 4–12 shows a BASIC program in the Microsoft BASIC language.

Pascal and Modula–2. Niklaus Wirth of Zurich developed **Pascal** in the late 1960s and named it after Blaise Pascal, the French mathematician and philosopher who invented the first practical mechanical adding machine. The Pascal language is suited to both scientific and file-processing applications. Pascal was originally designed to teach the concepts of structured programming and top-down design to students. Because of its structured

FIGURE 4–11

A PL/1 program that computes the sum and average of 10 numbers.

```
START: PROCEDURE OPTIONS (MAIN);
 DECLARE (N, K) DECIMAL FIXED (2),
         VALUE (N) DECIMAL FIXED (5,2) CONTROLLED,
         SUM         DECIMAL FIXED (6,2) INITIAL (0.0),
         AVERAGE     DECIMAL FIXED (6,3);
 GET DATA (N); ALLOCATE VALUE;
     GET LIST (VALUE);
     DO K = 1 TO N; SUM = SUM + VALUE (K); END;
     AVERAGE = ROUND(SUM/N,3); PUT DATA(N, SUM, AVERAGE);
 END START;

DATA:

N=10; 1.0 2.0 3.0 4.0 5.0 6.0 7.0 8.0 9.0 10.0
```

FIGURE 4–12

A BASIC program that computes the sum and average of 10 numbers.

```
10   REM COMPUTE SUM AND AVERAGE OF 10 NUMBERS
20   LET SUM = 0
30   FOR I = 1 TO 10
40     INPUT N(I)
50     LET SUM = SUM + N(I)
60   NEXT I
70   LET AVG = SUM / 10
80   PRINT "SUM = ",SUM
90   PRINT "AVERAGE = ",AVG
999  END
```

FIGURE 4–13

A PASCAL program that computes the sum and average of 10 numbers.

```
PROGRAM average(input, output);
{ Compute the sum and average of ten numbers }
VAR num, sum, avg : real;
    i : integer;

BEGIN
    sum:=0.0;
    FOR i := 1 TO 10 DO
    BEGIN
       read(num);
       sum:=sum + num;
    END;
    avg:=sum/10;
    writeln('Sum =',sum);
    writeln('Average =',avg);
END.
```

nature, some schools have replaced BASIC with Pascal in introductory programming classes. Like BASIC, Pascal is not standardized and has many different versions. An example of a short Pascal program is shown in Figure 4-13.

Because Pascal was originally designed as a teaching tool, it lacks some features of a good application-software development tool. To add the required additional features and correct the existing problems of Pascal, Niklaus Wirth redesigned Pascal and called it **Modula-2**. Modula-2 improves the modularity, the input and output capabilities, and the file-handling capabilities of the language. Figure 4-14 shows an example of a short Modula-2 program. Pascal also remains in use and has been greatly enhanced since its initial development.

RPG. RPG (Report Program Generator) was developed in the mid-1960s. Since most people at that time had no programming experience, RPG was designed to be especially easy to learn and use. A programmer uses coding sheets (Figure 4-15) to specify input, output, processing operations, and file specifications, all of which are then entered into the computer for processing. Although it is easy to learn, RPG has limited capabilities. It can be used for producing reports and processing files on tape or disk, but it is not well-suited to mathematical or scientific applications.

C. The C programming language, developed at Bell Laboratories in the early 1970s, incorporates many advantages of both low-level and high-

FIGURE 4-14

A Modula-2 program that computes the sum and average of 10 numbers.

```
MODULE averageNum;
FROM InOut IMPORT WriteLn, WriteString, ReadCard;
FROM RealLnOut IMPORT WriteReal;

VAR
    i:CARDINAL;
    sum, average:REAL;
    Nmbs:Array[1..10] OF CARDINAL;

BEGIN
    WriteLn;
    WriteString("Enter number: ");
    WriteLn;
    FOR i := 1 TO 10 BY 1 DO
        ReadCard(Nmbs[i]);  (* get numbers from keyboard *)
        WriteLn;
    END;
    sum := 0.0;
    FOR i := 1 TO 10 BY 1 DO (* sum numbers *)
        sum := sum + FLOAT(Nmbs[i]);
    END;
    average := sum / 10.0;  (* calculate average *)
    WriteLn;
    WriteString("Sum = ");
    WriteReal(sum,10);
    WriteLn;
    WriteString("Average = ");
    WriteReal(average,10);
END AverageNum.
```

FIGURE 4-15

RPG coding sheets. (Courtesy of International Business Machines Corporation)

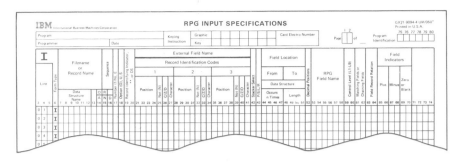

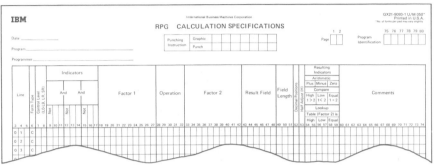

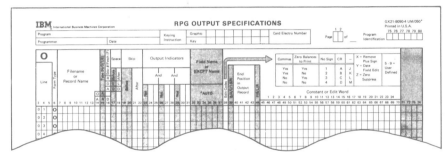

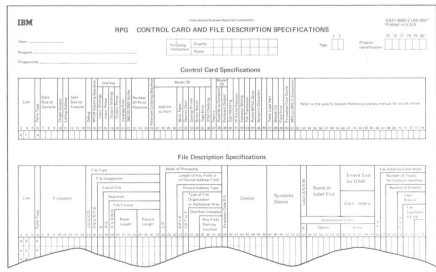

level languages. Like assembly language, it enables the programmer to have extensive control over computer hardware. But because it uses English-like statements, which are easy to read, it is often classified as a high-level language. C also incorporates sophisticated control and data structures, which make it a powerful but concise language.

C is well-suited to the development of system software, which was its original purpose in design. The UNIX operating system was developed largely with C. However, C is also becoming a popular choice for developing application programs because of its power and structured nature. Figure 4–16 is an example of a brief C program.

Ada. The Ada programming language was developed in the late 1970s with the support of the U.S. Department of Defense. It was named for Augusta Ada, Countess of Lovelace, who is considered by many to be the world's first programmer. The goal was to build a very powerful, complete, and yet efficient structured language to be used in military applications, such as controlling weapon systems.

To accomplish this purpose, the language was designed with powerful control and data structures and with a set of commands that allowed it to control hardware devices directly. Currently, Ada is used primarily by the U.S. Department of Defense, but the powerful and efficient nature of the language suggests that it may see greater use in other applications in the future. Figure 4–17 is an example of a brief Ada program.

Choosing a Programming Language

With so many programming languages to choose from, a manager should consider several factors before selecting one language for the organization's programmers to use.

- The nature of the problem—Is the programming language designed for this type of problem? For example, COBOL is not suited

FIGURE 4–16

A C program that computes the sum and average of 10 numbers.

```
#include <stdio.h>

main ()
    {
        int i, num;
        float sum;

        printf("Enter numbers \n");
        sum = 0;
        for (i = 0; i < 10; i++)
          {
              scanf("%d",&num);
              sum = sum + num;
          }
        printf("Sum = %3.1f\n",sum);
        printf("Average = %3.1f\n",sum / 10.0);
    }
```

Software for Business Computer Systems

FIGURE 4–17

An Ada program that computes
the sum and average of 10
numbers.

```
PROCEDURE average number IS
    USE simple io;
    num, sum, avg: REAL;

BEGIN
    sum := 0;
    FORiIN 1...10 LOOP
      GET(num);
      sum:=sum + num;
    END LOOP;
    avg:=sum / 10;
    PUT("Sum ="); PUT(sum);
    PUT("Average ="); PUT(avg);
END average number;
```

to robotics since it doesn't have the vocabulary or features to control such things as robot arm movements.

- The speed at which the program needs to execute—If the program will be used frequently and requires efficient execution, a programming language such as an assembly language or C may be necessary to reduce execution time.
- The expertise of the programming staff—Do the programmers already know the language under consideration? If not, can they learn it in the required time period, and is the additional cost for training justifiable?
- The portability of the language—Will the program have to run on more than one type of computer? Machine and assembly languages are machine-specific and require extensive changes or complete rewrites if new hardware is used. High-level languages are more portable and can usually be run on different computers with few or no changes.
- The amount of program maintenance expected—Will the program be subject to periodic updates and revisions? If so, a structured, high-level language may be the best choice.

SUMMARY

A program, or software, is the series of instructions that directs the hardware to perform various tasks. The two types of software are system and application software.

The set of programs that controls a computer system's hardware and provides services to users of the system is called an operating system. It is composed of two types of programs: control and service programs. Control programs manage the computer hardware and resources. Service programs provide a service to the user or programmer of a computer system.

An operating system for a microcomputer often resides on a diskette and is called a disk operating system (DOS). Popular microcomputer operating systems include MS-DOS, UNIX, Apple PRODOS, the Apple Macintosh operating system, and OS/2.

Many tasks that people perform manually can be done faster and more efficiently with a computer. An application package is a program that interacts with the system software to direct the computer hardware to complete a task for the user. The five most popular application packages for microcomputers are word processors, data managers, spreadsheets, graphics, and communication packages. A user-friendly application package is one that is easy to learn and use.

The main sources of application packages are purchased prewritten software, in-house custom-developed software, and outside custom-developed software.

Software developers have found a way to integrate several application packages. Integrated software is designed so that data can be easily shared among the separate programs. Ideally, integrated applications have a familiar set of functions, a common command set, and common keystrokes.

In order to instruct a computer to perform specific tasks, a set of written symbols called a programming language is used. Each programming language has a set of rules, or syntax, governing the use of its symbols. There are many programming languages, but each includes the following basic instructions: input/output, arithmetic, logic, control, data movement, and specifications. Programming languages are divided into four categories: machine, assembly, high-level, and fourth-generation languages.

The following factors should be considered in the selection of a programming language: the nature of the problem, the speed at which the program needs to execute, the expertise of the programming staff, the portability of the language, and the amount of program maintenance expected.

MINICASE 4–1

Ace Pharmaceutical Company is installing a supercomputer for its scientists to use in research. Ace has laboratories located in several parts of the country; the supercomputer will be located at the current data center in Cincinnati, Ohio. Many of the Ace scientists will need to access and run programs on the computer at the same time. In addition, Ace's management wants to make the supercomputer available to users outside the organization to help defray the cost of the hardware.

Most of the Ace scientists are not computer programmers. Although professional programmers will be utilized for some tasks, the scientists want a language available that will permit easy creation of applications to manipulate the data they need.

1. What characteristics will an operating system need to support Ace's intended use of its supercomputer? Explain the need for each characteristic.

2. What category of programming language will best suit the scientists' needs for quick and easy creation of applications to manipulate data? Why?

The Timber Woods Public Library has just received a donation of a microcomputer system. The system includes a hard disk and a letter-quality printer but no software. The operations manager at the library has called a local computer store to inquire about the kinds of software that she should purchase. In talking to the store representative, the operations manager has indicated that she would like to use the computer system to prepare the library's budgets, produce memos and reports, develop graphical information from financial data to present to the director, and maintain employee and volunteer information, such as names, addresses, phone numbers, and hours available for work. She has also indicated that some of the financial data, graphs, and information on employees and volunteers needs to be incorporated into the memos and reports she creates. In addition, the operations manager wants to use the computer to record appointments and notes from phone conversations.

1. As the computer store salesperson what types of software will you tell the operations manager that she needs and why?
2. Would integration be appropriate for the manager's needs? What type of integrated packages would you suggest?

Key Terms

Ada
all-in-one integrated package
application
application generator
application package
application software
assembler
assembly language
background integration
BASIC
business and analytical program
C
COBOL
communication package
communication parameters
compiler
concurrent operating system
control program
database
database management system (DBMS)
database query language

data manager
design program
disk operating system (DOS)
fifth-generation language
file-management system
formatting
FORTRAN
fourth-generation language
graphics package
high-level language
high-resolution graphics
integrated family of programs
integrated operating environment
integrated software
interpreter
interprocessing
interrupt
job
job control language (JCL)
language-translator program
low-level language

machine language

mnemonic

Modula–2

multiprocessing operating system

multiprogramming

multitasking

multithreading

natural language

nonprocedural language

operating system

painting and drawing program

Pascal

PL/1

presentation graphics

procedural language

program

programming language

program swapping

real-time operating system

report generator

RPG

service program

single-program operating system

spreadsheet

supervisor program

syntax

system resident device

system software

text editing

text graphics

time-sharing operating system

user-friendly

utility program

virtual-machine (VM) operating system

virtual-storage operating system

windows

word processing

word-processing system

word processor

Review Questions

1. What is a program?
2. Describe system software and give an example.
3. How can system software be helpful?
4. Describe application software and give an example.
5. Give an example of application software that you might use in your personal life.
6. Discuss the purpose of an operating system. Why is it needed?
7. What is the function of control programs?
8. What is the function of an interrupt?
9. What is the function of a supervisor program?
10. Describe the purpose of service programs.
11. Why are system resident devices useful?
12. What is the purpose of application software?
13. Describe some uses of a spreadsheet that help explain why it is classified as a generalized application package.
14. Describe the three main sources for acquiring application software.
15. Briefly describe the five major microcomputer applications discussed in this chapter.
16. Define integrated software.

17. Describe why you might prefer an integrated software package to a stand-alone package.

18. What is meant by the syntax of a programming language?

19. Describe the six basic types of instructions found in a programming language.

20. What characterizes a low-level programming language?

21. Why must a high-level language be converted to machine language?

22. What is the difference between a procedural and nonprocedural programming language?

23. What are fifth-generation languages?

24. Discuss some of the factors to consider when choosing a programming language.

Data Communication

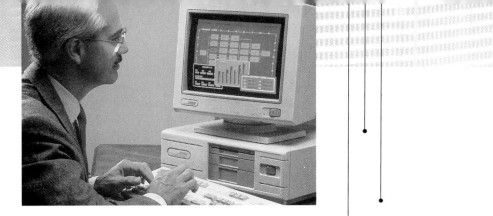

Chapter 5

Management Profile: Jack Garber
GARBER OFFERS KNOW-HOW

Jack Garber firmly believes in the value of learning from experience—particularly harrowing sink-or-swim experiences that force people to develop new skills and make hard decisions in a hurry. When he took over Fidelity Investment's telecommunications services group in early 1987, Garber brought to the job the know-how gleaned from 18 years of challenging work in the data-processing and communications fields. He has set himself the goal of instilling in his staff some of the lessons he has gained from his experience.

With lean, sharply defined features and a no-nonsense haircut, Garber comes across at first as the classic take-charge executive—one who comes into a new operation with his game plan mapped out and ready to go. In fact, however, his management style seems characterized by a strong willingness to hear out the other side before he goes ahead. Garber does not blindly assume that his way is the best but checks out why things are done a certain way before changing them.

He learned this lesson the hard way at Wells Fargo Bank NA, where he directed the telecommunications aspects of that company's acquisition of Crocker Bank. The biggest job at Wells Fargo was "integrating the cultures of the two groups," Garber recalls. "Just saying, 'You'll all work together,' didn't work."

Garber says his trial-by-fire at Wells Fargo stood him in good stead when he took over telecommunications at Fidelity. "I think I was brought in because I had spent a lot of time in the financial industry managing network costs and resources, making value judgments on what to buy, and fitting the network plan with the organization's financial and strategic goals."

Initially, Garber found that many users saw his group as "technical gurus spending all the profits" without providing high-quality, reliable service. Garber has been trying to make telecommunications people at Fidelity more responsive to the needs of the users in Fidelity's 19 companies. "I'm trying to instill the idea that we are not necessarily the users' sole source; that they are allowed to get the same services elsewhere if it's cheaper and more reliable." Garber says the department has become more user-oriented since he came on board but still has a ways to go before he will be satisfied. He now spends half of his time meeting with users, obtaining feedback about their needs. "I think it's one of the key things I was brought here to do."

"Greater responsiveness to user needs is something we started focusing on [in 1986]; [Garber] has taken it to the next plateau," says Michael Simmons, president of Fidelity Information Services Company. Simmons says he hired Garber "because of his reputation and because I liked his management style. He's continually looking for other, better ways to do things and testing to make sure the parameters we're using are the right ones." Simmons says Fidelity needs someone who is "continually changing the way we do business, to ensure we're not getting fat, dumb, and happy."

"He came in and took a growing operating division, realigned responsibilities, and put people in different jobs. He's generally up, with a bounce in his step. I see him as a positive influence," Simmons says.

In Chapter 1 you were introduced to the different categories of computers—supercomputers, mainframes, minicomputers, and micro-computers. These computers offer a wide range of computing power. Thus, if more computing power is needed, one way to get it is to buy a larger system. That option may be fine if the necessary money and facilities are available, but many businesses simply can't afford to purchase a larger system.

Another problem arises for organizations whose units are geograph-ically dispersed. They may need to send data to or use data in many different locations. One answer to this problem is to keep separate data files at each location, but this method can be a costly and potentially disastrous solution. It is expensive to maintain redundant data files and difficult to ensure their continuing accuracy.

What then are the answers to these problems? Solutions to the need for more power and for data exchange and sharing can be found in data communication technology. In this chapter we examine some basic con-cepts related to data communications. We also examine some ways in which data communication is used in an information system, including local-area networks, wide-area networks, and distributed data processing.

IMPACT ON MANAGEMENT PROBLEM SOLVING AND DECISION MAKING

In today's business world, data communication technologies are as impor-tant as the computer technologies that support them. Many organizations, including banking and financial firms, could not exist as they do today without data communications. Managers use data communications to communicate with a wide variety of individuals—other managers within the same organization, banking and financial services personnel, custom-ers, suppliers, shareholders, government officials, consumer groups, adver-tisers, and more. Communications can take place locally, nationally, or internationally.

Managers need to send and receive data and information in a timely fashion in order to identify and solve problems and make effective deci-sions. Often, in today's fast-paced electronic environment, even the slight-est delay can mean a missed opportunity. However, getting data to a de-sired destination in a timely manner is not a manager's only concern. Communication systems must transmit the data accurately and in a form that can be understood and used by the receiving system.

Managers are faced with numerous decisions concerning data com-munications. They must decide which data communications hardware and software options are right for their organizations. This crucial decision must take into account a number of factors, including cost and perfor-mance. In addition, managers must be aware of current or emerging data communications standards in their industry so that selected hardware and software will be compatible with their firms' current and future needs.

DATA COMMUNICATION

Data communication is the process of sending data electronically from one point to another. Linking one computer to another permits the power and resources of both computers to be tapped. It also makes possible the sharing and updating of data in different locations.

Computers that are physically close to each other, either in the same room or building, can communicate data through a direct-cable link. Computers that are far apart use a special form of data communication called telecommunication. **Telecommunication,** or teleprocessing, is the process of using communication facilities, such as the telephone system and microwave relays, to send data between computers.

Analog and Digital Data Transmissions

The two forms of data transmission are analog and digital. **Analog data transmission** is the transmission of data in a continuous waveform (Figure 5–1a). The telephone system is an example of a system designed for analog data transmission.

Digital data transmission is the transmission of data using distinct on and off electrical states (Figure 5–1b). Remember that data in digital form are represented as a sequence of 1s and 0s. Because the computer understands and works in digital form and because digital data communication is faster and more efficient than analog, it would seem that all data communication between computers would be in digital form; however, that is not the case. A completely digital system is possible, but the telephone system, an analog system, is used for a great percentage of data communication because it is the largest and most widely used communication system already in place. To avoid the expense involved in converting to a digital system or running a duplicate digital system over a large geographic area, a method was devised that allows a digital signal to be transmitted over telephone lines. This method is called modulation-demodulation.

FIGURE 5–1
Analog and digital data transmissions.

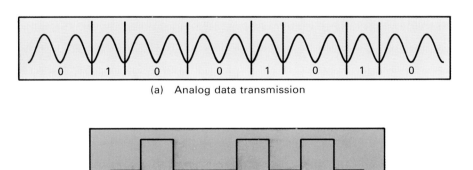

(a)   Analog data transmission

(b)   Digital data transmission

Modulation, Demodulation, and Modems

Data in a computer are formatted as digital signals. Because telephone lines were designed to transmit the human voice, they format data as analog signals. Thus, for communication between computers to take place via a telephone line, the digital signal must be converted to an analog signal before it is transmitted. After its journey along the telephone lines, the analog signal must then be reconverted to a digital signal so that it can be used by the receiving computer. The process of converting a digital signal to an analog signal is called **modulation** (Figure 5–2a). **Demodulation** is the process of reconverting the analog signal back to a digital signal (Figure 5–2b). The device that accomplishes both of these processes is a **modem,** short for *mo*dulator-*dem*odulator.

The three basic types of modems used with microcomputers are acoustic, external direct-connect, and internal direct-connect. An **acoustic modem,** or acoustic coupler as it is sometimes called, has two cups into which the handset of a telephone is placed (Figure 5–3). This type of modem sends data through the mouthpiece and receives data through the earpiece of the handset. An acoustic modem is not used very often today because its signal is much more susceptible to distortion than that of other types of modems and the carbon microphones used in a telephone handset limit the rate of data transmission.

An **external direct-connect modem** is external to the computer and connects directly to the telephone line with a modular phone jack (Figure

FIGURE 5–2
Modulation is the conversion of a digital signal to an analog signal. Demodulation is the conversion of an analog signal to a digital signal.

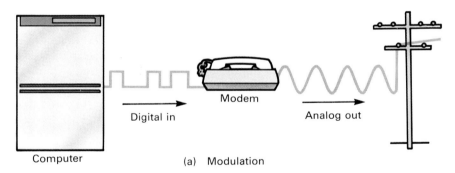

Computer   Digital in   Modem   Analog out

(a) Modulation

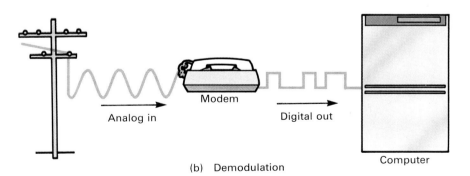

Analog in   Modem   Digital out   Computer

(b) Demodulation

FIGURE 5–3

An operator uses an acoustic modem to send data via telephone lines to another computer. (Photo courtesy of Hewlett-Packard Company)

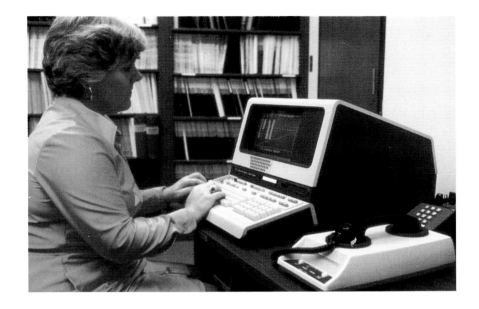

FIGURE 5–4

External direct-connect modems connect to a computer via a serial interface cable and to a telephone line via a modular phone jack.

5–4). The direct connection greatly reduces the signal's distortion and permits faster data transfer rates. A popular external direct-connect modem is the Hayes Smartmodem. Most external direct-connect modems have a variety of capabilities not found on acoustic modems:

- checking the operating status using status lights and speakers
- changing the speed at which data are transmitted
- dialing and answering the phone automatically
- responding to commands from a communications program
- self-testing their own ability to correctly transmit data

Because the specialized circuitry in these modems allows them to perform such functions, they are often called smart or intelligent devices.

Both the acoustic modem and the external direct-connect modem require that a computer be equipped with a communications adapter or other serial interface, which provides a standard method for serial transmission of data. A modem cable to connect the modem to the serial interface is also needed. For example, the RS–232C serial interface is used on most microcomputers. It has 25 pins, called a male connector, to which a modem cable is connected; the modem has 25 receptacles, called a female connector, to which the other end of the modem cable is connected.

An **internal direct-connect modem** has all the needed communications circuitry on a plug-in board that fits into one of the expansion slots (empty spaces) inside a computer (Figure 5–5). A separate communications board or serial interface is not needed. Internal direct-connect modems also link directly to a telephone line with a modular phone jack. These modems have many of the same special features that the external direct-connect modems have. In addition, they take up no desk space and are ideal for use in portable computers.

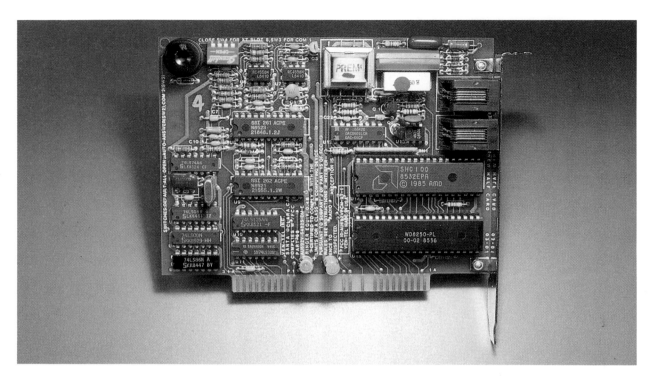

FIGURE 5–5
Internal direct-connect modems contain the necessary serial interface circuitry
and plug directly into a computer's main circuit board.

**COMMUNICATION
CHANNELS**

A **communication channel** is the medium, or pathway, along which data
are transmitted between devices. Communication channels fall into three
basic types: wire cable, microwave, and fiber optics. **Wire cable** includes
telegraph lines, telephone lines, and coaxial cables; it is the most common
type of data communication channel in use today. Telegraph and telephone lines are often referred to as twisted-pair lines because they consist
of a pair of wires, each wrapped in a protective coating and twisted around
each other. Television cable is a form of coaxial cable. Coaxial cable consists of a single wire surrounded by a layer of insulating material and then
by a metal sheath or tube for protection.

There are two basic categories of coaxial cables: baseband and broad-
band. Baseband coaxial cables carry a single digital signal at a rate between
1 million and 50 million bits per second. Multiple devices can use this
channel by combining their signals through a multiplexer, hardware that
permits two or more devices to share a common communication channel.
Broadband coaxial cables can carry multiple analog signals together (voice,
data, and video) at speeds between 20 million and 50 million bits per
second. Broadband is the more expensive of the two categories.

Because it is easier and cheaper to use the extensive wire-cable networks that already exist, wire-cable channels are the most popular. Another reason for their popularity is that the technology used to transmit data along wire cables is standardized, thus reducing compatibility problems. One disadvantage of wire cables is that data must be transmitted in analog form. Conversion of digital data not only requires special hardware but also slows down the transmission of the data. Another disadvantage is that wire cable is subject to electrical interference, making it less reliable than other types of communication channels. In addition, it is difficult to create the necessary physical links where users are separated by large distances or by natural barriers, such as mountains or large bodies of water.

Another type of analog communication channel is **microwave**. Microwave signals are transmitted through the atmosphere rather than through wire cables, much as radio and television signals are transmitted. However, microwave signals must be transmitted in a straight line because they cannot bend around corners or follow the curvature of the earth. You've probably seen microwave transmitter stations as you've driven to various places; they have to be strategically located about every 30 miles to accommodate the curvature of the earth. The transmitter stations redirect and boost the signals.

Satellites are also used to direct microwaves over large, geographically dispersed areas. A communication satellite is an electronic device that receives, amplifies, and then transmits signals from space to earth. Microwave signals are sent from a transmitter station to an earth station and then are beamed to an orbiting satellite. From there they are beamed directly back to another earth station if a direct line of sight is possible. If direct transmission is not possible, the signal is transmitted first to another satellite that does have a direct line of sight and then back to an earth station. Only three satellites are required to send a signal anywhere on earth.

Compared to wire cable, microwave has a much lower error rate, making it more reliable. Also, because there are no physical connections between the sending and receiving systems, communication links can span large distances and rough terrains. One disadvantage, however, is the high cost of transmitter stations, earth stations, and satellites to support a microwave network.

The third type of communication channel is **fiber optics** (Figure 5-6). Unlike wire cable and microwave, a fiber-optic channel transmits data in digital form. It uses light impulses that travel through clear flexible tubing, which is thinner than a human hair. Hundreds of these tubes can fit in the same amount of space required for one wire cable.

Fiber optics are reliable communication channels; data can be transmitted at high speeds (several billion bits per second) with few or no errors. And unlike wire cables, fiber-optic cables are not subject to electrical interference. They do, however, require repeaters to read and boost the signal strength because light pulses lose signal strength over long distances. Technical developments continue to drive down the cost of installing, using, and manufacturing fiber optics so that they are becoming competitive with traditional cabling. Some long-distance telephone companies, such as

Sprint, have already converted to a fiber-optic system, and others are in the process of converting.

Channel Configurations

The two principal configurations of communication channels are point-to-point and multipoint (Figure 5–7). In a **point-to-point channel configuration** a device (e.g., a terminal or a computer) is connected directly to another device by a dedicated communication channel, giving those devices sole use of that channel. Point-to-point can be an inefficient and costly configuration if a terminal is not active enough to keep the channel busy. Large computers that communicate with each other continuously often use point-to-point channel configurations.

An alternative configuration is the **multipoint channel configuration,** in which three or more devices are connected to the same line. The multipoint configuration uses a communication channel more efficiently and reduces the amount of intercabling needed, thus lowering costs. Two methods are used to determine which device gets access to a channel: polling and contention. In **polling,** the computer checks with each device, one at a time, to see whether the device has a message to send. If the device has a message ready, transmission begins; if not, the computer moves on to poll the next device. After all devices have been individually polled, the process begins again. A disadvantage to polling is that the computer's processor will be idle, wasting expensive processor time, if there are no messages to be sent by the device being polled.

FIGURE 5–6
Tiny fibers of transparent glass in fiber optics cables transmit data at the speed of light. A beam of light sent through these fibers can be turned on or off about one billion times per second. These cables are replacing traditional telephone lines and are used to connect computers in telecommunications systems. (Courtesy of United Telecommunications)

FIGURE 5-7
Two communication channel
configurations.

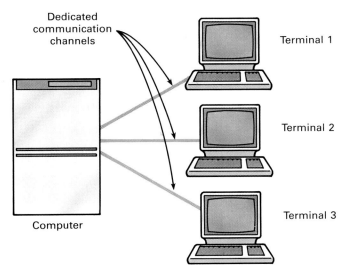

(a)   Point-to-point channel configuration

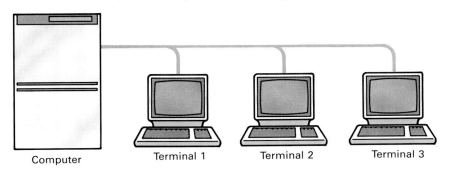

(b)   Multipoint channel configuration

A second method, **contention,** puts the devices in control; that is, each device monitors the communication channel to see whether the channel is available. If it is, the device sends its message. If the communication channel is being used, the device waits a predetermined amount of time and tries again, repeating this process until the channel is available. One problem with this approach is that a single device can tie up the communication channel for long periods of time.

Channel Sharing

Two methods are used to regulate the flow of data from communication channels into a computer: multiplexing and concentration. Their purpose is to increase the efficiency of channel use.

Multiplexing. Multiplexing is the process of combining the transmissions from several devices into a single data stream that can be sent over a single high-speed communication channel. A **multiplexer** is the hardware that provides multiplexing. It is used on the sending end to collect data from several devices and send them over one channel; it is used on the receiving end to separate the transmissions back into their original order for processing (Figure 5–8). The rationale behind this process is that most communication channels can transmit much more data at one time than a single device can send. Thus, a multiplexer allows a communication channel to be used more efficiently, thereby reducing the cost of using the channel.

There are two basic ways in which multiplexing is accomplished—frequency-division multiplexing and time-division multiplexing. In **frequency-division multiplexing** a high-speed channel is divided into multiple slow-speed channels of different frequencies. Each attached device is assigned a different frequency so that it can transmit whenever it has traffic. Each frequency assigned for traffic is surrounded by guard bands of unassigned frequencies to prevent adjacent signals from overlapping or interfering with each other.

In **time-division multiplexing** each device sharing a channel is assigned an equal time period, or slot, in which to transmit data. The multiplexer delays all incoming transmissions until their assigned time slots. With this method the assignment of time slots is static. That is, when a device has no data to send, the portion of the channel capacity assigned to that device is wasted. To avoid this situation, statistical time-division multiplexers were developed. **Statistical time-division multiplexing** dynamically reassigns unused time slots to devices with data waiting to be sent.

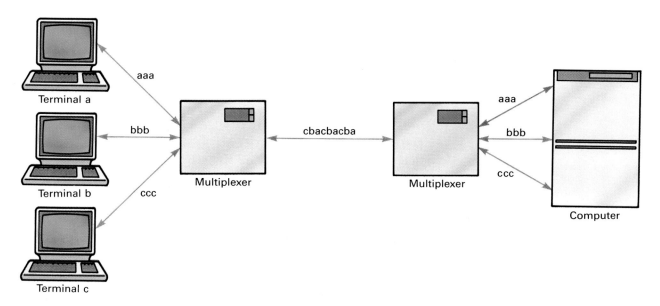

FIGURE 5–8
A multiplexer allows several terminals to share one communication channel.

Concentration. Frequently it is necessary to connect more devices to a computer than a communication channel can handle at one time. **Concentration** is the process of connecting and serving these devices; a **concentrator,** often a minicomputer, is the hardware that provides the concentration (Figure 5−9). When the number of transmitting devices exceeds the capacity of a communication channel, data are stored in a buffer for later transmission. Many multiplexers also provide concentration.

Front-End Processors

A **front-end processor** is a special purpose computer that handles all data-communication control functions (Figure 5−10). Thus, while the CPU in a front-end processor handles all communication tasks, the CPU of a main computer is free to work on other tasks. The two processors interact only when data need to be passed between them. A typical front-end processor might control scores of communication channels of varying types and speeds coming from a number of diverse remote terminals.

A front-end processor can be programmed to perform a variety of functions, such as concentration, error control, code conversion, buffering, channel sharing, and other activities related to data and message control. Front-end processors can also contain their own secondary storage devices to log (record) the communications activities for billing and audit trails.

Micro-to-Micro Link

Microcomputers are often connected for data communication in a **micro-to-micro link** so that microcomputer users with incompatible data formats can share data. A micro-to-micro link can be established with modems and telephone lines or by directly connecting the microcomputers. For example, users of an Apple Macintosh and an IBM PS/2 cannot swap data disks because the data are not saved on the disks in the same format. However, data that are in standard format, such as ASCII, can be interchanged via a modem and telephone lines. Transmission of data is possible in either direction—Apple to IBM or IBM to Apple. If the two computers are near each other, another option is to directly connect, or hard wire, them using a null modem cable. A **null modem** cable uses a different pin configuration from that of a modem cable and eliminates the need for a modem by directly matching the data transmit pin from one computer to the data receive pin on the other computer. Hard wiring with a null modem cable allows incompatible computers to transfer data at speeds up to 9600 bits per second and eliminates the need for modems at each computer. However, there are no error detection capabilities with hard wiring.

Micro-to-Mainframe Link

In order to share data and computing power, microcomputers can also be connected to large systems in a **micro-to-mainframe link**. As the number of microcomputers used in business increases, this connection is being seen

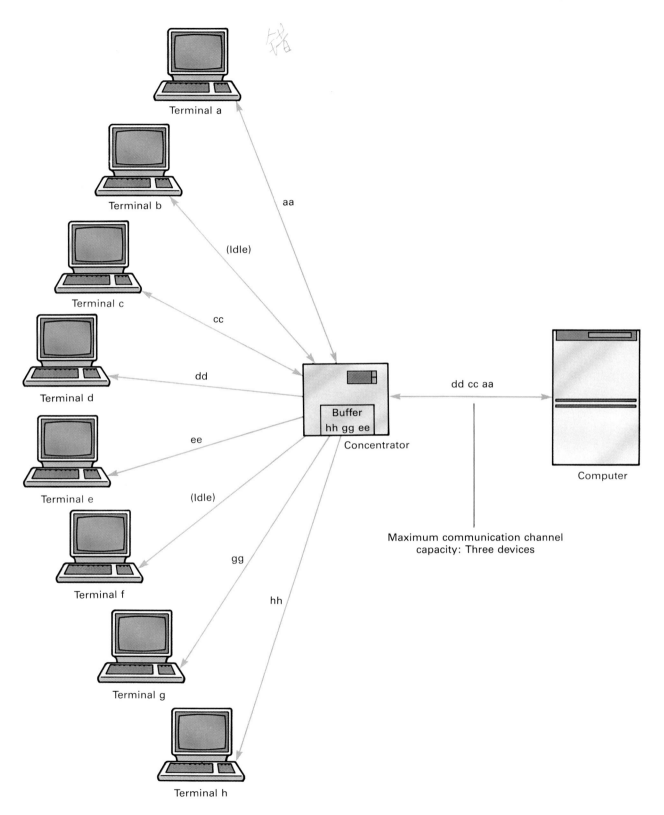

Terminal a

Terminal b

(Idle)

aa

Terminal c

cc

Terminal d

dd

Terminal e

ee

Concentrator

Buffer
hh gg ee

dd cc aa

Computer

(Idle)

Terminal f

gg

Maximum communication channel
capacity: Three devices

Terminal g

hh

Terminal h

FIGURE 5–9 (opposite)
A concentrator allows connection and service for a greater number of devices than a communication channel can handle at one time.

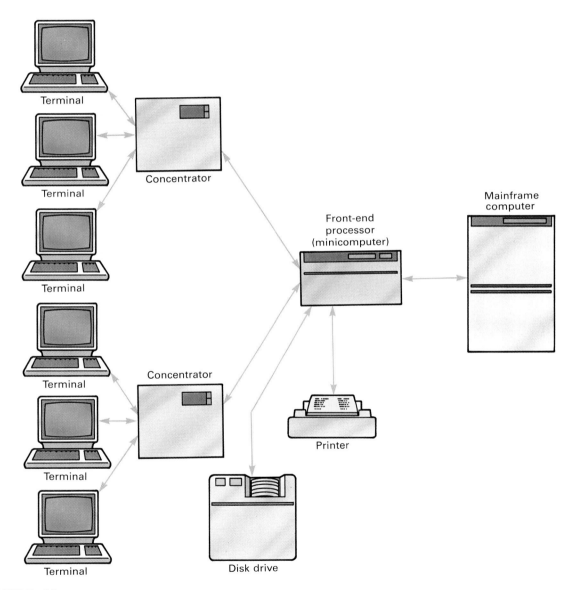

FIGURE 5–10
A front-end processor processes and routes all input and output operations.

more and more. As with micro-to-micro communication, micro-to-mainframe communication can be accomplished with modems and telephone lines or by hard wiring.

However, the connection of microcomputers and mainframes is not so simple because the larger systems use different formats for communication and handle data differently from the way their micro counterparts do. To complicate the problem even further, the communication and data formats used by the various mainframes also differ. Specialized hardware designed for the particular type of computer involved is usually needed to make the data compatible. Before a microcomputer can communicate with a mainframe, three facts must be known: (1) the type of mainframe being linked, (2) the mainframe's specific data format, and (3) the mainframe's specific communication protocols (or handshaking signals).

Common Carriers

A **common carrier** is a company that is licensed and regulated by federal or state government to transmit the data-communication property of others at regulated rates. There are thousands of licensed common carriers of data communications. Three of the largest are American Telephone and Telegraph (AT&T), Western Union, and General Telephone & Electronics (GTE). All common carriers dealing with communications are regulated by the Federal Communications Commission (FCC) and by various state agencies.

Specialized common carriers and value-added carriers are two alternatives to the major common carriers. A **specialized common carrier** is a company that supplies only a limited number of data-communication services. It is usually limited to communication in and between selected areas. MCI Communications, for example, is a specialized common carrier. A **value-added carrier** is a company that leases communication channels from the common carriers and adds extra services over and above those that the common carriers provide. Such services might include electronic mail and voice messaging, information retrieval services, time-sharing, and distributed data processing. Tymnet and Telenet are both value-added carriers.

RATE OF DATA TRANSMISSION

As people become accustomed to the speeds at which computers can transfer data, they seem to want even faster transfer. Information that once took days to receive now seems slow if it has taken a few minutes by computer. The rate at which data are transferred is the **baud rate;** it is the number of times per second that the signal being transmitted changes (modulates or demodulates). Baud is often equated with bits per second (bps); however, that comparison is not entirely accurate because a signal does not always carry one bit.

Although higher speeds are possible, typical data transmission speeds are 300, 1200, 2400, 4800, and 9600 baud. Modems used with microcomputers typically use 300, 1200, or 2400 baud. Larger computer systems used for business communications typically transmit data at speeds of 4800 baud or higher, using high-speed modems. Two factors that determine the rate at which data can be transmitted are the bandwidth of the communication channel and the method of data transmission—asynchronous or synchronous.

Communication Channel Bandwidths

The bandwidth, or grade, of a communication channel determines the rate, or speed, at which data can be transmitted over that channel. The term *bandwidth* is often shortened to *band*. There are three bands of communication channels: narrow-band, voice-band (also called voice-grade), and broad-band.

The slowest of these bands is the **narrow-band channel,** which transmits data at rates between 40 and 100 bps. A telegraph line is a narrow-band channel. A **voice-band channel** can transmit data at rates between 110 and 9600 bps. Telephone lines are voice-band channels. The fastest of these channels is the **broad-band channel,** which can transmit data at rates up to several million bps. Advances in technology will soon allow data to be transmitted on some types of broad-band channels at speeds of more than a billion bps. Microwaves, coaxial cables, and laser beams are broad-band channels.

Asynchronous and Synchronous Transmissions

Asynchronous transmission of data is a method that sends one character at a time. The transfer of data is controlled by start bits and stop bits; thus, each character is surrounded by bits that signal the beginning and the end of the character. These characters allow the receiving terminal to synchronize itself with the transmitting terminal on a character-by-character basis. Asynchronous transmission, the less expensive of the two methods, is often used in low-speed transmission of data in conjunction with narrow-band and some slower voice-band channels (less than 1200 baud) for which the transmitting device operates manually or intermittently.

In **synchronous transmission,** blocks of characters are transmitted in timed sequences. Rather than using start and stop bits around each character, each block of characters is marked with synchronization characters. The receiving device accepts data until it detects a special ending character or a predetermined number of characters, at which time the device knows the message has come to an end.

Synchronous transmission is much faster than asynchronous transmission. It commonly uses the faster voice-band (greater than 1200 baud) and broad-band channels and is usually used when data-transfer requirements exceed several thousand bps. Synchronous transmission is used in the direct computer-to-computer communications of large computer systems because of the high data-transfer speeds required.

The equipment required for synchronous transmission of data is more sophisticated than that needed with asynchronous devices. The special characters used by asynchronous and synchronous transmissions to alert a modem that data are being sent or that transmissions are complete are called **message characters**. Before data are transmitted, however, a set of traffic rules and procedures called **protocol** must be established. The purpose of protocol is to perform such tasks as getting the attention of another device, identifying all the devices involved in the communication, checking to see whether a message has been sent correctly, and initiating any necessary retransmission and/or error recovery. Protocol may vary depending on the devices being used, but the same protocol must be followed by all devices participating in a communication session. Highlight 5–1 takes a look at communication standards. Prearranged signals defining the protocol are sent between computers in an exchange called **handshaking**.

MODES OF TRANSMISSION

The transfer of data over communication channels occurs in three modes: simplex, half-duplex, and full-duplex. In the **simplex mode,** data can be transmitted in only one direction (Figure 5–11a). A device using the simplex mode of transmission can either send or receive data, but it cannot do

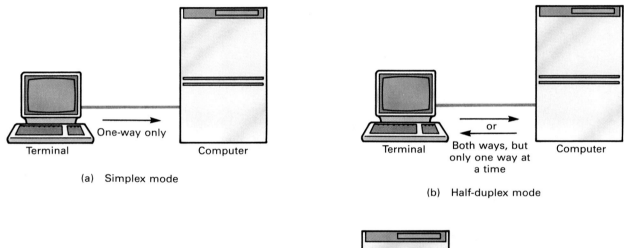

(a) Simplex mode

(b) Half-duplex mode

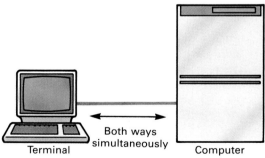

(c) Full-duplex mode

FIGURE 5–11
The transfer of data along a communication line can take place in one of three modes: simplex, half-duplex, or full-duplex.

both. This mode might be used in a burglar alarm system, with the source located in a building and the destination being the local police station. The simplex mode allows no means of feedback to ensure correct interpretation of the received signal. In the burglar alarm example, police officers would have no way of knowing whether the alarm had been set off by a test, a malfunction, or a burglar.

The **half-duplex mode** allows a device to send and receive data but not at the same time. In other words, the transmission of data can occur in only one direction at a time (Figure 5−11b). An example of half-duplex transmission is a citizens band (CB) radio; the user can talk or listen but cannot do both at the same time.

The most sophisticated of these transmission modes is the **full-duplex mode,** which allows a device to receive and send data simultaneously (Figure 5−11c). For example, a telephone system using a full-duplex mode allows the user to talk and listen at the same time. Telephone systems use either the half-duplex or full-duplex mode.

NETWORKS AND DISTRIBUTED DATA PROCESSING

One application of data communication technology is the development of computer networks. A **computer network** is created when several computers and other devices, such as printers and secondary storage devices, are linked by data communication channels. Each computer in a network can have its own processing capabilities and can also share hardware, data files, and programs. The two basic types of networks are wide-area and local-area.

Network Topology

Each computer or device in a network is called a **node**. How these nodes are connected is the network's **topology**. A network can be arranged in one of four different topologies.

Star Network. A **star network** consists of several devices connected to one centralized computer (Figure 5−12). All communications go first through the centralized computer, allowing it to control the operation, workload, and resource allocation of the other computers in the network. For example, a bank with several branch offices would typically use a star network to control and coordinate its branches. The advantage is relative simplicity, but the single-point vulnerability of the network may be a problem. If the central computer breaks down, none of the other computers can communicate with each other.

Ring Network. A **ring network** consists of several devices connected to each other in a closed loop by a single communication channel (Figure 5−13). There is no central or predominant computer in this network. Data must travel around the ring to each station in turn until they arrive at the desired station. A unidirectional ring moves data in one direction only; a bidirectional ring moves data in both directions, but in only one direction

FIGURE 5–12

A star network.

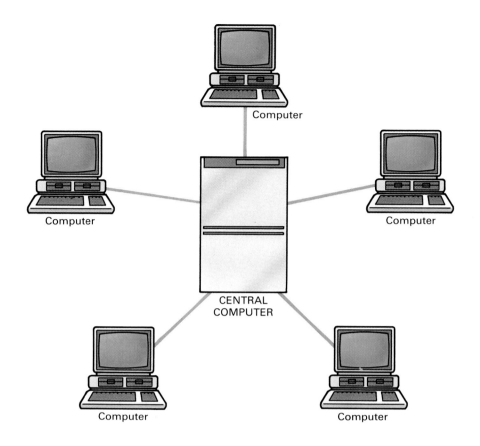

at a time. When one node malfunctions in a bidirectional ring, a message from an adjacent node can usually be sent in the opposite direction, still allowing communication among all the active nodes in the network.

Tree Network. A tree network links computers in a hierarchical fashion and requires data to flow through the branches (Figure 5–14). To move from the computer at Node 1 in Figure 5–14 to Node 7, data would have to go through Nodes 3, 5, and 6 before arriving at 7. One advantage of a tree structure is that functional groupings can be created. For example, one branch could contain all the general ledger terminals, another branch all the accounts receivable terminals, and so on. Also, if one branch stops functioning, the other branches in a tree network are not affected. However, data movement through this network can be slow.

Bus Network. In a **bus network** each computer is connected to a single communication cable via an interface; thus, every computer can communicate directly with every other computer or device in the network (Figure 5–15). Each node is given an address, and a user simply needs to know the address to access a particular node. This topology is frequently used with local-area networks. Going through a hierarchy of nodes is not necessary here, as it is in a tree network.

FIGURE 5–13
A ring network.

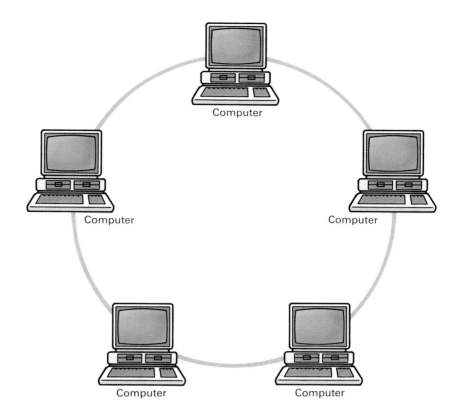

Wide-Area Networks

A **wide-area network (WAN)** consists of two or more computers that are geographically dispersed but are linked by communication facilities provided by common carriers, such as the telephone system or microwave relays. This type of network is often used by large corporations and government agencies to transmit data between geographically dispersed locations. Satellites are often used to transmit data across large distances divided by geographic barriers, such as oceans or mountains. The National Science Foundation (NSF) in Washington, DC, has linked six supercomputers together in a wide-area network that eliminates logistical problems and links schools and research centers around the nation to the supercomputers.

Several methods are used to move data through a wide-area network, including circuit switching, message switching, and packet switching. **Circuit switching** opens up a complete predetermined transmission route from sender to receiver before a message is transmitted. An entire message is then transmitted at once. This method guarantees exclusive use of the transmission route and an uninterrupted message transmission. If all the possible transmission routes to the receiver are being used, the sender must wait for a link to become free.

Message switching also involves sending an entire message at one time over a predetermined transmission route. However, in this case the

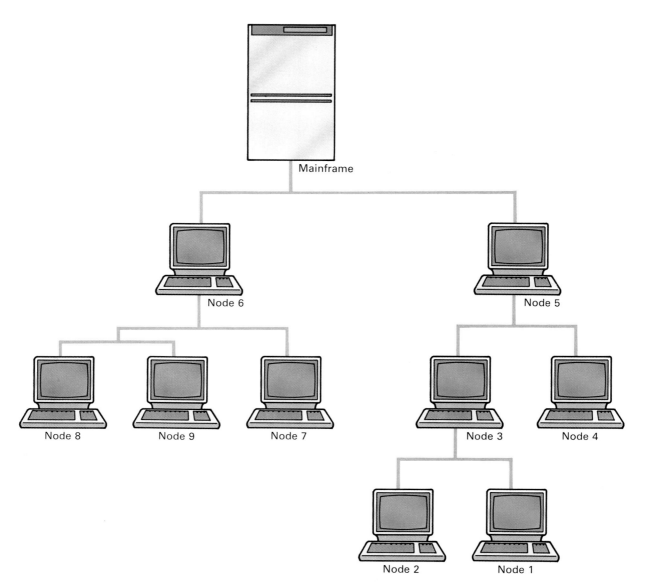

FIGURE 5–14
A tree network.

transmission route is not dedicated to just one message. It is possible that somewhere along the transmission route the message will encounter a portion of the route that is not available. When this happens, the message is temporarily stored. When that part of the route becomes available, the message is removed from storage, and transmission continues.

Packet switching is the most complex of the data movement methods discussed here. Its advantage is that it can increase the utilization of the network, thus decreasing the cost of using the network. In packet switching there is no temporary storage of messages in secondary storage devices.

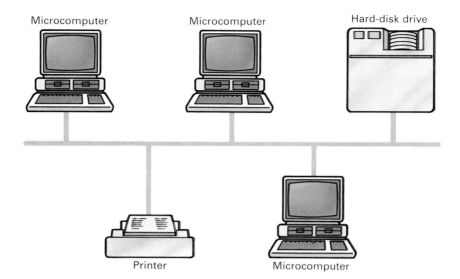

FIGURE 5–15
A bus network.

Instead, messages are divided up into packets, or blocks, of standard size; a single message may be made up of one or more packets. Each packet is sent along a transmission route that is determined in one of two ways. It may be predetermined at the time of transmission, or it may be dynamically determined at transmission time and at each node, depending on the amount of traffic and the availability of portions of transmission routes. Value-added common carriers use packet switching.

Local-Area Networks

A **local-area network (LAN)** consists of two or more computers directly linked within a relatively small, well-defined area, such as a room, building, or cluster of buildings. A LAN may include only microcomputers or any combination of microcomputers and large systems. Popular LANs available for microcomputer users include Ethernet (DEC, Xerox, and others), EtherLink (3Com), StarLAN (AT&T), and Token Ring (IBM).

The difference between a LAN and a multiuser system is that a LAN is made up of stand-alone computers, whereas a multiuser system typically has one computer that is shared among two or more terminals. A LAN usually includes the following:

- two or more computers, one or more of which act as a server, providing file, print, or communication services to other network devices
- peripheral devices, such as printers and hard-disk drives
- software to control the operation of the computers or other devices connected to the LAN
- special twisted-pair, coaxial, or fiber-optic cables to connect the computers and other devices
- a plug-in board to handle the data transmissions (usually when a microcomputer is part of a LAN)

One benefit of a LAN is reduced hardware costs because several computers and users can share peripheral devices, such as laser printers, hard-disk drives, color plotters, and modems. Another advantage is that users can share data and software. LANs also allow an organization to have control over a communication channel without having to deal with common carriers.

The security and privacy of data are two concerns of LAN users. The LAN must get data to the proper destination, transmit the data correctly, and prevent unauthorized users from gaining access to the data. These tasks are accomplished through both the hardware and the LAN software.

Bus and ring topologies are frequently used for LANs. Sometimes a LAN is also implemented in a star network, using an organization's existing telephone switching system in what is called a **private branch exchange (PBX)**. If this network is computer-based, it is often called a **computer branch exchange (CBX)**. A CBX is economical to install since it uses existing telephone wires instead of rewiring a building with other cables. However, because it uses twisted-pair wires, data transmission speeds are slower, and error rates are higher than they would be with coaxial or fiber-optic cables.

LANs also vary in the type and number of computers that can be connected, the speed at which data can be transferred, and the type of software used to control the network. Some LANs require that all computers be of a certain brand, whereas others allow a variety of brands to be connected. The number of computers in a LAN varies widely, from smaller LANs that typically connect 2 to 25 computers to larger LANs that can connect as many as 10,000 computers.

The length of the cable connecting a computer to the network also varies, depending on the LAN. Most LANs allow cables of about 1 thousand feet, but some allow cables of several miles to be used. The data transfer speeds range from several thousand bps to around 50 million bps. The programs that control the LANs also vary in the features they offer. Some programs allow the use of more than one operating system; others allow only one. In some LANs, file access is limited to one user at a time; in others more than one user can access a file simultaneously.

LANs also employ different access methods for devices wanting to gain access to the network. LANs that use a bus topology can use the **carrier sense multiple access (CSMA)** method. With this method a device listens to the channel to sense whether it is in use. If the channel is not being used, the device can send its message. If the channel is in use, the device waits a specified period of time and then checks again to see whether the channel is available. It is possible with this method for two or more devices to send messages at the same time, creating the possibility that messages may collide and become lost or incorrectly transmitted. To avoid this situation, the CSMA method is also available with collision detection capabilities. When these methods are combined, the access method is referred to as **carrier sense multiple access/collision detection (CSMA/D)**.

LANs that use a ring topology often use a **token passing** access method. A **token** is a string of bits that is passed around the network.

Toward a Data Communications Standard

With the growth in importance of data communications in the past decade came an onslaught of new products and vendors. Many of these products had different ways of interconnecting and different protocols. It was becoming nearly impossible to interconnect disparate systems; even individual vendors such as IBM had numerous data communication products that were incompatible with each other. In an effort to bring some standardization to the data communications world, many organizations and vendors began to consider standard models for connecting devices.

The object of standardization was to separate the user from the data communications hardware by letting standardized software serve as an interface. An organization could then change its data communication hardware without changing its programs or retraining the users. In effect, the user might not even realize that there had been a change. The ability to insulate the user from hardware changes has become increasingly important as the pace of technological improvements has continued to soar. Businesses must be able to implement the new technologies needed to stay competitive and gain a strategic edge without the associated costs of changing programs and retraining users.

Two of the first data communications models were IBM's System Network Architecture (SNA) and DEC's DEC Network Architecture (DNA). These and other models were designed primarily to link a vendor's own hardware. In response to the numerous vendor models, the International Standards Organization (ISO) developed the seven-layered Open Systems Interconnect (OSI) model, hoping to standardize the entire industry (Figure A). Both IBM and DEC have said that their models will be compatible with OSI.

The seven layers of the OSI model describe what happens when a terminal communicates with a computer or when a computer communicates with another computer. The model provides a set of standards that define a common language with which computers and terminals can talk to each other over a network. Protocols describe how the data are to be transferred between different parts of the model.

Let's briefly examine each of the seven layers. First, there's the physical layer, which enables the electrical connections and signaling to take place. This layer is made up of wiring and cables, such as twisted-pair wiring, coaxial cable, RS–232C cables, and fiber-optic strands. All communication signals from higher levels travel through the physical layer.

The second layer, or data-link layer, is responsible for controlling the data stream between the sending and receiving nodes. Its job is to string characters together into messages, check them for errors, and start their transmission. It also checks to see whether the message arrives at its destination, and it initiates any necessary retransmission. Many

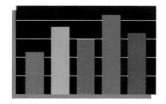

different protocols are used in this layer including High-Level Data-Link Control (HLDLC), bisynchronous, and Advanced Data Communications Control Procedures (ADCCP). The data-link functions for PC-based communications are usually performed by special integrated circuits that reside on an interface card. In larger systems these functions are performed by separate software.

The third layer, or network layer, determines the physical pathway the data will take when they are communicated. This decision is based on network conditions, priorities of service, and other factors.

The transport layer is the fourth layer of the OSI model. Its functions include looking for alternate routes or saving transmitted data in the event the network fails. It's also responsible for quality control of data received; data are checked for proper order and format. A popular protocol used in the transport layer by many PC-based networks is the Transmission Control Protocol (TCP).

The fifth layer, or session layer, initiates, maintains, and terminates each session. It allows two applications or two pieces of the same application to communicate across the network and is responsible for such functions as logging, administration, name recognition, and security. NetBIOS and Advanced Program-to-Program Communications (APPC) are two commonly used session-layer software products; programs such as these reside in every network station and pass calls between application programs in the network.

The presentation layer is the sixth layer, and its function is to format data so that they can be used by the application program or communication device. This layer controls such screen features as blinking characters, reverse video, special data-entry formats, and graphics. It may also control encryption and other special file formatting. All control codes, special graphics, and character sets reside in this layer. The operation of printers, plotters, and other peripherals is also controlled by the software in this layer.

The seventh and final layer is the application layer. The network operating system and application programs reside in this layer and are directly controlled by the user.

Each layer in this model performs a service for the layer above it. The bottom three layers are concerned only with data transmission from one node to the next, that is, moving the message from one end of the network (the sender) to the other (the receiver). Levels 4 through 7 allow the host node and user node to "talk" to each other.

Standards were motivated by the proliferation of data communication products and by user demands to interconnect different types and brands of computer equipment and systems. The advent of standards has begun a movement in the right direction. However, the number of emerging standards can still leave a user confused. Even

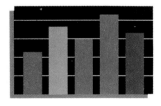

within the OSI standard much work still needs to be done to define the details of each layer. Barriers to the successful completion of the OSI standard include the political battles being waged over whose ideas should prevail. Much more work is still needed, and only time will tell which standards will become standard.

FIGURE A
The seven-layered OSI model for network communications.

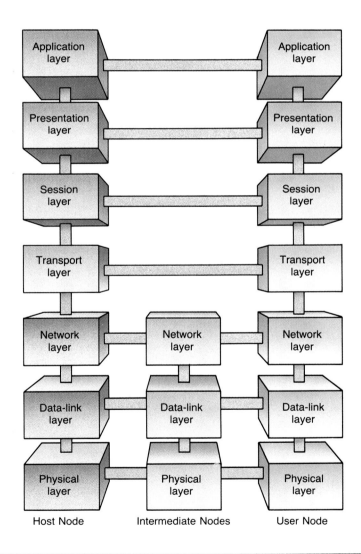

When a device wants to transmit a message, it must wait for a token. When a token appears, the device holds the token and then transmits its message. When the device is finished transmitting, it returns the token to the network. With only one token, message collisions do not occur. This method is most effective if the volume of network traffic is high; it ensures that use of the network will be balanced among all the devices. However, if traffic is low, devices on the network must still wait for a token before they can transmit, even if the network is available.

LANs can be connected to WANs through the use of gateways. A **gateway** is an interface that converts the data codes, formats, addresses, and transmission rates of one network into a form usable by another network.

Choosing a LAN. You may someday be faced with the task of selecting a LAN; they are widely used in business, small offices, churches, civic organizations, clinics, and so on. The selection task can be very difficult and confusing, given the number of LANs available. Current and future needs must be examined, as well as corporate strategy and user needs. The following questions are a start in the right direction.

Is it easy to install the LAN?

How long will it take to install it?

How many copies of documentation are provided for the operation of the LAN?

Can the documentation be easily understood?

Does the network cabling fit in with existing cabling?

How expensive is the cabling, and how much will be needed?

How many devices can be attached to the LAN?

Will each device need a network adaptor card?

What is the cost of network adaptor cards?

What different brands of PCs can be attached to the LAN?

What are the costs for each node?

Can other nodes be added easily at a later time?

Must one device be dedicated solely as the LAN controller?

How far from the file server can the printer be?

What other customers are using this vendor's LAN?

Is call-in service available?

How much does that service cost?

How quickly can this vendor respond to problems?

Can the LAN support existing software for multiusers?

If not, what application software will be required?

What will be the cost of upgrading software to a LAN version?

What password and security features are available?

Can the LAN software compile audit trails to account for the usage of each node?

Will the bandwidth support the anticipated traffic effectively?

What are the expected transfer and response-time speeds?

Are electronic mail and messaging features available?

Clearly, choosing a LAN is a very complex and difficult project. Often a private consultant is hired to help in the selection.

Distributed Data Processing

Distributed data processing (DDP) is a concept of dispersing into areas where they are used the computers, devices, software, and data that are connected by communication channels. The computers are distributed by function and geographical boundaries and work together as a cohesive system to support user requirements. DDP contrasts with a centralized system, where all data-processing resources are in one location. Typically, a centralized system has one large general-purpose computer with many terminals attached to it. Even though the centralized computer can do many tasks, it may not do many of them in the most efficient or cost-effective way. A DDP system allows many smaller, more specialized computers to be tailored to complete a particular task(s) efficiently and cost-effectively.

Three advantages of using DDP are cost-efficiency; user-controlled computing facilities, resulting in shorter response times; and shared resources. In the past the hardware costs of computing represented a major argument for not using DDP. However, most components in a computer system have decreased in cost and improved in performance, while the cost of using communication channels has not decreased as much. Consequently, many organizations have discovered that distributing computers and data storage to local areas can actually save them money by decreasing their use of expensive communication channels. In addition, because a DDP network allows remote sites to share equipment and data via telecommunications, proper management and control of the DDP system can reduce redundancy of both.

DDP has also become popular because users gain more control over individual information system needs. Users no longer have to count on a centralized computer staff that attempts to fulfill everyone else's needs. A DDP system typically uses many minicomputers and microcomputers, which are not as complicated and do not require as much maintenance as a larger, centralized system. Users of the smaller systems access them directly and take advantage of their full power. Nonetheless, for tasks such as managing extremely large and complicated databases, mainframes still play a vital role in many DDP systems.

Response times for many applications are also shorter in a DDP because there are fewer users and, thus, fewer demands on the system. The concept of distributing management is referred to as decentralized management. When a DDP system has its management decentralized, it is often referred to as a fully distributed system. Of course, there are varying degrees of both DDP and decentralized management.

Another advantage of DDP is that users share equipment, software, and data with other computers in the DDP system in order to meet their total information needs. For example, not all sites would need to maintain their own databases and database management software but could share these resources with other sites through telecommunication links.

On the other hand, DDP brings with it several disadvantages as well. First, problems can occur with a DDP system if it is not managed properly. If organizational control over data-processing resources is lost, management will have difficulty controlling costs and maintaining standards throughout the distributed areas of the organization.

A second problem that can arise is a redundancy of resources and data. Without proper management and control, each distributed site may try to develop information systems to meet all of the site's needs, and several systems that are the same, or nearly the same, may result. This duplicity can lead to higher hardware and software costs than would exist if the distributed sites shared these resources. Uncontrolled data redundancy can lead to differences in data among the distributed sites, causing discrepancies in reports. This problem can be difficult and expensive to resolve.

Third, if the distributed sites do not coordinate their selection of hardware and software, compatibility problems can arise. Different protocols at certain distributed sites may result in the inability of that hardware to communicate with hardware at other distributed sites. Designing software to solve compatibility problems can be time-consuming and costly.

A fourth problem can occur if a site falls under the control of untrained and inexperienced users, resulting in poor selection of hardware and software, inferior programming techniques, and little, if any, documentation. This circumstance can lead to a costly and overly complex system or, in some cases, to a system that is inappropriate for the job.

Finally, obtaining timely support for a computer system can be difficult at some distributed sites because they are too far from the vendor's or the organization's support staff. However, maintaining a separate support staff at each location may be too expensive for some organizations.

DDP is not appropriate for all situations. Large, centralized computing systems are still essential in some cases. However, many applications can be completed more efficiently and cost-effectively with distributed systems. To ensure that DDP meets an organization's needs, both central management and dispersed users should be integrally involved in the design of the system. Its success or failure ultimately depends on management planning, commitment, and control as well as user acceptance.

DATA COMMUNICATION AT WORK

In everyday situations the use of data communication is not without its challenges. Many computer systems are incompatible with each other and cannot easily establish communication linkages. Highlight 5−2 examines the issue of connectivity. In addition, data sent over communication channels are subject to various kinds of interference, which may alter or destroy some of the data. The privacy of data must also be protected. In this regard, passwords and access codes may be helpful. However, to prevent unauthorized access to highly sensitive data, they may have to be encrypted, or scrambled, before they are sent. Then, of course, they must be decoded or unscrambled when they are received.

Despite these concerns, however, numerous businesses make extensive use of telecommunication systems. One of the earliest and biggest success stories was that of American Hospital Supply Corporation and its installation of order-entry terminals on hospital premises in 1974. Hospitals could then simply enter or check the status of an order at any time.

Today Federal Express uses a parcel-tracking system it calls Cosmos. This on-line system enables inquiries about a parcel's status to be made from remote locations. In addition, it locates delayed shipments and automatically sends invoices to customers. The Federal Express delivery vans are even equipped with on-board terminals to improve customer service. With the use of telecommunications, drivers can call the Cosmos system directly and receive answers to customers' questions about package whereabouts.

On-line reservation systems have also revolutionized the travel industry, from car rentals to hotels to airlines. All of these organizations, as well as travel agencies, send and receive information on reservations and flight schedules through data communication channels. American Airlines' Sabre and United Airlines' Apollo are two of the largest reservation systems.

Many of the stories in newspapers and magazines are filed by journalists in remote locations, using portable computers and data communication channels. Many supermarket merchants and other retailers have their cash registers linked to their store's large computer in a remote location, to keep track of inventories.

Information systems technologies are also being used to automate and standardize the transactions between retailers and their suppliers. **Electronic data interchange (EDI)** is a communications protocol being used to achieve this. Its purpose is to allow retailers and their suppliers to conduct business transactions electronically instead of manually. It reduces the amounts of paperwork, human involvement, and time associated with processing a single order. Currently purchase order, invoice, advanced ship notice, inventory advice, and price/sales catalog applications have been developed. Mervyn's, a retailer in Hayward, California, reports that turnaround time for delivery of goods has decreased from a week to a day. Mervyn's is currently linked to 130 suppliers.

Electronic funds transfer (EFT), the electronic movement of money among accounts, is another widely used data communication application. A large portion of money in the business and financial community changes hands through EFT. One popular form of EFT is the automated teller machine. In fact, Society for Worldwide Interbank Financial Telecommunications (SWIFT), the most sophisticated private interbank system in the world, averages 750,000 transactions daily for 1,300 member banks in 46

Sometime after the onset of personal computers in the corporate world, organizations began noticing that little isolated islands of computing power were cropping up everywhere—from the corporate mainframes stuck in the back room, to departmental minicomputers, to an ever-growing number of personal computers on desktops. Often the disparate systems were the result of mergers that had incorporated technology from two different companies. With this realization came the notion that it would be great if all these computers, no matter what brand or model, could be linked to each other so that data and peripherals could be easily shared electronically. From this dream arose the concept of a three-tiered information system, in which personal computers were linked to departmental minicomputers, which were then linked to the corporate mainframe. In this model, data could travel throughout an organization.

The ability of different brands and models of computers to connect and share data and peripherals through data communication links was called connectivity. Like most buzzwords, *connectivity* tends to have slightly different meanings, depending on whom you ask. Simply accomplishing the physical links has been referred to as connectivity. However, ideal connectivity also implies that data transfers and the conversions needed to accomplish that kind of data sharing are transparent to the user, that is, do not require user attention to details. In other words, with ideal connectivity almost anyone within an organization can easily have immediate access to any piece of data, no matter where it is located. The intent behind the concept is that if corporate decision makers can have up-to-the-minute information from all pertinent areas, productivity will increase, and the company will gain a substantial competitive advantage.

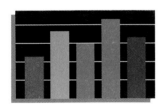

countries. After it is upgraded, the system's mainframe and communication network will process one million messages daily. Right now, approximately 1500 member banks in 46 states use the Cirrus banking network to process some 200 million transactions annually. The network provides such services as cash withdrawals and balance inquiries for checking, savings, and credit accounts and supports more than 6,500 automated teller machines.

Some companies have even adopted a method of employment, called **telecommuting,** that permits some personnel to work at home and use their own computers to communicate with an office computer. **Electronic mail** is a system used by computers and communication channels to store and send messages. Many businesses use electronic-mail systems to reduce paperwork and save the time it takes a message to reach its destination. A special form of electronic mail is facsimile. A **facsimile (FAX) machine**

Although the concept of connectivity sounds logical and simple on the surface, there are several problems that must be faced. Most companies have computers and data communication hardware from several different vendors or must communicate with other organizations that have different systems. Establishing communication links between disparate systems can be very difficult and costly because most computers were designed with little or no thought toward efficient data sharing. What exists is a jumble of communication protocols, programs, architectures, facilities, and standards. Currently, attempts are being made to develop standards that will allow greater connectivity. One such attempt is the Integrated Services Digital Network (ISDN). ISDN is a set of international standards designed to allow voice, data, facsimile, and video communication between disparate systems via a digital network using standard telephone lines.

Beyond these problems of creating the necessary physical links, corporate policies are also a stumbling block to achieving connectivity. In most organizations the information systems department is reluctant to give up any control of corporate information. In addition, there is a question as to whether certain individuals really need to have ready access to all or most corporate data and information. The fear is that problems of data security and data integrity will multiply as users are given more access to corporate data.

Thus, the benefits of connectivity are not always clear-cut for every organization. In many areas the need for users to communicate is not immediate enough to warrant a major system changeover. Connectivity, although appropriate for many organizations, is not a cure-all for every situation. As solutions to the physical links become less expensive and attitudes change, the concept of connectivity should find its proper place.

allows a user to digitize text, graphics, and photos and send them to another location electronically.

Information, database, and videotext services would not exist without data communications. These services use data communication so that their subscribers can access one or several large computers containing data banks on various topics. The services can be accessed easily from microcomputers equipped with the proper communication hardware and software. An **information service** is a business that supplies subscribers with information on numerous general-interest topics by using powerful, large computer systems that store millions of pieces of data. Information services require a subscription and payment of hourly access charges. Some may also require an initial sign-on fee.

The topics covered vary among the information services. Typical information offered by most of the services includes news, sports, weather, business, finance, and investment. Some also offer computerized shopping; games; teleconferencing facilities; forums on computers and computing; airline information; theater, restaurant, and hotel guides; on-line encyclopedias; word-processing capabilities; and computer programs. Several popular information services are The Source, CompuServe, Delphi, and Dow Jones News Retrieval.

In addition to information about general topics, commercial **database services** offer information on highly specialized topics. These services are collections of large-scale databases that contain millions of articles, abstracts, and bibliographic citations from thousands of books, periodicals, reports, and theses. A subscriber is permitted to search these collections electronically for needed information.

Several popular commercial database services are Dialog, Bibliographic Retrieval System (BRS), and NewsNet. The largest commercial database service is Dialog, a subsidiary of Lockheed Corporation; it offers approximately 200 databases. Topics include agriculture, business and economics, chemistry, current affairs, education, energy and environment, law and government, medicine and biosciences, science and technology, social sciences and humanities, and much more.

Some commercial databases are totally dedicated to special interests and can be subscribed to individually. For example, LEXIS, a specialized database of legal information, is offered by Mead Data Central. Many databases found in major commercial services also exist as stand-alone databases and can be subscribed to individually.

A **gateway service** buys large quantities of connect time at wholesale rates from an information or commercial database service and then resells the time to its own subscribers at retail rates. With one call to a gateway service, a subscriber can connect to several different services. A subscription to a gateway service waives the sign-up or monthly minimum fees charged by individual services. Charges are then made for only the actual connect time to each service at the service's regular rates. The Business Computer Network (BCN) is one popular gateway service; Searchlink is another.

Videotext is an interactive information service similar to other information services, but it uses color displays and graphics. The services discussed thus far transmit and receive data as text and have no graphic capabilities. Videotext is designed to heighten the appeal to and interest level of the information consumer with color and graphics. Users are required to have computer systems that display color and graphics.

France has had particular success with videotext systems. The government-controlled telephone system in that country funded the cost of the color/graphics terminals for those who wanted the system and met certain requirements. The telephone company did this primarily to help increase telephone usage. Services such as on-line banking and shopping are available.

Data communication has made the computer one of the most vital tools in our information-seeking society. It links two or more computers and enables users to send and receive electronic data with little regard for time or distance.

SUMMARY

Data communication is the process of sending data electronically from one point to another. Using communication facilities such as the telephone system and microwave relays to send data between computers is a type of data communication often referred to as telecommunications.

The transmission of data takes one of two forms: analog or digital. Analog data transmission is the passage of data in a continuous waveform. Digital data transmission passes data in distinct on and off pulses.

Modulation is the process of converting a digital signal into an analog signal. Demodulation is the process of converting an analog signal into a digital signal. A modem (*mo*dulator-*dem*odulator) is the device that converts the signals.

A communication channel is the pathway along which data are transmitted between devices. The three basic types of communication channels are wire cable, microwave, and fiber optics.

Multiplexing is the process of combining the transmissions of several computers or other devices so that the transmissions can share the same communication channel. Concentration allows a communication channel to be connected to and serve more devices than the capacity of that channel normally allows. A front-end processor is a computer that handles all data communication control functions, freeing the CPU of a main computer to work on other tasks.

Data communication has allowed the linking of microcomputer to microcomputer and microcomputer to mainframe so that data and capabilities can be shared.

Common carriers are companies that are licensed and regulated to transmit the data communication property of others. Specialized common carriers and value-added carriers are two alternatives to the major common carriers for data communications.

The baud rate of a communication channel is the number of times per second that the transmitted signal changes (modulates or demodulates). The bandwidth, or band, of a communication channel determines the speed at which that channel can transmit data.

Asynchronous transmission transmits data one character at a time. Synchronous transmission transmits data as a block of characters in timed sequences. Protocol is the set of rules and procedures defining the technical details of data transfer between two devices. Data transfer can occur in three modes: simplex, half-duplex, and full-duplex.

A computer network is created when several computers and other devices, such as printers and secondary storage devices, are linked together by data communication channels. Each computer or device in a network is called a node. The way in which these nodes are connected together is the network's topology. Network topologies include a star network, ring network, tree (hierarchical) network, and bus network.

A wide-area network (WAN) consists of two or more computers that are geographically dispersed but are linked by communication facilities provided by common carriers, such as the telephone system or microwave relays. A local-area network (LAN) consists of two or more computers directly linked within a small, well-defined area, such as a room, building, or cluster of buildings. LANs can be connected to WANs through the use of gateways, which convert the data codes, formats, addresses, and transmission rates of one network into a form that is usable by another network.

Distributed data processing (DDP) is the concept of dispersing into the areas where they are used the computers, devices, software, and data that are connected through communication channels. The computers are organized on a functional and geographical basis and work together as a cohesive system to support user requirements.

Data communication has allowed computers to share data in spite of the boundaries of time or distance and has found many applications in our society, including information services, database services, electronic funds transfer, electronic mail, facsimile (FAX) machines, telecommuting, reservation systems, and other business systems.

MINICASE 5–1

Mary Peterson is the manager of information services for a small clothing manufacturer that is beginning to experience some growth. All company data—accounting, financial, sales, and personnel—are gathered and processed on the firm's minicomputer. Mary receives constant complaints from all the other managers about how much time is required to receive information. Even the managers who carpool with Mary each day kid her about the "snail department."

During the last 2 years, most of the company's managers have acquired desktop computers, which they use primarily to analyze financial data on spreadsheets. The two shared printers have to be wheeled around on a cart from office to office and are often hidden in two of the managers' offices. Many of the managers keep their own databases on topics that concern them, such as product descriptions and prices; sales data; supplier addresses, prices, and terms; and employee information.

Often, reports from different managers have contained conflicting information because one manager may not have been informed of a change or may have failed to update his or her database. The plant manager once roared, "No two people ever give me the same answer to a question—does anyone know what's going on in this company?" As the company has grown, these problems have worsened. In fact, they have become so bad that managers are frequently making decisions without all the required information or with incorrect information. As a result, the company's growth and profit potential are now in jeopardy.

Today, the plant manager told Mary that she needs to find a way to improve the timeliness, reliability, and integrity of the information she sends to the managers. And she must accomplish these improvements with only a modest increase in her small budget, building any solutions around the current staff and computer equipment.

1. Are the managers' desktop computers a waste? Why or why not?
2. What specific data communication solution would help Mary with her problem?

Business Computer Systems

3. Are the two printers adequate? Explain.

4. What problems would be solved if a LAN linked all the microcomputers and the minicomputers? What problems would not be solved?

MINICASE 5–2

The North Shore Medical Center is a large research and teaching hospital. It consists of eight separate buildings that cover five city blocks in a downtown area. The hospital administrators have expressed concern over the billing of patients for services. Often as many as 9 days pass before patients' charges are brought over to the hospital data center and entered. This delay causes late billing of both patients and insurance firms so that a typical patient charge is not paid until 40 days after the service was rendered.

In addition, patients often see several doctors and have numerous tests in various locations of the hospital. The physicians would like better communication of patient data, which they need for diagnosis and treatment. The hospital uses a mainframe in its data center for administrative processing, and every physician currently has a microcomputer in his or her area.

1. Suggest a communications strategy that could solve the hospital's problems. Defend your choice.

2. For the strategy suggested in Question 1, what are some of the concerns that the hospital manager of information systems should address before choosing the hardware and software needed to implement the strategy?

Key Terms

acoustic modem

analog data transmission

asynchronous transmission

bandwidth

baud rate

broad-band channel

bus network

carrier sense multiple access (CSMA)

carrier sense multiple access/collision detection (CSMA/D)

circuit switching

common carrier

communication channel

computer branch exchange

computer network

concentration

concentrator

contention

database service

data communication

demodulation

digital data transmission

distributed data processing (DDP)

electronic data interchange (EDI)

electronic mail

external direct-connect modem

facsimile (FAX) machine

fiber optics

frequency-division multiplexing

front-end processor

full-duplex mode

gateway

gateway service

half-duplex mode

handshaking

information service

internal direct-connect modem

local-area network (LAN)

message characters

message switching

micro-to-mainframe link

micro-to-micro link

microwave

modem

modulation

multiplexer

multiplexing

multipoint channel configuration

narrow-band channel

node

null modem

packet switching

point-to-point channel configuration

polling

private branch exchange

protocol

ring network

simplex mode

specialized common carrier

star network

statistical time-division multiplexing

synchronous transmission

telecommunication

telecommuting

time-division multiplexing

token

token passing

topology

tree network

value-added carrier

videotext

voice-band channel

wide-area network (WAN)

wire cable

Review Questions

1. How does data communication differ from telecommunications?
2. Describe the difference between analog and digital data transmission.
3. When is a modem needed? Why would two modems be needed?
4. Why do most portable computers use internal direct-connect modems?
5. Describe the purpose of a communication channel.
6. What advantages have fiber optics as a communication channel?
7. Sketch how a point-to-point channel configuration works.
8. Describe how the polling process operates.
9. What is the process called in which each terminal monitors the communication channel to see whether it is available?
10. Describe the function of a multiplexer, and briefly describe the three different types of multiplexing discussed here.
11. Describe the process of concentration.
12. What is the function of a front-end processor?
13. List three factors that must be known in order for a microcomputer to communicate with a large-system computer.
14. What is a common carrier?
15. Define *baud rate*. How does it relate to bits per second?

16. What are the three bandwidths of communication channels? Discuss their differences.

17. Describe the difference between asynchronous and synchronous transmission of data.

18. Describe protocol.

19. List and describe the three modes in which data transfer can occur.

20. What is a computer network?

21. Name and describe the four different network topologies.

22. Define wide-area network and local-area network.

23. Explain distributed data processing, and discuss some possible advantages and disadvantages.

24. What is required to connect a LAN to another network?

25. How might you, via electronic communication, find out more about communications? Explain.

APPLICATION MODULE
Finance Information Systems

The major responsibilities of the finance function can be categorized in three activities:

1. determining how much funding is needed and when in order to meet a firm's goals and obligations
2. determining the best source(s) from which to obtain needed funds
3. determining how excess funds should be maintained and/or invested for the greatest benefit

These three activities require planning information, much of which can be obtained from a company's bread-and-butter applications—the transaction processing systems described in detail in Chapter 7. Here we will only highlight the information that is available from those applications and will examine how that information is used to support higher-level decision making within the finance function. Table A shows some of the finance-related data that can be obtained from the various transaction processing systems.

The higher-level decisions in this functional area relate to financial planning, which is supported by forecasting and funds management, and to financial control, which is supported by auditing.

FINANCIAL PLANNING

Finance managers must know where their companies are going in both the long and the short run. Transaction processing systems supply valuable information regarding today's activities, but financial planning tasks are future-oriented. Budgets for the various units (departments) are the financial plans that can give managers this future-oriented information. Either short-term (less than 1 year) or long-term department budgets can be rolled together to formulate an overall company budget, which then presents an estimate of future income and expenses for a specified time period. Financial managers use this information in their forecast of the future cash needs and surpluses of their companies.

Forecasting

Financial forecasts, or intelligent predictions of future cash positions, cover short-term time frames of, say, 90 days and long-term time frames of 10 years or more. There are, of course, different forecasts for each time frame, but each one tells when a firm is likely to need additional cash or may have surplus cash. Col-

TABLE A
Financial information available from transaction processing systems.

Transaction Processing System	Information
Billing	Number of units sold
Accounts payable	Money owed to others
Accounts receivable	Money others owe to firm
Payroll	Cost of labor
Inventory	Cost of manufacturing
Notes payable	Amount of money borrowed

lege students make similar, though less formalized, forecasts for each school year. For example, you and your financial supporters know that there may be a cash deficit associated with registration, books, and housing at the beginning of the semester, whereas there may be surplus cash at the end of the school year when housing and utility deposits are returned and perhaps some textbooks are sold. Financial forecasts are made more precise with the use of statistical models, which examine past data regarding such things as seasonal fluctuations (e.g., Christmas sales) and longer-term fluctuations (trends) and then suggest what values similar data will have in the future.

Forecasting cash flows is particularly important to firms since they must have enough cash on hand to pay employees, stockholders, and creditors at given points in time. An accurate estimate of the cash flow also aids a financial manager in planning for a firm's goals that require cash outlays. Financial managers use cash flow models to forecast cash surpluses and deficits over time. Such models are necessary because a firm must usually purchase inventories and pay employees before products are sold and money is collected. Cash outflows prior to cash

inflows result in an inevitable time lag. A computer, with financial modeling and statistical software, is an essential tool to experiment with changes in conditions that may affect cash flow models. Examples include the interest rate at which money can be borrowed, the length of time customers take to pay their bills, the costs of supplies used in the manufacturing process, and the costs of equipment and labor. Figure A shows the kinds of information used as input to and received as output from a cash flow model.

Although a substantial part of the data required for the cash flow model can be gathered from the information systems in Table A, not all of it can. First of all, financial statements produced by a firm's accounting system often present information on an accrual basis so that debts, prepayments, accounts receivable, and other transactions that have not yet affected a cash position are included. In addition, accounting statements include noncash expenditures, such as depreciation, which are not directly applicable to cash flow. Other data will need to be created, based on intelligent guesses or statistical estimates. The computer's special talent in this area is its ability to accept changes in given figures, quickly recompute how other figures

FIGURE A
A financial cash flow model.

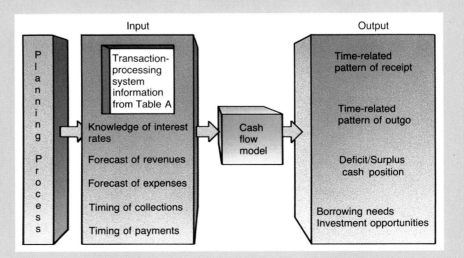

may have been affected by those changes, and apply time-tested mathematical techniques (e.g., exponential smoothing) to a stream of historical data in order to yield highly accurate future predictions.

Forecasting software packages use a variety of preprogrammed statistical techniques and formulas to turn historical data into a best guess at future values. Although human skill is valuable in forecasting tasks, human efficiency and effectiveness can be enhanced with software designed for financial modeling tasks. Execucom Corporation makes a widely used decision support system (DSS) for financial modeling; it is called an interactive financial planning system (IFPS), and it performs these tasks quite well.

Snapshots of Financial Health. Financial ratios provide clues to financial managers regarding the financial health of their firms. Ratios are quickly computed formulas that suggest how a firm is performing in a narrow area. For example, the average collection period ratio is equal to the accounts receivable figure divided by the average daily sales figure. The computed ratio indicates the average length of time between a sale and payment.

Ratios alone do not supply quick-fix answers to questions about what might be right or wrong with a firm's operations; instead, they supply information that can point to the source of a problem and indicate areas that require further analysis. A financial analysis can use more than 25 ratios, which fall under various general headings: operating performance, profitability, trading, common stock, credit analysis, liquidity, and activity. Some financial software packages not only automatically compute key ratios from accounting data, but also compare a firm's ratios with the average ratios for other firms within the same industry. FISCAL, which is used in business and education, is such a package.

Funds Management

Once a cash flow model has been generated to show when funds will be needed or will become available, funds management becomes the next planning task. Funds management examines two possible scenarios: insufficient cash and excess cash. In the first situation some possible plans are to borrow from a lending institution, sell bonds, or issue stock. Each of these activities has pluses and minuses, and each depends on the time frame for implementation. Financial managers faced with these decisions often use simulation techniques—that is, they pretend to choose each of the options and follow it through a variety of external economic variables, such as interest rates, tax rates, possible tax advantages, and so on. Here, too, a computer's strength in number crunching and recapitulation proves to be a valuable asset. Again, since these tasks are common to many firms, there are a number of preprogrammed software packages that are geared toward this type of decision making. Some financial managers use spreadsheets with formulas that they themselves have created.

The second situation is certainly preferred, but it, too, must be examined carefully—in light of given time constraints, the risk tolerance of top management, and the firm's liquidity needs (i.e., the ease and speed with which the investment can be converted to cash). A responsibility of the financial manager is to make as much from investment as possible while at the same time protecting the firm against unanticipated future events.

Auditing

The control function of financial managers is carried out through auditing. Audits are periodic examinations to determine whether procedures governing the processing and handling of money have been established and are being followed.

Audits can be performed by financial personnel within a firm (internal audits) or by professionals outside a firm (external audits). Audits are required for some firms but are recommended even when they are not required; they have frequently uncovered illegal and costly misdeeds as well as weak controls. Auditing also extends to computer processing of money transactions, an area with tremendous potential for mismanagement.

Whether internal or external, audits fall into two general areas: financial and procedural. Financial audits examine how cash and noncash transactions are recorded and processed. Financial audits answer such questions as, What documents (or other information) are available to show why an accounting entry was recorded as it was? Do the financial statements prepared by the firm accurately portray the true financial picture of the firm? Procedural audits, on the other hand, focus on how people perform certain tasks in their work environments to safeguard the assets of the organization. For example, a good cash-handling procedure would require one person to record the firm's cash deposits and another person to actually make those deposits in the bank. Separation of duties makes it more difficult, although not impossible, to mishandle cash without being detected.

Auditing responsibilities have become more difficult in the computer age and will continue to become more troublesome as the computer integrates financial information with information from different functional areas. Whereas paper documents provided written evidence of transactions in the past, many of today's transactions are keyed directly into a computer as a result of voice mail and other technologies. Thus, there is no paper audit trail to verify the accuracy of transactions. This problem is compounded because the computer manipulates much of its data in a "black box" environment: an auditor cannot really see what is going on inside the computer. In larger firms that are subject to massive complications if transactions are mishandled, these problems have prompted the creation of a position known as electronic data processing (EDP) auditor.

EDP auditors have special requirements for performing their work. Not only must they have a sound background in accounting, but they must also have considerable knowledge of the way in which computers process transaction data. Computer systems can be audited in two different modes: around the computer and through the computer. Auditing around the computer makes the sometimes-dangerous assumption that what goes on inside the computer must be right if the data going in look right and the data coming out look right. The fallacy of this approach is seen in the classic information-processing story of a computer programmer who wrote a program to round off the pennies from each employee's paycheck and insert the overage into his own check. The total payroll figures always balanced, and any employees who noticed the change believed that the figures in their own checks reflected only mathematical shortcomings, not programmed stealing.

Auditing through the computer typically uses test-case data as input to the computer. An examination then takes place of various files and documents to see whether they reflect that data. Many special software packages are available to help EDP auditors examine a firm's computer systems.

INTEGRATED FINANCIAL SOFTWARE

Financial managers are making extensive use of PCs and a number of generic software packages to analyze and report their firm's financial data. Data that are the most valuable to them are often contained in the corporate mainframes. To bridge the gap between where the data are located and where they can be used by financial planners, many companies are purchasing micro-mainframe link programs, which facilitate data communication between PCs and mainframes.

Integrated financial software packages, which share a common pool of financial data across different applications, are being created to accommodate foreign currency exchange, fixed asset accounting, cash management, and credit management, along with already-existing tie-ins to general ledger systems. Cullinet, a major software vendor, is even installing embedded artificial intelligence capabilities into its integrated financial software systems. Financial software is a big-ticket item. Information Systems of America in Atlanta received an award for $5 million of sales in 1 year for its PRISM investment management and accounting software package. PRISM's individual price tag is $400,000 to $2 million, based on the assets to be managed.

The sophistication required to manage finances in today's competitive business arena demands the use of a computer. Firms that continue to do financial planning, forecasting, and funds management without the aid of information technology will surely lose ground to those who surge ahead with quicker, more reliable, and more flexible computer-supported financial information systems.

Knight, Robert. 1987. Financial software permeates corporations. *Software News* (August), pp. 20–40.

Snyder, Christy. 1987. Artificial intelligence proves itself in business. *Business Software Review* (August), pp. 44–48.

PART THREE

Business
Information
Systems

File and Database Organization and Access

OBJECTIVES

- Understand the data storage hierarchy
- Understand the difference between batch processing and real-time processing
- Explain the difference between transaction files and master files
- Discuss when to use sequential files, direct-access files, and indexed sequential files
- Identify techniques to capture data entry errors
- Describe the difference between file management and database management
- Identify the advantages and disadvantages of the three database models and of database management systems in general
- Identify database design considerations
- Explain the function of a database administrator

OUTLINE

DATA HIERARCHY IN FILES
Bits and Bytes ǀ Fields ǀ Records ǀ
Files ǀ Databases
FILE TYPES
Master File ǀ Transaction File ǀ
History File ǀ Report, Input, and Output Files ǀ Print
File ǀ Backup File ǀ Sort File
FILE STORAGE AND ACCESS
Sequential-Access File Processing ǀ Direct-Access
File Processing ǀ Indexed Sequential File
Processing
DATA ENTRY MODES
On-Line/Off-Line ǀ Using PCs ǀ Remote Sites
FILE-UPDATING MODES
Batch Processing ǀ Real-Time Processing ǀ Batch
vs. Real-Time Processing
VALIDATING FILE INPUT
Examination Techniques ǀ Transposition
Errors ǀ Verification ǀ Check Digits ǀ Programming
Techniques
FILE-PROCESSING DISADVANTAGES
DATABASE PROCESSING
KINDS OF DATABASES
DATABASE STRUCTURES
The Hierarchical Model ǀ The Network Model ǀ The
Relational Model
DATABASE MANAGEMENT SYSTEMS
DATABASE DESIGN CONSIDERATIONS
Logical Design ǀ Physical Design ǀ Schema and
Subschema ǀ Data Definition Language ǀ Data
Manipulation Language ǀ Query
Languages ǀ Skeleton Reports
MANAGING DATABASES
Administering a Database ǀ Appointing a Database
Administrator ǀ Maintaining a Data
Dictionary ǀ Validating Input ǀ Providing for
Backups ǀ Providing for Security and
Privacy ǀ Controlling Concurrent Operations
DISTRIBUTED DATABASES

Chapter 6

Management Profile: Geri Riegger
FACING CHALLENGE

Some people just love a challenge. In Geri Riegger's case the drive is so strong that it carries over to her vacations, which have included a recent trek down the Amazon in Peru and four trips to Africa. Riegger is clearly not one to shy away from the unknown. Some 25 years ago she left the relative safety of a teaching post to pioneer in what was then the almost exclusively male bastion of data processing. Now, as vice president of the information services division of Empire Blue Cross/Blue Shield, she controls a budget of $40 million to $50 million and oversees computing and network departments that have a combined staff of about 300, serving roughly 10,000 users.

Riegger showed an early attraction to math and science. She began her career as a high school teacher, but that lasted just one year. Unable to find a position teaching the disciplines she had studied, she switched to teaching computers, a jump she describes as an unplanned but major turning point in her career. Riegger says she recognized the opportunities that computing, as a new industry, afforded women with the proper skills. And she was right. Her shift led first to 12 years with IBM, during which she moved from teaching to selling to product development, and then to a White House fellowship and selection as Manufacturers Hanover Trust Company's first female vice president, in charge of computing operations. She joined Empire Blue Cross/Blue Shield in 1982.

A no-nonsense, results-oriented approach on the job has helped Riegger get where she is today. She is known for being direct and assertive. "I am

definitely not laid back," Riegger says with a laugh. "I clearly believe in setting very high standards for my organization." Her job, as she sees it, is to define clear goals, set strategies, and direct the attention of her organization toward the goals. "I do get involved, but how someone implements those goals is not a concern of mine," she says. A colleague notes that Riegger is not one to drown in detail but is persistent in tracking those aspects of a project she cares about, such as costs.

Riegger's mix of technology and business knowledge allows her to hold her own in any planning or implementation environment—and a penchant for doing her homework doesn't hurt either, according to Dick DiFalco, a division vice president and Riegger's boss. MIS has recently become a corporate function rather than a divisional one. That makes it even more important for someone in Riegger's position to be able to relate to the business needs, DiFalco adds. "Her attitude on the job is always one of 'How does what we are doing help or hinder the business we are supposed to support?'" he says.

DiFalco describes Riegger as a "situation manager"—someone who can be counted on to take a project from start to finish and bring it in on time, within budget, and with the prescribed goals achieved.

Adapted from "Geri Riegger: Facing Challenge" by Patricia Keefe. Copyright 1988 by CW Publishing Inc., Framingham, MA 01701. Reprinted from *Computerworld,* Feb. 29, 1988.

In order for data to be used by an information system, it must be organized in a way that the computer can use. Transaction processing systems require that data be organized into files, which need to be structured to meet both user and processing requirements. In large organizations, information in different files overlaps, creating duplicate data in these files. Such overlap yields inefficiency and inconsistency, yet there is often a need to cross-reference related files. Problems like these created the need for database systems.

This chapter discusses the data storage hierarchy and examines how data are organized for storage. The concept of a file is introduced, and the different kinds of files that exist with a computer system are explained. We look at how data are used and what techniques are available for accessing data to create reports and generate information. We also discuss how people enter data into computers and how errors are captured. Various checking methods are available so that files can be error-free. Thereafter, our attention turns to the evolution of database systems and their connection to file systems. We show how database systems can be used to efficiently supply an organization's life blood—information.

IMPACT ON MANAGEMENT PROBLEM SOLVING AND DECISION MAKING

In order for managers to receive the information they need, they require a means to store the necessary data for use in application programs and for processing by the computer. Files are one way in which this is accomplished; databases are an alternate, more productive approach.

A manager counts on the data received from either a file or a database. The validity and accuracy of that data will have a tremendous impact on the manager's decisions. Therefore, the procedures designed to input data into files and databases must promote error-free entry, and appropriate security measures must be in place to protect the data. Making sure that file and database management systems function properly is important to ensure that the information generated will be correct and will meet a manager's problem-solving and decision-making needs in the most efficient and effective manner.

DATA HIERARCHY IN FILES

The main function of a computer system in a business environment is to process data and generate information to be used in making decisions. There are three main problems that most businesses face in generating this information:

1. capturing the data
2. inputting it into the computer system error-free
3. designing, writing, and maintaining programs to process the data into useful information

Before we can look at how a computer handles data, we must first look at the various levels of data, known as data storage hierarchy.

Bits and Bytes

A computer stores characters as bytes—one character to a byte. In fact, we frequently use the terms *byte* and *character* interchangeably. Since each byte is a combination of bits represented by 0s and 1s, the smallest bit combination for an 8-bit byte is 00000000, and the largest is 11111111. Remember that each place in the byte must be either a 0 or a 1; therefore, we have two possibilities for each of eight places, giving a total of 2^8, or 256, possible characters.

Fields

Groupings of characters are called fields; a **field** is simply any collection of related characters. For example, a person's name is composed of three fields: last name, first name, and middle initial. We can identify where someone lives using four fields: street address, city, state (or country), and zip code. We classify fields as being either alphabetic, numeric, or alphanumeric, much in the same way that we classify characters.

Records

A **record** is a collection of related fields. For example, a person's employment record might contain the following fields, shown with their respective lengths:

Field	Number of Characters (Bytes) in the Field
FICA number	9
Last name	25
First name	25
Middle initial	1
Street address	25
City	25
State	2
Zip code	5
Hours worked	3
Rate of pay	4
Number of dependents	2

Files

A **file** is a collection of related records in which each record contains related data fields. For example, an employee salary file contains a series of records, with each record representing data about a particular person and including fields related to that person's salary. Similarly, an inventory file contains a series of records in which each record contains data about a specific item in the company's inventory. Figure 6–1 contains sample files with multiple records and fields. Note that each of the nine records in each file is divided into multiple fields representing specific facts about the person identified in the record.

We create files by using

- vendor software
- in-house written software
- the operating system's general-purpose editor

```
Field 1  Field 2     Field 3   Field 4      Field 5
123456789Gregg       Charles   Gary         IN46401
234567890Robinson    Dale      Louisville   KY40247
345678901Morgan      Judy      Miami        FL33129
456789012Caldwell    Jerry     Plains       GA31752
567890123Walsh       LeRoi     Denver       CO80222
678901234Swartz      Ron       New York     NY10013
789012345Pellegrini  Anthony   Boston       MA02176
890123456Hutchins    Cheryl    Columbus     OH43213
901234567Coffey      Stella    Dallas       TX75277
(a)
```

```
Field 1  Field 2     Field 3   Field 4      Field 5  Field 6   Field 7   Field 8   Field 9
123456789Gregg       Charles   Gary         IN       0123.00   4         M         M
234567890Robinson    Dale      Louisville   KY       0234.44   5         M         M
345678901Morgan      Judy      Miami        FL       1000.00   1         M         F
456789012Caldwell    Jerry     Plains       GA       0500.00   2         M         M
567890123Walsh       LeRoi     Denver       CO       0250.00   3         M         M
678901234Swartz      Ron       New York     NY       0920.00   0         S         M
789012345Pellegrini  Anthony   Boston       MA       0005.00   0         S         M
890123456Hutchins    Cheryl    Columbus     OH       3000.00   0         S         F
901234567Coffey      Stella    Dallas       TX       0450.00   6         M         F
(b)
```

```
Field 1  Field 2     Field 3   Field 4      Field 5  Field 6   Field 7   Field 8
123456789Gregg       Charles   Gary         IN       780113    780213    20.00
234567890Robinson    Dale      Louisville   KY       671120    671120    30.00
345678901Morgan      Judy      Miami        FL       541201    550101    25.00
456789012Caldwell    Jerry     Plains       GA       560930    561030    20.00
567890123Walsh       LeRoi     Denver       CO       711129    721129    20.00
678901234Swartz      Ron       New York     NY       810104    810308    20.00
789012345Pellegrini  Anthony   Boston       MA       590305    650101    25.00
890123456Hutchins    Cheryl    Columbus     OH       631230    999999    00.00
901234567Coffey      Stella    Dallas       TX       700101    999999    00.00
(c)
```

FIGURE 6–1

Layout of several standard files containing employee identification numbers, last names, first names, and cities and states of residence. In addition, (a) includes zip codes; (b) shows amounts earned, number of dependents, marital status, and sex; and (c) gives dates hired, beginning dates of union membership, and union dues.

File Names. Each file has a name conforming to standards established by one or more of the following:

1. the manufacturer of the computer system
2. the developer of the vendor software in use
3. the manager of information systems
4. internal auditing guidelines, rules, or procedures
5. security personnel of information systems

To see the names of all the files on a disk, we use system software commands. On personal computers it can be as simple as entering the system command DIR or selecting a similar command from a menu. The listing typically contains the names of the files on the disk, the amount of disk space used by each file, and the date and time each file was created. On a mainframe a series of menu screens or commands is used to list the files in a particular account or on a particular disk. This listing typically contains the names of the files, the number of times each file has been modified, the date and time each was created, the name of the creator, and the amount of disk space used.

We must not assume that all the files on a secondary storage medium contain data relating to a business function. The vast majority of files in a computer system could be computer programs. In fact, a mainframe's operating system and supporting applications software contain hundreds and sometimes thousands of computer programs. Each performs a certain function, and each is classified as a file. Files containing only data are called **data files**, and those containing program instructions are called **program files**. Text files containing instructions or word processing documents might also be available.

Databases

A database is a cross-referenced collection of files designed and created to minimize repetition of data. Typically, a database is part of an overall system that includes special vendor software to manage the database files. Database files are like traditional files but with an ordered structure that links them logically together. Databases are discussed later in this chapter.

FILE TYPES

Data files are categorized according to how they are used. We consider here some of the major types of data files.

Master File

A **master file** includes data of a permanent nature. Employee salary files, inventory files, and customer files are typical business master files that are kept for long periods of time. They are updated from time to time or on an ongoing basis. The number of master files on a corporate mainframe can be enormous. In fact, the U.S. Department of the Treasury maintains more than 750,000 files on their computers. A typical insurance company would have multiple master files for each department in the company, as suggested in Table 6–1.

Note that Table 6–1 contains only a small portion of the actual files that could exist within a large company. Most of the files could be further subdivided into other master files. The simple task of generating a payroll involves creating files for salaried employees, hourly employees, and employees on commission since different types of employees get paid at different times during each month. Also, payroll programs must create files for deductions from employees' salaries (e.g., credit union, union dues, insurance, and local, state, federal, and FICA taxes). In addition, payroll programs must create files for unemployment insurance, vacation pay, sick pay, and other employee benefits supported by the company. And each master file is used by one or more program files to update or generate a number of reports.

Transaction File

A **transaction file** is a temporary file used to update master files. Data in transaction files are not dynamic in nature; that is, they can be stored for a brief period of time before the master files are actually updated. That brief period of time can range from a few hours to many months, depending on the nature of the file and the way it is used. For example, weekly updating might be a timely schedule for a payroll system, whereas immediate updating would be more appropriate for a bank's savings account system.

History File

If the data to update a master file need to be kept for some reason, a **history file** can be created for long-term storage. Suppose a manufacturer wants to keep track of who ordered which items from inventory. After each order is filled and shipped, the computer could create a history file containing data about the order and the shipment. Such a file could later be used for marketing research, resolution of problems or complaints, and various statistical or demographic studies. In essence, the manufacturer's history file becomes an ongoing record of all shipments the company has made. A company like Sears, however, would not create a history file of all of its transactions. Since the company's sales volume is so massive, the cost to maintain such a file would be prohibitive.

Report, Input, and Output Files

In many companies the volume of reports to be printed is so large that separate computers are used to perform the printing. For large companies like K mart and Kroger, which have thousands of stores and hundreds of thousands of items in inventory, it might take days to print out an inventory list for each store, even with high-speed printers. The federal government issues millions of checks each month for social security, payroll, and other types of payments, keeping multiple printers busy for many days or weeks just printing checks. To facilitate the printing process, a main com-

TABLE 6–1

Types of files in an insurance organization.

Department	Examples of File Types
Insurance products	Health, life, accident, home, liability, dental, disability; clients, payments, claims (for each type of insurance)
Accounting and auditing	Accounting, internal audit, stockholders, taxes, budget, accounts receivable, accounts payable
Marketing	Advertising media, statistical analysis, pricing policy, cost/payback, mass mailing, sales, products
Legal	Case, legal decisions
Investment	Stocks, bonds, land acquisition, investment strategy, commercial tenants, depreciation, equities, securities, mortgage loans, stock evaluation
Building and facilities	Maintenance, security, vendors, fixed assets, equipment inventory, supplies
Medical/health	Employee addresses, employee medical histories, medicine and drugs, government regulations
Conference planning	Travel costs, expense analysis, hotels/airlines
Human resources	Salary scale, commission, performance review, employment histories, employee vacations, employee benefits, employee skills, government regulations, savings plans

puter can create a **report file**—a file of information on auxiliary magnetic tape or disk. Then a second special-purpose computer can use the report file as an input file to print the checks. An **input file** is one that is used by a program to input data. By off-loading jobs to smaller and cheaper computers, the mainframe is kept free to process other transactions, thus saving the company or the government money.

When a program creates a file to be used by another program, the created file is called an **output file**. Many software application programs produce data files that are later used by other computer programs. For example, a program might create a file to write checks to pay vendors, employees, or insurance claims. That same file might later be used as an input file for programs written by an internal auditing department to check for accuracy and to prevent fraud or embezzlement. The resulting file from the internal auditing programs would be considered a report file. A report file can be

1. off-loaded and used on another computer
2. used as an input file in another program
3. sent to the printer immediately

Print File

A file that is sent to the printer is called a **print file**. In reality, such a file is not physically sent to the printer. The computer makes a copy of the file on a disk and formats it by placing headers, footers, dates, and page numbers in their proper places; aligning the margins; and setting the font for the characters. This copy is called a print file and contains all the information the printer needs to print it. The system then places the print file in queue for printing.

Backup File

A **backup file** is simply a copy of a file to ensure that data are not lost if the original file is lost or damaged. When a file is inadvertently destroyed, the backup copy permits the original file to be recreated. Of course, any changes that had been made to the original file must be duplicated and may require hours or even days of additional work.

Let's suppose that a bank accidentally destroys its customer master file. It extracts the backup copy from its secure storage area and re-creates the master. However, all the transactions that have occurred from the time the backup was made must now be reprocessed to bring the file up to date. All transaction files for checking accounts and passbook savings deposits and withdrawals must be credited or debited. Any electronic transfer of funds must be reentered, as well as any automatic teller machine transactions affecting the customers' accounts. And finally, any holds on accounts for collateral, freezes on out-of-state checks, or other unusual activity since the backup was first created must be entered. The newly created master file must then balance with the money taken in and given out, and any discrepancies must be resolved to guarantee that the new file is indeed a valid statement of the customers' current financial positions with the bank.

Most computer installations have a daily schedule for backing up important files; they use magnetic tape or cassettes for storage. A large fireproof vault either on-site or at a disaster recovery center holds the backups until they are needed. Because a company's entire business operation resides on its master files, serious damage to the files could put the company out of business or seriously hinder its ability to function.

Sort File

A **sort file** is any file having one or more fields in some sorted order. For mailing correspondence to customers or potential customers, most companies sort the mailing file by zip code. The resultant sort file becomes an input file for the program producing letters and labels. An obvious advantage of such a program is that presorted mail receives significant postal discounts, saving substantial dollars. Even small insurance companies have postal bills exceeding $100,000 per month.

FILE STORAGE AND ACCESS

There are three primary methods of storing files in and retrieving them from secondary storage:

- sequential file organization, whereby records are stored in sequential order
- direct file organization, whereby records are stored in random order
- indexed file organization, a combination of the two whereby each record contains a key so that it can be accessed either sequentially or directly

Application and processing requirements dictate which organizational structure is most appropriate, and that decision is made by the computer professional who designs the system. The professional must consider available resources, access time, programming requirements, software products available, and both present and future needs.

Sequential-Access File Processing

The sequential-access file-processing method is used for files in which all records must be accessed when the files are processed. The records in a **sequential file** appear one after another in the order they were entered into the computer and subsequently stored on the media. The transaction file a bank creates with data from customer checks to area merchants is a sequential file. Also, a name and address file for creating mailing labels, sorted by zip code, is a sequential file. The records in a sequential file may also be ordered (sorted) by a **key field**, which uniquely identifies each record. Account numbers, employee identification numbers, and social security numbers are examples of key fields. However, no matter how the records are ordered in a sequential file, access to any one record requires access to all preceding records.

Direct-Access File Processing

Direct-access files, also called **random-access files**, are files in which records are stored in random order. These files have a key, called an access key or key field, which lets the computer use direct-access file processing to locate, retrieve, and update any record in the file without having to read each preceding record. Airline reservation systems and banks use direct-access files frequently. When a bank customer withdraws money from a savings account, the computer goes to the random file, accesses the record with the customer's account number, and updates the record with an amount withdrawn debit. Similarly, when a customer wants to reserve space on an airline, the reservation system accesses data on available seats on the desired plane, using the flight number and the day and time of the flight as the combined access key. This example concatenates, or links, several fields to get the access key.

Processing data using direct-access files is much faster, thereby making the computer more convenient to use and more vital to a company's performance. In fact, the ability of the computer to instantaneously store and retrieve data via random files has created new businesses and industries whose main function is the dissemination of information. Credit card companies, credit bureaus, travel agencies, airlines, banks, insurance companies, telephone companies, and most government agencies would offer greatly reduced services if they did not have the ability to access files directly.

Direct-access files are used to randomly store a record in or retrieve it from a file. Typically, we enter a key field via a computer terminal or other input device that is controlled by a computer program. When we retrieve data from the file, the computer verifies that the entered key matches a key in the random file and directly retrieves the record. To store the new record, we enter the appropriate key, and the computer stores the new record at a calculated location on disk.

To determine where to place the record on the storage medium, the computer uses a technique called **hashing**, whereby a mathematical operation on the key field transforms it into a disk location. There are many hashing techniques, but the goal of all is to transform a record key into a disk location. Figure 6–2 illustrates hashing with the division-remainder

FIGURE 6–2

The process of hashing produces a unique storage location on a disk.

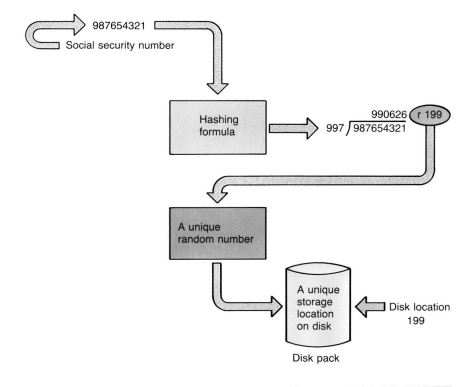

method. Once the record is stored and we later try to access it, the computer performs the same calculation, giving us the same unique location for the record.

Indexed Sequential File Processing

Indexed sequential file processing is a combination of sequential and direct file processing. In the event that a customer forgets his or her account number, we need the ability to look at a file sequentially (by name) to determine the account number and then to access the file directly by that number. In other words, we want to be able to access a single record, a whole file, or any part of a file. In the case of the forgotten account number, we want to list all our customers and their account numbers, beginning with the first letter of the customer's last name. An **indexed sequential file** lets us do just that by permitting both direct and sequential access.

For indexed files the computer must know which field(s) are to be included in the index. It stores the records sequentially in the file and then loads their locations into an **index directory**, which contains the key and the location of each record. When we try to access the record, the computer first looks in the index directory for the key, finds the location of the record, and then accesses it. Since we can have multiple indexes on the same record (e.g., both name and account number), we have multiple index directories.

The disadvantage of indexed sequential files is that the process of searching the index for the key creates an additional, time-consuming step. However, even though indexed files are slightly slower for random access than are direct files, their versatility is a significant advantage and makes them a popular form of storage.

DATA ENTRY MODES

One of the main problems that businesses face in generating information is **data entry**—the input of data into the system—in a timely manner, at a reasonable cost, and with a minimum of errors. Many different types of people enter data into computers in many different ways.

- a data entry clerk who sits in front of a terminal entering facts into a computer
- a car salesman entering sales price and cost into a PC after a sale
- a manager supplying data to a mainframe for a department budget
- a bank customer supplying data at an ATM to withdraw money
- a sales clerk at a department store entering charge card numbers and purchase amounts into a cash register—computer terminal
- a grocery store clerk passing UPC bar codes on food containers past an optical scanner
- a bank clerk processing checks through a magnetic ink character recognition reader
- a company president entering his account number into the system to make queries on databases

On-Line/Off-Line

Anyone supplying data to a computer system is performing data entry. The device used to enter the data can be either on-line or off-line. **On-line** refers to terminals that are directly connected to the CPU; **off-line** refers to devices that are not directly connected. The facts that a data entry clerk enters into a computer do not necessarily have to be processed as they are entered. The computer program monitoring their entry may allow the data to be edited and then placed into a transaction file for later processing. However, the clerk's terminal is connected to the computer, it is therefore on-line, even though processing against a master file does not occur.

A typical on-line data entry job is the processing of checks and invoices that customers send to credit card companies. A clerk opens a letter, extracts the check and the invoice, validates the amounts on both, and places each in a separate stack. After a period of time the clerk computes the total amount of money represented by the stack of checks and uses the invoice stack to enter the account numbers and amounts paid into the computer. A computer program then sums all the entered amounts and prints out a listing of the data with that sum. The sum obtained from the checks and the sum obtained from data entry are then compared and any discrepancies resolved.

Using PCs

An alternate form of data entry is to enter data into a PC and store it on a floppy disk. PC data entry is becoming popular because PCs are relatively inexpensive, readily available, and able to process data independently of the mainframe. In addition, data processing on PCs releases the mainframe for other processing activities.

When we use a PC, we are on-line to its CPU, but we are not on-line to the mainframe. Since a PC can perform only one job at a time, it cannot at the same time be on-line to both itself and the mainframe. However, with special hardware adapters and communications software, the PC can serve as a terminal and become on-line to the mainframe.

Remote Sites

If the data entry site is separate from the main computer center, the site is a **remote job-entry site**. In that situation, clerks use a smaller computer system to enter data off-line onto disks, magnetic tape, magnetic tape cassettes, or diskettes. Companies can thus use regional offices, postal-drop sites, location with cheaper labor costs, places more convenient to the source of the data, or other advantageous sites for data entry. On a timely basis these off-line data entry sites can then transfer the media (disks, tapes, diskettes) containing the data files to the main computer for processing. For many companies off-line remote job-entry is an attractive, cost-effective alternative to on-line processing.

Obviously, data capture and data communication with a central office are critical to the survival of certain industries. A PC or lap-top computer for every person in a sales force may be necessary for a company to be competitive in the marketplace. The sales staff can accumulate data at their homes or offices and upload the data to the regional or district office; **uploading** is the process of sending a file from one computer to another. To receive files from the main office, the salespeople download files from the mainframe to their computers; **downloading** is the process of receiving a file from another computer. By scheduling transmissions at predefined times or by mailing floppy disks, communications between a sales force and the home office can produce significant sales gains.

FILE-UPDATING MODES

Depending on the urgency of the information needed, one of two file-updating modes is used: batch processing or real-time processing.

Batch Processing

A transaction file on disk, tape, or diskette, either on-line or off-line, is a batch file. **Batch processing** is the collecting of data over time into a file that is later processed as a collection, or batch. During batch processing a computer program reads the file and processes data without any interaction with users, clerks, or other individuals. Most transaction files, sort files, and report files are batch files. Several advantages of batch processing are that (1) the computer does not have to interact with users, (2) the programming function is rather simple, (3) computer processing time is held to a minimum, and (4) it is cheaper than real-time processing because less hardware and software are needed to handle batch files.

In most companies the main computer activity during the second and third shifts is batch jobs executing on the system. A **batch job** is a computer program using a batch file(s) as input and output. Batch files are not just data files; they are also instruction files. All batch programs that run in a batch mode on mainframes execute by means of an instruction file—a batch file containing instructions to the computer on how to run the program. The instructions are written in a computer language called job control language (JCL) on some systems and command language on others. Programmers write control commands for each job that is executed on the computer, including both batch and non-batch jobs. These commands tell the computer which data and files to use, when to execute, where to send output, and so on.

Even on PCs, batch files control and run programs. If it exists, the AUTOEXEC.BAT batch file on a PC automatically executes each time the PC is powered on. Vendor-supplied software also contains batch files that control a computer and software.

Real-Time Processing

A common form of data entry is to enter data on-line and add, delete, or modify records instantly, a technique called **real-time processing**. Processing data in a real-time mode requires the user terminal to be on-line, that is, directly connected to the computer's CPU. Data entered into a system in a real-time environment are processed immediately, an ideal arrangement for airlines and banks. It permits customers to reserve seats on flights, cancel them if plans change, or change the dates if necessary. Bank customers can have their funds immediately available or can instantly determine their balances.

Real-time processing does have some problems, however. Keeping terminals on-line is very costly; the mainframe must constantly monitor each terminal even if it is inactive. Real-time systems are also expensive. Additional hardware (terminals, modems, more hard-disk space, controllers), communications software, and perhaps even database software must be purchased to allow all authorized personnel to maintain a dialogue with the computer via a terminal.

Batch vs. Real-Time Processing

Most installations use a combination of batch and real-time processing. When the computer is not busy processing on-line real-time jobs, a software scheduler gives the computer a batch job to execute. In fact, most computers work on real-time jobs only 60 to 80 percent of the time. During the remaining time the CPU remains idle, or in a **wait state**. Hence, programs with batch files can easily use the CPU's free time economically.

The main advantage of real-time processing is its speed. Most customers demand immediate attention, and speed may be critical for a company to remain competitive. Thus, the expense of maintaining on-line systems may be minor or even incidental to the overall operation of the business.

A secondary advantage of a real-time system is that the process permits continual updating of master files. For example, the buying and selling of securities on the major stock exchanges require instantaneous processing of orders. With hundreds of millions of shares being traded daily and with a market value in billions of dollars, the on-line system must handle trading, update brokerage house files of both buyers and the sellers, keep track of prices and volume, and transmit that information worldwide.

Several problems exist with mixing batch and real-time systems or, for that matter, with mixing multiple real-time systems. Let's suppose that a bank has a series of automatic teller machines that allow customers to withdraw money from either a checking or a savings account. The bank has a real-time system for updating the master file of savings accounts and a batch system to update the master file of checking accounts. If the systems are not properly linked or if the checking account batch files update the master file after the customer withdraws money from the ATM, the customer may find that she is overdrawn. Even if the customer received an account status report from the ATM before withdrawing the money, that information may not have been accurate because some batch files may not yet have updated the master files.

In this example, communication among several systems may be too difficult, too expensive, or nearly impossible, given the computer environment at the installation. The bank may have purchased the ATM system from a vendor who is unwilling to provide software support to the bank.

The bank's computer system may not have the capacity to link all the systems together. Both time and money may restrict the bank's ability to design a proper system. In addition, the bank may not have the time to write the programs because of other pressing needs.

VALIDATING FILE INPUT

Given the vast amount of data entered into business computer systems and the humanness of data entry personnel, errors are bound to occur. This section looks at several ways to validate file input and thus reduce the number of errors.

Examination Techniques

A major problem with data entry is ensuring that data are error-free. One of the main jobs of programmers is to write programs that will identify and trap errors before they enter files. If a data entry clerk spells a person's name wrong, it may be difficult for a computer program to capture the error because of the many possible name spellings.

However, when only a limited number of spellings exist, we can easily store all possible spellings in a file and compare the input data with the file to identify misspellings. A file containing the two-character postal codes of the 50 states would usually have 52 records, including DC and PR for Washington, DC, and Puerto Rico, respectively. Similarly, a file containing 50,000 to 100,000 words from a dictionary serves as a way to prevent misspellings in documents. A spelling program checks every word in the text with the words in the program dictionary and identifies the various mismatches.

Transposition Errors

The second type of input error is a **transposition error**, which occurs when characters are reversed or juxtaposed. This is the most common type of data entry error. One customer orders an item with the stock number R453 and receives item R435; another reserves a hotel room for June 21 but later finds that the reservation was made for June 12. These are transposition errors. More serious problems arise when the error is made in a key field. If a customer with account number 3849 pays $50.00 on his account but the data entry clerk credits account number 3894, both records become contaminated with errors. The customer who paid the amount will surely complain after receiving the next billing statement. However, the customer who was erroneously given an extra $50.00 may not even notice the error.

Verification

Many errors can be eliminated by cross-referencing the data in the file. After a clerk enters an account number into the system, the customer's name and other data are displayed on the screen. With visual **verification** the clerk can inspect the data to determine its accuracy. Of course, this assumes that the clerk is looking at the screen. As businesses demand faster and cheaper data entry environments, data entry personnel, under pressure to perform, may give only a cursory view toward such screens. The standard for some data entry shops is 2 to 3 percent total errors in data entry. Hence, if a large data entry department is processing a hundred thousand transactions a day, on average there will be 2,000 to 3,000 errors. (Here a transaction is defined as pressing the enter or return key, which represents entering one piece of data.) Another verification technique for ensuring error-free data is machine verification. In this process a second operator rekeys important data, which are compared against the data keyed by the first operator on a character-by-character basis.

For small transaction files visual verification or eyeballing may be the easiest way to find errors. For files like those in Figure 6–1, the simple process of visual inspection to see whether things look correct can stop many errors from entering the processing stage. For example, if a state abbreviation is listed as XX, the error is easily detected. The more difficult errors to detect are those where data entry used two entries for the same item. For example, if the clerk entered GREGG, CHARLES in one instance and CHARLES GREGG in another, both entries would appear to be valid. Also, since the computer treats uppercase and lowercase letters as two separate items, the mixing of uppercase and lowercase letters in names can also have an adverse effect on errors in data entry.

Check Digits

One way to prevent the transposition of numbers is to use a technique called check digits. **Check digits** is a mathematical calculation that uses the place location and value of the digits in a number to verify that the number was entered correctly. The process assigns an additional digit to a number so that it equals some predetermined value. There are more ways to compute check digits than this text can cover; however, the example that follows illustrates one way.

The mathematical calculation, in this case, requires summing all even-place digits (counting from right to left) and then adding a check digit to make that sum a number that ends in 9. The account number 123456 would be assigned the check digit 0 so that the sum of its even-place digits (9) and the check digit (0) remains 9. The account number 123465 would be assigned the check digit 9 to make the check digit sum 19 (10 + 9). These two account numbers would then become 1234560 and 1234659, respectively. If someone transposed the digits in one of the account numbers, the check digit total would not end in 9, and an error message would be displayed for the data entry clerk.

Original number: 123456	Original number: 123465
Sum of even-place numbers (from right):	Sum of even-place numbers (from right):
$5 + 3 + 1 = 9$	$6 + 3 + 1 = 10$
$9 + 0 = 9$	$10 + 9 = 19$
↓	↓
Check digit	Check digit
Revised number: 1234560	Revised number: 1234659

Business Information Systems

Programming Techniques

Application programs monitor all data as they enter computer systems. Many of these programs verify that an account number is valid, using check digits, and is indeed an account in the file. After the program checks for accuracy in the account number, it then displays the customer name and some other data to allow the data entry clerk to visually inspect the record, if needed.

Most fields that are entered into a system pass through an **edit check**, which verifies that

- numeric fields contain numeric characters
- fields that are required to be entered are indeed entered
- specific values are entered for certain fields (e.g., only *M* or *F* for the sex of a customer)
- lengths of fields are accurate

In addition, many fields pass through a **range check**, which verifies that the data fall within a particular range of values. If a two-character postal code is used for states, for example, a range check verifies a two-character field as valid. Similarly, numeric fields may have to fall within a certain range before a system will accept them as valid. For example, if a program considers only department numbers 110 through 399 to be valid, then numbers outside this range will produce an error message.

To prevent values from exceeding certain limits, many fields also pass through a **limit check**, which verifies that the field does not exceed some minimum or maximum value. Credit card companies restrict the amount customers can charge by placing a limit on the amount-charged field. Payroll checks, government checks, and other financial instruments may also have a limit on their dollar value. Once the value exceeds that limit, the computer fails to print the check, prints the check but displays an error message at the terminal, or prints the check and prints an error-exception report on the printer.

Finally, computer programs can check for impossible or infeasible values in fields. Employees cannot work 500 hours or -3 hours in a week. An unemployed person cannot receive 15 unemployment checks at once; an employee cannot have 395 dependents in her payroll record. City names are not just one character long, and people have both a first name and a last name, not just one name. In a real-time system entered data must be valid (i.e., acceptable to the computer), even if they are not correct. Correctness is a subjective concept that computers cannot handle; to a computer MQRSL may be a valid city.

FILE-PROCESSING DISADVANTAGES

As noted earlier, files are collections of records that are related in some way. These files reside on secondary storage devices, either on tapes, tape cassettes, hard disks, or floppy disks. The file access system of the operating system manages the files by

- storing them on the storage media

- retrieving them when they are accessed
- updating them when properly instructed to do so
- creating and using keys, depending on the types of files
- providing some sort of security mechanism
- providing communication routines among files and programs

At this point it probably seems that files, along with their access systems, are the greatest thing since sliced bread. The truth is that files do have some limitations for data storage in businesses. These disadvantages result from the fact that business data are often related. For example, payroll data files are related to personnel data files, and accounts receivable data files are strongly related to billing data files. Connecting these related files and ensuring that the related data within them are consistent is a difficult task.

The disadvantages of standard file processing (see Figure 6–1) include the following:

- The same data are often duplicated in multiple files; if the data change, all occurrences of the data must be located and updated.
- Programs are dependent on the arrangement of the fields in the records, called the file format. The data in a file must be stored in the exact format that the program expects.
- Programs to manage data in multiple files at the same time are difficult to create and maintain.
- Files are independent and are not integrated.
- Users have difficulty accessing files without the aid of prewritten programs.

DATABASE PROCESSING

To remedy some of the pitfalls found in using standard file structures, many businesses now rely on databases to store their vital data. Earlier we defined a *database* as a collection of related and cross-referenced files, designed and created to minimize the repetition of data. Database processing uses conventional files with some enhancements for cross-referencing and integration purposes. These integrated files are part of an overall system, including software, to manage the creating, accessing, updating, and deleting of database records.

Using a Database

A database is more than a sophisticated arrangement of data and the use of specialized software. It also includes hardware, procedures and standards for using the database, and people resources to increase productivity. All of these factors must be considered in determining the cost of a database system.

For businesses with large databases, the amount of hardware needed to store the data has increased dramatically as the size of the databases has expanded (this is also a problem with large file systems). In addition, many companies must upgrade from a minicomputer to a mainframe or must buy a second mainframe to handle the increased internal workload generated as a result of databases. Companies continually purchase additional disk drives to handle the massive amounts of data that must remain on-line. And they must develop standards, procedures, and security measures to keep the data error-free and available to authorized users but secure from unauthorized users. Companies must also train their user departments to use the database systems and their programming staff to develop and write effective and efficient systems. These expenses might prompt you to wonder whether databases can be justified on a cost-benefit basis.

Advantages of Databases

Using a database instead of standard files has numerous advantages. First of all, **data redundancy** is reduced. For example, a customer's name and residence location may appear only once in a database (Figure 6–3). A certain amount of redundancy in a database can be tolerated, and even encouraged, to support some data manipulation tasks. However, in standard file processing, each file needs the name and address of the customer since the files are not related and have no integrating structure. In a standard file system, therefore, a customer's name and related residency information may appear in 20 to 30 files (see Figure 6–1). Whenever a customer address changes, updating all the necessary files is both time-consuming and error-prone.

    Data integrity is also improved with the use of databases. Since a particular piece of data appears in only a limited number of locations, future reports are more apt to reflect any data change or addition. For example, if a customer notifies a bank of an address change and the address is stored in only one location, then all other data—checking account, savings account, outstanding loans, bank-issued credit card, tax reporting, and solicitation—will reflect the new address.

    Furthermore, **data independence** is maintained. The structure of the database requires that data be independent. That is, deleting or changing selected data in the database does not affect other data in the database. If a manager quits his job, for example, data concerning office furniture, telephone number, travel expenditures, and other nonsalary items are not destroyed when the manager is deleted from the current employee database. Also, data dependency between the data and the software is eliminated. A file organization might be changed from indexed sequential to random, requiring program changes with the file access system. But database software stores data independently of the programming language or file access method used to access the database.

    Another advantage is that security is improved. Since most database systems maintain their own security environment and the data are all in one place, security is easier to maintain. Ensuring security for redundant data in standard multiple files stored on multiple disks or tapes is difficult.

    In addition, **data consistency** is maintained. The kind, type, and size of data are consistent for all applications. For example, the size of the LASTNAME field is the same for all applications using the database.

    Finally, data are easier to use with a database. Since data are available for all applications, capturing and entering the data do not have to be

```
NAME TABLE

123456789Gregg        Charles    Gary        IN46401
234567890Robinson     Dale       Louisville  KY40247
345678901Morgan       Judy       Miami       FL33129
456789012Caldwell     Jerry      Plains      GA31752
567890123Walsh        LeRoi      Denver      CO80222
678901234Swartz       Ron        New York    NY10013
789012345Pellegrini   Anthony    Boston      MA02176
890123456Hutchins     Cheryl     Columbus    OH43213
901234567Coffey       Stella     Dallas      TX75277
(a)


DEPENDENTS TABLE

123456789 0123.00 4   M M
234567890 0234.44 5   M M
345678901 1000.00 1   M F
456789012 0500.00 2   M M
567890123 0250.00 3   M M
678901234 0920.00 0   S M
789012345 0005.00 0   S M
890123456 3000.00 0   S F
901234567 0450.00 6   M F
(b)


UNION TABLE

123456789 780113 780213 20.00
234567890 671120 671120 30.00
345678901 541201 550101 25.00
456789012 560930 561030 20.00
567890123 711129 721129 20.00
678901234 810104 810308 20.00
789012345 590305 650101 25.00
890123456 631230 999999 00.00
901234567 700101 999999 00.00
(c)
```

FIGURE 6–3

Layout of several relational tables containing employee identification numbers.
In addition, (a) includes last names, first names, cities and states of residence,
and zip codes; (b) shows amounts earned, number of dependents, marital
status, and sex; and (c) gives dates hired, beginning dates of union
membership, and union dues.

duplicated or repeated tasks. Most relational databases also contain a query language so that users can query the database without programmer intervention.

Disadvantages of Databases

There are also several disadvantages to using databases.

1. Mainframe databases are highly complex and require specialized designers and programmers to implement them.

2. Mainframe databases are expensive in terms of their purchase price, the hardware needed, and the personnel required to design and maintain them.

3. Since all data are in one location, databases are vulnerable to hardware failure or software errors. Even though databases provide increased security, massive damage to the database can occur if an unauthorized person penetrates the system.

4. Databases may be large, making recovery from a disaster very time-consuming and costly. Making a backup copy of an entire database poses problems and challenges for the data-processing staff, particularly if the database spans several disks, each containing multiple gigabytes of disk space.

A database system is not for everyone. There must be a real need to switch from standard file to database usage. A small company with simple needs and relatively few files may not need a database system. However, other companies could not exist or function efficiently without their database system and the information it provides.

KINDS OF DATABASES

The database software needs of a single-user PC system are different from those of a multiple-user mainframe system. There are four kinds of database systems available.

1. Single-user with single-application database (Figure 6–4), commonly found on PCs—the single-user uses a PC database software package for a specific application (e.g., payroll).

2. Single-user with multiple-application database, also found on PCs—the general ledger and accounts receivable programs, for example, could access each other's databases.

3. Multiple-user with single-application database, commonly found on either networked PCs using a LAN or on a minicomputer—multiple users of accounts receivable programs, for example, would access the same databases.

4. Multiple-user with multiple-application database (Figure 6–5), commonly found on minicomputers and mainframes—multiple users with varying needs use application software to perform a variety of processing tasks using multiple databases.

A single user with a single application database who wants or needs to switch to a multiple-user environment can purchase the necessary hardware and software and perform the migration. With multiple-user systems

FIGURE 6–4

An example of a single-user single-application database.

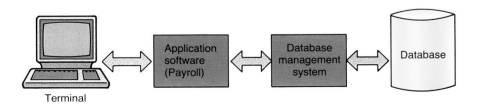

File and Database Organization and Access

FIGURE 6–5
An example of a multiple-user
multiple-application database.

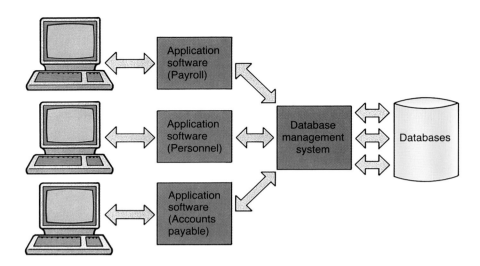

the main problem in implementing databases is degrading system performance. As more people and applications become active on a computer
system, performance levels decrease until response time at terminals becomes intolerable. When system performance decreases substantially, major changes in hardware, software, and database structure may be necessary.

DATABASE STRUCTURES

There are three types of database structures: hierarchical, network, and
relational (Figure 6–6). The type of database model that a company uses
is dependent on many factors. Hierarchical and network databases have
been available since the early 1970s, whereas relational databases became
popular in the early 1980s.

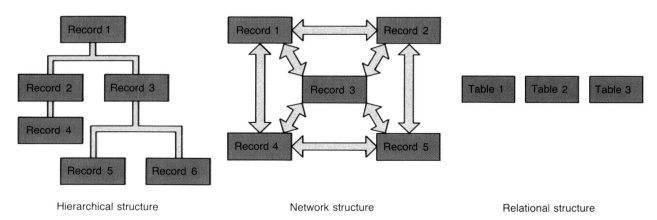

Hierarchical structure   Network structure   Relational structure

FIGURE 6–6
Examples of hierarchical, network, and relational databases.

The Hierarchical Model

In a **hierarchical database**, data relationships follow hierarchies, or trees, which reflect either a one-to-one or a one-to-many relationship among record types (Figure 6–7). The uppermost record in a tree structure is called the **root record**. From there, data are organized into groups containing **parent records** and **child records**. One parent record can have many child records, called siblings; but each child record can have only one parent record. Parent records are higher in the data structure than child records; however, each child can become a parent and have its own child records. Figures 6–8a and 6–8b illustrate a four-tiered parent-child relationship with the root record being a city.

The parent record City contains three records—Dallas, Houston, and El Paso. The parent Dallas has three child records—Downtown, Highlands, and Lowlands. Each of these child records is the parent of its own child records. The Downtown parent has the child records John Doe, Pete Smith, and Mary Johnson. The John Doe child record is the parent record of two accounts, 14163 and 14199, and a series of loans (House, Car, Boat, and 90-day note). Each Transaction record is a deposit to or withdrawal from the respective accounts.

With special software, users can access each parent record, each child record, each child record within a particular parent, all siblings, or any combination, including all records. Also, any record can be accessed according to a condition or fact within the record (e.g., all child records with less than $100.00 in savings account).

The Network Model

A **network database** is similar to the hierarchical model except that each record can have more than one parent, thus creating a many-to-many relationship among records (Figure 6–9). For example, a customer may be called on by more than one salesperson in the same company, and a single salesperson may call on more than one customer. Within this structure any record can be related to any other data element.

The main advantage of a network database is its ability to handle sophisticated relationships among various records. However, these relationships must be identified, established, and described to the database management system. Thus, the network complexity limits users in their ability to access the database without the help of programming staff.

FIGURE 6–7
Hierarchical data relationships.

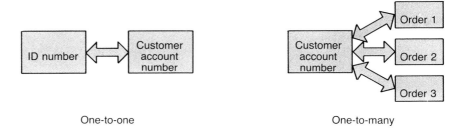

One-to-one   One-to-many

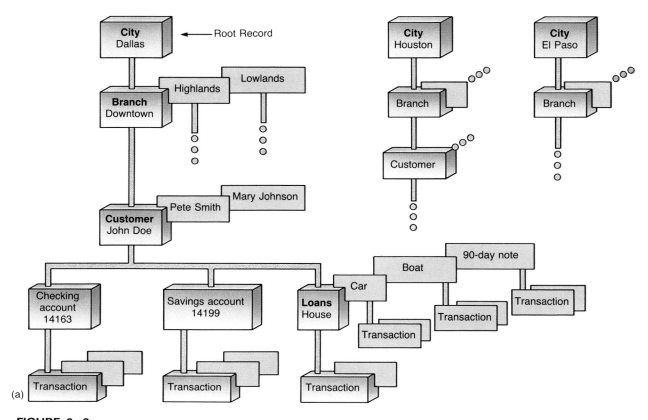

FIGURE 6–8
(a) A sample of a typical bank's general hierarchical structure. (b) Sample records from a typical bank's hierarchical database.

The Relational Model

A **relational database** is composed of many tables in which data are stored. Those **tables** contain rows and columns; the rows are called **tuples** (pronounced like *couples)*, and the columns are called **domains** (Figure 6–10). Tables contain related tuples, just as files contain related records. A file in a file management system may correspond to one or more tables in a database management system. Since most end-users are already familiar with the concepts of rows and columns in their reports, they quickly learn how to use a relational model.

In a table each row contains the same number of columns, and data in the columns are of the same type (alphanumeric, numeric) and size. Since tables are relatively easy to design, end-users need only a little training to design simple tables. However, for very large databases table design should be left to information systems professionals, to guarantee data independence and reduce data redundancy.

```
City Record

CODE      CITY        MAIN OFFICE ADDRESS     ZIP        PHONE

001       Dallas      1234 5th Street         75265      (214) 555-4322
002       Houston     67 E. 8th Ave.          77210      (713) 555-9100
003       El Paso     90 W. Broad             79945      (915) 555-0194


Branch Record

CODE      BRANCH MANAGER     # EMPLOYEES      ADDRESS

01        Gary Harrison      34               1234 5th Street
02        Ruth Bristol       27               34 Highlands Center
03        Paul Scott         31               121 Lowlands Center


Customer Record

CUSTOMER #     CUSTOMER NAME     CUSTOMER ADDRESS

9333           George Mendes     123 Fairland Ct.
8444           Julie Fowler      811 89th St.
7555           David Ramey       1234 Lincoln Ave.
6666           Cletus Yarsky     89 Coffey Lane


Checking Account Record

ACCOUNT #     DATE OPENED     TYPE ACCOUNT     OVERDRAFT PROTECT

9333          870322          Personal         VISA 12345678345456
8444          671201          Personal         NONE
7555          740203          Business         ACCT 3404
6666          820409          Personal         MC   43939834847474
```

FIGURE 6–8

(Continued)

FIGURE 6–9

Network data relationships.

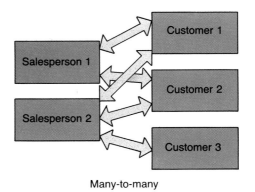

Many-to-many

FIGURE 6–10
A relational database table.

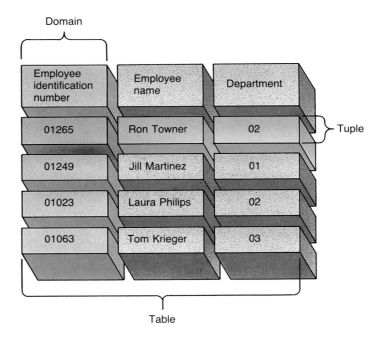

Let's look at a small employee-salary database with the following data: employee FICA number, last name, first name, address, city, state, zip code, hours worked, rate of pay, number of dependents, date employed, union membership, date of union membership, union dues, and department name. We can create the four tables in Figure 6–11 using these data descriptions. We use four tables instead of one because (1) the database management system can cross-reference two or more tables whenever needed, (2) we reduce the duplication necessary to maintain the database, and (3) database design principles recommend that all data within each row relate directly to the key of the row. Because the department name and the department manager relate more to the department than to any one employee, we build a separate table for department.

The tables in Figure 6–11 can be cross-referenced easily. Let's look at two inquiries and see how the process works. For the first inquiry, finding the name of the department where John Doe works, we use the employee's FICA or social security number (123456789) to access the salary table and extract the employee's department code (001). Next, we access the department table, using the department code, and extract the name of the department (electronics).

For the second inquiry, finding the name of John Doe's manager, we again access the salary table, using John Doe's FICA number (123456789), and extract the department code (001). Again we access the department table, using the department code, but this time we extract the department manager's number (345678901). Finally, we use the department manager's number to access the name table and extract the department manager's name (Mark Johnson).

```
Name Table

EMPLID          LASTNAME        FIRSTNAME       ADDRESS                 CITY            STATE   ZIP

123456789       McPherson       Aaron           123 3rd St.             Dunlap          TN      37306
234567890       Higgins         Nancy           321 Key Ave.            Ratee           MI      49278
345678901       Willard         Steve           Rt. 2                   Pirock          TX      78322
456789012       McPherson       Bonnie          123 3rd St.             Dunlap          TN      37306
(a)


Salary Table

EMPLID          HOURSWORKED       RATEPAY       NUMBDEPEND      DEPTCODE

123456789           40.0            12.45            3              001
234567890           35.0            10.80            1              001
345678901           46.5            13.55            2              003
456789012           40.0            11.00            0              004
(b)


Union Table

EMPLID          HIREDATE        UNIONDATE       DUESPAID

123456789       780101          780201          20.00
234567890       730412          741201          25.00
345678901       830207          830407          15.00
(c)


Department Table

DEPTCODE   DEPTNAME      DEPTMANAGER

001        ELECTRONICS   345678901
002        PLUMBING      890123456
003        FREIGHT       123456555
004        OFFICE        345678901
(d)
```

FIGURE 6–11
Four relational tables for an employee payroll.

Relational databases are useful because users can cross-reference data in them without relying on a particular structure. Thus, user-departments have a tool to solve their own problems and create their own reports, and it is the members of user-departments who are the experts in their departments' needs, not the programming staff. Since users can access the data and generate reports without involving the programming staff, relational databases can quickly increase productivity. This capability is particularly critical in dynamic business environments, where quick cross-referencing of data is crucial to company profits.

In both hierarchical and network structures the data relationships must be predefined. That is, all relationships between record types must be defined and entered into the system before data in the database can be used. Making changes to the structure of either of these types of databases is difficult and time-consuming. In a relational database, however, data relationships do not have to be predefined. Hence, end-users can query a relational database and establish data relationships spontaneously by joining common fields.

In spite of relational database advantages, mature businesses may have their entire database operations already established in a hierarchical or network structure. With programming staff and end-users already trained in using other structures, converting to a relational database structure might have some serious cost handicaps. With thousands of programs and hundreds of databases already on-line, scrapping them and starting anew with a different database structure might not be cost-effective.

DATABASE MANAGEMENT SYSTEMS

A database management system (DBMS) is the software that manages the storage in, access to, retrieval from, and use of a database, in much the same way that a file manager manages files. However, a file manager accesses or manages only one file at a time, whereas a DBMS can access and manage multiple files at the same time, linking them together if needed. Typical examples of mainframe DBMSs are IBM's IMS (Information Management Systems), Cullinet's IDMS/R (Integrated Data Management System), and IBM's DB2 (DataBase II), all three of which are explored in more detail in this chapter (Table 6–2).

Accessing a DBMS

A user who is authorized to access a DBMS can log-on to the DBMS directly or indirectly through other software. To **log-on** is to enter an account number into the system, followed by a password. The computer matches the account number and the password with a master list found in a system master file. Usually, master file data are encrypted (secretly coded) to provide maximum security. If the account number and the password are in the master list, the authorized user has access to certain software on the system. If they do not match, the user is denied access to the system. On many systems multiple unsuccessful attempts result in that

TABLE 6–2
Selected DBMS software and prices.

Supplier	Name of Product	Structure	Approximate Cost
Cincom	TOTAL	Network	$500–1500/month
IBM	CICS	—	$1000/month
IBM	IMS	Hierarchical	$1000–4000/month
IBM	DB2	Relational	$500–1500/month
Relational Software	ORACLE	Relational	$10,000–50,000 purchase
Relational Technology	Ingres	Relational	$800–3000/month
Cullinet	IDMS/R	Network	$1000–3000/month

account number's access privilege being frozen until it is released by the security manager or other authorized person.

Features of a DBMS

The routines and programs within a DBMS perform a variety of tasks and have numerous features that make the product attractive to user-departments. A typical DBMS product has the following features:

1. It provides the vehicle for application programs to access database files. Specific commands within a program code pass information to DBMS routines, which actually find, retrieve, delete, and update database records.
2. It provides a report generator for end-users. The end-user uses a language within the report generator to access the database, format the data, and print or display reports.
3. It creates the databases and their structures, using information provided by the database designer.
4. It provides reports to management on who accessed the database and what activity was performed.
5. It provides security for the databases, denying access to an entire database, selected records within a database, and specific fields within each record.
6. It provides reports to operators on hardware utilization, status of current users, and other monitoring data.
7. It provides automatic backup routines for data in the databases.

Many PC-based DBMS systems lack several of these features because they are not multiple-user systems. Highlight 6–1 presents an application in which construction and operation rely on DBMSs.

DATABASE DESIGN CONSIDERATIONS

Most database design is done by programming staff, usually a senior systems analyst, or, in larger companies, by a database designer or a database administrator. The design of a particular database must consider the needs of each user-department, the type of DBMS software already in use, the training of the staff, and the availability of system resources. Also, each department's request must be compatible with the company's long-range plans for DBMS usage.

A feasibility study, usually performed by a systems analyst, identifies the needs and wants of the user-departments (see Chapter 9). The analyst must then identify what data are needed, how to capture the data, and how to merge the data into the framework of existing databases. The analyst must also design methods, procedures, and standards for the maintenance and sharing of the data. Because the database must restrict access to sensitive data, such as an employee's or a customer's medical history, the analyst may have to consult with other departments, the company's upper management, or the legal department to guarantee security. After analyzing user needs and understanding data requirements, the analyst can begin database design.

Atom Smasher's Construction and Operation Rely on DBMS

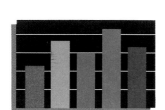

DBMSs are helping 13 European nations build the world's most powerful atom smasher. These nations belong to the Organization for Nuclear Research (better known as CERN, from its French acronym), which is involved in nonmilitary nuclear research. The 30-mile-long doughnut-shaped supercollider is called the Large Electron Positron Supercollider. The DBMS being used is that of Oracle Corporation. It was selected because of its ability to support the multivendor environment that resulted from the mix of nationalities and equipment coming from the 13 member nations, as well as visitors from the United States and the Eastern bloc.

One application of the DBMS is on a VAX cluster, dedicated to managing the logistics of construction. The system developed around the DBMS tracks the people and equipment involved and the details of getting the equipment into the underground tunnels. The DBMS is also being used to analyze the vast amounts of data captured in nuclear experiments. In addition, it is being run on a mainframe computer in order to supply a central general-purpose database for business, engineering support, and physicists' use. This database is accessed by more than 3,000 users. Without the use of DBMSs it would be difficult, if not impossible, to ensure the efficient construction and operation of the collider.

Logical Design

A **logical design** is a detailed description of the database in terms of how user-departments will use the data. It is during this phase that the analyst performs a detailed study of the data, identifying how they are grouped together and how they relate to each other. The analyst must also determine which fields have multiple occurrences of data, which will be keys or indexes, and what will be the size and type of each field.

Physical Design

After identifying all the data that will be included in a database, the analyst enters the database information into a **data dictionary**, which is a data file containing a technical description of the data to be stored in the database. The dictionary includes the field names; their type (e.g., alphanumeric or numeric), size, and descriptions; and their logical relationships. The data dictionary is a tool the developer uses to communicate with other members of the development staff about the database description. The dictionary also provides a means of standardizing the names and lengths of data within the database structure.

An analyst, a database designer, or a database administrator then transforms the logical design into a **physical design**, the actual structure of the database, in keeping with the DBMS software already in use. If multiple DBMS systems are available, the feasibility study should have identified which DBMS system is to be used for the development of the application. The analyst designs the database according to the database structure (hierarchical, network, or relational) of the recommended DBMS.

Schema and Subschema

The DBMS software must know the structure of the database and the relationships among the data in it. Consequently, the database administrator, who has the primary responsibility for providing this information to the database software, creates a schema and subschema for the database. A **schema** is a complete description of the content and structure of the database; it defines the database to the system, including the record layout; the names, lengths, and sizes of all fields; and the data relationships. The **subschema** defines each user's view or specific parts of the database. The subschema definition is the security envelope that restricts each user to certain records and fields within the database. Every database has one and only one schema, and every user must have a subschema.

Data Definition Language

We use **data definition language (DDL)** to enter the database structure into the DBMS. The commands permit us to create, alter, and drop (delete) databases and their entities. An entity is an item or area of interest—such as a person, place, thing, or event—about which data are stored. Each DBMS software product has different commands to define a schema. The subschema definition also uses different commands, dependent on the DBMS product. In DB2 the subschema definition uses the control language commands of GRANT and REVOKE. We would GRANT users access to DB2 database entities (database, tables, columns) but REVOKE that authorization when circumstances changed. Figure 6–12 gives the control commands to authorize access to the weekly disk, the payroll database, and the employee table.

Data Manipulation Language

A second type of language for databases is **data manipulation language (DML)**, which contains the commands SELECT, INSERT, UPDATE, and DELETE. Whereas the DDL commands deal with defining the structure of the database entities, DML commands deal with the data that are added to, deleted from, or changed in the database. Thus, after the structure of the database is established, using DDL commands to create a schema for the database and subschemas for the users, DML commands are used to load data into the database.

Generally, the programming staff designs and writes programs to aid data entry clerks in inputting data into the database. Programmers imbed

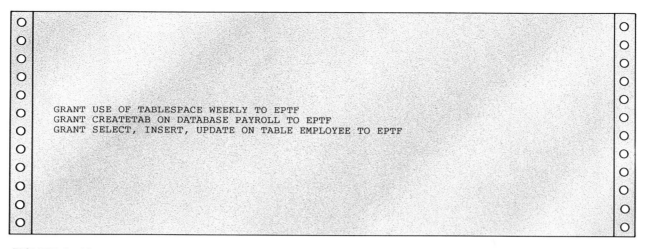

```
GRANT USE OF TABLESPACE WEEKLY TO EPTF
GRANT CREATETAB ON DATABASE PAYROLL TO EPTF
GRANT SELECT, INSERT, UPDATE ON TABLE EMPLOYEE TO EPTF
```

FIGURE 6-12
Control commands to grant specific authorization.

DML commands within their code, typically using COBOL, a business-oriented language, to write the code. However, the standard COBOL language does not have the DDL, DML, and control language commands of CREATE, INSERT, GRANT, and so on. (**Control language** is used to grant and revoke access to the database.) To resolve this dilemma, the DBMS vendor provides a routine to convert the DDL, DML, and control language instructions into standard COBOL; the routine is called a precompile. The programming staff writes the code, precompiles it using the vendor-supplied precompiler, and then proceeds to process the code normally, using the installation's standards and routines. Any additional interfacing between the code that programmers write and the software on the system must be supplied by the DBMS vendor.

Query Languages

There are two ways to manipulate data in a DBMS—with a query language or a programming language. Most DBMS systems come with a **query language** that allows end-users to make inquiries into the database. The most common query language is **structured query language (SQL)**. It contains DDL commands (CREATE, ALTER, DROP), DML commands (SELECT, INSERT, UPDATE, DELETE), and control commands (GRANT and REVOKE) and is becoming a standard for the industry. However, these commands simply access database records or perform some other activity on the database. End-users also need a product that allows them to access selected records in the database and generate reports. Hence, DBMS software must also include a report generator for end-users. For most network and hierarchical databases, reports and other requests must be written by the programming staff because of the complex structures involved with these types of databases and the considerable amount of time required.

One of the many benefits of relational databases is the ability of end-users to make inquiries and generate reports without the aid of the programming staff. Most PC-based databases have a report generator as part of the PC's DBMS. The report generator for the relational database DB2 is the Query Management Facility (QMF). End-users enter SQL commands into the QMF, format screens using relatively easy codes and commands, and then display, print, or store the resulting reports. Training end-users to write queries and use report writers typically takes 3 to 5 days and is done by a company's end-user support center. Such a center's main function is to train and help end-users in computer usage. Many companies include both mainframe and PC training.

Skeleton Reports

It is common for database developers or programmers to generate a series of skeleton reports for end-users. Such reports contain most of the commands and formatting instructions for a report and are saved in an end-user's account. End-users can quickly generate a report by accessing a skeleton report that is similar to the one they need, making minor changes in the skeleton, and printing the report. If no skeleton exists for a needed report, the user can generate her own report, call a support programmer for help, or enlist the aid of a specialist in the end-user support center.

MANAGING DATABASES

The objectives of managing databases are listed here.

- Avoid unnecessary redundancy
- Provide access flexibility
- Provide reliability
- Maintain data independence
- Allow for growth and changes in needs
- Preserve data integrity
- Ensure data security

Administering a Database

Databases are managed by a **database administrator (DBA)**, who may be one person or a group of people. A DBA has been specially trained in the DBMS software package currently in use and in the construction of database structures. A DBA's skills, coupled with DBMS software, should provide for efficient database management. If a company has multiple DBMS packages on its system, there is usually at least one DBA for each DBMS package.

A DBA's main functions are these:

- Implementing the database. A DBA coordinates the input of the intended users of the database through both the logical and the physical design phases. He works with user-departments and an analyst in creating an effective and efficient database structure.

- Providing security on the database. A DBA is responsible for designing and implementing security standards for the database. He controls who uses the database and what data are available to the users. The DBA works with middle and upper management to create corporate goals and guidelines for long-term usage of the database.
- Monitoring performance. A DBA continually oversees the performance of the database. When problems develop, it is the responsibility of the DBA to fix them. When necessary, the DBA consults with a systems team and/or a DBMS technical support team for problem resolution. If database performance lessens, the DBA makes recommendations for modifying software and/or purchasing additional hardware and software.
- Designing standards. A DBA creates standards and procedures for using the database. He also distributes and enforces the standards and procedures relating to the database. In addition, the DBA must distribute any literature, memos, and other documents on changes or modifications associated with the DBMS, both to user-departments and the programming staff.
- Providing backup and recovery. A DBA is responsible for establishing controls and procedures for the systematic backup of the database. He is also responsible for planning and implementing disaster recovery for the database.

Appointing a Database Administrator

The database administrator of each DBMS has the responsibility of maintaining and coordinating the use of the DBMS. After a company acquires a DBMS product, it must select an individual to be the administrator of that product. The vendor company then trains the selected individual in the use and management of the DBMS. Usually this initial training lasts from 1 to 3 weeks. An ongoing educational program for the database administrator involves attending timely conferences and seminars and attending user support groups on the DBMS. These groups consist of other users of the same DBMS product, who meet to exchange suggestions with each other and the DBMS vendor. When the vendor releases a new version of the DBMS, the DBA is the first to attend workshops on the new release, usually at the vendor's corporate headquarters.

Maintaining a Data Dictionary

Some large companies have a data dictionary product that contains the entire description of the DBMS, including all record descriptions of the database. The data dictionary is a tool that many DBAs, database designers, and systems analysts use to coordinate the activities of application development. Since the data dictionary contains a complete description of all data fields in the database, developers can access the data dictionary to find information about any field—its name, type, size, editing criteria, structure, and so on.

However, maintaining a data dictionary to include any and all changes in data descriptions is time-consuming and costly. Some DBMS products have a data dictionary as an integral part of the product (e.g., IDMS/R's Integrated Data Dictionary). But for those DBMS products that do not include an active data dictionary, the user-company must purchase or license a data dictionary product from another vendor. Unfortunately, many of the data dictionaries on the market today do not fulfill all programming needs, such as charting data relationships and automatically inserting data changes into the software. For that reason, many companies do not have an active data dictionary installed. In addition, for a data dictionary to be of value, it must contain a description of all records in the database, but installations with IMS may have already had that product for 15 or more years. Entering 15 years of database design into a data dictionary would not be a worthwhile endeavor for most companies.

Validating Input

One of the critical challenges associated with data entry is entering error-free data into the system. For hierarchical and network databases, programmers write codes containing edit routines to monitor the entry of data. An edit routine captures invalid data before they are stored in the database. However, with relational databases end-users can access and change the database without programmer involvement. And since most end-users do not write edit routines, the data they enter may not be electronically edited by a program. Thus, trash, or garbage, may enter the database through unedited data entry. Garbage refers to any data in a database that are invalid (e.g., 12TY4 for a zip code or 12345YY77 for a FICA number).

To solve some of the editing problems with data, many relational DBMSs permit the programming staff to write procedures to ensure data integrity and then attach those procedures to the data description. Thereafter, all data entering the DBMS system pass through those routines, which are transparent, or invisible, to the user but guarantee the validity of the data.

Providing for Backups

All databases have backup procedures to guarantee the recovery of data in case things go wrong with the system. For most DBMS products the database is removed from active status before the backup procedure starts so that additional processing cannot occur. These backups are usually made on second and third shifts to minimize interference with regular company business.

Other products provide for automatic backups during real-time operation. In other words, as a transaction enters the database, the DBMS makes an immediate backup of the data being affected. The advantages of a transaction-by-transaction backup are that the DBMS system does not have to be taken off-line, thereby permitting 24-hour operations, and the transactions can be reposted electronically to a backup copy of the database in the event of data contamination.

Providing for Security and Privacy

Security for the computer system is handled through a log-on process whereby a user enters an account number and a password. Generally, security specialists handle the security for a system; however, once the user accesses DBMS software, the subschema controls security for the database. A database administrator manages the security framework for the DBMS. She writes the subschema for each user, indicating what data are available to which users. Thus, it is the responsibility of the DBA to identify sensitive data and place restrictions on their access via the subschema. If the database administrator fails in this endeavor, sensitive data become vulnerable. Ethics and corporate philosophy have a tremendous impact on whether users identify mistakes and inform management of existing or potential problems. Highlight 6−2 examines some of the potential problems related to the large database maintained by the FBI.

Controlling Concurrent Operations

On real-time systems many users access the same database at the same time. On occasion, two users may attempt to access the same data simultaneously, a situation called **concurrent access**. If both are simply viewing the data, the system should allow multiple users to view the exact same data simultaneously. However, if one user wants to change the data, the system must temporarily lock the data from further access until the change occurs or the access is abandoned. Consider a typical college course registration process, where each class added or dropped changes the number of available seats in that class. While one student is adding or dropping a class, other students must be locked out of the database; otherwise, the class might be overloaded, or a student might be turned away when a seat exists in the class. To handle this potential problem, programming staff place locking instructions in the codes they write. In addition, most DBMS products permit a DBA to write locking strategies in schemas or subschemas and also permit a user to temporarily lock data.

DISTRIBUTED DATABASES

Distributive data processing is a network of decentralized computers, possibly with a central or host computer. Databases can also be distributed. A **distributed database** can exist in the following forms: (1) the database can be on-line at the host computer in a central location but also available to remote locations; (2) part of the database at the host computer can be duplicated and placed in a remote computer, a type of distributive database processing called **segmentation**, or (3) copies of the entire database and DBMS can be at each remote location, a type of distributive processing called **replication**. Any of these methods might be used with an inventory database for various chain units of a large department store, for example.

The cost benefits associated with distributed databases vary, depending on many factors within a company. For example, a database on a computer system in Atlanta that contains only data used by a San Francisco office will incur considerable data transmission expense. In addition,

FBI Database Expansion Seen as Threat to Civil Rights

The Federal Bureau of Investigation (FBI) maintains the National Crime Information Center (NCIC) database. Housing the necessary hardware to operate the system requires a room half the size of a football field. The NCIC database consists of 12 main files and a total of about 19.4 million individual files. These files contain information on criminal arrests and convictions, missing persons, individuals with outstanding warrants, stolen vehicles, and individuals suspected of plotting against high-level government officials.

Law enforcement officials access the NCIC files more than 700,000 times a day, checking on everything from routine traffic violations to information on felony suspects. The database is a valuable resource for law enforcement, but many groups and individuals are worried about violations of civil rights, which may result from inaccurate or false information stored in such databases. Even the FBI, which spends $1 million a year auditing the 20-year-old system, admits that "a lot of things can happen" with so many queries being made on the system each day.

Such was the case of Terry Dean Rogan of Michigan, who was arrested five times for crimes he did not commit after his wallet was stolen. He was even mistaken for a murder suspect who had used his identification. Eventually, Mr. Rogan received a settlement in the amount of $55,000 from the city of Los Angeles for failing to remove his name from its database. But the results could have been much worse.

Another worry is that the FBI cannot provide adequate security for the information stored there. For example, the FBI's listing of drug informers could be devastating for many individuals if it fell into the wrong hands. The recent incident of a computer virus that brought the Internet computer system to a standstill is a further reminder that most computer systems have serious security vulnerabilities, especially from within.

With these facts in mind, the Computer Professionals for Social Responsibility (CPSR) and the American Civil Liberties Union (ACLU) have teamed up to oppose a proposed expansion of the NCIC database. They believe that the scope of the expansion—which includes information on credit card transactions, telephone calls, airline passenger lists, and nonpublic information such as ongoing investigations—is too broad and only serves to increase the chances of civil rights violations. In response to public pressures, the FBI has narrowed its scope somewhat, but not to the satisfaction of the CPSR or the ACLU. As of this writing the issue has not been resolved.

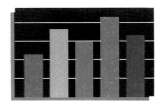

the differential in time between the two time zones may require the host site to keep the DBMS on-line during second shift operations, thus impacting the resources available for other processing at the central site. Furthermore, keeping key personnel (e.g., a systems team, DBA, and programmer) on-site in Atlanta for extended hours may be costly in terms of both money and loss of key personnel for other activities.

The expense of duplicating a DBMS at a remote site includes purchasing additional hardware, purchasing or licensing software for multiple sites, and maintaining key personnel at the remote site. As microcomputers and minicomputers are becoming more powerful, DBMS vendors are making their products available for them (e.g., ORACLE, FOCUS, IDMS/R). As costs decrease, distributive database processing may be an economical option for many businesses.

SUMMARY

Data form a hierarchy, from bits at the bottom through a cross-referenced collection of files, a database, at the top. The two major types of data files are master files, which are permanent, and transaction files, which are temporary and are used to update master files. In addition to data, files can contain programs, text, and instructions.

The three methods used to store data in files are sequential, direct, and indexed sequential. Sequential storage is most appropriate when most or all master file records need to be accessed. Direct storage has the advantage of quick access to a single record. Indexed files have some of the advantages of each of the other two methods.

Files can be processed on-line when the needed devices are directly connected to the computer or off-line when some human intervention is needed for processing. Processing may take place in a batch mode, with transactions collected and stored as a group prior to being processed, or in a real-time mode, with instantaneous updating taking place as the transactions occur.

A primary concern of information-processing specialists and managers alike is maintaining error-free data. Errors can be reduced by sight or machine verification, use of check digits, and a number of programming techniques, including edit, range, limit, and presence checks.

Databases provide an alternative to file-processing systems. Some of the advantages of databases are that (1) redundant data are eliminated, (2) data integrity is ensured, (3) data independence is maintained, (4) security is improved, (5) data consistency is maintained, and (6) data are easier to use. The major disadvantages of using databases are that (1) they are highly complex, (2) they are expensive, (3) they are vulnerable, and (4) backups and recovery are complicated. The four kinds of databases are single-user with single-application, single-user with multiple-application, multiple-user with single-application, and multiple-user with multiple-application.

There are three types of database structures: hierarchical, network, and relational. Both hierarchical and network databases have been available since the early 1970s, whereas relational databases became available in the early 1980s. Both hierarchical and network databases require the data relationships to be predefined before the data can be accessed. The data relationships in relational databases need not be predefined.

A database management system (DBMS) is the software that manages the storage in, access to, retrieval from, and use of a database. The main DBMS vendor software for mainframes is IMS, IDMS/R, and DB2.

A database administrator (DBA) is responsible for converting a logical database design into a physical design. The DBA creates the schema, which is the complete description of the content and the structure of the database, and a subschema for each user's access to the database. Data definition language (DDL) is used to define the structure of the database. Data Manipulation Language (DML) is used to access and change data in the database. Control language is used to grant and revoke access to the database. A query language—the most common is structured query language (SQL)—makes inquiries simple and, in conjunction with a report writer, gives end-users the ability to make queries and produce reports without programmer intervention.

A DBA, in conjunction with DBMS software, implements the database, provides for its security, monitors its performance, designs standards and procedures for its use, and provides for both backup and recovery. A database system can reside with a host computer or be distributed to remote locations.

MINICASE 6–1

Will Farnsworth was recently elected president of his college's marketing club. Almost every marketing major joins because the club has a great reputation, conducts several social functions, and puts on two successful fund-raisers each year. Will was excited about the year and believed the experience would look good on his résumé.

One week into the fall semester, however, Will's challenges began. The student association requested the name, address, and phone number of all marketing club officers. The campus news editor called to get a picture of all committee chairpersons, and the campus yearbook wanted to set up a time for a group picture. The faculty advisor had also mentioned to Will that the department needed a listing of all club members who were seniors so that it could select one of them to receive the department's annual scholarship.

Fortunately, last year's president had saved a listing of the names and addresses of all members—it lacked only the information on new freshmen members. With difficulty, Will was able to complete a roster of the club's membership and, along with the other officers, call most of the members to set up committees, announce the time and location for the group picture, and determine which members were seniors. It was not an easy task, and Will decided that next year's president should have a computer to help manage the organization's membership.

1. List the fields and field sizes that will be required to store membership information.

2. Should Will try to set up a file system or a database system to help with other requests later in the year? Explain.

3. How should the data be updated each year?

4. How can errors in the data be identified?

MINICASE 6–2

Tony's Louisville Video Emporium rents video tapes to customers. Thousands of empty tape cartons with elaborate graphic designs to appeal to customers fill the store's walls and standing racks. Customers who enter the store can browse through the aisles for the exact movie to satisfy their craze. The business is open from 8:00 A.M. to midnight every day of the week.

Once a customer selects a movie to rent, he takes the empty video carton from the rack and hands it to the cashier. In addition, the customer must also supply his membership card, which contains his name and membership number. The cashier takes the empty carton from the customer and finds the matching video cassette in the stack of cassettes behind the counter. The cashier then extracts the tape cassette from the stack, places the empty box in its slot, fills out a combination sales form and short rental agreement, has the customer sign it, gives the video cassette to the customer, collects the fee for the rental, and gives the customer a receipt.

New members must also fill out an application form for membership, for which there is no charge. The cashier reviews the application form, assigns a membership number to the new customer, and fills out a membership card. The card is laminated to prevent damage and is given to the customer, who can then rent tapes from the store.

1. What questions should be on the new-member application form?

2. From a data entry point of view, what fields are vital on the new-member application form?

3. How many files should be maintained for Tony's Emporium?

4. Should a database approach be used? Explain.

Key Terms

backup file	data definition language (DDL)
batch job	data dictionary
batch processing	data entry
check digit	data file
child record	data independence
concurrent access	data integrity
control language	data manipulation language (DML)
database administrator (DBA)	data redundancy
data consistency	direct-access file

distributed database

domains

downloading

edit check

field

file

hashing

hierarchical database

history file

index directory

indexed sequential file

input file

key field

limit check

logical design

log-on

master file

network database

off-line

on-line

output file

parent record

physical design

print file

program file

query language

random-access file

range check

real-time processing

record

relational database

remote job-entry site

replication

report file

root record

schema

segmentation

sequential file

sort file

structured query language (SQL)

subschema

table

transaction file

transposition error

tuples

uploading

verification

wait state

Review Questions

1. Explain the differences among a field, a record, and a file.
2. Name 10 files that your school could maintain for your records.
3. What is a master file?
4. How can a master file be destroyed?
5. Are all transaction files also sort files? Why or why not?
6. Describe the sequential-access file-processing method, and identify an application for which it is well suited.
7. Describe the direct-access file-processing method, and identify an application for which it is well suited.
8. What is hashing?
9. What is meant by uploading everything to a mainframe?
10. Explain the difference between batch processing and real-time processing.
11. Describe each of the following programming techniques, which help validate file input: edit check, range check, and limit check.
12. What is the difference between a database and a file?
13. What are the advantages of using a database?

14. What are the disadvantages of using a database?

15. What is a database management system?

16. What is the difference between logically and physically designing a database?

17. What is a data dictionary and how is it used?

18. What is a schema and a subschema? How do they differ?

19. What is the difference between data manipulation language and data definition language?

20. What is SQL?

21. What is the difference between a query language and a report generator?

22. A company currently has a hierarchical database and is investigating converting to a relational database. However, the company has only 20 to 30 different reports to generate, and none of the user-departments needs to make inquiries into the database. Should the company convert to a relational database? Explain.

23. What are the differences among tables, rows, and columns in relational databases?

24. Does a database administrator need programming experience? Why or why not?

25. If many people have access to a database, how are the data secured against unauthorized use?

Principles of Business Information Systems

OBJECTIVES

- Define transaction processing systems, management information systems, decision support systems, and knowledge-based (expert) systems
- Understand the characteristics, functions, and business uses of transaction processing systems
- Understand the characteristics, functions, and business uses of management information systems
- Understand the characteristics, functions, and business uses of decision support systems
- Understand the characteristics, functions, and business uses of knowledge-based (expert) systems

OUTLINE

IMPACT ON MANAGEMENT PROBLEM SOLVING AND DECISION MAKING

TRANSACTION PROCESSING SYSTEMS AND THEIR FUNCTIONS
Data Collection | Input Validation | Information Processing | Updating | Output Generation

COMMON TRANSACTION PROCESSING SYSTEMS
Accounts Payable | Order Entry | Accounts Receivable | Inventory Control | Payroll | General Ledger

MANAGEMENT INFORMATION SYSTEMS
TPSs in Relation to MISs

ROLE OF MANAGEMENT INFORMATION SYSTEMS
Management Functions | Management Hierarchy and Information Needs

MIS PRESENTATION OF INFORMATION
Reports | On-Line Retrieval

DECISION SUPPORT SYSTEMS
Primary Functions of a DSS | Components of a DSS

PROCESSING FUNCTIONS OF A DSS
Financial Calculation | What-If Analysis | Sensitivity Testing | Goal Seeking | Analysis | Simulation

DSS REPORTS AND APPLICATIONS

EXECUTIVE INFORMATION SYSTEMS

KNOWLEDGE-BASED (EXPERT) SYSTEMS
History | Conventional Programs vs. Knowledge-Based Systems

COMPONENTS OF A KNOWLEDGE-BASED SYSTEM
User Interface | Knowledge Base | Inference Engine | Working Memory | Explanation Subsystem | Knowledge Acquisition Subsystem | Shells

ROLE OF KNOWLEDGE ENGINEERS

BUSINESS USES OF KNOWLEDGE SYSTEMS

DIFFERENCES BETWEEN DSSs AND EXPERT SYSTEMS

Chapter 7

Management Profile: Thomas R. Gaughan
MIS CHIEF WALKS POINT ON DECENTRALIZATION

Tom Gaughan has seen and overseen changes in his years at Primerica Corporation. For instance, Primerica was called American Can Company and drew 85 percent of its revenue from manufacturing when Thomas Gaughan joined the firm as vice president of corporate information systems and services in 1982. Today, Primerica is a diversified services company, focusing on financial and retail businesses. The centralized mainframe operation is gone, and the hardware and day-to-day decision making have been shifted out to operating units.

Gaughan was brought in to change the structure of the information systems group, to keep it consistent with the structure of the evolving company. Today, his focus is to ensure that the information systems maximize their contribution to business objectives. The Primerica MIS strategy is one of decentralization and reaction to the strategic reorientation of business. "We had to dramatically change the way information services were provided in the organization. Basically, we've changed from a centralized operation to where we provide—I hate to call it consulting—value-added support to our companies," Gaughan notes.

The man who hired Gaughan, Jerry N. Mathis, recalls, "Tom turned out to be a terrific performer. He has fine interpersonal skills and is very user-oriented, which is very important in the systems business. He reorganized the entire department and reduced staff, but at the same time he maintained high morale."

Gaughan's responsibilities have included providing transitional support to manufacturing groups as they were divested and evaluating the MIS operations of companies considered for acquisition. Gaughan manages a group that sets the direction for MIS operations in subsidiary companies. That direction setting includes doing research on leading-edge technology (e.g., artificial intelligence and image-processing) for individual business units and then ensuring that the other business groups benefit from that technology whenever possible. Gaughan also coordinates volume-purchase discounts, deals with vendors on national accounts, and sets telecommunications strategies. In addition, Gaughan is responsible for managing different cultures. "One thing that became clear early on was that as we acquired companies, we acquired those different cultures," he notes.

Gaughan describes himself as "results-oriented but also somewhat flexible" and stresses that one of his key objectives is to motivate his people. That means being driven by project management and looking for opportunities and challenges. He has had to change his approach from that of hands-on operations. "There you plan and execute. Now, I plan and facilitate," he says.

He says his transition from an operations person to a businessman came two jobs ago, when he was director of systems at Celanese Corporation. There he had to become aware of how an entire factory operated, not just the MIS organization. He says that today's age of specialization may make it harder for younger people to make such a transition, because they focus so much more tightly on a single technology or application. "I was interested in how information systems are used to support the business function. Another thing that interested me was the constant change in technology. And it has never stopped changing," he says of the magnet that drew him to computers.

Adapted from "Thomas R. Gaughan: MIS Chief Walks Point on Decentralization" by James Connolly. Copyright 1988 by CW Publishing Inc., Framingham, MA 01701. Reprinted from *Computerworld,* May 16, 1988.

Business information systems provide information to individuals at various levels in an organization, and information requirements differ depending on the level and responsibilities of those individuals. For example, the information needs of the president of a company are different from those of a payroll clerk or a financial planner. To accommodate these differences in information needs, several different levels of business information systems have evolved. On the operational level there are transaction processing systems (TPSs); management information systems (MISs) support the tactical level; and decision support systems (DSS) can be found on both tactical and strategic levels. In addition, executive information systems operate on the strategic level; and a type of business information system, known as a knowledge-based (or expert) system, provides solutions to business problems that are usually solved by human experts. This chapter discusses each of these business information systems in order to clarify their characteristics, functions, and uses in business organizations.

IMPACT ON MANAGEMENT PROBLEM SOLVING AND DECISION MAKING

TPSs, MISs, DSSs, and knowledge-based (expert) systems are today's major tools that enable managers to detect and solve problems and assist in making decisions. To know when and how to use these tools effectively, managers must understand the nature and purpose of each. Within an organization, information from routine transactions flows through the various levels of management for use in operational, tactical, and strategic decisions. Information systems can filter and enhance that information so that it truly instructs the decision-making process. In addition, valuable human knowledge can be captured in systems and then reused to support decisions at different management levels. Well-designed information systems that are effectively used can improve both decision making and overall productivity, both of which are critical to business organizations.

TRANSACTION PROCESSING SYSTEMS AND THEIR FUNCTIONS

Chapter 1 defined a *transaction* as a business activity or event. It is difficult to describe precisely the transactions of an organization because they are different for different organizations. However, examples of transactions include buying a product or a service, such as gas at a gas station or food at a grocery store. The responsible organization needs to collect, record, and process information about such events; the information system that records and helps manage these transactions is known as a transaction processing system (TPS). A TPS performs several functions, including data collection, input validation, information processing, updating, and output generation.

Data Collection

In order to record and manage transactions, data must first be collected. The term **data collection** refers to the activity by which transactional data are collected for entry into a computer system. Transactional data are collected in two major ways—indirect and direct. Indirect data collection involves collecting data from source documents, which are primarily paper documents on which data have been manually recorded for later keying into a computer. Sales data that are first manually recorded on a sales receipt and are later keyed into a computer are an example of the indirect method of data collection. Direct data collection involves collecting data directly, without going through source documents; the process involves very little manual work. Examples of direct data collection include the data collected by a bank's computer system from its automated teller machines (ATMs) and the sales data collected by a large department store from its point-of-sale (POS) terminals. Today, more and more organizations are collecting transaction data directly because of the obvious time and cost savings.

Input Validation

It is extremely important that transactional data going into a computer system are valid. Every precaution should be taken to ensure that invalid data do not get into a computer because invalid data make the results of processing also invalid (as noted earlier, garbage in, garbage out).

Most organizations perform an activity called **input validation**, whereby input data are examined for all possible errors. This activity allows only valid data to enter a computer for processing, whereas invalid data are rejected. Validation is accomplished through computer programs that are a part of the TPS. They check the input data through a series of validation tests, which are discussed in Chapter 6.

Information Processing

After data are collected and validated, they are processed. A few common tasks comprise the bulk of the information-processing activity in an organization.

Classification. In many commercial applications **classification** is necessary to group business transactions according to preselected criteria. For example, a student master file might be classified according to the year of study (freshman, sophomore, and so on). Classification is necessary because business transactions that have the same criterion are often processed in the same way, and it is much faster to process these transactions if they are grouped together.

Calculation. Calculation involves performing a mathematical operation on the data. In most business TPS applications the computer performs simple calculations, such as addition, subtraction, multiplication, and division. However, some TPSs do require complex mathematical calculations. The following are typical examples of the calculations required of a TPS:

- addition operations, such as asking the computer to determine a student's total credits to date

- subtraction operations, such as figuring a customer's account balance after a monthly payment
- multiplication operations, such as calculating the gross pay of an hourly employee, based on the pay rate and the number of hours worked
- division operations, such as calculating the GPA of a student, based on total credit points and total credit units

These basic calculations are often combined—for example, adding the items in a list and then dividing by the total number of items to give an average.

Sorting. When a number of records are to be arranged in a specified order, a sorting operation is performed by the computer. Sorting is one of the most useful data-processing functions. For example, if a sales manager wants to rank order her salespersons on the basis of their total sales or a professor wants to rank order his students according to their GPAs or several marketing managers want to rank order their products on the basis of total product sales, a sorting function is necessary. The data field by which the records are to be sorted (e.g., the last name field) must be specified; it is called the sort key. The order of sorting can be either ascending (from lowest to highest) or descending (from highest to lowest). For example, a list of names sorted in ascending order would start with those names that begin with *A* and end with those that begin with *Z*. If that same list was sorted in descending order, it would begin with those names that start with *Z* and end with those that start with *A*. Figure 7–1 shows an unsorted student grade report; Figure 7–2 shows the same report sorted in a descending order of GPAs.

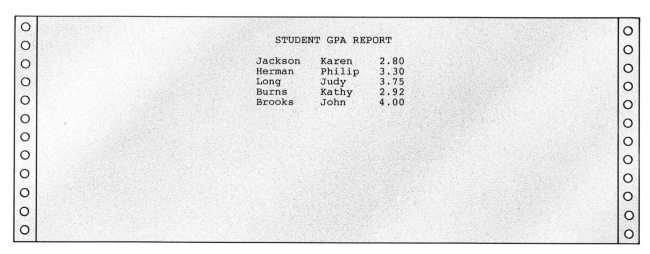

```
                    STUDENT GPA REPORT

         Jackson    Karen     2.80
         Herman     Philip    3.30
         Long       Judy      3.75
         Burns      Kathy     2.92
         Brooks     John      4.00
```

FIGURE 7–1
An unsorted GPA report.

```
                    STUDENT GPA REPORT

              Brooks      John      4.00
              Long        Judy      3.75
              Herman      Philip    3.30
              Burns       Kathy     2.92
              Jackson     Karen     2.80
```

FIGURE 7–2
A student report sorted in descending order of GPAs.

Summarization. **Summarization** is the process of transforming a mass of information into a reduced, or aggregate, form. For an overall view of an activity, summarized information is most useful. Many business managers are not interested in the details of an activity but want a general idea of it. To meet their requirements, detailed information needs to be summarized by the computer system. For example, if a professor is interested in knowing the grades earned by all students in one particular course, detailed information is needed. On the other hand, if she wants to know the total number of students receiving each of the letter grades, summarized information is needed. Figure 7–3 and Figure 7–4 show the two different types of information needed in this example.

```
                    STUDENT GPA REPORT

              Jackson     Karen      C
              Herman      Philip     B
              Long        Judy       B
              Burns       Kathy      C
              Brooks      John       A
              Murphy      Peter      D
              Haskins     Kevin      F
              Smith       Annie      A
              Schultze    Mark       D
              Patton      Kim        B
```

FIGURE 7–3
A detailed student grade report.

Principles of Business Information Systems

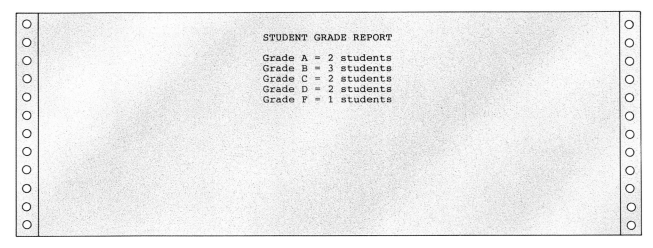

FIGURE 7–4
A summarized student grade report.

A well-known rule of thumb is that the higher the level is in an organization, the more summarized the information needs to be. All business managers need summarized information. Sales managers, inventory managers, marketing managers, financial managers, plant managers, engineering managers—all need summarized information of various types.

Updating

Updating is the process of changing the data that are stored in the computer. As new information becomes available, it is used to update old information. If someone moves, a new address replaces the old address; at the end of a school term, students' total credit units change, and so do their GPAs; if you work, your year-to-date earnings change at the end of each pay period. Because data are constantly changing, updating is one of the most useful functions performed by a TPS.

Computer-based sequential-file updating involves three primary files: an existing master file, a transaction file, and a new master file. The existing master file is the permanent repository of all data relating to an entity, such as an individual or an item. The transaction file contains all business transactions that occur during a specific time period—daily, weekly, or monthly. The data found in the transaction file indicate what kind of updating is to occur. Three common updating functions are (1) changing the value of a data field in the master file, (2) deleting a record in the master file, and (3) creating a new record in the master file. With data from the transaction file, the existing master file is updated, and a new master file is created. If the transaction file contains invalid data, an edit (error) report is generated during the updating process to inform management of the invalid data. Invalid data might result from trying to delete a nonexistent record, trying to add an existing record, and so on. The updating process is illustrated in Figure 7–5.

FIGURE 7–5
The process of updating a
master file with a transaction
file.

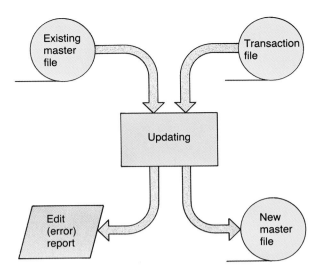

Output Generation

The end result of a transaction processing system is the production of output. Several types of output can be generated, most of which are paper. Figure 7–6 presents various outputs of transaction processing systems.

TPS reports include edit (error) reports and monitoring and control reports. As mentioned previously, edit (error) reports are generated during an updating function and supply a record of any invalid data contained in

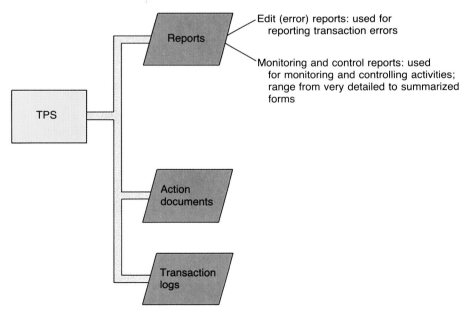

FIGURE 7–6
The outputs of a transaction processing system (TPS).

the transaction file. These reports can be generated by every transaction processing system, including those used in accounts payable, accounts receivable, payroll, inventory, general ledger, and so on. Edit reports would typically accompany updates of customer transactions, inventory, accounts payable, and the like.

Monitoring and control reports account for most TPS output. They supply operational level managers with the information needed to control and make decisions about the operational aspects of an organization. For example, a monitoring report of accounts payable might show the total amount paid out of each of the firm's checking accounts.

Another type of TPS output, an action document, is not a report but is a paper document that provides proof of transactions. Examples include purchase orders, tickets, and bank deposit and withdrawal slips.

Transaction logs, a third type of TPS output, are simple listings of transactions that occur during a specific time period. For example, a transaction log might list every check written by the accounts payable system during May. Each functional area within the system generates transaction logs that provide detailed information on all transactions. Because of their great detail, transaction logs offer little assistance to managers; however, they are quite valuable to persons who interact with the TPS on a daily basis.

COMMON TRANSACTION PROCESSING SYSTEMS

Certain transaction processing systems are commonly seen in business organizations: accounts payable, order entry, accounts receivable, inventory control, payroll, and general ledger. These systems are grouped into one broad category—accounting information systems.

Accounts Payable

When one organization purchases materials and services from other organizations, purchases are generally made on credit. The organizations to whom money is owed are commonly referred to as the vendors or suppliers, and the money that is owed is part of the debtor organization's accounts payable, until it is paid.

An accounts payable system is designed to keep track of and pay bills. The system can be used to determine such things as who gets how much and when, how much cash will be needed during a specific time period to pay vendors and suppliers, how much cash was disbursed during the last time period, and how large a discount each vendor or supplier is offering for prompt payment. An accounts payable system can generate a series of reports detailing this information for an organization.

Order Entry

The order entry function within an organization handles customer orders from the time an order is received until the time the product is sent. Since most orders are on credit, this function also approves or denies these orders based on the customer's payment history and capability. In addition, the order entry function ties in with the inventory function to ensure that a customer-ordered product is available.

The order entry system is designed to verify a customer order, perform credit checks on the customer in order to approve or deny the order, and dispose of the order accordingly. Because customer orders are the primary activity generating the sales for an organization, the order entry system is very important. With the numerous reports that this system produces, management can analyze sales to determine, among other things, what total sales were for a certain period, which products are the most popular, and which customers are the largest buyers.

Accounts Receivable

Accounts receivable is the opposite of accounts payable. It refers to the money owed to an organization by its customers for purchases made on credit. Until the money is fully paid, the customer's balance is part of accounts receivable.

Because it involves cash receipts, the accounts receivable system is one of the most critical applications. The system is used to generate customer bills and keep track of customer purchases, payments, account balances, and payment history. Several reports produced by this system are extremely important; they help managers better control accounts receivable and transform them into cash more quickly.

Inventory Control

The term *inventory* refers to the quantity of material that an organization has in stock or on order at any given moment. There are two types of inventory—raw materials and finished goods. The raw materials inventory represents the quantity of materials in stock that the organization uses to produce its products. The finished products inventory represents the quantity of finished goods available for sale to customers. For example, a furniture manufacturer keeps wood, metal, sandpaper, varnish, and so on as raw materials to produce its finished goods—tables and chairs.

Too much or too little inventory can have disastrous effects. It costs dollars and space to keep each item in inventory, but sales may be lost or production slowed if there is too little in inventory. The goal of an inventory control system is to minimize these effects. The system can be used to determine not only the level of inventory, but also the optimum inventory strategy. Several reports are generated by such a system, including the stock status of all inventory items, the fast-moving and the slow-moving items, items on back order, and the lead times (between order and receipt) for different items. Such reports help management control and minimize the cost of inventory.

Payroll

Every organization has employees who are paid wages at the end of a specific time period. The payroll function handles this activity. Depending on the type and size of the organization, this function can be very simple or very complex. The payroll system performs various calculations to compute taxes, insurance payments, other deductions, and net salary. The system then generates the paychecks and keeps records of various year-to-date amounts, such as earnings, taxes deducted, and amounts of vacation and sick leave accrued and used. In addition, this system produces various year-end documents (e.g., W-2 forms) and reports for the organization and the government.

General Ledger

The general ledger refers to a document that contains summarized information from each functional area of an organization. The general ledger information system generates an organization's general ledger with summary inputs from other transaction processing systems. This relationship is shown in Figure 7−7. Among the reports produced by the general ledger system are a balance sheet, income statement, and general ledger balance. These reports depict the financial health of an organization and are, therefore, the most important to its top management.

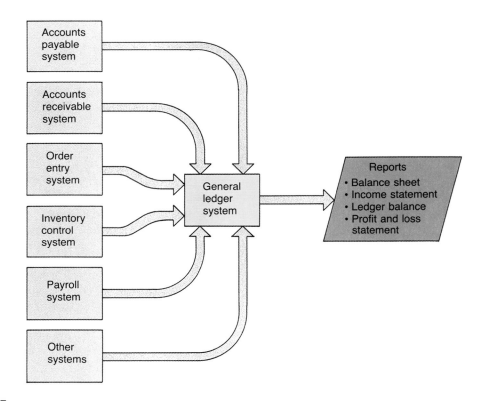

FIGURE 7−7
The relationship between the general ledger system and other transaction processing systems.

MANAGEMENT INFORMATION SYSTEMS

A management information system (MIS) generates information to help managers detect and solve problems in all areas of their responsibility. Although it is possible to have an MIS without a computer system, this text considers a computer system an essential element of an MIS.

TPSs in Relation to MISs

Transaction processing systems provide information on past transactions. They perform routine record-keeping functions to provide information for operational level management. A management information system provides information in the form of management reports that are used for problem detection and assistance in problem solving. An MIS serves the information needs of tactical- and strategic-level managers.

Often, TPSs feed information to an MIS. For example, the sales information gathered by the order entry TPS over several years can be used by an MIS to forecast the sales for the following year. The actual sales performance is provided by the transaction processing system, but the sales prediction is furnished by the management information system. With the sales forecast the manager can attempt to detect and solve any problems regarding purchase of materials, plant capacity, manpower requirements, and the like.

Let's consider another example. The accounts payable TPS identifies the cash requirements for the materials and services received from vendors and suppliers. The financial manager uses an MIS with data from the accounts payable TPS. The MIS helps the financial manager determine how much cash is needed and when and then analyze the cost of cash acquisition from several sources. Similar examples can be provided in other areas of the business organization, such as inventory, accounts receivable, and payroll.

ROLE OF MANAGEMENT INFORMATION SYSTEMS

During the early days of computers in business, routine record-keeping of an accounting nature was the only activity performed by computer systems. Later, the realization that a computer system could be used for purposes other than simple transaction processing led to the introduction of management information systems.

Management information systems are being used by more and more organizations for problem identification and problem solving and decision making in all areas of activity, including planning, marketing, finance, manufacturing, human resources, and project management. So successful has the use of MISs been, that today most organizations have an MIS department headed by a vice president. Spurred by the introduction of smaller, more powerful, yet inexpensive hardware; user-friendly programming languages; and database technology, organizations have started to develop innovative MIS applications in an effort to gain greater control over their activities, thus gaining advantages over their competitors. Highlight 7–1 takes a look at how retailers are using MISs. Today, there are few organizations that do not use an MIS. MISs provide more and better in-

To the average shopper the use of information systems in a retail store may not be readily noticeable. However, information systems are involved in most aspects of retailing. For example, when customers shop in the relaxed environment of Nordstrom stores in Seattle, they are probably unaware that a computer-aided design and manufacturing (CAD/CAM) system was used to plan the store's layout—with items arranged for easy access and aisles that allow smooth and easy traffic flow.

Information systems are also being used to improve customer service and to gather customer information for marketing efforts. One approach to improving customer service is through the use of video kiosks. A video kiosk is a single upright cabinet that contains a video disk player linked to one or more personal computers. For smaller retail stores like the Florsheim shoe store in San Francisco, which doesn't keep every item it sells in stock, a video kiosk offers customers a chance to view all the styles and colors offered. Customers who want items that are not in stock can place their orders on the terminal and have the shoes delivered to their homes.

Other retailers, such as the large all-purpose department stores, want to maintain a full stock of all their items on their premises. In order to do this cost-effectively, they need to employ an inventory control system. Such a system can inform them of when an item needs to be reordered so that they have enough in stock to satisfy customer demands but not so many that inventory costs get out of hand. These systems often use point-of-sale terminals equipped with bar code scanners; these terminals are on-line with the company's mainframe computers, which contain the inventory database. When an item is purchased, the data are recorded by the point-of-sale terminal and sent to the mainframe. The item is then deducted from inventory, and a check is made to see whether that item should be reordered.

formation so that management can more easily identify problems and solve them with better and wiser decisions.

An MIS not only makes internal operations more efficient, but also extends its impact to external operations, such as customer and vendor relations, to make them more efficient and beneficial. For example, an MIS at Mobil Oil Corporation supplied information that led to the development of a computer-based system to market gasoline in California. Point-of-sale terminals were installed at the gas pumps that could be used with the automated teller machines of two leading banks.

Information system technology is also being used to automate and standardize the transactions between retailers and their suppliers. Electronic data interchange (EDI) (also known as the ANSI X12 standard) is a communications protocol being used to allow retailers and their suppliers to conduct business transactions electronically instead of manually. EDI reduces the amount of paperwork, human involvement, and time associated with processing a single order. Turn-around time on orders has been reduced in some cases by as much as 50 percent. Currently, purchase order, invoice, advanced shipment, inventory advice, and price/sales catalog applications have been developed. Retailers such as Mervyn's in Hayward, California, report that turn-around time for delivery of goods has decreased from a week to a day. Mervyn's is currently linked electronically to 130 suppliers.

Information systems are also being used to improve customer service at the checkout counter; retailers want to reduce the amount of time customers must spend waiting in line to pay for their items. Many stores are now incorporating price management systems, which maintain the current prices on all items that a store stocks. In some stores this total can be close to several hundred thousand items. Price management systems allow clerks to look up the price of any item electronically, without having to thumb through catalogs or newspaper ads to check for sales prices while customers wait.

Retail stores are also using information systems to create databases containing customer information, such as where they shop, what items they purchase, and how often they use checks or credit cards. This information is being used for a variety of purposes. A store can provide better customer service by knowing which items shoppers purchase most often and then informing them through mailers of sales on those items. In addition, some retailers, such as Sears, Roebuck and Company, are trying to build a single profile of their customer to help them target their marketing efforts more effectively. Information on which items customers are buying can also help retailers identify which products are selling well and decide which merchandise to continue selling.

Management Functions

The function of management is to see that desired objectives are accomplished through others. What the objectives are and how they are to be accomplished must first be decided by top management. Then, as resources are organized to accomplish the objectives, constant communication and controlling are necessary to ensure that efforts are expended effectively.

Chapter 1 outlines the functions of a manager; planning, staffing, organizing, directing, and controlling. Figure 7−8 reviews these functions.

Principles of Business Information Systems

FIGURE 7–8
The functions of a manager.

• Planning	developing courses of action to meet short- and long-term goals of the organization
• Staffing	assembling and training personnel
• Organizing	providing resources and a structure in which personnel are responsible and accountable
• Directing	supplying leadership through communication and motivation
• Controlling	developing procedures to measure actual performance against goals and making any necessary adjustments

Management information systems play an important role in every function of management. Let's look at planning. At each level of an organization, a plan is developed after careful analysis of several alternatives. That analysis consists of evaluating the impact of each alternative on the organizational objective(s); an MIS facilitates the analysis by providing information to management.

An MIS also plays a significant role in the staffing function by enabling management to identify, recruit, train, and retrain the best personnel for the organization. In addition, staffing levels can be adjusted, depending on the sophistication of the MIS. Studies have shown that with an effective MIS an organization can reduce its levels of management.

The role of an MIS is also important in the organizing function. The allocation of resources among various departments can be difficult and is prone to problems. An MIS can help analyze allocation strategies and, in turn, help resolve problems related to resource allocation.

An increasingly important role is being played by MISs in the directing function, through the improvement of communications. MIS technology facilitates communication not only within but also outside the organization. This improvement has been achieved through the use of electronic mail and data communications technology in MISs.

One of the most important roles played by an MIS is in the controlling function. MISs provide performance feedback to management on all activities in the organization. Much MIS reporting is based on the idea that planned activity minus actual activity equals variance. And it is the variance that informs management to take the necessary corrective actions.

Management Hierarchy and Information Needs

Every organization has several levels of management; the number of levels depends primarily on the size and type of the organization. The structure of management is known as **management hierarchy**, with the president of an organization at the highest level, followed by the executive vice president, other vice presidents, directors, managers, and supervisors. Each level of the management hierarchy has different information needs. The information needed at the highest level is strategic, whereas the information needed at the middle level is more tactical, and that needed at the lowest level of management is more operational.

Strategic Management. Strategic management refers to those individuals who are at the highest level of the management hierarchy: the president, the executive vice president, and all other vice presidents of the organization. These individuals establish the goals of the organization and the strategies through which the goals will be achieved. Goals identify where an organization would like to be in the future; strategies are the vehicles that carry an organization to its goals.

Since the job of top management is strategic in nature, the information needed is also strategic. Information that is used in planning, organizing, directing, and controlling at the highest level is considered strategic. Not all information needed by top management comes out of the computer system. In fact, most of it comes from noncomputer sources.

Generally speaking, the higher the level an individual holds in an organization, the more summarized is the information that person needs. For example, the president of an organization does not need sales information about each salesperson. Rather, the president is more interested in the total sales of the organization. A regional sales manager, on the other hand, is very interested in the details about each salesperson within the region.

Tactical Management. Tactical management includes the individuals reporting directly to a vice-president of an organization. Tactics are the mechanisms with which the organizational strategy is accomplished. There may be several tactics to achieve one organizational strategy. For example, the strategy may be to become the largest organization (saleswise) in the industry. The tactics to achieve this strategy may be for each of the operating departments to contribute equally to the strategy. If there are five departments, each department should contribute 20 percent to the sales strategy. Thus, each department manager will need to develop tactics to meet the department strategy, monitor the performance of these tactics, and take corrective actions if necessary.

The information needs of middle management are tactical; middle managers need information that helps them achieve department objectives. Most of this information comes from an organization's MIS, and that information comes in semisummarized forms. For example, a department manager may not want to know the sales output of each salesperson in the department but will be interested in knowing the total sales of the department.

Operating Management. Operating management refers to those individuals who are responsible for managing the routine operations of an organization. They report to tactical (middle) management, and their functions are more operational in nature. A regional sales manager is an operating manager, responsible for the sales operation of the region.

Operating management needs operational information, which presents the details of a business operation. The information is primarily detailed although some of it may be summarized at the first level. For example, a regional sales manager is interested in sales information about each salesperson (detailed) as well as total sales information about the region (summarized at the first level).

<table>
<tr><td>

MIS PRESENTATION OF INFORMATION

</td><td>

The basic purpose of an MIS is to present information to managers for problem detection and problem solving. The information is presented in the form of reports and on-line retrieval. The reports are hard-copy printouts containing a mass of information, whereas on-line retrieval generates a small amount of information as a result of a manager's inquiry.

</td></tr>
</table>

Reports

Reports are the primary form of presenting information to all levels of management in an organization. Most of the time, these reports appear as hard-copy printouts. Reports are often classified according to their schedule of production and their contents. **Scheduled reports** are generated on a regular basis, following a well-established schedule. Some reports are generated weekly, and others monthly. Most accounting reports are scheduled reports, such as inventory stock status, accounts receivable aging, accounts payable aging, sales, production cost, budget, cash disbursements, and cash requirements reports. Scheduled reports are useful primarily to operating managers and their staffs. The reports may be detailed or summarized, depending on their use.

Demand reports are generated only on the demand of an individual. In other words, these reports are not produced unless someone asks for them; the reports are needed for special purposes. A personnel manager may want to know which employees have shown unsatisfactory job performance for 2 consecutive years. Such a report is not produced on a regular basis but may be required at special times, such as prior to staff layoffs.

Exception reports highlight activities that are out of control and thus need management action. These reports allow more efficient use of managers' time by focusing in on activities that seem to have problems. Exception reports might target late activities for a project manager, delinquent customers for a credit manager, slow-moving items for an inventory manager, or absentee workers for a manufacturing manager.

On-Line Retrieval

In many situations a manager may have specific questions about something that does not warrant a full report, but the manager wants answers very quickly. The on-line retrieval feature of a management information system offers this capability. It works like this: a manager asks a question by keying in a request in a user-friendly command language, and the computer responds to the question immediately. On-line retrieval applications include inquiries by a credit manager on the credit status of an applicant or a customer, by an airlines reservation manager on flight schedule information, and by an inventory manager on the status of an item in inventory.

Regardless of format, an MIS presents information to a manager only in a predetermined form. It cannot provide any other views of the information or incorporate new information without first being reprogrammed. To give managers greater flexibility in entering, retrieving, and analyzing the data they need, decision support systems (DSSs) are used.

DECISION SUPPORT SYSTEMS

A decision support system is an interactive, computer-based decision system that helps solve semistructured or unstructured management problems. The key terms in this definition are important. An **interactive system** allows a user to communicate with the computer through dialogue. The term *decision system* means that this system is used for decision making. *Unstructured problems* refer to those without any clear-cut solutions—these may be one-time problems that do not repeat or problems that cannot be predicted in advance. Structured problems have well-known solutions and are repetitive, whereas *semistructured problems* fall in between structured and unstructured problems. The term *management* suggests that managers are the ones who use decision support systems.

Primary Functions of a DSS

The primary function of a DSS is to assist managers in solving unstructured and semistructured problems. Its function is not to make decisions for managers, but to support them in their decision making. Managers need to evaluate the solutions proposed by a DSS, using their judgment, intuition, and experience to make their own decisions.

Since a semistructured or unstructured problem does not have a clear-cut solution, a DSS presents several tentative solutions for one problem. A manager then evaluates each of the proposed solutions. Thus, there are several cycles of information processing. The first step may involve the computer in mathematical calculations or manipulations of varying complexity. However, if the data for generating the necessary information already exist in the database, all that is needed is to access that database. This instantaneous retrieval of information after a few keys are pressed on a keyboard is an important feature of a DSS. A DSS allows a manager to enter, retrieve, and analyze data in an ad hoc manner. The manager does not have to rely on the systems department to make changes in the program, create new relationships among existing data, or analyze the data. As a result, information can be available almost immediately, and the typical MIS delays are avoided.

Components of a DSS

A decision support system has three basic components, called subsystems: the interface, model, and data subsystem. The **interface subsystem** is the component that links the manager and the computer. It handles all user inputs to and responses from the DSS. This subsystem consists of one or

FIGURE 7–9

Major components of a decision
support system (DSS).

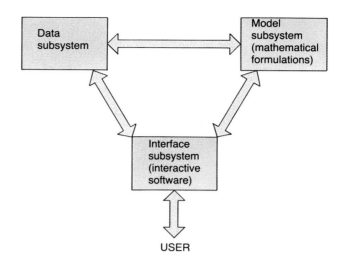

more computer programs and must be user-friendly so that managers will
not have difficulty using the DSS.

The **model subsystem** represents the mathematical formulations that
define a real-life problem. Many DSSs are based on quantitative models of
varying complexity. The computer uses these models to develop solutions
to a problem. For example, if a manager is trying to determine the best
location for a new plant, a complex mathematical model can be used to aid
in determining that location. Different mathematical models are necessary
for different problems. For certain problems an existing model can be used
directly by the DSS. For other problems the model may need to be developed first.

The **data subsystem** represents the data that are necessary to solve a
specific problem. Most of the data are input by a manager; some are
provided by either the developer of the model or the programmer. This
subsystem includes the database and the tools that are necessary to manage
the database; it handles the processing and the retrieval of the data. The
components of a DSS are shown in Figure 7–9.

PROCESSING FUNCTIONS OF A DSS

Of the different types of processing functions employed by DSSs, the following are the most important.

Financial Calculation

The financial function of a DSS consists of tools that are necessary in
common financial and economic analysis:

- present-value calculation
- future-value calculation
- return-on-investment calculation

- depreciation calculation
- loan amortization
- corporate tax structure
- statistical analyses

What-If Analysis

The what-if analysis, perhaps the most useful feature of a DSS, uses a model and several assumptions that are associated with it. If the data in the model or the assumptions are changed, the DSS generates a different solution. This ability to generate different solutions based on different data and assumptions is known as what-if analysis. For example, let's suppose that several managers are trying to decide whether their organization should acquire a new company. Their decision will depend on whether the new company is profitable. The profitability of the new company depends, in turn, on several factors: purchase price, projected sales in future years, cost of borrowed money, amount of down payment, and so on. The managers can enter a value for each of these variables and see the resulting profit. Then they can enter a different value for one or several of the variables and see the resulting profit in that case. They can continue in this way as long as they want to and then decide whether the acquisition would be profitable. The impact of these changeable variables can be seen instantaneously on the monitor, permitting the managers to make a much more informed decision than would otherwise be possible. Spreadsheets can also be used for DSS what-if analysis.

Sensitivity Testing

The sensitivity testing function is a special form of what-if analysis. In some situations managers are not sure of the data used in a variable of the model. In such situations they may want to change the data and find out how sensitive the result is to the change. In the previous example the managers would be able to determine the sensitivity of profit to a change in projected sales.

Goal Seeking

The goal-seeking function of a DSS provides an answer to the value of a certain variable once a target goal is specified. The function may be stated in this way: If the manager's goal is X, what should be the value of Y? In this statement X specifies the goal the manager wants to achieve, and Y specifies the variable whose value the manager wants to know. For example, the manager may ask, "What sales volume is needed to achieve a profit of $5 million, assuming that profit is 15 percent of sales?" In this example, the goal is $5 million profit, and the variable whose value the manager wants to learn through the goal-seeking function is the sales volume.

Analysis

The analyzing function of a DSS provides detailed explanation of the result of using a DSS. In cases where managers are intrigued by results, they may ask for an explanation. The DSS uses statistical analyses to provide that explanation. This function is not usually present in simple DSS packages but is available with the more sophisticated and expensive decision support systems.

Simulation

The simulation function of a DSS generates solutions to a problem by using various combinations of values for the variables in the model. For example, if the model consists of three variables and each variable can assume 10 possible values, simulation will generate solutions with 30 possible sets of values. A manager can then evaluate all 30 solutions before making a decision. When the decision model consists of several variables and each variable can have a large range of values, simulation is a useful DSS function. Since the DSS offers a solution for every possible set of variables, the risk associated with decision making is reduced.

DSS REPORTS AND APPLICATIONS

Reports generated by a decision support system are known as predictive reports and are useful in suggesting what might happen, given certain planning decisions. These reports are prepared on the basis of quantitative techniques, such as statistical analysis, and the tools of management science. Predictive reports are of two types—batch and interactive. Batch reports are produced by batch processing, which was described earlier. Interactive reports, which represent a large majority of DSS reports, are generated instantaneously while a manager interacts with the DSS.

There are numerous DSS applications in business organizations. Some of the most important and widely used are in financial planning, manufacturing, mergers and acquisitions, new product development, plant expansion, and sales forecasting. In financial planning DSSs are used by banks for budgeting and for analyzing the impact of changes in money market rates, financial regulations, and interest rates. Manufacturing firms use DSSs to study the impact that different combinations of production processes, labor rates, and machine capacities have on production costs. DSSs are used in new product development to analyze the impact that different marketing strategies and competitive actions have on the success of a new product. In plant expansion the application of a DSS involves analyzing the effect of different expansion alternatives on cost and production. Sales forecasting incorporates DSSs to evaluate various estimates of the profit of a company being considered for acquisition.

Astute managers are beginning to use the power of DSSs together with communications technology to support so-called group decision support systems (GDSS). Coopers and Lybrand include typical external conditions, costs, revenues, and so on and then let their key managers add in from their keyboards, additional information to be examined in important decisions.

EXECUTIVE INFORMATION SYSTEMS

Executive is usually synonymous with *strategic* or *top-level*. An executive has the responsibility to set long-range planning goals and a strategic course for an organization for the years ahead. Although different levels of management can benefit from decision support systems, DSSs are used predominately by middle management for assistance in decision making. An executive information system (EIS) is a specialized decision support system for use by executives. Figure 7–10 illustrates the relationships of TPSs, MISs, DSSs, and EISs for various levels of management.

An executive information system incorporates large volumes of data and information gathered from an organization's external environment. That information is used in conjunction with the information generated by MISs within functional areas of the organization to accommodate the specialized information needs of executives. An EIS plays a vital role in summarizing and controlling the volume of information that an executive must read. An executive can assign values to the various sources of information from which data for an EIS are drawn. This helps assure that the executive will receive information from sources deemed most important for decision making. Thus, EISs can be tailored to meet the specific needs of each executive in an organization.

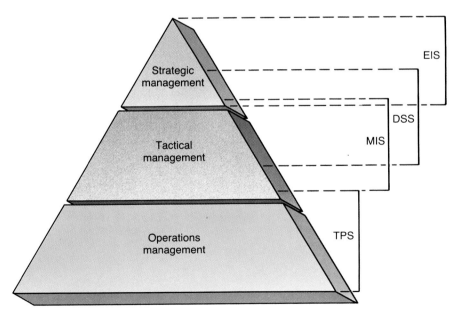

FIGURE 7–10
Relationship between TPSs, MISs, DSSs, EISs and the levels of management.

Principles of Business Information Systems

KNOWLEDGE-BASED (EXPERT) SYSTEMS

As mentioned previously, knowledge-based (expert) systems comprise a class of information systems used to help determine problems and assist in arriving at solutions. The popularity of these systems has grown significantly in recent years. More and more government and business organizations are developing expert systems to assist managers in an increasing number of areas of operation. According to Edward Feigenbaum, a professor at Stanford University and a leading researcher in expert systems, a knowledge-based (expert) system is defined as

> an intelligent computer program that uses knowledge and inference procedures to solve problems that are difficult enough to require significant human expertise for their solution. Knowledge necessary to perform at such a level, plus the inference procedures used, can be thought of as a model of the expertise of the best practitioners of the field.

From this definition it is clear that a knowledge-based system functions somewhat like an expert in a field, solving problems that require knowledge, intelligence, and experience. Since the system depends primarily on the knowledge of human experts, it is called a knowledge-based, or an expert, system. This book will use those terms interchangeably. It should also be clear that the source of information for an expert system is quite different from that of the other systems we have discussed. Table 7–1 depicts the sources of information for the various types of information systems.

History

Expert systems are the by-products of artificial intelligence (AI) research that has been going on since World War II. Although AI research is not a new discipline, its popularity and that of expert systems are a recent phenomenon. Once solely a topic among AI researchers, expert systems are

TABLE 7–1
Primary sources of information for TPSs, MISs, DSSs, EISs, and knowledge-based systems.

Type of System	Primary Sources of Information
Transaction processing	Business transactions from the functional areas
Management information	Summarized TPS data
Decision support	Internal database data External supporting data Internal MIS data
Executive information	External databases External environmental scans Internal DSS DATA
Knowledge-based (expert)	Human experts from the appropriate specialty area

now seen in offices, hospitals, research laboratories of various types, industrial plants, manufacturing shops, repair shops, oil wells, and the like.

During the second World War, computers were developed to perform complex numeric calculations. However, a small group of computer scientists were exploring the possibility of having computers process nonnumeric symbols. At about the same time psychologists who were studying human problem solving wanted to create computer programs to mimic human intelligence. The efforts of these two groups seemed to be directed at somewhat the same objective—to create machines that would act like humans. Together these two groups laid the foundation of a new discipline, termed artificial intelligence. In the early 1970s a number of corporations attempted to apply AI principles to the solution of business problems, and several of the companies set up AI research groups to develop practical business applications of AI research. However, these efforts did not prove successful at the time. AI applications were

- too costly to develop
- too slow in execution
- not sufficiently practical
- too complex to be run on existing hardware

With the introduction of microelectronics technology came a new generation of faster, more powerful, and relatively inexpensive computer hardware. This technology, combined with the development of programming languages suitable for AI applications, revived AI research interests and transformed AI applications such as knowledge-based systems into viable applications for business.

Conventional Programs vs. Knowledge-Based Systems

A knowledge-based system is a set of computer programs; however, there are certain differences between conventional computer programs and knowledge-based systems. The following are the most important of these differences.

- The task performed by an expert system resembles one performed by a human expert or specialist, whereas the task performed by a conventional computer program is a routine human task.
- An expert system is developed and maintained by a knowledge engineer and experts, but a conventional computer program is developed and maintained by a computer programmer.
- A conventional computer program relies heavily on algorithms, whereas an expert system relies on knowledge and rules of thumb (known as heuristic techniques).
- The algorithm of a conventional computer program remains unchanged, whereas the knowledge that is incorporated into an expert system usually changes constantly, thus changing the reasoning outcome.
- An expert system mimics human reasoning; no such reasoning is present in a conventional computer program.

COMPONENTS OF A KNOWLEDGE-BASED SYSTEM

A knowledge system has three major and three minor components. The major components are user-interface, a knowledge base, and an inference engine. The minor components are working (or short-term) memory, an explanation subsystem, and a knowledge acquisition subsystem. These components are depicted in Figure 7–11.

User Interface

The **user interface** consists of a set of computer programs that links a knowledge-based system and its user. All user inputs and system-generated outputs are handled by this software. Through a keyboard the user enters inputs in the form of commands and data entry operations. The expert system outputs are returned to the user in the form of messages and output displays.

Knowledge Base

The **knowledge base** is the most important component of an expert system. The performance of an expert system is a function of the size and quality of that knowledge base. A knowledge base resembles a database: a knowledge base contains knowledge just as a database contains data. However, a knowledge base contains the knowledge of an expert in a certain field. Rule-based knowledge representation enjoys high popularity today although expert knowledge can be represented by other methods. With the rule-based approach the expert's knowledge is transformed into rules and associations that are stored in the knowledge base. The greater the number of these rules and associations, the larger the knowledge base will be.

The rules and associations may be constructed in the form of conditional statements, such as the following: If sales are rapidly increasing and the long-range outlook is excellent, then consider hiring more production employees. Whatever precedes the comma forms the left-hand side of the rule, and whatever follows the comma forms the right-hand side of the

FIGURE 7–11
The components of a knowledge-based system.

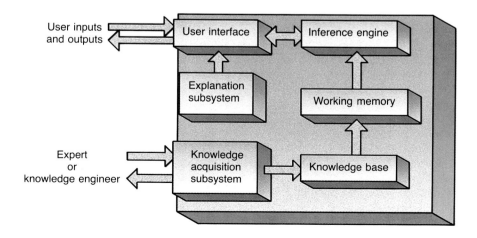

rule. In some expert systems rules have probabilities associated with them to indicate the degree of confidence in the conclusions. Let's consider another version of the previous example: If sales are rapidly increasing and the long-range outlook is excellent, then consider hiring more production employees (.7). This version claims a 70 percent chance that hiring more employees is the correct action if both conditions are true.

Inference Engine

The **inference engine**, an integral part of every expert system, is the software that applies the rules from the knowledge base to the data provided by the user to draw a conclusion. There are two types of inference engines, determined by how the conclusion is drawn. In a **data-directed inference procedure** the engine checks the left-hand side of a rule, matches it with user-provided data, and draws a conclusion by looking at the right-hand side of the rule. In a **goal-directed inference procedure** the engine forms a hypothesis and then tries to prove that hypothesis by looking at the right-hand side of the rule and checking the left-hand side to see whether it matches the user-provided data.

Working Memory

Working memory (also known as short-term memory or dynamic knowledge base) is that part of the computer memory in which the appropriate rules and data are stored for an instant during the execution of an expert system. Since these rules and data must be readily accessible by the expert system, they are removed from the knowledge base and maintained in the working memory. The contents of the working memory constantly change during the execution of an expert system.

Explanation Subsystem

Most expert systems incorporate an **explanation subsystem**, which has the capability to respond to user requests and inquiries while the system is executing. For example, if an expert system requests additional data from the user during execution, the user might want to ask the expert system why the additional data are needed. Typically, the user would ask why by pressing a key on the keyboard or typing the word *Why*. In response, the expert system would use the explanation subsystem to give the reason for the additional data. This component of the expert system can also be used to learn the reasoning behind the expert system's conclusion. Knowing the reasoning may help the user determine whether the conclusion is valid.

Knowledge Acquisition Subsystem

The heart of every expert system is the knowledge transferred from an expert to the knowledge base. This transfer is accomplished by the software component known as the **knowledge acquisition subsystem**. If the knowledge in the knowledge base needs to be updated or retrieved, this subsystem can perform these functions.

Shells

At present, several commercial tools are available to help build expert systems, making it unnecessary to build such systems from scratch. These tools are known in the industry as **shells**, or expert system shells. Most shells contain all of the components of an expert system except the knowledge base. Thus, buyers need to add only a knowledge base to create their own expert systems. Shells are available for both personal and mainframe computers. The low-end price of personal computer shells is approximately $50.00, whereas some mainframe computer shells cost more than $80,000.00.

ROLE OF KNOWLEDGE ENGINEERS

The process by which an expert's knowledge is transformed into a knowledge base is called **knowledge engineering**. Special skills are required to capture an expert's knowledge and put it into a programmable form; and a new group of professionals, known as **knowledge engineers**, are trained to perform that role.

The role of knowledge engineers is extremely critical in the design and development of expert systems; the power and success of the systems depend on the skills of the knowledge engineers who build them. As a result, the work of knowledge engineers requires an intimate association with the experts. Unfortunately, the experts themselves are often unable to explain the reasoning process they employ in solving complex problems, making the task of knowledge engineers even more difficult. In such cases knowledge engineers must ask the right questions to get the right information from the experts and then develop the appropriate rules for an expert system.

BUSINESS USES OF KNOWLEDGE SYSTEMS

Many businesses have been using knowledge systems to provide quicker and easier problem detection as well as assistance in problem solving and decision making, thereby improving productivity and reducing the costs of operation (Highlight 7–2). Both the number of business organizations using expert systems and the number of knowledge systems being developed are on the rise, testifying to the usefulness and effectiveness of expert systems in business (Figure 7–12). It is neither practical nor possible to identify all of the expert systems being used in business; businesses that employ expert systems for competitive purposes are reluctant to discuss their specific applications. However, we can describe a few well-known systems in diverse business organizations.

DENDRAL is an expert system that examines the spectroscopic analysis of an unknown chemical compound and predicts its molecular structure. Developed in 1965 through the joint effort of three scientists—Joshua Lederberg (a Nobel Prize winner in chemistry), Edward Feigenbaum, and Bruce Buchanan—DENDRAL has been a successful system, leading AI scientists to pursue business applications. DENDRAL is available on a Stanford University computer that can be accessed by outside chemists through time-sharing.

FIGURE 7–12
The recently developed Ford expert system enables plant electricians to maintain robots without undergoing lengthy and expensive training. Plant personnel are led to robot problems by pictures and instructions on the expert system's computer screen, shown in the center of the photo. At the left is the robot arm lifting three 40-pound automatic transmission torque converters. (Courtesy of Ford Motor Company)

MYCIN is a landmark expert system used to diagnose infectious diseases and suggest possible therapies. The system was developed by Edward Feigenbaum and Edward Shortliffe, both of Stanford University. MYCIN was the first expert system to use the rule-based inference procedure now used by most expert systems. It has a knowledge base of 500 rules that describe expert knowledge about diagnoses. Each rule has a probability figure associated with it to indicate its level of certainty. MYCIN's performance is almost as good as that of physicians, a real indication that this new technology has practical business applications. EMYCIN, or essentially MYCIN, is an expert system shell; it is MYCIN without the knowledge base and is marketed as a shell that can be used with other knowledge bases.

PROSPECTOR is a geological expert system used by geologists to help find valuable mineral deposits. Developed in the late 1970s by the Stanford Research Institute, this expert system provides consultation services regarding the investigation of a site for ore-grade deposits. PROSPECTOR is capable of generating graphic responses in the form of maps and providing a conclusion. With this expert system geologists discovered a molybdenum deposit at Mt. Tolman worth $100 million, a deposit that had been overlooked for many years.

INTERNIST is an expert system that helps analyze difficult clinical problems. Developed in 1974 by a computer scientist and a physician, INTERNIST was developed to model a clinician's diagnostic reasoning for a large number of diseases and their possible combinations. The system begins by asking the user to describe the manifestations of the disease. Its diagnostic process involves examining each of the manifestations to determine which types of diseases could be associated with that manifestation.

Development of the American Express Credit Authorization Expert System

As is the case in most organizations, the American Express Company got involved with expert systems not because of an interest in technology but because of a need to improve efficiency and ensure that business functions continued to support the company's fundamental business objective. In this case the target function was credit authorization for credit card users.

Because American Express does not assign preset credit limits to its cardholders, the acceptability of a charge has to be dynamically determined each time a card is used. This process of credit authorization must be concerned with several major issues. It attempts to detect fraud, such as the use of a stolen credit card. It also attempts to determine a cardholder's ability to pay. For example, if the cardholder has been consistently delinquent in paying or has had excessive outstanding balances, then credit might be denied. However, the authorization process must also protect against the loss of business resulting from an improper denial of customer credit.

American Express uses an automated IBM MVS/XA mainframe credit authorization system (CAS), which is capable of resolving simple credit-approval transactions without human intervention. However, the volume of transactions to be authorized grew beyond the system's capacity, and additional human authorizers had to be hired. Unfortunately, along with the increased transaction volume came an increase in fraud as well as credit losses, many of which were attributed to faulty authorization decisions made by less experienced authorizers. As a result, American Express began to consider an expert system to assist in authorization decisions.

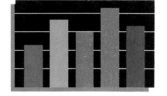

The company found that an expert system offered a number of potential benefits, including more consistent decision making, reductions

Each of the identified diseases is then given a composite score—a positive score for each of the patient's manifestations that can be attributed to the disease and a negative score for each of the manifestations that cannot be attributed to the disease. The highest-scoring disease is investigated first, in detail, to determine whether manifestations that should be present are present. Thus, all competing diseases are examined, and the most likely disease is identified.

XCON is an expert system that was developed at Carnegie-Mellon University for Digital Equipment Corporation (DEC). This system is used to ensure that the different components of a computer system chosen by DEC customers are compatible as one system. If the components are not compatible, the expert system recommends necessary adjustments. Before this expert system was developed, only a handful of DEC experts knew enough about computer components to be sure that the components chosen by a in the amount of credit and fraud loss, improved service to both customers and merchants, control and possible reduction in the expenses associated with processing credit cards, and a reduced learning curve for new authorizers. The firm's decision was to use an Inference Corporation expert system shell called Automated Reasoning Tool (ART); a group of expert authorizers was selected to provide the basis for the rules that would be used in the ART knowledge base. The initial design was a prototype including 520 rules and dealing only with the green card, American Express's basic card. The system was validated using actual case data from expert authorizers. Eventually, the system was fine-tuned and grew to 850 rules, proving to be very accurate at that stage of development. It demonstrated a 76 percent reduction in bad authorization decisions and was accurate 96.5 percent of the time, as compared with 85 percent accuracy for an average human authorizer.

The next phase in the development of the American Express expert system was called Authorizer's Assistant and was intended to integrate the system into the CAS environment. That phase was successfully completed in early 1987, and the system has been in use ever since. The expert system is now transparent, or invisible, to the human authorizer. It automatically reduces 12 screens of data to 2 screens of relevant information and then either recommends approval or denial of credit or asks that more data be gathered. If more data are to be gathered, Authorizer's Assistant guides the human authorizer through conversations with merchants and card members. As additional data are entered, Authorizer's Assistant uses them immediately to update the recommendations. All in all, the expert system has increased the efficiency and accuracy of credit authorizations for American Express and has proven its worth on the bottom line.

customer would work together. Since its development, XCON has generated considerable savings for DEC and has improved company decisions. A second expert system, XSEL, is being used by DEC salespersons to help them choose the right computer configuration for their customers.

DELTA (Diesel-Electric Locomotive Troubleshooting Aid) is an expert system used to help maintenance people repair diesel-electric locomotives. It was developed in 1983 by General Electric. DELTA is also known as CATS-1 (Computer-Aided Troubleshooting System−1). Before this expert system was developed, GE could fix its locomotives in two ways: either fly its only locomotive repair expert, David Smith, to the locomotive or transport the locomotive to David Smith. Both methods were expensive. DELTA was developed to transfer David Smith's repair knowledge to a computer-based system so that it could be used by GE's less expert personnel. The system has a knowledge base of 1200 rules and is capable of printing diagrams to show the locations of the various parts of a locomotive. It can also display, at the request of the user, a training film that shows the step-by-step procedure to fix a problem.

United Airlines is using an expert system developed by Texas Instruments to reduce travel delays and solve operating and scheduling problems at several airports. The system, called Gate Assignment Display System (GADS), has incorporated the knowledge of scheduling experts and has eliminated the wall-sized control boards and magnetic stick-on aircraft used to schedule incoming aircraft at different air terminal gates. Now the scheduler who becomes aware of weather interference or delays can move aircraft gate arrivals on a computer screen and have the system automatically adjust other aircraft to other available gates. The changes can be examined on the computer screen before the actual plan is set in motion.

DIFFERENCES BETWEEN DSSs AND EXPERT SYSTEMS

Many people think of expert systems and decision support systems as being the same; they think of expert systems as extensions of decision support systems. However, there are important differences between these two tools. Decision support systems almost always employ a model that formulates a real-life problem as a mathematical expression; such an expression rarely exists in most expert systems. And most decision support systems involve some mathematical calculations, whereas such calculations are few, if they exist, in expert systems. On the other hand, the reasoning procedure used by the processing component of an expert system, the inference engine, is nonexistent in decision support systems. In addition, the database used by a decision support system remains unchanged during execution, whereas the knowledge base of an expert system can be dynamically updated during execution. Finally, decision support systems are primarily used by managers, whereas expert systems can be used by any level of staff within an organization.

SUMMARY

A transaction processing system (TPS) is an information system that records and helps manage business transactions. The functions of a TPS include data collection, input validation, information processing, updating, and output generation. Data collection is the gathering of transactional data for entry into the computer system. Input validation is the process of checking input data for possible errors. Information processing includes the tasks of classification, calculation, sorting, and summarization. Updating is the process of changing data that are stored in the computer. Output generation includes the production of reports, action documents, and transaction logs. Common TPS applications include accounts payable, order entry, accounts receivable, inventory control, payroll, and general ledger.

A management information system (MIS) generates information for managers to use in problem detection and in problem solving and decision making. The information used by an MIS is often based on data generated by a TPS.

The functions of management are planning, staffing, organizing, directing, and controlling in order to get others to accomplish a desired objective. There are three basic levels of management: strategic or top-level, tactical or middle-level, and operational or low-level. Each level has specific information needs.

An MIS presents information through reports (scheduled, demand, and exception) and on-line retrieval. The data presented, their relationships, and their form are all predetermined in an MIS. To change or add data or relationships, the MIS must be reprogrammed by a systems department.

A DSS is an interactive, computer-based decision system that assists management in solving semistructured and unstructured problems. A DSS consists of three basic components: the interface, model, and data subsystems.

A DSS incorporates the following functions: financial calculation, what-if analysis, sensitivity testing, goal seeking, analysis, and simulation. A DSS generates predictive reports that are useful in planning. DSS applications include mergers and acquisitions, new product development, plant expansion, and plant financing.

A knowledge-based (expert) system provides suggested solutions to problems that require the knowledge, experience, and intuition of humans. Expert systems are a by-product of artificial intelligence research. The components of a knowledge-based system include a user interface, knowledge base, inference engine, working memory, explanation subsystem, and knowledge acquisition subsystem. A shell is an expert system without a knowledge base. Knowledge engineering is the process of transforming an expert's knowledge into a database. The specialist that performs this process is a knowledge engineer. Knowledge-based systems are useful for decision making in areas that have traditionally been handled by human experts.

MINICASE 7–1

Consumer Products Inc. (CPI) has developed a concept for a new product and is considering introducing that product. First, however, the company needs to determine whether the new product would be profitable. Several options are available to CPI. It can sell the concept to another company for a large sum of money and thus escape any risk, or it can do a market study and then, based on the results of the study, decide whether to introduce the product. The market study would cost some money, and the product might not succeed even if the market study indicated profitability. Numerous factors could influence the product's success or failure; however, the probabilities can be reasonably estimated by existing models.

1. The company is faced with a decision-making problem. Can an information system help? Which type of information system?

2. If you suggested an information system, how could it help in this decision-making situation?

Principles of Business Information Systems

The sales staff at Ray's Insurance Center deals with numerous types of insurance policies, and each customer comes to Ray's with different needs. It takes a salesperson a long time to help a customer select the right insurance policy to meet the constraints imposed by the customer—for example, price, amount of coverage, items to be covered, and numerous other factors. Often, customers end up waiting for a salesperson to become available. The sales staff is interested in a way to reduce the negotiating time needed to sell a customer a policy.

1. Can an information system help increase the salespersons' productivity and ensure the customers' satisfaction? Explain.
2. What type of information system, if any, would be appropriate?

Key Terms

calculation	knowledge acquisition subsystem
classification	knowledge base
data collection	knowledge engineer
data-directed inference procedure	knowledge engineering
data subsystem	management hierarchy
demand reports	model subsystem
exception reports	scheduled reports
explanation subsystem	shells
goal-directed inference procedure	summarization
inference engine	updating
input validation	user interface
interactive system	working memory
interface subsystem	

Review Questions

1. What is a transaction? Give several examples.
2. What is a transaction processing system?
3. Name five typical applications of transaction processing systems that are found in most businesses.
4. What are the functions of a transaction processing system?
5. Which four information processing functions are involved in transaction processing systems? Describe each.
6. Name and describe the three types of output generated by a transaction processing system.
7. What are management information systems?
8. What role does an MIS play in the controlling function of a manager?
9. Describe the three basic levels of management and their information needs.
10. Based on frequency and content, what are the different types of reports generated by an MIS? Provide an example of each type.

11. Describe a situation in which a manager might want to perform an on-line retrieval of information from an MIS.

12. What is a decision support system? To whom is such a system most useful?

13. Why are unstructured problems difficult to solve?

14. What are the components of decision support systems? State the function of each component.

15. What are the processing functions performed by decision support systems? Cite a real-life example of each function.

16. Give an example of a situation in which a DSS could be useful.

17. Define a knowledge-based system. Why is it also called an expert system?

18. Where would knowledge-based (expert) systems fit on Figure 7−10?

19. Describe the differences between conventional programs and knowledge-based systems.

20. Describe the three major and three minor components of an expert system.

21. Why are expert system shells valuable?

22. What is knowledge engineering? Why is it so important in an expert system?

23. What is the function of a knowledge engineer?

24. What rules should be included in an expert system to help you decide how long to study for your next test?

25. Provide an innovative problem situation in which an expert system could help solve the problem.

Office Information Systems

OBJECTIVES

- Understand the purpose of an office information system
- Define the role of word processing in an office information system
- Describe several major components found in office information systems
- Understand why human factors are important in the design of an office information system

OUTLINE

IMPACT ON MANAGEMENT PROBLEM SOLVING AND DECISION MAKING

DEFINITION OF AN OFFICE INFORMATION SYSTEM

WORD PROCESSING
Components of a Word-Processing System

DATA PROCESSING, STORAGE, AND RETRIEVAL
Automated Records Management I Micrographics I Optical Storage and Retrieval

IMAGE PROCESSING
Office Copiers I Scanners I Desktop Publishing as a Business Tool

COMMUNICATION SYSTEMS
Electronic Mail I Facsimile I The Telephone and Voice Messaging I Electronic Teleconferencing I Telecommuting

OFFICE SUPPORT SYSTEMS

INTEGRATION

HUMAN FACTORS

Chapter 8

Management Profile: George Perara
RYDER'S TEAM DRIVER

Twenty years ago George Perara worked for Ryder Truck Rental as a keypunch operator to put himself through college. Now, as Ryder's director of operations technology and administration, Cuban-born Perara remains true to his humble beginnings with a management style that seeks the advice of workers at every level.

That style, which Perara has dubbed "participatory management," is also adopted by Dennis Klinger, Ryder's vice president of MIS and Perara's boss. "We don't talk to him like he's the boss and we are the subordinates. He is kind of one of the group," Perara says of Klinger.

That is the very same approach Perara has established with those who report to him. According to Perara, simply asking for employees' advice can be a powerful motivator. The way it works is simple: "I don't follow a lot of the traditional organizational lines. It is not unusual for me to stop in the computer room at 7:00 at night, talk to the printing operator, and ask, 'What do you think if we did this?' "

In another case Perara had the job of redesigning Ryder's complex network command center. "It was a terror in the way cables were laid out. I wondered if I really understood what was under the floor," he says. So Perara did something that seemed obvious to him but which some managers questioned. He brought in the people who had been under the floor and asked their advice. The payoff was almost instantaneous. "I got back the most detailed plan I had ever seen," he says. "Those individuals volunteered to come in at midnight to make the thing work. They worked the entire weekend, and by Monday it was done."

Besides adding perspective to Ryder MIS decisions, participatory management gives all employees something to strive for, a chance to rise, like Perara, toward the top of the MIS heap. "I believe that promotions from within work," Perara explains.

The Klinger/Perara management style does place particular demands on employees. The key requirement for success is to be a team player. "That is a requirement to work for George Perara. You must be a team player," Perara says. For those who do not catch on, there is coaching and counseling on how to be more cooperative. If these lessons fail to sink in, the person may be left behind as the team marches on.

However, the Ryder MIS style is not as freewheeling as it may appear. Another element of Perara's approach is what he calls management by objective. This approach consists of weekly and monthly reports that state and track the company's objectives as well as detailed reports of specific projects.

Perara also ferrets out the views of the people whose jobs are directly affected by automation—the accounting staff, the marketing departments, and the purchasing groups. And being with a nationwide truck rental firm, Perara must also keep in touch with Ryder's field operations. "We get involved where the rubber meets the road," he notes.

Adapted from "George Perara: Ryder's Team Driver" by Douglas Barney. Copyright 1988 by CW Publishing Inc., Framingham, MA 01701. Reprinted from *Computerworld,* June 27, 1988.

In the late 1800s the invention of the typewriter brought automation and increased productivity to the typical office. Later, accounting machines and calculators added to office speed and efficiency. In a modern office of a large company prior to the 1960s, you probably would have seen a large, open space with rows of secretarial desks, topped with typewriters and adding machines, and lines of filing cabinets.

In that office, letters, reports, memos, and other data were written or typed and sorted manually. Any of the originals that needed to be distributed outside the office were sent via the U.S. Postal Service, and a carbon copy was filed in the filing cabinet. Memos, reports, and other data that needed to be distributed between offices were hand carried. Recordkeeping was usually handled right in the business office by clerks and accountants who processed the company's data and oversaw the office's information needs.

In recent times computers have had a powerful impact on the office environment and the way in which offices operate. In fact, with the acceptance of computer and communications technology, the whole concept of general office work and the business workplace changed in the 1970s and 1980s. Computers and communication technology made possible the concept of office information systems (OISs). This chapter defines an OIS and looks at some of its components.

IMPACT ON MANAGEMENT PROBLEM SOLVING AND DECISION MAKING

As we have noted throughout this text, managers need information to identify and solve problems and make decisions. That information needs to be prepared, stored, retrieved, and communicated; but all of these activities take time and can slow down a manager's receipt of needed information in a usable form. An office information system helps improve a manager's ability to control these processes. It enables the manager or an assistant to access information more quickly, prepare it in the desired form, and distribute it to those who need it. All of this translates into more productive time for both manager and staff.

Office information systems increase the productivity of office workers much as factory equipment has increased the productivity of factory workers. However, offices probably employ larger numbers of more highly paid people, so the gains from office information systems can be even greater. OISs allow managers more time to concentrate on the primary activities of problem detection and solution and decision making.

DEFINITION OF AN OFFICE INFORMATION SYSTEM

An office information system (OIS) is used to help knowledge workers manage the preparation, storage, retrieval, reproduction, and communication of information within and among business offices (Figure 8-1). A knowledge worker is a person who creates, processes, and distributes information. In the present Information Age these activities are the predominant tasks of most business workers, making an office information system very important to the efficient management of information in today's business world.

FIGURE 8–1

Office information systems have a variety of functions, including word processing, data processing, and sending and receiving electronic mail. The application functions of an individual system can change from time to time depending on the program being implemented. (Courtesy of Honeywell)

In their early development OISs were primarily concerned with automating the preparation of documents and other clerical functions; the term *office automation* (OA) was used to describe the automation of those functions. As the scope of an automated office grew, however, the term *office information system* became favored. An office information system involves more than simply introducing new hardware and software to automate tasks. It involves changing the procedures and attitudes of the personnel who will use the OIS. Careful planning is required to determine what type of OIS will meet an organization's goals; careful design is needed to meet the wide range of user needs.

It is also important that top management support any proposed OIS. Top management needs to be convinced that an OIS will not simply introduce new technology into the office, but will also result in changes to help achieve the organization's goals. Later chapters cover the analysis, design, and implementation phases involved in developing this or any information system.

It is important to realize that automation is not necessarily the answer or an appropriate solution for all information problems within an office. However, in many cases an OIS that is designed and used effectively can increase productivity in an office environment by making the production and flow of information more efficient, cheaper, and faster. Let's look at some of the technologies incorporated in an OIS.

WORD PROCESSING

It is generally agreed that the introduction of word-processing machines in the 1960s was the pivotal factor in changing the way that offices were operated. Today, word processing is the most widely adopted of all the new office technologies. Chapter 4 explained that a word processor allows text to be input into a computer, stored, edited, and printed. Thus, it assists a knowledge worker in the electronic creation of documents.

There are many reasons to use word processors. They help generate documents faster than traditional typewriters because there is no need to retype pages or white-out words and lines. Typographical errors can be corrected, and editing changes can be made on the screen before the text is actually printed. Words and paragraphs can be moved anywhere in the text, and characters can be changed, inserted, or deleted with just a few keystrokes. Many word processors also have a windowing feature that permits the user to work with two documents at once (Figure 8–2).

If there is a dictionary feature in the software, spelling can also be automatically checked. If there is a thesaurus, overused words can be automatically replaced by different words with the same meanings. Revisions can be made in the document until it is exactly right. Then it is printed electronically, clean and neat and needing no revisions. A word processor cannot tell writers what to say, but it can give them the freedom to concentrate on that creative aspect of their work—developing ideas. From a manager's perspective, word processors have the advantage of increasing the accuracy and speed with which documents are prepared and in some cases reducing the staff needed to prepare documents.

Components of a Word-Processing System

Because the purpose of a word processor is to accomplish a specific task—that is, to produce a written communication—specific pieces of equipment and software are required.

- A computer with sufficient RAM in primary storage is needed. RAM specifications are listed on the word processor packaging.

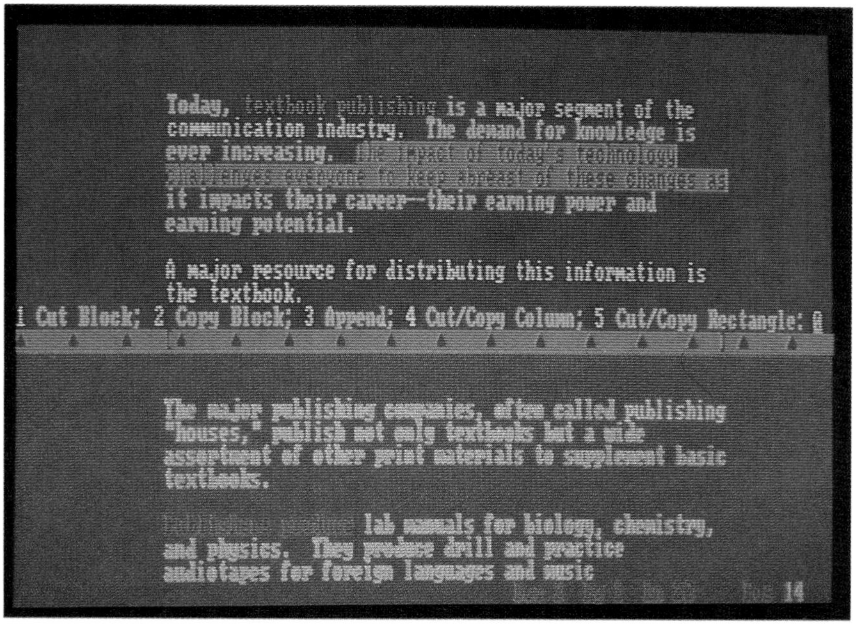

FIGURE 8–2
Many word processors offer a split-screen function so that a user can see and edit two different parts of the same document or two different documents at the same time.

- A video display screen, or monitor, is required to view the document as it is typed and edited. A high-resolution monitor gives the best results for word processing and is often required to take full advantage of the graphic capabilities of some of the newer word processors.
- Most word processors suitable for business tasks require two floppy-diskette drives or one floppy-diskette drive and one hard-disk drive.
- A printer is needed to produce hard-copy output. An appropriate interface card is also needed.
- A word processor (the software) to load into the computer is the final essential item. WordPerfect, XyWrite, Microsoft Word, WordStar, MultiMate, and PFS:Write are typical word processors available for various brands of computers. Many of these are available in network versions that allow the word processor to be used by several individuals on a LAN. LANs help integrate the various components of an office information system but require specific LAN hardware and software.

It is important for a manager to know the type of system on which the word processor will be used so that the processor selected will meet current needs and accommodate anticipated future needs. Once all of these components are assembled, they must be coordinated in a work environment that offers comfort for the user and promotes productivity. A later section on human factors describes some conditions that make a workstation more comfortable for users.

DATA PROCESSING, STORAGE, AND RETRIEVAL

Computer technology has changed the way data are processed, stored, and retrieved in a business office. An office information system helps tie the various technologies together so that they work as a system to improve the efficiency of data handling.

Automated Records Management

New and faster ways to handle an office's information needs came with the arrival of computers. The introduction of computerized equipment automated and in many cases separated data-processing activities from general office activities. Most of a company's records are now stored electronically in separate data-processing departments. Some records need to be stored for many years; and electronic media, such as tapes and disks, take up much less space than filing cabinets. OISs link data-processing departments electronically to other department offices, permitting secretaries, managers, executives, and others to access relevant data and information while remaining at their desks.

Mainframe and minicomputers play the dominant role in storing and processing most of an organization's data. Microcomputers are used as workstations and play a vital role in connecting end-users to an office information system and organizational data. These microcomputers allow users to enter data into and access data from another computer, but they are also capable of processing and storing their own data. Office workstations are linked to departmental minicomputers and corporate mainframes through LANs, PBXs, and gateways or in some cases through direct device-to-device connections.

Workstations need to be able to access all the applications and data that any potential user may need. A secretary or assistant may need access to word processing and scheduling software, a manager may need access to database management and spreadsheet software, and so on. Executive workstations are those that allow access to applications specifically designed to meet the information needs of executives. In all cases appropriate security measures should be taken to assure that users have access only to data and information for which they are authorized.

Micrographics

Micrographics refers to the process of photographing paper records and maintaining and storing the images on microforms. A microform is a medium used to store images; two of the most common types are microfilm and microfiche. Microfilm can take several different forms. Roll microfilm uses film wrapped in rolls; approximately 4000 images can be held on a 100-foot roll. Such rolls must be loaded onto and threaded into a roll microfilm reader. Microfilm cartridges are easier to use because they are self-threading in a cartridge microfilm reader. The cartridge also provides protection for the film and makes handling easier.

Microfiche is another type of microform; it consists of sheets of 105-mm film mounted on a 4-by-6-inch card. A single microfiche card may contain as many as 420 images. The card usually has title and index information printed at the top of the card so that it can be read without magnification.

In the past, micrographics were used by business primarily for archival purposes. Today, micrographic technology has been integrated with computers into a **computer-assisted retrieval (CAR) system** to allow random and fast retrieval of information stored on microforms (Figure 8–3). Micrographics can benefit an organization by reducing information storage and distribution costs and improving access.

Optical Storage and Retrieval

One of the newest technologies enhancing the storage and retrieval of information is optical storage systems. Optical disk systems can store gigabytes—billions of bytes—of information. These devices provide on-line mass storage with fast access. Optical disks that allow users to record their own data, and in some cases erase and rerecord data, allow greater flexibility with data that are prone to change. Optical storage media are further discussed in Chapter 3.

FIGURE 8–3

A computer-assisted retrieval (CAR) system. (Reprinted courtesy of Eastman Kodak Company.)

IMAGE PROCESSING

A business often needs to create duplicate images of documents so that they can be distributed to users who require that information. Much of the needed information consists of both textual and graphic images that need to be stored, combined, manipulated, and distributed. Several technologies that work toward those ends are office copiers, scanners, and desktop publishing systems.

Office Copiers

Reprographics is the term used to describe the process of reproducing hard copies through various duplicating methods, the most common of which is probably the use of an office copier. An office copier has become an integral part of an overall OIS and plays an important role in the management and distribution of documents within an office. Even with all the electronic technology available to transmit and duplicate data on soft-copy devices, humans still prefer to work with hard copy. People like to deal with information in a tangible form that they can carry with them, write comments and corrections on, and show to others. Copiers fulfill this need.

Modern office copiers offer a number of features. Automatic document feed allows numerous documents to be stacked in a feeder tray and then automatically fed into the copier one at a time. A reduction and enlargement feature allows a user to reduce or enlarge the size of the original copy. Some copiers also allow duplexing, which is the ability to make two-sided copies. Many businesses require high-volume copying of documents, which then need to be sorted or collated. Consequently, many office copiers provide attachments that collate output. Some also permit the attachment of an electronic editing device that can be used to edit copies without altering the original.

Some of today's copiers can even be linked directly to a computer or LAN to tie them into an OIS network. Information can then be sent directly from a computer to a copier, where multiple documents can be printed without waiting for the computer system to print out the original. These devices are sometimes referred to as intelligent printers. Some have internal storage capabilities that allow them to store thousands of pages of information. Thus, entire documents or portions of documents that are used repeatedly can be stored and printed when needed.

Scanners

A fairly new technique for duplicating documents involves the use of a scanner to digitize text or graphic images so that they can be stored on magnetic media. A scanner is connected directly to a computer and uses optical technology to digitize and store a document or image (Figure 8–4). The text and images can then be retrieved, modified, and output as needed. Once digitized and stored, text, numeric data, and graphic images can all be easily combined into one document by using the appropriate software. For example, a scanner can easily incorporate company logos, letterhead designs, and product photographs into documents. Because graphic images can be so quickly incorporated into documents, organizations benefit from increased productivity. And once captured, images may be rotated, sized up, or sized down to fit with the other material in a particular document.

FIGURE 8–4

The Kodak reader of optical character-recognition (OCR) forms, coupled with a personal computer, can capture data from forms at rates up to 750 forms per hour. The forms reader can read a variety of standard type styles; commonly used, proportionally spaced type styles; output from most dot-matrix printers; and hand printing according to instructions on the forms. (Reprinted courtesy of Eastman Kodak Company.)

The need for graphic artists is also decreased because numerous graphic images are available on commercial disks and because original art, once created, doesn't have to be redrawn for later use. It can simply be digitized, stored, and retrieved whenever needed.

Desktop Publishing as a Business Tool

Desktop publishing is a concept that combines the use of a microcomputer with page-composition (graphics-oriented) software and high-quality laser printers (Figure 8–5). Anyone can use such a system to create and publish documents—corporations that want to publish in-house, small businesses, and writers who like the idea of self-publishing.

FIGURE 8–5
A magazine page prepared with desktop-publishing software.

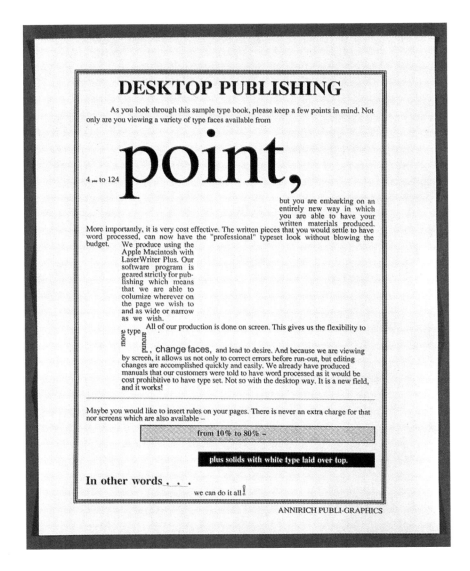

Booklets, newsletters, advertisements, forms, and letters are various items that can be produced with desktop publishing software. The uniqueness of such a system lies in the page-design and composition software. Desktop publishing is basically a graphics-oriented software because it involves the positioning and repositioning of graphics and other elements on the screen. An important feature of this software is that it enables a user to see on the screen what an entire page will look like when it is printed—in other words, what you see is what you get, or WYSIWYG (pronounced "wizzywig").

Some page-composition software has limited word-processing capability. Usually, the text is created and formatted with a word processor first and then is transferred to the page-composition software to be manipulated. Some of the art is also created with separate graphics software and is then transferred to the page-composition software to be positioned on the particular page being "pasted up." The final product can be printed either as camera-ready copy for mass printing or as copies ready for distribution directly from the computer. Laser printers produce type and graphics nearly as crisp and detailed as those in professionally published magazines and textbooks.

Most page-composition software was first developed for the Apple Macintosh; however, programs have subsequently been developed for the various IBM and compatible microcomputers. The term *desktop publishing* was coined by Paul Brainard of Aldus Corporation when that company's software, PageMaker, was introduced. With the combination of the Apple Macintosh microcomputer, Apple LaserWriter (a laser printer), and Aldus's PageMaker software, the concept of desktop publishing took off. Today, other software developers, such as Graphics Corporation and Xerox Corporation, offer desktop publishing packages such as Ready, Set, Go and Ventura Publisher, respectively, for microcomputers. In addition, many word-processing programs—such as WordPerfect 5.0, WordStar 2000, and Microsoft Word—have incorporated sophisticated graphic manipulation features that give these program some desktop publishing capabilities.

You may someday be faced with the decision of whether to use desktop or traditional publishing to produce such items as annual reports, press releases, forms, letters, and product catalogs. You will need to be familiar with the components of a desktop publishing system and understand the factors that affect its appropriateness.

Desktop Publishing Systems. Desktop publishing provides a means of creating camera-ready copy through the use of various computer hardware and software. Together the hardware and software components make up a desktop publishing system. Camera-ready copy is the final page layout from which a printer produces a publication. A typical desktop publishing system consists of several major components.

- A high-speed microcomputer—to perform the required operations to manipulate text and graphics. To run powerful page-layout software efficiently, a microcomputer should have at least

640 KB and preferably 1MB or more of internal memory as well as a fast hard-disk drive.

- A high-resolution graphic monitor—to display graphics and page layouts.
- A laser printer for final copy—to produce near-typeset-quality publications.
- A dot-matrix printer for draft copy—to produce inexpensive draft copies.
- Peripheral hardware, such as scanners or video cameras—to digitize and store images from two- and three-dimensional sources, respectively.
- Word-processing software—to produce text.
- Graphic software—to produce graphics.
- Page-layout software—to combine text and graphics and lay out a page design.

Desktop publishing systems can be configured in a number of different ways to suit a user's needs. Some factors to consider are budget constraints, current and expected needs, and organizational buying preferences. To incorporate an in-house desktop publishing system, managers must do more than buy technology. They must also

- identify their needs
- establish a corporate plan
- design standards
- train personnel
- consider the impact on job structures (whether jobs are created, eliminated, or redefined)

Simply having a desktop publishing system does not guarantee effective publications. Even though almost anyone can master the basic operations of a desktop publishing system, understanding how to design effective presentations requires some skill that's not as easily learned.

Choosing Between Desktop Publishing and Traditional Typesetting.
To decide whether a desktop publishing system is suited to the needs of your organization, you should analyze current and future publishing requirements. One of the first things to determine is the volume of material that needs to be published: what publications need to be produced, how often each is published, how long each publication is, and how many of each are needed. Here are some additional questions that should be addressed before reaching a decision.

- Is the original material created in-house or by an outside service?
- Is the current publishing done in-house or by an outside service?
- What are the typical schedules?
- Are the schedules adequate, or are they often missed—and why?
- How are revisions handled?
- How is accuracy ensured?
- Who has the final say on what gets published and when?
- What type of quality is needed now and in the future?

- What form will each publication take in the future?
- What changes should be made?
- How much will publishing volumes change in the future?
- Will training, hardware, and additional staffing needs fit within your budget?

Many jobs are not suited to desktop publishing because they are too big or too complex or require higher quality than can be produced with a desktop system. The following circumstances generally call for traditional publishing.

- When very high quality is of the utmost importance—traditional typesetting offers resolutions of 2,500 dots and more per inch.
- When an organization does not have the experienced personnel to accomplish desktop publishing.
- When documents are very long—for example, more than 100 pages in length.
- When documents are very complex and contain numerous elements, such as text, graphics, half-tones, scanned images, and formulas.
- When the publishing volume is very large—traditional typesetting is better able to maintain speed and equipment. In addition, economies of scale in large print runs make the cost savings from using desktop publishing to produce the original master insignificant.
- When color output is needed—color is still on the horizon for desktop publishing.

Nonetheless, in some cases desktop publishing offers a number of attractive benefits. First, it can result in lower costs by reducing production and printing costs. Production expenses associated with producing near-typeset-quality print are usually only a fraction of the costs associated with traditional typesetting methods. Often, the difference in quality is not important enough to justify the higher cost of typesetting. Desktop publishing systems typically offer 300-dots-per-inch resolution, and many readers cannot tell the difference.

Desktop publishing can also help a business create a better-looking publication than could be accomplished with typewriters, letter-quality printers, or dot-matrix printers. The ability of laser printers to produce numerous professional-quality typefaces as well as high-quality graphics can give materials a more polished professional appearance. A publication often conveys as much with its appearance as it does with its content. In addition, for documents that require only simple graphics and illustrations, desktop publishing software eliminates the need for an experienced artist.

In other cases desktop publishing can provide an economical solution for low-volume projects. Even with some moderate-volume products desktop publishing can be used to produce inexpensive camera-ready copy, which is then sent to a printer to be reproduced. A desktop publishing system can reduce the amount of time needed to prepare camera-ready copy: word processor, graphics, and page-layout programs allow text and graphics to be easily created and combined on a page and revisions to be performed quickly and easily.

Desktop publishing can also give a great deal more control over the scheduling and artistic aspects of a publication. Outside services generally have numerous projects in process. But an in-house publisher can monitor and adjust progress as well as change design or graphic components immediately, without waiting for a project to return from an outside service.

Business Publications and Desktop Publishing. Desktop publishing can be an economical means of producing many different types of business materials. For instance, a business can use a desktop publishing system to create advertisements for newspaper and other printed media. Desktop publishing can create numerous mock-up ads for review as well as the final camera-ready copy.

Press releases, newsletters, product catalogs, and technical documents in addition to business cards, forms, and letters are other ideal uses of a desktop publishing system. Such documents can be produced inexpensively and quickly, yet with a professional appearance. Near-typeset-quality print is adequate for these publications. Desktop publishing improves the output quality of in-house materials while only minimally increasing costs. It also gives creative control to the user.

Some documents such as annual reports and brochures reflect an organization's image and demand extreme attention to content and high-quality printing. In these cases final materials should be sent to professional typesetters. However, desktop publishing systems can be used to inexpensively mock-up numerous drafts for review before the final content is sent to a typesetter.

COMMUNICATION SYSTEMS

Many of the components of an office information system are concerned primarily with the communication of information.

Electronic Mail

An early form of electronic mail, or E-mail, was the telegram, which sent coded signals by electric transmission over wire. **Electronic mail** includes a variety of methods used to transmit mail and messages electronically, in streams of 0s and 1s, directly to a recipient's computer or terminal almost anywhere in the world. Electronic mail can be sent short distances, such as between offices, or long distances—even around the world—by satellite. At its destination the communication is placed in a file inside the recipient's computer to be read immediately or stored for later use.

E-mail is faster and usually cheaper than overnight mail delivery. Some overnight carriers such as Federal Express now offer a commercial electronic mail service. The Radisson Hotel in Nashville, Tennessee, is the first major hotel to offer electronic mail service to its guests. The service, Hotelcopy Inc., allows the Radisson's guests, a large portion of whom are business people, to send up to 10 pages to other users worldwide in less than a minute. Highlight 8–1 examines Kodak's E-mail system.

Kodak Develops E-Mail Networks

Kodak has developed an electronic messaging system that is currently used by nearly 50,000 employees. For Kodak the E-mail system has proved to be cheaper than conventional messaging systems, with an average E-mail message costing about 10 cents.

Kodak's E-mail system has been built over time. It began with Kodak's desire to message anyone in the company at any location from any terminal at any time. The system required an increased number of terminals since each E-mail user must have a terminal on his desk. The company outlined the following specific benefits that it wanted to achieve:

reliable 24-hour worldwide communications

access to all of Kodak's personnel and subsidiaries

two-way electronic access to anyone, anywhere

ability to move acquisitions, such as Sterling Drug, on-line quickly

Kodak's total communication system is a mix of different mail packages and multivendor systems; it encompasses voice, E-mail, and file transfer along with telex and cablegram. Kodak's total system allows 24-hour-a-day, seven-days-a-week service to a variety of users in a variety of networks. To ensure the security of the messages sent, Kodak has had elaborate security facilities built into the system—for example encryptions, user identifications, and password protection. Kodak has devised a single, unified directory that lists users of voice and E-mail and also lists phone numbers for those not located on any messaging system. Currently, about 80,000 users of voice and E-mail are listed.

Kodak uses IBM's Professional Office System (PROFS) for about 45,000 users, who send 180,000 messages per day. The company also developed and uses KMX Voice Mail (recently sold to Taigon Corporation) to provide field personnel with communication services. That system is now used by 26,000 users worldwide, who send 75,000 messages per day. Kodak also uses several other systems for messaging.

Kodak has faced formidable challenges in supporting this network of mixed systems at 100 worldwide locations with a variety of messaging needs, from voice and data to paper and electronic, operating both within and outside the company. Currently, 30 percent of Kodak's employees are using the overall system, and Kodak estimates that some 80 percent could benefit from it. The company is still expanding its network, hoping to link up with outside suppliers and research networks and to provide electronic image transfer.

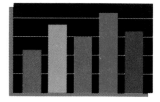

How It Works. To send and receive electronic mail, a computer must be equipped for communication. There are two ways to create E-mail messages to be sent: (1) use a microcomputer and have an on-line editor available in the electronic mail system; or (2) use a microcomputer and a word processor and then upload the message to the electronic-mail service. A typical transmission might proceed as follows:

- The sender accesses an electronic mail system.
- The sender keys or uploads the message into the computer.
- The sender tells the computer where to send the message.
- The sender issues the command to mail the message.
- The message is transmitted to the specified destination.
- The message is received and can be read immediately or placed in the recipient's file space (mailbox), where it can be retrieved and displayed or printed at any time.

There are two general types of electronic mail networks: an in-house network, which connects all or some of the employees within a business and an external network connecting people at different locations around the world. In-house systems are generally configured in one of three ways:

1. As a local-area network (LAN), in which the personal computers don't need to be equipped for telecommunications to be included in the network—the LAN is typically located in a single building or in a group of closely placed buildings, with each computer linked by a direct cable. Messages can be sent and received anywhere in the building or group of buildings.
2. As an internal communication system in which each personal computer uses a modem and telephone lines instead of LANs—this arrangement is useful if different brands of computers are used.
3. As a dedicated system in which special devices are used exclusively for the transfer of electronic mail and voice transmissions.

External systems take one of two different forms:

1. As Telex and TWX printing machines—messages are received and then printed.
2. As part of a commercial information service—for example, SourceMail is available from The Source and EMAIL from Compuserve. Electronic mail can be sent between subscribers of the same service and sometimes between subscribers of different services.

Benefits and Drawbacks. Electronic mail has several notable benefits.

- It is faster than traditional mail and less expensive to prepare and send.
- A single message can be sent simultaneously to multiple addresses.

- Unlike a telephone call, the receiver of the message and the sender don't need to be on the line at the same time.
- A busy person doesn't need to be interrupted to receive a message.
- The message can be printed on paper.

However, electronic mail also has some drawbacks.

- It is expensive to set up, and it can be expensive to operate if used indiscriminately.
- There is no guarantee that electronic mail systems will be compatible.
- Privacy and security can also be a problem. It is difficult to ensure that only the recipient reads the mail.
- Electronic junk mail has emerged.

Facsimile

Facsimile is a specialized type of electronic mail. **Facsimile** transmission, often referred to as fax, allows a copy of an original document containing alphanumeric data, graphics, and photographs to be sent electronically to another location. Many fax units are directly connected to phone lines. Otherwise, a phone receiver must be placed into a coupler. The sender can insert an original document into a fax unit. The fax machine then scans the document and sends the document text, pictures, even handwriting over the telephone lines (Figure 8–6). Another fax machine at the receiving end accepts the electronic signals and converts the document back into its original form, producing a hard-copy duplicate of the original document. Fax machines must be compatible in order to communicate with each other, and fax standards are beginning to emerge.

Facsimile communication is rapidly growing in popularity, so much so that many already consider junk fax mail a problem. One of the newest developments is fax boards that allow a personal computer to function as a fax machine. Through the use of facsimile technology, documents that are urgently needed can now be sent between offices anywhere in the world in a matter of minutes.

The Telephone and Voice Messaging

Even with the introduction of many new forms of electronic communication, the telephone is still the most frequently used device for communicating information between business individuals. It is simple, efficient, and easy for individuals to understand and use. Highlight 8–2 examines how the automobile has been transformed into an office by cellular technology.

A telephone can be combined with a computer in a **voice messaging** system, which is a computer-supported system that allows a message to be sent in a human voice without the receiver's being present at the same time to accept the message. The message can be sent and received from a standard push-button telephone. When first recorded, the message is stored by the voice messaging system and can be reviewed and edited before being sent on. When instructed to do so, the computer sends the message to the

FIGURE 8-6
A fax machine sends a
document electronically to a
branch office in another city.

recipient's voice mailbox for storage. A receiver can then dial the mailbox and hear the message whenever it is convenient.

Voice messaging systems have several advantages:

- ability to leave messages for one or more persons
- elimination of multiple calls when a receiver is not available
- convenience of push-button phones
- no need for concern with time schedules and time zones
- the personal touch of a message sent in the sender's own voice

Electronic Teleconferencing

Voice teleconferencing, in which three or more people could talk to each other on the phone simultaneously, was an early form of teleconferencing. That method, however, did not convey charts and graphs, and it required all participants to be available at the same time.

When video teleconferencing became possible voices and images were combined and transmitted to different locations. However, equipment remains expensive, difficulties can arise in arranging participants'

The Office Takes to the Road

It's a common occurrence today for executives to communicate with their offices from their automobiles, which are equipped with cellular mobile phones. Cellular phones offer the traveling businessperson high-quality mobile communications.

In a cellular mobile telephone system transmitters are placed in a checkerboard pattern throughout the system service area. The geographical area that each transmitter covers is referred to as a cell, and each cell has frequencies assigned to it that are not available to other cells in the network. When an individual places a call, it is detected by the local cell (from which the person is calling) and is assigned specific frequencies for transmitting and receiving calls. A computer system is used to monitor the strength of the signal. As a caller moves out of a cell, the signal gets weaker. When the signal strength falls to a predetermined level, the computer detects that the caller has left the cell and checks all surrounding cells to determine which cell is picking up the transmission. The call is then taken over by that cell, and the user's mobile telephone is assigned new frequencies for transmitting and receiving. Usually this handoff between cells happens so fast that it goes undetected by the user.

Business use of cellular telephones is growing rapidly. Executives who travel by car can stay in touch with their offices and receive last-minute information on the way to meetings. Supervisors and repair technicians who work at remote sites can stay in touch with their offices, too. Portable computers can be connected to the home office through modems connected to cellular phones, and information can thus be conveniently exchanged. Terminals are also available that enable facsimile images to be transmitted over a cellular network. In addition, portable cellular computers are available to transmit data directly over a cellular network without a modem or cellular phone.

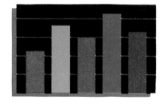

Many types of public transportation that cater to a large business clientele, such as commuter trains and ferry boats, are beginning to make cellular phones available to their patrons. Cellular networks are found in most major cities, but the networks are not all compatible. The trend, however, is toward nationwide compatibility that will enable cellular devices to be used in any cellular network across the country.

schedules, and others' perceptions of those appearing on the video can be a problem.

The latest and most promising technology is **electronic teleconferencing**, which electronically links participants in different locations through their computers. Participants can enter information at their own terminals which is then transmitted to the other participants and displayed on their terminals. The information is also stored so that it can be recalled if it is needed at a future time. Electronic teleconferencing allows managers in remote locations to meet and share ideas without the expense and time required to travel to a central location. It also allows them to have access to all the available information in their own locations.

A device often used in electronic teleconferencing is the **electronic blackboard**, which is a pressure-sensitive chalkboard used with ordinary chalk. An image is digitized and transmitted electronically by telephone lines to one or more conference locations and displayed on monitors. The image gradually appears on each monitor as if an invisible hand were writing it.

Telecommuting

Telecommuting allows people to work at home by connecting their home computers or terminals to computers in the office through communication channels. The benefits of this approach are still being argued, but the trend is growing. According to the New York research firm Electronic Services Unlimited, approximately 100,000 people telecommuted to work in 1985. That firm predicts that by 1990 as many as 10 million people, including those who use telecommuting for overtime work, will be involved in this method of communication.

OFFICE SUPPORT SYSTEMS

Many office information systems incorporate a number of applications into an office support system, which can be used to help individual users better organize many of their daily office activities. An **office support system** typically includes applications such as an electronic calendar and time management, tickler files, and electronic scratch pad files. Such systems also include applications discussed earlier, including electronic mail, word processing, and document storage and retrieval. These applications help increase individual efficiency by reducing reliance on telephones, standard mail, and written documents. Office support systems can greatly reduce the time spent preparing, sending, and receiving information among individuals.

An electronic calendar and time management application is used like an ordinary appointment book to schedule appointments and events. But it has more flexibility because it can be available to several people through a computer network. In this way participants' calendars can be checked prior to scheduling a meeting to find the best available times. Electronic calendars can also be used as a log of activities by engineers, lawyers, and other professionals using time-billing systems. For example, a psychologist might use an electronic calendar to log time spent with each patient and later use it for precise billing.

A tickler file allows users to enter information about meetings or other important items that they want to be reminded of. The file can be set to display that information each time the computer is turned on or at specified times during the day.

An electronic scratch pad can typically be accessed from any other application in the office support system, to allow users to quickly jot down thoughts, comments, and ideas before they are forgotten. One example of an office support system is IBM's Professional Office System, or PROFS.

INTEGRATION

An office is not really fully automated until all electronic elements are linked. Office information systems link, or integrate, all of the equipment and people within and among offices so that they can communicate electronically, using all of the electronic data and hardware resources within an organization. Of course, actual access to certain hardware and files may be limited to specific workstations and controlled through passwords and access codes. Departments thus share company data and equipment, such as laser printers, large computers, and databases. LANs, PBXs, and gateways are used to connect and integrate the various components of an OIS. Gateways connect the larger systems to those networks.

Total office automation and integration is a gradual occurrence in most organizations. Little by little, new technology is introduced until finally the entire system is integrated within the organization. Everyone in an office is affected by an office information system—salespeople, order-entry clerks, typists, accountants, managers, and executives. Office information systems have the potential to make a company's operation more productive, efficient, and competitive.

HUMAN FACTORS

All benefits and productivity gains accompanying office information systems can be lost if the high-tech physical environment doesn't meet the emotional and physical needs of the people working in it. Concern for workers' comfort has brought attention to **ergonomics**, or **human engineering**, the science of designing the workplace for the comfort and safety of the workers. For example, office equipment and furniture manufacturers can design their products according to the needs of the people who will use them. Chairs can be constructed to prevent backaches, and computer screens can have special monitors to prevent eye strain.

Some of the generally agreed-upon standards for preventing discomfort or pain in a modern electronic workstation include

- placing the keyboard at a height of 24 to 27 inches
- keeping the computer screen about 18 to 24 inches from the eyes
- positioning the computer screen to avoid glare from lamps or windows
- covering windows to diffuse the light coming through
- installing wood floors or antistatic fiber carpet
- using a posture chair with the seat height and back tilt adjustable
- using a glare-free desktop
- using a stable computer stand
- arranging a handy storage area
- having workers place feet flat on floor
- having workers maintain a horizontal arm position

FIGURE 8–7

A design for an ergonomically sound work area.

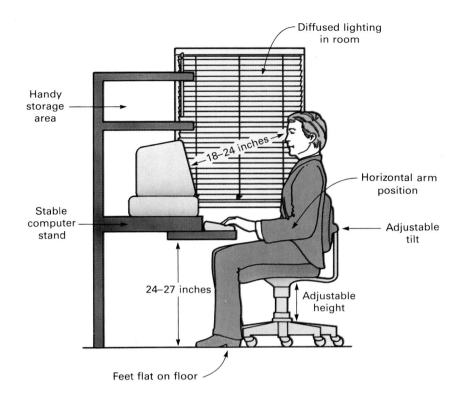

Figure 8–7 is a diagram of a workstation that has taken these ergonomic features into consideration.

Office designers are also trying to combat the coldness and impersonal feel of a plastic and metal high-tech environment. They suggest sound-absorbing materials and softer lighting (fewer overhead lights and more area lighting). Designers are also using colors and materials—fabric and wood—that more closely resemble a home environment.

Studies show that people are more productive in well-designed work areas; therefore, some companies are willing to spend a lot of money to make their workers comfortable. Pacific Bell's experiment in using office design to improve performance in the El Segundo, California, office cost the company approximately $11 million. Before the money was spent, however, employees were polled about their preferences on everything from color combinations to ventilation. According to a company spokesperson, the extra attention to employee comfort and safety paid off; workers are pleased, and productivity has increased.

SUMMARY

An office information system (OIS) is a system that is used to manage the preparation, storage, retrieval, and communication of information within and among business offices. An OIS includes a number of different automated functions.

Word processors were developed to speed up the process of written communication and are now the foundation of today's office information system. Word processors are used in businesses to generate letters, memos, and reports as well as many other types of documents.

Reprographics is the process of reproducing hard copies through various duplicating methods. Modern copiers can be linked to computers either directly or through a network to tie them into the OIS. Scanners allow a document containing text, numeric data, graphics, and pictures to be digitized and stored on magnetic media. The stored document can then be retrieved, manipulated, and printed.

Desktop publishing combines the use of a microcomputer with page-composition software and laser printers to produce high-quality documents that incorporate text, graphics, and pictures.

Electronic mail, or E-mail, refers to the methods used to transmit mail and messages electronically almost anywhere in the world. Facsimile transmission allows a copy of an original document containing alphanumeric data and graphics (including pictures and handwriting) to be scanned and digitized and sent electronically to another location using telephone lines. Another facsimile machine then receives the signals, converts them into the document's original form, and prints it.

Voice messaging incorporates the use of push-button telephones and a computer system to allow messages to be sent in a human voice, stored, and then retrieved by the recipient. Electronic teleconferencing electronically links through their computers conference participants located in remote locations. Telecommuting allows people to work at home by using communication channels to connect office computers to home computers or terminals.

Office support systems combine applications such as electronic mail, word processing, document handling, electronic calendars and time management, tickler files, and electronic scratch pads into a single system to help increase workers' efficiency in completing these office activities. To be the most effective, all the components of an OIS need to be integrated. LANs, PBXs, and gateways are common methods of linking the various components.

Ergonomics, or human engineering, is the science of designing the workplace for the comfort and safety of the workers. Studies have shown that an office environment that addresses human factors can result in improved employee morale and productivity.

MINICASE 8–1

Nick Rowback manufactures quality tennis shoes and has numerous plant locations across the nation. Currently, the manufacturing information system (MIS) and the office information system (OIS) in each location are not integrated. The OISs incorporate electronic teleconferencing, which management uses to hold some meetings among the various plants. Often, someone using the electronic teleconferencing system and needing information from a plant database about the manufacture or distribution of tennis shoes must make a special request to the information systems personnel. This process often results in substantial delays and frequently postpones the conference until the needed information is received.

The company has decided to look into integrating its OISs with the databases of the various information systems to allow users quick and easy access to any information they need. The development team has determined that there are no cost or technical reasons to prevent this integration.

1. Do you think it is a good idea to integrate the OISs with the databases of the information systems? Why or why not?

2. If the systems are integrated, what types of controls, if any, should be placed on the users of the OISs when they access a database from a functional area? Explain.

MINICASE 8–2

Ms. Johnson is the manager of a very large marketing department. She has numerous supervisors under her control, and the demands on her time are heavy. Often she has to stay late or take work home to finish it. Most of the work requires use of the company's computer system, forcing her to complete the work in the office. Much of Ms. Johnson's time during the day is consumed in short, informal meetings with individual supervisors or in telephone calls to pass along information. In addition, needed individuals are frequently unavailable, and time is wasted walking to their offices or making phone calls.

Ms. Johnson has her secretary create memos for more formal messages but would like a way to quickly and efficiently deliver short, informal ideas and suggestions to appropriate supervisors. Even with memos, messages sometimes get lost, misdirected, or delayed in getting to their destinations. Ms. Johnson would like to ensure that everyone who is supposed to get a message receives it in a timely fashion and that the message is conveniently available no matter where the recipient is. Some messages are detailed enough that a written copy is needed; others could be handled by telephone if she could just get through. In addition, Ms. Johnson must communicate several times a week with corporate headquarters, which is located 100 miles away. She would like a convenient way to leave messages there.

1. Which component(s) of an OIS could help Ms. Johnson communicate her messages more efficiently?

2. List several ways in which the component(s) you listed in question one could help solve Ms. Johnson's problems.

Key Terms

computer-assisted retrieval system (CAR)

desktop publishing

electronic blackboard

electronic mail

electronic teleconferencing

ergonomics

facsimile

human engineering

microfiche

micrographics

office support system

reprographics

voice messaging

Review Questions

1. What is an office information system?
2. What is the most widely adopted computerized technology in an OIS? Why do you think it is so popular?
3. List some of the tasks for which a business might use word processors.
4. What are some of the advantages of using a word processor rather than a standard typewriter?
5. What might you use to economically store the price and description of every item in your sales catalog?
6. Define reprographics and describe its importance to an OIS.
7. Describe the purpose of a scanner.
8. How could desktop publishing be useful as a business tool in an OIS?
9. What tools would you use to incorporate a black-and-white picture of yourself with some text?
10. What is electronic mail?
11. Describe the two general types of electronic mail networks.
12. List several benefits and drawbacks of using an electronic mail system.
13. What is facsimile transmission? How can it benefit a business?
14. What advantage does facsimile transmission have over E-mail?
15. Describe voice messaging.
16. Why is voice messaging preferable to written memos?
17. Describe electronic teleconferencing, and tell what it can do for a business.
18. What is an electronic blackboard?
19. Define telecommuting.
20. What is an office support system?
21. What OIS feature would be useful in scheduling a 2-hour meeting with members of your sales staff?
22. What is the purpose of integrating an OIS?
23. What is meant by the terms *ergonomics* and *human engineering*?
24. What are some considerations when planning an ergonomically appropriate office?
25. What do you see as the advantages of having an OIS?

APPLICATION MODULE
Human Resource Information Systems

Appreciation for and utilization of the personnel function has been minimal until the last 20 years or so. Reasons for the earlier lack of concern were related to the intense concentration on productivity and profit motives that existed at that same time. Those concerns are still important, but there has been an increasing movement toward concern for individual health, safety, and other needs. The personnel function has recently seen dramatic changes in the workplace, including increased government regulations, large numbers of minorities in the work force, an ever-increasing number of women entering the job market, better educated employees, and more mobile employees. These changes have generated an explosion of interest in the acquisition, involvement, and development of humans in the workplace. So pronounced have these changes been that many traditional managers in the personnel area have been renamed human resources managers, representing an apparent recognition of the importance of managing a firm's human resources.

INTERNAL USES OF HUMAN RESOURCE INFORMATION SYSTEMS

Information systems within the personnel function must support the basic needs of a firm, such as payroll and employee benefits. Timely recording and reporting of changes in payroll and benefits information is of great importance to a firm and its employees. The payroll subsystem of the human resource information system (HRIS) produces paychecks for employees but must also keep up with much other data never seen by a typical employee. For example, the HRIS must keep track of the individual deductions taken by all employees for contributions to a credit union so that the combined total deductions, along with any matching or supporting company contributions, can be written as one big check to the credit union. Similar records must be maintained for other employee benefit programs, such as stock purchase, life insurance, health insurance, U.S. savings bonds, and retirement plans. In addition, financial figures must be maintained for reports to local, state, and federal governments. Payments of social security taxes, income taxes, workman's compensation, and so on are required from all firms on a quarterly basis; and that information must be collected and summarized on an annual basis to produce such documents as W-2 forms. The computer's power to sort, classify, and summarize makes it an ideal tool for these personnel tasks.

Although the payroll subsystem of an HRIS is the most visible, it is only one of several subsystems included in a comprehensive HRIS. Performance monitoring subsystems of an HRIS are used to keep track of an employee's performance over time. Today's HRISs can quickly identify employees who have been consistently written up or formally reported for undesirable conduct. Some say that early identification of undesirable conduct and appropriate disciplinary actions show other employees the results of detracting from the team effort. Human resource managers who see this function as a benefit to both firm and employees contend that other employees appreciate having trouble makers handled by management rather than permitting them to diminish overall productive efforts. Performance monitoring subsystems also provide useful information for the evaluation and compensation of employees when companies decide to reward employee performance periodically with raises and/or promotions.

Education/skills monitoring subsystems of an HRIS are valuable for maintaining information on the education and skills of each employee of the firm. Although this information is not required for all firms, it is valuable for those that must identify skills and educational levels for government-sponsored projects. Some companies, called government contractors, are paid on a cost-plus basis (the firm's actual cost to do a project plus an additional overhead percentage of that cost). In some instances, costs are allowed to be higher if highly educated workers are used, but the burden of proof is on the contractor.

The benefit of maintaining an employee skills inventory is more obvious. Companies can qualify for certain contracted jobs if they have employees who possess the skills required by the contract. Such companies send contract bids that may include not only summarized skill and/or education information, but also the names and résumés of particular employees who have the desired skills. Additionally, the education/skills subsystem can be used to select employees for undertakings within the firm that require a certain skill or educational level. The HRIS provides skill-matching software to support these special needs. A sophisticated software program for this purpose might let the manager make a computer inquiry requesting the names and departments of all employees with the skills needed for a particular project.

A subsystem devoted to training and developing a firm's human resources proves beneficial for many firms. Employees are more productive and safer in their work when they have been trained in the proper use of the best methods and tools for their work. Computers are playing a vital role in reducing the costs associated with training. Lots of job training is taking place with computer-aided instruction (CAI) and its newer relative, intelligent computer-assisted instruction (ICAI), which couples the technology of

knowledge-based systems with traditional CAI. Many experiments have demonstrated that students learn an equal amount of material in a shorter time frame when CAI is used rather than more traditional types of training. This speed benefit is thought to occur because CAI allows students to learn at their own pace, whereas traditional instructor-oriented training must permit the slowest student to keep up. Currently, about 50 CAI authoring packages (used to prepare specific training) are on the market.

THE IMPACT OF GOVERNMENT

Government legislative interest in the 1960s concentrated on a collection of legal measures and guidelines called antidiscrimination efforts. These efforts prohibited people from being treated differently because of their religion, sex, race, or national origin; and that focus forced many firms to concentrate on efforts to ensure that their employment practices were in compliance with the new rules and regulations. Human resource managers had to defend their selection of one particular applicant rather than another. However, a large firm, with perhaps 2,000 applicants for 200 positions annually, could not possibly maintain adequate manual records to justify responsible hiring and promotion decisions. Thus, the complexity of personnel record-keeping tasks led to the development and installation of many computer-controlled HRISs during the 1960s.

Recent Government Regulation

Government continues to promote legal measures to further protect and enhance the lives of employees. One such recent act was H.R. 3128, tax reform legislation better known as Cobra, which went into effect in 1987. Cobra requires firms with 20 or more employees to continue benefits for terminated or retired employees and their dependents for a period of up to 36 months. These requirements dictate extensive changes in the record-keeping practices of personnel managers, who must now identify qualifying events; identify, track, and notify qualifying dependents; bill and collect for participatory benefits; process delinquent accounts; set rates; and report to carriers and management. Because all of this information is needed for people who are not even employed by the firm, the HRIS must maintain and process benefit records for both current and former employees.

Firms that purchased HRIS software packages with separate maintenance agreements could have the necessary software changes to implement Cobra handled for them. Those firms that elected to develop their software packages in-house or that purchased or leased HRIS software without an annual maintenance agreement suffered major program modification headaches. Changes like Cobra will undoubtedly continue as our nation concentrates on protection of individual rights and a better life-style for all.

Data Requirements

In order to track the educational and skill information related to employees and to maintain adequate data for payroll and employee benefit purposes, firms collect considerable biographic and demographic data on their employees. Figure A identifies some of the types of information now being computer-collected and -maintained for each employee. With the computer's power to sort and summarize data, standard as well as special-purpose reports and employee tabulations (by age, sex, race, salary range, and so on) are readily available for any divisions/ departments within a company. Thus, computers allow human resource managers to provide information that would otherwise be very difficult, if not impossible, to assemble.

Since personnel managers collect employees' birthdates to support required reporting functions, some firms reuse that data to gener-

```
FICA number
Name
Sex
Race
Birthdate
Marital status
Address
Telephone number
Electronic mail ID
Company mail address
Bank account number
Education: degree, major, location, date
Special training: area, vocation, date
Foreign language skills
Current employment information
    Department/division
    Position
    Salary
    Effective date
Historical employment information
    Department/division
    Position
    Salary
    Effective date
External employment information
    Date
    Position
    Salary
    Employer
Benefit information
Dependent information
Evaluation information
In-house training information
Health history
Drug test results
```

FIGURE A
Selected employee data.

ate birthday greetings and individualized benefits for employees on their birthdays. The up side of this application for some employees is the feeling that the company really cares about them, but a possible negative reaction is that the employees have been computer-manipulated.

SUPPORT FOR THE HUMAN RESOURCES FUNCTION

Available Software

As with software targeted toward other special-purpose areas, human resources software may be developed in-house by a firm's computer programmers, or it may be leased or purchased from companies that manufacture special-purpose software. Both software and hardware companies develop HRISs for distribution. *Software News* (January 1987) listed 45 companies that produce software products specifically targeted to human resource information systems—all at the mainframe or minicomputer level. Of course, many more systems are being developed today for increasingly powerful and functional microcomputers. HRIS software vendors boast microcomputer packages that are flexible enough to accommodate acquisitions

and mergers, which are becoming increasingly common in today's workplace.

MUTUAL BENEFITS OF HRISs

Even though the major intent of today's HRISs is to benefit and protect firms, such systems often benefit employees as well. One example of this mutual benefit is the flexible compensation plan that is experiencing increased popularity among both firms and employees. The plan allows flexible costs and benefits to employees with different needs. A young married employee beginning to raise a family and a single employee nearing retirement have different insurance and medical protection needs, and neither should be required to pay for benefits that they really don't need. A flexible compensation plan, which may be just one small part of an HRIS (Figure B), is said to reduce costs to both the firm and its employees, resulting in a no-lose outcome.

FIGURE B
Human resource database.

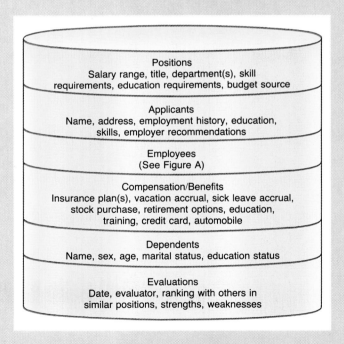

Positions
Salary range, title, department(s), skill requirements, education requirements, budget source

Applicants
Name, address, employment history, education, skills, employer recommendations

Employees
(See Figure A)

Compensation/Benefits
Insurance plan(s), vacation accrual, sick leave accrual, stock purchase, retirement options, education, training, credit card, automobile

Dependents
Name, sex, age, marital status, education status

Evaluations
Date, evaluator, ranking with others in similar positions, strengths, weaknesses

In the areas of available positions and interested applicants, a firm's interest is in attracting the most qualified persons to fill any job vacancies, whereas a current or potential employee's interest is in obtaining a working position that is satisfying and appropriate to that employee's skills and education. A personnel manager can use a computer-supported HRIS to satisfy both needs by identifying job skill requirements and existing employee skills for the employer and by outlining career plans for the employee. More sophisticated HRISs list the skills required to advance to a particular type of job and provide a matching list of company training programs designed to provide those skills. Thus, the computer is providing information to help fill a gap between job position requirements and individual employee skills. In addition, that same system can pinpoint skill deficiencies within a company that may become significant if the company decides to introduce new positions or technologies.

One company used its HRIS and identified an engineer who spoke Russian. As a result, the engineer was sent to Russia on an assignment that provided an exciting boost to his career. Skill-matching modules of HRISs are common today and, if used effectively, can increase employee morale and effect cost savings by eliminating the need for expensive external recruiting efforts.

FUTURE CONSIDERATIONS FOR HRISs

HRISs are considered by many to be a double-edged sword. On one side, such systems can quickly provide a wealth of selected and filtered information to support the decision making required by a firm. On the other hand, the vast amount of personal information stored by an HRIS clearly holds the potential for an invasion of employee privacy. The *Wall Street Journal* (April 19, 1989) reported a study that found misuse of employees' personal data. A key challenge for personnel managers in the future is to draw the fine line between necessary personal information and information that is not critical and/or could cause employee embarrassment. Diverse opinions are involved in this distinction.

Another area for future deliberation is the ever-increasing emphasis on ethical behavior within businesses, which has caused some companies to provide channels within their firms for employees to blow the whistle on some activity that is injurious to the general public or is morally or ethically wrong. No one had to blow the whistle on Exxon's oil spill in Alaska's Prince William Sound, but incidents in other companies and other places may be less visible. Internal whistle blowing allows a firm to make the necessary changes to correct a problem without publicizing it to the outside world. Evidence suggests that an established and firmly supported internal whistle-blowing channel is more likely to be used than an external channel.

Responsibility for establishing whistle-blowing procedures often falls within the personnel function. Personnel managers then have a dual responsibility to protect the rights of the whistle blower and of the person(s) accused of improper action. The information obtained from the whistle blower must be recorded and acted upon without violating the legal rights of the accused. This process requires skillful management and may involve sensitive or secret data.

American Information Technologies (Ameritech). 1988. Annual report.

Major, Michael E. 1987. Can software technology develop human potential? *Business Software Review* (August): 49–53.

Major, Michael E. 1987. HRMS: When the rules change. *Software News* (January): 39–42.

PART FOUR
Development of Business Information Systems

System Analysis

OBJECTIVES

- Explain why replacement information systems must be developed
- List and discuss the seven stages of the system development life cycle (SDLC)
- Explore the role of the systems analyst in the development of new information systems
- Describe the tasks required in the development of new information systems
- Describe some of the traditional and automated tools that systems analysts use in the system analysis phase of the SDLC
- Discuss the need for project management in the development of new information systems

OUTLINE

IMPACT ON MANAGEMENT PROBLEM SOLVING AND DECISION MAKING

WHY NEW SYSTEMS NEED TO BE DEVELOPED
The Life Cycle of Information Systems | Why Information Systems Die | The Piggybacking Concept

THE TRADITIONAL LIFE CYCLE OF SYSTEM DEVELOPMENT
Prototyping and Its Effects on the System Development Life Cycle

QUALIFICATIONS AND ATTRIBUTES OF THE SYSTEMS ANALYST
Differences in Position Responsibilities | Systems Analyst Skills and Qualifications

PROBLEM DEFINITION
Problem Sources | Nature of Systems Problems

REQUIREMENTS ANALYSIS
The Current Information System | The Ideal Information System | Types of New Information Systems

PROJECT JUSTIFICATION
Cost/Benefit Analysis | The System Study

SYSTEM ANALYSIS TOOLS
System Flowcharts | Data Flow Diagrams | Tabular Techniques

AUTOMATING SYSTEM ANALYSIS

PROJECT MANAGEMENT

Chapter 9

Management Profile: Albert E. Collins Jr.
HBO BREEDS MIS STAR

To excel in an industry marked by bloody competition, entertainment companies need MIS executives who are as crafty as film directors or editors and as daring as on-camera talent. The successful MIS executive, therefore, combines a keen understanding of the entertainment business with a deep-seated love of technology. Add a creative management style to that potent mixture, and the countenance of Albert E. Collins, Jr., vice president of information services at Home Box Office (HBO), comes into focus.

Collins is the first to admit that advanced technology is not sufficient in itself to deliver useful information. Collins spends a lot of time roaming HBO's offices to ascertain user needs. "His role is to interface with the business side, find out what is going on and come up with ideas for information services and delivery mechanisms," says Doug Spitz, HBO's vice president of systems development and planning and the architect of Collins's systems.

Collins runs a 90-member MIS department that places as much emphasis on entertainment industry knowledge as it does on technical skills. It is a shop in which teamwork is rewarded and people work hard without spending every waking hour on the job. "The key is to give people interesting work and let them do it," Collins says in an understated fashion. "In other words, don't overmanage. Be there to assist and monitor, but don't sit over their shoulder and direct."

Collins eschews charge-back mechanisms, saying they put too much emphasis on costs and not enough on developing useful, efficient systems. Accountability with end-users, he says, is gained through hard work, trust, and mutual respect.

Collins came to HBO from Pepsico, where he had spent 10 years working his way up through the data-processing ranks before becoming corporate MIS director. Before that he had headed systems services at W.R. Grace & Company and had spent time at AT&T as a management trainee and at IBM as a service bureau salesman.

Upon joining HBO, Collins discovered that similar data were compiled and maintained differently by various departments. Consequently, ownership of information was established to make one group or another responsible for data gathering and input, thus eliminating a large number of redundant data elements. In addition, requirements for all systems were evaluated. A three-dimensional triangle was used to track system status from three perspectives: executive information, decision support and management control, and transaction processing. Each side of the triangle represented a different functional area: network programming, sales and marketing, and finance and personnel.

Collins also transformed HBO's woebegone batch-billing system into a powerful sales information resource, allowing HBO to respond to trends as they developed. "You need to be careful with technology. You can fight it for a little bit, and you may win the battle, but you won't win the war. The secret is how you amend, change, modify, and optimize so you don't lose your position," Collins concludes.

Adapted from "Albert E. Collins, Jr.: HBO Breeds MIS Star" by Alan Alper. Copyright 1988 by CW Publishing Inc., Framingham, MA 01701. Reprinted from *Computerworld,* July 18, 1988.

Managers depend on information systems for the successful operation of their businesses. Often, the success or failure of an information system can make or break a business. Consequently, it is extremely important that information systems be carefully designed and developed to successfully accomplish their intended purposes.

This chapter begins to look at how information systems are designed and developed. We'll examine the system development life cycle (SDLC), including the system analysis, design, and implementation phases. Each phase is composed of several stages. This chapter examines the system analysis phase; Chapter 10 discusses the system design and implementation phases.

IMPACT ON MANAGEMENT PROBLEM SOLVING AND DECISION MAKING

System analysis affects management problem-solving and decision-making activities in several ways. Managers are the ones who control the process and make the final decision of whether to proceed to the next phase of system design. In order to make a sound decision, they and we must understand what should take place during the system analysis phase.

The system analysis phase is crucial in developing an information system that will satisfy management's need for information. Managers must work with system personnel so that the true nature of a problem or opportunity can be identified and a system developed to provide the necessary information for solving that problem or exploiting that opportunity. If a problem or new opportunity is not correctly analyzed, the resulting system may be useless or even detrimental to the organization's goals.

WHY NEW SYSTEMS NEED TO BE DEVELOPED

All systems deteriorate, whether those systems are biological (the human body), mechanical (an automobile), or social (the Roman Empire). In addition, all systems have a life cycle that proceeds through the stages of development, growth, maturity, and decay (Figure 9–1). Information systems are no different; we just use different terms to describe the life cycle stages. No matter how much you love that old car, no matter how much you are willing to spend to patch it, mend it, and fix it, someday that beloved old car will collapse, and you'll have to replace it with a new car. That's also the way it is with information systems. They eventually grow

FIGURE 9–1
General life cycle of systems.

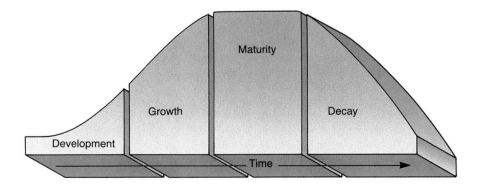

old and don't perform well. Then they must be replaced. Highlight 9– i takes a look at the aging IRS information system and the steps that are being taken to update it.

New systems are also developed in response to new opportunities that have been identified. For example, consider a 16-year-old who has just received her driver's license. She currently rides the bus (the old system) but can now drive (the new opportunity) and wants to purchase an automobile (the new system) to take advantage of the new opportunity.

Design of new or replacement information systems is not the major undertaking of information specialists. It is estimated that only about 15 percent of the dollars spent annually on business computer programming is devoted to new or replacement system development. The other 85 percent of the dollars are spent on maintaining current, still-satisfactory systems. There are even indications that the 15 percent now spent on new system development may be decreasing. Continuous technological advances are providing ways to make old information systems faster, to connect systems of different designs and manufacturers, and to cosmetically make aging systems seem young again. A vice president for McDonnell Douglas, a leading aerospace firm, recently stated that his firm had not developed a completely new information system in the past 7 years.

Nonetheless, it is difficult to imagine a world in which we will never have to buy new cars. In the same way it is difficult to imagine an information world in which no new systems need to be developed. Despite technological advances, information systems deteriorate in the same manner that cars, houses, and our own bodies do.

The Life Cycle of Information Systems

The **information system life cycle** represents the life span of an information system from its inception to its removal or redesign. The stages of the typical information system life cycle are shown in Figure 9–2.

1. *Design*—when the new information system is conceived and built to the specifications of the end-users.
2. *Implementation*—when the designed system is introduced into the workplace as a completely new system or as a replacement for an unsatisfactory system. A new system is rarely perfect, and minor flaws need to be corrected until the system operates properly.
3. *Maintenance*—when the new system is operating smoothly and only minor adjustments are made as minor flaws are discovered or small changes are desired.
4. *Replacement*—when the new system begins to perform in an unsatisfactory manner, for reasons discussed later in this chapter. A failing system must be replaced by a new information system.

An information system life cycle is a simple concept. However, a typical business firm has many different information systems—one to handle payroll, another to handle warehouse stocks, still another to process customer orders, and so on. And all of these different information systems are usually in different stages of their own individual life cycles. In the

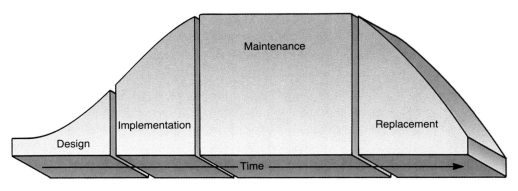

FIGURE 9–2
Information system life cycle.

fictional firm illustrated in Figure 9–3, System A is in the replacement stage, Systems B and C are in the maintenance stage, System D is being implemented, and System E is being designed. Thus, a typical information systems department may have a difficult time managing the variety of systems in different life cycle stages. It is always a rather traumatic event to discover that an old, reliable information system is beginning to deteriorate and a new information system must be designed to take its place.

FIGURE 9–3
Life cycles of multiple systems.

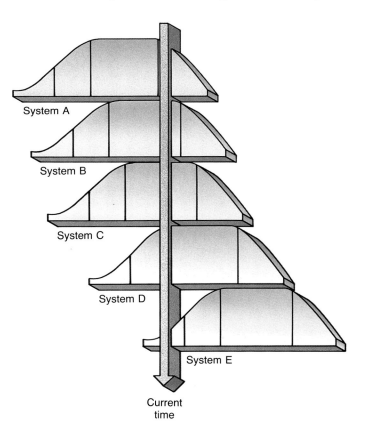

Why Information Systems Die

Business information systems become obsolete and need to be replaced for one or more of the following reasons:

1. *Physical deterioration.* Occasionally, computer systems deteriorate physically, as do automobiles or buildings. However, given the current state of dependable hardware manufacturing, such deterioration is rare.

2. *Technological obsolescence.* A perfectly healthy information system may be made competitively obsolete by new computing technologies, such as voice input, optical character recognition, or graphic display systems. For example, it would be hard today to imagine a new grocery chain entering into serious competition with other chains without automatic laser register systems. Old cash register systems did not deteriorate, but they did become technologically obsolete.

3. *Change in user expectations.* Many drivers like to buy a new car every year, even when the old one is running perfectly well. So it is with computer systems. A system may be designed so that an end-user can receive a response to an inquiry in 10 seconds (referred to as terminal response time). However, after 2 years with this information system, users believe that 10 seconds is now too slow and want a response time of 5 seconds or less. This information system has been made obsolete by changed user expectations.

4. *Accounting practice.* The average life of a business information system is only about 5 years for commercial firms, yet this life expectancy stretches well beyond 10 years for nonprofit firms. Why? Commercial firms typically depreciate capital investments, such as computers, over a 5-year period to secure the best possible tax advantages; one-fifth of the purchase cost can be deducted each year from taxable income. Nonprofit firms, including government agencies, do not pay taxes and therefore do not write off, or depreciate, their computer systems in this way. Commercial firms find it easier to justify purchasing a more technologically advanced computer to replace a model that has been written off the books.

5. *Outside influences.* Sometimes pressures from outside a firm force the replacement of a perfectly healthy information system. For example, if McElmore Industries acquires the Long Beach Drilling Company, executives at McElmore may demand that Long Beach Drilling change its information system hardware and software to match what the parent company has.

It is difficult to predict the life expectancy of a business information system, since it can die from many causes. Nevertheless, it is certain that every information system will eventually be replaced, and it is important to predict when the complex task of designing a replacement system should begin.

IRS's Information System Taxed to the Limit

One of the reasons that new systems need to be developed is that old systems can no longer handle the volume of data that needs to be processed. The IRS information systems are rapidly approaching this point. The agency expects to process more than 100 million tax returns for the 1989 filing season, adding up to a whopping $12 trillion in tax revenues. Each year that volume continues to increase, and according to a government watchdog agency, the system could reach overload as soon as 1992.

The current system has had some modifications but is essentially the same system that was approved by Congress in 1959 and put into place during the 1960s. The technology used in the current system is sorely outdated. Even though on-line access to information is commonplace in most businesses today, the IRS still uses magnetic tape and paper documents. Because the magnetic tape or paper document is stored at a central storage facility and must be shipped to a service center if an inquiry is made, the current system can take several weeks to answer the most routine questions about a tax return. In addition, according to the General Accounting Office (GAO) (the government agency that evaluates the IRS information systems), the IRS telecommunications system is basically airplanes and trucks—not a very efficient system for today's fast-paced electronic society.

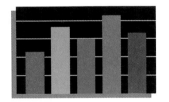

The IRS has recognized this problem and has tried numerous times to revamp its system. As far back as the 1960s, the IRS attempted to modernize its system for the future, but Congress considered the proposal too costly and denied the request. In 1982 the IRS again addressed the problem by formulating a modernization program called Tax System Redesign. That program is an effort by the IRS to replace its

The Piggybacking Concept

The concept of predicting information system decline is called **piggybacking**. It would be ideal if a replacement information system could be ready to operate just when the old system fails. This would be analogous to having a new car delivered to your house at the exact moment when your old car dies. In both cases such perfect timing is more dream than reality.

In the real world, replacement information systems require a long lead time for development—typically from 1 to 3 years. Therefore, it is essential to predict well in advance (Point [1] in Figure 9–4) when a current system is going to fail (Point [2] in Figure 9–4) and begin to design a replacement system while the current system is still healthy. Selling this concept to management may take some doing!

A **performance measurement system (PMS)** is used to predict an information system's demise or even a minor ailment that needs doctoring.

central, tape-based master files with an on-line database system. The agency also plans to use optical technology to capture and store images of tax returns. It currently costs the IRS $34 million per year to store the paper documents; the change would not only cut costs but would also dramatically improve response time by having the returns on-line. In addition, the agency plans to install a communications network that would allow on-line accessing and updating of taxpayer accounts. This system is to be developed incrementally and is targeted for completion by the year 2000.

The IRS has also been exploring the use of AI since the mid-1980s. The hope is that by the early 1990s expert systems might be able to help identify potential taxpayer audits and capture the expertise of the IRS personnel who are leaving or retiring from the agency.

Although solving certain problems, a new system will also bring different ones to the agency. Some of the implemented changes have already led to disaster, such as the 1985 switch to new computer systems in the IRS service centers. The switch experienced problems and was not accomplished in time for the filing season, thus disrupting both processing and taxpayer services. The delays cost the IRS several million dollars in interest on late refunds and spurred allegations that IRS employees were throwing out backlogged returns.

Furthermore, because of a virtual lack of a telecommunications network in the antiquated system of the past, the IRS has not had to worry about unauthorized access to taxpayer accounts by hackers. The installation of a full-scale telecommunications network will pose greater security concerns even as it improves access to data. The business environment of the IRS is constantly growing and changing, and the agency must continually reevaluate its information systems to ensure their ability to handle the information needs of the future.

A PMS keeps track of the daily operations of an information system and signals management when the system appears to be deteriorating, much as a doctor gives periodic checkups or a mechanic tests an automobile every 5000 miles. To illustrate how a PMS works, let's assume that information system users demand a terminal response time of less than 30 seconds. Currently, terminal response time is at 25 seconds, well within user expectations. However, the performance measurement system has stored past response times in computer memory. The PMS response time trend (Figure 9–5) shows that 6 months from now terminal response time will not meet user expectations. Management should now realize that there is a potential problem with the current system, perhaps requiring it to be replaced. Thus, the piggybacking concept deals with predicting current information system decay far enough in advance to allow sufficient time to develop a replacement system. The concept assumes the use of some sort of performance measurement system (PMS).

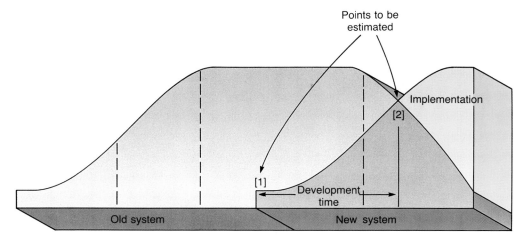

FIGURE 9–4
An illustration of piggybacking.

Information systems naturally die and need to be replaced. This natural phenomenon should not be cause for alarm but instead subject to systematic planning. The sections that follow present a structure that allows the orderly replacement of business information systems.

FIGURE 9–5
Predicting response time with a performance measurement system.

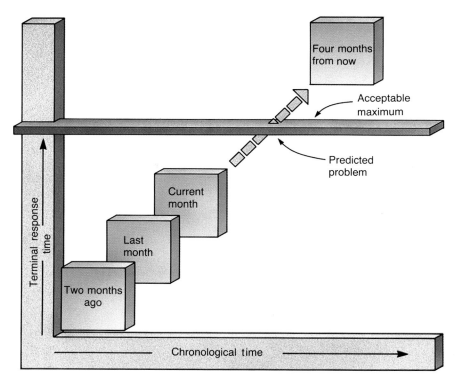

THE TRADITIONAL LIFE CYCLE OF SYSTEM DEVELOPMENT

The **system development life cycle (SDLC)** is the structured sequence of operations required to conceive, develop, and make operational a new information system. The term *cycle* stresses that a newly designed system will not last forever; ultimately, it will have to be replaced, and the development cycle will start again.

The system development life cycle consists of seven sequential stages grouped into three phases, the first of which is considered here. This first phase is known as **system analysis** and includes three separate stages.

1. The **problem definition stage** begins when a problem with the current information system is detected and is serious enough to lead to the question, "Should we start planning for a new system to replace the current system?"
2. The **requirements analysis stage** involves the analysis of the current system's performance. System users are interviewed to determine what the ideal system would be. The gap between the current system and the ideal system is explored to determine what is the best new system to close the gap (Figure 9-6).
3. During the **project justification stage** many alternatives are considered for the design of a new system; each alternative has differing costs and differing benefits (Figure 9-7). Information system personnel analyze the costs and benefits of the various alternatives and recommend to management either no changes or a new system configuration, in what is commonly called a system proposal.

At this point management must decide whether to accept the new system proposal, reject it and continue with the current system, or ask that the analysis be redone to address specific management concerns.

Even though the other two phases of the SDLC—system design and implementation—are discussed in the next chapter, let's look at them briefly to understand the scope of the entire system development life cycle (Figure 9-8). Steps 4 and 5 are collectively referred to as system design; Steps 6 and 7 are collectively referred to as implementation.

4. The **logical (conceptual) systems design stage** is the blueprint phase of designing a new information system. Descriptive tools (graphs, charts, and tables) are used to describe what the inputs, outputs, and files of the new system will look like. The products of this stage will be turned over to information construction workers (called applications programmers), who will convert the conceptual blueprint into an actual working system.
5. During the **physical (detailed) system design stage** the logical (paper) design is transformed into an actual working system that can process paychecks, customer orders, or whatever else the system is intended to do. This phase of the design includes programming—determining the series of steps necessary to convert system input (e.g., a time card) to system output (e.g., a paycheck).

FIGURE 9-6
Analysis of the gap between
current and ideal information
systems.

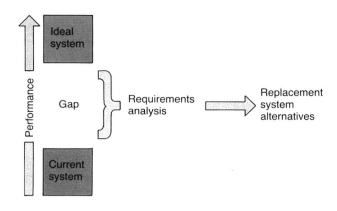

FIGURE 9-7
Identification and analysis of replacement system alternatives.

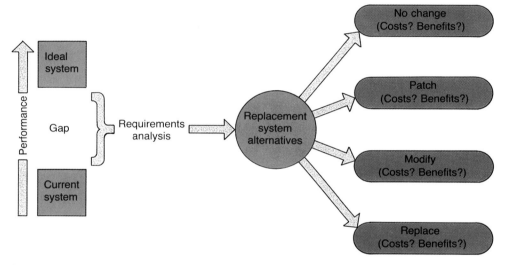

FIGURE 9-8
The seven stages of the system
development life cycle.

System analysis
- Problem definition
- Requirements analysis
- Project justification

System design
- Logical (conceptual) design
- Physical (detailed) design

Implementation
- Testing, installation, and training
- System changeover and maintenance

6. The **implementation stage** of the SDLC includes testing of system programs, installation of new computer equipment, and training of persons who will be operating the new system.
7. During the **system changeover stage** the old information system is discontinued, and the newly developed system is placed in operation. Fine tuning continues until the new system fully meets user expectations. Then the new system is signed over from the systems analyst to the user organization, and the maintenance period begins, with continual updates to meet the changing needs of the users until the system finally needs to be replaced.

As stated earlier, this traditional life cycle typically has a long development lead time of 1 to 3 years. However, these long lead times have become more and more intolerable to information users, who are unwilling to wait for such long periods of time.

Prototyping and Its Effects on the System Development Life Cycle

A **prototype information system** is defined as "a real, working, and usable system, built economically and quickly with the intention of being modified." It is similar to using a wind tunnel to develop the first stages of a new aircraft model. The advantages of prototyping over traditional development methods include the following:

1. The ultimate users play an active role early in the development of a new system. Thus, the system becomes *our* system for the users rather than *their* system, and users are more tolerant of flaws that may occur once the new system is operating.
2. New system errors are caught earlier in the development process, reducing the major changes required after the new system becomes operational.
3. Users begin training on the new system earlier in the development process, reducing user fears of the new system.
4. Often, new system users don't really know what they need until they gather some computer experience, much as a new driver doesn't know the type of automobile he wants until he has acquired some driving experience. Prototyping presents the new user with an experimental model that can be used to discover which features of a new information system are really needed.

The process of using prototypes is shown in Figure 9–9. A typical prototyping effort might follow these steps:

1. The business user identifies the need for a new information system, perhaps to accomplish some specific task.
2. The user communicates that need to a prototyper, who is a systems expert in the design of quick, cheap systems that users can change easily to accommodate their specific needs.
3. The prototyper uses fourth-generation software (see Chapter 4) on a microcomputer to quickly design a model that the user can play with.

FIGURE 9–9
The prototype cycle.

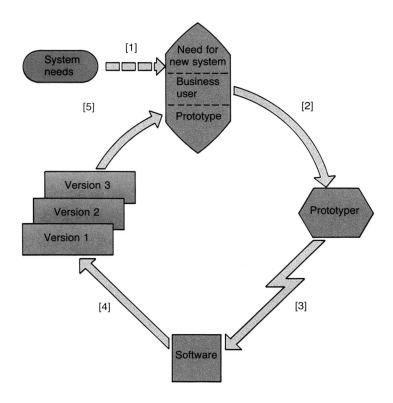

4. The user suggests changes to the first version of the prototype. The changes are made, and the user experiments with the second version. More changes are made, and more versions of the prototype are quickly produced.

5. Finally, the user likes a prototype, and that model becomes the working blueprint from which the new information system will be developed.

The concept of prototyping is not new; it has been used in other fields for many years. Wind-tunnel models of aircraft have been tested since the 1920s, and architects have constructed scale models of buildings for centuries. In the information systems field, however, it took the advent of the microcomputer and fourth-generation languages (4GL) for prototyping to become an efficient development tool. Effective use of prototyping cannot substantially change the tasks that must be accomplished to produce a new information system, but it can significantly decrease the time generally taken to develop such a system. Even though prototyping still seems to be in the experimental rather than the traditional mode of system development, it promises soon to become an accepted part of the SDLC.

QUALIFICATIONS AND ATTRIBUTES OF THE SYSTEMS ANALYST

Let's pause for a moment to examine an essential fact: the development of a new information system is not an automatic process, despite the growing number of automated design tools to assist in that process. New system development is accomplished by people, often referred to as systems analysts. Systems analysts are business professionals who (1) detect information system problems or new opportunities, (2) devise the means (e.g., new systems) to correct those problems or exploit those opportunities, and (3) implement those solutions in a business environment.

Many different job titles are given to information system specialists. Among these are programmer, project leader, data control analyst, systems analyst, and programmer/analyst. It is important to differentiate among the four most common titles: systems analyst, programmer, programmer/analyst, and project leader.

Differences in Position Responsibilities

The differing roles of these four information specialists are shown in Table 9–1 and explained here.

1. *Systems analyst.* The systems analyst is a problem solver who compares the performance of the current information system with the performance it should deliver and then determines the appropriate means to bridge any performance gap (Figure 9–10). The systems analyst also prepares the schematics of the inputs, files, and outputs of a new system during the logical design phase of the SDLC. Those schematics become the new system blueprint that is delivered to the programmer.
2. *Programmer.* This individual enters the scene during the physical design phase of the SDLC, receiving the new system blueprint

TABLE 9–1
Roles of information specialists.

SDLC Stages	Information Specialist Roles			
	Systems Analyst	Programmer	Programmer/ Analyst	Project Leader
Problem definition	A		A	A
Requirements analysis	A		A	O
Project justification	A		A	O
Logical design	A		A	O
Physical design		A	A	O
Implementation		A	A	A
Changeover				A

A = active role
O = overseer role

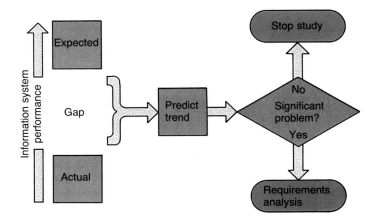

FIGURE 9–10

The problem-solving role of the systems analyst.

developed in the logical design phase. The programmer transforms the blueprint into a programming language code that will enter business data (transactions), update the necessary business files, and output the desired documents and reports. The programmer also tests (debugs) the programs to ensure that they are working properly in all circumstances.

3. *Programmer/analyst*. For small- to medium-size firms or business applications, the position of systems analyst and programmer are often combined and given the label **programmer/analyst**.

4. *Project leader*. At the other end of the size spectrum, when the firm housing the computerized application is so large that many systems analysts and programmers are involved, a **project leader** is often designated. A project leader supervises a development project through all phases of the system development life cycle.

The typical career progression for an information system specialist would begin with the position of programmer, continue to programmer/analyst, then to systems analyst, and finally to project leader. Our attention in this chapter is directed to the systems analyst.

Systems Analyst Skills and Qualifications

A successful systems analyst must possess the following characteristics:

- Communication skills, both oral and written. Unlike the programmer, who often works only with other information specialists, the systems analyst must communicate with a wide variety of personnel, ranging from nontechnical clerical personnel to top management.

- Analytical and logical skills. The systems analyst must be able to look at complex, often fuzzy, situations and reduce them to their simplest terms and structures. The systems analyst must also be adept at using the various analytical tools presented in this and the following chapters.

- Knowledge of business processes. The systems analyst must be familiar with inventory, payroll, order entry, and all other basic business functions, as well as the philosophy of the particular business.
- The ability to work independently.
- An information systems education that is future-oriented so that the systems analyst is not locked into old solutions.

A career as a systems analyst can be profitable and emotionally rewarding. It is also a demanding position for which the faint of heart should not apply.

PROBLEM DEFINITION

The first stage in the system development life cycle is that of problem definition. Here the systems analyst must act as a systems doctor, quickly detecting symptoms that indicate that the system is becoming unhealthy, or ineffective. However, just as a reputable doctor would not prescribe major surgery until all other options had been explored, so too must the systems analyst carefully gather all the facts relevant to the problem at hand. The initiation of a new system or a major system modification is costly and time-consuming and should not be begun in an offhand manner. People in the information field too often operate by the law of the hammer, which states, "Give a kid a hammer, and you'll be surprised what needs to be hammered." Problem definition, instead, should carefully gather the facts to determine the nature, scope, and seriousness of any alleged problem with an information system.

Problem Sources

Notification of an alleged information system problem can come from several sources:

- user complaints, either direct to the information center staff or through functional supervisors
- performance measurement systems, which reveal statistically deteriorating performance trends
- systems analyst "scouting," the periodic visiting of user work areas to see whether everything is all right
- performance audits by internal company auditors or by hired outside consultants

Nature of Systems Problems

There are six performance categories within which most information systems problems fall.

1. *Accuracy.* Output from the information system may be inaccurate. For example, a failing payroll system may be incorrectly computing overtime pay or omitting certain employee paychecks.

2. *Responsiveness.* System users may not be receiving computer products in a timely manner. Management reports may be 3 days late, or the user may have to wait 5 minutes before the system responds to a question.
3. *Currency.* System files may not be updated in a timely manner because there is a growing backlog of transactions that have not been entered. For example, a firm may be losing customer sales because receipts of inventory from vendors are not being input into the inventory system from the receiving area. In such a case, when a salesman processes a customer order, the inventory record may show no inventory on hand, even though dozens of units may be sitting on a receiving dock.
4. *Economy.* The costs of an information system may be increasing rapidly. Costs include people, supplies, and hardware/software changes.
5. *Consistency.* An information system's accuracy, responsiveness, currency, and economy may be are unpredictable. In other words, the information system may run smoothly *when* it runs. However, erratic equipment failures may make the entire system inoperative at unpredictable times.
6. *Security.* An organization's critical information may be lost or routed to unintended parties. At its worst this class of information system problem can include cases of military or industrial espionage.

Whatever type of information system problem is detected from whatever source(s), the problem should be brought to the attention of the information systems department, where it should be formally recorded to ensure that it won't be ignored or forgotten. Then the potential problem should be assigned to a specific systems analyst to investigate the problem in more detail (e.g., interview unhappy users) and then write a **preliminary problem report**, containing the following elements:

- the nature and source of the information system problem
- the systems analyst's more detailed analysis of the problem
- the analyst's recommendation as to whether the problem is (1) minor or imagined and therefore able to be treated through normal day-to-day, system maintenance (Band-Aid) operations or (2) substantial, requiring either a major modification of the information system or the complete replacement of that system.

If the latter recommendation is accepted by management, the systems analyst must then continue to the second stage of the system development life cycle.

REQUIREMENTS ANALYSIS	Once again, this stage of the SDLC determines how the present information system performs, how the best possible system might perform, and what types of new systems might be designed to bridge the gap between these two performance levels.

Development of Business Information Systems

The Current Information System

Much of the required description of the current system will have been completed during the systems analyst's preliminary investigation conducted during the problem definition stage. It is difficult to define a problem without thoroughly describing the current situation. That description will most likely have been at least partially achieved with the graphics tools described later in this chapter.

The Ideal Information System

The systems analyst interviews (with great oral communication skills) the system users to determine what would be their ideal information system. The systems analyst asks questions such as these:

- What type of reports do you really need to do your job?
- Do you need those reports every day? once a week? once a month? or only when you ask for them?
- What level of inaccuracy can you really tolerate and still do your job well?
- How current do your records have to be? (For instance, does an employee payroll record have to be kept current with each hour of that employee's work, when that employee's check is produced only once each month?)

The systems analyst will typically interview a number of information system users, each with an individual idea of the ideal system. The analyst must then consolidate those interviews into one composite picture of the user group's ideal information system. The composite portrait must, of course, be approved by key management personnel within the user group.

The analyst might also choose other methods to support the interviewing process. Among the more common techniques are surveys, document review, policy and procedure review, and direct observation.

Types of New Information Systems

At this point the systems analyst should have a good idea of where the current system and the users' ideal system stand in regard to the key performance categories of accuracy, responsiveness, currency, economy, consistency, and security. The analyst must then determine which types of replacement information systems will bridge the gap between the current and the desired systems.

A Cadillac system might be very fast and have tight security, but its cost would exceed management's limits. The systems analyst must creatively balance all performance objectives and identify alternative information systems in a process too complex to be discussed here. Suffice it to say that a journeyman systems analyst will arrive at a narrow range of new information systems that will bridge the gap between current and ideal system performance.

PROJECT JUSTIFICATION

This phase of the SDLC is intended to systematically compare alternative information systems and decide which of them to propose to management. This is the last stage of the systems analysis portion of the SDLC, and it is a critical stage that will end with management's approval or denial of the design of a new information system. Thus, the SDLC could be aborted here. Indeed, in a large percentage of cases, solutions have been found to patch the current system, and the replacement project idea is not pursued. The project justification stage includes the cost/benefit analysis of alternate systems, selection of the best system, preparation of a system study for submission to management, and management's final go/no-go decision.

Cost/Benefit Analysis

Often referred to as the feasibility study, the objective of the **cost/benefit analysis** is to compare both costs and benefits of alternative new information systems and the current system to determine which system should be recommended to management. An example of a cost comparison is shown in Figure 9–11. Note that the new system has both one-time developmental costs required for start-up and recurring operating costs, which must be paid for over some reasonable period of time. In this case the new system generates benefits beyond its cost in 4.9 years.

Cost/benefit analysis of alternative information systems can be a difficult task for several reasons.

1. As seen in Figure 9–11, costs must be projected many years into the future. Such forecasting is always more art than science.
2. Costs can be stated in numbers, but benefits are more difficult to quantify. For example, how much will profit be increased in dollars by increasing system accuracy? Or what is the dollar value of providing faster service to customers?
3. The systems analyst must show that one alternative information system is better than all other alternatives and that investment in that system is preferable to all other company alternatives. For example, the analyst's new information system may be competing with a manufacturing plan to retool the production line.

Thus, cost/benefit analysis is not nearly so clear-cut as it appears in Figure 9–11. Typically, cost analysis is used to narrow down the alternative systems to two or, at most, three. Then the systems analyst qualitatively (no numbers involved) considers the relative benefits of those two or three systems and selects the one she feels will do the best job.

Having done so, the systems analyst must then sell that chosen information system to management.

The System Study

The **system study** is an extensive report that is sent to management and is generally accompanied by a formal oral presentation. The study contains these materials:

	Current Year	+1	+2	+3	+4	+5
New System Costs						
Developmental costs:						
Personnel	$ 60,000	$ 10,000				
Hardware/software	32,000	6,000				
Training	10,000	8,000				
Supplies	3,000	500				
Overhead	5,500	—				
Total development costs	$110,500	$ 24,500				
Operating costs:						
Personnel		$ 38,500	$ 27,000	$16,250	$ 18,000	$ 19,200
Hardware/software		35,000	25,000	26,000	27,000	28,000
Supplies		3,400	3,600	3,500	4,000	4,200
Overhead		3,500	4,000	4,500	5,000	5,500
Total operating costs		$ 80,400	$ 59,600	$50,550	$ 54,000	$ 56,900
Current System Costs						
Personnel	$ 44,000	$ 46,200	$ 48,000	$50,500	$ 53,250	$ 56,000
Hardware/software	25,000	26,000	27,000	29,000	30,000	32,000
Supplies	9,000	10,000	12,000	14,000	15,000	17,000
Overhead	4,500	5,000	5,500	6,000	6,500	7,000
Total current system costs	$ 82,500	$ 87,200	$ 92,500	$99,500	$104,750	$112,000
Net Operating Benefits						
Operating costs:						
Current system	—	$ 87,200	$ 92,500	$99,500	$104,750	$112,000
Proposed system	—	80,400	59,600	50,550	54,000	56,900
Savings		$ 6,800	$ 32,900	$48,950	$ 50,750	$ 55,100
Developmental costs:						
Previous years	—	$110,500	$128,200	$95,300	$ 46,350	$ (4,400)
Current year	$110,500	24,500	—	—	—	—
Total	$110,500	$135,000	$128,200	$95,300	$ 46,350	$ (4,400)
Applied savings	—	6,800	32,900	48,950	50,750	55,100
Unrecovered costs	$110,500	$128,200	$ 95,300	$46,350	$ (4,400)	$ (59,500)

$$\text{Payback} = 4 + \frac{46,350}{50,250} \text{ years} = 4.9 \text{ years}$$

FIGURE 9–11
Cost/benefit analysis.

- A summary of current information system problems and the reasons the study was initiated.
- Specific constraints that affect the choice of a new information system. Typical constraints are funds, time, and lack of qualified systems personnel. Such constraints generally prevent a systems analyst from proposing the users' ideal information system to management.
- Specific objectives of the new information system, stated in terms of the key performance characteristics already discussed.
- A thorough presentation of the method (cost/benefit analysis) by which the proposed new information system was selected from among other alternatives.
- Recommendations as to which information system should be designed and a project plan including time and cost specifications.

At this point, management must decide whether to accept the systems analyst's recommendations. That conclusion is often referred to as the go/no-go decision because it determines whether the systems analyst is authorized to *go* ahead with designing a replacement information system. Management may choose any one of several options at this point.

- Accept the systems analyst's recommendations to proceed with the design of the new information system. In this case the remaining steps of the SDLC are activated.
- Retain the present information system. This option may be chosen because (1) there is a cash-flow problem in the firm, making necessary funds unavailable for initial investment in the new system; (2) some other department's recommendation shows more profit potential; or (3) management finds the system study to be so poorly prepared that it cannot be repeated.
- Repeat the system study because one or more aspects seem to require further analysis. In this case the systems analyst must reenter the SDLC at an earlier stage.
- Table the study for future consideration, a variant of the second option listed here. The systems analyst's recommendation for a new information system may not be the right idea at the right time.

The project justification stage ends with the systems analyst continuing the SDLC, abandoning the project entirely, or polishing the project for presentation to management at a future date. However, before we consider the remaining stages of the SDLC, we need to look in more detail at how the tasks of the systems analyst are actually accomplished.

SYSTEM ANALYSIS TOOLS

During the system analysis phase of the SDLC, a number of graphic and tabular system analysis tools are used.

System Flowcharts

A **system flowchart** is a tool that shows the flow of information through a system and all the ways that information is altered as it flows through that system. Figure 9–12 shows the flow of a customer order as it is processed; the meanings of the specific flowchart symbols are shown in Figure 9–13. The rectangle labeled "PROGRAM W23—Order Processing Module" that appears in the middle of the system flowchart describes the identification of a specific computer program to convert input into output in this order processing system. The step-by-step manner in which this conversion occurs is not specified in the system flowchart but is included in the program flowchart discussed in Chapter 10. The system flowchart is a means of communication between technical-information specialists and is not intended to be used by nontechnical-information users.

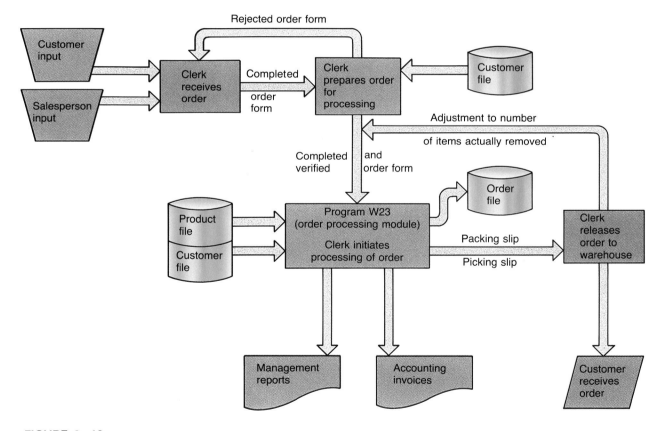

FIGURE 9–12
System flowchart for customer order processing.

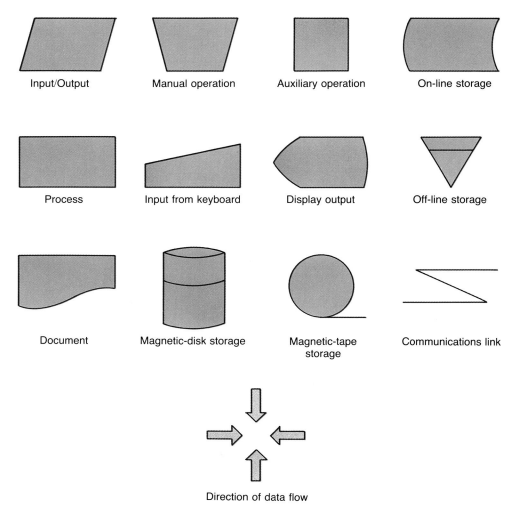

FIGURE 9–13
System flowchart symbols.

Data Flow Diagrams

A graphic technique that is more user-oriented is the data flow diagram. A **data flow diagram (DFD)** is a picture of the system that concentrates on information flow rather than on the treatment of that information during the flow. A data flow diagram for the same customer order processing shown earlier is illustrated in Figure 9–14; the meanings of the symbols are given in Figure 9–15.

There are two variations of the data flow diagram—the physical DFD and the logical DFD. The physical data flow diagram is used during the problem definition stage and shows what the current system looks like. It demonstrates to users that the systems analyst really understands how the current information system works. The logical data flow diagram is used

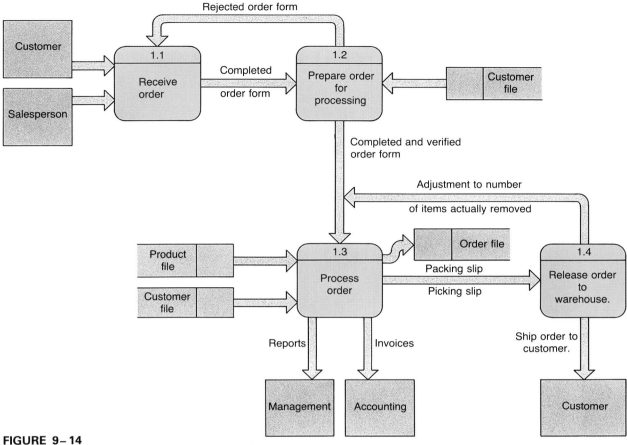

FIGURE 9–14
Data flow diagram for customer order processing.

FIGURE 9–15
Data flow diagram (DFD)
symbols.

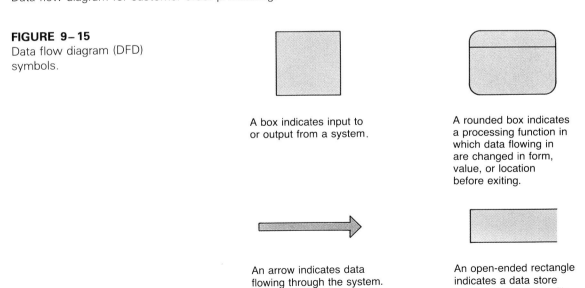

A box indicates input to
or output from a system.

A rounded box indicates
a processing function in
which data flowing in
are changed in form,
value, or location
before exiting.

An arrow indicates data
flowing through the system.

An open-ended rectangle
indicates a data store
such as a data-base file.

Input data element \ File	Sales File	Inventory File	Supplier File	• • •				
Item number	✓	✓	✓					
Item price	✓							
Current quantity in stock		✓						
Supplier number			✓					
Supplier name			✓					
Supplier address			✓					
•								
•								
•								

FIGURE 9–16
An input to file matrix.

during the requirements analysis stage of the SDLC; it shows what an ideal information system would look like. For example, the physical DFD might show that there are two current customer files, one for active customers and the other for past customers. The logical DFD might consolidate these two files into one integrated customer file.

The data flow diagram is a valuable analysis tool that paints a systems picture system in terms that nontechnical end-users can understand. However, a DFD is rarely detailed enough to satisfy technical information specialists. Therefore, when a systems analyst wishes to communicate with end-users, data flow diagrams should be used. When the analyst wishes to communicate with other systems analysts or technical personnel, system flowcharts should be used. Often, a system study contains both types of graphic descriptions.

FIGURE 9–17
A data element to report matrix.

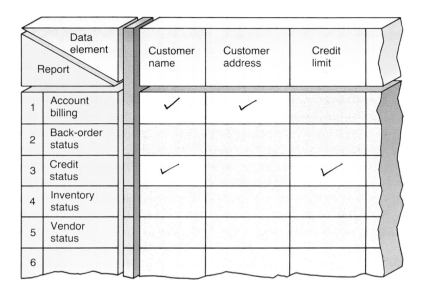

Report	Data element	Customer name	Customer address	Credit limit
1	Account billing	✓	✓	
2	Back-order status			
3	Credit status	✓		✓
4	Inventory status			
5	Vendor status			
6				

Tabular Techniques

Tables are often used in the system analysis phase to show relationships among information elements. Two of the more common tables are the **input to file matrix** (Figure 9–16) and the **data element to report matrix** (Figure 9–17). The input to file matrix shows which input documents update which system files; the data element to report matrix shows which data elements are printed out on which reports.

Such tabular techniques allow a quick cross-reference for changes. For example, if we change the length of the customer name field in Figure 9–16, we can easily see that this change would affect the composition of the first and third reports. Therefore, the computer programs that produce those two reports would also have to be changed.

There are several other tools that are used in the systems analysis phase, but those discussed here are the most common. Graphic and other tools used in the system design phase of the SDLC are discussed in Chapter 10.

AUTOMATING SYSTEM ANALYSIS

Until recently, systems analysts were in a rather bizarre situation regarding the tools they used. These analysts were designing large, complex computer information systems with pencil and paper. In other words, the automators were not automated, and circumstances could prove quite frustrating. For example, the system flowchart tool just described might produce a final flowchart of 50 or more pages with a dozen or more symbols per page, all of which had to be drawn in pencil, using flowchart templates. If the systems analyst discovered that a process step had been omitted in the middle of page 34, imagine the work involved to modify the total flowchart to insert the omitted symbol.

In recent years automated system analysis programs that run on microcomputers have been marketed. These programs are designed to automate many of the systems analyst's trivial but time-consuming tasks. The approach is similar to that of computer-aided design (CAD) in aiding architectural design and computer-aided manufacturing (CAM) in helping production designers. The entire class of programs (software) that automates system analysis tasks is referred to as **computer-aided systems engineering (CASE)**. CASE products offer the following automated capabilities:

- graphics to produce and change automatically such analysis tools as data flow diagrams
- integration of other productivity tools, such as word processors and spreadsheets
- quality assurance functions, which evaluate graphs and other CASE products for completeness, consistency, and accuracy
- data sharing, which allows systems analysts to use several different microcomputer workstations to share graphics and data
- rapid prototyping, which allows quick and automatic generation of user input screens and output reports and forms

The use of CASE products has made the design of business information systems faster and easier and of greater quality. The investment required for CASE software purchases is typically less than $10,000, yet increases in systems analyst productivity typically exceed 35 percent. As CASE products become more available and more comprehensive, their price is likely to decrease. As a result, the use of CASE products should dramatically increase during the next several years. Highlight 9–2 looks at how CASE products have helped improve productivity in several businesses.

PROJECT MANAGEMENT

During the first three stages of the system development life cycle, and during the remainder of the stages as well, there must be careful coordination.

- There will probably be several or even many systems analysts and programmers working on the design of a new information system.
- The design must be accomplished within a specified time frame and an agreed-upon budget.
- The beginning of any one stage in the SDLC depends on work being partially or wholly completed in one or more preceding stages. For example, a system study cannot be completed unless a feasibility analysis has been done.

Such a situation calls for the use of project management techniques. **Project management** is the structured coordination and monitoring of all activities involved in a one-time endeavor or project. Three basic functions are required for the management of a system project.

1. *Planning.* Detailed task lists are developed that specify timing, sequencing, and responsibilities. This function often involves the use

Many businesses are beginning to report positive results in productivity from the use of computer-aided systems engineering (CASE) software products. One such business is the BDM Corporation in McLean, Virginia. That company reports that user complaints about information system software have declined by 75 percent since the company started using CASE analysis and design tools several years ago. Other benefits have included a decrease of 50 percent in the number of errors in documentation and in program code.

Another user reporting positive benefits from CASE products is Royal Insurance Company in Charlotte, North Carolina. CASE tools have helped that firm standardize corporate reports and unify them in a relational database. The company has also reported a 30 to 50 percent time savings in repetitive drawings done by system personnel.

First Capital Life Insurance Company in La Jolla, California, reported the ability to complete the programming and testing portions of their pilot projects four to five times faster or with one-fourth to one-fifth of the personnel traditionally required. In addition, CASE tools can be used to both prototype and generate usable COBOL code. The advantage of this capability is that a working prototype can be quickly constructed while discussing user requirements for a system, and the user can determine whether it meets company needs.

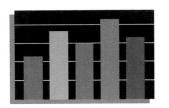

Hercules Computer Technology, based in Delaware, has reported productivity increases of about 10 percent in the development of new systems and 25 percent in system maintenance through the use of CASE tools.

Nonetheless, many organizations are still wary of the CASE claims and are waiting for more information. As CASE products evolve and measures of productivity become more understood and standardized, more organizations are likely to jump into the CASE arena.

of such scheduling tools as PERT or CPM. Another useful planning tool is the **project accountability chart (PAC)**, as shown in Figure 9–18. Such a chart organizes a project by time on the horizontal axis and by responsible agency or department on the vertical axis.

2. *Monitoring.* All project tasks are periodically measured to determine completion progress, both in terms of time and costs.

3. *Resource control.* Planned progress is compared with actual progress to determine whether resource or schedule adjustments must be made. The project manager assures that all project activities have sufficient personnel, material, and finances to complete work in the required time.

In very large development projects a special project manager is assigned to coordinate efforts. A project manager is rarely assigned other

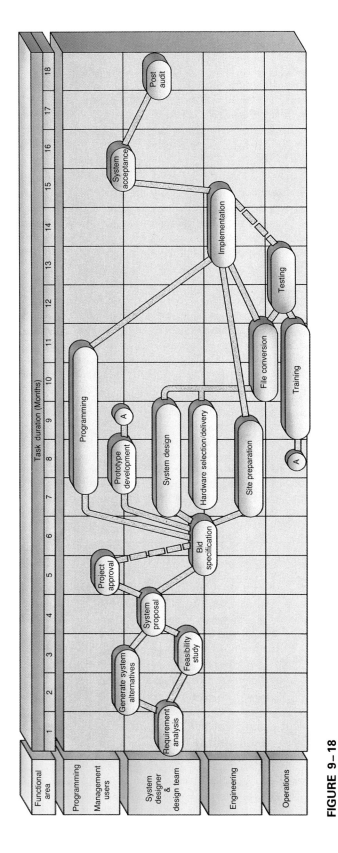

FIGURE 9–18

A project accountability chart (PAC). (Reprinted by permission from M. Martin and J. Trumbly, "A Project Accountability Chart," *Journal of Systems Management* [March 1987]: 9.)

project tasks, such as flow charting or programming, because careful management of a large development project is considered to be a full-time job. In development of smaller information systems, management of the overall project is usually not considered a full-time job. Often, project responsibilities are added to the development tasks performed by the senior systems analyst, who is then designated as the project leader.

Whatever the size of the information system development project or whoever is assigned project management responsibilities, coordination of development activities is not an easy task for several reasons.

1. There are many talented analysts and programmers involved, each with an individual opinion of how the project should be handled.
2. Development of an information system takes years, increasing the chances that key project people may leave or that some major design error will occur.
3. The costs of long-lead-time projects are rarely underestimated. Instead, it is more common for the budget of the project to be drained before the system is fully implemented. The project manager is then faced with equally dangerous alternatives—asking management for more funds or cutting corners in the design of the new system.
4. Too often, ultimate users of a new information system change their minds about what they want after a project is well into the design cycle. The project manager must either say no to such changes or demand a new project budget.

Even though management of an information system development project is difficult, it is not impossible. New information systems are implemented regularly, some on schedule and some within original budgets. The key principle in successful projects is that the project leader immediately notify management if and when it first appears that the project will be late or that it will be over the budget. The history of information system development has shown that a majority of projects are over-budget, late, or both. Management is usually tolerant of such development situations if the reasons are understandable and key personnel were notified early that such a situation would probably occur.

SUMMARY

New information systems are developed in response to problems in an existing system or identification of new opportunities. Development of new information systems comprises about 15 percent of the information processing dollars spent annually. Information systems proceed through a natural life cycle of development, implementation, maintenance, and then replacement. An information system must be replaced when it has physically deteriorated, has become technologically obsolete, has experienced a change in user expectations, has exceeded its accounting (tax write-off) life, or is under pressure from influences outside the firm (e.g., acquisition).

It is important to predict well in advance when an information system is beginning to deteriorate in order to start the development of a replacement system. A long lead time is associated with the development of a new information system. The concept of predicting a system's demise and planning early for its replacement is called piggybacking.

Development of a new information system proceeds in seven stages, called the system development life cycle (SDLC). The first three stages are problem definition, requirements analysis, and project justification; they are referred to collectively as system analysis.

The system development life cycle continues with Stage 4 (logical system design) and Stage 5 (physical system design), which comprise the system design phase. The implementation stage (Stage 6) and the changeover stage (Stage 7) are called collectively implementation.

A traditional system development life cycle can take 2 to 3 years. Rapid prototyping of a new system can significantly reduce this extensive development time. Prototyping is the rapid, quick, and inexpensive development of a model of a new information system. It allows early user evaluation and modification of a new system before implementation.

The person who diagnoses the condition of an old information system and prescribes a replacement system is called a systems analyst. That person is an artistic problem solver and superb communicator, who can bridge the gap between the technical information-processing world and the less technical, more pragmatic world of the end-user.

During the systems analysis phase, several tools are necessary to produce a system study. Among these are system flowcharts, data flow diagrams, and various tabular techniques. The development of a new information system through the seven stages of the system development life cycle is a complex undertaking requiring the structured planning and scheduling skills of project management.

MINICASE 9–1

Brock Enterprises produces high-quality videos for a number of musical artists. The new CEO has mandated that the company incorporate and take advantage of information system technology at all levels of management. The systems analyst at Brock Enterprises has been asked to develop a system to assist top managers with their decisions. The managers at Brock have little or no computer experience and are unsure of what a computer system could or should do for them. Many of the managers are skeptical about a computer system's ability to help them with the types of decisions they make. They were unable to tell the systems analyst what type of user interface they would prefer and had no idea how the information should be presented or exactly what types of information they would want from the system. The managers gave the analyst plenty of generalized information, but because of their unfamiliarity with systems of this type, they couldn't identify the features or requirements in advance.

1. As the new systems analyst, what type of development approach would you suggest for a system to help Brock managers in their decision making?

---

2. How would the development approach you suggested improve your chances of designing a successful information system?

MINICASE 9–2

Miler, Inc. manufactures and distributes apparel for both women and men. Despite the company's beachfront location and excellent program of employee benefits, there are some disgruntled employees. The group of systems analysts at Miler is experiencing a high turnover rate because of poor morale, the result of being overworked and poorly managed.

The company started several years ago with just a few employees, all friends of the owner. Since then the company has experienced continuous growth. Jack Bodner, the manager of the systems group and one of the initial employees, rose to his position as the company grew.

There is currently a large backlog of information systems projects that need the attention of the systems group. The analysts spend many nights in the office finishing flowcharts and other time-consuming tasks. Numerous projects are in various stages of completion. Each project involves several systems analysts, and some analysts are working on multiple projects.

Mr. Bodner has not set up any formal plans to monitor and control the projects, so each project team is left basically on its own. Often, systems analysts who are assigned to a project cannot begin when they are supposed to because information needed from another analyst is not complete. There is poor communication and a lack of direction in the systems group. As a result, many projects are late and are way over budget.

Jack has just been given early retirement, and you have been hired as the new manager of the systems group.

1. Describe what techniques you would use to bring the systems group's projects under control.

2. How could the charting, graphic, and other manual functions of the systems analysts be speeded up to help relieve the backlog? Explain your answer.

Key Terms

computer-aided systems engineering (CASE)

cost/benefit analysis

data element to report matrix

data flow diagram (DFD)

implementation stage

information system life cycle

input to file matrix

logical (conceptual) system design stage

performance measurement system (PMS)

physical (detailed) system design stage

piggybacking

preliminary problem report

problem definition stage

programmer/analyst

project accountability chart (PAC)

project justification stage

project leader

project management

prototype information system

requirements analysis stage

system analysis

system changeover stage

system development life cycle (SDLC)

system flowchart

system study

Review Questions

1. What are the four stages of an individual information system life cycle?
2. How does an information system life cycle compare with a human life cycle?
3. Describe the reasons that information systems die.
4. Why do information systems have a longer life in nonprofit firms than in commercial firms?
5. Explain the concept of information system piggybacking.
6. What are the seven stages of the SDLC?
7. Which SDLC stages are included in the phase called system analysis?
8. What is the difference between logical and physical system design?
9. What are the components of the implementation stage of the SDLC?
10. What is prototyping? How does it affect the system development life cycle (SDLC)?
11. What are the advantages of prototyping versus traditional development methods?
12. What are the essential differences in the roles of programmers and systems analyst?
13. What are the specific skills and attributes of a successful systems analyst?
14. List the sources of alleged problems relating to a current information system.
15. What is the difference between system accuracy and system consistency?
16. What are the contents of a preliminary problem report?
17. What is the purpose of the requirements analysis stage of the SDLC?
18. What technique can be used to provide a financial evaluation of a proposed information system?
19. Explain the significance of a go/no-go decision.
20. What is the difference in usage of system flowcharts and data flow diagrams?
21. Which come first—logical or physical data flow diagrams? Why?
22. What are the primary purposes of the tabular techniques discussed in this chapter?
23. What is CASE? Why is it important to the development of new information systems?
24. What capabilities do CASE products offer?
25. What are the components of project management?

System Design and Implementation

OBJECTIVES

- To learn the tasks involved in the design of input, output, and file components of business information systems
- To understand the role of prototyping in system design
- To generally describe the different charting techniques used in system design
- To understand the importance of automation in system design tasks
- To understand the purpose and methodology of testing an information system
- To know the tasks that need to be completed before an information system is installed and the various approaches to and the organizational impact of installing an information system
- To understand the need, responsibilities, and management issues associated with the maintenance of an information system

OUTLINE

IMPACT ON MANAGEMENT PROBLEM SOLVING AND DECISION MAKING
LOGICAL DESIGN CONCEPTS
The System Blueprint I Principles of Well-Designed Systems I Design Sequence
OUTPUT DESIGN CONSIDERATIONS
Types of Documents I Types of Reports I Output Media
INPUT DESIGN CONSIDERATIONS
Source Documents I Coding I Error Checking I Interactive Screen Design I Input Media
FILE DESIGN CONSIDERATIONS
File Media I File Access Methods I Record Format I File Size I File Retention and Recovery I Database Management System (DBMS) I Designing Files for the Future
PHYSICAL DESIGN
Organizing the Programming Effort I Developing Program Logic I Prototyping in System Design
CHARTING TECHNIQUES FOR SYSTEM DESIGN
Logical Design I Physical Design
AUTOMATING SYSTEM DESIGN
TESTING
Purpose of Testing I Testing Methodology I Automated Testing I Auditor's Role in Testing I Debugging a Program
INSTALLATION
Planning I Installation Tasks I Conversion I Organizational Impact
TRAINING
User Training I Operator Training I Management Training
MAINTENANCE
Need for Maintenance I Maintenance Programmers I Factors Facilitating Maintenance

Chapter 10

Management Profile: Michael S. Heschel
TAKING THE PULSE OF MIS

At Baxter Healthcare Corporation's 250-acre complex, Michael S. Heschel is corporate vice president of information resources for the worldwide computer operations of this hospital supply company. Heschel believes that one key element in his information systems strategy doesn't have a price tag—the creation of ongoing and effective communications with senior management, end-users, and 750 staffers. "I've tried to create an esprit de corps by providing a challenging work environment, a good career path, and some rewards. We have an open atmosphere, because people have to feel good about what they're doing to be productive," says Heschel.

Heschel communicates with information systems staffers in several ways: by holding quarterly all-center meetings that are attended by all information systems employees; by writing a biweekly newsletter called *FYI*; and by making himself available for discussion. He also attends departmental social gatherings and drops in on after-hours pizza parties. Longtime associate Carl Steiner, who is Baxter's vice president of planning and administration, says Heschel's extra effort to communicate pinpoints problems before they surface.

Heschel does this communicating via monthly breakfast meetings attended by 10 to 15 people with a variety of job titles. "I have some unwritten rules about the breakfast meetings," Heschel notes. "I give them my personal commitment that no names will be used, and their staff managers are not present." That promise makes interchanges lively, something Heschel encourages even in larger meetings.

The quarterly all-center meetings feature 2 hours of formal discussions, followed by a question-and-answer period. But, Steiner notes,

Heschel doesn't like the sessions to end in polite silence. "There have been times," Steiner says, "when he didn't let the audience go until they asked a few more questions."

What Heschel encourages is an environment in which quality and cost-effectiveness are highly prized commodities. "Good people want a challenge, and I give them the responsibility," Heschel says. The best efforts are sometimes rewarded with an evening on the town, paid for by Heschel, or with a $2,500 check for outstanding work on a project.

Getting the funds for new technology is one of Heschel's priorities. "Mike has been able to show senior management how MIS could contribute to the business," said Bob Kretz, vice president of systems development. "He raised the visibility of the information systems function and showed the executives how the corporation's business plans could be tied into those of the information resources group."

To sharpen his information systems strategy, Heschel spends about 30 percent of his time traveling to user sites, meetings with hardware vendors, and meetings with his peers in other large corporations. Heschel describes his role as being made up of four primary components: providing an architectural vision; ensuring that information systems meet end-users' computing needs; providing cost-competitive information services; and ensuring that the information systems infrastructure keeps pace with changing needs.

Adapted from "Michael S. Heschel: Taking the Pulse of MIS" by Jean S. Bozman. Copyright 1988 by CW Publishing Inc., Framingham, MA 01701. Reprinted from *Computerworld,* April 4, 1988.

Chapter 9 described a systems analyst and the first three stages of the system development life cycle (SDLC). Those stages, collectively known as the system analysis phase, included identifying an information system problem (Stage 1), specifying user requirements for the system (Stage 2), and justifying a replacement system project to management (Stage 3).

The next phase, the **system design** phase, is comprised of two stages—logical design and physical design. Logical design is the development of a paper blueprint for a new system. Physical design is the translation of that blueprint into the specific programming logic that will cause a new system to operate as planned. Sometimes the logical design phase is called conceptual design, and the physical design phase is called detailed design.

Once a system is designed, it is then implemented. In short, implementation brings the system to its useful life, by way of testing, installation, training, and maintenance. Before a system can be used in a "real" environment, it must be tested and installed on the hardware it will use, and its users must be trained. Then the system must undergo continued maintenance to conform it to changes in user requirements.

IMPACT ON MANAGEMENT PROBLEM SOLVING AND DECISION MAKING

The design of an information system is very important to its effectiveness in supporting management's problem solving and decision making and thus the organization's success. Managers should be intimately involved in the design process so that the final system supplies them with the information they need in a form they can use to accomplish their activities. Managers need to communicate the type, content, and frequency of the reports and screen displays they need so that the information included will be well received by those who use it. The acceptance of those individuals is crucial for the success of the information system. It is also important that managers as well as users be involved in the design of the software interfaces so that the information system is easy to use. An information system that goes unused because it is too difficult or awkward to use will not help managers identify and solve problems or make decisions. In addition, managers need to be aware of the automated tools available to improve the efficiency and effectiveness of the system design process. Those technologies, when appropriately used, will help create better and less expensive systems and will get them into the hands of the users more quickly. By understanding the system design phase, managers can better control the processes and can make more effective contributions to the design effort.

Managers must ensure that systems are thoroughly tested and as error free as possible to help build user confidence and acceptance. Frequently, managers must also budget for the type and amount of training that information system users should have, and managers may also be called on to decide which implementation strategy should be used.

LOGICAL DESIGN CONCEPTS

Logical design tasks must be carefully planned; the remaining SDLC stages are dependent on the logical design stage. Even the smallest error in this stage can be magnified throughout the SDLC and may become a major problem when the new system is implemented. In addition, design errors identified early in this stage can be corrected much more quickly and cheaply than they can be later in the development cycle.

The System Blueprint

Much like the architect's blueprint, the systems analyst's **system blueprint** is a series of charts, graphs, and data layouts that describe in detail the following:

- The input documents that the information system will process and the exact way these documents will look. For example, the analyst might decide that a vendor invoice document must be processed in an accounts receivable information system. The analyst might also decide that the vendor invoice should have a field for vendor identification numbers and that this field should be the first on the invoice document (top left-hand-corner)
- The computer records that will be needed to store data generated by the input documents just described. Each computer record will include a list of data elements to be included in the record.
- Output documents and reports required by users of the information system. Items to be decided include how the outputs will look (format), which users will receive the outputs (distribution), and how often the outputs will be produced (frequency).
- The sequence and method by which documents are input and used to update computer records and then to produce user-desired output documents and reports.

These components of the system blueprint are shown graphically in Figure 10–1.

Principles of Well-Designed Systems

Regardless of the type of information system being designed, certain principles appear to be common among most successful systems.

1. **Modularity**. The system should be designed in relatively small chunks (Figure 10–2) to allow assignment of different programmers and analysts to separate tasks and also to allow modules to be developed independently of each other. (Team A doesn't need to wait for Team B to complete a module before Team A can start work on a different one.) Perhaps most important is that small modules of program code can later be repaired with minimal disruption to other modules, much as a mechanic removes only the ignition module to repair it, rather than having to remove the entire electrical system of an automobile.

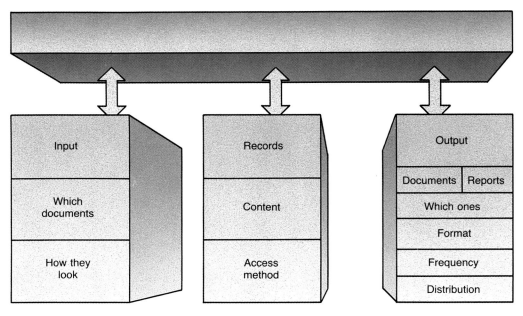

FIGURE 10–1
Contents of a system blueprint.

2. **Interdependence**. Information systems rarely operate independently. The output from one system is likely the input required for one or more other systems. For example, one output of the purchasing system is a purchase order, which becomes input for the receiving system when it is returned by the vendor with the shipped material. The design of any information system must be highly coordinated to ensure that any changes do not adversely affect the operations of other information systems

3. **Decoupling (independence)**. At the same time a systems analyst must provide safeguards so that one system is not at the mercy of another system. For example, the designer of the receiving system must have a contingency plan so that the receiving system can operate, even when the purchasing system has problems.

4. **User involvement**. The ultimate information system is only as successful as its users believe it to be. Early and active involvement of users in the design of information systems provides the users with a sense of ownership and dramatically increases the chances of system success because the users will then be more tolerant of system flaws.

5. **Future orientation**. All information systems, no matter how well designed, undergo numerous modifications and repairs during their lifetimes. Consequently, each information system should be designed for such change.

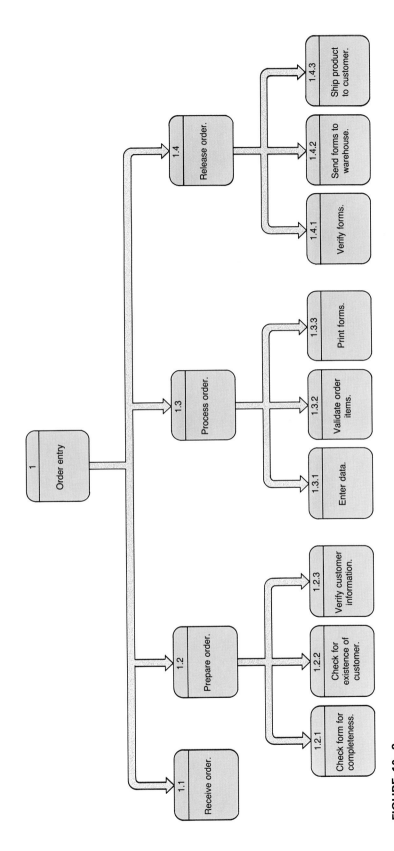

FIGURE 10–2
The concept of modularity, breaking a system into small chunks.

Design Sequence

The sequence of information processing is input, record update (processing), and then output. Thus, it would seem natural that information system design should proceed in the same sequence. However, it does not. Instead, the design sequence proceeds from output documents and reports to input documents and then to storage records. The reason for this seemingly unnatural sequence is that output is the real purpose of any information system; it is what users need to fulfill their clerical or management duties. Therefore, we design the output first and then see what types of data need to be input into and stored within the computer in order to produce the desired output. We design the output the user really needs and then find ways of acquiring the data required to yield that output.

OUTPUT DESIGN CONSIDERATIONS

A systems analyst must consider several topics when designing output documents and reports during the logical design stage.

Types of Documents

An **action document** is a computer-produced document that will later become an input document for another information system. Examples of typical action documents are shown in Table 10–1. Because action documents are used by more than one system, a systems analyst must coordinate design activities with analysts and users of other systems to be sure that documents will work across all systems.

A special type of action document is the **turnaround document**, which can be used as input to one or more systems without keystroke entry. For example, most credit card billings are in machine-readable format, such as the strange characters printed on your gasoline credit card bill. If you pay the full amount of the bill and return your billing stub, your payment can automatically be read into the computer without human intervention.

Types of Reports

A systems analyst must determine the format, distribution, and frequency of every report to be produced by a business information system. The

TABLE 10–1
Typical action documents.

Information System	Action Document	Input to Another System
Payroll	Paycheck	Disbursements
Purchasing	Purchase order	Receiving
Order entry	Picking slip	Accounts receivable
Accounts receivable	Customer statement	Cash receipts

report format is how the report will look, including the numbers of lines and columns, headlines, and the type of information to be included in the report. **Report distribution** is concerned with the office(s) or person(s) receiving the report. **Report frequency** identifies how often the report is produced. These concerns must be addressed for all three types of reports found in most business information systems.

1. **Detail report**—a listing of all transactions that have been entered during the day and the change each transaction has made in a stored record. For example, a detail report for an accounts receivable system would show each customer payment that was entered during a given day and the way in which customer records were changed for each payment entered (e.g., the balance owed decreased). Detail reports are used for auditing purposes to determine whether an information system is functioning properly.

2. **Status report**—a listing of the current and future status of a particular type of resource. For example, for the office supply items he sells, a salesman may request a status report on the amount of stock in the warehouse (current) and due to come in from vendors (future). Status reports are typically generated as they are needed, rather than at periodic intervals.

3. **Management report**—a composite of ratios, averages, totals, and other statistical devices for summarizing data. A management report might, for example, give the total of customer payments for a given day, whereas a detail report would list each customer payment received during that day. As the name implies, management reports are periodically sent to managers who oversee a firm's operations.

An example of the format, distribution, and frequency of these three types of information system reports is shown in Table 10–2.

Output Media

The different types of output media are described in Chapter 3. A systems analyst must select the type of output medium to be used, based on costs and user desires. A modern trend in business information processing is the design of inquiry-based systems, in which user-desired reports are generated on demand through video display terminals (VDTs). With such systems no paper is produced on a daily, weekly, or even monthly basis.

TABLE 10–2
Format, distribution, and frequency of reports.

Type of Report	Format (type of content)	Distribution	Frequency
Detail	All items	Auditing	Daily
Status	Selected items	Clerical	As requested
Management	Statistics, ratios	Management	Monthly

System Design and Implementation

INPUT DESIGN CONSIDERATIONS

In designing system input, a systems analyst must consider the following topics:

- source documents
- coding
- error checking
- interactive screen design
- input media

Source Documents

A **source document** contains data pertaining to a business event (transaction). The source document for a payroll system might be a time card, on which employee working hours are recorded. The source document for a customer order entry system would be a customer order.

Source documents are important because they are used by both information processing personnel and end-users. Consequently, they must be designed to fit two sets of people with different backgrounds. Source documents are also important because any inaccuracies will flow through the remainder of the information processing cycle—input, processing, and output. The principles involved in designing source documents are too complex to be discussed here. However, it is important to note that design of forms is an additional skill demanded of a business systems analyst.

Coding

Often, information fields on a source document must be coded before they can be entered into the computer. **Coding** is the substitution of a short, structured field for a longer field. For example, instead of entering the gender status of MALE or FEMALE, we might choose to enter M or F instead. There are several reasons that coding is used in business information processing.

1. Storage space is decreased. Instead of having to store six characters for the word FEMALE, we need store only one character for the letter F.
2. Data entry time is decreased. A one-character code can obviously be entered faster than a six-character field.
3. Data entry errors are decreased. With a six-character entry a data entry operator has six chances to type in an incorrect character. With a one-character code the operator has only one opportunity to make a mistake.

There is an associated and important disadvantage to coding. Codes are less English-like and therefore are more difficult for humans to understand. This disadvantage can be reduced by avoiding numeric codes, in which numbers are substituted for letters. For example, instead of using the F and M gender code, we could have chosen to use 1 and 2 instead; that would be a numeric code. But then the user might have become confused about which was the code for which gender.

Often it is best to use mnemonic codes, which approximate (resemble) the phrases that they represent. M is a mnemonic code for male, and F is a mnemonic code for female. Mnemonic codes provide all the advantages of coding but take a step closer to human understanding in the process. A systems analyst must determine which of the information fields on a source document should be coded and what the code structure will be.

Error Checking

There is an old acronym in information processing known as GIGO. It stands for garbage in—garbage out and stresses the important fact that unless data are purified before being entered into an information processing system, the output from that system will be nothing but quickly and expensively produced garbage.

A systems analyst must design into an information system a series of comprehensive tests to detect data errors. Some of the more commonly checked errors are for incomplete fields (e.g., missing a customer address), inaccurate fields (e.g., a letter typed in a quantity field), and unreasonable values (e.g., a paycheck issued for $10 million). Tests for these errors are discussed in detail in Chapter 6.

Interactive Screen Design

In most modern information systems a human operator is communicating with the computer almost instantaneously through a video display terminal (VDT) or a PC screen and keyboard. An information system that emphasizes such continuous conversation between humans and machines is called an interactive system.

The design of the screens that function as the communicator between humans and machines is critical. A systems analyst has no idea which human—of what sex, age, or background—will be using the screen at any particular moment in time and must therefore design the computer's conversation for a human that is essentially unknown.

Many experiments have been conducted to determine which types of interactive screens are best for different types of people and different work situations. Principles of interactive screen design are a topic within a discipline called **human factors**, which studies the interface between humans and machines in general and computers in particular.

Input Media

A systems analyst must decide how source document data are to be physically entered into a computer system. Some of the more common input media are identified here.

- Keystroke entry. An operator enters through a typewriter-like device certain fields from the source document. Although keystroke entry has its place for some applications, automated data entry should be used whenever it can be economically justified.

- Character scanning. A reading machine automatically translates field entries without human intervention. Many variations on this option include the following:

    1. Optical scanning, in which the machine can decipher typed or handwritten entries. For example, the U.S. Post Office uses optical scanning equipment to sort and categorize mail by the zip code typed or written on the envelope.
    2. Laser scanning, such as that seen in supermarkets, where a purchased item is pulled over a laser scanner that reads the universal product code (UPC) posted on the item. Computer memory is then searched for the price of the item, and that price is recorded on an electronic cash register.
    3. Computer input microfilm (CIM), on which small pictures of documents can be recognized by the computer automatically and read into computer memory.

- Voice. A computer accepts data and instructions directly from a human voice—undoubtedly the input medium of the future.

FILE DESIGN CONSIDERATIONS

Information system files are comprised of records, which are made up of fields of information, which will be output in reports or documents at a later date. Input source documents are the means by which files are updated, or changed. When designing system files, a system analyst must consider numerous elements.

File Media

Several hardware media are used in information systems and are discussed in Chapter 3. These can be segregated into on-line and off-line devices. As was noted earlier, on-line devices, often called auxiliary storage devices, are connected directly to a computer's central processing unit (CPU). Therefore, files can be updated and accessed without human intervention. The most common on-line media type is magnetic disk.

Off-line storage devices operate independently of the CPU; human intervention is required to access information. The most common medium is magnetic tape, which must be placed on a reading device operated by a computer operator before file information is available for update or access. Another example of an off-line storage device is a floppy diskette for microcomputers.

On-line storage devices provide rapid access to information, but they are relatively expensive. Off-line storage devices, although less expensive, provide relatively slow information access. A systems analyst must balance needs and costs when selecting file media. Often, on-line and off-line file media can exist concurrently in one information system. Typically, magnetic disks are used for file updating, whereas magnetic tapes are used for file backup.

File Access Methods

A systems analyst must determine by what method file records are accessed. The three record-access options are discussed in Chapter 6 and are briefly reviewed here.

1. Sequential. A file is searched from the top, one record at a time, until the desired record is found. This type of access is generally used for off-line storage devices, such as magnetic tape.
2. Direct. A formula, or hashing routine, is used in a field in the input source document to compute where the desired record is located in the file (record address). Direct access provides the fastest means of finding a desired record, but its complexity requires greater design and programming costs and time.
3. Index-sequential. A compromise between sequential and direct access, this method operates much like a telephone directory, in which the correct listing page is found directly, but the correct entry is then located sequentially. As a compromise between cost and speed, index-sequential has become the most common business access method.

A systems analyst must decide which of these access methods is most appropriate for the information system being designed. Often the analyst selects a mixed strategy, using direct access for important files that need rapid retrieval (e.g., customer or inventory files) and sequential access for seldom-used files (e.g., payment history).

Record Format

A systems analyst must also decide (1) which information fields are to be included in each file record, (2) how many characters must be in each field, and (3) in what sequence the fields will occur on the record. An analyst uses a record layout sheet as a means of determining what the record will look like.

File Size

A systems analyst must determine how much file storage space will be required so that sufficient units of file media can be acquired. Computation of file size follows these guidelines:

- A maximum size is set for each information field. For example, a last name field may be set at a maximum of 20 characters.
- The maximum size of all fields belonging to a particular record is totaled to arrive at the record size. For example, an employee record may total 240 characters, including the 20 characters allowed for a last name.
- The maximum record size is multiplied by the maximum number of records expected in a file to arrive at the file size. For example, if there are 240 characters for each employee record and 10,000

employee records are expected, there will be 240 times 10,000, or 2,400,000, characters in the employee file.

File Retention and Recovery

A systems analyst must then decide how long inactive records should be retained. For example, how long after the last customer activity (e.g., purchase) should the record for that customer be kept in the active file?

In addition, a systems analyst must develop a contingency plan in case file data are lost or destroyed. Such a plan should include saving on-line file data on magnetic tape at periodic intervals and, if there are subsequent problems with the on-line file data, reloading the magnetic tape data back onto the on-line file medium. This process is called **file recovery**.

Database Management System (DBMS)

Database management systems are discussed in Chapter 6. These systems are comprised of several information files, and access to and from the contents of these files is tightly and centrally controlled by a database administrator.

In dealing with a DBMS, a systems analyst has little responsibility or control over the determination of file media, access methods, size, format, retention, or recovery. An analyst can recommend changes to a DBMS, but those changes must be accepted by the database administrator. With a DBMS file design is mostly a fixed rather than a variable activity for a systems analyst.

Designing Files for the Future

Business organizations, circumstances, and needs change. Therefore, business information systems need to change. Files should be designed so that future changes can be made with minimum disruption and cost to an organization. A systems analyst must design information system files with the future in mind. Field lengths should be expanded to meet future, rather than current, needs. For example, a total sales field should be stretched to reflect projected sales expansion over the next several years. In the same manner unused space may be placed in current records so that, when new data fields are needed in the future, the system will not have to be disrupted when they are added.

PHYSICAL DESIGN

Several products developed during the logical design stage are needed to accomplish the physical design phase:

1. detailed specifications of all system output, to include all action documents and all reports
2. detailed specifications (format) of all source documents to be entered (input) into the information system

3. layouts of all storage files in the system
4. a data dictionary of all data fields in the system, including where they are located, what their coding structures are (if any), and how the fields are edited upon input
5. system processing sequence, identifying how and when input documents are entered, records are changed, and output is produced

The purpose of the physical design stage of the system development life cycle is to convert these products (the system blueprint) into the specific detail required by programmers to develop the computer code that can transform the logical design into a working business information system.

Organizing the Programming Effort

A typical business information system is comprised of hundreds of thousands of lines of code. Each line of code represents a separate instruction for the computer to perform an operation. A good many programmers are needed, and their efforts must be coordinated. In addition, the programming project must be broken down into modules, as discussed earlier.

Organizing the programming effort into workable modules is accomplished with a **top-down approach**. In other words, the entire programming effort is separated into natural parts, each of which is further divided into subparts, and those subparts into sub-subparts, until each part, called a programming module, is small enough to be coded by one programmer within the required time frame. There are other approaches to system design—bottom-up, to name one—but most design experts believe the top-down approach to be superior. An example of this top-down approach to programming organization is shown in Figure 10–3. The graphic tool shown in the figure is called a **hierarchical chart**. Each module of the chart is given a program name and is assigned to a specific programmer.

Developing Program Logic

For each program module a specific sequence of steps must be developed to perform the module's assigned information processing task. Developing that specific sequence is an appropriate focus for a computer programming course and cannot be covered here. However, the final products of the physical design stage should be known:

1. the specifications produced during the logical design stage
2. organization of the programming effort into program modules
3. a detailed sequence of computer operations (program instructions) to perform each information processing activity

The logical and physical design of business information systems has been rather mechanical and traditional during the past 25 years. However, two recent developments have made that design more rapid and of better quality. One of these developments, the automation of system design tools, is discussed later in this chapter. The second development is the use of prototyping.

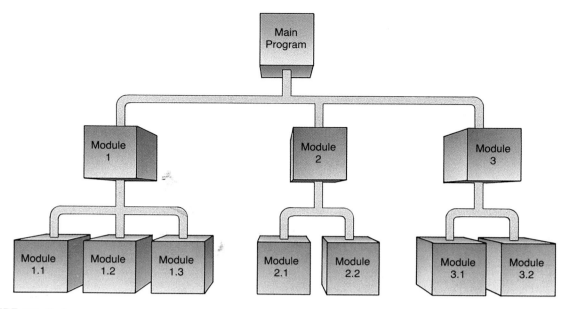

FIGURE 10-3
A hierarchical chart.

Prototyping in System Design

The use of prototyping in the system analysis phase of the SDLC is described in Chapter 9. Prototyping is the construction of an experimental information system to stimulate early user changes in a proposed system. In the system analysis phase, prototyping is used to find out what the uncertain end-user really wants in an information system. In the system design phase, a systems analyst uses a prototype for varied reasons.

1. *To fine-tune system specifications.* For example, users are given copies of system output. Any desired changes can be made before any further effort is put into programming that output.
2. *To train end-users* earlier in the development process.
3. *To involve end-users* so that they have a sense of system ownership and will therefore be more tolerant of minor system faults after the new system is operational.
4. *To demonstrate the system to management* so that key personnel can see how the long and expensive information system project is progressing.

As stated in the previous chapter, the growing use of prototyping promises to streamline the development of information systems in general and the system analysis and system design phases in particular.

CHARTING TECHNIQUES FOR SYSTEM DESIGN

Whether or not prototyping is used, charting techniques are used in the system design phase as well as in other stages. Different charting techniques are used for logical and physical designs.

Development of Business Information Systems

Logical Design

The first group of charting techniques used during this stage includes layouts (facsimiles) of inputs, outputs, and files—action document layouts, report layouts, input source document layouts, and file (record) layouts.

The second group of charting techniques depicts system processing sequences—how input is processed and converted to system output. The most common of these techniques are the system flowchart (SFC) and the data flow diagram (DFD), discussed in Chapter 9 and used there to describe the old system. During the logical design stage the SFC and DFD are used to describe what the new information system will look like.

Physical Design

Two groups of charting techniques are also used in this stage of the SDLC. The first group, used to organize programming efforts according to a top-down methodology, includes three techniques: a hierarchical chart, a Warnier-Orr diagram, and menu maps. A hierarchical chart was discussed earlier and is shown in Figure 10–3. A **Warnier-Orr diagram** (Figure 10–4) is similar to a hierarchical chart except that the Warnier-Orr diagram follows a horizontal rather than a vertical organization. A **menu map** (Figure 10–5) is used for interactive information systems. It provides a top-down structure for selection menus, which allow end-users to communicate processing choices.

The second group of charting techniques used in the physical design stage shows graphically the step-by-step logic used in developing specific computer programs. The most common of these techniques is the program

FIGURE 10–4
A Warnier-Orr diagram.

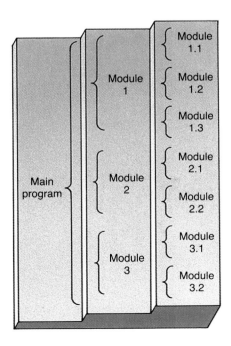

System Design and Implementation

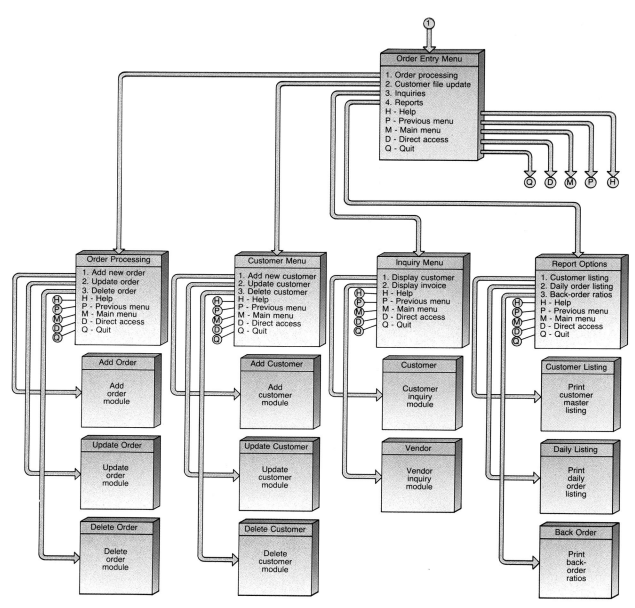

FIGURE 10–5
A menu map.

flowchart. A **program flowchart (PFC)** details the processing steps of a particular program. It is used to

- clarify program logic
- identify alternate processing methods
- serve as a guide for program coding
- serve as documentation

Figure 10−6 shows some standard program flowcharting symbols; Figure 10−7 shows a flowchart constructed for a program that checks client payment records.

A variation of a standard flowchart is the structured flowchart, also called a **Nassi-Shneiderman chart** for its developers, Isaac Nassi and Ben Shneiderman. A Nassi-Shneiderman chart uses the three basic program control structures (sequence, selection, and repetition) to illustrate the processing steps of a program. Boxes of various shapes represent each control structure in a box-within-a-box format. Figure 10−8 illustrates the logic patterns of a Nassi-Shneiderman chart; Figure 10−9 shows the flowchart from Figure 10−7 in a Nassi-Shneiderman format.

Another tool used to formulate the processing steps of a program is **pseudocode**, which uses English phrases to describe the processing steps of a program or module. Often, the phrases resemble the programming language code, hence the name pseudocode. Pseudocode, designed as an alternative to flowcharts, expresses processing steps in a simple, straightforward manner so that the pseudocode can be easily converted to a program code. Most programming departments establish rules and conventions to be followed with pseudocode so that others are able to read and interpret its meaning. Figure 10−10 gives an example of pseudocode as it might be written for the program in Figure 10−7.

FIGURE 10−6
Programming flowchart symbols.

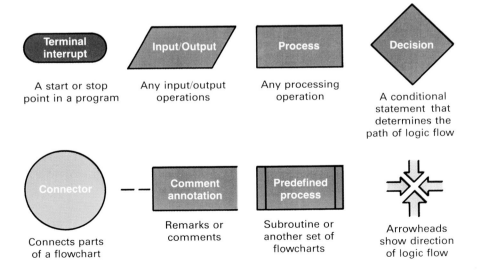

Terminal interrupt — A start or stop point in a program

Input/Output — Any input/output operations

Process — Any processing operation

Decision — A conditional statement that determines the path of logic flow

Connector — Connects parts of a flowchart

Comment annotation — Remarks or comments

Predefined process — Subroutine or another set of flowcharts

Arrowheads show direction of logic flow

System Design and Implementation

FIGURE 10–7
A program flowchart.

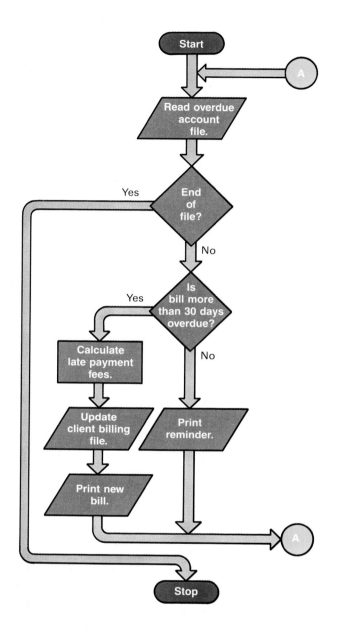

Clearly, the system design phase of the system development life cycle is dominated by graphic techniques. Until a few years ago a systems analyst produced these graphics with paper and pencil. Today, automated aids allow a systems analyst to design and produce graphics in a more rapid and efficient manner.

FIGURE 10–8

Logic patterns of a Nassi-Shneiderman chart.

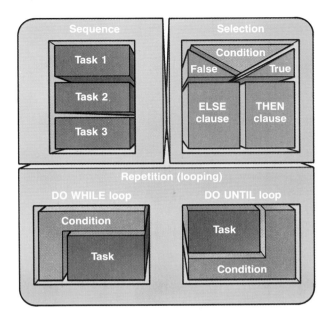

FIGURE 10–9

A Nassi-Shneiderman version of the program in Figure 10–7.

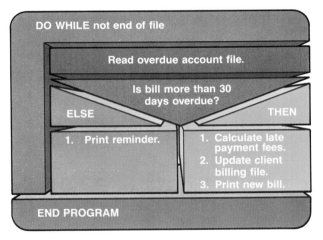

FIGURE 10–10

Pseudocode for the program in Figure 10–7.

```
Begin
   Read overdue billing file.
   DO WHILE not end of file
      IF bill more than 30 days overdue
         THEN
            Calculate late payment fees.
            Update billing file.
            Print new bill.
         ELSE
            Print payment reminder.
      End-if
      Read overdue billing file.
   End
```

AUTOMATING SYSTEM DESIGN

The automation of system design tools is an extension of the computer-assisted system engineering (CASE) technology discussed in Chapter 9. Workbench packages allow a systems analyst, sitting at a microcomputer or at the video display terminal of a mainframe computer, to perform automatically several design functions that were previously done manually:

- charting aids for development of data flow diagrams, system flowcharts, program flowcharts, and many other design tools
- screen/document design for input and output design tasks
- file modification to facilitate addition or deletion of and changes to data fields in files (records)
- changes in data dictionary whenever file changes are made
- code generation, allowing automatic generation of language code from program flowcharts

Continued development and use of automated system design tools will lead to faster, better-quality products emanating from the system design phase.

TESTING

The system implementation phase of the SDLC includes testing, installation, training, and maintenance. **Testing** is the activity through which a new information system is checked to ensure that all of its parts are correct. Testing is one of the most important activities in the development of an information system. Any system—whether a bridge, a piece of equipment, or an information system—can bring disastrous results to its users if it is not thoroughly tested and found to be satisfactory. The development of an information system incurs a huge expenditure of money and is important to an organization's success. Therefore, a system should not be handed over to its users without a thorough testing.

Purpose of Testing

Every information system performs information processing of some type. The overall purpose of testing such a system is to be sure that it processes data correctly and produces information that is useful to its users. Testing is conducted with each computer program module to ensure that its results are correct and that it has sufficient documentation.

Testing Methodology

The testing of an information system should be conducted with extreme care and thoroughness. Most information developers follow a well-established procedure, known as **testing methodology**, which specifies a plan and criteria for and an approach to testing.

Test Plan. A **test plan** is a document that describes an overall testing plan for an information system. During the design phase a test plan is developed jointly by a system development team and the system users. A plan should be developed very carefully because it directs the testing. If a plan lacks details, the test is apt to be incomplete. A test plan should identify the test approach, criteria, data to be used, administrator of the test, and the like. The following important items should be specified:

- User-acceptance criteria. These are the criteria by which the users decide the success of the system. Included might be system response time, system transaction volume, turn-around time, system reliability, and error tolerance.
- Data to be used in the test. These data may be generated by programmers (artificial data) or from user files (real data).
- Documentation standards. These standards will be followed by the programmers and include program design charts (such as hierarchy charts), program flowcharts or pseudocodes, in-program documentation, and so on.
- Levels of testing. This element indicates the levels at which testing is to be conducted, such as individual program testing, subsystem testing, and system testing.

Testing Criteria. Testing criteria are those by which information system users determine its success. Since users are the ultimate judges of a system, these criteria are very important and should be carefully considered by system developers. The criteria should be quantitative and definitive so that a system can be measured against them.

- System response time is the amount of elapsed time between user input and system response.
- Transaction volume is the number of transactions a system can process in a given time period.
- Turn-around time or responsiveness is the time that elapses between data arrival at a computer center and availability of the system output to users.
- Reliability is the degree to which a system performs its functions over a period of time.
- Error tolerance is the ratio of errors detected and/or corrected by the system to the number of errors that are undetected.

These criteria are quantitative and definitive; users could easily test an information system against them.

Test Approach. As was mentioned earlier, the basic purpose of testing is to be sure that a system works. An information system is composed of numerous individual program modules, several of which work together as a subsystem and all of which work together as a single system. Thus, to ensure the correctness of the entire system, three levels of testing are commonly employed with commercial information systems:

1. **unit testing**, in which each program module is tested to ensure its correctness

2. **subsystem testing**, in which several related program modules are tested as a single unit to ensure the correctness of the unit
3. **system testing**, in which all program modules are tested as a single unit to ensure the correctness of the entire unit

These three levels of testing are illustrated in Figure 10–11.

Test Data. The data used for testing are known as **test data**. They should be selected carefully because the thoroughness of the testing depends on them. Test data should ensure that each and every segment of a program module is tested, both regularly used and seldom-used segments. A module that is not thoroughly tested may contain bugs that may show up later when the module is operational.

There are two types of test data: artificial (or hypothetical) and real. Artificial test data are selected by programmers, whereas real data are selected by users. Artificial data are those that programmers consider necessary to test a program module; they may or may not test a module thoroughly, depending on the abilities of individual programmers. If the programmers select data that check each and every segment of a module, the test is thorough; otherwise, it is not. Real-life test data are user-selected

FIGURE 10–11
Levels of testing for an information system.

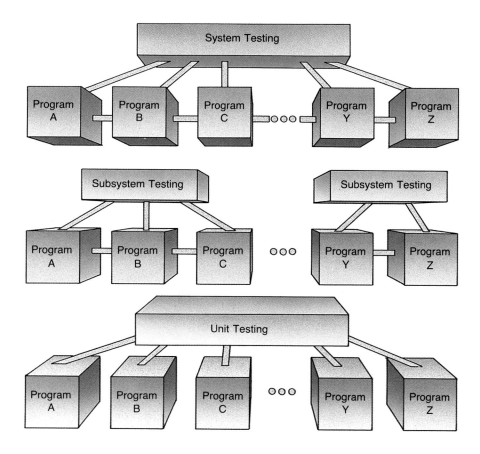

from actual data files; they represent the real content and volume of the functional system. Whether artificial or real-life, test data must include every possible type and combination of data that could possibly, not necessarily typically, occur.

Automated Testing

A few software tools can be used to automate software testing and thus to improve the productivity of programmers in testing software. **Automated testing** involves using software tools to mark all the paths in a program module and to report on which paths were or were not executed in a test. The use of these tools—one is known as TEST-XPERT—offers both tangible and intangible benefits. The tangible benefits include time and cost savings in testing. Among the intangible benefits are these:

- reduced production failures
- improved software quality
- improved programmer morale
- faster diagnosis and solution of software problems
- adherence to software schedules

Auditor's Role in Testing

Many business organizations employ the services of an **electronic data-processing (EDP)** auditor to test an information system. The role of the EDP auditor is to ensure that business transactions are processed by a computer system in accordance with desired procedures. The test conducted by the auditor is additional to that performed by system developers and/or users. An EDP auditor, often an official member of a development team, usually tests an information system with invalid data to see whether the system detects them as errors.

An auditor also tests a system for unauthorized use, inadequate program documentation, and inadequate disaster recovery plans. Testing for unauthorized use determines whether a system can be used by someone not authorized to use it. Testing for inadequate program documentation assesses whether each program module has enough documentation so that a user can understand the purpose of the module. Testing for inadequate disaster recovery plans checks whether a system has adequate plans to recover from a potential disaster, such as a flood, earthquake or fire.

The test performed by an EDP auditor is very important. In most organizations management considers the auditor's testing to be the most thorough and valid of all tests. If the auditor's test does not find any deficiency in a system, both user and management confidence in the system is increased. In some organizations information systems are not implemented unless an auditor's test is performed and fails to find any serious deficiencies in the systems. Highlight 10–1 examines another element, that of quality assurance, which many organizations are recognizing as important in improving the development, testing, and maintenance of information systems.

Quality Assurance

Information systems departments, recognizing the importance of the quality assurance function, are beginning to incorporate such a position into their area. Quality assurance is concerned with improving the processes involved in developing, testing, and maintaining information systems. The individuals who oversee that function are responsible for establishing the methodologies used in those processes, fine-tuning them, and administering them. In addition, quality assurance personnel attempt to create awareness of quality, stop poor-quality systems from going into production, implement problem reporting, and conduct training programs. Such individuals are sometimes known as development center managers or standards managers.

Organizations are placing more importance on quality assurance, as witnessed by the higher salaries being attached to the quality assurance position. According to a survey conducted by the Quality Assurance Institute, most companies fill the quality assurance position from the ranks of systems analysts with computer science backgrounds. The survey also found that such individuals have little quality assurance training when they begin their jobs but acquire their skills on the job and through outside seminars. A quality assurance manager needs skills in trend analysis, regression analysis, and the creation of cause-and-effect charts. Frequently, quality assurance professionals rely on standards, training, reviews, communication skills, and common sense.

Barriers to a quality assurance position in some organizations include difficulty in obtaining top-management support and involvement, getting adequate staff and budget to meet the needs, responding to high expectations from top management, and counteracting the view of a quality assurance position as a police function. Despite these difficulties, however, more and more organizations are realizing the importance of this position to the development, testing, and maintenance of quality information systems.

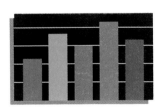

Debugging a Program

Three types of program errors may be encountered during the testing phase: syntax, run-time, and logic. The syntax of a programming language is the set of rules and conventions to be followed in writing a program; these rules are similar to the grammatical rules of the English language. When these rules are violated, a **syntax error** occurs. All syntax errors must be found and corrected before a program will execute.

The second type of error that can occur during testing is a **run-time error**, which stops the execution of a program. It may be that invalid data were entered. For example, if the program was set up to expect numerical data and alphabetical data were entered instead, a poorly designed program would "crash," that is, stop executing. A properly written program would identify the problem, prompt the user with an error message, and then permit the data to be reentered.

The third type of error, and the most difficult to find, is a logic error. A **logic error** does not stop the execution of a program but the results will not be accurate. With luck the error will be obvious. However, often it is not. If the problem is to add 2 apples to 4 apples and determine the total number of apples, the formula should be $2 + 4 = 6$. But if the wrong symbol, perhaps a multiplication sign, is typed into the computer, an answer of 8 will be correct for the formula as entered ($2 \times 4 = 8$) but not for the problem intended to be solved—adding 2 apples to 4 apples. Finding the logic error in this example is easy; however, finding a logic error in a complicated program can be like trying to find the proverbial needle in a haystack.

The process of finding any type of error and correcting it is called **debugging** (Figure 10–12 and Highlight 10–2). After a program is debugged, it can be installed and used.

INSTALLATION

After the successful testing of an information system comes the **installation** task, in which the system is made operational and is put to work for the users. This is a significant component of the development of an information system and may require considerable capital, in support of both people and equipment. In some cases the cost of installation has exceeded the cost of system design. However, the ultimate success of an information system may depend on how well the various parts of this task are carried out.

Planning

Planning is the first subtask that needs to be completed for the installation of an information system. Many information systems cause significant changes in the operating procedures of a business organization, and such changes are filled with many technical and human problems that must be solved. For an installation that is as trouble-free as possible, careful planning is an essential activity.

A plan for installation should be prepared by a team that consists of the users, system developers, and managers. The different tasks that need to be completed, the completion dates for those activities, and the individuals responsible for their completion are included in the plan. The following tasks should be accomplished as part of the planning process:

- organize a team of individuals to carry out the installation activity
- identify all installation tasks
- estimate completion dates for all activities
- identify individuals responsible for each activity
- prepare an estimated budget for the installation
- develop a project control system to monitor the progress of the installation effort

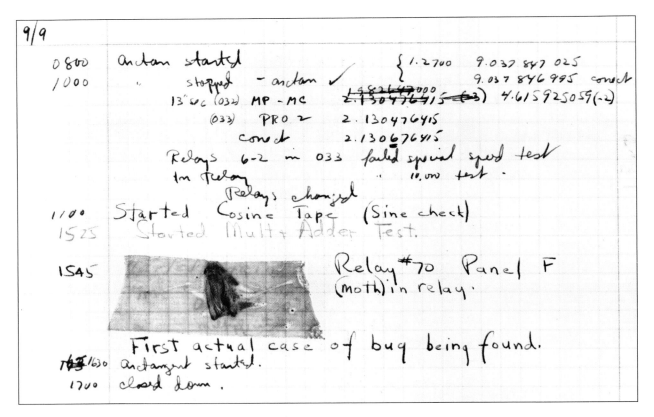

FIGURE 10–12

Grace Hopper relates the story that she and a team of programmers were working on the Mark II back in 1945 when the computer simply quit. They couldn't determine what was wrong; finally, they looked inside the computer and saw a large, dead moth in one of the signal relays. The moth, the first computer "bug," was removed and saved for posterity in a log book now located at the U.S. Naval Museum in Dahlgren, Virginia. After that incident, when naval officers came in to check on the progress of a nonoperating computer, the personnel advised that they were debugging the program. (U.S. Navy photo)

Installation Tasks

Although the installation of each information system is unique in respect to size and organizational characteristics, certain tasks are common to all system installations.

- Develop procedures for installation, specifying the routines that are to be followed by each person working with the new system—who fills out which forms, how the data are captured by the computer system, how problems are to be resolved, and the like. These procedures are established by systems analysts.
- Develop a training plan for users and important others. This involves a training plan for different users and often includes a short

training program for managers. The plan should establish the level, duration, and schedule of training for each individual.

- Design forms with which data are collected and input into the computer system. The forms should be clear and understandable to users and should be as limited in number as possible.
- Generate all files and databases necessary for processing data with the new system. Often, existing files need to be converted into new files and databases; at other times data from manual files may be converted to computer-based files and databases. This activity may require a long period of time, depending on the size of the files and databases, the current form of the data, and the type of information system being installed.
- Acquire needed resources for the new information system— personnel, equipment, supplies, office space, and so on. Computer hardware, included among the resources, must meet the organization's specifications. The interrelationships of some of the resources and their lead times are also important and must be taken into consideration. For example, if computer hardware is to be acquired, its lead time—that is, the time between its being ordered and received—must be considered by the installation planning team, and adequate floor space must be made available before its arrival. Hardware evaluation and selection represent a process too complex to be considered in detail in this text.

Conversion

Conversion refers to the replacement of an existing system, whether manual or computer-based, with a new information system. There are four approaches to conversion: direct, parallel, phased-in, and pilot conversion (Figure 10–13). Which conversion approach is appropriate for a particular information system depends on several factors.

Direct Conversion. With **direct conversion** (also called crash conversion) an existing information system is replaced by a new information system as of a certain date, and the old system is no longer used. This approach has advantages and disadvantages. Direct conversion is economical because only one system is operational. It does not create confusion because everyone knows that only one system is operational and everyone knows the same system. However, this conversion approach is risky because there is no backup system if the new system does not work. An organization could run into operational chaos if something went wrong with the new information system. Information would not be available, reports would be delayed, management decisions would not be made, user confidence in the new system would be questionable, and user acceptance of the new system would be in jeopardy.

The direct conversion approach may be appropriate when the information system being implemented is not critical to the organization's operation and there is not expected to be much resistance to the new system or when the size of the organization is small. In such instances it is an easy

FIGURE 10–13
Conversion strategies for
information systems.

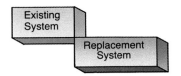

Direct Conversion
End existing system and begin replacement system immediately.

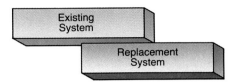

Parallel Conversion
Existing system and replacement system are both run for a specified
period of time and then the existing system is dropped.

Phase-In Conversion
Gradually phase out existing system as replacement system is gradually phased in.

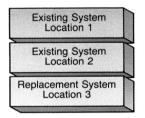

Pilot Conversion
Replacement system is installed in one location and tried out
before being installed in other locations.

job to recover from the loss that is incurred if something goes wrong with
the new system. For example, a new accounts payable system for a small
business would be an appropriate application for direct conversion.

Parallel Conversion. With **parallel conversion** both new and old information systems are used for a certain period of time, after which the old
system is no longer used. Of all conversion approaches, parallel conversion
is the safest and is therefore most appropriate for critical business applications, such as customer billing and payroll. This approach provides a
backup system for users, which is useful in the event of problems with the
new system. In addition, the new system can be checked out against the
old, thereby permitting all bugs to be removed from the new system and
making it error-free by the time it becomes the only operational system.

Nonetheless, there are disadvantages to this conversion approach. It
is expensive because two systems are used in parallel. It may also create
confusion among users because some are using the old system with its

procedures, forms, files, and the like, whereas others are using the new system with its different requirements. In addition, there may not be enough skilled personnel available to operate two systems simultaneously.

Phased-In Conversion. With **phased-in conversion** the new information system is installed in phases, or segments. As individual segments of the system are developed, they are installed and used. This is not a common approach since most segments cannot be installed and used as independent units. The different segments of most information systems are interrelated and cannot work in isolation.

However, if an existing computer-based information system is being upgraded or enhanced, phased-in conversion may prove beneficial. In such a situation the change brought about by the upgraded system would not be overwhelming, and the users would be exposed to the system gradually. A gradual changeover could provide advance lessons for the users so that they would be ready for the total system when it became operational. However, extreme caution should be taken to ensure that the installed segments can really work in isolation.

Pilot Conversion. If an information system is to be used in multiple locations, pilot conversion may prove safe and economical. With a **pilot conversion**, a new system is installed in one location and is tried out there before it is installed in other locations. This approach is safe and economical because the impact of any bugs is felt in only one unit of an organization, thereby also reducing user frustration.

Sometimes pilot conversion is used in combination with other conversion approaches. For example, if an organization is installing a billing system in several subsidiary organizations, it might employ a pilot conversion approach in combination with parallel conversion. The organization could use the new billing system in parallel with the old system in one of its subsidiaries. The experiences learned in that pilot location could provide valuable lessons for installing the system in other locations.

Organizational Impact

As already mentioned, the installation of a new information system results in changes in operating procedures. System users need to adjust themselves to these changes. Depending on the degree of change, users may exhibit resistance, and other organizational issues may surface during the installation of a new system.

Resistance to Change. People in general resist change. It means something new and unknown and therefore causes skepticism and uncertainty. When a new information system is installed, users are not sure how the system will affect their work procedures, career growth, level of responsibility, and the like. Some users are not sure whether the new system will help them in their work; others are not sure whether they can work with the new system. As a result of the skepticism and uncertainty associated with a new system, users may resist it.

Bugs are the flaws that find their way into a computer or its software and lie in wait to cause trouble. In some cases bugs are merely bothersome, but they can also be enormously expensive to businesses and catastrophic to military systems. Our increasing knowledge about computer construction and programming makes it easier to spot bugs; however, the spread of computers into all facets of business gives bugs more places to hide.

According to one poll, computer glitches have complicated the lives of at least 91 percent of us, whether at work, at the bank, with credit card companies or airlines, or with computerized appliances at home. Bugs have delayed federal tax returns, wiped out financial records for an entire town, delayed space launches, caused gigantic overdrafts that have sent banks reeling, and raised the question of whether a life-or-death military system such as the Strategic Defense Initiative can ever be considered foolproof in its operations.

To reduce the likelihood of bugs, designers are turning to computers to build computers and software, instead of leaving those tasks in the hands of more fallible human beings. Large computer programs may use as many as 100,000 lines of code; the space and defense program use millions of lines. Without computer aid even a seasoned programmer might be able to write only 20 permanently usable lines of code a day.

In 1979 the General Accounting Office looked at computer use and reliability in government and learned that less than 2 percent of the $6.89 million spent for software programs could actually be used as bought. To address problems like this, there are now companies that test programs for buyers before the programs are put into use.

Another defense against bugs—and probably the most realistic one—is to put safeguards in place to catch them. For example, the nearly 100 computers needed to fly the Boeing 767 duplicate essential operations so that another computer can compensate if a bug ruins a function.

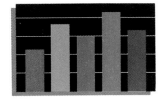

Another reason for resistance may be the new information system itself. A poorly designed system that does not incorporate human elements is apt to generate resistance in users. For example, a technologically so-phisticated system designed for nontechnical users will meet with resis-tance. The system may be excellent from a technical standpoint but poor from the users' standpoint. Every effort should be made by system design-ers to develop user-friendly systems.

Resistance to change may be expressed by employees in different ways: avoidance, apathy, and even open aggression. The most effective ways to combat user resistance to change are user involvement and user education. Keeping the users involved from the very beginning of the development process reduces their fear of the new system. This involvement may range from answering the system designers' questions to suggesting improvements to the system. Explaining the benefits of the new system over the old also reduces user resistance. And proper training of users should be a prerequisite to system installation. Knowing how to use a new system reduces user frustration and, hence, user resistance.

Reorganization. A new information system may streamline operating procedures, resulting in a new organizational structure. This reorganization may bring about several organizational changes, and authority, responsibility, and employee-supervisor relations may change. For example, if a manual operation involving several employees is automated, thereby reducing the number of employees needed, the supervisor's level of responsibility is reduced. That reduction in responsibility may lead to supervisor dissatisfaction. In addition, any change in an employee's supervisor may cause employee dissatisfaction, which may lead to employee turnover. And some employees may be so valuable to an organization that their departure would result in temporary organizational instability.

TRAINING

Training is one of the most important tasks in the implementation of a new information system. The primary purpose of **training** is to make users and others familiar with the system so that they are able to work with it effectively. Training is normally provided for three levels of employees: users, operators, and managers.

User Training

User training is provided to those employees who work with a new system on a regular basis—accounts payable clerks, inventory clerks, payroll clerks, accounts receivable clerks, and the like. The purpose of **user training** is to make users thoroughly familiar with the operation of a new system. This training is the most elaborate and extensive of all and typically includes topics like the following:

- which forms to fill out
- how to enter data into the computer
- what the commands are
- how to run the system
- what the password is
- what the functions of the system are
- what the user inputs are
- what the report outputs are

User training must be hands-on and may last several days or weeks, depending on the complexity of the system. Hands-on training need not be on the actual system but may be on a prototype, thus reducing risk to the actual system. The training may be in-house or outside and should be conducted by those who know the system very well. Because users learn at different speeds, patience and good communication skills are essential on the part of the trainers.

Hands-on training is supplemented with a **user's manual**. Users may come up with numerous questions while using a new system, and a user's manual should answer those questions. To be most effective, the manual should be well written and should have an easy reference guide. It must have answers to common user questions and should be organized so that users can find answers quickly and easily.

Operator Training

Operators are those employees who work in the computer center of an organization and are responsible for running the computer system. When a new information system is implemented, operational details must be made known to the operators. **Operator training** deals with communicating those operational details to the operators.

- Which files and databases to use. When an information system is run, operators must know which files and databases the system needs so that they can mount the right tape or disk on the proper disk unit.
- How long the system will run under normal circumstances. Knowing the average length of a system run helps operators determine whether the system is running as expected or has run into some problems.
- Which systems precede and follow the new system. A complete information system consists of several subsystems running in sequence. Problems with one subsystem hold up all succeeding subsystems. However, if operators know the sequence of the subsystems, they can better answer user questions. For example, if the general ledger subsystem of an organization is run after all other subsystems are run and the accounts payable subsystem runs into problems, the general ledger subsystem cannot be run. If users ask why reports are not coming out of the general ledger subsystem, the operators can provide an explanation.
- Which reports are to be produced and how many copies of each. Knowing which reports are to be produced and how many copies of each are needed helps an operator ensure that all reports are generated and that the correct number of copies are printed.
- What the average length of each report is. Reports generated by an information system are of varying lengths. Because of programming errors, a printer may sometimes be printing a report for an unusually long period of time. Knowing the average length of a report helps the operator detect a problem in the printing, terminate the printing process, and secure help.
- Which type of printer is to be used. A computer center normally has more than one type of printer. An operator needs to know which printer is used for which reports so that each report output is directed to the correct printer.

- What the schedule of the system run is. Most organizations have a fairly regular schedule for running different subsystems of a complete information system. This schedule should be known by the operator.
- Whether there is any special output, such as microfiche or microfilm. Some reports, because of their length, are produced in microfiche or microfilm. Special measures are necessary on the part of an operator when running a system that outputs reports on microfiche or microfilm.
- What some of the potential problems are and what to do in each case. During the running of a subsystem, problems may arise, and an operator needs to take certain steps to resolve those problems. Although it is not possible to know all potential problems that may arise with a specific subsystem, operators should be made aware of the more common problems and the measures to solve them.
- Who the responsible programmer is. In most organizations a programmer is responsible for one or more subsystems of an information system. If problems occur during the running of a subsystem, the responsible programmer is called in to resolve them. Operators need to know the responsible programmer for each subsystem in case a problem develops.

Management Training

Whereas user and operator training deal with operational details, **management training** deals with an overview of a new system. The main purpose of this training is to familiarize management with a system's major strengths and weaknesses and its impact on organizational goals. Such training normally lasts a short time and is conducted with the help of presentation slides. It should not cover any details unless management requests them.

MAINTENANCE

Maintenance is the last stage in the implementation of an information system. After a system has been tested and installed and its users trained, the system enters the maintenance phase. The maintenance of a system may span several years, during which time the system is continually updated to meet the changing requirements of its users. It is not unusual for a system to be maintained for more than 20 years and then be replaced with another new system. Most often, the maintenance costs of an information system are considerably higher than its development costs.

Need for Maintenance

All information systems are designed and developed to meet user information requirements in the present and the future. As information requirements change, the information system must also be changed accordingly.

Some of the reasons that information requirements change are identified here.

- Government regulations change. A change in government rules and regulations demands a change in information systems. For example, a payroll system calculates an employee's net salary by deducting income taxes, social security tax, and other items. Of these deductions the social security tax limit and rate change every year. To reflect this change, the payroll system must be modified annually.
- Company policy may change. A change in company policy necessitates a change in its information system. For example, a company may have an existing policy that refuses credit sales to a customer whose unpaid balance is more than $10,000. The accounts receivable system of this company incorporates this credit policy. If the company decides to relax its credit policy and approve credit sales to customers whose unpaid balance is not more than $15,000, the accounts receivable system must be modified to accommodate this change in the company's credit policy.
- A company may need new information. New information needs require modification in a company's information system. For example, let's suppose that a company needs a new report on employees whose job performance has been below a certain level for 2 consecutive years. This report is not available at this time, but the company will need it on a regular basis from now on. This need for new information requires that the company's human resource information system be modified to produce the new report.

Maintenance Programmers

Information systems are maintained by a special group of programmers known as **maintenance programmers**. After an information system is installed, it is handed over to maintenance programmers, who are responsible for its maintenance. Most college graduates with a degree in information systems or related disciplines start their careers as maintenance programmers.

Each maintenance programmer is responsible for one or more application systems (also known as production systems), such as accounts payable, accounts receivable, payroll, general ledger, order entry, and inventory control. It is the maintenance programmer's responsibility to communicate with the users on an ongoing basis to determine their changing requirements and modify the production system(s) accordingly. Production systems are run by a computer center at regular intervals to produce reports for users.

During its run a production system may face unexpected problems, resulting in abnormal termination. A maintenance programmer is responsible for fixing these problems so that the system can run uninterrupted. It is common for a maintenance programmer to be called on to fix production system problems in the middle of the night and be expected to keep working until the problems are fixed.

Maintenance programmers have challenging responsibilities and are critical to the operation of a business organization. Although they are compensated for their difficult duties, maintenance programmers are often frustrated. As a result, the turnover rates among these professionals are considerably higher than they are for other information system specialists.

Factors Facilitating Maintenance

Although nothing can be done to completely remove the frustration of maintenance programmers, several steps can be taken to minimize the level of that frustration.

- Install a thoroughly tested information system. Often, information systems are installed without a thorough testing, resulting in a production system that is full of bugs. When such systems are run, frequent problems occur, raising the frustration of the responsible maintenance programmer. Installing a system that is thoroughly tested reduces the number of bugs and consequently the amount of programmer frustration.
- Develop excellent program documentation. Being responsible for a production system requires understanding thoroughly each and every program module that is a part of that system. However, to understand a program module that has been written by someone else is a difficult task. What makes it even more difficult is a lack of good documentation. When changes are made to an existing program module, good documentation helps a programmer considerably. It minimizes frustration and reduces the time needed to make the change. In addition, good documentation helps a maintenance programmer understand the impact of a change in one module on other modules.
- Develop program modules according to good programming standards. A program module may be constructed in several ways, some of which are more desirable than others. If a module is constructed according to good programming standards, it is easy to understand and maintain. Most information system management teams establish programming standards that all programmers are required to follow. However, it is necessary to enforce compliance with these standards before a program module is accepted as a final product.
- Obtain management understanding. Production systems are critical to the operation of most organizations. For example, the payroll and billing systems are the most critical computer applications. Maintenance programmers who are responsible for these systems are under intense pressure to keep them running smoothly. It is important for management (both information system and user) to realize that maintenance programmers are human and are capable of making mistakes. Programmers should

not be subjected to harsh punishment for occasional mistakes. Instead, management must be sympathetic to and tolerant and supportive of maintenance programmers.

- Keep user expectations reasonable. Users of information systems request service from maintenance programmers in providing new information or changes to existing information. Sometimes a request that may seem simple to a user is not so to a maintenance programmer, and compliance with that request may take a longer time than the user thinks acceptable. In another situation a maintenance programmer may be working on other, more important user requests, and their priority may mean a longer waiting time for another user. If users understand the workload of maintenance programmers, the former will add less to the latter's frustration.

- Develop a good scheduling system. Maintenance programmers may receive several requests from users at the same time. Since the number of requests are often more than programmers can handle, there is usually a backlog of user requests. A good prioritization and scheduling system helps maintenance programmers decide the order in which user requests are to be serviced. The prioritization of user requests should be decided by the users themselves.

- Develop career growth plans for maintenance programmers. Maintenance programmers do not want to remain maintenance programmers forever. They must know how long they have to work as maintenance programmers before being promoted. Staying in the same position for more than 3 years results in increased programmer frustration and reduced productivity. A well-defined career growth plan for maintenance programmers helps reduce programmer frustration and facilitates maintenance programming.

SUMMARY

The system design phase of the system development life cycle is comprised of two stages—logical design and physical design. Logical design is the development of a paper blueprint for a new system. Physical design is the translation of that blueprint into the specific programming logic that will cause the new system to operate as planned.

The logical design of an information system is accomplished according to certain principles common to most successful systems: modularity, interdependence, independence (decoupling), user involvement, and future orientation. A design looks first at system output, then system input, and finally required storage records.

Once a logical design blueprint is completed, physical design of the new system begins. It has two objectives. The first is to organize the structure of the programming effort, which follows a top-down approach and culminates with the development of a hierarchy of program modules. The second objective is to develop the program logic for each of the program modules identified. This logic is the sequence of specific computer operations required to perform the information task assigned to the program module. A programmer converts the logic to a computer-understood language.

A systems analyst has many tools and techniques available to accomplish the logical and physical design of business information systems. The newest of these tools is prototyping. Many of the more traditional tools have now been automated with computer-assisted system engineering (CASE) methodology.

The implementation phase follows system design. Implementation brings a new system to its productive life and includes testing, installation, training, and maintenance. Testing ensures that all program modules, subsystems, and the system as a whole function as intended. A test plan specifies the details and levels of the testing.

In installation an information system is transferred from designers to users. In other words, users start using the system in their daily work. An installation plan should describe how an organization is to convert to a new system. There are four basic approaches to conversion: direct, parallel, phased-in, and pilot. All approaches have advantages and disadvantages that must be considered before a selection is made.

Several organizational issues arise during the installation of a new information system. The two most important issues are resistance to change and reorganization. With user involvement and user education, resistance to change can be minimized. User education is provided through training, which needs to be thorough and complete so that users feel comfortable in using the new system. Besides user training, operator and management training are also necessary.

Maintenance is the last activity in the system development life cycle. After an information system is installed, it enters the maintenance phase, during which it is continually updated to meet the changing requirements of users. That continuing update is accomplished by a special group of programmers known as maintenance programmers. This group plays a very important, but difficult role and suffers from frequent frustration.

MINICASE 10–1

The Birch Company has a number of transaction processing systems and management information systems designed to supply the needs of operational and middle-level managers. Top management has recently gone to the director of information systems and asked for a decision support system that would supply them with information to help support their unstructured decisions. The system should accommodate internally generated information as well as external information about the competition, the economy, and the like. The managers would like the system to supply them with information on their VDTs in response to ad hoc inquiries. No paper reports would be required from the system at this time, but it should be able to process their requests and generate the relevant information quickly.

1. What type of output and input design considerations would be appropriate for this system?

---

2. Would you recommend a file system or a DBMS for this information system? Why?

MINICASE 10–2

Software Design, Inc. (SDI) is an information system consulting company that develops and sells business application software. The company has just developed a billing system that has not yet been fully tested. Nonetheless, SDI has begun a full-scale marketing effort. Four organizations have reviewed SDI's billing software and have contracted with the consulting company to buy the billing system. These organizations have manual billing systems at the present time. The consulting company can take several approaches to implementing its billing system in the four organizations: direct, parallel, pilot, or a combined approach.

1. Which approach would you recommend, and why?
2. As the manager of information systems at one of the four organizations, what would you do to make the transition from a manual to a computerized system as smooth and trouble-free as possible?

Key Terms

action document
automated testing
coding
conversion
debugging
decoupling
detail report
direct conversion
electronic data-processing (EDP) auditor
file recovery
future orientation
hierarchical chart
human factors
independence
installation
interdependence
logic error
maintenance
maintenance programmer
management report
management training

menu map
modularity
Nassi-Shneiderman chart
operator training
parallel conversion
phased-in conversion
pilot conversion
program flowchart (PFC)
pseudocode
report distribution
report format
report frequency
run-time error
source document
status report
subsystem testing
syntax error
system blueprint
system design
system testing
test data

testing   turnaround document
testing criteria   unit testing
testing methodology   user involvement
test plan   user's manual
top-down approach   user training
training   Warnier-Orr diagram

Review Questions

1. What are the different objectives for the logical and physical design stages?
2. What is a system blueprint?
3. What is meant by the design principle of modularity?
4. Why is user involvement important in the design of information systems?
5. How does a turnaround document differ from an action document?
6. What is a source document?
7. What are the differences between numeric and mnemonic codes?
8. Describe the sequence of steps required to compute file size.
9. Describe the top-down approach to physical design.
10. What is the role of prototyping in the system design stage?
11. What is the essential difference between a hierarchical chart and a Warnier-Orr diagram?
12. What system design aids are provided by CASE technology?
13. Why do we code data fields?
14. List five important testing criteria for an information system. Why do these criteria need to be quantitative and definitive?
15. Differentiate unit, subsystem, and system testing for an information system. Cite a common application (other than an information system) for which this concept of testing is appropriate.
16. What is automated testing? Describe some of its benefits.
17. What role does an auditor play in the testing of an information system?
18. Describe five important tasks that are necessary in the installation of an information system.
19. What is conversion? Describe four conversion approaches.
20. When would you select each of the conversion approaches in the installation of an information system?
21. Installing a new information system may present an organization with certain problems. What are some of these problems? How can an organization solve them?
22. Describe the type of training users need.
23. What is the main purpose of management training?
24. Describe three reasons that an information system requires maintenance.
25. What is maintenance programming? Why is it difficult and important?

Manufacturing Information Systems

Manufacturing as a functional area of business is responsible for producing finished products from raw materials. The days of smokestack industries are numbered, as today's newer industries take advantage of high technology for the sake of ecological concerns and production efficiencies. Even older industries are making changes in their plants and production facilities, where jobs can be performed more efficiently with the assistance of automated tools. Thomas Gunn, author of *Manufacturing for Competitive Advantage: Becoming a World Class Manufacturer,* suggests that manufacturing today involves a series of data-processing operations: sorting, analyzing, transmitting, and modifying data. Further, Gunn says that hardware is the essential commodity but that software provides the competitive advantage. These changes are largely the result of the impact of technology but also reflect consumers' demand for quality and the intense pressure brought about by foreign competitors.

COMPUTER INFLUENCE ON MANUFACTURING DECISIONS

The primary decisions facing manufacturing managers are
1. product design
2. facility design
3. production
4. quality control

Computer influence is rapidly increasing in each of these decision areas. Let's examine the expanding use of computers in the automotive industry, where the impact can be seen in all four decision areas.

Not all automotive companies have automated their manufacturing facilities, but there is an ever-increasing pressure for them to do so if they are to be competitive. Much automated manufacturing will be aided by larger mini- and mainframe computers, but some will also benefit from PCs.

Product Design

For the basic layout and structural analysis of all 3-D interior and body parts, Mazda uses a modeling layout and design system that runs on a pair of IBM3090 mainframe computers. That Japanese manufacturer uses American software—Lockheed's CADAM—for two-dimensional design, and Mazda Net is used for global communication of information between dealers and manufacturers.

Facility Design

America's largest automobile manufacturer, GM, has experimented with the use of small and less expensive PCs in their assembly line facilities. An assembly line facility is designed to move parts along at a pace that permits a different stage of their manufacture to be completed at various stations along the line. Initial experiments were at the Packard plant, which builds dash harnesses—the bundle of wires used in a car for dash and signal lights, lighter, radio, and so on. All related jobs had long been performed by humans, but PCs now serve as monitors, testers, and pressers in the Packard plant.

Production

At the Packard plant just described, the computerized monitor times the assembly line movement to see whether its speed needs to be increased or decreased to meet the production goal. When humans handled this job, some simply made errors in judgment, whereas others were subject to favoritism or prejudice. The computer easily overcomes these faults and maintains an electronic log of the average line movement speed throughout the work shift.

Quality Control

The job of the tester on an assembly line is to simulate harness inputs (e.g., switches turned on) and outputs (e.g., a shining light). The common purpose of these tests, whether performed by humans or computers, is to see whether the harness works for repeated inputs and outputs. The computer is proving to be faster and more reliable with these tasks.

The presser starts a press to cut and/or crimp wires on an exact mark to ensure an exact fit. The cuts must be made within 1/8 inch of the mark while the wires are moving along the assembly line. The movement causes 1 of 10 human-activated cuts to be the wrong length, whereas the computer's error rate has been 1 in 800. Clearly, the costs involved with the manufacture of these products can be dramatically reduced with automation. And when one company comes up with a good idea, others follow suit. Toyota, Nissan, Ford, and Chrysler are now testing PC-controlled and -staffed assembly lines.

OPERATIONAL PLANNING

A major information output of manufacturing is an operation plan, which contains the day-by-day activities required to produce a certain product quantity over a given time period. To aid in operational planning, a company must have an inventory system to maintain supplies that support the manufacturing and office processes as well as those that enter the production process directly as raw materials. The Japanese developed the just-in-time (JIT) inventory concept, which saves some of the inventory costs involved in maintaining an inventory, such as carrying costs and ordering costs. Carrying costs include the storage and maintenance of inventory, whereas ordering costs cover placing an order, having the shipment made, and moving the goods to a storage location. The JIT concept means that raw materials arrive just in time to be used in the next stage of the manufacturing process so that inventory carrying costs are reduced or eliminated. Many American firms are successfully using JIT concepts by encouraging suppliers to make deliveries at the appropriate times. A stockpile of raw materials is no longer needed.

Data to Support Manufacturing Operational Plans

The total output of the manufacturing process is dictated by sales forecasts that come from the marketing information system. Let's suppose that your firm produces the Super Look II rear-window louver for Cameros and Firebirds, and marketing information indicates that 20,000 of these units can be sold during the next time period. The materials to support the production of 20,000 units come from an exploded bill of materials. Figure A shows the louvers and a bill of materials required for the product. That single-unit bill of materials is exploded to produce a list of the material requirements necessary for 20,000 units (Figure B). The data from Figure B must then be compared with an inventory of materials on hand to identify how many units of each part (raw materials) must be ordered to support the operations plan. Routine capture and

FIGURE A
Manufacturing materials
required for rear-window
louvers.

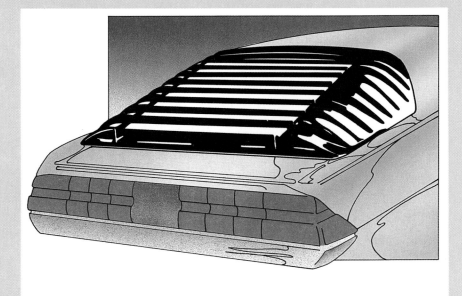

```
 O                                                    O
 O   Bill of Materials for Louvers                    O
 O                                                    O
 O         Component              Quantity            O
 O                                                    O
 O   top slats                       10               O
 O   side supports                    2               O
 O   1/4" screws                      6               O
 O   side-mounting brackets           2               O
 O   10" adhesive strips              4               O
 O   shipping box                     1               O
 O                                                    O
 O                                                    O
```

calculation of these data have been handled by computers for years, but now the data are captured at the front end of the planning process—rather than at the end, to document the process—so that they can enhance inventory management and manufacturing control.

AUTOMATED MANUFACTURING

Planning and controlling the manufacturing process with the aid of a computer is called materials requirement planning (MRP). MRP has helped lower manufacturing costs by improving the flow of work on the plant floor, reducing inventory investment, and forcing more timely supplier delivery schedules. A more comprehensive automated manufacturing system is computer-integrated manufacturing (CIM). The idea behind CIM is to use computers to automate all functions of the factory. With this concept a computer is used to design a product via computer-aided design (CAD); successfully designed products are then produced by computer-

```
Super Look II Rear Window Louvers

                          Unit        Production        Total
Component               Quantity         Goal        Requirements

top slats                  10          20,000          200,000
side supports               2          20,000           40,000
1/4" screws                 6          20,000          120,000
side-mounted brackets       2          20,000           40,000
10" adhesive strips         4          20,000           80,000
shipping box                1          20,000           20,000
```

controlled machinery. Computers are also used for timely movement of materials to appropriate locations in the factory and for movement of finished products to a location where they can be shipped out for sale. The direct use of a computer in the manufacturing operation is called computer-aided manufacturing (CAM). Vendors supply the tandem information systems as CAD/CAM systems.

Data Automation

Successful CIM operations have data available to tell the amount and cost of the raw materials acquired, the amount of raw materials used in the manufacturing process, and the number of units produced by the process in any time period. This information does not have to be recaptured but can be directly communicated to other affected information systems, such as inventory, purchasing, and accounting. Production savings in automated manufacturing are fairly apparent, but savings also result from automated data collection. The data entry function has accounted for about 25 percent of the budget of an information system department in the past, but automated data collection in all functional areas is quickly driving down the data capture expense and increasing the accuracy of the data recorded as well.

Quality Control in Manufacturing

The computer, along with statistical and operations research techniques, supplies quality control information to help manufacturing managers ensure that manufactured products meet acceptable standards. Those standards may or may not be at the highest possible level, but they will always be consistent. Inspection activities tell the story. No doubt you've reached into the left pocket of your new Levis and pulled out that small slip of paper declaring that they were inspected by Helen or #8. Much inspection of manufactured products is now accomplished faster and with equal care by using a computer. In addition, a computer can perform some inspections that are dangerous for humans.

Software

Information systems are more than hardware; software must be used to make the systems functional. MRP software has been defined by the American Production and Inventory Association as a method for effectively planning all resources at a production facility. More than 200 software packages are available to manufacturers seeking such a tool. These packages can be installed on mainframes, minicomputers, and microcomputers. For low-end microcomputers, packages run from $4,000 to $40,000. Mid-range minicomputers use MRP software ranging in cost from $4,000 to $315,000. Mainframe software starts at $300,000 and can be considerably more expensive, depending on the number of users and the complexity of the software.

Organizational Impact of Automated Manufacturing

Information Executive reported a study that showed 64 percent of manufacturers using MRP during the early 1980s. More recently, manufacturers have begun using capacity requirement planning (CRP), also called MRP II, to manage material, labor, and production facilities. Now the computer can massage data and facts and arrive at decisions that once required humans. This application, which is predicted to increase, reduces the need for many of the clerical tasks required in the manufacturing environment. Also revised are the requirements for many of the analytical tasks so that there is said to be a flattening of the middle management structure within the manufacturing function. In other words, middle management's role has been reduced, and fewer middle managers will be needed.

IMPORTANCE OF HUMAN INVOLVEMENT

It might seem that spending more than a quarter of a million dollars on software should quickly solve any manufacturing problem. However, Christopher Gray, president of Oliver Wright Software Research and author of a book on choosing MRP II software (*The Right Choice*), says that many software packages must be modified before their benefits can be seen on the shop floor. A generic package cannot always accommodate the peculiarities of every firm. Gray emphasizes that software solutions have many available modules, but the typical manufac-

turer can use only a few of them. He adds that people are the key to successful automated manufacturing facilities; computers can't do it alone. Managers must be committed to motivating and training everyone to work as a team if MRP II is to be successful.

Many automated manufacturing applications have failed to lower operations costs and improve product quality. A major barrier to successful automation is a manager's lack of understanding of a company's business environment. Automated manufacture cannot improve poorly conceived or understood business strategies.

John Deere Harvester in Moline, Illinois, the company that invented the tractor 150 years ago, claims to be in love with its $1 million CIM facility. Spokespersons claim that it is partially responsible for their maintaining a 23 to 34 percent return on investment (ROI). Deere officials further state that the ROI would not be possible with the CIM facility alone. They spent $15,000 on program design and another $10,000 on software linkup costs before the CIM system was selected. They also had to figure out just how the system would communicate with accounting, finance, inventory management, and engineering. All of these tasks required a lot of human skill but were absolutely essential to make CIM a success at Deere.

Information technology will undoubtedly have an increasingly significant impact on manufacturing for years to come. Nonetheless, automation cannot be applied without the study, care, and understanding of skilled human managers.

Brady, Sharon. 1987. No longer an ugly duckling. *Software News* (June): 37–42.

Jones, W. Frank. 1989. Fiscal failure despite technical success. *Information Strategy* (Spring): 34–37.

Knight, Robert. 1987. Plan first; then use CIM. *Software News* (December): 61–65.

Yaeger, Judy, and Andrew Targowski. 1989. The flattening of middle management in the computer-based environment. *Information Executive* (Spring): 47–50.

PART FIVE

Implications of Computers in Business Information Systems

Impact of Information Systems and the Information Resource

OBJECTIVES

- Describe the effects that the incorporation of information systems can have on corporate strategy
- Describe the new kinds of crimes that have been created or accelerated by the increasing use of computer-based information systems
- Discuss how computer use in business information systems has shifted traditional labor and employment patterns in the United States
- Discuss concerns related to electronic work monitoring, health and safety hazards, computer ethics, privacy, and other legal issues
- Explain the concept of information resource management
- Discuss the impact of end-user computing on organizational communication and structure

OUTLINE

IMPACT ON MANAGEMENT PROBLEM SOLVING AND DECISION MAKING
CORPORATE STRATEGY
COMPUTER CRIME
Difficulty of Detection and Prevention | Types of Computer Crimes
INFORMATION SYSTEMS AND THE RIGHT TO PRIVACY
How Information Systems Increase the Danger | What Society Is Afraid Of
JOB SECURITY
ELECTRONIC WORK MONITORING
A Tool for Productivity | The Potential for Probing
HEALTH AND SAFETY
COMPUTER ETHICS
LEGAL ISSUES AND LEGISLATION
Privacy and Electronic Eavesdropping | Liability for Incorrect Information and Software Workability | Copyright and Infringement
THE INFORMATION RESOURCE
DATA AND INFORMATION FILTERS
END-USER COMPUTING
INFORMATION CENTERS
THE CHIEF INFORMATION OFFICER
FLATTENING OF THE ORGANIZATION

Chapter 11

Management Profile: Janet L. Barnes
FIRST IN GOVERNMENT

Step by step, inch by inch, Janet L. Barnes is starting to build the first chief-information-officer operation in the federal government. The site is the Pension Benefit Guaranty Corporation (PBGC), the pension insurance agency that hired Barnes in 1987 as director of information resources management and CIO. Barnes says the addition of the CIO title—the first in the federal sector—was a senior management decision based on the recognition that information processing is vital to the agency's mission.

PBGC is just beginning to think about involving information systems in its business strategy. "I'm still trying to understand the business," Barnes says. "I'm going to be learning a lot so I can figure out how to formulate an information strategy. I can't say we have one today." However, Barnes is preparing for the full-fledged CIO role by first strengthening the traditional MIS operation. "I've been trying to structure an organization that's well positioned to carry out the CIO function when it's been defined," she explains.

Barnes is asserting control over the first half of her title, director of information resources management (IRM), before tackling the second. IRM calls for the management of information as a valuable resource. "The CIO function definitely encompasses what IRM is all about, but it also stresses the broad, strategic view [of information systems]," Barnes says. "The CIO is business-oriented. What direction is PBGC headed in? How do we provide better service to our retirees and pensioners, and how do we use information to help us do that?"

Much of the CIO literature talks about using information systems for competitive business advantages, namely, profits. In the public sector, she points out, it is more appropriate to ask how information systems can improve service to the public. Barnes is in a good position to compare MIS life in the public and private sectors. Before joining PBGC, she worked in systems development at Arthur Young and MCI Communications Corporation and helped to start a small MIS consulting business.

The biggest difference between the private sector and government is the lack of flexibility that managers have to hire and reward employees, she says. But Barnes views these problems as challenges to be overcome with creative approaches, not as insurmountable obstacles. "Who says my job is supposed to be easy?" she adds.

Personnel problems aside, Barnes speaks with excitement about the possibility of a strong CIO operation and the support she gets from PBGC executives. "Just seeing how upper management is so motivated and energized stimulates you to do your best. It's almost addictive," she says.

Adapted from "Janet L. Barnes: First in Government" by Mitch Betts. Copyright 1988 by CW Publishing Inc., Framingham, MA 01701. Reprinted from *Computerworld,* Aug. 1, 1988.

Significant inventions, such as the computer, alter how things are produced, how they are used, and how they are protected by law. Very often, these inventions cause us to revise our ethical values, too.

Business and society never fully adjust to new inventions. For instance, the appearance of the automobile still raises arguments about the need for drunk-driving, seat-belt, and airbag legislation; about the legality of radar detectors; and about destruction of farmlands by interstate highways. As a result of computers, business and society in general are now experiencing just the first big wave of change and controversy.

This chapter looks at how computer-based information systems are affecting corporate strategy, computer-related crimes, concerns about privacy, and the existence and security of huge banks of personal data. You'll read about the effects of computers on the job market and about issues in the workplace, including health, safety, and electronic work monitoring. You'll learn that the emergence of computers has created some ethical questions for today's computer users. We'll examine some of the legal issues and legislation that have arisen as a result of the widespread use of computer-based information systems. Finally, the chapter investigates the increasing importance of information in our society and, in particular, the concept of information resource management (IRM). Specific future impacts of the IRM concept are addressed as well.

IMPACT ON MANAGEMENT PROBLEM SOLVING AND DECISION MAKING

The proliferation of computer-based business information systems has enabled managers to improve their abilities to identify and solve problems and make decisions. But these systems have also forced management to consider a number of problems and issues that were not of concern before the proliferation of information systems. Managers must now continually examine if and how information systems can be used to give their organizations a strategic advantage over the competition. They must deal with potential crime and with problems of privacy, security, health and safety, ethics, and law brought on by the increasing use of information systems. In many cases managers are being held responsible—legally, ethically, or both—for problems in these areas. Today's managers must be informed about these issues so that they can identify potential problems and effectively deal with them. Failure to do so could result in costly consequences to managers and to their organizations.

The Information Age has brought an increased emphasis on managing information, in addition to the more traditional resources of the organization—materials, machines, labor, capital, and so on. Concern for this new area—information resource management (IRM)—is leaping into academic course offerings and is a must for managers who enter today's fast-paced, hi-tech workplace.

CORPORATE STRATEGY

In the past, information systems were used only to support the operating and administrative functions of an organization. Firms were simply concerned with increasing the efficiency of transaction processing and controlling the vast amounts of paperwork created by their operating and administrative activities. In recent years, however, organizations have begun to recognize the strategic value that information systems can have in the marketplace.

A **strategic information system** is one that changes the way an organization competes in the marketplace. Organizations need to consider ways in which information systems can help differentiate them from their competitors. As cited earlier, the American Hospital Supply Company was particularly successful in accomplishing this goal. That company's direct-order entry system lowered costs while improving services to customers. It also changed the way the company competed in the marketplace. Instead of sending out salespersons to the various health care institutes or manually placing orders with numerous suppliers, the company received and placed orders electronically. This change lowered costs, increased customer convenience and satisfaction, and gave American Hospital Supply Company a larger customer base and a competitive advantage over the competition.

The change also imposed switching costs on customers. A **switching cost** is incurred when a company or an individual changes from one supplier to another. That cost may represent money, time, or simply the irritation of getting used to a new way of doing things. Even after other hospital supply companies followed suit and established their own direct-order entry systems, most hospitals remained with American Hospital Supply Company because that system was established and had proven to be reliable.

Another example cited earlier illustrates an organization's using its information system to a strategic advantage. American Airlines' Sabre system was the first airline reservations system. It allowed the airline easy access to customers, who no longer had to go to the airport to buy a ticket but could go to their neighborhood travel agencies. Because of the convenience this information system afforded customers, American Airlines was able to substantially increase its market share. The Sabre system was also used by other airlines, who paid American for the service, and American was able to keep track of what the competition was doing in various travel markets. Some say that American makes more from the Sabre system than from its airline operations.

This example also illustrates the significant impact that one company's strategic information system can have on its competitors. Such a system can make it virtually impossible for new contenders to enter the marketplace. In the area of airline reservations, an airline must have or pay to be a part of an automated reservation system to be a top competitor. However, development of such a system is difficult and costly, yet paying to use another airline's reservation system can also be costly. In addition, the reservation systems are often set up to favor the airline that owns the system. Legal questions are still being resolved on this issue of fairness.

On the other hand, information systems can also help an organization enter a new market. For example, the use of information systems and communications allowed many nonbanking institutions, such as insurance companies and brokerage firms, to enter the cash management account market that had traditionally been held by banks. Federal Express is a more recent example of strategic information system use. That company developed an information system that modified its existing strategy as an overnight package delivery service by providing a new product to customers and opening up a new market for Federal Express. The company's new information system provided customers with electronic delivery of messages in less than 2 hours anywhere in the country. The system also took Federal Express into the electronic mail market.

Many firms also use their own information systems to market information services to organizations unable to implement their own systems. TRW, the largest credit rating service in the United States, maintains credit histories for millions of people; their records are both updated by and sold to other businesses. As technology marches forward and provides new and less expensive options, more and more organizations are examining ways in which information systems can be strategically used to benefit their businesses.

COMPUTER CRIME

The increasing use of computers in business information systems and the increasing integration of these systems has led to an increase in computer crimes. A **computer crime** is generally defined as one that involves the use of computers and software for illegal purposes. Many of these crimes—such as embezzlement of funds, alteration of records, theft, vandalism, sabotage, and terrorism—can be committed without a computer. But a computer permits these offenses to be carried out more quickly and with less chance of being discovered.

Computer crimes have been on the rise for the last 15 years. Just how much these computer crimes cost businesses is in dispute, but estimates range from $3 billion to $5 billion annually. Even the FBI, which attempts to keep track of the growth or decline of all kinds of crimes, is unable to say precisely how large a loss is involved. However, it estimates that the average amount taken from a company hit by computer crime is $600,000. This figure is considerably higher than that for non–computer-based crimes.

A number of reasons are given for the increase in computer crime: (1) more computers are in use, and thus more people are familiar with basic computer operation; (2) more computers are tied together in satellite and other data-transmission networks; and (3) the easy access of microcomputers to huge mainframe databases is now quite common.

Difficulty of Detection and Prevention

Movies and newspaper stories might lead us to believe that most computer crimes are committed by teenage hackers—brilliant and basically good young people who let their imaginations and technical genius get them into trouble. But a realistic look at computer crimes reveals that the offender is likely to be an employee of the firm against which the crime has been committed, that is, an insider.

Given this description of the computer criminal and the environment in which the crime occurs, it is often difficult to identify the criminal. First of all, the crime may be so complex that months or years go by before anyone discovers it. Second, once the crime has been revealed, it is not easy to find a clear trail of evidence leading back to the guilty party. There are no weapons or fingerprints as there might be in the investigation of more conventional crimes. And third, there are usually no witnesses to computer crime, even though it may be taking place in a room filled with people. Who knows whether the person at the next terminal, calmly keying in data, is doing company work or committing a criminal act (Figure 11–1)?

Unfortunately, not enough people in management and law enforcement know enough about computer technology to help prevent computer crimes. Management and legal authorities have to be familiar with a computer's capabilities in a given situation to guard against its misuse. In some large cities, such as Los Angeles, police departments have now set up specially trained computer crime units. However, even when an offender is caught, investigators, attorneys, judges, and/or juries may find the alleged crime too complicated and perplexing to handle. Fortunately, more attorneys today are specializing in computer law and studying the computer's potential for misuse.

Another complicating factor is that many companies do not report computer crime or prosecute the person responsible even after a crime has been discovered. These companies may hide the crimes out of fear that the public will lose confidence in their organizations when it discovers the weaknesses of their computer systems. Banks, credit card companies, and investment firms are especially sensitive about revealing their vulnerabilities because they rely heavily on customer trust. Thus, to avoid public attention, cautious companies often settle cases of computer tampering out of court. And if cases do go to trial and the offenders are convicted, they

FIGURE 11–1
Large computer rooms with many terminals make it difficult to deter or detect
an individual who is fraudulently using the system. (Courtesy of Honeywell)

may be punished only by a fine or a light sentence because the judge or jury may not be fully trained to understand the seriousness of the crime.

Not all companies are timid in apprehending computer criminals, however. For example, Connecticut General Life Insurance Company decided that it had to get tough on violators. So when the company discovered that one of its computer technicians had embezzled $200,000 by entering false benefit claims, it presented its findings to the state's attorney and aided in the prosecution of the technician. The technician was found guilty and was sentenced to prison, not just for computer misuse but also for grand theft and insurance fraud. Connecticut General now has a policy of reporting all incidents of theft or fraud, no matter how small.

Types of Computer Crimes

Numerous types of computer crimes have emerged with the proliferation of computers and information systems.

Data Manipulation. Altering the data that enter or exit a computer is generally called **data manipulation**. Examples include changing school grades by putting false data into a school's computer system and changing credit standing by accessing credit-bureau computer files and entering or deleting information. Another type of data manipulation is called **salami slicing**, that is, skimming off a tiny bit of money from a number of accounts and diverting it into the manipulator's own account.

Time Bomb. Coding a computer program to destroy itself after it has been run a certain number of times is called a **time bomb**. This method of sabotage is sometimes used by disgruntled employees. It is also used by software developers as a protection against companies that buy software on credit. If the buyer doesn't pay for the software by the time agreed upon, the program self-destructs. When the bill is paid, the developer defuses the bomb.

Computer Virus. A **computer virus** is a program that is embedded in what seems to be legitimate software (e.g., a word processor or a computer game). However, when unsuspecting users run the software, the virus can attack their systems. Computer viruses have been programmed to scramble data, erase a hard-disk index, or even erase all data on a hard-disk drive. If the user does not have backup copies, the contents of the disk may be irretrievably lost. Some viruses act immediately; others are programmed to activate after a certain number of uses or with a certain combination of keystrokes. Even when a program is copied, a virus can reproduce itself and be carried to another computer. In the fall of 1988 the Internet network was brought to a standstill by a virus (Highlight 11–1). Programs are currently available to fight viruses.

Trap Door. A special password that is created and keyed in to give access to a system is called a **trap door**. With a trap door a programmer can get back into a program without anyone else's knowing about it, and the entry is not documented. A trap door approach might be used by programmers involved in coding programs to which they wished to gain illegal entry after the programs were installed.

Data Stealing. Using a computer to steal data that have been gathered for an organization's legitimate purposes and using that data for one's own purposes is called **data stealing**. One example is taking a client list from one company and selling it to a competitor.

Time Stealing. Time stealing is using someone else's computer without authorization and thus stealing the amount of money that would have been paid in rent for the time used or stealing the money that it takes to keep the computer in operation for its intended purpose.

Electronic Eavesdropping. Tapping, without authorization, into communication lines over which computer data and messages are sent is called **electronic eavesdropping**.

Industrial Espionage. Using a computer to steal designs, marketing plans, or other trade secrets from one company and sell them to another is a form of **industrial espionage**. As information systems have made it easier to collect, process, and distribute information, they have also made it easier to illegally acquire and use that information.

An organization must identify and then secure any information of strategic value, but this process is often a complex and difficult proposition. Organizations frequently operate in varied and changing competitive situations. For example, a defense contractor may fiercely compete against a particular company for one contract and yet work with that same company as a co-contractor on another project. For the common project, access to information must flow freely, and systems must interconnect. However, elaborate security measures must be installed on that same computer system to prevent access to information about competing projects.

Having company secrets stolen can mean disaster. But for one little-known firm, the Saxpy Computer Corporation, it has meant increased interest in their product and national media attention that has enhanced their image. Saxpy manufactures and markets the Matrix 1, a $1.5-million supercomputer. The Matrix 1 has processing speeds of 250 million to 1 billion floating-point operations per second and can create synthetic images based on radar and sonar data. Saxpy was originally getting only two or three calls a day about its computer until a former employee was arrested by the FBI and charged with stealing company secrets and selling them to the Soviet Union. Since that story broke, the company has been receiving two to three times that number of calls. According to one Saxpy official, ''It doesn't hurt to have articles saying our technology is so powerful the Soviets want it.''

Piracy. As more people learn to use computers and as more uses are found for them, there is a corresponding growth in software piracy. In this case **piracy** means making unauthorized copies of copyrighted computer

Virus Attacks Internet Network

The Computer Fraud and Abuse Act of 1986 outlaws unauthorized access to and tampering with federal computer systems and gives the Secret Service and the FBI joint jurisdiction over investigations. Nonetheless, a computer virus planted in the nationwide Internet network brought thousands of computer systems to a near standstill. The Internet network ties together several networks throughout the nation and is predominantly used by universities, research laboratories, federal agencies, and other institutions. The virus caused hundreds of research institutions to shut down their computers. The three primary networks included in Internet are Advanced Researched Projects Agency Network (Arpnet), which connects military and civilian computers; Military Network (Milnet), which is reserved for the military; and National Science Foundation Network (NSFnet), which links universities, research labs, and other institutions.

The type of virus that infected the network is called a worm. A worm has the ability to slip into a computer system and propagate itself. As it does so, it ties up computers, eventually shutting them down. This particular virus did not damage or destroy files. Without human intervention a worm virus moves rapidly from one program to another, replicating itself. In contrast, most viruses attach themselves to a program.

A virus has a multipronged attack. In the Internet case it entered a targeted machine through a debug feature in a widely used mailer

programs. Highlight 11–2 looks at how some software companies are responding to this issue.

INFORMATION SYSTEMS AND THE RIGHT TO PRIVACY

Amendment IV of the Bill of Rights guarantees U.S. citizens that the right to be secure in "their persons, houses, papers, and effects against unreasonable searches and seizures shall not be violated." The privacy of personal data stored in computers, of course, is not mentioned in the Bill of Rights. So the issue of exactly how much privacy citizens have a right to has naturally arisen. For the discussion in this text, **privacy** means the right of control over one's personal data.

Privacy is a much easier issue to deal with if you conduct your life within the walls of your own home, beyond the eyes and ears of passersby. But once you reach beyond those walls by installing and using a telephone, setting up a bank account, filing an insurance claim, applying for a loan, enrolling in a school, admitting yourself to a hospital, or performing any of hundreds of other such actions that involve business information systems, your privacy is endangered.

program called Sendmail. The virus shut off the system's security and copied a short program from the host machine to the targeted machine. The virus then rummaged through the computer's files, attempting to identify user names and programs, especially automated log-on procedures. It compiled a list of possible passwords and attempted to find out to which network the computer was linked. The virus then came up with a list of machines that might be vulnerable to attack and infection, and it simply ground away at every possibility until it penetrated the system.

A second component of the virus made use of a bug in the network facility in the UNIX operating system to launch its attack inside the machine. It did not result in malicious damage of files or data, but it used up memory and storage space, quickly bringing the machine to a near standstill.

The Internet virus was stopped when a message was sent over the network telling what to do to fix the virus. The fix came from someone who disassembled the code and figured out what the virus did, what route it used to bypass security, and how to patch systems so that its route was cut off. The virus was estimated to be about 50,000 lines of executable code.

Various opinions have circulated about the origin of the virus. The *New York Times* claimed that an anonymous caller credited it to a graduate student's viral program experiment that went out of control. Some good was derived from the episode: it highlighted the need for a secure nationwide network for research and encouraged renewed concern for tightening security on computer networks.

Most people are somewhat aware of George Orwell's classic book *1984*, in which he describes a society where all information about individuals is locked in the state's database. Individual freedoms have been violated and are no longer in existence in that society. Even though that Orwellian society seems impossible it could be supported with today's technology.

How Information Systems Increase the Danger

Today's information systems alone don't invade our privacy, but they enable businesses and individuals to do so with greater ease and frequency than ever before. Information systems assist in the invasion of privacy in two primary ways: (1) they enable users to stockpile and categorize a lot of information in a very small space, and (2) they allow other users quick access to anything and everything that is in the stockpile.

The federal government is the biggest stockpiler. Its various departments, bureaus, and offices have more than 3½ billion files about U.S. citizens. If the computerized files of all state agencies (health, welfare, education, law enforcement, and so on) and such private institutions as

**Software Firms Take Stand Against
International Piracy and Trade Barriers**

In response to the growing problems of international piracy and trade barriers, several major software companies have formed the Business Software Association (BSA). The goal of this association is to maintain a small group, focused narrowly and intensely on fighting these problems. BSA was formed by Aldus Corporation, Ashton-Tate Corporation, Autodesk, Lotus Development Corporation, and WordPerfect Corporation. The U.S. Trade Commission reported that in 1986 31 U.S. hardware and software firms lost $4.1 billion because of piracy.

BSA has been instrumental in several raids on groups that pirate software internationally. One of these was in Hong Kong's Golden Shopping Arcade, which is known as one of the world's most notorious markets for illegally copied software. In a raid conducted in July 1988, officials succeeded in closing several outlets that were selling pirated software. BSA is also fighting to ensure that the software markets in Europe and Brazil are kept open to U.S. software products.

BSA is using several means to reach its goals: lobbying U.S. and foreign governments, working with law enforcement agencies, pursuing private lawsuits, conducting educational programs, and working with other trade associations. The focus of the organization is entirely on international concerns. The organization says it will leave the pursuit of domestic piracy cases to the Software Publisher's Association (SPA) and the ADAPSO, an association of computer software and services firms, but will work closely with these groups on international affairs. BSA hopes that focusing all its attention and effort on the problems of international piracy and trade barriers can help to resolve these problems more swiftly.

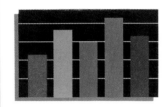

banks, hospitals, insurance companies, and credit bureaus are added in, it becomes clear that no one has a lot of privacy left. Information on what we buy, how we pay for it, what we read, what we watch on television, what our sicknesses are, and how much we earn is valuable information for those who want to sell us things—whether products or ideas. And if there is money to be made, some businesses and individuals will proceed without regard for laws or ethics. The danger is that businesses and individuals will use our preferences, weaknesses, and habits to their advantage and not to ours.

Still, there are organizations and institutions that need to know something about us if they are going to work toward our own good. Often, doctors must have quick access to our complete medical history if they are to cure us or save our lives. Banks need proof that our credit record is good so that they can loan us the money for a new car or house. Basically, then, the question of privacy boils down to the *fair* collection and use of personal data.

What Society Is Afraid Of

Listed here are some of the specific dangers that society sees in the huge personal data banks stored by government agencies and large private organizations.

- To begin with, the data collected may be inaccurate. A computer doesn't know which data are true and which are false. All it tells is what is in the file. Yet the data may be wrong for any number of reasons: (1) a mistake on the part of the person who gathered the data or keyed them into the computer; (2) a mismatch of the right data but the wrong name; or (3) data that were once correct but are now out of date.
- The personal data collected may not be secure from illegal access and use. Private data sent over communication lines may be illegally intercepted. Although many organizations do establish elaborate security systems, computer-related crimes and theft have increased in the last few years.
- One giant database with all the personal data about every member of society in it might be compiled. If all agencies put all their data banks together into one, for example, it would include almost everything about everyone that anyone would ever want to know.
- A computer's great ability to store and classify vast amounts of data leads to a tendency to collect and keep more data about people than are actually needed to fulfill the original function. Because data are often very useful and sometimes very profitable, the temptation is to amass as much of it as possible.
- Data collection agencies commonly combine and exchange their data. This practice enables anyone with access to get not only credit records, for example, but also health, insurance, and employment records.

Even though there is legislation against federal agencies using information for a purpose other than that for which it was intended, there is a system called matching. With **matching**, one agency compares its data with another's for a specific purpose. For example, Internal Revenue Service files are matched against the welfare rolls to catch welfare cheaters. There are advantages to this practice as well as a potential for misuse.

In general, the fact that an individual, business, or agency has personal data may cause no particular harm, but interpretation of data can be hazardous. The combination of potentially inaccurate, out-of-date, and irrelevant information is quite dangerous.

JOB SECURITY

One of the most apparent effects of computer-based information systems is the way in which they have altered the job market. The incorporation of computers has changed the way work has traditionally been done at every level of production—from design to manufacture to distribution. When computers were still in their infancy, labor union leaders predicted that they would take jobs away from people. And, to some degree, those predictions have been correct. As of 1986 more than 100,000 industrial robots were used throughout the non-communist countries of the world. In addition, there are more robots and fewer people on auto assembly lines now (Figure 11–2). General Motors alone has more than 40,000 programmable devices, 4,000 of which are robots. And GM plans about 200,000 programmable devices (14,000 of them being robots) for two new plants.

Office jobs have also been eliminated because a few workers using word processors and database management systems are now able to turn out more letters and reports than a roomful of secretaries, laboring away at old-fashioned typewriters and file cabinets. A few years ago a large law firm might have had a staff of several dozen people typing briefs and other legal documents. Today, a few individuals with word processors can produce the same output. In addition, newspaper reporters can prepare their own articles to be set in type as they compose them at a computer terminal. Just a few years ago typesetting was done by skillful and well-paid linotypists, who are no longer needed (Figure 11–3).

The W. E. Upjohn Institute, in a report to Congress, predicted that by 1990, 200,000 workers could be displaced by robots and computers. As many as 50,000 of those lost jobs could belong to auto workers. Others think the threats of unemployment are overstated. The Office of Technology Assessment, in a report to Congress, said that programmable automation probably won't create massive nationwide unemployment in this decade.

The plus side to robots is that they can do some jobs faster and cheaper than human beings. Better still, robots never become ill, never need breaks, and can work 24 hours a day. These facts mean not only economy for the manufacturer, but also lower prices for consumers. Because robots are not susceptible to human ills and are not inclined to sue for physical injuries, they are especially valuable in performing high-risk and monotonous jobs, such as mining, diving, painting, working with toxic chemicals, and assembling parts. Furthermore, robots do create some

FIGURE 11–2
Many automobile assembly line jobs, such as painting and welding, are being automated with the use of robotics. This trend has eliminated some jobs but has also created others. Here, the chassis are spray painted as they roll down the assembly lines. (Courtesy of Honda of America, Marysville, Ohio)

FIGURE 11-3
News stories can be entered and stored directly in the computer. The files can then be transmitted electronically to a typesetting machine, eliminating the need for a linotypist. (Courtesy of *Chicago Tribune*)

jobs. After all, someone has to design, build, sell, and maintain them. Some newer industries would never have been possible without them.

Nonetheless, even though predictions of the disastrous effects of computers on employment have not yet come to pass, many jobs, especially in manufacturing and the auto industry, are being eliminated. Thus far, the effect of these job shifts has been to weaken the labor union—not just because machines can do the work of people, but also because computers enable one worker to do a variety of related jobs well instead of specializing in one task. Unions were organized on the principle that a worker had a specific job and was therefore protected. In response to union and societal concerns, heavily computerized companies often try to soften this reality by waiting for workers to retire or simply not replacing workers who resign. Some companies offer retraining and job-placement help for those who have been nudged out by computers.

ELECTRONIC WORK MONITORING

The National Institute of Occupational Safety and Health (NIOSH) estimates that more than 8 million video display terminal (VDT) operators are being watched by their own computers. The term for this new way of supervising workers is **electronic work monitoring**. Computers can count keystrokes, track data entry errors, record the length and frequency of breaks, and measure the time it takes an operator to handle a customer service transaction. In short, the computer can measure the quantity and, in some ways, the quality of an employee's work.

It used to be that this kind of monitoring was found only on a factory assembly line as a way of calculating each worker's productivity. Or a supervisor may have been looking over a worker's shoulder to see whether a job was being done. With electronic work monitoring, white-collar

Impact of Information Systems and the Information Resource

workers are now faced with the same situation that assembly-line workers have been facing.

A Tool for Productivity

Is there anything wrong with electronic work monitoring? Surely, an employer has a right to know who is producing and how well. How else, employers argue, can they decide whom to promote, reprimand, or fire? They claim that this system is fair and objective, for with electronic work monitoring employees can have a detailed, electronic record of productivity right there in their permanent files. Companies see this as a cost-effective way to measure job performance, provide incentive pay to workers who perform beyond minimum requirements, and make the most of new technology in bringing costs down.

The Potential for Probing

Many workers see the work-monitoring issue as an invasion of privacy and a not-so-subtle way of speeding up performance. But companies say that workers who use company equipment necessarily give up some privacy rights. And so the arguments continue. Certainly, there is room in this practice for company misuse if, for instance, managers take note only of an operator's speed in completing a transaction and give no weight to the quality of the work. Furthermore, employees may never get a chance to see the data compiled about them and, thus, have no chance to correct any inaccuracies.

Electronic work monitoring, since it is easy and automatic, may tend to replace human evaluation of job performance, but some employees say that machine measuring only appears to be objective. Companies using electronic work monitoring, on the other hand, say that the computer *is* objective. When it registers an employee's performance and puts that record in an electronic file, it is really protecting an individual's privacy, not violating it, the companies say. This productivity-versus-privacy argument may never be settled without laws to govern the monitoring or a formal agreement between a company's management and worker representatives.

| HEALTH AND SAFETY | Are computers hazardous to your health? The jury is still out on this question. Some people are worried that the radiation coming from VDTs may cause cataracts, cancer, miscarriages, visual problems, stress, and/or sterility. These charges have been researched by such agencies as the Food and Drug Administration's Bureau of Radiological Health, the Occupational Safety and Health Administration, the National Institute of Occupational Safety and Health, and the Canadian Radiation Protection Bureau. One Japanese report recommends that pregnant workers not use VDTs until more conclusive studies can be conducted. However, the American and Canadian studies have failed to demonstrate any connection between VDT radiation and disease. The House Education and Labor Subcommittee |

on Health and Safety reported to Congress that it, too, found no connection. But it did suggest that employers and employees work together to set up satisfactory operation and work guidelines.

Workers' fears continue, and other private and government studies are underway. Among the other common complaints of VDT operators are eye strain, neck strain, backache, and fatigue. Studies confirm that these ailments can result if users aren't provided with proper lighting, adjustable chairs, and frequent breaks away from their terminals. Mental stress is another common complaint. Many people who work at terminals feel that they are expected to produce more and do it faster because computers themselves are so fast. Workers who are aware of being monitored by a computer frequently feel additional pressure.

Other people are concerned about the emotional and personality changes that might result from being isolated from other workers. In today's high-tech, automated society, people can conduct business and communicate without ever coming face to face. Computer operators can work an entire shift, taking their instructions from a terminal screen. Employees can send and receive memos to each other electronically, seldom engaging in personal conversation.

In 1985 the National Association of Working Women and the Service Employees International Union campaigned strongly on behalf of VDT safety. Many states—such as Washington, California, New Mexico, Rhode Island, Wisconsin, and Massachusetts—have passed VDT-safety laws. Although all the laws are slightly different, they generally deal with more comfortable workstations, medical checkups, and employer/employee discussions. For example, in Suffolk County, New York, the law dictates that workers at terminals must be given 15 minutes away from the monitor for every 3 hours in front of it.

In the meantime, ergonomics, the study of adjusting the machine and the workplace to the worker, has been applied to the electronic office. Efforts are continually being made to incorporate human factors into the design of the workplace so that it is safe and comfortable.

COMPUTER ETHICS

It may not be immediately apparent that computers pose any particular ethical problems; but **computer ethics**, a standard of behavior governing the use of computers by individuals and organizations, is needed. As long ago as 1970, the American Federation of Information Processing Societies (AFIPS) saw the need for standards and thus established a code of computer ethics for its members. In addition, the Institute for Certification of Computer Professionals (ICCP) requires that an applicant for a certificate meet ethical standards as well as fulfilling education and experience criteria.

The observance of ethics is a way of self-regulating conduct when the law or a particular situation doesn't indicate a clear course of action. Here are some persistent ethical questions regarding computers.

- Is it an invasion of privacy to monitor employees through their own computers?

- Is it fair for employers to use the data collected from electronic work monitoring as the only basis for evaluating employees?
- Does a company owe a worker who has been replaced by a computer any consideration other than that prescribed by labor law or contract?
- Is it right for someone who buys a software program to make a copy for a friend?
- Should computer operators regard all data they process as completely confidential?
- Is it fair to tap into someone else's computer data files?

LEGAL ISSUES AND LEGISLATION

Because information is often randomly gathered, carelessly guarded, and easily accessible with computer technology, the assaults on personal and corporate privacy are difficult to detect and legislate against. Much of our safety under present conditions depends on the thoroughness and ethics of those who compile the data in the first place. However, new laws are being made. Of the 400 laws passed by the 98th Congress, 58 were related to information technology. Most states have also passed laws to discourage computer crime or privacy invasion.

Privacy and Electronic Eavesdropping

One difficulty arising from the increased use of computer-based information systems is that laws have to take into account the rights of all the people who might be affected. For example, is information about a person the property of that person or the company that gathers it; does the person have any right to or ownership of it? If someone gains access to information that an individual has freely provided to someone else, does that constitute theft or ethical misuse? In the 1960s and 1970s some federal agencies and Congress became aware of the seriousness of the information problem. Congress passed the **Freedom of Information Act of 1970** to allow citizens to find out which federal agencies are keeping records on them and to secure copies of those records to see whether they are correct.

This legislation was the forerunner of a series of acts to stop unnecessary and unauthorized snooping into credit ratings (the Fair Credit Reporting Act of 1970), educational records (the Education Privacy Act of 1974), and personal finance (the Right to Financial Privacy Act of 1978). Most federal privacy legislation prior to the mid-1980s related to the behavior of the federal government and the organizations to which it supplied funds. Now, legislation is appearing that reaches into the private sector.

To affirm the position that the federal government has no right to keep secret records about any citizen and to protect citizens from privacy abuses by the federal government, Congress enacted the **Privacy Act of 1974**. Some of the provisions of this act are listed here:

- It allows individuals to find out what data concerning them have been collected, filed, and used by government agencies.

- It forbids personal data collected for one purpose to be used for another purpose without the consent of the individual(s) involved. However, the government's more frequent use of matching decreases the power of this provision.
- The act specifies that individuals must be allowed to have a copy of all records that pertain to them and must have a way to correct incorrect data.
- It says that the government agency involved must ensure that records are up-to-date and accurate and must protect them from misuse.

The refinement of computer technology in the 1980s led to the passage of other federal laws to protect privacy. Some of them are cited in Figure 11−4. Computer-related areas that may require better protective laws include electronic mailboxes and bulletin boards, data communication lines, and unattended computer terminals. The Electronic Communications Privacy Act of 1986 makes illegal the interception of data communications. Another related law is the Computer Fraud and Abuse Act of 1986, which gives the federal government jurisdiction over interstate computer crimes and crimes involving computers used by the federal government.

Liability for Incorrect Information and Software Workability

Have you ever been the victim of a computer error? Perhaps you have received a check with the wrong amount printed on it, or you received your class-registration form with the wrong classes listed. These errors result more in inconvenience than in anything else. But some errors and losses are so great that the courts are trying to discover just who is legally responsible for them—whether the fault is in the information or in information system software that is used.

Incorrect Information. Although it is not yet clear to what extent any agency or company can be held accountable for the accuracy of information it gives out, organizations are becoming more vulnerable to large claims. The question of blame is quite complex, as shown by these two examples of litigation:

- The family of victims in an airplane crash in Alaska sued the airline and its chartmaker. The pilot had relied on graphically drawn charts that included faulty government data. The family won and collected damages.
- A federal court in Boston ruled that the U.S. Weather Service was not liable for an erroneous forecast that resulted in the deaths of four lobster fishermen.

Society is becoming aware of just how deep the effect of incorrect information can be. For example, incorrect data provided to air traffic controllers or drug manufacturers can have life and death consequences for hundreds or thousands of people. Some providers of information and in-

FIGURE 11–4
Key federal legislation related to computers.

PRIVACY

Freedom of Information Act of 1970
Allow citizens to find out which federal agencies are collecting and storing data about them and to secure copies of the records to see whether they are correct.

Fair Credit Reporting Act of 1970
Provides that people have the right to inspect their credit records. If a citizen challenges data in the record, the credit agency is legally required to investigate the accuracy of that data.

Crime Control Act of 1973
Stipulates that those responsible for maintaining state criminal records developed with federal funds must ensure the security and privacy of the data in those records.

Privacy Act of 1974
Establishes laws to prevent federal government abuse of individual privacy: forbids data on individuals to be collected for one purpose and used for another without the individuals' consent; gives individuals the right to find out what information the government has collected about them; allows individuals to have copies of these files and a way to correct erroneous data; requires the government agency involved to ensure that records are up-to-date and correct and to protect them from misuse; establishes other provisions as well.

Education Privacy Act of 1974
Restricts access to computer records of grades and behavior evaluations in private and public schools. Students have the right to examine and challenge the data in their records.

Tax Reform Act of 1976
Puts limitations on the IRS in its access to personal information in bank records and in its provision of that information to other agencies.

Right to Financial Privacy Act of 1978
Establishes restrictions on government access to customer files in financial institutions and gives citizens the right to examine data about themselves in those files.

formation system software are working within their own companies and trade organizations to prevent both potential tragedies and lawsuits. They are using two basic approaches: (1) testing and verification of data and software to create a more reliable product or service and (2) limiting their liability in advance through contract provisions and disclaimer statements.

Software Workability. There is an ongoing battle between software manufacturers and those who purchase software as to who must bear the cost of damages if the software doesn't work. Currently, software suppliers give no performance guarantee. Manufacturers say they can't possibly an-

FIGURE 11–4
(Continued)

Privacy Protection Act of 1980
Prohibits government agents from making unwarranted searches of press offices and files.

Electronic Funds Transfer Act of 1980
Stipulates that those who offer electronic funds transfer (EFT) check service must tell customers about third-party access to customer accounts.

Debt Collection Act of 1982
Sets up due-process conditions that federal agencies must follow before releasing any information about bad debts to credit bureaus.

Cable Communications Policy Act of 1984
Requires cable television services to tell their subscribers whether any personal information about them is beingcollected, used, or disclosed.

Electronic Communications Privacy Act of 1986
Makes it illegal to intercept data communications, such as electronic mail.

Computer Fraud and Abuse Act of 1986
Gives federal jurisdiction over interstate computer crimes in the private sector; applies to computers used by the federal government and federally insured financial institutions.

COPYRIGHT PROTECTION

Copyright Act of 1976
Protects creative and intellectual property, such as books, plays, songs, photographs, and computer programs from the moment of creation.

Semiconductor Chip Protection Act of 1984
Intended to prevent one company from reproducing the chip pattern of another. The act gives an original developer a 10-year period of exclusive rights.

ticipate or ensure usefulness in all software applications. Consumers argue that the software should do what it says it can do.

The question of responsibility becomes even more acute in the case of expert systems. Because they are designed for specific and complex uses, such as medical diagnosis, and because the results of any defects could be catastrophic, the legal implications are more serious. In reality, any accident or financial loss that arises from the use of any information system might be blamed on the hardware manufacturers, the database or knowledge base, the software, and/or the user—all of which share responsibility for the system and its operation. It is not surprising, then, that the laws applying to liability are in the early stages of evolution.

Copyright and Infringement

Because computer software is protected by federal copyright law, many of the ethical and legal problems surrounding computer technology today are perceived to arise from copyright violations. The only way in which software manufacturers can recover their development expenses and make a profit is to sell their programs in large numbers. Since pirates have to pay only the copying costs—and none of the research and development expenses—they can sell the programs more cheaply than the developers can. And naturally, each pirated copy sold reduces the number that the developers can sell.

To discourage unauthorized copying, software developers use a variety of methods.

- Licensing one or several manufacturers to produce the programs. The manufacturer(s) then pay the developer a royalty fee on each program produced.
- Putting a seal on the software package and stating that, when the seal is broken, the buyer automatically guarantees that only the number of users stated in the agreement will use the software. The assumption here is that breaking the seal is the same thing as signing an agreement (Figure 11–5).
- Building locks into the programs to prevent them from being copied or permitting only a limited number of backup copies to be made. Unfortunately for program developers, these locks are not unbreakable, and many organizations refuse to purchase copy-protected programs.

In the United States the **Copyright Act of 1976**, which went into effect January 1, 1978, specifically lists computer programs among the works protected from the moment of their creation—instead of from the time of their official registration. The standard notice includes the copyright symbol ©, the date of creation, and the name of the author or copyright owner—for example, © 1988 SSMP Software Co. The copyright notice usually appears on the computer monitor when the computer is turned on and the software is installed (Figure 11–6). Espionage incidents involving chip design led Congress to pass additional legislation, the Semiconductor Chip Protection Act of 1984, to prevent one company from reproducing the chip pattern of another. That act gives the original developer a 10-year period of exclusive rights.

The more effective software manufacturers became in thwarting copying, however, the more complaints they got from customers with legitimate needs for extra copies of a program. Some needed the copies for backup; others needed to load the program onto large-capacity disk drives. The result was that some customers, including the U.S. Department of Defense, quit buying copy-protected software. As a consequence, manufacturers began dropping the anticopy features of their software packages but, to compensate for the setback, stepped up their prosecution of those suspected of copying and selling the software. People familiar with the variety and cleverness of computer criminals agree that there needs to be

FIGURE 11–5
A software license agreement outlines the terms and conditions that a buyer automatically accepts upon opening a software package.

FIGURE 11–6
Copyright notices inform users that programs are protected by the Copyright Act of 1976 and cannot be duplicated.

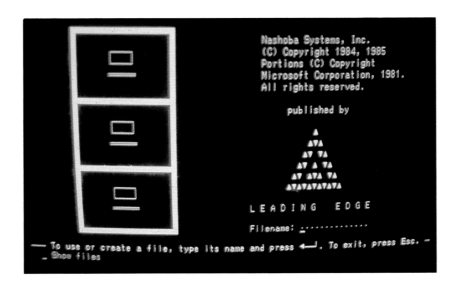

Impact of Information Systems and the Information Resource

more specific legislation. Present laws cannot be stretched to cover all of the criminal opportunities that a new technology creates.

State and federal lawmakers are finding computer-related questions a regular part of their legislative sessions. In 1986 the U.S. Congress passed the Computer Fraud and Abuse Act, giving the federal government jurisdiction over interstate computer crimes in the private sector. Among its several provisions, the act makes it a federal misdemeanor to use stolen passwords to defraud or gain entry into a "federal-interest computer" to inspect or obtain data. The act makes the accessing of such a computer a felony if (1) the aim is to steal by computer; (2) computer data are changed or destroyed; (3) the loss is at least $1,000; or (4) the data involved are medical records. It hardly requires a crystal ball to see that more legal issues are being raised and more legislation is being passed as the computer continues to imbed itself in our lives.

THE INFORMATION RESOURCE

Information is the lifeblood of corporate America. Without some form of prior knowledge, it would be impossible to make informed choices about what kind of product to make, how much product to make, how to sell the product, and on and on—the decisions that enable corporate America to decline or prosper. However, information has not always been recognized as a valuable resource. In fact, it is only in recent times that people have begun to recognize the true value of good information in determining the success of a firm. Information is now becoming one of the most critical elements in the survival of competitive businesses.

An interesting concept regarding the information resource is that it retains its value as it is consumed. Most resources decrease in value or at least change forms as they are utilized. Information is somewhat unique among resources in that it does not necessarily diminish either in economic value or in significance to a firm as it is consumed. In fact, if used in a reasonable manner, a firm's information may actually increase in value.

Information forms part of a cycle that helps to demonstrate the uniqueness of this valuable resource (Figure 11–7). As was noted earlier, information is derived from processed data. Processing data into information and then combining that information with other information in a useful form ultimately leads to knowledge. Knowledge is essential to make good decisions; the most valued decision makers, or managers, are those who are knowledgeable about the activities they are considering. Knowl-

FIGURE 11–7
The information-knowledge cycle.

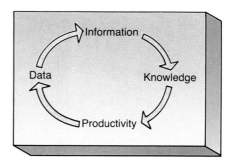

FIGURE 11–8

The relation of information to a firm's other resources.

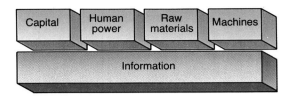

edge leads ultimately to productivity, and it is this productivity that makes our business economy flourish. Yet even in the midst of this productivity, or business activity, more data are generated, and the cycle begins again. In truth, it never ends.

If we reflect for a moment on this cycle and remember that information is nonconsumable, it becomes clear that as more and more data are processed, more and more information is being generated and made available for decision-making purposes. Thus, decision makers are acquiring an enormous amount of information from the historical as well as the daily activities of business firms. Better management of the information resource has become a necessity.

Initial use of the term **information resource management (IRM)** is generally attributed to John Diebold, who issued the Diebold Research Program report (No. 187545) of the Administration of Information Resources. Diebold used the term to explain that information was indeed an asset that was valuable and costly. He went further to explain that, like all other assets, information needed to be closely managed if a firm was to maximize its use of that resource.

The information resource is truly the bedrock on which other resource allocations can be made. It would be impossible for business management to decide how to allocate its human resource or its capital resource or its material or machinery resource without this foundation. Information appears to be the one resource that is required for the generation and maintenance of all others (Figure 11–8).

DATA AND INFORMATION FILTERS

Another area of information resource management that has become critically important in recent times is the use of data or information filtering. This term, which was recently coined in reference to information systems, implies that information resource managers must communicate relevant information to decision makers. Technology has enabled firms to maintain enormous quantities of data for fairly reasonable sums of money, leading to a problem that is becoming ever more severe—**information overload.**

Essentially, **information filtering** is the process of removing trivial or nonessential information from the total amount of information generated for a given decision (Figure 11–9). Data filtering can be done from within an information system through the judicious use of various techniques. However, these techniques must have been well thought out and well defined by the information resource manager. Many of the concepts of data filtering are still in their infancy because the problem of information overload has only recently become one of major consequence.

FIGURE 11-9
The process of information filtering.

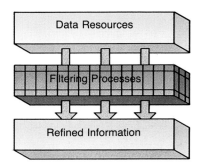

END-USER COMPUTING

Probably the most obvious area in information systems processing that has affected information resources and their distribution is the tremendous growth in end-user computing. This phenomenon, which is currently sweeping information areas, has had one of the most significant impacts on information systems during the past decade.

The advent and geometric growth of microcomputers and associated software applications in business has driven the push toward end-user computing. Most persons have the capability to use these computing systems with a modicum of effort. They like the immediacy of the results and the feeling of control over their own processing activities. The microcomputer may well be the most important personal productivity tool ever devised and used in business.

End-user computing supports the notion that the person who is responsible for the computing output should be the person who is going to utilize that output. In other words, the person who needs the information should be the person who obtains it from the system. Similarly, the end-user who is responsible for obtaining the correct output should be actively involved in the development of the system.

Although most information system managers accept and encourage the idea of end-user computing, many new problems are created by this emerging practice. End-users must be given the resources necessary to complete their own activities—the hardware and the software as well as extensive training, support from systems experts, and freedom to use the information resource. If end-users are to be successful, they must have unlimited access to the data files and/or information required to do the job. Certainly, this rapidly emerging and expanding area will impact IRM managers.

INFORMATION CENTERS

Closely associated with end-user computing and with the concept of information resource management is the information center. Information centers were first described by IBM as a way of distributing information system resources throughout a firm. An **information center** is to be used within a firm to distribute information, provide instruction in the use of the information system, distribute computing hardware, and provide information systems experts and other useful functions in a support role. Generally speaking, the information center is responsible for overseeing many different activities.

- Technical support—helping end-users with software, hardware, communications, and other technically related processes
- Education—training end-users on new software and hardware
- Systems consulting—helping end-users define and solve their systems problems
- Resource allocation—carrying out the functions of software, hardware, and information distribution
- Evaluation—looking at the possible applications of new products
- Marketing—promoting the services of the information center to the potential users

Information center services should be provided to all employees of a firm. The major function of an information center is to encourage the use of distributed processing and end-user computing throughout the firm. Clearly, these activities create an even greater need for good management of information resources.

THE CHIEF INFORMATION OFFICER

One of the most interesting factors affecting IRM is the emergence of a chief information officer. A **chief information officer (CIO)** is the designated individual responsible for the overall management of information and its delivery system. Thus, a CIO must see that all other members of an organization receive the information necessary for the adequate functioning of the business. With such awesome responsibilities, a CIO should be given a great deal of authority to direct and control the functions of the information resource area.

In many organizations the CIO is given a position not unlike that of either an executive vice president or at least a line vice president. Many people have suggested that a CIO, because of the importance of the position, must report directly to the chief executive officer of a firm. This relationship brings out the importance of information to the firm and also provides an efficient way of delivering information to all other functional areas within the firm.

Regardless of the CIO's position within a firm, the function is one of great importance. Not all firms, however, have readily embraced the concept of a CIO. Many traditional businesspersons believe that such a position gives undue power to a specific individual. Others have criticized the title of the position, believing that the function is not well defined or, again, represents too much individualized power.

FLATTENING OF THE ORGANIZATION

Another interesting phenomenon associated with information resource management is the general flattening of the management pyramid within many American firms. For years, corporations have functioned with multiple levels of managers, starting with the top, or strategic, management and arriving ultimately at the lower levels of operational management.

This management hierarchy served a necessary function until the time of an information processing group; that is, many levels of individuals were required to pass information up to or down from top management. In essence, these multiple levels of management were serving as information movers, data and information filters, and other roles currently seen in information systems. However, because of the automation now available and the sophistication of information resource management, the need for middle managers has diminished greatly in many firms in the last decade. Many believe that this trend will be expanded in the next decade and project a flat rather than a pyramidal organizational structure in corporate America in the next two decades.

If this trend is successful, information systems and information resource management must play a critical role in the functioning of these organizations. Corporate America may become a model of a few top managers directing, through the information system, the many specialists working under them. Only time will tell whether these predictions come true, but they are supported by the changing distribution of information and the high regard for the information resource within corporate America.

SUMMARY

Initially, information systems were used to support the operating and administrative functions of organizations. In recent years organizations have begun to recognize the strategic value of information systems. A strategic information system is one that changes the way an organization competes in the marketplace.

Along with computer-based information systems has come computer crime. Computer crimes, most often committed by an insider, are usually difficult to detect. Many of these crimes are not reported because businesses fear that the weaknesses in their computer-based information systems will be made public. Computer crime takes several forms: data manipulation; time bomb; computer virus; trap door; data stealing; time stealing; electronic eavesdropping; industrial espionage; and piracy.

The issue of privacy has emerged since the appearance of huge data banks and reported incidents of misuse of personal information. Some people think that computer-based information systems put our privacy at risk because (1) they permit the stockpiling of a lot of information in one place and (2) they allow users to access everything in the stockpile. Many are concerned that (1) the data may be incorrect; (2) the data may not be secure from illegal access; (3) there will be one giant data bank where all information about an individual is stored; (4) more information will be collected and kept than is needed; and (5) information may be exchanged among organizations.

The use of robots and other computerized devices in information systems in the workplace has workers and managers trying to find ways to handle displaced workers. Both are also debating the issue of electronic work monitoring. Managers say that they need this efficient measurement tool, but workers consider it an invasion of privacy.

Reports that VDT radiation causes disease have not yet been confirmed, but people are still worried about this and other health and safety concerns related to computer use. Further concerns about the use of computers include physical stress, mental stress, and worker isolation.

A firmly established code of computer ethics is needed in addition to current legislation to assure that data are handled in a way that will not deprive citizens of their right to privacy.

As information systems become more complex and intensive, managing the information resource becomes increasingly important. The role of information resource management is to provide a foundation for the sound maintenance and protection of this resource.

Many of the current information system trends have impacted information resource management, and vice versa. End-user computing has placed great demands on information being distributed in a timely and accurate fashion throughout a firm. The evolution of the CIO will continue to put great emphasis on the importance of good IRM practices. As firms become more dependent on information systems for proper functioning—as illustrated by flatter organizations—IRM becomes a mandate for proper administration.

MINICASE 11–1

Beth and Bill Bateson, computer programmers and accomplished home entertainers, recently developed a neat recipe program for use on their personal computer. They wrote the program for fun but later found it to be useful in their home entertainment activities. The recipe program provides 1500 recipes and can be accessed by ingredient, recipe name, or food category (e.g., dessert, main course, after-dinner drinks). Beth and Bill even added a feature so that the ingredients were automatically adjusted whenever the number of servings was changed. They shared the program with some friends in their bridge club and received many favorable comments.

The Batesons then decided that they should try to sell the program for $24.95, hoping not only to recoup their time investment, but also to make some extra money. Bill wants to sell the program through a popular entertainment magazine and has installed a time-bomb routine in the program to handle any customers who fail to make timely payments. Beth is not sure that the magazine is the best way to market the program or that the time-bomb routine is a good idea.

1. What other possible marketing channels could the Batesons use to sell their program?
2. Do you think the time-bomb routine is legal? Explain.
3. Should Beth and Bill give credit for the recipes, which came from friends, relatives, and magazines?

MINICASE 11-2

Midtown Savings and Loan Corporation is a small, locally owned institution. It competes with numerous larger, well-established savings and loans and banks in the area. Midtown's marketing effort has focused mainly on personal service and the fact that the company is locally owned and operated by long-time residents—"neighbors you can trust."

Recently, Midtown's management uncovered a scheme by several employees in the computer department to divert small amounts of interest income from the accounts of numerous patrons into their own accounts. Management is now faced with the decision of whether to publicly prosecute the employees or quietly dismiss them.

1. Discuss the reasons for and against publicly disclosing the vulnerability of the Midtown computer system.

2. Does Midtown's management have an ethical responsibility to inform its patrons of the crime? Explain.

Key Terms

chief information officer (CIO)

computer crime

computer ethics

computer virus

Copyright Act of 1976

data manipulation

data stealing

electronic eavesdropping

electronic work monitoring

end-user computing

Freedom of Information Act of 1970

industrial espionage

information center

information filtering

information overload

information resource management (IRM)

matching

piracy

privacy

Privacy Act of 1974

salami slicing

strategic information system

switching cost

time bomb

time stealing

trap door

Review Questions

1. Discuss several ways in which an information system can give an organization a strategic advantage over its competition.

2. Why is computer crime increasing?

3. Give three reasons that computer crime is difficult for management to detect and thus prevent.

4. Why are some companies reluctant to report incidents of computer crime?

5. Briefly describe several types of computer-related crimes.

6. Do you think time-bomb programs are fair? Why or why not?

7. What is the computer-crime called in which a computer is used to steal trade secrets?

8. How does the commission of crimes such as computer fraud and theft differ from the traditional crimes of fraud and theft?

9. What does privacy refer to in regard to computers and data?

10. How does increased use of computer-based information systems increase the danger to individual privacy?

11. Why does the concept of several agencies' matching files concern some people?

12. How can a computer monitor a worker's productivity?

13. Is electronic work monitoring fair? Why or why not?

14. What are some of the ethical questions relating to computers?

15. What landmark legislation in 1970 allowed citizens to find out which federal agencies were keeping records on them and to get copies of those records?

16. Of what significance is the Privacy Act of 1974?

17. How is the issue of who is responsible for computer mistakes being resolved?

18. How does U.S. copyright law protect computer software against piracy?

19. How does information differ from other resources?

20. How has end-user computing impacted IRM?

21. What are the activities of an information center? How may such a center impact IRM?

22. Why do flatter organizations require better information management?

Trends in Business Information Systems

OBJECTIVES

- Describe some of the new directions in technology that will affect computer-based information systems of the future
- Discuss some of the changes and trends occurring in our society as a result of the Information Revolution
- Discuss the major international competitors of the United States in the information technology arena
- Describe some of the trends occurring in information system use in business

OUTLINE

IMPACT ON MANAGEMENT PROBLEM SOLVING AND DECISION MAKING

NEW DIRECTIONS IN TECHNOLOGY
Artificial Intelligence | Josephson Junction | Parallel Processing | Chip Technology | Communication Technology | Optoelectronics | Software Innovations

THE INTERNATIONAL SCENE

SOCIETY'S RESPONSE TO THE INFORMATION REVOLUTION

TRENDS IN INFORMATION SYSTEM USE

Chapter 12

Management Profile: Karl J. Swanseen and Matthew Meldon
TRUMP PLAZA PULLS ROYAL FLUSH ON INFORMATION BOARDWALK

The name of the game in the cavernous, mirrored casino is staying ahead. In the cramped computer room and generic MIS offices off the corridors in Atlantic City's Trump Plaza Casino and Hotel, the same theory prevails.

MIS director Karl J. Swanseen, 34, is responsible for keeping Trump Plaza's customers happy and keeping the company's computer users content. Happy customers—perhaps gamblers whose credit lines, ranging from $500 to $1 million, are approved within minutes or casual tourists whose check-in and check-out are trouble-free—are more likely to spend their gambling money where they get the best service. Swanseen's mandate is to give Trump Plaza computer users the hardware and software they need to get their jobs done and ultimately to keep customers happy.

The relatively low competition for data-processing jobs in Atlantic City permitted the energetic Swanseen to advance from being a computer operator at a local hospital 11 years ago to his current position. The same situation afforded college dropout, former parking lot attendant, and self-taught personal-computer guru Matthew Meldon the opportunity to climb the ranks in the city casinos to become the microcomputer manager at Trump Plaza at the age of 27.

For Swanseen one way to retain employees such as Meldon is by giving the talented workers what they want: "Staying state-of-the-art is one way to draw the best talent and keep the talent that you have." The MIS strategy downplays technological gambles in favor of cautious spending on proven technologies, Meldon says. The local competition is tough because most of the casinos are working on similar systems, so gaining the edge

by using computers more effectively than the others is important, he adds.

One way Meldon sees the Plaza using technology to gain an edge is through its credit-card-like Trump Card system, which allows gamblers at approximately 50 percent of the casino's slot machines to receive credit toward meals and rooms, Meldon says. A computer is also used to handle the complex schedules of casino dealers, who work 9-hour stints with 20-minute breaks.

For in-house security, Plaza employees are issued cards that act as time cards for hourly wage employees; grant admittance to the cafeteria, where each employee receives free meals; and allow controlled access to various parts of the building. An employee holds the card in front of a beam of light, which allows or denies access to an area. If granted, the access is automatically recorded with the employee's identification number on a printout in the computer room.

Another Trump Plaza challenge is to keep people coming back. "Direct marketing seems to be the most effective way to reach people today, and it is a big issue for us," Swanseen says. "We have a half million people on our international database, so we try to establish a rapport with them." Direct mailing for Trump events is coordinated according to the types of players they are most likely to attract. The system tracks such players by colors, which correspond to the chips they typically shuffle across the felt-covered gaming tables.

Adapted from "Karl J. Swanseen, Matthew Meldon: Trump Plaza Pulls Royal Flush on Information Boardwalk" by Alan J. Ryan. Copyright 1988 by CW Publishing Inc., Framingham, MA 01701. Reprinted from *Computerworld*, Nov. 7, 1988.

Some people suggest that the computer advances of the last 40 years are only the beginning—that even more dramatic breakthroughs in electronics, computers, and information systems are looming on the horizon.

About 100 years ago the United States had progressed from an agricultural society/economy to an industrial one. The Industrial Revolution, centered on the steam engine and similar technologies, had resulted in a dramatic change in methods of factory production, which led to an urbanization of population patterns and major changes in American life-styles.

Now, according to the experts who study trends, we are seeing an Information Revolution, one that also affects economic and societal patterns. Starting in about 1947 with the ENIAC (one of the first general-purpose, electronic digital computers), the United States began to experience a tremendous increase in its ability to collect and store information; and Americans began to develop new technologies and information systems to collect, manipulate, and communicate that information.

Some people claim that the revolution is actually over. They say that the most important discoveries have been made—computers and communication technology—and that we are now in a stage of evolving or refining those technologies and adjusting to the changes they have brought. Regardless of the revolution, we are still clearly in the midst of the Information Age, living in an information-centered economy with all its rewards and problems.

Although some changes have occurred relatively fast, progress has been very slow in giving computers true intelligence, and no major breakthrough, or intelligence revolution, has yet occurred. This chapter looks at some of the areas to watch closely and at some of the forecasts for the future that will affect business information systems.

IMPACT ON MANAGEMENT PROBLEM SOLVING AND DECISION MAKING

Managers of the future must be aware of improvements and developments in technology. Many, more mature and established managers are untrained in and afraid of new technologies. But they are being replaced every day. Managers of the future will want to use information technology to provide significant improvement in strategic advantage and increased efficiency in problem solving and decision making for their organizations. As the competitive nature of business increases, information technology will provide advantages more quickly and less expensively. Failure to utilize the new technologies will grant the competitive edge to the competition.

NEW DIRECTIONS IN TECHNOLOGY

The discovery and harnessing of electricity, coupled with the development of vacuum tubes, brought us to the first generation of computers. Then, semiconductors (transistors) brought in the second generation. Integrated circuits, containing thousands of switches on one chip, were the key to the third generation. Microscopic-sized circuits on a chip (LSI and VLSI) were the elements of the fourth generation. Each generation gave us greater capabilities to process and store information. Now, scientists are looking for the technological breakthrough to propel us into the fifth generation of computers, which many people believe will be marked by the development of artificial intelligence.

Currently, scientific research is being conducted on several fronts, all with the purpose of (1) increasing the speed, memory, and power of computers; (2) teaching them to think like humans; (3) making them easier to use; and (4) finding practical applications for existing technology. Advances in technology will eventually result in new uses for information systems. Astute managers will keep abreast of these advances so that their organizations' information systems can benefit.

Artificial Intelligence

It may seem that no frontiers are left. After all, computers are inexpensive and are quickly becoming available to almost everyone in the United States who wants to use them. Computers can calculate many times faster than humans; computerized robots can work longer hours; and data banks can remember much more data than the human mind. Most experts think that the next breakthrough will be **artificial intelligence (AI)**—the ability of machines to think and reason like humans—which, futurists predict, will change the way we use computers and information systems. What it will take to accomplish this technological leap is more computer speed, more power, and more memory than ever before in order to accommodate the sophisticated programming that AI requires.

Although it started in the mid-1950s, research in artificial intelligence is still in the early stages of development, and progress is slow. Several specific areas of artificial intelligence are apt to have the greatest impact on information systems in the near future.

Expert Systems. Expert systems (discussed in Chapter 7) are software programs that store the knowledge of human experts and are then used as consultants in particular fields—for example, to help doctors diagnose illnesses or service/repair engineers determine equipment malfunctioning (Figure 12−1). Most of these systems do not come close to replacing human experts and are not considered by most AI experts to be true artificial intelligence. As technological advancements continue in both hardware and software design, expert systems will continue to improve their capabilities and impact on the business environment.

Robotics. Robotics is concerned with the design, construction, and operation of robots. Robots are still used mainly for simple, repetitive tasks on factory assembly lines. However, they have become sophisticated enough for important and dangerous jobs, such as bomb disposal, ocean exploration, outer-space probes, coal mine excavation, and cleanup of chemical or nuclear accidents. Denning Mobile Robotics in Woburn, Massachusetts, makes robots that function as prison guards. These 4-foot-tall robots detect human movement with sensors. If a prisoner is detected in an unauthorized area, the robot alerts authorities and tells the prisoner to return to the proper cell.

FIGURE 12–1
Honeywell service people use expert systems to maintain industrial and computer equipment. These conversational programs are important in diagnostics, professional assistance, emergency management, and other uses. (Courtesy of Honeywell)

MIT, Stanford University, and Carnegie-Mellon University are among several institutions and private companies that are heavily involved in robotics research. They are (1) making robots intelligent by using the latest in AI research (i.e., giving them the ability to make decisions); (2) giving them highly sensitive tactile capabilities; (3) providing them with a capacity to see in great detail; and (4) designing them with dependable stabilizing systems. As robots fully acquire these capabilities, they will begin to play a larger role in the information systems of many organizations.

Natural Language Processing. Finding ways to communicate with the computer as one would with a colleague depends not only on the right hardware and an immense primary memory, but also on sophisticated software in the form of a natural language processor. **Natural language processing** denotes a computer ability to understand and translate natural, everyday language. Many people consider natural language processing to be the fifth generation of programming languages. Researchers have been trying for more than 40 years to make machines that recognize and process natural language, but they have had only limited success. Even a simple word like *on* creates problems: a book can be *on* business computers, *on* the table, *on* fire, or *on* the bestseller list. Humans can detect the specific changes in meaning, but such understanding is difficult for today's software programs.

The development of this capability may one day make information systems as easy, understandable, and convenient to use as the telephone. Future systems using natural language processing software will be able to understand input in any human language and perhaps translate it into any other. This capability should greatly enhance the cooperation and exchange of information among organizations and governments of different nations.

Voice Recognition. Most systems with voice recognition capability recognize only a few words. The computer must first be trained to recognize the user's voice; then it will accept data or instructions spoken into the computer microphone. However, the speaker must pause after each word. And there are other difficulties: (1) many words sound like other words; (2) different people pronounce the same word differently; (3) one word can have multiple meanings; and (4) the tone in which something is said may carry more meaning than the actual words do. Any programming that improves on these limiting factors will have to be able to interpret all of the characteristics that make up conversation, such as inflection, sentence structure, and speed.

Kurzweil's VoiceWriter and IBM's Talkwriter are current devices that transform human speech into printed text. Voice recognition capability may ultimately be the method of giving computers instructions or robots commands. In addition, computers that can recognize and react properly to the human voice will make information systems and other computerized applications accessible to people who can't enter data in traditional ways or who require both hands to accomplish a task simultaneously.

Voice Synthesis. Machines that talk—that is, have the capability of voice synthesis and respond to an inquiry in a simulated human voice—are not new. Banking and retail food industries have long incorporated limited voice synthesis into portions of their information systems. You may have heard a computerized bank teller give your account balance in a human-like voice, or you may have witnessed talking cash registers, soft drink machines, or automobiles.

A typical audio-response system speaks fewer than 200 words and is limited in its ability to combine them into sentences. As sophisticated as these devices now seem, they are primitive compared to what inventors visualize. The machines that Apple Computer is working on will speak while doing other tasks. They will read numbers aloud as they are entered into an electronic spreadsheet or repeat words as you type them. This capability will help individuals who are visually impaired access and use information systems.

Computer Vision. Scientists hope to develop computers that will process and interpret light waves just as the human brain does. Such a system would use scanning devices to sense and interpret objects, graphics, and text-character shapes. This ability could be used to guide robots in their movement and selection of objects. It would also allow a computer to see as humans do and to read and interpret text in almost any format, including handwriting.

Josephson Junction

The **Josephson junction**, developed by Brian Josephson of the University of Cambridge, is a very fast electronic switch. Its key feature is that it works at low temperatures—near absolute zero—where there is little resistance to electricity. With a lack of resistance on and off switching operations can occur about 1,000 times faster than they can with silicon transistors.

This technology has been perfected slowly, but in 1986 Hypres revealed the world's first commercial system using the Josephson junctions. One of the earlier problems in developing the technology had been that the chips had to be immersed in liquid helium to achieve the low temperatures needed for superconductivity. **Superconductivity** refers to the flow of electricity through certain materials with no resistance. Hypres found that it could simply spray liquid helium on just one corner, where all the logic circuits are located, rather than totally immersing the circuitry.

The search is continuing for elements that offer superconductivity at higher temperatures. Finding a low-cost, practical way to achieve superconductivity could eventually lead to faster, more powerful computers and thus to new ways of using them in information systems.

Parallel Processing

Although progress is slow in the search for significantly increased computer speed and power, one technique looks promising—**parallel processing**. This technology links many processors, allowing them to process volumes of data simultaneously.

Since von Neumann revealed his principles of computer design in 1945, all stored-program computers have been serial computers; that is, they access and execute only one instruction at a time. A computer using parallel processing accesses several instructions at once and works on them at the same time, using multiple CPUs. Parallel processing differs from multiprocessing, in which several programs can run at the same time, but each on a separate processor. Parallel processing assigns different portions of a single program to various processors. When programs run concurrently, parts of different programs share the same processor (Figure 12-2).

Several companies are working on parallel-processing computers. Thinking Machines Corporation has a version called the Connection Machine 2; it holds 64,000 silicon chip processors to simulate the brain's 40 million processing cells. The Cray-2, released in 1986 by Cray Research, also uses this technology to some degree. It is believed that someday, by using many millions of processors all communicating with each other, a computer will come close to simulating human thought processes. For now, even though these complex computers are being built, it will be some

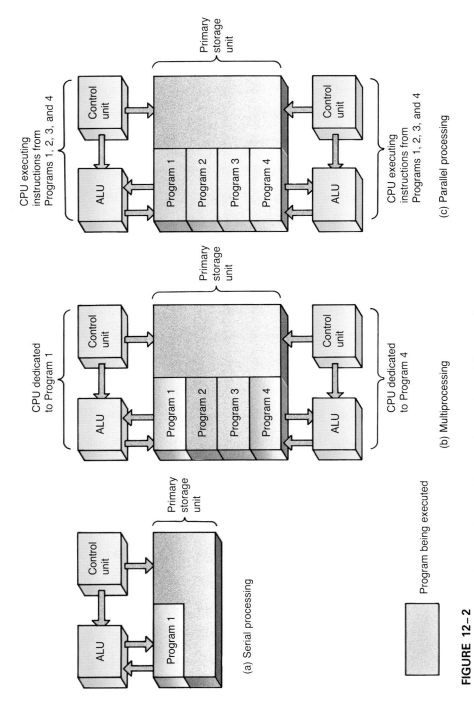

FIGURE 12-2

A comparison of serial processing, multiprocessing, and parallel processing.

(a) Serial processing

Control unit

ALU

Program 1

Primary storage unit

(b) Multiprocessing

Control unit

ALU

CPU dedicated to Program 1

Program 1

Program 2

Program 3

Program 4

Primary storage unit

Control unit

ALU

CPU dedicated to Program 4

(c) Parallel processing

Control unit

ALU

CPU executing instructions from Programs 1, 2, 3, and 4

Program 1

Program 2

Program 3

Program 4

Primary storage unit

Control unit

ALU

CPU executing instructions from Programs 1, 2, 3, and 4

Program being executed

time before they are perfected and widely used. Early users will have to spend a lot of time developing new programs and new ways to use the many processors.

Chip Technology

Some experts think that the secret to the next generation of computers lies in new chip designs to increase speed, power, and memory. Since the first silicon chip was produced, improvements in chip technology have occurred at a tremendous pace, and each improvement has squeezed more circuitry into smaller spaces.

Building so many circuits and packing them so densely onto a chip have brought a new set of problems, however. First of all, tremendous heat is generated when a chip is in use—enough to actually burn out the chip. Thus, large computers require special cooling systems, and even microcomputers need built-in fans to cool them. Since the heat is generated by a chip's resistance to the flow of electricity, finding a practical superconductor material from which to make chips might eventually solve this problem.

Another problem is that the circuits on these tiny chips are so small that the slightest particle of a foreign substance (e.g., a bit of dust) left on the circuit during its manufacture ruins the chip. And faulty connections are also a major problem. Several chips are placed on a ceramic or metal cartridge with tiny gold wires connecting the chips to pins on the cartridge. In turn, the cartridge is connected to a circuit board, and in that linkage a faulty connection can occur. In addition, because circuits are packed so tightly onto chips, sometimes there is cross talk, a condition in which one circuit picks up signals from another nearby circuit.

Much of the current research and experimentation is aimed at finding remedies for these problems. A variety of solutions are being considered.

Smaller Features. The circuits on a chip are called its features. A chip's speed and power are determined by how much etched-in circuitry is on the chip and how closely it is packed. There can be more circuitry on a chip if it is tightly packed; and the smaller the features, the more densely they can be packed. Some scientists are experimenting with ways to decrease the width of the features. Researchers at Sub-Micron Structures Laboratory at MIT are exploring methods to create features 1/10 of a micron wide—so thin that a human hair would cover 500 of them.

Larger Chips. Since the first chip was made, scientists have been building miniature chips to save space and make computers smaller. They have refined the process to the point that a chip is now less than 1/3 of an inch square and is very densely packed with circuitry. The only way to get any more circuitry on chips is to make the features smaller, the chips larger, or both.

A large chip appears to be a step backward in technology. However, it is actually more difficult to build a large chip because the flaw rate is increased. In any chip-making process the most minute manufacturing flaw—a speck of dust or a flake of skin—renders the entire chip useless. Even with the sterile labs, called clean rooms, in which chips are made, a large percentage of them are unusable (Figure 12–3). Therefore, making a larger chip presents a greater chance of contamination.

Several U.S. companies, including TRW and Motorola, are experimenting with **superchips**—larger chips with smaller features—with support from a $1 billion Defense Department program called VHSIC (Very High Speed Integrated Circuits). This kind of chip will be essential wherever data from various sensors must be processed almost instantaneously, that is, in real-time processing. The Defense Department plans to use these powerful chips in complex weapons systems being designed. For example, they could be used in space-based computers that might some day control antimissile weapons.

TRW's new superchip will perform the work of more than 10,000 ordinary chips. The product is a 1.4-inch-square, paper-thin chip, which has not gone into mass production yet and may not be available commercially until sometime in the 1990s.

New Superconducting Materials. Although silicon is the foundation of current chip technology, scientists continue to look for materials to replace silicon as the film of conducting material used in chips. They are looking for a material that offers conductivity at the speed of light and one that is also feasible to produce. It seems that there just might be a substance better than silicon for conductivity.

One compound under consideration, **gallium arsenide**, is made by combining arsenic and gallium. Although not perfected, gallium-arsenide elements have been used for more than 10 years on a small scale in applications where silicon is too slow, as in transistors and small circuits in high-frequency microwave radio and satellite communication systems and

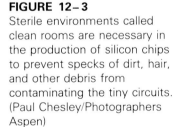

FIGURE 12–3
Sterile environments called clean rooms are necessary in the production of silicon chips to prevent specks of dirt, hair, and other debris from contaminating the tiny circuits. (Paul Chesley/Photographers Aspen)

in some satellite-dish antennas and radar detectors. In the future, gallium arsenide will probably compete with silicon in data-processing and opto-electronics applications. However, implementation of the gallium-arsenide chip will be gradual because its components are expensive to acquire and manufacture and because its technology is behind silicon technology by a few years.

Other materials being considered as superconductors are semiconducting oxides, basically ceramics, which are made from inexpensive elements, such as calcium and lutetium. Because ceramic oxides can become superconductors at high temperatures, they would not have to be cooled. They are also easily and inexpensively manufactured. These oxides could be used as a thin coating that would form the foundation of computer circuits instead of silicon. The main property of these superconductors is that they can conduct electricity with no power lost to resistance.

Another approach mixed methane and hydrogen in a simple and inexpensive process and produced a thin, synthetic diamond coating that could be used on chips as a base for circuitry. The Soviets discovered this technique more than 10 years ago, but it is just now being applied in the United States.

Biochips. Many experts think that chips with circuits made from living matter, **biochips**, and a molecular computer will be the technology that breaks through to the fifth generation of computers and to artificial intelligence. Some scientists are using biomolecular technology to develop a biochip. They think that eventually they will be able to grow tiny circuits from the proteins and enzymes of living material. The circuits would use oxygen and send signals similar to those sent and received by the human brain.

Of course, the molecular computer has not been built yet, but the model for it is the human brain. Perhaps these biochips, because they are living, might be connected to the cells (neurons) in the brain to replace damaged cells. Scientists are looking at implanted biochips as a possible way to restore sight to blind people.

Communication Technology

Telecommunications has sometimes been called the backbone of the Information Age. It has been the largest growth area in high technology during the past few years and is expected to continue to grow. Highlight 12–1 looks at how automakers are using satellite communications to gain a competitive edge. Because of the demand for this technology, futurists predict these trends:

- We'll see more use of telecommunication and information networks.
- Eventually all communication will be digital transmission.
- The number of communication satellites in orbit will continue to increase.

Satellite Communications Help Automakers Gain Competitive Edge

Automakers are beginning to incorporate satellite communication technologies to gain a competitive edge. With this technology automakers are able to provide their dealers with up-to-date customer records, information about the latest service offering, pricing changes, and other important data. Chrysler Corporation and Toyota Motor Corporation are both using very-small-aperture terminal (VSAT) dishes from Hughes Aircraft Company in a satellite network that links them to their dealers.

These automakers plan to use the system's data and video capabilities to offer customers and dealers services not found in most of the auto industry. For example, a customer's records are currently available only from the seller. However, by using a national database and a satellite communication system, an automaker is able to supply to any dealership on-line information about a customer's car, including its complete maintenance history. In addition, inventory information for both cars and parts can be transmitted. And the video capabilities of the system allow an automaker to keep its dealers up-to-date with live broadcasts from top management, technical service information, and parts announcements.

The drive behind this system is an improvement in customer service. Automakers, especially those in the high-end markets, see service as one way in which a manufacturer can differentiate itself from the competition. Toyota's system links together the dealers for its new Lexus LS400 luxury sedan and its main office in Torrance, California. The network includes a hub satellite station and a video broadcasting studio at company headquarters. Each dealer is equipped with a VSAT satellite dish; the hardware needed for the network and the satellite are provided by Hughes Network Systems in Germantown, Maryland. In addition, each of the dealers (the network nodes) is equipped with an IBM Application System/400 computer to handle computing needs. The company hopes that improved customer service will provide a strategic advantage over the competition.

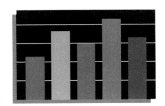

- There will be both more use of fiber optics as it becomes cheaper and a phasing out of wire cable in phone systems.
- Gallium arsenide will be used not only in computers, but also in telecommunication networks because it can handle both electronic and light signals.
- The number of electronic funds transfer (EFT) transactions in banking and other business applications will increase.
- The type of telephone in use today will merge with the computer and other communication technology into a new device for communication.

Optoelectronics

Optoelectronics, the combination of electronics and optics, may eventually become the basis of information technology. When the electron is united with the photon (a particle of light), greater efficiency is possible in communication and in data processing than electronics can achieve alone. Thus far, this technology has been used mainly for communication. And fiber optics, the communication channel for the photon, will continue to be improved because this type of channel has the tremendous benefit of both speed and clarity of signal. Optical communication networks are already in place around the country. According to some scientists, when this technology is perfected, a single fiber may be able to handle all of the world's telephone calls.

Scientists in the physics department of Heriot-Watt University in Edinburgh, Scotland, are conducting research to bring optics technology inside the computer. Their efforts are focused on circuits that process data with laser beams instead of electronics. Optical computers will use chips that combine electronic data processing with photonic switching and transmission. In the United States, Bell Labs has built the first optical counterpart of the transistor and has thus brought us just a little closer to the day of the optical computer. An optical computer should be able to operate 1,000 times faster than an electronic one.

Software Innovations

Software development has always lagged behind hardware technology. Powerful computers already exist, but they are not always used to their potential because the software doesn't exist for them yet. Software engineers and developers are working in several areas, and changes are expected in the next few years.

- Software will be more versatile and easier to use. Many programs are very difficult to use, and some require extensive study of the documentation. Future software will be easier to install in the computer and will need fewer commands to use. For very sophisticated programs the program itself will teach the user the skills needed to operate it.
- More application software will be available. Designers are reluctant to create software for a new machine that may not stay in the marketplace. Some supercomputers mentioned earlier do not yet have software that takes advantage of their power. When the Compaq 80386 microcomputer entered the marketplace in 1986, software developers had not had enough time to design programs to take advantage of the powerful 32-bit microprocessor. Although users could run existing IBM PC and compatible software on it, little was available that challenged its high speed, larger available memory for program use, and ability to complete several tasks at once.
- Another aim is to expand programming in natural languages.

- Researchers are developing techniques to program **neural networks**, that is, programs that attempt to mimic the neural connections in the human brain.
- Developers are working to find ways to mathematically prove that programs are correct.
- They want to produce new types of applications and programs that can write other programs. New software solutions are continually being applied to the design and development of information systems. Products such as computer-aided software engineering (CASE) programs are being improved to help increase the accuracy and speed up the design of information systems.

THE INTERNATIONAL SCENE

Several countries are racing for the lead in high-tech development. It is generally agreed that the countries that lead in the development of the most sophisticated computers and information systems and have control over the Information Revolution and the electronics industry will have an economic and political edge on the rest of the world. Competition is so fierce that IBM brought action against China for misbranding Chinese-made computers with the IBM logo.

Several factors determine leadership in computer technology. Countries that are already in the lead can set goals to keep that lead. And much depends on the level of financial support the government and private industry are willing to put into research. The United States has always dominated advanced-computer technologies. Until 1983 all the world's supercomputers were American made. The United States has also been the leader in the innovation and design of microprocessors. Consequently, when Japan announced its $300 million Fifth Generation Project in 1982, the United States became concerned about losing its supremacy in the computer industry. Private industry and the U.S. Defense Department provided enormous funds for research in new computer architectures, software, and artificial intelligence. Although the United States still maintains the lead in the computer industry, which is the largest segment of the electronics industry, Japan is a formidable opponent.

Japan's ambitious Fifth Generation Project was a 10-year plan to develop a new computer, using a type of parallel processing and artificial intelligence, that would be radically different from then-current supercomputers. Japan's goal is to build a faster, more intelligent computer. Always the world leader in printers (with Epson and NEC), Japan is also at the front line in robotics, owning two-thirds of the world's robots. Japanese factories are the most automated in the world; Japan excels at manufacturing and leads in the development of gallium arsenide. Even though scientists in the United States brought forth the modern electronics age with the invention of the transistor, Japan put it to best use in consumer products. Japan's strength lies in its efficient manufacturing rather than its innovation and design. Japan is the leader in computer chip production and sales, but South Korea and Taiwan are close behind.

Western European countries lead in some areas of semiconductor technology. For example, West Germany was the first supplier of a line of components for transmitting data, voice, and video over the same communication channels. Holland leads the way in erasable optical storage technology. And both Great Britain and France are moving ahead in artificial intelligence research.

In Eastern Europe, the U.S.S.R. has launched a fifth-generation project, START, with plans to build a massive parallel-processing computer. Because of its scientists' traditional strength in mathematics and logic, the Soviet Union may make significant progress. In 1987 the Soviets announced the completion of a supercomputer and claim that it surpasses the capabilities of the other supercomputers (fewer than 200) operating in the rest of the world. The Soviet supercomputer, described by the Moscow Institute of Precise Machines and Computer Technology, contains 16 processors, uses the parallel-processing approach, and performs 10 billion operations per second. In comparison, the Cray-2, often considered to be the world's fastest supercomputer, has only 4 processors and performs 1.2 billion calculations per second.

Before the development of this supercomputer, it was generally agreed that the U.S.S.R. was about 10 years behind other high-tech countries in most areas of electronics and in software. The Soviets have not been innovators in electronics, but followers. The same is true of Bulgaria, Czechoslovakia, Hungary, Poland, Romania, and East Germany.

China has about 100 computer companies and is making a serious attempt to upgrade its 400,000 factories with automation. Personal computers are already playing a big role in education and industry. Because China buys as many personal computers as it can get, many American companies are moving into the Chinese market; both IBM and Apple have set up Chinese subsidiaries.

SOCIETY'S RESPONSE TO THE INFORMATION REVOLUTION

Because the Information Age is still in its infancy, it is not easy to predict all of its effects on our way of life. There has been unprecedented progress in medical research and diagnosis, education, sea and space exploration, and removal of human beings from dangerous or dull jobs. In addition, we have instant communications with the rest of the world. And computers have challenged and surpassed us in some intellectual games and technical skills, such as chess, mathematical computations, and some assembly-line work. Yet most of us view this technology as a contribution and a benefit to society, not as a threat.

Here are some predictions that forecasters are making for the next few years.

- Efforts will be made to find more practical uses for the technology that has already been developed. The technological advances made during the last 20 to 40 years have been overwhelming. In fact, they have exceeded our ability to adapt to them; some technologies that have been in existence for several years are just now being put to use. Many organizations are focusing on this situation as they try to adapt existing information system technology to improve their strategic positions in the marketplace.

- We will continue to move from a brawn to brains society as the Information Age progresses. Factories will become more automated, adding to our fears of unemployment. The nature of our work life and leisure time will change.

- Education will have to gear itself to training students in computer-assisted services, rather than teaching them physical or industrial skills. Traditional jobs will change or disappear, just as the office typing pool has. We can hope and plan for more interesting and challenging jobs to replace the ones that are lost.

- There will be an increase in the number of people telecommuting. These changes will have significant effects on day-care centers, public transportation, and office and parking lot design, as well as on many other institutions.

- The use of computer-based information systems in retail and service industries—such as shopping, banking, and EFT—will increase and move us closer toward a cashless society.

- The issues of computer crime, privacy, health and safety, and computer ethics will continue as major ethical and social concerns for at least the next few years. No major technology is ever introduced into a society without causing waves, and these issues are not going to be resolved quickly.

- In many ways the economies of nations have always been connected, and computers and information systems will help make the long-talked-about global village a distinct possibility. Because of computer and communication technology, worldwide communication (and the associated tightening of social bonds) is immediate.

- Thinking machines are a long way off, but concerns about their reality have been with us since the birth of science fiction. If, indeed, computers can be made to program, repair, and reproduce themselves, there will be upheavals in law, ethics, sociology, and all the sciences that deal with social relationships. At present, fears of computers taking over seem groundless. However, as computers gain more autonomy of operation and become more versatile, they can become a social menace in the wrong hands.

TRENDS IN INFORMATION SYSTEM USE

Continuing technological advances should result in cheaper and more powerful computers in the future, a trend that has characterized the development of the computer. Today's microcomputers have greater speed and power than the early mainframe computers and are significantly cheaper. Greater power will open up new uses, and cheaper prices will provide an incentive to develop those new uses. Because of the rapid advances in technology and the number of new computer products presented each year, a manager needs to stay abreast of changes so that informed decisions can be made about which new technologies to pursue and when to update.

Even though the power and use of personal computers continue to grow, mainframes are expected to remain the predominant computers for processing transactions in organizations. For large volumes of transaction data, mainframes still provide the best option in terms of processing speed and storage capacity.

Communication technologies will continue to improve and be applied to the communication of information to and from an organization's mainframe as well as among its various minicomputers and microcomputers. Microcomputer proliferation will increase the accessibility of information and will continue to fuel the movement toward end-user computing. Continuous developments, coupled with a move toward standards and a need or desire to connect information systems, will see a growing number of communication systems put into operation over the next decade.

Changes in productivity will result from information systems that are easy to use and able to supply needed information quickly and efficiently. The development of artificial intelligence and expert systems will influence the role of information systems in the future. As these technologies are perfected, they will change the way we interact with information systems and the kind of information they supply us with. For example, artificial intelligence may eventually let us use voice or handwritten text as the predominant means of inputting data into a computer. It may also allow expert systems to truly mimic a human expert's intuition, judgment, hunches, and all the rest.

In addition, organizations will begin to develop organization-wide information systems. That is, information systems will be planned and developed for the organization as a whole, rather than serving only specific functions within the organization. This integration of the various information systems will improve the overall performance and benefit of an information system to an organization. This emphasis can currently be seen in many manufacturing plants that have developed computer-integrated manufacturing (CIM) information systems.

As was mentioned earlier, organizations will also be expanding their strategic use of information systems. Not only will these information systems enhance existing business opportunities and provide a competitive edge, but in many cases the information systems themselves will become the business as organizations that are proficient in information systems market their skills and facilities to other organizations. The development and use of strategic information systems has become so important that many organizations are beginning to patent their systems. Highlight 12−2 examines this trend.

As corporation-wide and strategic information systems continue to increase in businesses, top managers will see a number of changes in their responsibilities. Managers in all areas will benefit from increased knowledge of information technologies. However, good management and organizational skills will also be of prime concern to information system managers. These individuals will have to be sure that system goals are in line with organizational goals, not just with individual department goals. Greater communication and cooperation will be necessary among all functional areas.

Patenting the Strategic Information System

This text has noted the importance of strategic information systems. Just how important they are becoming is witnessed by the fact that many organizations, especially in the financial services industry, are beginning to seek patents to protect their strategic information systems. In much the same way that computer vendors use patents to protect their hardware, organizations are finding that patents can prohibit other organizations from using a protected strategic information system for 17 years. This protection ensures a longer and more profitable life for strategic information systems.

The Advest Group, located in Hartford, Connecticut, is an example of one firm that has already patented a strategic information system. The company is a financial services firm that developed a system to move money from an investor's bank account to cover stock transactions. The service is called Bank Link and was granted U.S. Patent No. 4,694,397. According to Advest Group's vice president and director of MIS, the patent was sought to protect the competitive advantage of the system. In addition, because the system is used every day by the Advest Group, the company was concerned that someone else might patent this type of system first. Advest plans eventually to determine whether other firms are using the process and, if so, to charge them royalties. Some patent attorneys believe that we may be about to see an onslaught of patent applications for strategic information systems.

Expert systems are another popular system for which patent applications are being filed. U.S. Patent No. 4,736,294, for example, was issued to the Royal Bank of Canada in Toronto for an expert system that manages car loans. Other patents already received include U.S. Patent No. 4,346,442 to Merrill Lynch & Company in New York City for a securities brokerage cash management system; U.S. Patent No. 4,674,044, also to Merrill Lynch, for an automated securities trading system; and U.S. Patent No. 4,642,768 to Peter A. Roberts in New York City for an insurance investment program. These patents have not been unchallenged, however. For example, Paine Weber challenged the legality of Merrill Lynch's patent for a cash management system. The courts, however, upheld the patent.

This trend makes it clear that information systems management will need to work on securing patents and developing intelligence strategies that will enable them to find out which competitors are applying for patents. If aggressive moves are not taken, an organization may find itself paying royalties to a competitor in order to continue using an important strategic information system. And of course, those firms holding patents will need to find out who might be violating their patent rights.

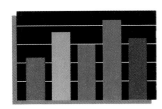

Managers will also be held responsible for criminal or unethical use of information or information systems. Top managers will need to set corporate policies to ensure that government regulations are followed. Top managers will also be responsible for evaluating the benefits of developing and using new information systems. And they will need to identify the risks to their organizations if these systems fail.

SUMMARY

Artificial intelligence will probably be the breakthrough to the fifth generation of computer technology. However, more computer power, speed, and memory are required before AI software can be developed. Expert systems, advanced robotics, voice synthesis, natural language processing, voice recognition, and computer vision are areas of artificial intelligence that are being incorporated into business information systems. More expert systems are being designed; robots will become more sophisticated, with humanlike qualities; ways to communicate with a computer are being refined and made easier; and computer vision, the ability to process and interpret light waves, is a very real goal.

Ways to improve computer power, speed, and memory might include the use of Josephson junctions, parallel processing, and new kinds of chips. Research is being conducted with superchips, biochips, chips made from smaller features, and chips made from gallium arsenide and other superconducting materials.

Some experts say that the largest growth area in high technology will remain telecommunications. Optoelectronics is a relatively new technology, but it has made fiber-optic communication networks a reality. In the future optical switching and data transmission inside a computer will be possible. Researchers are constantly searching for ways to improve the design process and performance of software used in information systems.

The United States and Japan are the key participants in the ongoing race for leadership in computer and information technology. Government's and private industry's financial support of research will be one of the driving factors in determining who will lead the way in future technological advances. Computers and information systems have had a tremendous impact on businesses and thus on society in general.

MINICASE 12–1

As the senior vice president of information systems, you have promoted and backed the use of computer-based information systems throughout your entire organization. Information systems are now used in all aspects of the company's operations and at all levels of management. Because of your influence the organization has been quick to adopt new technologies. The foundation of the organization now rests on computer-based information systems and data communications technology. The CEO, although not against incorporating these new technologies, has asked you to come to a meeting to discuss the organization's current dependence on technology.

1. How would you address the CEO's concern that increased reliance on information systems has made the organization overly vulnerable to the failure of these systems?
2. Do you believe that it is important for organizations to invest in new technologies quickly? Why or why not?

MINICASE 12-2

Because of heavy competition in the marketplace, Tower Industries, which manufactures industrial machinery, needs to find ways to reduce costs and improve quality. The company's current facility is not automated. Many of the parts that Tower manufactures must be made to very high tolerances. Lately, some parts have been experiencing microfractures, which have caused them to fail quickly. These flaws were not visible to human inspectors. Management would like to increase the efficiency of the design and manufacturing processes as well as improve quality by better identifying minute flaws in various parts before they are assembled.

1. What information system technologies might you suggest to help management accomplish its goals?
2. What human factors must management be concerned with if various processes at the plant are automated?

Key Terms

artificial intelligence (AI)
biochip
gallium arsenide
Josephson junction
natural language processing
neural networks

optoelectronics
parallel processing
robotics
superchip
superconductivity

Review Questions

1. What do some people think will be the breakthrough that will propel computer technology into a fifth generation?
2. What does the phrase *artificial intelligence* imply in reference to computers?
3. What are the six areas of AI research that will probably have the greatest impact on information systems in the near future?
4. Describe four ways in which scientists in robotics research are trying to improve robots.
5. Describe a business application that could be aided with natural language processing.
6. What might be the advantages in using natural language processing?
7. Why do computers have trouble recognizing voice input?

8. Which area of artificial intelligence might ultimately be used to give robots and computers instructions or commands?

9. How can voice synthesis be used in information systems? Give an example.

10. What is computer vision, and how might it improve the use of computers and information systems?

11. What is the advantage of using Josephson junctions in computers?

12. What does the term *superconductivity* mean?

13. Describe the significance of parallel processing.

14. Name four improvements being considered in the production of chips.

15. Why would smaller circuits increase chip power?

16. Describe some of the problems of packing many circuits on a chip.

17. What characteristics of gallium arsenide make it better suited than silicon for use in chips designed for communications and optoelectronic applications?

18. What are biochips?

19. What are some of the changes or trends forecast in communication technology?

20. What is optoelectronics, and what advantages will its use in information systems have?

21. What are the implications of the statement that software development has always lagged behind hardware development?

22. Describe some trends in software development.

23. Describe some of the forecasts of major changes and trends in our society as a result of the Information Age.

24. Describe some of the trends in information system use.

APPLICATION MODULE
Marketing Information Systems

Marketing executives have long appreciated the value of information systems in developing, pricing, promoting, and distributing commercial products. Marketing information systems come in two varieties: (1) operational systems that use transaction processing data to support routine tasks and decisions and (2) analytical systems that use higher levels of intelligence or information to support long-range and strategic decisions.

OPERATIONAL MARKETING INFORMATION SYSTEMS

The use of customer names and addresses for mass mailings is one example of the operational use of marketing information systems. No doubt you have seen the impressive-looking envelope that declares you the possible winner of thousands of dollars.

Similar efforts, but on a smaller scale, are directed daily by marketing specialists in a wide variety of firms across the country. Many companies even use their computer-controlled monthly billing service to include "specials" that can be ordered by mail when customer pay their bills. Other channels direct marketing efforts toward specific customer populations. Based on data captured by their order entry systems, some companies are using recorded messages to sell additional products and maintenance agreements over the telephone. Tremendous labor savings can be realized if sales are secured via recordings.

Transaction processing systems provide extensive operational data for the marketing function. Retail firms that have sales strategies other than cash-and-carry always have two files or databases of valuable marketing information (one of customers and one of orders) that support their order entry system. A sample of the information contained in these files can be seen in the customer invoice in Figure A, which shows a paper document. Newer technologies, such as scanning devices and electronic voice messaging, have given us faster and less error-prone methods of invoice preparation, but the essential data are the same. From data like that shown in Figure A, a firm can produce a variety of information and reports that suggest marketing strategies. For example, the following infor-

FIGURE A
A customer invoice.

mation can be identified for weekly, monthly, or annual time periods:

- which customers spend the most
- how much each customer spends on the average
- which products move slow/fast
- which salespersons sell the most/least
- which geographic areas purchase the most of a given product
- how current sales of a product compare to its last year's sales
- names and addresses for each customer

Output from this order entry system becomes input to the accounts receivable system, which provides customer credit and payment information that is valuable to the accounting, finance, and marketing functions. Likewise, the order entry information regarding the numbers and types of products or services sold gives a clear signal to the manufacturing function about how many units of what to produce and when. Thus, even basic transaction processing systems (TPSs) provide considerable decision making information for a firm's functional areas. Figure B shows the data-sharing relationships among several transaction processing systems that exist in most firms.

ANALYTICAL MARKETING INFORMATION SYSTEMS

Since almost all firms utilize order entry and other transaction processing systems, these systems, by themselves, don't provide a competitive advantage. To gain a competitive edge, a firm must have a better way of doing things, and the computer has been extremely valuable as a tool for marketing in a new and/or better way. The following examples tell how Metropolitan Life Insurance (MLI) and the retail industry have put the computer to work in analytical information systems to gain a competitive edge in marketing.

MLI's use of computer technology has had a definite impact on the company's marketing efforts. MLI's system maintains insurance policies and automatically processes claims and premiums much faster than was done by clerical methods. Moreover, it is common to find the sales staff equipped with lap-top computers that can custom-tailor personal insurance/financial planning information on the spot. No longer is it necessary for a salesperson to collect data from a potential client, mail them to the central office to be entered into a mainframe computer and analyzed, and finally receive a response the following week. Now, data can be analyzed while a client is present to answer any other questions, all in a single visit. Quicker analysis, thus, produces more, better, and quicker information for clients and results in an increased customer base.

The American retail industry has taken a tip from its customers, who have always tried to obtain faster service, and has capitalized on a textile and apparel industry idea to combat the intense competition of foreign imports. Point-of-sale (POS) register information can be translated into marketing and ordering data, and orders can then be electronically transmitted to suppliers. This new process is called electronic data interchange (EDI) and is responsible for reducing local inventories as well as ordering time. Arthur Andersen's Philip Dolden says that EDI will be the biggest hit in the retail industry since Cabbage Patch Kids. He claims that some retailers are experiencing average sales increases in the 20 to 40 percent range. So fast moving is the EDI effort that more than 25 percent of small firms (under $50 million in annual revenues) will be using the technology by 1991. The percentage of larger retail firms using EDI is predicted to be even higher. Revco, a 20,000 chain retail drug store, has been installing POS terminals in its various locations. Revco plans to use EDI for exchanging purchase order information also, and the company's MIS manager suggests

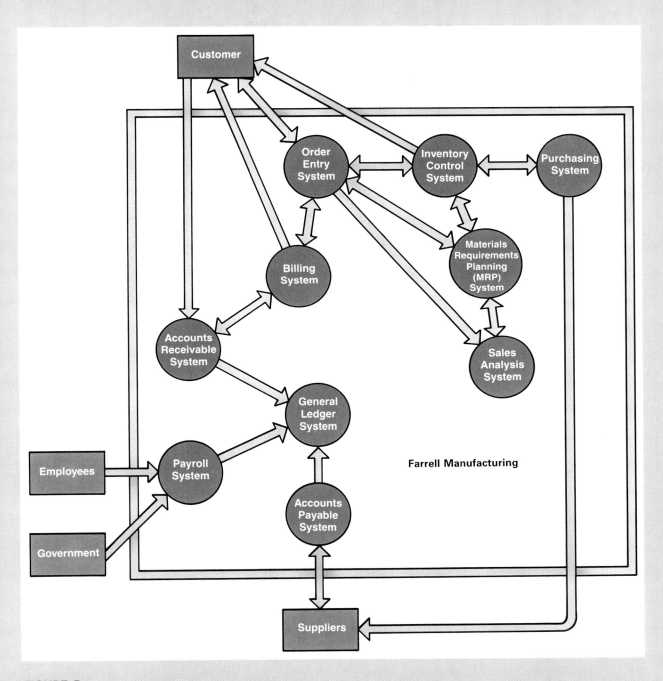

FIGURE B
Data sharing within business information systems.

at least two benefits—increased speed and reduced error rates.

MARKET SEGMENTATION

A market represents a group of people that can purchase particular products and services or are able to influence such purchases. Sellers can now segment markets to appeal to differences in consumer preferences and thereby increase sales. Coca Cola has at least six different Coke soft drink products because of recognized market segments.

Markets can be divided or segmented along several dimensions. Geographic, demographic, and behavioral variables form the basis of the majority of market segmentation strategies. Geographic segmentation involves cities, states, regions, climates, and so on and explains why snow skis aren't promoted in Florida. Human demographic variables—such as age, sex, race, family income, and religious preference—dictate differentiated strategies. Clearly, Grecian formula advertisements need to be directed toward older consumers. Behavioral segmentation is the most interesting because it is concerned with the personalities and life-styles of consumers. The wide array of automobiles, from small sports cars to large luxury cars, provides an example of products targeted toward market segments defined by personality and life-style.

To take advantage of market segmentation, marketing managers need information to make product, price, promotion, and place decisions. Internal information systems provide demographic variables for existing customers, but there is a whole world of potential customers to be attracted. Their demographic and life-style variables must be captured from personal interviews and externally produced market research data. The expense of capturing data for a large, geographically dispersed group of potential

consumers persuades many firms to purchase market research data. Once obtained, the data can be integrated into decision support systems (DSSs) to aid marketing managers in their decision making regarding segmented market strategies.

Campbell Soup's U.S. president, Herbert Baum, says that Campbell products are, or have been, in 99 percent of all American households. Those "umm umm good" Campbell kids are familiar to American consumers in all age brackets, but Campbell's is into more than soup. Some of their nonsoup products are V-8 vegetable juice, Prego spaghetti sauce, Franco-American canned products, Campbell's pork and beans, and Le-Menu and Swanson frozen food lines. Baum credits Campbell's strategic decentralization movement with responsibility for specifically targeted marketing efforts and products for different areas of the country. For example, Campbell distributes a recipe for quick jambalaya in the New Orleans district and, based on employee suggestions, successfully markets a low-cost enchilada frozen dinner in southern California. A computer-based marketing information system is used to evaluate the effectiveness of a particular product in a particular market. Data can be partially derived from the order entry system and sales staff reports but must be supplemented with external data, such as what the competition is doing, to become an analytical marketing information system, which can lead to decisions to expand, reduce, or eliminate particular products.

The Product Life Cycle

The concept of a product life cycle is similar to that of a system life cycle, described earlier. Of the four distinct stages—introduction, growth, maturity, and decline—the last three are determined by sales volume, which is higher in the growth and maturity stages. As with the system life cycle, a firm is likely to track the life cycle of several products, each introduced at a different time. Another complication is that the length of each stage differs among products. The growth stage of a new video game is less than a year, whereas the growth stage of a video camera may be several years. Analysis of the life cycle is important because marketing management has a defined set of strategies to promote and price products during each different stage. For example, low prices might be used in the decline phase to stretch out the market life of a fading product. Computer-supported marketing information systems can readily accommodate life cycle analysis, using unit and dollar sales data collected on products over time.

American Information Technologies (Ameritech). 1988. Annual report.
Baum, Herbert M. Speech. April 21, 1989.
Davis, Leila. 1989. Retailers go shopping for EDI. *Datamation* (March 1): 53–60.

Appendix
Structured Programming Concepts
The BASIC Programming Language

WHY YOU NEED TO KNOW ABOUT PROGRAMMING

You may have no intention of becoming a programmer or of programming your own software. You may be interested only in knowing how to use commercially available application programs, such as word-processing, database, or spreadsheet packages. Why then should you take the time to learn about programming concepts?

First of all, your basic knowledge of how a computer works and what it can do will increase. As your understanding increases, computers will become less threatening and more useful. Second, the chance that you will have to communicate with a programmer, directly or indirectly, is increasing as computers become more prevalent. Your understanding of a programmer's work and the information needed to do that work will help the two of you work more effectively together. And third, many application programs, particularly databases, incorporate fourth-generation languages (4GL) that can be easily used by nonprogrammers to take greater advantage of a program's power. Therefore, knowledge of the basic concepts of good program design and development can be beneficial even if you don't intend to do much traditional programming.

Qualities of a Good Program

A good program should have these characteristics:

- Correct and accurate
- Easy to understand
- Easy to maintain and update
- Efficient
- Reliable
- Flexible

A correct and accurate program will do without error what it was designed to do in accordance with the specifications laid out during program design. The program should be designed so that anyone who works with it finds its logic easy to understand. It should also be designed and documented in such a way that program maintenance and updating can be achieved with relative ease. In addition, the program should run efficiently by executing quickly and using computer resources, such as primary storage, conservatively. The reliability of a program is its ability to operate under unforeseen circumstances, such as invalid data entries. For example, if a program expects a yes or no response but a user types in a number, the program should recognize the error, inform the user that an invalid entry has been made, and indicate what is expected. Nonetheless, a flexible program operates with a wide range of legitimate input. For example, if a program requests a yes or no answer, it should accept any combination of capital and lowercase letters for the words *yes* and *no,* in addition to the single letters *Y, y, N,* and *n.*

STRUCTURED PROGRAMMING CONCEPTS

As uses for computers become more sophisticated, the software required to accomplish these tasks becomes more complicated. A method is needed to control the development of programs and assure their quality. Edsger Dijkstra, one of the major proponents of structured programming, thinks that, ultimately, programming will be tested mathematically rather than by trial and error. According to Dijkstra, the presence of bugs, or errors, may be merely annoying in many programming situations, such as fouled-up airline reservations; but in others, such as the launching and guidance of space flights, that presence may be a life-and-death matter. An example of such a situation occurred in 1981 when the first launching of a U.S. space shuttle was halted because software errors caused the shuttle's computers to fall out of synchronization.

Dijkstra and others think that traditional programming is sloppy in design. Commonly, such programming relies on specific GOTO commands, which tell the computer to go to another, sometimes distant, point in the program. The use of this command in extended programming results in enormous structural complexity and creates innumerable opportunities for errors. Structured programming is a step toward improving the design process testing to ensure that a program is error-free.

Need for Structured Programming

In the early days of computers, programming was more an art than a science, and developing a quality program was more a hit-or-miss proposition than a planned goal. Programmers were given a task to program and were left on their own to come up with a solution in any way they could.

Three major problems arose from this free-form method of programming: (1) long development time, (2) high maintenance costs, and (3) low quality software. Managers found that many software projects were taking too long to complete; they wanted to increase the productivity of programmers. In addition, software development costs were getting out of hand. As the computer age moved forward, hardware costs began to decrease, but software development costs, especially personnel costs, were rising sharply. Most of the money invested in a computer system was spent on software-related costs and, in particular, on maintaining software. Many organizations were spending more than 60 percent of their time repairing and enhancing systems that were already installed. And not only was the cost of developing, testing, and maintaining programs too high, but it was also continuing to increase. To avoid these high costs, program designs had to be right the first time.

Many of the programs were also of low quality; they were too complex and had poor documentation. As a result, they were difficult to test and maintain, and numerous errors went undetected. In many cases programmers also lost sight of user requirements; consequently, the programs did not meet user needs.

These problems forced people to search for solutions. The work of Edsger Dijkstra and others led to the development of the structured programming concept. **Structured programming** stresses the systematic design and management of the program development process. The purpose and overall goals of structured programming are to

Decrease development time by increasing programmer productivity and reducing the time to test and debug a program

Decrease maintenance costs by reducing errors and making programs easier to understand

Improve the quality of software by providing programs with fewer errors

Structured programming attempts to accomplish these goals by incorporating the following concepts:

Use of limited control structures (sequence, selection, and repetition)

Top-down design and use of modules

Management control

Control Structures

In the late 1960s two mathematicians, Corrado Bohm and Guiseppe Jacopini, proved that even the most complex program logic could be expressed with three control structures: sequence, selection, and repetition (also called looping or iteration). Edsger Dijkstra put forth this same theory in his article "Notes on Structured Programming." A control structure is a device in a programming language that determines the order of execution of program statements.

A **sequence control structure** executes statements one after another in a linear fashion, as illustrated in Figure 1. The **selection control structure** presents a number of processing options. The option chosen depends on the result of the decision criterion. Figure 2 depicts some variations of a selection control structure. A **repetition control structure** is used to execute an instruction(s) more than once without having it recoded. The two basic variations of this type of structure are DO WHILE and DO UNTIL. If the decision criterion, or condition, is placed before the statements, or instructions, to be repeated, then it is a DO WHILE loop, as illustrated in Figure 3. A DO UNTIL loop places the decision criterion at the end of the statements to be repeated, as shown in Figure 4. In this particular structure, statements are always executed at least once.

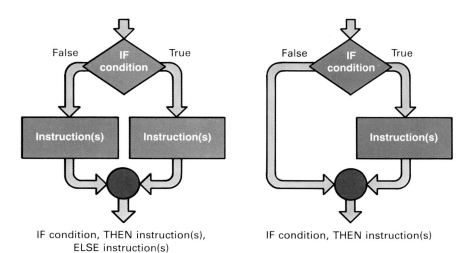

IF condition, THEN instruction(s),
ELSE instruction(s)

IF condition, THEN instruction(s)

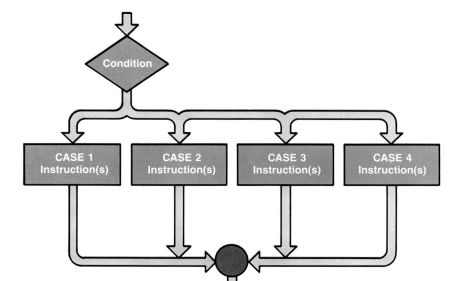

CASE condition: CASE 1, CASE 2, CASE 3, CASE 4

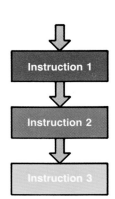

FIGURE 1
A sequence control structure.

FIGURE 2
Selection control structures.

A fourth type of control structure commonly used in early programs was the unconditional branch. In many programming languages this structure took the form of a GOTO statement. It allowed program execution to jump indiscriminately to other points in the program. Programs designed with several of these unconditional branches were very confusing and difficult to follow, thereby earning them the name spaghetti code. Avoid-

FIGURE 3
A DO WHILE control structure.

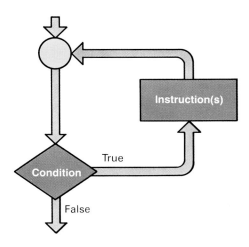

ance of unconditional branching was part of the first step toward a structured programming methodology.

Top-Down Design and Use of Modules

Structured programming also advocates a top-down approach to problem solving. Top-down design starts with the major functions involved in a problem and divides them into subfunctions until the problem has been divided as much as possible. Top-down design involves three major steps:

1. defining the output, input, and major processing steps required
2. step-by-step refining of the major processing steps
3. designing the algorithms

The first step involves three separate processes. First, the desired outputs are defined; then, the required inputs are determined; and finally, the major processing tasks are specified. In the second step each of the major processing tasks is broken down into smaller and smaller tasks until one unit is small enough to be programmed by an individual programmer in the required time frame. This approach forces an examination of all aspects of a problem on one level before considering the next level. A programmer is left with a small group, or **module,** of processing instructions that is easy to understand and code. Working from the top down (from the general to the specific) rather than from the bottom up avoids partial solutions that deal with only part of a problem.

In addition, a program broken into smaller modules is easier to read, test, and maintain. In structured programming, modules ensure these qualities with the following features:

- Has only one entrance and one exit
- Performs only one program function
- Returns control to the module from which it was received

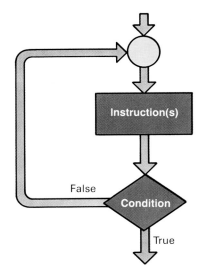

FIGURE 4
A DO UNTIL control structure.

FIGURE 5
Coding by level and by path.

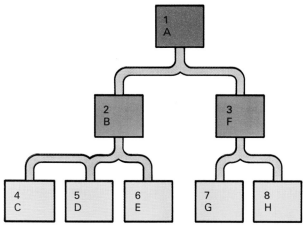

Coding by level: 1 2 3 4 5 6 7 8

Coding by path: A B C D E F G H

The third step in top-down design involves designing the algorithm for each module. An **algorithm** is the finite set of step-by-step instructions that solves a problem. The main module is considered first and development then moves down by level or by path. In programming by level, each complete level of modules is coded before the next lower level is considered. In Figure 5, coding by level would follow a numeric order. In programming by path, all modules along a path are coded in sequence before other paths are considered. In Figure 5, coding by path would follow an alphabetic order. Top-down design has often resulted in a lower error rate and shorter program development time.

Management Control

Management control is an essential part of structured programming. It prevents a project from being sidetracked, keeps it on schedule, and assures that user needs are being met. When many people are involved in the design and development of a large program, different ideas and methods surface. To avoid conflict, a **chief programmer team** is established, consisting of specialized personnel to design and develop the program. Although the type of specialists may vary depending on the project, a typical team might consist of the following:

- Chief programmer
- Assistant programmer
- Librarian
- Other specialists as needed

A chief programmer defines and assigns portions of program development to various team members and also takes responsibility for a project (Figure 6). The chief programmer reviews each member's work, coordi-

nates the integration of the work, and serves as liaison between management and the project. It is the chief programmer's responsibility to be sure that the appropriate personnel are on the team and to make changes in or additions to the team as needed.

The assistant programmer works directly with the chief programmer. Depending on the size of the project, there may be more than one assistant programmer. For very large projects separate teams of programmers are sometimes established. Each team might have a group leader who would report to an assistant programmer or directly to the chief programmer.

A librarian's responsibility is to maintain and make available the records of a project, such as program listings, the results of testing, and so on. Other specialists, such as systems analysts or financial analysts, may also be a part of a chief programmer team. The nature of each project determines their involvement. Thus, the makeup of a chief programmer team depends on the nature of the problem, in addition to management philosophy and cost factors.

One technique a chief programmer team may use before beginning to code a program is a **structured walk-through** with a systems analyst, user(s), and possibly other system personnel. With team members present, the systems analyst discusses, or walks through, the program design. The rationale is that errors may be caught and corrected before programming begins.

The Importance of Documentation

Documentation is the text or graphics that provide specific instructions about or records the purpose or function of a particular step or instruction in a program. Each step throughout the programming process should be documented. Sometimes, however, documentation is done as an after-thought rather than as an ongoing and integral part of a project. Approached belatedly, it can become an overwhelming burden of paperwork. If documentation guidelines are established and followed from the beginning of a project, the process takes less time and effort.

There are two good reasons to document the program development process. First, documentation leaves a clear record that enables someone else to understand what was done. Such a record is extremely important in a business environment because the person who originally designs or codes a program is not apt to be the same person who later corrects or modifies it. Second, documenting steps as they are developed forces a reexamination of the actions taken. Problems might be discovered early enough to avoid costly alterations later. However, for documentation to be of value, it must be clear and concise, and it must be available to those who need it. Many organizations maintain a library where copies of all documentation are accessible to authorized personnel.

Several types of documentation are kept during the course of program development and life.

- program specifications
- program description
- program design charts (flowcharts, pseudocode, and so on)
- description of testing done and errors found
- operator's manual (user's guide)
- maintenance record

Program specifications describe what a program is intended to accomplish; they help the programmer design the program. A program description details what the completed program actually does; it can be found in the programming code itself in addition to a separate document. Program design charts outline the specific steps used in the program to produce the desired results. The types of testing done and the data used, as well as the errors found, are typically recorded separately. Details on how to operate a program are presented in an operator's manual. Maintenance documentation records and explains in detail the changes made to a program. The type of documentation actually kept depends on each programming department's various requirements.

The concepts of structured programming and documentation are important to remember and follow when using any programming language, whether for business or personal use. A program that adheres to these concepts will be much easier to maintain and modify than one that doesn't. The remainder of this appendix introduces a particular programming language known as BASIC.

BASIC

BASIC stands for **B**eginner's **A**ll-Purpose **S**ymbolic **I**nstruction **C**ode. It was developed in the early 1960s at Dartmouth College by John G. Kemeny and Thomas E. Kurtz. The first version of BASIC was formally introduced in 1966. It was intended to be an easy-to-learn interactive language that could be used to teach beginners how to program. Initially designed to run in a time-sharing environment, BASIC's time-sharing, interactive nature made it ideal for teaching an inexperienced user because the results of a student's program were available almost immediately, thus providing positive feedback if the program worked or a timely chance for error correction if it did not.

BASIC gained popularity on minicomputers in the 1970s and was the first high-level language used on microcomputers. Today, almost all microcomputers have a version of BASIC available. Most of those versions use an interpreter, which converts one line at a time of BASIC code into machine language for the computer. Some BASICs use a compiler, which translates an entire program at a time into machine language. Although the compiler approach creates a smaller machine language program that executes faster, that approach can also make it more difficult for inexperienced users to create and debug a BASIC program. An interpreted BASIC program gives users immediate feedback on whether something they have just typed has the correct syntax. Because it is easier to use, this appendix will refer to an interpreted version of BASIC.

It is not possible to cover the many versions of BASIC in this supplement. Our reference version is Microsoft GWBASIC version 3.11. Also, it is not our purpose to teach the entire BASIC language. Instead, we cover only a basic subset of the language, but that subset is useful in illustrating some of the basic structures and concepts involved in any programming language.

STARTING BASIC

If you are using a hard disk with Microsoft GWBASIC or IBM BASIC stored in a directory, the steps shown here can be used to load the BASIC programming language. We will assume that the directory name is BASIC. If your directory name is different, substitute the appropriate name.

1. Be sure drive A does *not* contain a diskette.
2. Turn the computer on. MS-DOS is loaded.
3. Type **CD\BASIC** at the C prompt to make the directory BASIC the current directory.
4. Type the file name **BASIC** and press the enter key (IBM BASIC: type **BASICA** to load the full version of **BASIC**). (Note: On older-style keyboards the enter key may be labeled *Return*.)

If you are using a hard disk with Microsoft GWBASIC or IBM BASIC stored on a floppy diskette, the steps shown here can be used to load BASIC.

1. Be sure drive A does *not* contain a diskette.
2. Turn the computer on. MS-DOS is loaded.
3. Insert the GWBASIC diskette into drive A (IBM BASIC: Insert the diskette containing the BASIC and BASICA files into drive A).
4. Type **A:** at the C:> prompt and press the enter key. (Note: On older-style keyboards the enter key may be labeled *Return.)*

5. Type **BASIC** and press the enter key (IBM BASIC: type **BASICA** to load the full version of BASIC).

If you are using Microsoft GWBASIC or IBM BASIC with a system that has only two floppy-diskette drives, the steps that follow can be used to load BASIC.

1. Insert an MS-DOS diskette into drive A.
2. Turn on the computer. MS-DOS is loaded.
3. Remove the MS-DOS diskette from drive A.
4. Insert the GWBASIC diskette into drive A (IBM BASIC: Insert the diskette containing the BASIC and BASICA files into drive A).
5. Type **BASIC** and press the enter key (IBM BASIC: Type **BASICA** to load the full version of BASIC). (Note: On older-style keyboards the enter key may be labeled *Return*.)

An Ok prompt appears on the screen after BASIC is loaded (Figure 7); it indicates that BASIC is ready to accept commands. When you see the Ok prompt, you can begin to create, change, or run a BASIC program.

TYPES OF COMMANDS

BASIC includes two types of commands—programming statements and system commands. Programming statements make up a program; they direct the computer to perform the desired tasks. System commands direct the operating system to perform various operations on existing programs or programs currently being created. The BASIC programming statements

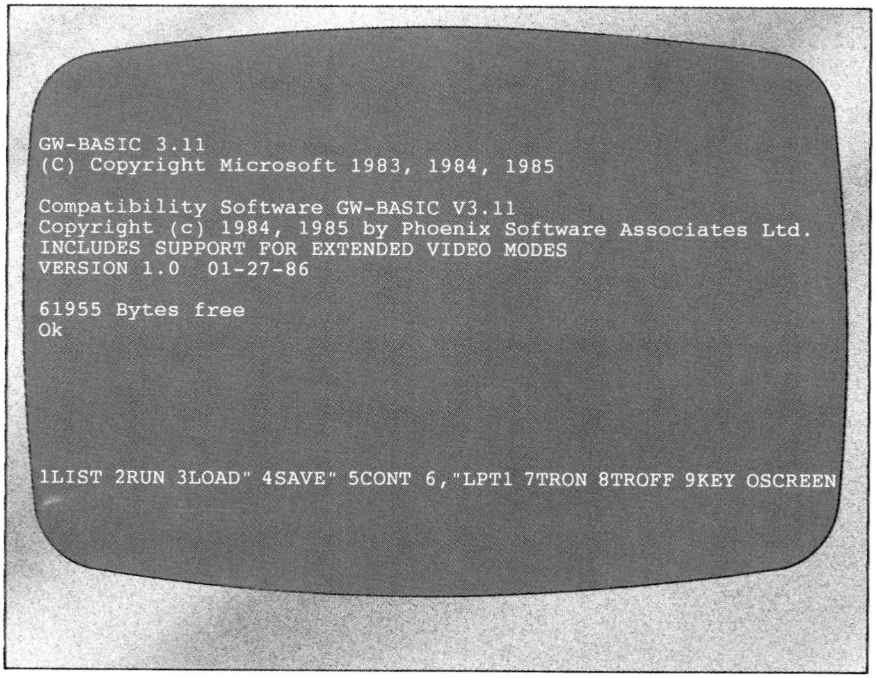

FIGURE 7
An Ok prompt indicates that BASIC is ready to accept commands.

```
GW-BASIC 3.11
(C) Copyright Microsoft 1983, 1984, 1985

Compatibility Software GW-BASIC V3.11
Copyright (c) 1984, 1985 by Phoenix Software Associates Ltd.
INCLUDES SUPPORT FOR EXTENDED VIDEO MODES
VERSION 1.0   01-27-86

61955 Bytes free
Ok




1LIST 2RUN 3LOAD" 4SAVE" 5CONT 6,"LPT1 7TRON 8TROFF 9KEY OSCREEN
```

that we will examine in this appendix are PRINT, LPRINT, LET, END, REM, INPUT, CLS, READ, DATA, RESTORE, FOR, NEXT, WHILE, WEND, IF . . . THEN, IF . . . THEN . . . ELSE, GOTO, GOSUB, ON . . . GOSUB, and RETURN. The BASIC system commands that we will examine are LIST, LLIST, RUN, SAVE, LOAD, NEW, DELETE, and RENUM.

MODES

BASIC has two modes—the command (direct) mode and the program (indirect) mode.

Command Mode

In the command mode programming statements and system commands are not preceded by a line number. The statements and commands are executed immediately after the enter key is pressed. BASIC system commands for handling files and displaying the contents of a program are usually executed in this mode.

Program Mode

When you precede a programming statement or a system command with a line number, BASIC automatically goes into a program (indirect) mode. In that mode programming statements and system commands that are preceded by a line number are stored in memory before being executed. To execute them, you must type the system command RUN and press the enter key. After they are executed, the program instructions stay in memory; they can be assigned a name and saved for later use.

BASIC PROGRAM LINES

A BASIC program line (also called a program instruction) always begins with a line number, which is used to indicate the order in which the program lines are stored in memory. In addition, a line number is used as a reference in branching and editing. Line numbers must be between 0 and 65529. They are typically followed by programming statements, although system commands can also be used in program lines. Programming statements and system commands are followed by any appropriate expressions, the maximum length of a program line in BASIC being 255 characters or spaces. The following examples illustrate typical program lines:

Line Numbers	Program Statements	Expressions
30	LET	X = 10
40	LET	Y = 100 * .06
100	PRINT	X + Y

BASIC'S CHARACTER SET AND RESERVED WORDS

The characters that can be used with BASIC include alphabetic characters (uppercase A to Z and lowercase a to z), numeric characters (0 to 9), and the special characters found in Table 1.

TABLE 1
BASIC's special characters.

Symbol	Name
	Blank
=	Equal sign or assignment symbol
+	Plus sign
−	Minus sign
*	Asterisk or multiplication symbol
/	Slash or division symbol
∧	Exponentiation symbol
(	Left parenthesis
)	Right parenthesis
%	Percent sign
#	Number (or pound) sign
$	Dollar sign
!	Exclamation point
,	Comma
.	Period or decimal point
'	Apostrophe (or single quotation mark)
;	Semicolon
:	Colon
&	Ampersand
?	Question mark
<	Less than sign
>	Greater than sign
\	Back slash or integer division symbol
" "	Double quotation mark
_	Underscore

Reserved words are words or abbreviations that have a special meaning to BASIC. All of BASIC's commands, statements, function names, and operator names are reserved words. A list of these words is found in Figure 8. Reserved words cannot be used as variable names; however, they can be used as part of variable names. For example, NAME is a BASIC system command and thus is a reserved word. Consequently, NAME cannot be used as a variable name, but LASTNAME is an acceptable variable name. Delimiters such as commas or spaces always separate reserved words from other BASIC elements.

THE PRINT STATEMENT

The PRINT statement is used to display output on the display screen. It can be used to display blank lines, constants, variables, and the results of expressions.

Printing Blank Lines

To display a blank line, the PRINT statement is used alone as follows:

```
10 PRINT
```

Blank lines can help improve the visual appearance of output and make it more readable.

FIGURE 8

BASIC's reserved words.

ABS	DELETE	IOCTL	OPEN	SIN
AND	DIM	IOCTL$	OPTION	SOUND
ASC	DRAW	INT	OR	SPACE$
ATN	EDIT	KEY	OUT	SPC
AUTO	ELSE	KEY$	PAINT	SQR
BEEP	END	KILL	PALETTE	STEP
BLOAD	ENVIRON	LCOPY	PEEK	STICK
BSAVE	ENVIRON$	LEFT$	PEN	STOP
CALL	EOF	LEN	PLAY	STRIG
CDBL	EQV	LET	PMAP	STR$
CHAIN	ERASE	LINE	POINT	STRING$
CHDIR	ERDEV	LIST	POKE	SWAP
CHR$	ERDEV$	LLIST	POS	SYSTEM
CINT	ERL	LOAD	PRESET	TAB
CIRCLE	ERR	LOC	PRINT	TAN
CLEAR	ERROR	LOCATE	PRINT$	THEN
CLOSE	EXP	LOF	PSET	TIME$
CLS	FIELD	LOG	PUT	TIMER
COLOR	FILES	LPOS	RANDOMIZE	TO
COM	FIX	LPRINT	READ	TROFF
COMMON	FNxxxxx	LSET	REM	TRON
CONT	FOR	MERGE	RENUM	USING
COS	FRE	MID$	RESET	USR
CSNG	GET	MKDIR	RESTORE	VAL
CSRLIN	GOSUB	MKD$	RESUME	VARPTR
CVD	GOTO	MKI$	RETURN	VARPTR$
CVI	HEX$	MKS$	RIGHT$	VIEW
CVS	IF	MOD	RMDIR	WAIT
DATA	IMP	MOTOR	RND	WEND
DATE$	INKEY$	NAME	RSET	WHILE
DEF	INP	NEW	RUN	WIDTH
DEFDBL	INPUT	NEXT	SAVE	WINDOW
DEF FN	INPUT#	NOT	SCREEN	WRITE
DEFINT	INPUT$	OCT$	SEG	WRITE#
DEFSNG	INSTR	OFF	SGN	XOR
DEFSTR	INTER$	ON	SHELL	

Printing Constants

A constant is a value that does not change throughout the execution of a program. There are two kinds of constants—string constants and numeric constants.

String Constants. A string constant is a sequence of up to 255 alphanumeric characters enclosed in double quotation marks. The following are all examples of string constants:

```
"HI MOM"
"$2,000,000.00"
"NET SALES"
```

String constants must be enclosed in quotation marks. When used with the PRINT statement, whatever is inside the quotation marks will be displayed on the screen when the statement is executed. The quotation marks do not display. For example:

```
100 PRINT "GROSS PAY"
```

would display on the screen as

```
GROSS PAY
```

Numeric Constants. Numeric constants can be positive or negative numbers but cannot contain commas. BASIC allows five types of numeric constants: integers, fixed point, floating point, hexidecimal, and octal. Integers are whole numbers between -32768 and $+32768$. As whole numbers, they do not have decimal points—for example, 12, -2034, 10000, 3, -2, and 346. Fixed point constants are positive or negative real numbers. A real number is one that does contain a decimal point—for example, -1.35, 2.00, 10.5679, -3.01, 100.45, and 50.00.

Floating point constants are positive or negative numbers that are represented in exponential form (also called scientific form). Such a constant is made up of three parts: a mantissa, the letter *E*, and an exponent. The mantissa may be a positive or negative integer or a positive or negative fixed point number. The exponent may also be a positive or negative integer. Floating point constants must be in the range of $10E-38$ to $10E+38$—for example, 12E06 ($12E06 = 12,000,000$) and 3.26E-06 ($3.26E-06 = .00000326$).

Hexadecimal numbers are those preceded with the prefix &*H* (e.g., &H32F and &H2B, which equal 815 and 43, respectively). Octal numbers are preceded with the prefix &*O* and & (e.g., &O143 and &72, which equal 99 and 58, respectively).

Numeric constants can be printed using the PRINT command. However, a numeric constant is placed after the PRINT command without any quotation marks. The statement 100 PRINT 30 will print on the display screen as 30 when the statement is executed.

Precision of Numeric Constants

BASIC provides for either single- or double-precision numeric constants. A single-precision numeric constant (1) has seven or fewer digits, (2) uses the exponential form with E, or (3) has a trailing exclamation point (!). These constants are stored with seven digits of precision and are displayed with up to seven digits. The following are examples of single-precision numeric constants: 12.4, 3.21E-05, and 53.1!.

For many applications single-precision numeric constants do not supply sufficiently accurate results. For example, when there are many dependent calculations, rounding errors can significantly alter the final result. To help alleviate this problem, BASIC allows the use of double-precision numeric constants. A double-precision numeric constant (1) has eight or more digits, (2) uses the exponential form with D (which works just like the floating point constant except that D is substituted for E, and the numbers are stored with double precision), or (3) has a trailing number sign (#). These constants are stored with 17 digits of precision and require up to 16 digits for display. The following are examples of double-precision numeric constants: 54369813852, −4.032693D-03, 6.089#, and 8912523.4632.

Printing Variables

Variables are symbolic names representing values that may change as a BASIC program is executed. A variable can be assigned a specific value, or it can be assigned a value that results from calculation. A variable name must begin with a letter, but it can contain letters, numbers, and a decimal point. BASIC recognizes no more than 40 characters in a variable name. Names may be larger, but only the first 40 characters will be used by BASIC. Thus, if one variable name is 40 characters long and another is 48 but the first 40 characters in each are exactly the same, BASIC would see them as the same variable.

As noted earlier, reserved words cannot be used as variable names; however, they can be included in a variable name. For example, the abbreviation *FN* is a reserved word that indicates a call to a user-defined function. Therefore, FN cannot be used to start a variable name, but it can be used elsewhere in a variable name. Thus, FNAMOUNT (for finance amount) is an illegal variable name, but CUSTFNAMOUNT (for customer finance amount) is a legal variable name.

String Variables. A string variable must end in a dollar sign ($). That sign indicates that the variable represents a string. Again, the actual string must be enclosed in quotation marks. A string variable is assumed to be null before being assigned a string value in a program.

A PRINT statement can be used to print the value of a string variable. For example, let's suppose that the string variable *A$* represents the string *HELLO.* When executed, the statement 100 PRINT A$ would print HELLO on the display screen.

Numeric Variables. The last character in the name of a numeric variable can be used to indicate whether the numeral represented by the variable name has an integer, single-precision, or double-precision value.

> % indicates an integer variable (e.g., QUANTITY%).
>
> ! indicates a single-precision variable (e.g., PRICE!)
>
> # indicates a double-precision variable (e.g., PI#)

If one of these symbols is not used as the last character, then the numeric variable is defaulted to single precision (e.g., TOTAL represents a single-precision value). Before a numeric variable is assigned a value, its value is assumed to be zero (0).

A PRINT statement can also be used to print the value of a numeric variable. For example, if the numeric variable *TOTAL* represents the value

365, then the statement 100 PRINT TOTAL would appear as 365 on the display screen.

Printing Values of Expressions

In BASIC an expression can be (1) a variable, (2) a string constant, (3) a numeric constant, or (4) a combination of constants and variables with operators to produce a single value. Operators perform mathematical or logical operations on values. BASIC divides operators into five different categories: arithmetic, relational, logical, functional, and string. In this appendix we will consider only arithmetic and relational operators.

Arithmetic Operators. BASIC maintains an order of precedence when evaluating expressions that use arithmetic operators. Table 2 shows the operators in order of precedence. Exponentiation operations, which involve raising a number to a power, are performed first. In BASIC X^Y would be represented as $X^\wedge Y$, and 3^2 would be represented as $3^\wedge 2$. Negation is the use of a negative sign to give a number a negative value (e.g., $-X$ or -4); it is performed after exponentiation. Multiplication uses the symbol * (e.g., X*Y or 3*4) and is the next operation performed. Floating point division is performed next. It is division with real numbers and uses the slash symbol (/) (e.g., X/Y or 5.00/2.23).

The next operation performed is integer division. Before such division can take place, numbers must be rounded to integers. The quotient is also truncated to an integer, and the process is denoted by a back slash (\). For integer division, numbers must be in the range of -32768 to $+32767$. Here are two examples:

$$10 \backslash 4 = 2 \qquad 25.68 \backslash 6.99 = 3$$

Modulo arithmetic gives the integer value that is the remainder in integer division. The process is denoted by the operator MOD. You need to remember that numbers are rounded to integers before the division occurs. The following are two examples of modulo arithmetic:

$$10.4 \ \text{MOD} \quad 4 = 2 \qquad (10 \backslash 4 = 2 \text{ with a remainder of 2})$$

$$25.68 \ \text{MOD} \ 6.97 = 5 \qquad (26 \backslash 7 = 3 \text{ with a remainder of 5})$$

TABLE 2
Order of precedence of arithmetic operators.

Operator	Operation
$\wedge$	Exponentiation
$-$	Negation (e.g., -4)
*	Multiplication
/	Floating point division
\	Integer division
MOD	Modulo arithmetic
+	Addition
$-$	Subtraction

TABLE 3
Relational operators.

Operator	Relationship
=*	Equality
<>	Inequality
<	Less than
>	Greater than
<=	Less than or equal to
>=	Greater than or equal to

*The equal sign has a dual role in BASIC. In addition to being a relational operator, it is also used to assign a value to a variable using the LET command.

Addition operations are next in the order of precedence, and finally subtraction operations are performed.

One factor that complicates this arrangement is that operations enclosed in parentheses override the order of precedence and are performed first. However, within the parentheses operations follow the normal order. Let's consider this expression:

$$5*2/2 + 1$$

According to the order of operations, multiplication is done before division, which is done before addition. Therefore, $5*2 = 10$ and $10/2 = 5$ and $5 + 1 = 6$. Thus, $5*2/2 + 1 = 6$. Now let's change this expression as follows:

$$5*(2/2 + 1)$$

Operations within parentheses are done first, but within the parentheses operations follow the normal order. Thus, division is done first, followed by addition and then multiplication. Therefore, $2/2 = 1$ and $1 + 1 = 2$ and $5*2 = 10$. Clearly, the expressions are different.

Relational Operators. Relational operators are used to compare two values. The relational operators used by BASIC are listed in Table 3. The result of a comparison using a relational operator is either true (-1) or false (0). This result can then be used to redirect program flow. Whenever arithmetic and relational operators are combined in the same expression, the arithmetic operators are performed first. For example, in the expression A*B>C*D the arithmetic operations A*B and C*D are performed first. If the result of A*B is greater than C*D, the expression is true; otherwise the expression is false.

Strings can also be compared using these relational operators: =, <>, <, >, <=, and >=. When strings are compared, the ASCII code of each character is compared, starting with the first character in each string. String comparisons are used to test values and to alphabetize strings. All strings must, of course, be enclosed in quotation marks.

The values of expressions can be printed by the PRINT command. For example, if the numeric variable X represents the value 10 and the numeric variable Y represents the value 20, then the statement 100 PRINT X + Y would print on the display screen as 30. The expressions in a PRINT statement are evaluated according to the hierarchy of operators.

Formatting Output with the PRINT Statement

BASIC divides an 80-column screen into 5 print zones of 14 columns (Figure 9). The number of columns in each zone may vary with different versions of BASIC. To print values in columns, we separate them with commas. For example, the statement

```
100 PRINT "Gross Pay","Net Pay", "Year to Date"
```

would print Gross Pay in print zone 1, Net Pay in print zone 2, and Year to Date in print zone 3, as shown in Figure 10.

If a string extends into the next print zone, then the next string to be printed must start in the first full print zone available. A semicolon is used to print values next to each other instead of in columns defined by the print zones. For example, the statement 100 PRINT "ANY";"PLACE" would print ANYPLACE on the display screen. However, the statement 100 PRINT 10;20 would print 10 20 (and not 1020) because positive numbers, when printed, are preceded by a blank space.

Because BASIC uses the comma as a delimiter, numeric constants cannot contain commas. If we wanted to print the number 10,564, the statement 100 PRINT 10,564 would not produce the desired result. Instead, BASIC would print 10 in the first print zone and 564 in the second print zone. The appropriate statement to print the numeric value 10,564 would be 100 PRINT 10564.

FIGURE 9
The five print zones in BASIC.

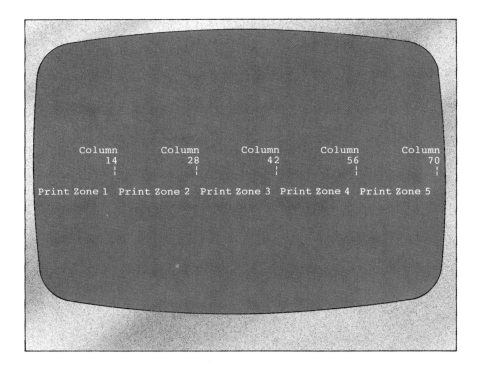

FIGURE 10
The result of executing the
program line 100 PRINT "Gross
Pay", "Net Pay", "Year to
Date".

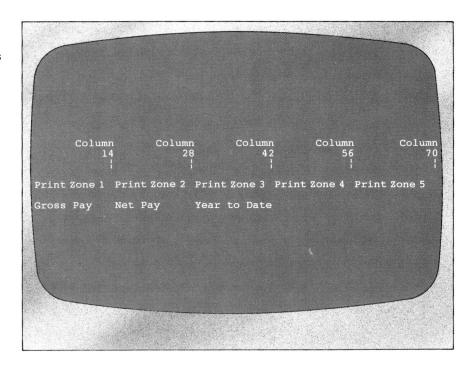

OTHER BASIC STATEMENTS

The LPRINT Statement

Output can be directed to a printer instead of a display screen by using the LPRINT statement. LPRINT assumes an 80-column printer and follows the same syntax as that used for the PRINT statement. For example, the program line

```
100 LPRINT "HELLO WORLD"
```

would print the string HELLO WORLD directly to the printer. However, the printer must be on and ready before the LPRINT statement is executed.

The LET Statement

The LET statement, or assignment statement, is used to store a value in variables. In a LET statement a variable name is placed on the left side of an equal sign, and the value to be placed in that variable is placed on the right side of the equal sign. Here are two examples:

```
100 LET X = 200    200 LET A$ = "HELLO"
```

Since the equal sign has two meanings in BASIC, it should be read "becomes" instead of "equal to" in an assignment statement to avoid confusion. The statement

```
200 LET X = X + 1
```

would not make sense if we read it "X equals X + 1" but is sensible as "X becomes X + 1."

The LET statement is optional in an assignment statement. The two examples cited first could also be written

```
100 X = 200    200 A$ = "HELLO"
```

The following program uses the LET statement to assign values to variables and then uses the PRINT statement to display the results.

```
30 LET X = 5
40 LET Y = 6
50 LET N = X + Y
60 PRINT "X","Y","X + Y"
70 PRINT X,Y,N
```

When executed, this program would appear on the display screen like this:

```
X              Y            X + Y
 5             6             11
```

The END Statement

The END statement tells BASIC to stop execution of a program. It can appear anywhere in a program but is usually the last line. Often, it is identified with a line number made up of all 9s— for example,

```
999 END
```

Use of the END statement is optional. If it is not used, BASIC stops executing a program when there are no more program lines to execute.

The REM Statement

In order to make it easier for people to understand what a program does and how to debug or make changes in a program, BASIC allows a program to be documented with the REM statement.

```
100 REM CALCULATE GROSS PAY
200 LET GROSSPAY = HRLYRATE * TOTALHRS
```

In this example the REM statement identifies the purpose of the assignment statement. The REM statement can also be used to make a program listing more readable. Segments of a program that accomplish specific tasks can be set off from the rest of the program for easy identification by REM statements used alone or with symbols, such as an asterisk.

```
100 REM ********************************
110 REM Calculate Gross Pay
120 LET GROSSPAY = HRLYRATE * TOTALHRS
130 REM ********************************
140 REM
```

The REM statement can also be used to document the meaning of variable names.

```
10 REM CUSTADD$ = customer address
20 REM CUSTNAME = customer name
```

The REM statement is not used by the computer; it supplies information only to the person reading it. BASIC ignores all other characters in a program line after a REM statement. An apostrophe can be substituted for the REM statement. For example, the following two program lines are equivalent:

```
100 ' Calculate Gross Pay
100 REM Calculate Gross Pay
```

It is a good idea to document all written programs. The following program illustrates the use of REM statements in this capacity.

```
10 REM Program Adds Two Numbers and Prints Sum
20 REM
30 REM Assign Values to Variables
40 LET X = 5
50 LET Y = 6
60 REM Calculate Sum of X and Y
70 LET N = X + Y
80 REM Display Output
90 PRINT "X","Y","X + Y"
100 PRINT X,Y,N
999 END
```

Multi-statement Lines

In some instances it is desirable to place several statements in a single program line. This task can be accomplished by separating the statements with a colon (:). For example, if you wanted to print three blank lines, you could use the following statements:

```
10 PRINT
20 PRINT
30 PRINT
```

You could also use one multi-statement line:

```
10 PRINT:PRINT:PRINT
```

The colon is also useful for placing REM statements after other statements to document them.

```
100 LET GROSSPAY = HRLYRATE * TOTALHRS:REM
      Calculate Gross Pay
```

Since BASIC ignores all characters after a REM statement, no other statements can be added after a REM statement. Otherwise, a program line can contain any number of statements up to a maximum of 255 characters in one program line.

SYSTEM COMMANDS

System commands operate on BASIC program files. The commands are usually used in the command (direct) mode, although in some cases they can be used in a program mode. We will examine the most common commands used in the command mode: LIST, RUN, SAVE, LOAD, NEW, DELETE, and RENUM.

If someone types a program statement that is preceded by a line number and then presses the enter key, that program line will be stored in computer memory. A BASIC program consists of a series of such program lines, just like those that make up the sample program at the end of the REM discussion. Let's see how system commands can be used to act on that program.

LIST

The LIST command is used to display the program that is currently in memory. If the program that concludes the REM discussion is currently in memory, typing **LIST** and then pressing the <Enter> key should display the entire program.

```
10 REM Program Adds Two Numbers and Prints Sum
20 REM
30 REM Assign Values to Variables
40 LET X = 5
50 LET Y = 6
60 REM Calculate Sum of X and Y
70 LET N = X + Y
80 REM Display Output
90 PRINT "X", "Y", "X + Y"
100 PRINT X,Y,N
999 END
```

LIST also has several other options that allow only specified portions of a program to be displayed. These are useful if a program listing is too long to fit on the display screen. The following examples illustrate the options that can be used to view selected lines.

```
LIST          Lists the entire program
LIST 30-50    Lists lines 30 through 50
LIST -50      Lists all lines from the beginning of the program
              through line 50
LIST 60-      Lists all lines from line 60 to the end of the program
LIST 70       Lists only line 70
```

The LLIST Command

The LLIST command allows a program listing to be printed on a printer. It operates just as LIST does except that it directs the listing to a printer instead of a display screen. Again, the printer must be on and ready to use the LLIST command.

RUN

The RUN statement is used to execute a program. With our program still in memory, typing **RUN** and pressing <Enter> should produce the following output on the display screen.

```
X              Y              X + Y
 5              6              11
```

Naming and Accessing Files in BASIC

Some system commands store and retrieve files. A file is a collection of information, such as a program, stored on a floppy or a fixed disk. Each file must be given a unique file name, which is used to access the file. In addition to the file name an optional extension may be used to help identify the file. The following list states the rules that apply to naming a file in BASIC.

- The file name can be from one to eight characters long.
- An extension consists of a period (.) and one to three characters.
- The file name and the extension can consist of numbers, letters, and the following special characters: $ # & @ ! % ( ) - _ { } ' ^
- If an extension is omitted, BASIC assumes that the file has a .BAS extension and automatically appends it to the file name. However, the commands KILL, NAME, and OPEN do not assume an extension.
- If a file name is longer than eight characters and doesn't specify an extension, BASIC terminates the file name after the first eight characters, adds a period, and uses the next three characters as an extension. If the file name is longer than eight characters and does specify an extension, the file name is truncated to eight characters, and the original extension is retained.
- If an extension is specified with more than three characters, BASIC truncates it to the first three characters.

In a BASIC command or statement the word *filespec* calls for the following information to be supplied:

```
[d:][path]file name[.ext]
```

where [d:] represents the name of the drive where the file is or will be stored (e.g., A:, B:, or C:). If a drive is not indicated, BASIC saves or looks for the file on the default drive. [path] indicates the route, or list of subdirectories, that leads to where the file is to be saved or located. If no path is specified, BASIC saves or looks for the file in the current directory.

SAVE

When a computer is turned off, everything stored in primary memory is lost; therefore, a program must be reentered in order to be executed again. To avoid this situation, especially with longer programs, BASIC provides a way of storing programs in secondary storage with the use of the SAVE command.

The SAVE command requires that a program have a file name. In GWBASIC and IBM BASIC the file name must be enclosed in quotation marks. To save our sample program under the name SUM, the command would appear as

SAVE "SUM"

If drive A is the current drive and you want to save the file to a diskette in drive B, the command would appear as

SAVE "B:SUM"

There is no line number because we want the command to execute as soon as the enter key is pressed.

LOAD

When a user wants to put back into the computer's primary memory a copy of a BASIC file that is stored on disk, BASIC uses the LOAD command. To load the SUM file back into memory, the command would be

LOAD "SUM"

If drive A is the current drive and the file SUM is stored on a diskette in drive B, we could load the program with this command:

LOAD "B:SUM"

After the enter key is pressed, the file SUM would be retrieved from disk and loaded back into memory.

NEW

After a program is executed it still resides in computer memory. Before a new program can be created, the existing program must be removed from memory. Otherwise, anything entered would be added to the existing program. To clear the computer's memory, this command is used:

NEW

When the enter key is pressed, the computer's memory will be cleared.

Editing Program Lines

We humans are prone to occasional errors. If we catch an error before the enter key has been pressed, we can simply use the backspace key to delete the error and then retype the program line. If the program line has already been entered, the error can be corrected in several other ways. One approach is to retype the entire line with the desired correction. If a new program line has the same line number as an existing program line, the new will replace the old. For example, if the value of Y in line 50 of our program should really be 4 and the program SUM is still in memory, we could simply type **50 LET Y = 4** and press <Enter>. The program in memory would then be changed. However, the permanent copy on disk would still contain the old line 50; the SAVE command must be used to update the disk file.

A second way to correct an error is to use the screen editing capabilities of BASIC. This approach lists just the portion of the program to be edited. For our small program we could list the entire program since it fits on one screen, but for larger programs we would list only the line(s) that we wanted to edit. With our original program the command LIST 50 followed by <Enter> would display only line 50: 50 LET Y = 6. We could then move the cursor to the 6 and type **4** as the correction. At this point the number would appear correct on the screen, but the program line in primary memory would not have been updated. To update it in memory, we would need to press the enter key while the cursor was somewhere in the program line being edited. To confirm that our changes had been made to the program in memory, we could use the LIST command to view the program.

Sometimes, editing a program requires adding a line. That task is accomplished by typing the new program line with a line number that has not been used and that places the new line in proper sequence. For example, if we wanted to add the heading SUMMATION OF X AND Y to the output of program SUM, we might choose the line number 85 so that other lines could be added in front of and behind it if necessary. For that same reason program lines are initially numbered by 10s—to leave room for additional program lines. Our addition would be typed as follows:

```
85 PRINT "SUMMATION OF X AND Y"
```

After pressing the enter key, we could type **LIST** and press <Enter> again to view our corrected and amended program.

```
10 REM Program Adds Two Numbers and Prints Sum
20 REM
30 REM Assign Values to Variables
40 LET X = 5
50 LET Y = 4
60 REM Calculate Sum of X and Y
70 LET N = X + Y
80 REM Display Output
85 PRINT "SUMMATION OF X AND Y"
90 PRINT "X","Y","X + Y"
100 PRINT X,Y,N
999 END
```

The DELETE Command. In some cases it is necessary to delete one or more program lines. There are two ways to delete a single line. Simply typing a line number and pressing the enter key will delete that line, or the DELETE command can be used. Thus, to delete line 20 of our program, we could type **20** and then press <Enter> , or we could type **DELETE 20** and then press <Enter>. The DELETE command can also be used to delete a range of program lines. For example, DELETE 20—50 would delete lines 20 through 50. DELETE 20— would delete all lines from line 20 to the end of the program. DELETE —50 would delete all lines from the beginning of the program through line 50.

The RENUM Command. Sometimes the increment between line numbers is not sufficient to accommodate the necessary additions to a program. At other times a programmer may wish to renumber program lines simply to make the increments between line numbers consistent. The RENUM command by itself renumbers an entire program, starting with 10 and incrementing each line by 10. In addition, a programmer can specify the new line number with which to begin the renumbering, the line number from which the renumbering will start, and the increment to be used. The format for the RENUM statement is RENUM n,n,n. For example, the statement

```
RENUM 1000, 500, 10
```

renumbers lines 500 and up so that they start with 1000 and increment by 10. The statement

```
RENUM 100,, 20
```

renumbers the entire program so that the first line number is 100 and the lines increment by 20.

The RENUM command cannot be used to change the order of program lines; it can only renumber them in the same sequence. And program line numbers cannot be greater than 65529.

The SYSTEM Command

The SYSTEM command is used to exit BASIC and return to DOS. When executed, the SYSTEM command erases any BASIC program that may still be in RAM, removes BASIC from RAM, and returns the system to the DOS prompt. The command is typed in the command mode, and the enter key is pressed.

THE INPUT STATEMENT

Using an assignment (LET) statement to assign values to variables is not very efficient if the values change. A more flexible way to assign values is to use the INPUT statement, which is placed where data are needed in a program. It allows a user to enter data as a program is executing. The INPUT statement can take several forms.

Let's consider the following program.

```
10 REM Calculate Sales Price
20 REM ***********************
30 REM SALESP = Sales Price
40 REM DISCOUNT = Sales Discount
50 REM ITEMP = Price of an Item
```

```
60 REM ************************
70 INPUT ITEMP
80 INPUT DISCOUNT
90 LET SALESP = ITEMP - (ITEMP * DISCOUNT):REM
   Calculate Sales Price
100 PRINT "Sales Price = $";SALESP
999 END
```

When the INPUT statement in line 70 is executed, BASIC will display a ? on the screen and wait for the user to input data. The value entered must match the data type of the variable, in this case a numeric variable. When that value is entered, it is assigned to the variable.

Since BASIC displays only a question mark, it can be difficult for the user to know which data are being asked for by the computer. To get around this problem, the INPUT statement allows a prompt, or message, to be printed with it. The prompt is placed in quotation marks and is followed by a semicolon. For example, lines 70 and 80 in this program could be written as follows:

```
70 INPUT "What is the item price";ITEMP
80 INPUT "What is the sales discount";DISCOUNT
```

Then, when line 70 is executed, the user would be prompted with this line: What is the item price? A prompt could also be added with a PRINT statement placed in the program line before the INPUT statement. However, because this operation is so common, BASIC allows the prompt to be incorporated into the INPUT statement.

A single INPUT statement can be used to enter data for more than one variable. For example, lines 70 and 80 could be combined into a single statement as follows:

```
70 INPUT "What are the item price and sales
   discount";ITEMP,DISCOUNT
```

When this statement is executed, the user would be prompted with this line: What are the item price and sales discount? It is important that data are entered in the same order in which they appear in the INPUT statement, separated by a comma.

The user would then enter the values—let's assume the item price is $6.35 and the sales discount is 10 percent (.10)—and would follow up by pressing the enter key.

Both string and numeric values can be entered with the INPUT statement. If incorrect values are entered (e.g., numeric data for a string variable), the computer responds with the message "Redo from start," redisplays the ? (or prompt and ?), and waits for the user to enter the correct data type.

THE CLS STATEMENT

The display screen can sometimes get cluttered with prompts and become difficult to read. BASIC provides the CLS, or clear screen, statement to remove the clutter. When the CLS statement is executed, all characters on the display screen are erased, and the cursor is placed in the upper left corner of the display screen. An example of such a statement is:

```
100 CLS
```

THE READ AND DATA STATEMENTS

In some programs the data remain relatively constant and do not need to be input by the user as the program is executing. In these cases the data can be coded directly into the program. Earlier we saw that the LET statement can be used to assign data to variables. However, if data have to be changed, locating the appropriate LET statements can be difficult in a large program.

BASIC allows users to group data together with a DATA statement. DATA statements can be placed anywhere in a program as long as the data appear in the same sequence as that needed by the READ statement(s). The values stored in DATA statements are then assigned to the variables listed in the READ statements. However, before any statements in a program are executed, all of the values stored in DATA statements must be placed in a data list; they are stored sequentially in the same order in which they appear in the program. A READ statement, when executed, takes the first datum in the data list and assigns it to a variable. For example, let's consider this program segment:

```
100 DATA 100, 200
200 READ NUM1, NUM2, NUM3, NUM4
300 DATA 300
400 DATA 400
```

A computer will place those data in a data list as follows:

```
100
200
300
400
```

When the READ statement is executed, it will assign 100 to the variable NUM1, 200 to NUM2, 300 to NUM3, and 400 to NUM4.

Both numeric and string data can be used in READ and DATA statements. Let's look at the following example:

```
100 REM Example Program Using READ and DATA
    Statements
110 REM N1$, N2$ = Product Description
120 REM P1, P2 = Product Prices
130 READ N1$, P1
140 READ N2$, P2
150 PRINT "PRODUCT: ";N1$,"PRICE: ";P1
160 PRINT "PRODUCT: ";N2$,"PRICE: ";P2
170 DATA "Laser Printer",4000,"Letter Quality
    Printer",1200
999 END
```

Before the program is executed, the values listed in the DATA statement are placed in a data list, as follows:

```
"Laser Printer"
4000
"Letter Quality Printer"
1200
```

When the READ statement is executed in line 130, the string value "Laser Printer" is assigned to the string variable N1$, and the numeric value 4000 is assigned to the numeric variable P1. When the READ statement in line 140 is executed, the string value "Letter Quality Printer" is assigned to the string variable N2$, and the numeric value 1200 is assigned to the numeric variable P2. The order of the variable types in the READ statements must match the order of the value types in the data list, or an error will occur. INPUT, READ, and DATA statements can all be combined in a single program.

THE RESTORE STATEMENT

The RESTORE statement causes the READ statement to start reading data from the top of the data list again. If, in our earlier example, a RESTORE statement had been used in line 135, then the READ statement in line 140 would have taken data from the top of the data list, and both N1$ and N2$ would have been assigned the string value "Laser Printer," and both P1 and P2 would have had the numeric value 4000. If a READ statement is executed but there are no more data in the data list and a RESTORE statement is not executed, the computer will respond with this message: Out of data in [line number where error occurred].

LOOPING

Often the same series of program instructions needs to be executed more than once in a program. That series could be repeated in sequence as many times as necessary, but BASIC provides a loop control structure to accomplish this task more efficiently. A loop control structure allows a program segment to be repeated as often as needed. This structure can be implemented in BASIC with FOR and NEXT statements or WHILE and WEND statements.

FOR and NEXT Statements

FOR and NEXT statements are used together to execute a series of instructions a specific number of times. The following example demonstrates these statements.

```
100 REM A FOR...NEXT Example
200 FOR X = 1 to 5
300 PRINT "The value of X = ";X
400 NEXT X
500 PRINT "End of Loop"
999 END
```

When that program is executed, these results are displayed:

```
The value of X = 1
The value of X = 2
```

```
The value of X = 3
The value of X = 4
The value of X = 5
End of Loop
```

In the FOR statement in line 200, X is called the control variable, or loop index. The number 1 is the initial value, and 5 is the terminal value. The statement(s) between the FOR and the NEXT statements constitute the loop body. In this example the loop body is only one instruction, although the body can contain any number of instructions. When line 200 is executed, the control variable (X) is set to the initial value (1). A test is performed to determine whether the value represented by the control variable is greater than the terminal value. If it is, then control is transferred to the statement following the NEXT statement, and the loop is terminated. However, if the control variable is not greater than the terminal value, then the statements in the body of the loop are executed. Thereafter, the NEXT statement is executed. During that execution the control variable is incremented by +1. (It can also be incremented by other values, using the STEP clause, as we will see shortly.) After the loop body has been executed, the control variable is compared to the terminal variable. If the control variable is greater, control transfers to the first statement after the NEXT statement. If the control variable is not greater, control transfers again to the first statement in the body of the loop, which is then executed once more.

The STEP clause that was mentioned allows the control variable to be incremented by a positive or negative value other than +1.

```
100 FOR X = 1 TO 10 STEP 2
200 PRINT X;
300 NEXT X
```

This program would result in this output:

```
1    3    5    7    9
```

A negative STEP value causes the value of the control variable to diminish.

```
100 FOR X = 10 TO 1 STEP -2
200 PRINT X;
300 NEXT X
```

This program would result in this output:

```
10   8    6    4    2
```

FOR and NEXT statements can also be nested, that is, placed inside one another.

```
100 REM Outer Loop
110 FOR X = 1 TO 3
120 PRINT "Outer Loop Execution Number";X
130 TOTALOUT = TOTALOUT + 1
140 REM Inner Loop
150 FOR Y = 1 TO 2
160 PRINT "Inner Loop Execution Number";Y
```

```
170 TOTALIN = TOTALIN + 1
180 NEXT Y
190 NEXT X
200 PRINT
210 PRINT "Outer Loop Was Executed";X;"Times"
220 PRINT "Inner Loop Was Executed";Y;"Times"
9999 END
```

After the user types **RUN** and presses <Enter>, the output of this program would look like this:

```
Outer Loop Execution Number 1
  Inner Loop Execution Number 1
  Inner Loop Execution Number 2
Outer Loop Execution Number 2
  Inner Loop Execution Number 1
  Inner Loop Execution Number 2
Outer Loop Execution Number 3
  Inner Loop Execution Number 1
  Inner Loop Execution Number 2


Outer Loop Was Executed 3 Times
Inner Loop Was Executed 6 Times
```

The following program uses nested FOR and NEXT statements to print multiplication tables for 2s, 4s, 6s, and 8s.

```
100 REM This Program Prints Multiplication Tables
110 PRINT "Multiplication Tables For 2s, 4s, 6s,
    and 8s"
120 PRINT
130 FOR X = 1 TO 12
140 FOR Y = 2 TO 8 STEP 2
150 PRINT Y;" x";X;" =";Y * X,
160 NEXT Y
170 PRINT
180 NEXT X
999 END
```

After the user types **RUN** and presses <Enter>, the output of this program would appear as follows:

```
2 x  1 =  2     4 x  1 =  4     6 x  1 =  6     8 x  1 =  8
2 x  2 =  4     4 x  2 =  8     6 x  2 = 12     8 x  2 = 16
2 x  3 =  6     4 x  3 = 12     6 x  3 = 18     8 x  3 = 24
2 x  4 =  8     4 x  4 = 16     6 x  4 = 24     8 x  4 = 32
2 x  5 = 10     4 x  5 = 20     6 x  5 = 30     8 x  5 = 40
2 x  6 = 12     4 x  6 = 24     6 x  6 = 36     8 x  6 = 48
2 x  7 = 14     4 x  7 = 28     6 x  7 = 42     8 x  7 = 56
2 x  8 = 16     4 x  8 = 32     6 x  8 = 48     8 x  8 = 64
2 x  9 = 18     4 x  9 = 36     6 x  9 = 54     8 x  9 = 72
2 x 10 = 20     4 x 10 = 40     6 x 10 = 60     8 x 10 = 80
2 x 11 = 22     4 x 11 = 44     6 x 11 = 66     8 x 11 = 88
2 x 12 = 24     4 x 12 = 48     6 x 12 = 72     8 x 12 = 96
```

WHILE and WEND Statements

WHILE and WEND (**W**hile **END**) statements are also used in BASIC to implement a loop control structure. The following example illustrates a WHILE . . . WEND loop.

```
100 REM A WHILE...WEND Loop
110 REM ITEMP = Item Price
120 REM TOTALP = Total Price of All Items
130 REM
140 INPUT "Enter Item Price (Enter 0 to
    Quit)";ITEMP
150 WHILE ITEMP <> 0
160 LET TOTALP = TOTALP + ITEMP
170 INPUT "Enter Item Price (Enter 0 to
    Quit)";ITEMP
180 WEND
190 PRINT "Total Price of All Items = ";TOTALP
999 END
```

A WHILE statement contains a condition. In line 150 the condition is ITEMP <> 0. When the WHILE statement is executed, the condition is tested. However, the variable ITEMP must have a value assigned to it before the WHILE statement is executed, and the INPUT statement in line 140 calls for this value. If the condition is true (i.e., if the value of ITEMP does not equal zero), the statements between WHILE and WEND are executed. When the WEND statement is executed, control is returned to the WHILE statement. On the other hand, if the condition in the WHILE statement is false (i.e., if the value of ITEMP does equal zero), then control is passed to the first statement following the WEND statement.

THE IF . . . THEN STATEMENT

The IF . . . THEN statement provides a conditional transfer. That is, it is used to redirect the flow of processing according to the result of a condition. It is used to select a specific course of action to be taken during processing if a condition is true. If the condition is not true, no action is taken, and the program continues with the next line. Let's look at an example.

```
100 IF TOTAL >= 100 THEN TOTAL = TOTAL * .90
120 PRINT "Total Purchases = ";TOTAL
```

The IF clause in line 100 is followed by the condition that TOTAL >= 100. During execution this condition is evaluated. If the condition is true—that is, if the TOTAL is greater than or equal to 100—the program statement(s) following the THEN clause are executed. In this case a 10 percent discount is given to those individuals purchasing 100 dollars' worth or more of merchandise. Program execution then continues with the next line. If the condition following the IF clause is false—that is, if the TOTAL is less than 100—the THEN clause is not executed. Instead, control passes immediately to the next program line.

THE IF . . . THEN . . . ELSE STATEMENT

The IF . . . THEN . . . ELSE statement allows one action to be taken if a condition is true and another, if it is false.

```
100 IF AMOUNT > CREDIT THEN PRINT "Reject Credit
     Card" ELSE PRINT "Accept Credit Card"
```

The IF clause in line 100 is followed by the condition AMOUNT > CREDIT. That condition checks to see whether the amount of purchase is greater than the credit available on a customer's credit card. If the condition is true—that is, if the amount of the purchase is greater than the customer's credit limit—the statement following the THEN clause is executed, and the message "Reject Credit Card" is printed. Control would then go to the next program line. If the condition is false—that is, if the purchase amount is less than or equal to the customer's credit limit—the statement following the ELSE clause is executed, and the message "Accept Credit Card" is printed.

To improve readability, the IF . . . THEN . . . ELSE statement can be broken across several lines.

```
100 IF AMOUNT > CREDIT
        THEN PRINT "Reject Credit Card"
        ELSE PRINT "Accept Credit Card"
```

IF . . . THEN . . . ELSE statements can also be nested.

```
100 IF BALANCE <> 0
        THEN IF AGE < 30
        THEN PRINT "Account Current"
        ELSE PRINT "Account Overdue"
ELSE PRINT "Account Paid in Full"
```

In this example if a customer's balance is equal to zero, processing goes to the ELSE clause associated with the first IF statement and displays the message "Account Paid in Full." If the balance is not equal to zero, then the statements following the THEN clause are executed. In this case that step involves another IF statement, and the condition AGE < 30 must be tested. If the account is less than 30 days overdue, the statement after the THEN clause is executed, and the message "Account Current" is displayed. If the account is more than 30 days past due, the condition is false, and the statement(s) after the ELSE clause are executed; in other words, the message "Account Overdue" is displayed.

THE GOTO STATEMENT

In a BASIC program a GOTO statement allows the unconditional transfer of control to the line number specified in the statement. For example, in this instruction— 100 GOTO 420— control would transfer from line 100 to line 420 without executing any line in between.

Indiscriminate use of the GOTO statement can create programs in which the logic is very difficult to follow, test, or modify. Many programmers recommend that GOTO statements not be used; others say that limited and controlled use is acceptable. However, a GOTO statement should never be used to transfer control into or out of a loop or subroutine. The following program illustrates how a GOTO statement could be used to implement a loop.

```
10 REM Program Using GOTO
20 REM
30 INPUT "Enter Item Price";PRICE
40 INPUT "Enter Total Number of Items
   Purchased";NUM
50 LET TOTAL = PRICE * NUM
60 INPUT "Any More Items (Enter Y or N)";A$
70 IF A$ = "N" THEN GOTO 999
80 GOTO 30
999 END
```

Line 70 tests the condition A$ = "N." If A$ is not equal to "N," the condition is false, and control passes to line 80. Line 80 then performs an unconditional transfer and sends control back to line 30. However, if the condition in line 70 is true, then control is transferred to line 999, and the program terminates. The GOTO statement in the THEN clause in line 70 is optional. The statement could also be written as follows:

```
IF A$ = "N" THEN 999
```

GOSUB and RETURN Statements

The GOSUB and RETURN statements work together as a team. The GOSUB statement allows control to be transferred to a specified line in a program. Execution begins at that line and continues until the RETURN statement is encountered. The RETURN statement sends control back to the line that follows the GOSUB statement. Thus, the GOSUB and RETURN statements allow the construction of modules, or subroutines.

Modules help structure a program, making it easier to read, modify, and debug. A common use of the GOSUB and RETURN statements is to implement a menu in a program. When a menu selection is entered, the GOSUB statement directs processing to the appropriate module. When that module is finished executing, control returns to the main program module. The following example illustrates this process.

```
10 REM This Program Illustrates the use of the
   GOSUB Statement
20 REM
30 LET A$ = "Y"
40 WHILE A$ = "Y"
45 CLS
50 INPUT "Enter First Number";X
60 INPUT "Enter Second Number";Y
70 GOSUB 1000
90 IF MENU = 1 THEN GOSUB 2000
100 IF MENU = 2 THEN GOSUB 3000
```

```
110 IF MENU = 3 THEN GOSUB 4000
120 IF MENU = 4 THEN GOSUB 5000
125 PRINT:PRINT
130 INPUT "Enter Two More Numbers (Y or N)"; A$
140 WEND
150 END
160 REM ***************************************
1000 REM Subroutine for Displaying MENU
1005 CLS
1010 PRINT "Enter 1 for Addition"
1020 PRINT "Enter 2 for Subtraction"
1030 PRINT "Enter 3 for Multiplication"
1040 PRINT "Enter 4 for Division"
1050 RETURN
1060 REM ***************************************
2000 REM Subroutine to Perform Addition
2010 LET T = X + Y
2020 PRINT "The Sum of";X;" Plus";Y;" Is";T
2030 RETURN
2040 REM ***************************************
3000 REM Subroutine to Perform Subtraction
3010 LET T = X - Y
3020 PRINT "The Result of";X;" Minus";Y;" Is";T
3030 RETURN
3040 REM ***************************************
4000 REM Subroutine to Perform Multiplication
4010 LET T = X * Y
4020 PRINT "The Product of";X;" Times";Y;
     " Is";T
4030 RETURN
4040 REM ***************************************
5000 REM Subroutine to Perform Division
5010 LET T = X / Y
5020 PRINT "The Result of";X;" Divided by";Y;
     " Is";T
5030 RETURN
```

There are five subroutines in this program. The subroutine starting at line 1000 displays the menu. The subroutine starting at line 2000 performs addition; the one at line 3000, subtraction; the one at 4000, multiplication; and the one at 5000, division. The main program extends from line 10 to line 150. Lines 50 and 60 ask the user to input two numbers. Line 70 branches to the menu subroutine starting at 1000. When the RETURN statement in line 1050 is executed, control is passed back to line 90. The IF statements in lines 90 to 120 are used to determine which subroutine should follow. If any one of the conditions in the IF statements is true, the appropriate THEN clause is executed. The GOSUB statement directs processing to the appropriate subroutine. After one of these subroutines is executed, control is returned to line 125. Also, if the value of MENU does not equal 1, 2, 3, or 4, the THEN clauses are skipped, and processing continues with line 125.

THE ON . . . GOSUB AND RETURN STATEMENTS

The ON . . . GOSUB statement is used to branch to any one of a number of modules, depending on the value of the variable following the ON clause. The following example illustrates an ON . . . GOSUB statement.

```
90 ON MENU GOSUB 2000, 3000, 4000, 5000
```

When this statement is executed, the value of the variable *MENU* is evaluated. If it has a value of 1, processing branches to the first line number (2000). If it has a value of 2, processing branches to the second line number in the GOSUB list (3000), and so on.

An ON . . . GOSUB statement can be used in place of numerous IF statements and allows for more concise programs. For example, the ON . . . GOSUB statement just cited could replace the four IF statements located in lines 90 through 120 in the menu program cited earlier.

```
10 REM This Program Illustrates the Use of the
   GOSUB Statement
20 REM
30 LET A$ = "Y"
40 WHILE A$ = "Y"
45 CLS
50 INPUT "Enter First Number";X
60 INPUT "Enter Second Number";Y
70 GOSUB 1000
90 ON MENU GOSUB 2000, 3000, 4000, 5000
125 PRINT:PRINT
130 INPUT "Enter Two More Numbers (Y or N)"; A$
140 WEND
150 END
160 REM ******************************************
1000 REM Subroutine for Displaying MENU
1005 CLS
1010 PRINT "Enter 1 for Addition"
1020 PRINT "Enter 2 for Subtraction"
1030 PRINT "Enter 3 for Multiplication"
1040 PRINT "Enter 4 for Division"
1050 RETURN
1060 REM *****************************************
2000 REM Subroutine to Perform Addition
2010 LET T = X + Y
2020 PRINT "The Sum of";X;" Plus";Y;" Is";T
2030 RETURN
2040 REM *****************************************
3000 REM Subroutine to Perform Subtraction
3010 LET T = X - Y
3020 PRINT "The Result of";X;" Minus";Y;" Is";T
3030 RETURN
3040 REM *****************************************
4000 REM Subroutine to Perform Multiplication
4010 LET T = X * Y
4020 PRINT "The Product of";X;" Times";Y;
     " Is";T
4030 RETURN
```

```
4040 REM ******************************************
5000 REM Subroutine to Perform Division
5010 LET T = X / Y
5020 PRINT "The Result of";X;" Divided by";Y;
     " Is";T
5030 RETURN
```

Glossary

absolute cell reference A method of copying in which the exact formula is repeated, using the same cell references; used with spreadsheets.

accounting information system An information system using primarily transaction processing systems to record transactions that affect the financial status of an organization. It maintains a historical record of the organization's transactions and is used to produce reports that give a financial picture of the organization.

accuracy An attribute of information that refers to whether the information is accurate (true) or inaccurate (false).

acoustic modem Also called an acoustic coupler; a type of modem with two rubber cups into which the standard telephone receiver is placed to send and receive data.

action document A computer-produced document that becomes an input document for another information system.

active cell A cell in a spreadsheet that is currently being used for data entry or data manipulation; usually indicated by the cursor position.

Ada A programming language developed for the U.S. Department of Defense for use in military applications. Ada includes powerful control and data structures and a specialized set of commands that allows it to control hardware devices directly.

adding The process of entering new records in an existing file or database.

algorithm A finite set of step-by-step instructions for the purpose of solving a problem.

all-in-one integrated package An integrated application package that combines the features of several application programs into a single program.

analog computer A type of computer that recognizes data as a continuous measurement of a physical property (e.g., voltage, pressure, speed).

analog data transmission The transmission of data in a continuous wave form.

application The job or task that a user wants a computer to perform.

application generator A type of fourth-generation language that allows a user to enter data and specify how the data are to be manipulated and output.

application package See *application software.*

application software Software that interfaces between a user and system software to allow the user to perform specific tasks.

arithmetic and logic unit (ALU) The part of the central processing unit (CPU) that performs all mathematical and logical functions.

artificial intelligence (AI) The ability of computers to perform humanlike thinking and reasoning.

assembler A language-translator program that translates an assembly language code into a machine language code.

assembly language A low-level language that uses mnemonic codes instead of 1s and 0s.

asynchronous transmission A method of data transmission in which characters are sent one at a time over a communication channel. Each character is surrounded by a start-and-stop bit that controls the transfer of that character.

attributes The set of characteristics used to describe a data entry field or the appearance of output. These are often set by a user to fit a particular situation.

auditability An attribute of information, also referred to as verifiability, that refers to the ability of information to be checked.

audit trail   Documentation of all activity in a file, including what was done, what was affected, when it was done, and who did it.

automated testing   A testing process that involves the use of software tools to mark all the paths in a program module and report on which paths were executed in a test.

automatic page numbering   An application-software feature that automatically places a consecutive page number on each page.

automatic spillover   A spreadsheet option in which a cell label is allowed to continue, or spill over, into the next cell.

background integration   The placing of utility programs into memory to make them available to someone using other software packages.

backup file   A copy of a file to ensure that data are not lost if the original file is lost or damaged; a duplicate copy of a file.

band printer   A line-at-a-time impact printer similar to a chain printer but using a band containing characters instead of a chain.

bandwidth   A characteristic of a communication channel that determines the rate, or speed, at which data can be transmitted over that channel.

bar code   A series of thick and thin black bars and spaces of various widths that represent data; seen on many consumer products.

BASIC (Beginners' All-purpose Symbolic Instruction Code)   A high-level language developed at Dartmouth College as an easy-to-learn and -use language for beginning programmers.

batch job   A computer program that executes with a batch file(s) as input and output.

batch processing   The process of collecting data in a file that is later processed in a group, or batch.

baud rate   The number of times per second that a transmitted signal changes (modulates or demodulates).

binary system   The base-2 numbering system using the digits 0 and 1. Computer data can be represented by this numbering system.

biochip   A newer technology for designing integrated circuits; uses living protein and enzymes to grow circuits; exists in theory only.

bit   A binary digit; the smallest piece of data that can be recognized and used by a computer.

black box process   A transformation process that is not known in detail because it is too complex.

block editing   A word-processor feature that allows a user to edit large portions of text as a unit.

blocking factor   The number of records stored between a pair of interblock gaps.

broad-band channel   A communication channel, such as microwaves or fiber optics, that transmits data at rates as high as several megabits per second.

bubble memory   A type of nonvolatile memory in which data are represented by the presence or absence of magnetized areas (bubbles) formed on a thin piece of garnet.

buffer   A temporary holding place for data; may be part of a CPU or part of an input or output device.

built-in function   A function that is contained within an application program and that automatically performs a mathematical or logic function without a user's manually entering a formula.

bus   An electrical path for data flow from point to point in a circuit.

business and analytical program   A type of graphics program that is capable of extracting numerical data and presenting it in the form of a graph or a chart; often a separate program but one that may be integrated into another application program.

bus network   A computer network arrangement in which each device is connected to a single communication cable by an interface. Each device can communicate directly with every other device.

byte   A group of eight bits.

C   A programming language that uses English-like statements; uses sophisticated control and data structures, which make it a very concise, powerful language.

calculation   An information-processing task that involves performing a mathematical operation on data.

carrier sense multiple access (CSMA)   A local-area-network access method in which a device listens to a channel to sense whether that channel is in use.

carrier sense multiple access/collision detection (CSMA/CD)   The carrier sense multiple access (CSMA) method with collision detection capabilities.

cathode-ray tube (CRT)   A type of display that uses an electron beam to illuminate a phosphor-coated screen in order to form characters.

cell   A data entry point in a spreadsheet, defined by its row and column coordinates.

centering   A feature in application software that automatically places a word(s) in the center of a defined space, such as a spreadsheet cell or a document page.

central processing unit (CPU) The name given to the processing unit of a computer; contains the arithmetic and logic unit (ALU), control unit, and primary storage unit.

chain printer A line-at-a-time impact printer that uses a rotating chain containing all the characters.

character enhancements Features in application software that allow a user to alter text style, for example, by boldfacing or italicizing.

check digit A mathematical calculation using the place location and value of the digits in a number.

chief information officer (CIO) The designated individual in an organization who is responsible for the overall management of information and its delivery system.

chief programmer team A group of specialized personnel involved in designing and developing a computer program.

child record A record at a level lower than that of the parent record in a database structure.

chip Another term for microchip; see *integrated circuit.*

circuit switching A method of moving data through a wide-area network that opens up a complete predetermined transmission route from sender to receiver before a message is transmitted.

classification The information processing task that arranges business transactions according to preselected criteria and groups the transactions having the same criterion together.

COBOL (COmmon Business-Oriented Language) A high-level language used in business information processing; specifically designed to manipulate large data files.

coding The substitution of a short, structured field for a longer field; for example, using M or F instead of MALE or FEMALE.

column In a spreadsheet the alphabetic ordering from left to right that, along with the numeric row designation, locates the position of a cell.

command mode A mode of operation in which application program commands can be selected.

common carrier A company licensed and regulated by federal or state government to carry the data communication property of others at a regulated rate.

communication channel The medium, or pathway, through which data are transmitted between devices. This pathway may be wire cable, microwave, or fiber optics.

communication package An application package that allows the exchange of data between computers.

communication parameters The boundaries within which devices are able to communicate with each other. Four essential components are the baud rate, the number of bits used to create each character, the number of stop bits, and the type of parity checking used.

compiler A language-translator program that translates at once an entire high-level language program into machine language.

completeness An attribute of information that refers to how complete a set of information is. A complete set of information tells everything that is needed to be known about a situation.

computer A device that can accept data, perform certain functions on that data, and present the results of those operations.

computer-aided design (CAD) The integration of computers and graphics to aid in the design and drafting processes.

computer-aided manufacturing (CAM) The use of computers to control machines in the manufacturing process.

computer-aided systems engineering (CASE) An entire class of programs (software) that automates systems analysis tasks.

computer-assisted retrieval system (CARS) The integration of micrographic technology and computers in a system that allows random and fast retrieval of information stored on microforms.

computer-based information system A set of people, data, procedures, hardware, and software that work together to achieve the common goal of information management.

computer branch exchange A computer-based private branch exchange (PBX).

computer crime A crime that involves the use of computers and software.

computer ethics A set of codes or rules governing the conduct of individuals and corporations in their use of computers; an accepted standard of behavior when dealing with computers and the information they contain.

computer-integrated manufacturing (CIM) The linking and integration of manufacturing and all other aspects of a company by computers.

computer network A system of two or more computers linked by data communication channels.

computer numerical control (CNC) The controlling of milling or cutting operations by a computer.

computer output microform (COM) Hard copy in the form of photographic images recorded on microfilm or microfiche.

computer virus A program that is embedded in what seems to be legitimate software (e.g., a word processor or a computer game); when used, can attack a system. A virus may simply be annoying, or it can cause significant damage to a system. Computer viruses have been programmed to scramble data, erase a hard-disk index, or even erase all data on a hard-disk drive.

concentration The process of connecting and serving more devices on a communication channel than that channel was designed to handle.

concentrator A hardware device, often a minicomputer, that controls the process of concentration.

concurrent access An attempt by two or more individuals or groups to use the same data simultaneously.

concurrent operating system An operating system that allows one CPU to switch rapidly between two programs as instructions are received; appears as if both programs are executing simultaneously.

contention A method for determining device access to a communication channel. With this method each device checks a channel to see whether it is free before sending data. Once a device begins transmission, it maintains sole control of that channel until it completes its transmission.

control language The portion of a query language used to grant and revoke access to a database.

controlling A management function that develops procedures to measure actual performance against goals and to make any necessary adjustments to ensure that the organization is moving toward its goal.

control panel An area in an electronic spreadsheet that displays information about the current file and the command or activity being performed.

control program A computer program in an operating system that manages a computer's hardware and its resources, such as CPU time, primary storage, and input and output devices.

control unit That part of a central processing unit that controls the sequence of events necessary to execute an instruction.

conversion The replacement of an existing system with a new information system.

converting The process of changing the data storage format of one file so that the file may be used by another program with a different data storage format.

coordinate The intersection of a row and a column in a spreadsheet; used to define a cell's position in a worksheet.

copying (1) The process of making a duplicate file from an existing file. (2) The process of duplicating text or graphics on the screen for placement elsewhere while leaving the original text or graphics intact.

Copyright Act of 1976 A law that actually went into effect in 1978; specifically lists computer programs among the works protected from the moment of creation against illegal copying.

cost/benefit analysis Part of the project justification stage of the system development life cycle often referred to as a feasibility study; compares both costs and benefits for alternative new information systems and the current system to determine which system should be recommended to management.

cost-effectiveness An attribute of information that suggests that the benefit to be derived from using information must be more than the cost of producing that information. If the cost of the information is greater than the benefit, the information is not cost-effective and is usually not produced.

cursor A special character that indicates a user's present position on a computer display screen; also acts as a pointer to focus attention on a particular point on the screen.

daisy-wheel printer A type of printer that uses a print wheel resembling a daisy. At the end of each petal is a fully formed character.

data Numbers, letters, characters, or combinations thereof that are capable of being entered into and processed by a computer; raw facts before processing.

database A cross-referenced collection of files designed and created to minimize repetition of data.

database administrator (DBA) One person or a group of people who manage a database. A DBA is specially trained in the DBMS software package being used on a system and in the construction of database structures.

database management system (DBMS) The software that allows data to be readily created, maintained, manipulated, and retrieved from a database. It is the interface among programs, users, and the data in the database.

database query language A fourth-generation language that is used in conjunction with a relational database; acts as an interface between a user and a DBMS and helps the user easily access data without the use of a complex programming code.

database service An on-line computer service through which users may access large databases of information. Like information services, these are subscriber services, but they contain information on more specialized topics.

data collection The activity of collecting transactional data for entry into a computer system.

data communication The process of sending data electronically from one point to another.

data consistency The concept of using the same kind, type, and size of data for all applications.

data definition language (DDL) The commands used to enter a database structure into a DBMS. The commands permit users to create, alter, and drop (delete) databases and their entities.

data dictionary A data file containing the technical description of the data to be stored in a database; it includes the field names, types (e.g., alphanumeric, numeric), size, descriptions, and logical relationships.

data-directed inference procedure Use of an inference engine to match the left-hand side of a rule with user-provided data and then draw a conclusion by looking at the right-hand side of the rule.

data element to report matrix A tabular technique that shows which file-data elements are printed out on which reports.

data entry The input of data into a system.

data file A file that contains only data.

data flow diagram (DFD) A graphic depiction of a system that concentrates on information flow rather than on treatment of the information during the flow.

data independence A concept whereby deleting or changing selected data in a database does not affect other data in that database.

data integrity The idea that data stored in a file or database are correct and accurate.

data manager An application package that allows a user to manage (manipulate, store, retrieve, display, and print) data. A data manager may be a file-management system or a database management system.

data manipulation Altering data that enter or exit a computer.

data manipulation language (DML) Commands that deal with the data that are added to, deleted from, or changed in the database.

data processing The traditional term for the process of converting data into information; now often referred to as information processing.

data redundancy Refers to the number of times a datum is stored in a standard file-processing or database system.

data stealing A computer crime in which data gathered for a legitimate use are used in an unauthorized manner.

data subsystem The component of a decision support system (DSS) that represents the data that are necessary to solve a specific problem.

debugging The process of finding any type of error in a program and correcting it.

decision support system (DSS) An information system that is designed to allow managers to interact directly with a computer for assistance with relatively unstructured decisions.

decoupling The process of providing safeguards so that a system is not at the mercy of another system; also called independence.

default settings In application software a parameter that is automatically entered unless changed by the user.

deleting An application-software feature that allows existing text, data, fields, records, or files to be removed.

demand reports Management reports that are generated only at the request of an individual.

demodulation The process of converting an analog signal into a digital signal.

density The amount of data that can be stored in a given area of a storage medium. The higher the density, the more data are stored.

design program A graphics program that is used as a design tool to create and/or alter the image of an object; a computerized drafting table.

desktop computer Another name for a microcomputer; so called because it fits on the top of a desk.

desktop publishing A concept that combines the use of a microcomputer with page-composition (graphics-oriented) software and high-quality laser printers.

detail report A listing of all transactions that have been entered during a day and the way in which each transaction has changed a stored record.

digital computer   A high-speed, programmable electronic device that stores, processes, and retrieves data by counting discrete signals.

digital data transmission   The transmission of data as distinct pulses, or on/off electrical states.

digitizer   An input device that uses a tablet on which a special stylus is moved to provide data entry or indicate position; also called a graphics tablet.

direct-access file   A file where records are stored in random order; also called a random-access file.

direct conversion   A type of changeover in which an existing information system is replaced with a new information system as of a certain date; also called crash conversion.

directing   The management function that supplies leadership in the supervising of personnel through communication and motivation.

disk operating system (DOS)   An operating system for microcomputers in which all or part of the system resides on a disk and must be loaded into the computer; a set of programs that controls and supervises a microcomputer's hardware.

disk pack   A removable, hard-disk storage device containing multiple hard disks in a plastic case; provides increased storage capabilities for large computer systems.

distributed database   A database that exists in one of the following forms: (1) on-line at the host computer in a central location but also available to remote locations; (2) partially duplicated at the host computer and placed on a remote computer for processing, called segmentation; (3) entirely copied for processing, called replication, at each remote location.

distributed data processing (DDP)   The concept of dispersing computers, devices, software, and data connected through communication channels into areas where they are used.

documentation   (1) The written or graphic record of the steps involved in developing or maintaining an information system. (2) Written or graphic descriptions detailing the purpose and the operation of software.

domains   The name given to the columns in a relational database table.

dot-matrix printer   A type of impact printer that uses a print head containing pins, usually 9 to 24, that produce characters by printing patterns of dots.

downloading   The process of receiving a file from another computer.

draft-quality print   Lowest quality print; suitable for rough drafts; also called compressed print.

Characters are smaller than they are in standard-quality print and are formed with a minimum number of dots.

drum printer   A line-at-a-time impact printer that uses a rotating drum of 80 to 132 print positions, with each print position containing a complete set of characters.

dumb terminal   A stand-alone keyboard and display screen that can send or receive data but cannot process that data.

edit check   A programming technique to verify that (1) numeric fields contain numeric characters; (2) fields that are required to be entered are indeed entered; (3) specific values are entered for certain fields; and (4) lengths of fields are accurate.

editing   The process by which typographical errors, incorrect values, or erroneous formulas are corrected in an application program.

electrically erasable programmable read-only memory (EEPROM)   A type of memory that can be erased and reprogrammed electronically without removing a chip from the circuit board.

electronic blackboard   A pressure-sensitive chalkboard that digitizes and displays on a monitor whatever is written on it.

electronic data interchange (EDI)   A communications protocol that allows retailers and their suppliers to conduct business transactions electronically.

electronic data-processing (EDP) auditor   An individual who tests an information system to ensure that business transactions are processed by the computer system in accordance with the desired procedures.

electronic eavesdropping   Illegal tapping into communication lines that are used by computers to send and receive data.

electronic funds transfer (EFT)   A method of data communication that uses a communication channel to transfer money between accounts.

electronic mail   Any mail or messages transmitted electronically by computers using communication channels.

electronic teleconferencing   A method of communicating via computers connected through a telephone system. Each user or group of users participates in the conference by keying in their conversations.

electronic work monitoring   A process of measuring worker productivity with the use of computers.

encoding system   A system whereby alphanumeric characters are represented by patterns of 1s and 0s so that they can be recognized and used by a computer. The American Standard Code for Information Interchange (ASCII) and Extended Binary Coded Decimal Interchange Code (EBCDIC) are the two most widely used encoding systems.

encryption   A data-coding scheme that converts data into unintelligible characters so that they cannot be read or used by unauthorized persons.

end-user   A term that specifically refers to noninformation system personnel who use an information system.

end-user computing   The concept that supports and embraces the notion that the person who is responsible for the output of computing should be the person who is going to utilize that output.

erasable optical-storage disk   A type of optical-storage disk on which data can be written and erased and the disk can then be reused.

erasable programmable read-only memory (EPROM)   A type of memory that can be erased by removing it from the circuit and exposing the chip to ultraviolet light. It can then be reprogrammed.

ergonomics   The science of designing the workplace for the comfort and the safety of the worker; also referred to as human engineering.

exception reports   Management reports indicating activities that are out of control and thus need management action.

exchange mode   A condition in an application package that causes new text to take the place of, or overwrite, any existing text that occupies the same space.

execution cycle   The cycle during which an instruction is executed by the ALU.

executive information system (EIS)   An information system that specifically caters to an executive's special information needs in managerial planning, monitoring, and analysis.

explanation subsystem   The component of a knowledge-based (expert) system that has the capability of responding to user requests and inquiries in the course of the system's execution.

external direct-connect modem   A type of modem that is external to a computer and connected directly to a telephone line. This type of modem reduces distortion and allows for faster data transmission than the acoustic type permits.

external source of information   A source of information outside the organization (e.g., external

survey, annual report from another organization, government agency, and trade publication).

facsimile   A form of electronic mail that copies and sends text and graphics over long distances.

facsimile (FAX) machine   A communication device that allows a user to digitize text, graphics, and photos and send them to another location electronically.

feedback   A reintroduction of a portion of a system's output as an input to that same system; used as a control mechanism within a system to indicate the difference between a goal and the actual performance of the system.

fiber optics   A type of data communication channel in which data are transmitted and received as digital pulses of light.

field   Any collection of related characters.

fifth-generation language   One of the next generation of programming languages. Many consider natural languages to be fifth generation.

file   A collection of related records in which each record contains related data fields.

file locking   A file-protection procedure that allows only one user to access a file at a time.

file-management system   An application program that can manage (manipulate, store, retrieve, and print) data in separate files. In this system only one file can be accessed at one time.

file recovery   A contingency plan developed by a systems analyst to guard against file data being lost or destroyed. This plan includes (1) saving on-line file data on magnetic tape at periodic intervals and, if there are subsequent problems with the on-line file data, (2) reloading the magnetic tape data back onto the on-line file medium.

financial information system   A system designed to provide management with information concerning the acquisition of funds to finance a business and the allocation and control of the organization's financial resources.

fixed disk   A hard-disk storage system of one or more nonremovable hard disks protected in a permanently sealed case.

flat-panel display   A type of display that does not use a picture tube to display characters; includes liquid-crystal display (LCD) and gas plasma.

floppy diskette   A flexible, mylar magnetic diskette commonly used with microcomputers for magnetic storage of data.

footer   Text that appears at the bottom of a page; often a page number.

formatting (1) The setting of parameters such as margins or tabs that control the appearance of text or the setting of attributes to describe how data are to be displayed. (2) A term used to describe the preparation of a disk or diskette for use.

formula A mathematical or logical equation from which data values are calculated.

FORTRAN (FORmula TRANslator) A high-level language designed for scientists, engineers, and mathematicians to use in solving complex numerical problems.

fourth-generation language A class of programming languages in which a user needs very little programming knowledge to write computer instructions. Examples include database query languages, report generators, and application generators.

Freedom of Information Act of 1970 A law passed in 1970 that allows citizens to find out which federal agencies are collecting and storing data about them and to secure copies of the records.

frequency-division multiplexing A multiplexing method in which a high-speed channel is divided into multiple slow-speed channels of different frequencies.

front-end processor A special-purpose computer that controls the input and output functions of a main computer.

full-duplex mode A method of transferring data over a communication channel; permits data to be transmitted and received at the same time.

future orientation The principle that all information systems, no matter how well designed, undergo considerable modification and repair during their lifetimes.

gallium arsenide A material used to make semiconductors; replaces silicon because it allows faster transmission times, uses less power, is more radiation resistant, and can process both light and electronic digital data on one chip.

gateway An interface that converts the data codes, formats, addresses, and transmission rates of one network into a form usable by another network.

gateway service A service whereby computer time is bought from many information and commercial database services at wholesale rates and sold to subscribers at a retail rate. A gateway service provides users with the convenience of accessing many services through one central communication line.

glossary A word-processor feature that allows abbreviations to be typed instead of longer words or phrases. As the abbreviation is being typed, the full word or phrase appears on the screen.

goal-directed inference procedure Use of an inference engine to form a hypothesis and then try to prove that hypothesis by looking at the right-hand side of the rule and checking to see whether the left-hand side of the rule matches user-provided data.

grammar checker A software program that locates grammar and punctuation errors in a document.

graphical information Information represented pictorially.

graphics Representation of data in charts, graphs, or other pictorial forms.

graphics package An application program that allows a user to create, edit, display, and print graphic images; may be a separate software program or integrated into another software program.

half-duplex mode A method of transferring data over a communication channel; permits data to be transmitted and received but not at the same time.

hand-held computer A portable computer slightly larger than a pocket calculator that can be held in one hand.

handshaking The process of sending prearranged signals specifying the protocol to be followed when transmitting or receiving data.

hard copy A form of relatively stable and permanent output; for example, paper or computer output microform.

hard disk A hard metallic disk used for magnetic storage of data. Because of its rigid construction, it can be produced with higher storage densities, allowing more data to be stored. Data can also be accessed faster than they can with a floppy diskette.

hardware The physical components of a computer system, such as the computer itself, input devices, output devices, and data communication devices.

hashing A method whereby a computer performs a mathematical operation on a key field and transforms the key field into a disk location.

head crash The result of the read/write head of a hard-disk drive coming into contact with the hard disk; results in severe damage to the head, disk, or both.

header   Text that appears at the top of a page; often a title.

help window   A feature in many application programs that can provide users with information about commands or procedures.

hierarchical chart   A design aid that shows the purpose of a module, its relationship to other modules, and the overall program logic.

hierarchical database   A database structure in which data relationships follow hierarchies or trees, which are either one-to-one or one-to-many relationships among record types.

high-level language   A programming language using instructions that closely resemble human language and mathematical notation. BASIC and Pascal are two examples.

high-resolution graphics   A method of creating graphic images by turning on or off the pixels that make up the screen display.

history file   A file created for long-term storage of data.

human engineering   The science of designing the workplace for the comfort and safety of the workers; also called ergonomics.

human factors   The subject of a study of the interface between humans and machines in general and computers in particular.

human resources information system   A system designed to provide management with information involving the recruitment, placement, evaluation, compensation, and development of employees.

hyphenation   A word-processor feature that determines how a word will be hyphenated. There are three basic types: hard, soft, and nonbreaking hyphens.

impact printer   A type of printer that produces characters by using a hammer or pins to strike an ink ribbon against a sheet of paper.

implementation stage   The stage of the system development life cycle during which a designed system is introduced into the workplace as a completely new system or as a replacement system; includes testing, installation, training, and maintenance.

independence   See *decoupling*.

index directory   A directory that contains the key field and the location of a record in an indexed sequential file.

indexed sequential file   A file that permits both direct and sequential access.

industrial espionage   A computer crime in which a computer is used to steal trade secrets, such as design or marketing plans, from a company.

inference engine   The component of a knowledge-based (expert) system that uses the rules from the knowledge base together with the data provided by a user to draw a possible conclusion.

information   The result of processing data with a computer into a form usable by people.

information center   A center that is used within a firm to distribute information, provide instruction in the use of an information system, distribute computing hardware, and provide information system experts and other useful functions in a support role.

information filtering   The process of removing trivial or nonessential information from the total information generated for any given decision situation.

information overload   The problem of receiving trivial or nonessential information in any given decision situation.

information processing   Using the computer to transform data (raw facts) into information (an organized, usable form).

information resource management (IRM)   A concept that information is an asset that is valuable and costly and needs to be closely managed if a firm is to maximize the use of this resource.

information service   An on-line computer service through which users can access large databases of general-interest information. Information services are usually offered for a fee and require a password to gain entry.

information system   A set of people, data, and procedures that work together to achieve the common goal of information management. See also *computer-based information system*.

information system life cycle   The life span of an information system from its inception to its removal or redesign.

ink-jet printer   A type of nonimpact printer that forms characters on paper by spraying ink particles in character forms.

input   (1) The process of collecting, verifying, and encoding data in a machine-readable form for the computer. (2) The data before processing takes place.

input device   A peripheral device, such as a keyboard or a mouse, through which data are entered and transformed into machine-readable form.

input line   The place in a spreadsheet where data are typed before actually being entered into the program. An input line often allows a user to edit data before they are entered.

input to file matrix   A tabular technique that shows which system input documents update (change) which system files.

input validation   The process of validating input data against all possible errors.

insert mode   A condition in an application package in which the addition of new text results in all text to the right being moved over to make room for the new text.

installation   The second task in the implementation phase of the system development life cycle, during which an information system is made operational by being put to work for the users.

instruction cycle   The fetch and decode steps in the process of performing an instruction.

instruction set   The group of instructions that defines the basic operations of a computer, that is, the arithmetic, logical, storage, and retrieval functions.

integrated circuit (IC)   A single, complete, electronic semiconductor circuit contained on a piece of silicon; also called a microchip or chip.

integrated family of programs   A group of independent application packages that share the same data and use common commands and functions.

integrated operating environment   A program called a window manager, or integrator, that allows several different application packages to work concurrently and share data.

integrated software   Application software packages that can share the same data.

intelligent terminal   A stand-alone keyboard and display screen that can send or receive data and that incorporates a microprocessor, enabling it to process data independently.

interactive system   A system that allows a user to communicate with the computer through dialogue.

interblock gap (IBG)   The blank section of tape that separates groups of records. It provides a space for the tape to attain the proper speed for reading or writing.

interdependence   A situation in which the output from one system is the input required for one or more other systems.

interface subsystem   The component of a decision support system (DSS) that acts as the link between a manager and the computer.

internal direct-connect modem   Similar in function to the external direct-connect modem; has all the circuitry on one circuit board, which fits into an expansion slot inside the computer.

internal source of information   A source of information within an organization (e.g., internally generated document, observation, and internal survey).

interpreter   A language-translator program that translates a high-level language program into machine code one line at a time. Each line is executed after it is translated.

interprocessing   A type of processing (also called dynamic linking) that allows any change made in one application to be automatically reflected in any related, linked applications.

interrecord gap (IRG)   The section of magnetic tape between individual records that allows the tape to attain the proper speed for reading or writing.

interrupt   A signal that tells the operating system that (1) some action needs to be taken or (2) an action started earlier is now completed.

job   A collection of one or more related job steps (programs).

job control language (JCL)   A language used to tell an operating system what a job requires in terms of computer resources and operating system services; provides users with a means of communicating with the operating system.

joining   Also called merging; the process of combining records from two or more tables in a relational database management system.

Josephson junction   An electronic switching device that operates at extremely low temperatures; is much faster than a transistor and consumes less power.

jumping   A cursor movement used in a spreadsheet whereby a user may go directly to any designated cell.

justification   A feature of application software that allows a user to move text flush to the right or left margins.

keyboard   An input device, similar to a typewriter keyboard, that contains letters, numbers, special-character keys, keys that control cursor movement, and keys that can be programmed for other uses.

key field   A field used to uniquely identify each record.

knowledge acquisition subsystem   The component of a knowledge-based (expert) system that transfers the knowledge from an expert to a knowledge base.

knowledge base The component of a knowledge-based (expert) system that contains a collection of facts and the rules by which those facts relate.

knowledge-based (expert) system An information system that specializes in one area or application to help humans make a decision or solve a problem; acts as a consultant, or expert, for the user.

knowledge engineering The process by which an expert's knowledge is transformed into a knowledge base.

knowledge engineer A person involved in the gathering of facts, rules, and knowledge for the knowledge base of an expert system.

knowledge workers The people who create, process, and distribute information.

label An alphanumeric designator that describes the contents of an area or device, such as a title or a heading for a report.

language-translator program A program that translates a programming language into machine code for execution by a computer.

lap-top computer A portable computer, usually small enough to fit in a briefcase; so named because it is small enough to fit on a person's lap.

large-scale integration (LSI) The process of putting several thousand complete circuits on a single chip.

laser printer A nonimpact printer that produces images on paper by directing a laser beam onto a drum and leaving a negative charge to which positively charged toner powder will stick. The toner powder is transferred to paper as it rolls by the drum and is bonded to the paper by hot rollers.

letter-quality print Print of fully formed characters, similar to typewriter print.

light pen A light-sensitive input device that detects the presence or absence of light when touched to a screen; used to select an entry or indicate position.

limit check A technique used to verify that a field does not exceed some minimum or maximum value.

line printer A printer with a print mechanism capable of printing an entire line at a time; also called a line-at-a-time printer.

local-area network (LAN) A type of computer network in which two or more computers of the same or different sizes are directly linked within a small, well-defined area, such as a room or building.

logical (conceptual) system design stage The blueprint phase of designing a new information system. Descriptive tools (graphs, charts, and tables) are used to describe what the inputs, outputs, and files of a new system will look like. The products of this SDLC phase are turned over to application programmers, who convert a conceptual information system blueprint into an actual working system.

logical design A detailed description of a database based on how a user-department will use the data.

logic error A type of computer program error that is caused by improperly coding either individual statements or sequences. It does not stop program execution but produces inaccurate results.

log-on The process of entering into a system an account number followed by a password to control user access to the system.

low-level language A programming language, such as machine or assembly language; requires a programmer to have detailed knowledge of the internal workings of the computer.

low-level (operational) managers Managers who are involved with the day-to-day operational aspects of a business; mainly direct other personnel to implement the tactical decisions of middle-level management.

machine language A programming language that a computer understands; based on electronic states represented by 1s and 0s.

macro A file in some application programs that contains a series of previously recorded keystrokes or commands that can be executed with one or two keystrokes. A macro is used to increase the speed and efficiency of making repeated entries.

magnetic disk A mylar (floppy-diskette) or metallic (hard-disk) platter on which electronic data can be stored; suitable for both direct-access or sequential-access storage and retrieval of data.

magnetic-ink character recognition (MICR) A source data input technique in which data are represented by magnetic-ink characters that can be read into a computer either by special machines or by humans.

magnetic strips The thin bands of magnetically encoded data found on the backs of many credit cards and automatic banking cards.

magnetic tape A strip of mylar coated with iron oxide and used to store data magnetically; a sequential storage medium.

mail merge   The process of combining two documents into one. For example, a form letter can be merged with a file containing names and addresses, in order to personalize the letter.

mainframe computer   A large-scale computer with processing capabilities greater than those of a minicomputer but less than those of a supercomputer.

maintenance   The fourth task in the implementation phase of the system development life cycle, during which an information system is continually modified to meet the changing requirements of its users.

maintenance programmer   A special type of programmer responsible for the maintenance of an information system.

management hierarchy   The structure of management in an organization.

management information system (MIS)   A system that supplies managers with information to aid them in their decision-making responsibilities.

management report   An exception report that shows an unfavorable pattern in an organization's operation.

management training   An overview of a new system, intended to familiarize management with the system's major strengths and weaknesses and its impact on organizational goals.

manager   A person responsible for using available resources (people, materials/equipment, land, and money) to achieve an organizational goal.

manufacturing automation protocol (MAP)   A communication link, developed by General Motors, that allows different types of computers to communicate with each other.

margin settings   Specifications that describe the blank spaces around the left, right, top, and bottom sides of a document.

marketing information system   An information system designed to gather details about day-to-day sales transactions, management and control of operations, and sales and marketing strategies for the future.

master file   A file that contains data of a permanent nature, such as employee salary files and inventory files.

matching   The comparing of data in one computer database with those in another for a specific purpose; used by some government agencies to detect discrepancies that might indicate fraud.

menu   In application software a screen listing of commands, actions, or other alternatives from which a user may select at a particular point in a program. A menu selection may perform an action or bring up another menu.

menu map   A charting technique used with interactive information systems to provide a top-down structure for selection menus.

message characters   The start and stop bits of asynchronous transmission and the synchronizing characters in synchronous transmission that signal when data are being sent and when a transmission is finished.

message switching   A method of moving data through a wide-area network; involves sending an entire message at once over a predetermined transmission route that is not dedicated to just one message.

microcomputer   A small computer with processing capabilities that are less than those of a minicomputer; sometimes called a personal computer.

microfiche   A type of microform that consists of sheets of 105-mm film mounted on a 4 × 6-inch card.

micrographics   The process of photographing paper records and maintaining and storing the images on microforms.

microprocessor   A single chip that contains both the arithmetic and logic unit (ALU) and the control unit; may also contain the primary storage unit.

micro-to-mainframe link   A method of connecting a microcomputer to a mainframe computer; enables the microcomputer user to share the data and computing power of the larger system.

micro-to-micro link   A method of connecting microcomputers to one another so that they can share data; allows computers using incompatible data formats to share data.

microwave   A type of data communication channel in which data are transmitted through the air as analog signals for reception by satellites or microwave transmitting stations.

middle-level (tactical) managers   Managers who are generally concerned with short-term tactical decisions; allocate time to staffing, planning, organizing, directing, and controlling.

millions of instructions per second (MIPS)   A measure of computer speed; the number of instructions completed per second.

minicomputer   A computer in the large-scale category with fewer processing capabilities than a mainframe computer has.

mixed cell reference   A method of copying a formula in a spreadsheet; requires that each cell reference be specified as either absolute or relative.

mnemonic An alphabetic abbreviation used as a memory aid.

model name An identifying name given to a spreadsheet file; another term for *file name*.

model subsystem The component of a decision support system (DSS) that represents the mathematical formulations that define a real-life problem.

modem Acronym for modulator-demodulator; the device that converts signals from analog to digital form and from digital to analog form.

modularity The process of designing a system in relatively small chunks to allow assignment of different programmers and analysts to separate tasks. Modules can be developed independently of each other, and small modules of program code can later be repaired with minimum disruption to other modules.

modulation The process of converting a digital signal to an analog signal.

Modula-2 A version of Pascal with improvements in modularity, input and output, and file-handling capabilities.

module A group of related processing instructions; part of a larger program.

monitor A television-like device used to display data.

mouse A small input device that controls the position of a cursor on a screen. Two types are used: an electromechanical mouse, which rolls an enclosed sphere along a flat surface, and an optical mouse, which uses light beams to mark its position on a special tablet of grid lines.

multiplexer A hardware device that performs the multiplexing process.

multiplexing The process of combining the transmission from more than one device, character by character, into a single data stream that can be sent over a single communication channel.

multipoint channel configuration A type of communication channel configuration in which three or more devices, connected together, share the same communication channel.

multiprocessing operating system An operating system that allows a multiple CPU computer to execute more than one program at a time.

multiprogramming A type of processing in which a CPU switches its attention between two or more programs in primary memory, executing statements from one program and then from another; allows a single CPU to execute what

seems to be (but is not) more than one program at the same time.

multitasking A type of processing that allows several different applications to run simultaneously.

multithreading A type of processing that supports several simultaneous functions with the same application.

multiuser data manager A data manager that can be accessed by more than one user at a time.

narrow-band channel A communication channel, such as a telegraph line, that transmits data at 40 to 100 bits per second.

Nassi-Shneiderman chart A structured flowchart, developed by Isaac Nassi and Ben Shneiderman, that uses various-shaped boxes to represent the sequence, selection, and repetition control structures within program processing.

natural language A language that closely resembles human speech; eliminates the need for a user or programmer to learn a specific vocabulary, grammar, or syntax.

natural language processing The ability of a computer to understand and translate a natural language, such as English, into commands to perform a specific operation.

network database A database structure in which data use a many-to-many relationship among the records.

neural networks Programs that attempt to mimic the neural connections in the human brain.

node Each computer or device in a computer network system.

nonimpact printer A type of printer that produces characters without physically striking the paper.

nonprocedural language A programming language that describes the task to be accomplished without specifying the approach.

null modem A cable that eliminates the need for a modem when data are transferred between two computers located near each other.

numerical information Information represented by numbers.

office information system (OIS) An information system that includes a number of subsystems integrated together to perform office functions more efficiently and productively.

office support system A variety of applications that can help individual users better organize many of their daily office activities; typically includes an electronic calendar and time management, tickler files, and electronic scratch pad files as well as electronic mail, word processing, and document storage and retrieval capabilities.

off-line   Refers to devices that are not directly connected to a CPU.

on-line   Refers to devices that are directly connected to a CPU.

operating system (OS)   A set of programs that controls and supervises a computer system's hardware and provides services to programmers and users.

operator training   Communicating the operational details of an information system to the operators.

optical-bar recognition (OBR)   A data input method that reads and interprets bar codes.

optical card   A small card that stores data on a strip of special material that is similar to a magnetic strip. However, the data on an optical card are encoded by a laser rather than magnetically.

optical-character recognition (OCR)   The most sophisticated form of optical recognition; recognizes letters, numbers, and other optical character sets by their shapes, in much the same way that a human eye recognizes them.

optical laser disk   A type of storage medium on which data are stored and read by a laser. Optical-laser disks have much higher data densities than their magnetic disk counterparts.

optical-mark recognition (OMR)   A data input method that scans a series of pen or pencil marks on a special form and translates their positions into machine-readable code.

optical tape   A storage medium that is similar in appearance to magnetic tape but that stores data with optical-laser techniques.

optoelectronics   A combination of both electronic and optical technology for data processing and communication applications.

organizing   A management function that provides resources and a structure in which personnel are responsible and accountable for working toward an organizational goal.

orphan line   The first line of a new paragraph that stands alone at the bottom of a page.

outliner   A word-processor feature that helps a user organize ideas by representing them as headings or subheadings that can be rearranged in a logical pattern.

output   (1) The process of retrieving stored information, converting it into human-readable form, and displaying that information to a user. (2) The result of data processing.

output device   A peripheral device that translates machine-readable codes into a form that can be used by humans or other machines.

output file   A file created by one program that is to be used by another program.

packet switching   A method of moving data through a wide-area network; divides messages into packets, or blocks, and sends them over a transmission route.

page breaks   An application-software parameter that controls the number of lines on a page. After a set number of lines is reached, additional text is automatically placed on the next page.

painting and drawing program   A microcomputer graphics program that allows a user to "paint" an image by using an input device, such as a mouse, as the brush. The user can also draw, fill shapes, and change the color and texture of a painting.

parallel conversion   A conversion approach in which both new and old information systems are used for a certain period of time, after which the old system is discontinued.

parallel processing   A data-processing method in which a computer accesses several instructions from the same program at once and works on them at the same time, using multiple CPUs; much faster than traditional serial processing techniques.

parent record   A record at a level higher than that of a child record in a database structure.

Pascal   A high-level language originally designed to teach structured-programming concepts; suited for both file processing and mathematical applications.

password   An alphanumeric code that restricts data access to those with knowledge of the correct password.

performance measurement system (PMS)   A technique used to predict an information system's demise or minor ailment in need of treatment. A PMS keeps track of the daily operations of an information system and signals management when the system appears to be deteriorating.

peripheral device   Any hardware item that is attached to the main unit of a computer, such as an input or output device or a secondary storage device.

personal computer   A microcomputer that is used for the benefit of one person.

phased-in conversion   A conversion approach in which a new information system is installed in phases, or segments.

physical design   The actual structure of a database, based on the DBMS software on the system.

physical (detailed) system design stage A stage of the system development life cycle, during which a logical (paper) design is transformed into an actual working system.

piggybacking A concept of predicting information system decay so that a replacement system is ready to operate just when the old system fails.

pilot conversion A conversion approach in which a new system is installed in one location and tried there before it is installed in other locations.

piracy The illegal copying of copyrighted computer programs.

pixel The smallest part of a display screen that can be individually controlled.

planning A management function that involves developing courses of action to meet short- and long-term goals of the organization.

PL/1 (Programming Language One) A high-level language that allows powerful computations and sophisticated data structures. It was designed to replace FORTRAN, ALGOL, and COBOL and is used largely in the oil industry.

plotter An output device especially designed to produce a hard copy of graphics.

point-of-sale (POS) system A system that allows data to be captured automatically at the source of a transaction.

point-of-sale (POS) terminal A device that reads data at the source of a transaction and immediately translates them into usable information.

point-to-point channel configuration A type of communication channel configuration that directly connects a computer to a single device, giving those two entities sole use of the channel.

polling A method of determining which device needs to access a communication channel. The main computer checks, or polls, each device on the channel, one at a time, to see whether it has any data to send. Only one device can use that channel at a time.

portable computer A microcomputer that is small enough to be carried easily from place to place.

preliminary problem report A report created by a systems analyst that includes (1) the nature and source of an information system problem, (2) the systems analyst's more detailed analysis of the problem, and (3) the analyst's recommendation as to whether the problem can be treated through normal system maintenance operations or requires major modification or complete replacement of the system.

presentation graphics Graphics suitable for a formal presentation.

primary storage Also known as primary memory; the internal storage unit of a computer.

printer An output device that produces hard copy, usually consisting of text but sometimes including graphics as well.

print file A file that is sent to the printer.

printing The process of producing hard-copy output.

privacy In relationship to computer data, the right of control over one's personal data.

Privacy Act of 1974 Established that the federal government has no right to keep secret files about any citizen; allows individuals to find out which data have been collected about them and how the data are being used, among other provisions.

private branch exchange A local-area network that is implemented in a star network arrangement, using an organization's existing telephone switching system.

problem definition stage The first stage of the system development life cycle, which begins when a problem with the current information system is detected and is serious enough to lead to the question, Should we start planning for a new system to replace the current system?

procedural language A programming language that specifies how a task is to be accomplished.

procedures Lists of instructions that guide and direct the use of hardware and software.

process control Monitoring and controlling an operation.

processing The routine whereby a computer creates useful information from data by performing such operations as classifying, sorting, calculating, summarizing, and storing.

production/operations information system An information system designed to gather and process data about all activities involved in producing goods and services.

program A series of instructions that tells the computer what to do.

program file A file that contains program instructions.

program flowchart (PFC) A flowchart that graphically details the processing steps of a particular program.

programmable controller A computer-controlled unit consisting of a microprocessor, input and output modules, and a power supply; used to monitor and control machinery and processes.

programmable read-only memory (PROM) A type of memory that can be programmed only once and then cannot be further altered.

programmer A person who codes instructions in a programming language so that they can be used by a computer to solve a problem.

programmer/analyst A position that combines the functions of a programmer and a systems analyst.

programming language A set of written symbols that instructs the computer to perform specific tasks.

program swapping A technique that involves moving programs between primary storage and secondary storage.

project accountability chart (PAC) A planning tool that organizes a project by time on the horizontal axis and by responsible agency on the vertical axis.

projecting In a relational database management system a process by which a subset of a larger table is created with only the needed rows and columns.

project justification stage A stage of the system development life cycle in which the information system personnel perform cost/benefit analysis of the various alternative information systems that could bridge the gap between the current and the ideal information systems and select one system to recommend to management.

project leader An individual who supervises a development project through all phases of the system development life cycle.

project management The structured coordination and monitoring of all activities involved in a one-time endeavor, or project.

prompt line A line that appears when a software package is being used that asks, or prompts, the user for a response. It may be posed as a question or may be a listing of choices.

protocol A set of rules and procedures for transmitting and receiving data so that different devices can communicate with each other.

prototype information system A real, working, and usable system, built economically and quickly with the intention of being modified.

pseudocode A type of code that uses English-like phrases to describe the processing steps of a program or a module.

qualitative information Information that describes something using nonquantitative characteristics—for example, red, happy, excellent.

quantitative information Information that tells how much or how many—for example, twelve, small, every.

query language A language that allows end-users to make inquiries into a database. Such a language makes inquiries simple and, in conjunction with a report writer, gives end-users the ability to make queries and produce reports without programmer intervention.

random-access file A file in which records are stored in random order; also called a direct-access file.

random-access memory (RAM) A type of memory into which data and programs can be written and from which data and programs can be read. Data stored in RAM are erased when the computer's power is shut off.

range check A programming technique verifying that the data in a field fall within a particular range of values.

range of cells In a spreadsheet a method of selecting specific cells by identifying the upper-left cell and the lower-right cell; permits large blocks of cells to be manipulated together.

read-only memory (ROM) A type of memory, the contents of which are entered during manufacturing. The contents can only be read; they are permanent and cannot be changed.

ready/entry mode A mode of operation in which a spreadsheet program indicates that it is ready to receive information. When a character is entered, the program automatically switches to the entry mode.

real-time operating system An operating system that allows a computer to respond to input immediately or as soon as required.

real-time processing A common form of data entry in which data are entered on-line and the adding, deleting, or modifying of records in files can take place instantly.

record A collection of related fields.

register A temporary holding place for data or instructions that are to be worked on immediately; part of a CPU.

relational database A database that is composed of many tables in which data are stored.

relative cell reference A method of copying in which the formula is the same but the cells referenced in that formula are different; used with spreadsheets.

relevance An attribute of information that refers to whether information is needed and useful in a particular situation.

reliability An attribute of information that refers to the variance associated with the means of the other six attributes of information.

remote-job-entry site   A data entry site that is separate from a main computer center.

removable cartridge   A hard-disk storage system that utilizes a cartridge containing one or more hard disks. The cartridge can be removed from the hard-disk drive and replaced with another cartridge at any time.

repetition control structure   Also called looping; a programming control structure that allows a series of instructions to be executed more than once without having to be recoded.

replication   A type of distributive database processing in which copies of an entire database and DBMS are available in each remote location.

report distribution   A list of which reports are generated by an information system and who receives a copy of each report.

report file   A file of information to be printed; created on auxiliary magnetic tape or disk.

report format   How a report will look, including the numbers of lines, columns, and pages and a summary of the information to be included in the report.

report frequency   How often a report is produced.

report generator   A type of fourth-generation language that allows data to be extracted from a database and formatted into a report.

reprographics   The process of reproducing hard copies through various duplicating methods.

requirements analysis stage   A stage of the system development life cycle that involves the analysis of a current system's performance to determine what the ideal system would be. The gap between the current system and the ideal system is explored to determine which system will best close the gap.

resolution   The quality of a monitor's screen, measured by the number of pixels the screen contains.

ring network   A computer network arrangement in which each computer or device is connected in a closed loop by a single communication channel. Communication between the source and the destination must flow through each device in the ring.

robot   A reprogrammable machine that can be instructed to do a variety of tasks; often used to perform dangerous or boring tasks.

robotics   The area of study dealing with the design, construction, and operation of robots.

root record   The topmost record in a tree structure.

row   In a spreadsheet the numeric ordering from top to bottom that partially locates the position of a cell.

RPG (Report Program Generator)   A programming language designed for producing reports and processing files.

run-time error   An error that causes a program to stop executing.

salami slicing   A type of computer crime; data manipulation in which a small amount of money is skimmed from many accounts and put into one central account.

scanner   An input device that scans a printed surface and translates the image it sees into a machine-readable format.

scheduled reports   Management reports that are generated on a regular basis according to a well-established schedule.

schema   A complete description of the content and structure of a database.

screen form   A layout form created for the purpose of defining the position of data fields and providing an entry point for the data in a data manager.

scrolling   A feature that allows movement of the edit window in order to create or view text that is outside the display screen. Scrolling can take place horizontally and vertically.

search and replace   An application-software feature that allows a user to look for a word or phrase in a file and determine whether it should be replaced. One option permits it to be automatically replaced.

searching   The process of locating and retrieving data stored in a file.

secondary storage   Computer memory external to the computer that is typically used for long-term storage or for large quantities of data or programs.

sectors   A pie-shaped division of each magnetic-disk track, which further identifies the storage location of data.

segmentation   A type of distributive database processing in which part of the database at the host computer is duplicated and placed on a remote computer.

selecting   The process of retrieving only certain records from a table in a relational database management system.

selection control structure   A programming control structure that selects a processing option based on the result of decision criteria.

semiconductor memory   A memory type in which electronic circuits are etched onto silicon wafers.

sequence control structure   A programming control structure that executes statements in order, one after another.

sequential file   A file in which the records appear in the order in which they were entered into the computer and subsequently stored on the storage media.

service program   An operating system program that provides a service, such as a utility or language-translator program, to the user.

shells   In an expert system a general-purpose inference engine and a skeleton of the knowledge base into which users can add their own special data.

simplex mode   A method of transferring data over a communication channel in only one direction. Simplex mode devices can transmit or receive but not both.

single-program operating system   A type of operating system that allows only one program to execute at a time.

smart terminal   A terminal that allows limited editing and data storage without interacting with the main computer system; cannot be used to program or run sophisticated applications.

soft copy   A form of volatile output, usually a screen display.

software   The instructions that tell a computer what to do.

sort file   Any file having one or more fields in some sorted order.

sorting   The process of arranging data in numeric or alphabetic sequence, either in ascending or descending order.

source document   A document that contains data pertaining to a business event (transaction). For example, a source document for a payroll system might be a time card, where employee working hours are first recorded.

specialized common carrier   A common carrier that offers only a limited number of services, usually within only a limited area.

spelling checker   Also called a dictionary; a word-processor program that locates misspelled words or words not in its dictionary.

spooling   The process of sending output to a secondary storage device for temporary storage before printing.

spreadsheet   A paper form, divided into rows and columns, that can be used to keep track of and manipulate numeric data. The computerized version is called an electronic spreadsheet.

staffing   The management function that assembles and trains personnel who are to achieve an organization's goals.

standard-quality print   Print made from dots that is suitable for most informal applications; of lower quality than near-letter-quality print.

star network   A computer network arrangement in which each device is connected to one centralized computer. All communications must be routed through the central host computer.

statistical time-division multiplexing   A variation of time-division multiplexing, which dynamically reassigns unused time slots to devices with data waiting to be sent.

status line   One or more lines located at the top or the bottom of a display screen; provides information about the current file or operation in progress.

status report   A report that lists the current and future status (e.g., balances) of a particular type of resource.

strategic information system   An information system that changes the way an organization competes in the marketplace.

structured programming   A method of writing computer programs that emphasizes the systematic design, development, and management of the software development process. This type of programming increases programmer productivity, improves the quality of programs, and makes them easier to read.

structured query language (SQL)   A query language that allows end-users to make inquiries into a database.

structured walk-through   A procedure in which an analyst discusses, or walks through, the design of a computer program with members of the chief programmer team.

subschema   Defines each user's view or specific part of a database; a security envelope that restricts each user to certain records and fields within a database.

subsystem testing   A level of testing in which several related program modules are tested as a single unit to ensure the correctness of the unit.

summarization   The information processing task that transforms a mass of information into a reduced, or aggregate, form.

superchip   Larger in size than many chips and with significantly more circuitry; designed for increased processing capabilities.

supercomputer   The most powerful type of computer; used primarily by government agencies and organizations that process vast quantities of data.

superconductivity The flow of electricity through certain materials with no resistance.

supermicro A computer that bridges the gap between microcomputers and minicomputers.

supermini A computer that bridges the gap between standard minicomputers and mainframes.

supervisor program Also called monitor, executive, or kernel; the main control program in an operating system.

switching cost The cost incurred by a company or an individual when changing from one supplier to another.

synchronous transmission A method of data transmission in which blocks of characters are sent in timed sequences. Each block of characters is marked by special synchronizing characters. This method is much faster than asynchronous transmission.

syntax The rules by which a programming language is governed.

syntax error A type of error that occurs when a computer program is being coded and the rules of the programming language are violated.

system A set of components that interact with each other to form a whole and work together toward a common goal.

system analysis The term applied to the first three stages of the system development life cycle: problem definition, requirements analysis, and project justification.

system blueprint A series of charts, graphs, and data layouts that describe in detail the following: (1) the input documents that the information system will process and the way those documents will look; (2) the computer records that will be needed to store data generated by the input documents; (3) output documents and reports required by users of the information system; and (4) the sequence and method by which documents are input and used to update computer records and then to produce user-desired output documents and reports.

system changeover stage A stage of the system development life cycle in which the old information system is discontinued and the newly developed system is placed into operation.

system clock The portion of the control unit that sends out electrical pulses to synchronize all tasks in the CPU; instrumental in determining the speed of a processor.

system design A phase of the system development life cycle that is comprised of two stages: (1) the logical design, during which the paper blueprint for the new system is developed, and (2) the physical design, during which that blueprint is translated into the specific programming logic that will cause the new system to operate as planned.

system development life cycle (SDLC) A structured sequence of operations required to conceive, develop, and make operational a new information system; includes a system analysis phase, a design phase, and an implementation phase.

system flowchart A flowchart that shows the flow of information through a system and all the ways that the information is altered as it flows through that system.

system personnel The professionals responsible for designing and implementing an information system.

system resident device A device, such as a disk or a tape, on which control and service programs are stored when not being used by the computer.

systems analyst The specialist who works with users to determine their information needs and designs a system to fulfill those needs.

system software The programs that direct and control the operations of a computer system. An operating system is one example of system software.

system study An extensive report that is prepared by a systems analyst at the end of the system analysis phase; sent to management to promote a chosen information system.

system testing The level of testing in which all program modules are tested as a single unit to ensure the correctness of the entire unit.

table A relational database structure consisting of rows and columns in which data are stored.

tab settings An application-software feature that sets indentions in a file and aligns columns and decimal numbers.

telecommunication Also called teleprocessing; the process of using communication facilities, such as the telephone system or microwave relays, to send data to and from devices.

telecommuting A method of working whereby a person uses a computer and a communication channel to establish a link with a remote office computer. With a personal computer (or terminal) connected to a company's computer, an off-site employee can communicate with the office.

terminal The combination of a monitor and a keyboard used to view output and to enter and check input; also called a video display terminal (VDT).

test data The data with which the testing of a program is conducted.

testing The activity through which a new information system is checked to ensure that it is correct.

testing criteria Those standards by which the users of an information system determine its success.

testing methodology The plan, criteria, and approach according to which the testing of an information system is performed.

test plan A document that describes the overall testing plan for an information system.

text editing The process of adding, deleting, or otherwise altering text after it has been entered into a document.

text graphics A method of creating a graphic image, such as a shape or a line, with alphanumeric and other special characters.

thermal-transfer printer A type of nonimpact printer that uses heat to transfer ink to paper to form characters.

thesaurus A software program that provides alternative words (synonyms) for a given word in a document.

time bomb A method of sabotaging a computer program so that it will destroy itself after a predetermined time or action occurs.

time-division multiplexing A multiplexing method in which each device sharing a channel is assigned an equal time period, or slot, in which to transmit data.

timeliness An attribute of information that refers to two conditions: Is the information available when it is needed? and Is the information outdated when it is received or is to be used?

time-sharing operating system An operating system that allows more than one user to access a single computer system on a timed basis.

time stealing A computer crime in which time on the computer is used without proper authorization.

titles (1) A feature in a graphics package that allows a user to enter text information, such as a title, into the drawing. (2) A feature in a spreadsheet package that freezes row and column titles so that they remain stationary as the spreadsheet is scrolled.

token A string of bits that is passed around a network.

token passing An access method that utilizes tokens in a local-area network. A device must wait for and hold a token in order to transmit a message and then release the token when finished transmitting.

top-down approach A design methodology that organizes the programming effort into workable modules. An entire programming effort is separated into natural parts, which are further divided into subparts and then into subsubparts until each lower-level part (called a programming module) is small enough to be coded by one programmer within the prescribed time frame.

top-level (strategic) managers Managers who are involved in making long-range, strategic decisions. Most of top-level managers' time is spent in planning and organizing.

topology The arrangement by which a computer or a device is connected in a computer network.

touch screen An input device that allows a user to enter data or show position by touching the screen with a finger or other object.

tracks The concentric circles of a magnetic disk where data are stored; used by a computer to identify where data are stored.

training The third task in the implementation phase of the system development life cycle; intended to make users and others familiar with a system so that they are able to work with it.

transaction A business activity or event—for example, the receipt of an order or the sale of a product.

transaction file A temporary file used to update master files.

transaction processing system (TPS) An information system that processes data about transactions or other events that affect the operation of a business.

transferring The process of sharing a data file created in one application program with a file in another application program without having to convert the files.

transposition error An error that occurs when characters are reversed or wrongly juxtaposed.

trap door A special password created by the developer of a program; allows undocumented access to the program.

tree network A computer network arrangement in which devices are linked in a treelike manner through branches.

tuples The name given to the rows of a relational database table.

turnaround document An action document that can be used as input into the same or other systems without human keystroke entry.

typeset-quality print Top-of-the-line print; produced by computer-driven typeset machines. Examples can be seen in magazines and high-quality books.

undo A feature in application software that allows a user to cancel the action of the previous instruction.

unit testing A level of testing in which each program module is tested to ensure its correctness.

updating The process of changing the data that are stored in a computer.

uploading The process of sending a file from one computer to another.

user The person or group of people required to activate a system.

user-friendly A relative term generally implying that a particular computer or software package is easy to learn and use.

user interface A set of computer programs in a knowledge-based (expert) system that provides the link between the system and its user.

user involvement A principle of system design that states that an information system is only as successful as its users believe it to be and that early and active involvement of users in the design of information systems provides them with a sense of ownership, which increases the chance of system success because users are then more tolerant of system flaws.

user's manual Documentation designed to answer common user questions about an information system; organized so that a user can find answers to questions quickly and easily.

user training Training provided to those employees who work with a new system on a regular basis; intended to make users thoroughly familiar with the operation of a new information system.

utility program A program that performs common or routine functions on a computer, such as preparing a disk for use and saving or copying a program.

validating The process of checking data for appropriateness and accuracy as they are entered.

value-added carrier A type of carrier that specializes in leasing services from common carriers and then adding extra services beyond the leased services for their customers.

values Any numbers or formulas that are used to represent data in a program.

verification A technique used to inspect data to determine its accuracy; may be accomplished either visually or by machine.

very-large-scale integration (VLSI) The process of putting several hundred thousand complete circuits on a single chip.

video display terminal (VDT) The combination of a monitor and a keyboard used to view output and to enter and check input; also called a terminal.

videotext An interactive computer information service that can transmit monochrome text as well as colors and graphics; a service in which computers and phones are used for two-way communication to order goods and services.

virtual-machine (VM) operating system An operating system that can run several operating systems at a time; allows each workstation or terminal to choose the operating system applicable to its particular task.

virtual-storage operating system An operating system that makes use of a secondary storage device as an extension of primary storage.

voice-band channel A communication channel, such as a telephone line, that transmits data at 110 to 9600 bits per second.

voice messaging A combination of a telephone and a computer to create a computerized system that allows a message to be sent in human voice without the receiver needing to be present at the same time to receive the message.

voice recognition The capability of a computer to accept input in the form of human speech.

voice synthesis The capability of a computer to respond in a simulated human voice.

wait state The time that a CPU is idle and no processing occurs.

Warnier-Orr diagram A charting technique similar to a hierarchical chart except that the diagram has a horizontal rather than a vertical organization.

white box process A process that transforms an input into an output in a known way.

wide-area network (WAN) A computer network in which the computers are geographically dispersed.

widow line The last line of a paragraph that stands alone at the top of a page.

windows Separate, defined areas on a computer screen that can be used to display data, menus, or other software packages.

wire cable   A type of data communication channel; includes telegraph lines, telephone lines, and co-axial cables.

word   The number of adjacent bits that can be stored and manipulated as a unit by the computer.

word processing   The activity of entering, viewing, storing, retrieving, editing, rearranging, and printing text material using a computer and a word processor.

word-processing system   A combination of hardware and software used in computerized word processing.

word processor   An application package that creates, edits, manipulates, and prints text; generally used for writing documents such as letters and reports.

wordwrap   A word-processor feature that automatically continues a sentence on the next line without the user's pressing the return key at the end of the first line. Any words that extend past the right margin are moved down to the next line.

working memory   That part of the computer memory in a knowledge-based (expert) system in which the appropriate rules and data are stored at a given instant during the execution of the system; also known as short-term memory or dynamic knowledge base.

worksheet   The blank spreadsheet form used for entering and organizing numeric data; a paper form in a noncomputerized spreadsheet and a screen form in an electronic spreadsheet.

write-once-read-many (WORM) optical disk   A blank optical disk that allows a user to write data to the disk once. After part of the disk has been written to once, it can only be read from.

Index

Demodulation, 172
Denning Mobile Robotics, 439
Desktop publishing, 301–5
Detail report, 365
Didier, Mel, 39–40
Diebold, John, 429
Digital Equipment Corporation, 62, 66
Digitizer, 99
Direct-access file, 223–25, 369
Disks, magnetic, 116–20
    floppy, 116–18
    hard, 118–20
Distributed data processing, 195–96
Downloading, 227

Eastman Kodak Company, 81, 306
EBCDIC encoding scheme, 84
Eckert, J. P., 61
Edit check, 231
Education Privacy Act, 424
Electronic Communications Privacy Act, 425
Electronic data interchange, 197
Electronic Data Systems Corporation, 27
Electronic eavesdropping, 413, 422–23
Electronic funds transfer, 197, 198
Electronic Funds Transfer Act, 425
Electronic mail, 305, 307–8
Electronic Services Unlimited, 311
Empire Blue Cross/Blue Shield, 215
Encoding systems, 83–85
End-user computing, 430
Ergonomics, 312–13
Error checking, 367. *See also* Debugging
Errors, program. *See* Debugging
Errors, transposition, 229
Ethics, 421–22
Execution cycle, 93–94
Executive information system, 42, 279
Expert system. *See* Knowledge-based information
        system
Explanation subsystem, 283

Facsimile communication, 308, 309
Facsimile machines, 198–99
Fairchild Semiconductor, 62
Fair Credit Reporting Act, 424
Federal Bureau of Investigation, 251
Federal Express, 197, 409–10
Fiber optics, 175–76
Fidelity Investment, 169
Field, 217
Fifth-generation language, 154
File, 217–19
    access methods, 369

design, 368–70
input validation, 229–31
names, 219
retention and recovery, 370
size, 369–70
storage and access, 223–25, 369
types, 219–23
updating, 227–29
Financial information system, 45
First Capital Life Insurance Company, 351
Flat-panel display monitor, 112
FORTRAN, 62, 154, 155
Fourth-generation language, 153
Frankston, Bob, 63
Freedom of Information Act, 422, 424
Front-end processors, 179, 181

Garber, Jack, 169
Gates, Bill, 63
Gateway service, 200
Gaughan, Thomas R., 259
General Electric Company, 5, 61
General Motors Corporation, 47, 51
Graphics software, 141, 142–44
Grippo, George, 3

Hard-copy devices, 105–10
    computer output microform, 109
    plotters, 109, 110
    printers, 106, 107–9
Hardware, 11–12
Health concerns (and VDTs), 420–21
Hercules Computer Technology, 351
Hertz (Hz), 87
Heschel, Michael S., 359
Hierarchical chart, 371, 372, 373
Hierarchical database, 237, 238, 239
History file, 220
Hoff, Ted, 63
Home Box Office, 325
Hopper, Grace Murray, 62
Hudson, Katherine, 81
Human resources information system, 46

IBM, 52, 64
IBM personal computer, 64
IBM System, 360, 362
ILLIAC IV, 62
Image processing
    copiers, office, 299–300
    desktop publishing, 301–5
    scanners, 300–301
Indexed sequential file, 225, 369
Industrial espionage, 413